PREHISTORIC TIMES

PREHISTORIC TIMES

AS ILLUSTRATED BY

ANCIENT REMAINS

AND THE

MANNERS AND CUSTOMS
OF MODERN SAVAGES

BY

THE LATE RT. HON. LORD AVEBURY

D.C.L. (Oxon.), LL.D. (Cantab., Dubl. et Edin.), M.D. (Würzb.), F.R.S., V.P.L.S., F.G.S.,
F.Z.S., F.S.A., F.E.S., Trust. Brit. Mus. ; Assoc. Acad. Roy. des Sci. Brux. ;
Hon. Mem. R. Irish Acad., Amer. Ethnol. Soc., Anthrop. Soc. Wash. (U.S.), Brux., Fierenze,
Anthrop. Verein Graz, Soc. Entom. de France, Soc. Géol. de la Suisse, and Soc. Helvét. des Sci. Nat. ;
Mem. Amer. Phil. Soc. Philad. and Soc. d'Ethn. de Paris ; Corresp. Mem. Soc. Nat. des Sci.
Nat. de Cherb., Berl. Gesell. für Anthrop., Soc. Romana di Antrop., Soc. d'Emul. d'Abbeville,
Soc. Cient. Argentina, Soc. de Géog. de Lisb,, Acad. Nat. Sci. Philad., Numis. and Ant. Soc. Philad.,
Amer. Entom. Soc. ; For. Assoc. Mem. Soc. d'Anthrop. de Paris ;
For. Mem. Amer. Antiq. Soc.

SEVENTH EDITION, THOROUGHLY REVISED
AND ENTIRELY RESET

1969

ANTHROPOLOGICAL PUBLICATIONS

Oosterhout N.B. – The Netherlands

Photomechanic reprint of the edition of 1913

Exclusive distributor in the U.S.A., its possessions and territories, and Canada and Mexico:
HUMANITIES PRESS Inc.
303 Park Avenue South
New York, N.Y. 10010

Printed in The Netherlands

PUBLISHERS' NOTE

In the spring of the year, and only a few months before his lamented death, Lord Avebury subjected this work to a very thorough revision, making numerous additions dealing with recent discoveries and theories, and cutting out portions which seemed no longer essential.

Besides this a number of new illustrations have been added, to replace or supplement those of the earlier editions.

The book has been entirely reset, and, though the author was not able to pass the proof-sheets himself, every care has been taken to carry out his wish that the book should remain an accurate and up-to-date guide to the student of prehistoric times.

We wish to express our thanks to those who have assisted us in the preparation of this edition or have kindly given us permission to reproduce their work in the illustrations.

WILLIAMS & NORGATE.

November 1913.

PUBLISHER'S NOTE

In the spring of the year ... and only a few months before his honoured death, the author subjected this work to a very thorough revision, making numerous additional ... dealing with ... discoveries and theories, and cutting out portions which seemed no longer essential ...

Besides this, a number of new illustrations have been added to replace ... explain or those of the earlier editions.

The book thus being entirely reset, and though the author was not able ... to ... the proof-sheets himself, every care has been exercised ... ... has with that the book should remain ... ... up-to-date guide to the study of ... ...

We wish to ... our thanks to those who have assisted us ... ... and ... those authors or ... kindly given us permission to reproduce their work in these illustrations.

WILLIAM R. ... ...

... ...

CONTENTS

PREHISTORIC TIMES

CHAPTER I

INTRODUCTION

THE first appearance of man in Europe dates from a period so remote, that neither history, nor tradition, can throw any light on his origin, or mode of life. Under these circumstances, some have supposed that the past is hidden from the present by a veil, which time will probably thicken, but never can remove. Thus our prehistoric antiquities have been valued as monuments of ancient skill and perseverance, not regarded as pages of ancient history ; recognized as interesting vignettes, not as historical pictures. Some writers have assured us that, in the words of Palgrave, "We must give it up, that speechless past ; whether fact or chronology, doctrine or mythology ; whether in Europe, Asia, Africa, or America ; at Thebes or Palenque, on Lycian shore or Salisbury Plain : lost is lost ; gone is gone for ever." Others have taken a more hopeful view, but in attempting to reconstruct the story of the past, they have too often allowed imagination to usurp the place of research, and have written in the spirit of the novelist, rather than in that of the philosopher.

Of late years, however, a new branch of knowledge has arisen ; a new Science has, so to say, been born among us, which deals with times and events far more ancient than any which have yet fallen within the province of the archæologist. The geologist reckons not by days or by years ; the whole six thousand years, which were until lately looked on as the sum of the world's existence, are to him but one unit of measurement in the long succession of past ages. Our knowledge of geology is, of course, very incomplete ; on some questions we shall no doubt see reason to change our opinion, but, on the whole, the conclusions to which it points are as definite as those of zoology, chemistry, or any of the kindred sciences. Nor does there appear to be any reason why those methods of examination which have proved so successful in geology, should not also be used to throw light on the history of man in prehistoric times. Archæology forms, in fact, the link between geology and history. It is true that in the case of other animals we can, from their bones and teeth, form a definite idea of their habits and mode of life, while in the present state of our knowledge the skeleton of a savage could not always be distinguished from that of a philosopher. But on the other hand, while other animals leave only teeth and bones behind them, the men of past ages are to be studied principally by their works : houses for the living, tombs for the dead, fortifications for defence, temples for worship, implements for use, and ornaments for decoration.

From the careful study of the remains which have come down to us, it would appear that Prehistoric Archæology may be divided into four great epochs.

I. That of the Drift ; when man shared the possession of Europe with the Mammoth, the Cave bear, the Woolly-haired rhinoceros, and other extinct animals. This I have proposed to call the "Palæolithic" Period.

II. The later or polished Stone Age ; a period characterized by beautiful weapons and instruments made of flint and other kinds of stone ; in which, however, we find no trace of the knowledge of any metal, excepting gold, which seems to have been sometimes used for ornaments. For this period I have suggested the term "Neolithic." [1]

---

[1] These two names have met with general acceptance.

III. The Bronze Age, in which bronze was used for arms and cutting instruments of all kinds.

IV. The Iron Age, in which that metal had superseded bronze for arms, axes, knives, etc. ; bronze, however, still being in common use for ornaments, and frequently also for the *handles* of swords and other arms, though never for the blades.

Stone weapons, however, of many kinds were still in use during the Age of Bronze, and lingered on even into that of Iron, so that the mere presence of a few stone implements is not in itself sufficient evidence that any given "find" belongs to the Stone Age. In order to prevent misapprehension, it may also be well to state, at once, that, for the present, I only apply this classification to Europe, though, in all probability, it might be extended also to the neighbouring regions of Asia and Africa. The civilization of the south of Europe, moreover, preceded that of northern Europe. As regards other civilized countries, China and Japan for instance, we, as yet, know but little of their prehistoric archæology, though recent researches have gone far to prove that the use of iron was there also preceded by bronze, and bronze by stone. Some nations, indeed, such as the Fuegians, Andamaners, etc., are even now, or were very lately, in an Age of Stone.

It is probable that gold was the metal which first attracted the attention of man ; it is found in many rivers, and by its bright colour would certainly strike even the rudest savages, who are known to be very fond of personal decoration. Silver does not appear to have been discovered until long after gold, and was apparently preceded by both copper and tin ; for it rarely, if ever, occurs in tumuli of the Bronze Age ; but, however this may be, copper seems to have been the metal which first became of real importance to Man ; no doubt owing to the fact that its ores are abundant in many countries, and can be smelted without difficulty ; and that, while iron is hardly ever found except in the form of ore, copper often occurs in a native condition, and can be beaten at once into shape. Thus, for instance, the North American Indians obtained pure copper from the mines near Lake Superior and elsewhere, and hammered it at once into axes, bracelets, and other objects.

Tin also early attracted notice, probably on account of its great heaviness. When metals were very scarce, it would naturally sometimes happen that, in order to make up the necessary quantity, some tin would be added to copper, or *vice versâ*. It would then be found that the properties of the alloy were quite different from those of either metal, and a very few experiments would determine the most advantageous proportion, which for axes and other cutting instruments is about nine parts of copper to one of tin. No implements or weapons of tin have yet been found, and those of copper are rare, in Western Europe, whence it has been inferred that the art of making bronze was known elsewhere before the use of either copper or tin was introduced into Europe. Many of the so-called "copper" axes, etc., contain a small proportion of tin ; and the few exceptions indicate probably a mere temporary want, rather than a total ignorance, of this metal.

The ores of iron, though more abundant, are much less striking in appearance than those of copper. Moreover, though they are perhaps more easily reduced, the metal, when obtained, is much less tractable than bronze. This valuable alloy can very easily be cast, and, in fact, all the weapons and implements made of it in olden times were cast in moulds of sand or stone. The art of casting iron, on the other hand, was unknown until a comparatively late period.

In the writings of the early poets, iron is frequently characterized by the epithet πολύκμητος, and its adjective, σιδήρεος, is used metaphorically to imply the greatest stubbornness.

These considerations tend very much to remove the *a priori* improbability that a compound and comparatively expensive material like bronze should have been in general use before such a common metal as iron, and the evidence that it was so seems conclusive.

Hesiod, who is supposed to have written about 900 B.C., and who is the earliest European author whose works have come down to us, appears to have lived soon after the transition from the Bronze to the Iron Age. He distinctly states that iron was discovered later than copper and tin. Speaking of those who were ancient, even in his day, he says that they used bronze, and not iron.

τοῖς δ᾽ ἦν χάλκεα μὲν τεύχεα, χάλκεοι δέ τε οἶκοι
χαλκῷ δ᾽ εἰργάζοντο μέλας δ᾽ οὐκ ἔσκε σίδηρος,

It is also significant that the word χαλκεύειν, from χαλκος, bronze, means to work in metal. Moreover, the forms of early weapons indicate that those of iron were copied from bronze, not those of bronze from iron. Hesiod's poems, as well as those of Homer, show that more than three thousand years ago the value of iron was known and appreciated. It is true that, as we read in Dr Smith's *Dictionary of Greek and Roman Antiquities*, bronze "is represented in the *Iliad* and *Odyssey* as the common material of arms, instruments, and vessels of various sorts ; the latter (iron) is mentioned much more rarely." While, however, the above statement is strictly correct, we must remember that among the Greeks the word iron (σίδηρος) was used, even in the time of Homer, as synonymous with a sword, and that steel also appears to have been known to them under the name of ἀδάμας, and perhaps also of κύανος, as early as the time of Hesiod. We may, therefore, consider that the Trojan war took place during the period of transition from the Bronze to the Iron Age.

In the Pentateuch, excluding Deuteronomy, bronze, or, as it is unfortunately translated, brass, is mentioned thirty-eight times, and iron only four times.

Lucretius distinctly mentions the three ages. He says :—

> " Arma antiqua, manus, ungues, dentesque fuerunt
> Et lapides, et item sylvarum fragmina rami,
> Posterius ferri vis est, ærisque reperta,
> Sed prior æris erat, quam ferri cognitus usus." [1]

---

[1] V. 1282.

Coming down to more modern times, Eccard [1] in 1750, and Goguet in 1758, [2] mention the three latter ages in plain terms ; [3] the same idea runs through Borlase's *History of Cornwall* ; and Sir Richard Colt Hoare also alludes to "instruments of stone before the use of metals was known," and expresses the opinion that instruments of iron "denote a much later period" than those of bronze.

To the Northern archæologists, however—especially to C. J. Thomsen, the founder of the Museum at Copenhagen, and to Professor Nilsson—must be ascribed the merit of having raised these suggestions to the rank of a scientific classification.

The art of obtaining metal when once discovered offered no great difficulty. Dr Percy indeed tells us [4] that "nothing more easy can be conceived." In various parts of the world metal is still obtained by very simple methods. Dr Gowland quotes examples [5] from Japan and several parts of Africa, India, etc. Among the hill tribes of the Ghats in India "the furnace is first filled nearly half full of charcoal, and upon this, fire is put, after which it is filled to the top with charcoal. The blast is then applied. When the charcoal sinks at the top of the furnace, alternate charges of ore and charcoal are supplied until the proper charge of ore has been introduced, after which the blast is increased and maintained till the close of the operation. The greater part of the slag remains in the furnace and is taken out along with the iron. In from four to six hours a charge is completed, when, the front of the furnace being removed, a small mass of malleable iron, slag, and unburnt charcoal is drawn out." The iron is then hammered into a bar.

Even at the present day in Ceylon the bloom or mass of iron is taken out of the furnace with long tongs made

---

[1] Eccard, *De Origine et Moribus Germanorum.*
[2] Goguet, *De l'Origine des Lois, des Arts et des Sciences.* See ch. iv. and the Preface.
[3] See Rhind in *Arch. Ins. Jour.*, vol. xiii.
[4] *Metallurgy, Iron and Steel,* 1864.
[5] *The Metals in Antiquity*, Huxley Mem. Lecture, 1912, p. 279.

of greenwood sticks tied together at one end, and is then beaten a little into shape with thick sticks.

It is probable that a lump of ore chanced to be used as one of the enclosing stones of a hearth, and that metal was thus produced.

The North American Indians worked the native copper found near Lake Superior, and the Esquimaux made knives, etc., from the Ovifak masses of meteoric iron. In both these cases, however, the metal was used as a malleable stone.

M. Wibel[1] is of opinion that the ancient bronze was obtained, not by the fusion of copper and of tin, but directly from ore containing the two metals. This is also the opinion of Dr Gowland.[2] On the other hand, I was assured by the late Sir H. H. Vivian (afterwards Lord Swansea), than whom we had no higher authority in this country, that in his judgment it is almost impossible that bronze can ever have been so obtained. I cannot, therefore, but agree with those who maintain that the knowledge of bronze must necessarily have been preceded by the separate use of copper and of tin.

Copper and tin were perhaps discovered in Central Asia. The earliest evidence of their use is in Egypt. Neither of them, however, occurs in that country, though the copper mines of Mount Sinai were worked by King Dyezer of the IIIrd Dynasty, about 4000 B.C.,[3] and small implements of bronze occur in the tombs of Abydos, El Amreh, etc., which are referred to an even earlier period. The earliest piece of bronze at present known is said to be the rod found at Mêdûm in Egypt, and which is dated at 3700 B.C. The earliest metal dagger yet known is a copper weapon with two holes for rivets, found at Nagada in a necropolis dating from the period preceding the Ist Dynasty; but the oldest copper daggers from Cyprus and Syria cannot be very much later in date.

[1] *Die Cultur der Bronze-zeit Nord- und Mittel-Europas*, Dr F. Wibel, Kiel.
[2] *The Metals in Antiquity*, Huxley Lecture, 1912, p. 241.
[3] De Morgan, *Rech. s. l. Or. de l'Égypt*, p. 230.

The Museum of Gizeh contains an admirable bronze statue of Pepi I., who is supposed to have reigned about 3400 B.C. It seems probable that the use of metal was not discovered in Egypt, but that the Pharaonic Egyptians brought the knowledge of metals with them from the East.

As regards iron, Mr Budge informs me that in a passage in the funeral text of Pepi I., about B.C. 3400, it is said that this king will sit upon a "throne of iron ornamented with lions' faces," and the hoofs of the bull Sma-ur (see *Recueil de Travaux*, vol. vii. p. 154), and in several places in the texts of this period there is abundant reference to iron. Thus the abode of the blessed was in heaven, the floor of which was made of iron, and the Nile flowed across it. The earth below was lit by night either by lamps being suspended from holes which had been bored in it, or by the light which made its way through the holes. The recensions of these texts which we now have cannot have been made after B.C. 3800, and in his opinion they are much earlier.

There is a prayer in the Harris papyrus, written during the reign of Rameses III. (1300 B.C.), that the words of the king may be "firm as iron." In the same papyrus vessels of iron are mentioned, and the king is said to have made the wall of the temple of Horus like a "hill of iron." Objects of iron are also mentioned in the Karnac tribute. In the lists of Thothmes III. (1600 B.C.) iron comes third in the series of metals paid as tribute. These references, however, imply that the use of iron was already well known.[1] This renders less improbable the authenticity of the piece of iron said to have been found wedged in between two of the stones of the Great Pyramid.[2] Maspero, moreover, in 1882 found some pieces of iron in the Black Pyramid of Abousir (VIth Dynasty);[3] but no iron has been found in any of the tombs belonging to the earlier Egyptian dynasties.

The earliest evidence of iron in Assyria is an inscrip-

---

[1] I am indebted for these particulars to Mr Budge.
[2] Vyse, *Pyramids of Gizeh*, vi. p. 275.
[3] Maspero, *Guide du Musée de Boulaq*, p. 296.

tion of Tiglath-Pileser (1120 B.C.), who says : "In the desert of Mitani near Araziki, which is in front of the land of Hatti, I slew four mighty buffaloes with my great bow and iron arrows, and with my lance."

In China copper is said to have been used as far back as the reign of Yu Nai Hwang-ti, 2200 B.C. ; and iron in that of Kung Kiu, about 1900 B.C.[1] Copper axes of very simple type have also been discovered in India, but we have no means of determining their date.

The remarkable phase of archaic culture known as Mycenæan—when arms of bronze were beautifully inlaid with gold, when gems were cut, and the potter's art had attained a high degree of perfection—appears to have attained its zenith about 1500 B.C. It must, therefore, have commenced much earlier.

The date of the introduction of iron into the North of Europe cannot at present be satisfactorily determined ; nevertheless, it is most likely that the use of this metal spread rapidly. Not only does it seem *a priori* probable that such an important discovery would have done so, but it is evident that the same commercial organization which had already carried the tin of Cornwall all over our continent, would equally facilitate the transmission of iron. However this may be, the soldiers of Brennus were provided with iron swords, and when the armies of Rome brought the civilization of the South into contact with that of the North, they found iron already well known to, and in general use among, their new enemies. Nor is there any reason to suppose that arms of bronze were also at that time still in use in the North, for, had this been so, they would certainly have been mentioned by the Roman writers ; whereas the description given by Tacitus of the Caledonian weapons shows that in his time the swords used in Scotland were made of iron. Moreover, there are several cases in which large quantities of arms belonging to the Roman period have been found together, and in which the arms and implements are all of iron. This argument is in its very nature

[1] De Lacouperie, *Brit. Mus. Cat. of Chinese Coins*, p. 9.

cumulative, and cannot therefore be fully developed here, but out of many, I will mention a few cases in illustration.

Some years ago, an old battle-field was discovered at Tiefenau, near Berne, and described by M. Jahn. On it were found a great number of objects made of iron ; such as fragments of chariots, bits for horses, wheels, pieces of coats of mail, and arms of various sorts, including no less than a hundred two-handed swords. All of these were made of iron, but with them were several fibulæ of bronze, and some coins, of which about thirty were of bronze, struck at Marseilles, and presenting a head of Apollo on one side and a bull on the other ; both good specimens of Greek art. The rest were silver pieces, also struck at Marseilles. These coins, and the absence of any trace of Roman influence, sufficiently indicate the antiquity of these interesting remains.

A very similar collection of antiquities has been obtained from the ancient lake-village near La Tene, on the Lake of Neufchâtel. This interesting locality will be referred to again in the chapter on Swiss lake-villages, and I will here only observe that 50 swords, 5 axes, 4 knives, and 23 lances have been discovered, but not a single weapon of bronze. Nine coins have been also found here, while not a single one has been met with in any of the Stone Age or Bronze Age villages. Yet the Gauls had a coinage of their own nearly three hundred years before Christ, and the Britons, as Sir John Evans [1] has well shown, about a century or perhaps one hundred and fifty years later.

Some very interesting " finds " of articles belonging to the Iron Age have been made in the peat bogs of Slesvick, and described by M. Engelhardt, Curator of the Museum at Flensborg. One of these, in the Moss of Nydam, comprises clothes, sandals, brooches, tweezers, beads, helmets, shields, shield bosses, breastplates, coats of mail, buckles, sword-belts, sword-sheaths, 100 swords, 500

[1] *The Coins of the Ancient Britons*, 1864, by Sir John Evans, K.C.B., F.R.S.

spears, 30 axes, 40 awls, 160 arrows, 80 knives, various articles of horse gear, wooden rakes, mallets, vessels, wheels, pottery, coins, etc. Without a single exception, all the weapons and cutting implements are made of iron, though bronze was freely used for brooches and other similar articles.[1]

In the summer of 1862, M. Engelhardt found in the same field a ship, or rather a large flat-bottomed boat, 70 feet in length, 3 feet deep in the middle, and 8 or 9 feet wide. The sides are of oak boards, overlapping one another, and fastened together by iron bolts. On the inner side of each board are several projections, which are not made from separate pieces, but were left when the boards were cut out of the solid timber. Each of these projections has two small holes, through which ropes, made of the inner bark of trees, were passed, in order to fasten the sides of the boat to the ribs. The rowlocks are formed by a projecting horn of wood, under which is an orifice, so that a rope, fastened to the horn and passing through the orifice, leaves a space through which the oar played. There appear to have been about fifty pairs of oars, of which sixteen have already been discovered. The bottom of the boat was covered by matting. I visited the spot about a week after the boat had been discovered, but was unable to see much of it, as it had been taken to pieces, and the boards, etc., were covered over with straw and peat, that they might dry slowly. In this manner, M. Engelhardt hoped that they would perhaps, at least in part, retain their original shape. The freight of the boat consisted of iron axes, including a socketed celt with its handle, swords, lances, knives, brooches, whetstones, wooden vessels, and, oddly enough, two birch brooms, with many smaller articles. Only those, however, have yet been found which remained actually in the boat ; and as, in sinking,

---

[1] See Lubbock in *Nat. Hist. Rev.*, Oct. 1863, and Stephens in *Gent. Mag.*, Dec. 1863. On one of the arrows were some Runic characters. I had the pleasure of visiting this interesting spot with M. Engelhardt in 1862. See also *Denmark in the Early Iron Age*, by C. Engelhardt.

it turned partly over on its side, no doubt many more articles will reward further explorations. It is evident that this ancient boat was sunk on purpose, because there is a square hole about six inches in diameter hewn out of the bottom ; and it has been suggested that these objects were sunk as offerings to the Lake, but, on the whole, it seems more probable that in some time of panic or danger the objects contained in it were thus hidden by their owner, who was never able to recover them. Even in recent times of disturbance, as, for instance, in the beginning of last century, and in 1848, many arms, ornaments, household utensils, etc., were so effectually hidden in the lakes and peat mosses, that they could never be found again. Much interest is added to this vessel and its contents, by the fact that we can fix almost their exact date. The boat lies, as I have already mentioned, within a few yards of the spot where the previous discoveries at Nydam were made, and as all the arms and ornaments exactly correspond, there can be little doubt that they belong to the same period. Now, the previous collection included nearly fifty Roman coins, ranging in date from A.D. 67 to A.D. 217, and we cannot therefore be far wrong in referring these remains to the third century.

A very similar discovery has been made at Thorsbjerg in the same neighbourhood, but in this case, owing to some chemical difference in the peat, the iron has been almost entirely removed. It may naturally be asked why, then, this should be quoted as an instance of the Iron Age ? And the answer seems quite satisfactory. All the swords, lance-heads, and axe-blades have disappeared, while the handles of bronze or wood are perfectly preserved, and as the ornaments and other objects of bronze are well preserved, it is evident that the swords, etc., were not of that metal ; and it is therefore reasonable to conclude that they were of iron, more especially as the whole character of the objects resembles that of those found at Nydam, and the coins, which are about as numerous as those from the latter place, range from 60 A.D. to 197 A.D.; so that these two great "finds" may be regarded as almost contemporaneous.

Not only are the weapons in these finds all of iron, but their forms and the character of the ornamentation are very different from those of the Bronze

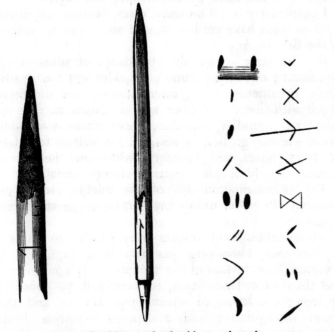

FIG. 1.—Ancient Danish arrow-head, with owner's mark.
FIG. 2.—Modern Esquimaux arrow-head, with owner's mark. In my collection, one-half natural size.
FIG. 3.—Owners' marks from various ancient Danish arrows.

Age; resembling in some respects Roman arms, in others they are quite peculiar, and evidently representative of Northern art.

Many of the arrows had owners' marks on them (figs. 1 and 3) resembling those on the modern Esquimaux arrows (fig. 2). The Nydam swords also bear seven inscriptions; three of them are illegible, the others are "ricus," "riccim," "cocillus," and "umored." On the umbo of one of the shields is inscribed, in dotted Roman letters, AEL. AELIANUS ; while another one has a short Runic[1] inscription, which Mr Haigh reads as Aisc Ah (Aisc owns) ;[2] two figures resembling Runic letters are also inlaid with golden wire on one of the sword blades. One of the Thorsbjerg scabbards also has a Runic inscription of two lines, each containing ten letters.

I particularly dwell on these cases, because no inscriptions or coins have yet been found which can be referred to the Bronze Age.

For the same reason the abundance of silver is very significant ; out of two hundred buckles and square silver girdle ornaments, the greater number are of bronze plated with silver, and silver was also used to ornament shield rims, sandals, brooches, breast-plates, sword-hilts, sword-sheaths, girdles, harness, etc., as well as for clasps, pendants, boxes, and tweezers, while one helmet was formed entirely of this comparatively rare metal.

The ornamentation also of the shields, etc., is of a character altogether unlike any that occurs in the Bronze Age.

An assemblage of objects very similar to those of Nydam and Thorsbjerg has also been found in the " Vimose," or " Moss of the Temple." It comprises no less than 1500 lance-heads, 40 axes, and 30 swords, all of iron ; abundance of silver ; one Roman and three Runic inscriptions ; and a coin of Faustina Junior. Here, again, bronze weapons are entirely absent, though bronze was used for ornaments, etc.

From these and similar discoveries, it appears evident that the use of bronze weapons had been discontinued in the North long before the commencement of our era. From the ease with which bronze could be worked, this metal was still used for brooches and ornaments ; but in the manufacture of swords, axes, and similar implements, it had been entirely superseded by iron. There are many cases on record of iron swords with bronze handles or scabbards, but scarcely an instance of the reverse.

---

[1] See Appendix No. I.   [2] *Archæological Journal*, 1863.

Conversely, as bronze weapons are entirely absent from the great "finds" of the Iron Age, so are iron weapons altogether wanting in those instances where, as for instance at Nidau, on the Lake of Bienne, and Estavayer, on that of Neufchâtel, large quantities of bronze tools and weapons have been found together.

To sum up this argument, though the discoveries of bronze and of iron weapons have been very numerous, yet there is hardly a single case in which swords, axes, daggers, or other weapons of these two different metals have been found together ; nor are bronze weapons found associated with inscriptions, or with coins, pottery, or other relics of Roman origin.

So, also, though no doubt stone weapons were used during the Bronze Age, there are many cases in which large numbers of stone implements and weapons have been found without any of metal.

In illustration of this argument, I must call attention to the following table. Objects found singly teach us comparatively little, but when numbers occur together they become much more instructive. The first ten localities are some of the Swiss lake-villages, which will be described in Chapter VI. ; to which I have added the Nydam find just alluded to, and two of the great French bronze finds.

Now from the ancient lake-village in the peat moss of Moosseedorf we have a list comprising 75 flint nuclei, 25 arrow-heads, 12 spear-heads, 90 scrapers, 30 saws, 96 axes, 310 long flakes and about 2000 small ones, 25 hammers, 45 grindstones, etc., 71 awls of bone, 12 pointed ribs, 160 bone chisels, 18 sharpened boar's teeth, 8 perforated boar's teeth, 2 perforated bear's teeth, 5 harpoons of horn, 8 chisels and 4 awls of horn, besides 30 axe-handles or sockets, without a trace of metal. The result, so far as six stations are concerned, is shown in the following table (p. 16).

If, for instance, we commence with the remains discovered at Wangen, on the Lake of Constance, we have an even more remarkable case. M. Löhle has found

	Stone Axes	Stone Arrows	Stone Flakes	Stone Other Objects	Stone Total	Bronze Axes	Bronze Knives	Bronze Lances	Bronze Sickles	Bronze Fish-Hooks	Bronze Ornaments	Bronze Sundries	Bronze Total	Iron Swords	Iron Axes	Iron Knives	Iron Lances	Iron Ornaments	Iron Sundries	Iron Total	Coins
SWITZERLAND.																					
Wangen	1500		2500	450	4450																0
Moosseedorf	100	25	2300	277	2702																0
Nussdorf	1000	100	100	30	1230																0
Wauwyl	43	36	200	147	426																0
Nidau	33	?	?	335 Corn-crushers	368	23	102	27	18	109	1420	805	2004								0
Cortaillod	?	?	?	?		13	22	4	2	71	515	208	835								0
Estavayer	?	?	?	?		6	14		1	43	403	150	617								0
Corcelettes	?	?	?	?		1	19	2	7		465	16	510								0
Morges	0	?	?	Many Corn-crushers		50	20	11	11	10	108	?	210						1	1	0
Marin			Some	12 Balls		1 Pierced					1	13	15								0
Larnaud						87	76	54	51	6	768	758	1800	50	5	4	23	More than 100	61	250	0
Réallon							1	2	2		44	1	453								0
DENMARK.																					
Nydam				A few Whet-stones								Ornaments very numerous		100	30	86	500 at least	?	300 at least	1000 at least	34

there more than 1500 axes, 100 whetstones, 150 corn-crushers, and 2500 arrow-heads, flint flakes, chips, etc. ; altogether more than 4450 instruments of stone, besides about 350 of bone, making, with 100 earthenware spinning-weights, a grand total of nearly 5000 objects, and yet not a trace of metal. The number of corn-crushers and spindle-whorls is interesting, when we remember that Wangen alone, among these four localities, has supplied us with specimens of carbonized grain, and flax fabrics.

Now let me ask the reader to compare with the four cases given in the table on p. 16 the list of remains from the Bronze Age settlements of Morges, Nidau, Estavayer, Cortaillod, and Corcelettes, and the two Bronze Age finds of Larnaud and Réallon. The manner in which the collections were made accounts, probably, for the absence of whetstones, and, perhaps, to a great extent, for that of the flint flakes, etc. On these points, therefore, I lay little stress ; but the total absence of stone axes at Morges, and their rarity at Nidau and Estavayer, is very remarkable. At the former, M. Forel, after the most careful search, has found but one object of iron. The large number of corn-crushers and the presence of spinning-weights are also significant.

Colonel Schwab's splendid collection from Nidau tells the same tale. When I saw it he had only 33 stone axes, and yet as many as 335 corn-crushers. The ruder articles of stone he had not apparently collected. He had nearly 200 spindle-whorls, and many earthenware rings, specimens of which have also been found at Morges, but which are entirely wanting at the Pont de Thiele, at Wauwyl, at Moosseedorf, and at Wangen.

It is, of course, possible that very different states of civilization may co-exist in different parts of the same country ; but in this case we must remember that the settlement at Nidau is only about fifteen miles from Moosseedorf. Nor can we suppose that the differences were merely a question of wealth ; the bronze fish-hooks, axes, small rings, pins, etc., which are found in such large numbers, show that bronze was used not for the articles of luxury only, but also for the ordinary implements of daily life.

Nor is it only in the presence or absence of bronze that the lake-dwellings differ from one another ; there are many other indications of progress. We cannot expect to find much evidence of this in the implements of bone or stone ; but, as has already been mentioned, the better forms of stone axe, and those which are perforated, are very rare, if not altogether absent, in the Stone Age, none having been found at the Pont de Thiele, at Moosseedorf, or at Wauwyl, and only two at Wangen.

Again, it is not only by the mere presence of bronze, but by the number, beauty, and variety of the articles made out of it, that we are so much struck. In a collection of objects made at any of the Stone Age settlements, no one can fail to remark the uniformity which prevails. The wants of the artificers seem to have been few and simple. In the Bronze Age all this is altered. We find not only axes, arrows, and knives, but, in addition, swords, lances, sickles, ear-rings, bracelets, pins, rings, and a variety of other articles. The list on page 16 gives an idea of the objects found in some of the Swiss lake settlements, whilst the number of bronze objects found in the lakes of Bienne and Neufchâtel alone exceeds 20,000. As regards France, M. Chantre gave the following numbers :—Celts, 9153 ; swords and daggers, 727 ; lances, 513 ; knives, 342 ; sickles, 225 ; pins, 1220 ; needles, 204 ; bracelets, 1086 ; rings and chains, 1572 ; arrow-heads, 213 ; hammers, 23 ; anvils, 5 ; chisels, 58 ; gouges, 31 ; razors, 62 ; saws, 8 ; hooks, 172 ; moulds, 74 ; and a variety of other articles, making altogether no less than 20,000 objects, since which time many more have been discovered. The bronze objects, therefore, evidently cannot be regarded as mere isolated and exceptional specimens, but represent a special and somewhat advanced phase of civilization.

The pottery also shows a considerable advance. The potter's wheel indeed seems to have been unknown during both the Bronze and Stone Ages, but the material of which the Stone Age pottery is composed is rough,[1] containing large grains of quartz, while that used during the Bronze Age is more carefully prepared. The ornaments of the two periods show also a great contrast. In the Stone Age they consist of impressions made by the nail or the finger, and sometimes by a cord twisted round the soft clay. The lines are all straight, or if curved are very irregular and badly drawn. In the Bronze Age all the patterns present in the Stone Age are continued, but in addition we find circles and spirals; while imitations of animals and plants are characteristic of the Iron Age.

So again the distinction between the Bronze and Iron Ages rests by no means merely on the presence of iron. The pottery is different, the forms of the implements and weapons are different, the ornamentation is different, the knowledge of metallurgy was more advanced, silver and lead were in use, letters had been invented, coins had been struck. The entire absence of silver, of coins, and of inscriptions, in the bronze finds, is very remarkable.

This class of evidence is by no means confined to the Swiss lake discoveries. In various parts of Europe more or less extensive deposits of bronze implements have been found. They may be divided into two principal classes—(1) treasures, which were hidden away by their owners and never recovered, and (2) founders' stocks. The former consist of implements, weapons, and ornaments, entire, and often almost new ; the latter principally of worn and broken objects, often with lumps of rude metal. In the table given on page 16 I have given two of these finds, one (Réallon) a treasure, the other (Larnaud) a founder's stock. These finds are particularly instructive, because the objects contained in them are evidently contemporaneous. It will be seen from the lists on pp. 16, 18, 25, and 47 that the numbers of bronze objects are

---

[1] The extreme coarseness of the Swiss lake pottery is, perhaps, partly owing to its having been intended for kitchen purposes ; for the vessels found in tumuli of the Stone Age, the material was often more carefully prepared.

very considerable ; indeed, for France and Switzerland
alone they amount to between 30,000 and 40,000, and
the number is continually increasing.[1]

The value of this evidence will be better appreciated
after reading the following extract from Mr Wright's
Essays on Archæology : [2]

"All the sites of ruined Roman towns with which I am
acquainted present to the excavator a numerous collection
of objects, ranging through a period which ends abruptly
with what we call the close of the Roman period, and
attended with circumstances which cannot leave any doubt
that this was the period of destruction. Otherwise, surely
we should find some objects which would remind us of
the subsequent periods. I will only mention one class
of articles which are generally found in considerable
numbers, the coins. We invariably find these presenting
a more or less complete series of Roman coins, ending at
latest with the emperors who reigned in the first half of
the fifth century. This is not the case with Roman towns
which have continued to exist after that period, for then,
on the contrary, we find relics which speak of the subsequent inhabitants, early Saxon and Mediæval. I will only,
for want of space, give one example, that of Richborough,
in Kent. The town of Rutupiæ seems to have capitulated
with the Saxon invaders, and to have continued until its
inhabitants, in consequence of the retreat of the sea,
gradually abandoned it to establish themselves at Sandwich. Now the coins found at Richborough do not end
with those of the Roman emperors, but we find, first, a
great quantity of those singular little coins which are
generally known by the name minimi, and which, presenting very bad imitations of the Roman coinage, are
considered as belonging to the age immediately following
the Roman period, and preceding that of the Saxon
coinage."

We may assume, then, on the authority of Mr Wright
himself, that if all the bronze arms which are so abundant

---

[1] Chantre, *Age du Bronze*, vol. ii. p. 275.
[2] *Essays on Archæology*, p. 105.

in our museums were really of Roman origin, many of them would have been found from time to time in conjunction with other Roman remains ; whereas bronze weapons are never found in association with coins, pottery, or other relics of Roman origin.

Elsewhere, indeed, he has called this fact in question, but in spite of his profound acquaintance with archæological literature, he has only been able to bring forward three cases in support of his argument, not one of which appears to me to be satisfactory.

For a full statement of his views I must refer to his " Memoir on Bronze Weapons," in the *Transactions of the Ethnological Society*,[1] which, in conjunction with my brother Frederic, I have endeavoured to answer before the same learned body.[2] I will, however, refer to the only three cases which Mr Wright has been able to discover.

The first is that of the bronze sword figured in Stuart's *Caledonia Romana*, pl. v. " This sword," says Mr Wright, " is stated to have been found at the Roman station of Ardoch, in Scotland, on the wall of Antoninus, and there appears no reason to doubt the statement." In truth, however, there is no such statement ; Mr Wright has been misled by the fact that the sword is figured on the same plate with some Roman remains from Ardoch.

The second case quoted by Mr Wright is that of a sword described by Mongez before the French Institute, on the " 16th Prairial, An. 9," *i.e.* 5th June 1801. It is stated to have been found in a peat-moss at Heilly, near Abbeville, with the skeletons of a man and a horse, and four coins of the Emperor Caracalla. " This sword, therefore," says Mr Wright, " was that of a Roman cavalry soldier, not older, and perhaps a little later, than this reign, who had sunk in the bog to which this turbary had succeeded."

Mongez, on the contrary, concluded that the skeleton

[1] *Transactions of the Ethnological Soc.*, N.S., vol. iv. p. 176.
[2] Ditto, N.S., vol. v. p. 105.

could not have been that of a cavalry soldier at all, because
a cavalry soldier would not have been armed with a short
sword ; and so far from regarding the sword as Roman,
" On ne pourroit," he says, " également pas l'attribuer
aux Romains, si l'on ne raisonnoit que d'après la matière
dont elle est faite."[1]   And in the next page he adds,
" We are therefore certain, that after the second Punic
war the Roman swords were made of iron."[2]

It is true that five months later he changed his mind,
and came to the conclusion that, after all, the bronze
swords were Roman ; but I cannot consider that much
weight should be attached to this opinion, which was in
direct opposition to that which he entertained a few
months previously.

Finally, Mr Wright cites an instance of a bronze
sword found with some Roman coins of Maxentius, who
reigned from 306 to 312 A.D. This sword was discovered in a turbary at Piquigny, near Abbeville, in a
large boat, which it would seem had been sunk, and in
which were several skeletons. The reason for referring
this bronze sword to the Roman epoch was the presence
in this case, as in the last, of Roman coins. But it is
somewhat remarkable that the antiquaries who recorded
the discovery attributed so little importance to the
presence of these coins that they did not in either case
take the trouble to specify the exact position which these
occupied with reference to the bronze weapons ; in fact
they only mention the coins casually, and as it were by
an afterthought, in a footnote. I may be pardoned,
then, if I do not myself look upon them as being certainly
of the same date as the weapons near which they are
said to have been discovered. But even if it be admitted
that in these two cases bronze weapons were actually
discovered near some Roman coins, still, when we consider the great abundance of Roman coins on the one
hand, and of bronze weapons on the other, we cannot be

---

[1] *Loc. cit.*, p. 193.
[2] " Nous voilà donc certains que l'épée des Romains, depuis la seconde
guerre Punique, fut fabriquée en fer," p. 194.

surprised that there should be one or two cases in which they have been found associated together.

Again, the geographical distribution of bronze weapons and implements does not favour such a theory. The Romans never entered Denmark ; it is doubtful whether they ever landed in Ireland ; no Roman road, masonry, or earthwork has ever been found there. Yet while more than 350 bronze swords have been found in Denmark,[1] more than 400 in France, and a very large number in Ireland,[2] the Italian museums only contain about 50. Indeed, the rich museums at Florence, Rome, and Naples do not appear to possess a single specimen of those typical, leaf-shaped bronze swords, which are, comparatively speaking, so common in the North. That the bronze swords should have been introduced into Denmark by a people who never occupied that country, and from a part of Europe in which they are very rare, is, I think, a most untenable hypothesis. I may add that no swords or celts of bronze have been found in the excavations of Pompeii.[3]

Moreover, the use of the word "ferrum" (iron) as synonymous with a sword, clearly proves that the Roman swords were made of that metal.

I have already mentioned that silver and lead do not occur in Bronze Age finds, that coins and letters are equally absent, and that the ornamentation of the Bronze Age, though sometimes very beautiful, is not of a Roman character.

Lastly, the bronze which was so largely used by the Romans for ornaments, etc., was composed partly of lead, whereas that of the Bronze Age consists of copper and tin only. Other metals, indeed, such as iron, silver,

[1] If daggers are included the number would reach nearly 1200, and 480 for Sweden.—Chantre, *Age du Bronze*, vol. i. p. 134.

[2] The Museum at Dublin contains 282 swords and daggers ; the number of swords is not stated separately.

[3] This statement has been questioned by Mr Wright, who pointed out that two bronze celts in the museum at Naples have been figured and described as coming from Pompeii. During a visit to Naples, I looked out these celts, and found that they did not come from Pompeii, but from an ancient tomb in Magna Græcia.

nickel, and lead itself, are present ; but in small quantities, not having been purposely introduced, but only occurring as impurities.

In Plutarch's Essay *On the Pythian Responses*, Philinus describes certain ancient bronze statues which were of a peculiar colour, and says : Was " there then some mode of alloying and preparing the bronze used by the ancient artificers, like the traditional tempering of swords, which process being lost, bronze obtained exemption from war-like employment " ?[1]

The reasons, then, which satisfy me that our bronze weapons cannot be referred to Roman times, may be summed up as follows :—

Firstly. They have never been found in company with Roman pottery, or other remains of the Roman period.

Secondly. They are very abundant in some countries, as, for instance, in Denmark and Ireland, which were never invaded by Roman armies.

Thirdly. The bronze swords do not resemble in form those used by Roman soldiers.

Fourthly. The Latin word " ferrum " was used as synonymous with a sword, showing that the Romans always used iron.

Fifthly. The ornamentation is not Roman in its character.

Sixthly. The bronze used by the Romans contained, generally, a large proportion of lead, which is never the case in that of the Bronze Age.

Nor is there any subsequent period to which we can refer the weapons and implements of bronze. Great numbers of Saxon interments have been examined both in this country and on the Continent, and we know that the swords, lances, knives, and other weapons of that time were all of iron. Besides this, if the bronze implements and weapons had belonged to post-Roman times, we should certainly, I think, have found some of them in the ruined towns, and with the pottery and coins of that period. Moreover, the similarity to each other of

[1] Plutarch, *On the Pythian Responses.*

TABLE C.

HALLSTADT.

GRAVES WITH BODIES BURIED IN THE ORDINARY MANNER.

	No. of the Graves.	Gold Ornaments.	Bronze.				Iron.		Ornaments.			
			Ornaments.	Vessels.	Sundries.	Weapons.	Weapons.	Other Objects.	Amber.	Glass.	Pottery.	Stone.
ANTIQUITIES.	527	6	1471	3	85	18	161	33	165	88	334	57

GRAVES WITH BURNT CORPSES.

	No. of the Graves.	Gold Ornaments.	Bronze.				Iron.		Ornaments.			
			Ornaments.	Vessels.	Sundries.	Weapons.	Weapons.	Other Objects.	Amber.	Glass.	Pottery.	Different Objects.
ANTIQUITIES.	453	58	1744	179	54	91	349	41	105	35	908	100
	980	64	3215	182	89	109	510	74	270	73	1242	157

Totals, 5985

the weapons found in very distant parts of Europe, implies more extended intercourse between different countries than any which existed in those centuries. On the whole, then, the evidence is conclusive that the use of bronze weapons characterizes a particular phase in the history of European civilization, and one which was anterior to the discovery of iron, or at any rate, to the general use of that metal for cutting purposes.

Evidently, however, the transition from the use of

bronze weapons to those of iron must have been gradual, and there must have been a time when the two were in use together. M. Ramsauer, for many years director of the salt-mines at Hallstadt, near Salzburg, in Austria, has discovered an extensive cemetery belonging to this transitional period. He has opened no less than 980 graves,

FIG. 4.—Copper (?) celt from Waterford—6 inches long, 3¾ wide at the broader end, and 1⅞ at the smaller, which is about 1-16th thick.

FIG. 5.—Winged celt, or Paalstave, from Ireland.

evidently of those who even at that early period worked the salt-mines which are still so celebrated. The objects discovered are described and figured in an album, which has unfortunately never been published, but of which Sir John Evans and I secured a copy. The foregoing table will sufficiently prove the importance of the discovery.

That the period to which these graves belonged was that of the transition between the Bronze and Iron Ages, is evident ; both because we find cutting instruments of iron as well as of bronze, and also because both are of somewhat unusual, and we may almost say of intermediate types. The same remark applies to the ornamentation.

Animals are frequently represented, but are very poorly executed, while the geometrical patterns are well drawn. Coins are entirely absent. That the transition was from bronze to iron, and not from iron to bronze, is clear ; because here, as elsewhere, while iron instruments with bronze handles are common, there is not a single case of a bronze blade with an iron handle. This shows that, when both metals were in use, the iron was preferred for blades. Another interesting point in the Hallstadt bronze, as in that of the true Bronze Age, is the absence of silver, lead, and zinc (excepting, of course, as mere impurities in the bronze). This is the more significant, inasmuch as the presence, not only of the tin itself, but also of glass, amber, and ivory, indicates the existence of an extensive commerce.

FIG. 6. — Socketed celt from Ireland, one - third of the actual size.

Moreover, as Morlot well pointed out, the absence of silver cannot be accidental, because the bronze of Hallstadt contains no lead, and the absence of lead entails that of silver, since the latter could not, at least in Europe, be obtained without the former.[1]

In the fifty years which have elapsed since this chapter was written much more evidence has accumulated, and archæologists are now agreed that the use of iron was preceded by that of bronze, and that iron dates back to a very early period, which in Egypt, Assyria, and the South of Europe may be estimated as at least 1500 B.C. In our own country I estimate the introduction of iron as having occurred about 1000 B.C.

[1] For further information on the subject of this chapter I may refer to Sir John Evans' admirable *Ancient Bronze Implements of Great Britain and Ireland,* which has appeared since the 4th edition of this work ; to Sir C. H. Read's *British Museum Catalogue, The Bronze Age* ; and to various works by Montelius.

CHAPTER II

ON THE USE OF BRONZE IN ANCIENT TIMES

THE commonest and, perhaps, most characteristic objects belonging to the Bronze Age are the so-called "celts" (figs. 4–18), which were probably used for chisels, hoes, war-axes, and a variety of other purposes. Implements

FIGS. 7, 8, 9.—The three principal types of celts, and the manner in which they are supposed to have been handled.

similar, though not identical, and made of iron instead of bronze, are even now employed in Siberia (fig. 10) and some parts of Africa.[1] The French Museums contain more than 10,000 bronze celts. More than 2000 are known to exist in the different Irish collections, of which the great Museum belonging to the Royal Irish Academy at Dublin contained in the year 1860 no less than 688,[2]

---

[1] Klemm's *Culturgeschichte der Menschen*, vol. iii. p. 160. *Horæ Ferales*, p. 77.

[2] In the Museum at Edinburgh are more than 100, at Copenhagen 350.

no two of which were cast in the same mould. They vary in size from an inch to a foot in length, and may be divided into three principal classes (figs. 7–9) according to the manner in which they were handled ; though we must remember that there were many intermediate forms. The first class (figs. 4, 7, 11, 13, 14, 15, 17, and 18) is the simplest in form, and evidently the oldest, being " formed on the type of the old stone celts."

FIG. 10.—Kalmuck Axe; iron. In the collection of the late Dr Klemm.

FIG. 11.—Copper (?) celt from Ireland, one-half of the actual size.

There can be little doubt that these simple celts were handled in the manner indicated (fig. 7). Fig. 19 represents a modern African axe in my collection. Here, indeed, the blade is of iron.

FIG. 12.—Half of a celt mould from Ireland. It is of mica slate, 6¾ inches long, 4 wide, and presents upon the surface the apertures by means of which it was adjusted by the other half.

Evidently, however, in such an axe the blade would tend to split the handle in which it was placed. To remedy this defect, a stop, or ridge, was raised across the celt, and the metal and wood were made to fit into one another (figs. 5, 8, and 20). This second form of celt is known as a Paalstab, or Paalstave, and has often a small loop on one side (which was probably used to attach the celt to the handle by a cord, as indicated in fig. 8), and a wing on each side. A still further improvement consisted (figs. 6, 9, 16) in reversing the position of the metal and the handle, making the axe hollow at one end, and so passing the handle into it.

Bronze celts are generally plain, but often ornamented with ridges, dots, or lines, as in figs. 6, 9, 13, 15, 16, and 20. That they were made in the countries where they are found is proved by the presence of moulds (fig. 12). It is difficult to understand why the celt-makers never cast their axes as we do ours, with a transverse hole, through which the handle might pass. No bronze implement of this description has, however, so far as I know, been yet found in Great Britain, though a few have occurred in Denmark, where they are of great beauty and highly decorated.

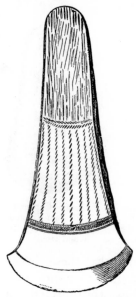

FIG. 13.—Decorated celt from Ireland—8½ inches long, 4 wide at the blade end, and half an inch thick.

The development of the beautiful leaf-shaped spears is also very interesting, and has been well described by Rev. W. Greenwell and Mr Brewis.[1] They are derived from the small and rather weak knife (commonly called a knife-dagger), so frequently found associated with early burials. This eventually passed into the true dagger, which was the immediate parent of the spear-head, the rapier, and the sword. The base of the dagger blade was first narrowed, and a flat tang with a peg hole at its termination was added to it, for the purpose of fixing it to the shaft. This tanged blade constitutes the first true spear-head of metal. The next change was the addition of a loose ferrule, which enclosed the wood through which the tang was carried. The object of this was to prevent the wood splitting and the head being

FIG. 14.—Simple celt from Denmark, one-third of the actual size.

[1] *Archæologia*, vol. lxi., 1909.

torn from the shaft. The head was then improved still further by the omission of the tang, and by the amalgamation of the ferrule with the blade.

FIG. 16.—Socketed celt from Denmark, one-third of the actual size.

This, however, did not materially alter the appearance of the head, though it added much to the firmness of the hold which the two parts of the spear had on each other. A head was thus produced which was provided with a socket, though at that time the cavity was not carried up into the blade. These apparent rivet heads are simulated, as also

FIG 15.—Ornamental celt from Denmark, one-third of the actual size.

the junction of the blade socket. The next step was the extension of the socket up into the blade.

The wings undergo many significant and interesting changes. At first the outline of the base of the wings, where it emerges from the socket, retains the old concave form, which is a survival of the period when the edge stopped at the simulated junction of the blade and ferrule. This is illustrated in fig. 21, representing a specimen from the Arreton Down hoard. The rivets which originally fastened on the sheath are

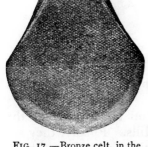

FIG. 17.—Bronze celt, in the Museum, Bergen.

indicated by knobs, which are of course mere survivals and of no use.

The next improvement was the addition of a pair of loops, by which the blade was still more firmly fastened to the shaft, as in fig. 22, which represents a specimen

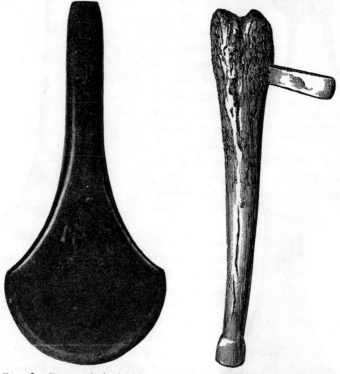

FIG. 18.—Bronze celt, in the Museum, Bergen.

FIG. 19.—Modern African axe. In my collection, one-sixth natural size.

from Rostrevor Down. The loops are some way down the shaft.

Gradually, however, they move up to the base of the wings, as in fig. 23 from Bush Mills. Finally, they are included in the sloping outline of the blade (fig. 24 from Dowris Hoard), into which also the shaft is carried.

The thongs attached to the loops were then found to be unnecessary and somewhat inconvenient.

The longer shaft rendered them less necessary, and they were replaced by a peg much reduced in size, so as to be practically useless, then simulated, and finally disappeared.

The angular break in the flow of the outline of the

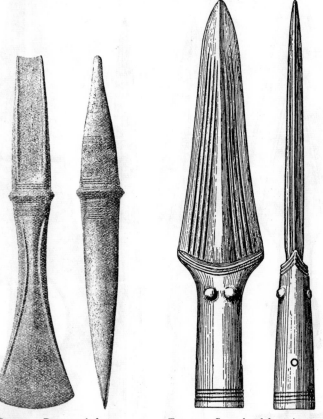

FIG. 20.—Bronze celt from Sweden. After Montelius.

FIG. 21.—Spear-head from Arreton Down.

wings, the upper part of the blade alone being provided with a sharp edge, is due to the fact that in the earlier examples the edge stopped at the simulated junction of the blade and socket.

This form is almost confined to the United Kingdom, though a few have been found at Mycenæ, in Hungary,

and elsewhere in Europe, though
our specimens are perhaps the most
beautifully proportioned, and grace-

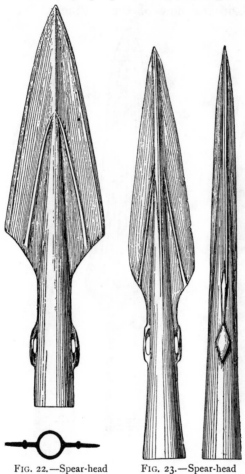

FIG. 22.—Spear-head
from Rostrevor Down.

FIG. 23.—Spear-head
from Bush Mills.

FIG. 24.

fully though simply decorated. The
loops are replaced by lunate openings,
mainly for ornament, though they
served also to lighten the spear without
seriously reducing the strength.

It is, unfortunately, impossible to date the specimens, or the changes, but the gradual development, the obvious advantages gained, and the simulation of old forms, leave scarcely any room for doubt as to the sequence through which the beautiful leaf-shaped spear-head has been evolved.

The swords of the Bronze Age (figs. 26–33 [1]) are more or less leaf-like in shape, double-edged, sharp-pointed, and intended for stabbing and thrusting rather than for cutting. This is evident, not only from the general shape, but also from the condition of the edges. They never have any hand-guards : the handles are sometimes solid (figs. 29–36) ; this is generally the case with those found in Denmark : sometimes (figs. 26–28) flat, thin, and evidently intended to be plated with wood or bone : while sometimes the sword expands at its base, and is fastened to a handle by from two to four rivets. Swords of this class are generally shorter than the others, and indeed we find every intermediate form between the true sword and the dagger (figs. 37, 38, 39) ;

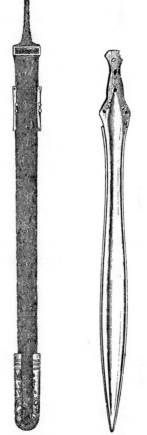

FIG. 25.—Iron sword from a cemetery at Brighthampton in Oxfordshire, one-eighth of the actual size.

FIG. 26.—Sword from Ireland— 23½ inches long, 1⅝ wide in the centre of the blade, which is margined by a grooved feather edge.

of the two classes together, the Dublin Museum contains

---

[1] In fig. 25 an ancient iron sword is represented, in order to show the difference in form.

nearly 300. The handles of the bronze swords are very short, a characteristic much relied on by those who attribute the introduction of bronze into Europe to a people of Asiatic origin, but is probably due to the manner in which they were held. The Museums of Denmark contain more than 1000 bronze swords, that of Stockholm, including daggers, over 500. At Mycenæ 150 swords were found, all of bronze.

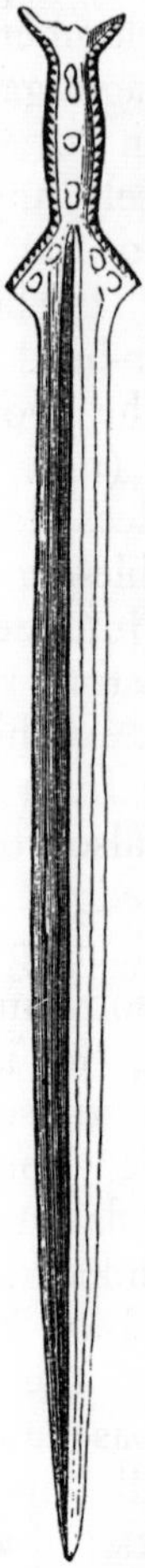

Bronze arrows are not very common in Northern Europe, probably because flint was so much cheaper, and almost as effective.

More than a hundred bronze *fish-hooks* have been found at Nidau in the Lake of Bienne, but elsewhere they appear to be rare ; the Museum at Dublin contains only one. *Sickles* are more numerous ; at Copenhagen there are 25, at Dublin 11 ; in the lake-village at Morges 11 have been found, at Nidau 18 ; they are generally about 6 inches in length, flat on one side, and raised on the other ; they were always intended to be held in the right hand.

FIG. 28.—Sword from Switzerland, one-fifth of the actual size. In the museum of Col. Schwab.

FIG. 27.—Sword from Sweden, one-fourth of the actual size.

Bronze *knives* (figs. 40–44) are frequently found in tumuli, and among the remains of the Swiss lake habitations ;

FIG. 29.—Sword from
Concise on the Lake
of Neufchâtel, ¼ of
the actual size. In
the museum of Col.
Schwab.

20, for instance, at Morges, 26 at Estavayer, and about 100 at Nidau ; in Ireland they appear to be very rare ; the Dublin Museum does not contain one. They were generally fitted into handles of bone, horn, or wood, and the blade was almost always more or less curved ; those of iron knives, on the contrary, being generally straight.

Fig. 48 represents a bronze knife figured in Lee's translation of Keller, page 276,[1] and said to have been found at Thebes by Sir Gardner Wilkinson. The type, however, is not Egyptian. It is just possible that the knife may have been carried to that country in ancient times, but it seems more probable that there is an error as to the locality.

The small bronze *razor-knives* (figs. 45, 46), indeed, have straight edges, but they are quite of a different character from the iron knives ; from the ornaments engraved on them, I am disposed to regard them as belonging to a late period in the Age of Bronze, if not in some cases to the

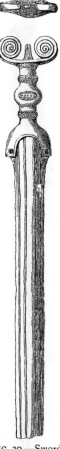

FIG. 30.—Sword from Scandinavia.

[1] See also for Egyptian bronze implements and weapons, Mr A. Arcelin's paper in the *Matér. p. sér. à l'Hist. Prim. de l'Homme*, 1869, p. 376.

beginning of that of Iron. Indeed, the Flensborg Museum contains a razor-knife, said to have been found together with objects of the latter metal. A somewhat similar pattern occurs on the knife fig. 42, which, from the human figure forming the handle, I should also refer to the Iron Age.

Ornaments of bronze do not, like the weapons of that metal, characterize a definite period, but may belong to any age. Some forms have maintained themselves almost unchanged for ages. The "safety - pin," for instance, was invented in the Bronze Age. Before, therefore, we refer any particular ornament to this period, we must know the circumstances under which it was found. The following illustrations are, however, principally from the Swiss

FIG. 31.—Sword from Denmark, found in the Treenhoi tumulus.

FIG. 32.—Bronze sword, Stockholm.

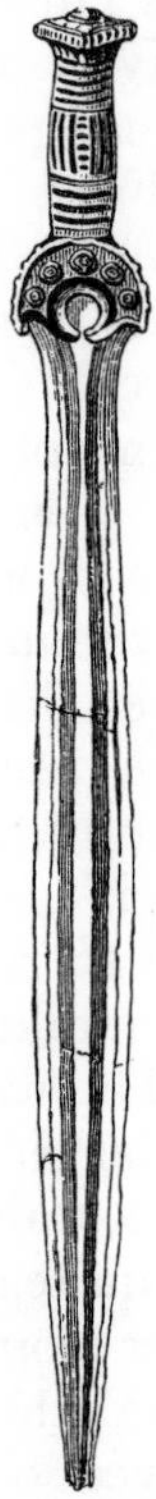

FIG. 33.—Sword from Denmark, one-sixth of the actual size.

lake-villages, and may be regarded as belonging to the Bronze Age.

The personal *ornaments* which may, I think, safely be referred to the Bronze Age, consist principally of bracelets (figs. 49, 50), pins (figs. 51–54), and rings. The bracelets are either simple spirals, or rings open at one side, and decorated by those combinations of straight and curved lines so characteristic of the Bronze Age. Like the weapons, they generally indicate small hands, but, like the bronze ornaments of various existing savages—for instance, of many Negro tribes, of the Khonds in Orissa,

FIG. 34.—Hilt of sword from Denmark, one-fourth of the actual size.

FIG. 35.—Hilt of sword from Denmark, one-fourth of the actual size.

etc. — they are often extremely heavy.

Bronze pins are very abundant : for instance, 239 from Estavayer, 600 from Nidau, and more than 6000 from the two lakes of Bienne and Neufchâtel.[1] They are also very frequently found in graves, where they were used, as pointed out by Sir R. C. Hoare, to secure the linen cloth which enveloped the bones. Although brooches of bronze are very common, they have generally been found in conjunction with iron, and during the Bronze Age their place seems to have been generally filled by mere pins. Many of the latter articles found in the

FIG. 36.—Hilt of bronze sword, Museum, Bergen.

[1] See Appendix.

Swiss lakes appear, however, to have been hairpins. Some of them are nearly a foot in length, and two found near Berne even as much as 2 ft. 9 in. Many of the pins have large hollow spherical heads, as in figs. 51, 52 ; the others vary so much that it is impossible to give any general description of them. There can be little doubt that these pins really belong to the Bronze Age; but the fact that similar ones continued in use long after the introduction of iron is equally well established. One of these later bronze pins is represented in fig.

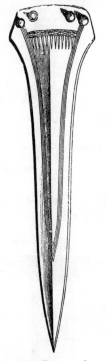

FIG. 37.—Bronze dagger-blade from Ireland—10¾ inches long by 2¾ wide. The four rivets by which it is fastened to the handle are still *in situ*.

194. Some other small objects of bronze, including two needles, from the Lake of

FIG. 38.—Bronze dagger from Ireland, two-thirds of the actual size.

Neufchâtel, are represented in figs. 55-60. Bronze hammers are very rare : it is probable that stones were used for this purpose. Gouges are more common. Small saws have been discovered in Germany and Denmark, but not, as yet, in Great Britain. Studs or buttons, though not very abundant, are found both in Switzerland and Scandinavia.[1]

[1] Further information as to the objects of bronze from Switzerland will be found in the chapter on Swiss lake habitations.

Brooches were very rare in Western Europe, if, indeed, they had been invented, during the Bronze Age. No English specimens have been discovered which can with certainty be referred to this period. Almost the same may be said as regards the Swiss Bronze Age lake-villages. They are said, on the contrary, to be common in Sweden. The earliest form resembled what is now known as a safety - pin.

FIG. 39.—Bronze dagger-blade from Ireland, $\frac{1}{3}$ of the actual size.

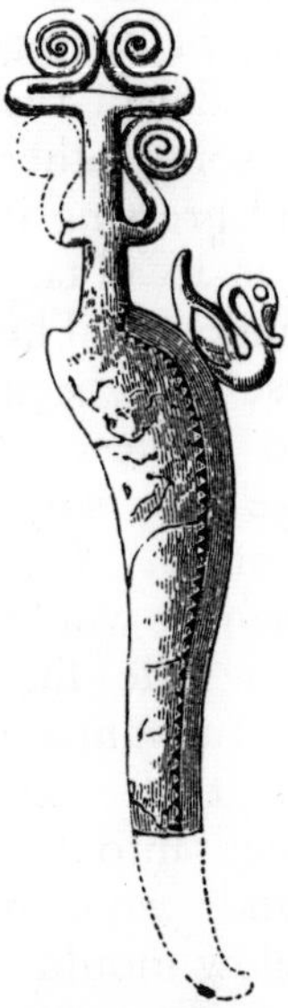

Silver, lead,[1] and zinc appear to have been unknown, or very rare, during the Bronze Age. Glass beads were in use, but no vessels of glass have yet been discovered; in the same manner there are barbarous tribes now which are well supplied with European beads, but which possess no glass vessels.

The weapons and ornaments of the Bronze Age are all cast, and show considerable skill in metallurgy.[2] Three modes of casting were employed. One was that in a mould, either of stone or metal. Of course in this case the mould was necessarily in two halves, and the line of junction was generally visible, as in fig. 61, representing a celt which has evidently been cast in this manner. This specimen was found in Kent, and presented to me by Sir George Dasent. It is clear, however that such an object as the knife in fig. 43 could not have been cast in this manner. Neither were

FIG. 40.—Bronze knife from Denmark, one-half of the actual size.

[1] Lead, however, is mentioned in the inscriptions of Karnak. See Lepsius, *Les métaux dans les Ins. Egypt*, p. 58.

[2] See Morlot's interesting memoir: *Sur le passage de l'Âge de la Pierre à l'Âge du Bronze et sur les métaux employés dans l'Âge du Bronze.* Copenhague, 1866.

the pins figs. 51-54, for if they had been, the line of junction between the two halves of the mould must have been traceable.

Indeed, this mode of casting was evidently unusual. This is proved by the condition of the objects, by the scarcity of moulds, and also by the fact that we seldom find any two bronze objects exactly similar to one another.

Thus, out of the 688 specimens in the Dublin Museum, no two were cast in the same mould, clearly showing that the moulds were not permanent.

The second mode of casting was by making a model of the object in wood or some other hard substance, and pressing it on fine sand, so as to obtain a corresponding hollow. The sand must of course have been contained in two boxes or frames, fitting like the solid moulds one on the other. Objects cast in this manner would therefore also show the line of junction. The advantage of this method is that sand can easily be worked into the required form, and wooden

FIGS. 41, 42.—Bronze knives from Denmark, one-third of the actual size.

models were much more easily made than hollow moulds, either of stone or metal. Like the former, however, this method was applicable to very simple castings only. Specimens in which the line of junction is not exactly central, or symmetrical, were probably cast in this manner, the model having been pressed into the one mould rather more deeply than into the other.

The third method of casting was with wax or wood. In this case, as in the former, a model was made and enclosed in prepared earth, made of some clayey soil mixed probably with cow-dung, or some other inflammable substance, in order that when subjected to heat it might become porous.   The frame was then heated until the wax or wood disappeared.   This mode of casting required fewer instruments, and did not, like the other two methods, involve a line of junction, which was a great advantage, because in the absence of steel the projecting ridge thus produced was very difficult to remove, especially when the objects were ornamented.   In one case M. Morlot observed on an object of bronze the mark of a finger, evidently resulting from an impression on the soft wax. Occasionally, again, when the

wax was heated carelessly, it burned and left a carbonized film, which of course produced a corresponding mark on the object cast.   The use of wax in this manner, though presenting many

FIGS. 43, 44.—Bronze knives from the lake-village of Estavayer, on the Lake of Neufchâtel, one-half of the actual size.

FIG. 45.—Razor-knife from Denmark, one-half of the actual size.

advantages, does not appear to have been frequent in Great Britain.

In some few cases the interiors of bronze vessels show the marks of the spatula with which the wax was worked.

The evidences of imperfect metallurgical knowledge and appliances are also very interesting ; the art of soldering appears to have been unknown.   M. Morlot has called attention to a striking instance of this presented by one of the large Schwerin brooches (fig. 62). This was evidently a *chef d'œuvre*, but the intermediate bow connecting the two great discs had been accidentally broken. In order to mend it again, the two pieces were put into their proper relative position, and the broken bow was covered with a layer of wax. The whole was then surrounded with the usual preparation of clay, etc.; the wax was melted out and replaced with bronze.

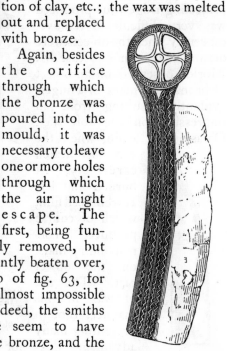

FIG. 46.—Razor-knife from Denmark, one-half of the actual size.

Again, besides the orifice through which the bronze was poured into the mould, it was necessary to leave one or more holes through which the air might escape. The first, being funnel-shaped, was easily removed, but the latter were frequently beaten over, as is seen at the top of fig. 63, for without steel it was almost impossible to cut them off. Indeed, the smiths of the Bronze Age seem to have been unable to pierce bronze, and the holes for rivets, as in the swords, etc., are cast, and not pierced.

FIG. 47.—Bronze knife, actual size, Denmark.

Even the ornamentation in circles, spirals, etc., on the bronze objects is mostly cast, and though beautifully drawn, was evidently done with the free hand ; compasses seem therefore to have been unknown.

In some cases, however, the ornamentation appears to have been engraved on the objects themselves. For this

purpose short instruments were used, in which there
was a much larger proportion of tin than usual. Such

FIG. 48.—Bronze knife, said to have been found by Sir Gardner Wilkinson,
at Thebes, but probably European.

implements are very hard, but at the same time very
brittle, and therefore not
suited for ordinary pur-
poses.   Instruments of this
character, though rare, have
been met with in the great
bronze find at Larnaud and
elsewhere.

On some of the bronze
vessels the ornamentation
has been produced by ham-
mering.   This, however,
indicates a considerable progress in metallurgy.

Soldering seems to have
been entirely unknown during the Bronze Age, and even
during the earlier times of the Iron
Age. Thus the Hallstadt bronze
vessels, when broken, were always
riveted together.

FIG. 49.—Bronze bracelet from Cortaillod, on the Lake of Neufchâtel,
one-third of the actual size.

FIG. 50.—Bronze bracelet from
Cortaillod, on the Lake of
Neufchâtel, one-third of the
actual size.

I have also figured a group (figs.
64–67) of Irish gold ornaments.
The earlier ones probably belong
to the Bronze Age ; a torque
much like fig. 64 formed part of
the great Larnaud find, but they
appear to have come down to a
much later period. The fact is interesting that very
similar ornaments, made, however, not of gold, but of

iron, are now worn by the natives of Africa. One of these is represented in fig. 68.[1]

The ornamentation on the objects of bronze is of a peculiar, and at the same time uniform, character ; it consists of simple geometrical patterns, and is formed by combinations of spirals, circles, and zigzag lines ; representations of animals, and plants being very rarely attempted. Even the few exceptions to this rule are perhaps more apparent than real. Thus, two such only are figured in the Catalogue of the Copenhagen Museum ; one is a rude figure of a swan (fig. 40), the other of a

FIGS. 51, 52, 53, 54.—Bronze hair-pins from the Swiss lakes, one-half of the actual size.

man (fig. 42). The second of these forms the handle of a knife, which appears to be straight in the blade, a type characteristic of the Iron Age, but rarely found in that of Bronze. As regards one of them, therefore, there is an independent reason for referring it to the period of transition, or at least to the close of the Bronze Age. There is, indeed, one type of pattern, usually found on the razor-knives, but sometimes also on others, intended probably for a rude representation of a ship (fig. 46). Even, however, if we admit this to be the case, and if we accept these objects as belonging to the Bronze Age, this will only show how little advance had yet been made in the art of representing natural objects.

[1] *Archæologia*, vol. xliii. p. 442.

	Nidau.	Mœrigen.	Estavayer.	Cortaillod.	Corcelettes.	Auvernier.	Other Places.	Total.
Celts and Fragments, .	23	7	6	13	1	6	11	67
Swords, ...	...	...	...	...	...	...	4	4
Hammers, . . .	4	...	1	...	...	...	...	5
Knives and Fragments, .	102	19	14	22	19	8	9	193
Pins, ...	611	53	239	183	237	22	22	1367
Small Rings, . .	496	28	115	195	202	14	3	1053
Ear-rings, . . .	238	42	36	116	...	3	5	440
Bracelets and Fragments,	55	14	16	21	26	11	2	145
Fish-hooks, . . .	189	12	43	71	9	2	1	248
Awls, ...	95	3	49	98	17	...	...	262
Spiral Wires, . .	...	...	46	50	5	...	...	101
Lance-heads, . .	27	7	...	4	2	5	2	47
Arrow-heads, . .	...	...	5	1	...	...	...	6
Buttons, . . .	...	1	28	10	10	...	...	49
Needles, . . .	20	2	3	4	1	...	...	30
Various Ornaments, .	15	5	7	18	3	1	...	49
Saws, . . .	...	...	...	3	...	...	...	3
Daggers, . . .	...	...	...	...	...	...	2	2
Sickles, . . .	18	12	1	2	7	1	4	45
Double-pointed Pins, .	75	...	...	...	...	...	...	75
Small Bracelets, .	20	...	...	11	...	...	...	31
Sundries, . . .	96	3	5	16	...	...	4	124
Total, . .	2004	208	618	835	539	73	69	4346

The foregoing table, which I owe to the kindness of Dr Keller, and the list given on p. 18, will give an idea of the relative numbers of the different objects. Since it was drawn up the numbers have considerably increased, and the

FIG. 55.—Bronze awl from the Swiss lakes, actual size.

total number of bronze objects recovered from the two lakes of Bienne and Neufchâtel alone now exceeds 20,000.

Dr Thurnam gives the following list of the bronze objects found by Sir R. C. Hoare in the Wiltshire tumuli.

Objects of Bronze.

	With Unburnt Bodies.	With Burnt Bodies.	Total.
Celts	4	1	5
Blades of knives, daggers, etc.	16	44	60
Awls and drills . . .	5	29	34
Crutch-headed screws . .	1	2	3
Large pin with rings . .	...	1	1
Prong with rings . . .	1	...	1
Rivets and pieces of bronze-mounted shield (?) . .	1	...	1
Bracelet	1	...	1
Buckle.	...	1	1
Bead	...	1	1
Total . .	29	79	108

As already mentioned (*ante*, p. 19), the bronze objects were evidently in many cases made by travelling pedlars

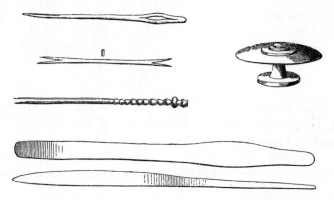

FIGS. 56–60.—Various small objects of bronze from the Swiss lakes.

who exchanged new ones for old, or for broken pieces. To save carrying about heavy and precious objects, they often concealed part of their stock, and many of their hoards have been discovered, in France alone over 400. These hoards are very instructive, and I shall refer to

them again when we come to consider the chronology of
the Bronze Age.

There is, I believe, only one case in which any bronze
weapon or implement bears an inscription ; a fact which
is the more significant when we remember how often
letters are met with on
those of iron. Fig. 71
represents this interesting
specimen, which is a winged
celt, and is in the Museum
Kircherianum of the Col-
legio Romano, at Rome.
No explanation of the
inscription has yet been
given, nor do we even
know to what alphabet
the letters belong. It was
found in the Campagna,
but there is unfortunately
no record of the circum-
stances under which it was
discovered.

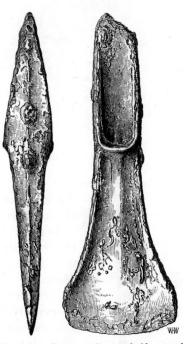

FIG, 61.—Bronze celt, one-half natural
size. Showing the line of junction of
the two halves of the mould in which
it was cast.

The skill displayed in
the manufacture of the
objects described in this
chapter, as well as the
beauty of their form and
ornamentation, shows a
considerable development
of art. The discovery of
a bar of tin at Estavayer, and of a mould for casting
celts at Morges, has proved that some at least of these
objects were made in Switzerland, just as evidence of
a similar nature shows that other countries in Europe,
as, for instance, Denmark, England, Scotland, and Ireland,
had also their own foundries. The similarity of form
and ornamentation appears also to indicate some communication between different parts of Europe ; but each
country presents special types ; but as Cornwall, Saxony,

and Spain [1] are the only known European sources from which tin can be obtained in any quantity, the mere

FIG. 62.—Bronze brooch, Mecklenburg, three-tenths natural size.   Showing the manner in which it has been mended.

presence of bronze is in itself a sufficient evidence not only of metallurgical skill, but also of commercial intercourse.

FIG. 63.—Bronze celt. Showing the air-vents bent over.

We should hardly, perhaps, have hoped to ascertain much of the manner in which the people of the Bronze Age were dressed.   Considering how perishable are the materials out of which clothes are necessarily formed, it is wonderful that any fragments of them should have re-mained to the present day.   There can be little doubt that the skins of animals were extensively used for this purpose, as indeed they have been in all ages of man's history ; many traces of linen tissue also have been found in English tumuli of the Bronze Age, and in the Swiss lakes.   Figs. 189–190 represent pieces of fabric from Robenhausen in Switzerland ; they belong, however, in all probability,

[1] Tin is said to have anciently been obtained in Pannonia, near the modern Temesvar, but I do not know whether the mines were extensive. See Howorth, *Stockholm Prehist. Congress*, p. 533.

to the Stone Age.   Even small fragments such as these throw much light on the manufactures, if we may call them so, of the period to which they belong ; but fortunately we need not content ourselves with any such partial knowledge as this, as we possess the whole dress of a chief belonging to the Bronze Age.

FIG. 64.—Gold torque, consisting of a simple flat strip or band of gold, loosely twisted, and having expanded extremities which loop into one another.   It measures 5½ inches across, and was found near Clonmacnoise, in Ireland.

On a farm near Ribe, in Jutland, is a tumulus known as Treenhoi, which was examined in 1861 by MM. Worsaae and Herbst.   It is about fifty ells in diameter and six in height, being composed of a loose sandy earth.   In it, near the centre, were found three wooden coffins, two of full size and one evidently intended for a child.   The coffin with which we are now particularly concerned was about 9 ft. 8 in. long and 2 ft. 2 in. broad on the outside ; its internal measurements were 7½ ft. long and 1 ft. 8 in. broad.   It was covered by a movable lid of corresponding size. The contents were peculiar and very interesting. While, as might naturally be expected, we find, in most

ancient graves, only the bones and teeth, all the soft parts having long ago decayed away, in some cases —and this was one of them—almost exactly the reverse has happened. Through the action of water, owing perhaps to the fact that it was strongly impregnated with iron, the soft parts of the body had been turned into a dark, greasy substance; and the bones, with the exception of a few fragments, were changed into a kind of blue powder.

FIG. 65.—Gold fibula, one-half of the actual size. The hoop is very slender; the cups deep and conical.

Singularly enough, the brain seems to have been the part which had undergone least change. On opening the coffin, it was found lying at one end, where no doubt the head had originally been placed, covered by a thick hemi-spherical woollen cap, about six inches in height (fig. 72). The outer side of the cap was thickly covered by short loose threads, every one of them ending in a small knot, which gave the cap a very singular appearance. The body of the corpse had been wrapped in a coarse woollen cloak (fig. 73), which was almost semicircular, and hollowed out round the

FIG. 66.—Smooth, massive, cylindrical gold ring, with ornamented ends, one-half of the actual size.

neck. It was about 3 ft. 8 in. long, and broad in proportion. On its inner side were left hanging a great number of short woollen threads, which gave it somewhat the appearance of plush.

On the right side of the body was a box, closed by a lid of the same diameter. It was $7\frac{1}{2}$ in. in diameter,

6¼ in. high, and was fastened together by pieces of osier or bark. In this box was a similar smaller one, without a lid, and in this again were three articles, namely,

FIG. 67.—Gold fibula, one-third of the actual size. The external surfaces of the cups are decorated with circular indentations surrounding a central indented spost. There is also an elegant pattern where the handle joins the cups. It is 8⅜ inches long, and weighs 33 ounces, being the heaviest now known to exist.

a cap 7 in. high, of simply woven woollen stuff (fig. 74) ; a small comb 3 in. long, 2½ in. high (fig. 75) ; and a small simple razor-knife.

After the cloak and the bark-box had been taken away,

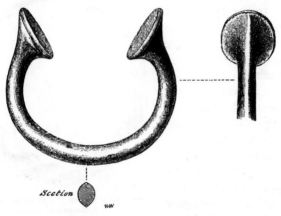

Section

FIG. 68.—Iron ornament, Africa.

two woollen shawls came to view, one of them covering the feet, the other lying nearer to the head. They were of a square shape, rather less than 5 ft. long, 3 ft. 9 in. broad, and with a long fringe (fig. 77). At the place where the body had lain was a shirt (fig. 76), also of

woollen material, cut out a little for the neck, and with a
long projecting tongue at one of the upper angles. It

FIG. 69.—Bronze necklet in Bergen
Museum.

was fastened at the waist by
a long woollen band, which
went twice round the body,
and hung down in front.
On the left side of the
corpse was a bronze sword
(fig. 31), in a wooden sheath.
It is 2 ft. 3 in. in length, and
has a solid simple handle.

At the feet were two pieces
of woollen stuff, about $14\frac{1}{2}$
in. long and $3\frac{1}{2}$ in. wide
(fig. 78), the use of which
does not seem quite clear, though they may be supposed
to have been leggings. At the end of the coffin were
found traces of leather,
doubtless the remains of
boots. In the cap, where
the head had been, was
some black hair, and the
form of the brain was still
recognizable. Finally,
this ancient warrior had
been wrapped round in
an ox's hide, and so com-
mitted to the grave.

The other two coffins
were not examined by
competent persons, and
the valuable information
which they might have

FIG. 70.—Bronze torque from Norway,
in Bergen Museum.

afforded was thus lost to us. The more indestructible
things were, however, preserved ; consisting of a sword,
a brooch, a knife, a double-pointed awl, a pair of tweezers,
a large double button or stud, all of bronze ; a small
double button of tin, and a javelin-head of flint.

The baby's coffin produced only an amber bead, and

a small bronze bracelet, consisting of a simple ring of metal.

Another tumulus on the same farm contained four wooden coffins, in which were bodies clothed in woollen garments, a bronze sword in a wooden sheath ornamented with carvings, two bronze daggers, a wooden bowl ornamented by a large number of tin nails, a vase of wood, and a small box of bark.

In another instance, near Aarhuus, the dress of a woman was discovered under similar circumstances. Over her head were two shawls, one rather fine, the other coarser. She wore a cloak with sleeves, and a long shirt tied round the waist by woollen cords. She also had been buried with a bronze dagger.

Fig. 71.—Inscribed celt, Museum Kircherianum, Rome, one-half of the actual size.

There can, therefore, be no doubt that these very interesting tumuli date from the Bronze Age, and I am inclined to place them somewhat late in that period, partly on account of the knife and razor-knife, both of which belong to forms which there are, as already mentioned, other reasons for referring to the close of the Bronze Age, and to the beginning of that of Iron. Bronze brooches are also very rarely found in the Bronze Age, and are common in that of Iron. The sword, again, belongs to a form which is regarded by Professor Nilsson as being of late introduction.

Fig. 72.—Woollen cap, one-sixth of the actual size. Found with the bronze sword (fig. 32) in a Danish tumulus.

The ancient Egyptians and Assyrians were both acquainted with the art of embroidery at a very early date.[1] Leviticus (about 1500 B.C.) mentions garments of linen

---

[1] See Cole on "Ancient Embroideries," *Soc. of Arts*, Feb. 1895. Also Yates' *Textimum Antiquorum*.

and wool.   Pliny attributes the invention of cotton weaving to the reign of Semiramis.   In one of the wall paintings at Beni-hassan on the Nile (about 2100 B.C.), a figure is represented in a spotted dress — apparently woven with a shuttle. On another tomb at Thebes, a personage is represented in a dress with red and blue spots, which, however, may have been darned on.   On a wall painting in the

FIG. 73.—A woollen cape, one-sixth of the actual size. Found with the preceding.

Ramesseum (about 1400 B.C.) an Egyptian being is represented in a dress striped with blue and yellow, while his horse carries a cloth striped with blue, yellow, red, and green. Herodotus describes a corselet sent as a present by Amasis to the Greeks as being of linen with " many figures of animals unwrought, and adorned with gold and tree wool."

From 1000 B.C. we have actual specimens of embroidery.

Finally, the mode of sepulture, though other similar cases are on record, is, to say the least, very

FIG. 74.—Another woollen cap, one - sixth of the actual size. Found with the preceding.

unusual ; in the Age of Iron, indeed, the corpse was generally extended, but in that of Bronze the dead were, with few exceptions, burned, or buried in a contracted attitude. In Denmark, cremation appears to have been almost universal; in England, I have taken out the statistics of 100 cases of tombs containing objects of bronze, 37 recorded by Mr Bateman and 63 by Sir R. C. Hoare; and the following table shows the manner in which the corpse had been treated.

	Contracted.	Burnt.	Extended.	Uncertain.
Bateman	15	10	5	7
Hoare.	4	49	2	8
	19	59	7	15

In 100 cases recorded by Canon Greenwell, all were contracted or burnt.

We may consider, therefore, that during this period the corpse was sometimes, though very rarely, extended on its back, and more frequently it was buried in a sitting or crouching position, and in a small chamber formed by large stones, but that the most usual practice was to burn the dead, and collect the ashes and fragments of bones in or under an urn.

FIG. 75.—A small comb, one-sixth of the actual size. Found with the preceding.

The ancient funeral customs, however, will be more fully considered in a subsequent chapter.

The people of the Bronze Age led a pastoral life, having cows, sheep, pigs, dogs, and horses. The cows were small, about the size of the present Kerry breed, standing 3 ft. 5 in. at the shoulder. Larger oxen sometimes occurred, but were not common. The sheep and horse were also small; but the pigs, though slender, were about the average size of modern specimens. There are indications that they cultivated the soil from the prevalence of lines of terrace near the camps, but on this point the evidence is not conclusive.

The camps were no doubt occupied for a long period, and from that day to this objects have been dropped in them, and especially in the ditch. General Pitt Rivers, however, has carefully recorded not only when, but at what depth, every object, even every bit of pottery, was found, and the result is most interesting and instructive. He has also given average sections of the camps and the ditches, showing the position of the relics projected into them.

We know as yet very little about the architecture of the Bronze Age. Rougemont[1] considers that the Round towers belong to that period, but I know no sufficient reason for this opinion. In the next chapter I shall give my reasons for

FIG. 76.—A woollen shirt, one-sixth of the actual size. Found with the preceding.

referring some at least of our so-called Druidical remains to that period, and many of the Swiss lake-villages certainly belong to it. These remains, indeed, give us little information as to the kind of houses then in use. Certain "hut-urns," however, or urns in the form of huts, which have been discovered in Italy and Germany, appear to belong to the close of the Bronze Age. The Italian "hut-urns" were discovered in 1817[2] at Albano, near Rome, under an undisturbed layer of peperino or consolidated volcanic ash, and belong, therefore, to a time when the volcanoes near Rome were still in a state of activity. The volume of

FIG. 77. — A woollen shawl, one-sixth of the actual size. Found with the preceding.

---

[1] *L'Age du Bronze*, pp. 12, 380.
[2] See *Lettera del Signor D. A. Visconti sopra alcuni vasi sepolchrali rinvenuti nelle vincinanze della antica Alba-Longa*, Roma, 1867.

the *Archæologia* for 1869 contains a full account by Professor Pigorini and myself of the numerous vases and other objects found with these hut-urns. The pottery is peculiarly dark and compact, and with it were found several bronze knives. The presence of some fragments of iron, however, appears to show that the huts belong quite to the close of the Bronze Age, or rather to the commencement of that of Iron. The following figure will give an idea of the urns themselves, as well as of the houses they were intended to represent.

FIG. 78.—A pair of leggings one-third of the actual size. Found with the preceding.

These cases are not isolated. In the year 1837 Dr Beyer found near Parchim a somewhat similar hut-urn in a tumulus, which, both from its form and as containing bronze, is considered by Dr Lisch as certainly belonging to the Bronze Age.[1]

In 1849 an urn, evidently intended to represent a house with a tall straw roof, was found in a tumulus at Aschersleben. From its colour and material Dr Lisch refers this urn also to the Bronze Age.

FIG. 79.—Hut urn. Albano.

The Museum at Munich contains a very interesting piece of pottery (fig. 80), apparently intended to represent a Lake-hamlet comprising seven small round huts. The huts are arranged in three rows of three each, thus forming three sides of a square. The fourth side is closed by a wall, in the centre of which is an opening leading into a porch, which is represented as being thatched. The platform on which the huts

[1] *Ueber die Hausurnen*, Schwerin, 1856.

stand is supported by four columns represented as consisting of logs, lying one upon the other. The roofs are unfortunately wanting. The sides are ornamented with the double spiral so characteristic of the Bronze Age.

In North Germany and Denmark also urns have been discovered somewhat resembling that in fig. 79. In some cases the "door" is in the roof. Dr Lisch considers that these last urns are the earliest, and represent a form of dwelling even more ancient than those in which the door is in the side. To me, I confess, it seems more probable that these urns belong to a later period, when the representation of the dwelling was more conventional, and the resemblance consequently less.

FIG. 80.—Urn apparently representing a lake-dwelling. In the Munich collection.

Many of the dwellings in use during the Bronze Age were no doubt subterranean or semi - subterranean. On almost all large tracts of uncultivated land ancient villages of this character may still be traced. A pit was dug, generally from 6 to 16 feet in diameter, and the earth which was thrown out formed a circular wall, the whole being then probably covered over with boughs.

True hut circles, however, occur in many places. In Anglesea a group of such have been well described by the Honourable Owen Stanley.[1]

On Dartmoor and elsewhere, where large blocks of stone abounded, the natives saved themselves the trouble of excavating, and built up circular walls of stone. In other cases, perhaps when concealment was an object, or for use in severe weather, the dwellings were entirely subterranean.

[1] *On Remains of the Ancient Circular Habitations in Holyhead Island*, by the Hon. W. O. Stanley, M.P.

Such ancient dwellings are in Scotland known as
"weems," from "Uamha," a cave.   In one of these, at
Monzie, in Perthshire, a bronze sword was discovered.[1]
Such underground chambers, however, appear to have
been used in Scotland as dwellings, or at least as places
of concealment, down to the time of the Romans ; for a
weem described by Lord Rosehill [2] was constructed partly
of stones "showing the diagonal and diamond markings
peculiar to Roman workmanship."   The so-called Picts'

FIG. 81.—Beehive house, Inishmurray, Sligo.

houses, which are so common in the north of Scotland,
are but slightly, and often not at all, sunk beneath
the surface, though, being covered with earth, they are
scarcely distinguishable externally from the larger tumuli :
but on digging into the green mound, it is found to
cover a series of large chambers, built generally with
stones of considerable size and converging towards the
centre, where an opening appears to have been left for
light and ventilation.   These differ little from many of
the subterranean weems, excepting that they are erected
on the natural surface of the soil, and have been buried

---

[1] Wilson, *Pre-Historic Annals of Scotland*, vol. i. p. 104.
[2] Lord Rosehill, *Proc. of the Soc. of Ant. of Scotland*, 1869, p. 109.

by means of an artificial mound heaped over them. It may seem improbable that a people living in such rude dwellings should possess a knowledge of metallurgy, but the Kaffirs and other existing African tribes present us with a similar case.

From these we pass naturally to the beehive houses, which are constructed of dry, thick walls in the form indicated by the name.[1] No doubt many of these are very ancient, and some probably date from the Age of Stone ; but on the other hand, they also come down to the present day, and fig. 82 represents a group in Long Island, on the shore of Loch Resort, which was inhabited

Fig. 82.—Group of beehive houses, Scotland.

down to the year 1823. Even now some few beehive houses are still occupied in the Island of Uig.

The celebrated "brochs" or "burghs" which abound in the north of Scotland, as well as in the Orkneys and Shetlands, are of a very peculiar character. They have been supposed by some to be Scandinavian, but no similar buildings occur in Norway, Sweden, or Denmark.

Fig. 83 is from a photograph of the celebrated Burgh of Moussa, in the Shetlands, the best preserved specimen of this curious style of architecture. I visited this most interesting building in 1867. It stands close to the sea, on the little Island of Moussa, and may be taken as a typical specimen. Some 300 are known, almost all in the north of Scotland or on the Islands. They are all circular, about 60 feet in diameter, with walls about

[1] See Captain Thomas on Beehive Houses, *Proc. Soc. Antiq. Scotland*, vol. iii. p. 133 ; vol. vii. p. 153. See also Petrie, *Proc. Soc. Antiq. Scotland*, vol. vii. p. 201.

15 feet thick, enclosing a courtyard about 30 feet in diameter. The walls contain a staircase, which leads to the top of the building, several horizontal galleries, and some small conical chambers, all opening on the inside ; the only external orifice being the door, which is about 7 feet high.

FIG. 83.—The Burgh of Moussa, Shetland.

The absence of trees and abundance of stone probably led to this curious style of architecture. Although, moreover, so archaic in character, these burghs continued in use down to historical times, in fact until the introduction of lime, and the knowledge of the true principle of the arch enabled the natives to construct buildings of a more modern character ; they are extremely numerous in Caithness, in the Orkneys, and the Shetlands ; but this Moussa Burgh is one of the few that are mentioned in history. Torfœus tells us that about the year 1150 Erling carried off the beautiful Margaret, mother of Harold, the then Earl of Orkney, and was besieged in Moussa by Harold, who, however, being unable to take the place, at length thought it politic to consent to the marriage. By far the greater number of the burghs are mere ruins, and the so-called Dun of Dornadilla, supposed to have been erected by the ancient Scotch king of that name, is the only one which is at all as complete as that of Moussa. Whether any of the burghs are referable to the Bronze

FIG. 84.—Staigue Fort, in the county of Kerry. From a model in the collection of the Royal Irish Academy.

Age it is impossible to say. It is remarkable, however, that in the Island of Sardinia there are archaic buildings known as "nurhags," which closely resemble the British burghs.

In a future chapter I shall endeavour to show that Stonehenge and Avebury belong to the Bronze Age. Some of the ancient fortifications also probably are of this period, but a large proportion, as well as many of the earthen forts known as Raths and Duns and the stone forts known as Cashels or Cahirs, as for instance the Staigue Fort, in the county of Kerry, fig. 84, belong in all probability to a much later period. In Sligo alone there are said to be no less than 1800 forts.[1]

[1] *T. R. Irish Soc. of Ant.*, 1891.

CHAPTER III

THE BRONZE AGE

THERE have been four principal theories as to the Bronze Age. According to some archæologists, the discovery, or introduction, of bronze was (1) due to Roman influence, (2) to the Etruscans, (3) to the Phœnicians, (4) to a new and more civilized people of Indo-European race, coming from the East, who, bringing with them a knowledge of bronze, overran Europe, and dispossessed—in some places entirely destroying—the original or rather the earlier inhabitants, or, lastly, was the result of gradual and peaceable development.

The Roman theory has been dealt with, perhaps under the circumstances at almost unnecessary length, and has now no adherents.

M. Wiberg attempted to show that the Bronze Age in Northern Europe was mainly due to Etrurian merchants. Without, however, altogether denying the influence of Etrurian art, we have not any evidence that Etruria ever enjoyed so extensive a commerce as would account for the great number of bronze objects which have been found in Northern and Western Europe.

The theory which attributed the Bronze Age civilization in Northern Europe to Phœnician influence was maintained by Professor Nilsson with great ability.[1] Since he wrote, however, the evidence has convinced archæologists that the Bronze Age commenced much earlier than was supposed fifty years ago. Marseilles was only

[1] *Skandinaviska Nordens Ur-invanare*, af S. Nilsson, Stockholm, 1862. English ed., ed. by Sir John Lubbock : Longmans.

65

founded in 600 B.C. ; Carthage in 800 B.C. ; and Utica, according to Strabo and Pliny, about 300 years earlier ; and, as we shall see, the Bronze Age commenced long before these dates.

Nor is there any sufficient evidence that bronze was introduced by a new superior or conquering race, which disposed, or destroyed, the previous neolithic inhabitants.

It would seem, therefore, that the knowledge of bronze was introduced from the East, and gradually made its way over Europe.

A circumstance which strongly militates against the theory of a gradual and independent development of metallurgical knowledge in different countries, is the fact which, though perhaps somewhat too strongly stated by Mr Wright, is substantially correct, that whenever we find the bronze swords or celts, " whether in Ireland, in the far west, in Scotland, in distant Scandinavia, in Germany, or still further east in the Sclavonic countries, they are the same, not similar in character, but identical." The great resemblance to each other of stone implements found in different parts of the world may be satisfactorily accounted for by the similarity of the material, and the simplicity of the forms. But this argument cannot be applied to the bronze arms and implements. Though there are certain differences, yet several varieties of celts found throughout Europe, as well as some of the swords, knives, daggers, etc., are so similar that they seem as if they must have been cast by the same maker. Compare, for instance, figs. 4, 6, and 13, which represent Irish celts, with 14, 15, and 16, which are copied from Danish specimens ; the three swords, figs. 26, 27, and 28, which come respectively from Ireland, Sweden, and Switzerland, and the two, figs. 29 and 30, of which the first is Swiss, the second Scandinavian. It would have been easy to multiply examples of this similarity, and it is not going too far to say that these resemblances cannot be the result of accident. On the other hand, it must be admitted that each country has certain minor peculiarities. Neither the form nor the ornaments are exactly similar.

In Denmark and Mecklenburg, spiral ornaments are most common ; farther south, these are replaced by ring ornaments and lines. The Danish swords generally have solid and richly-decorated handles, as in figs. 30–36, while those found in Great Britain (fig. 26) terminate in a plate which was riveted to pieces of wood or bone. Again, the British lance-heads frequently have loops at the side of the shaft-hole, as in figs. 22, 23, and 24, which is never the case with Danish specimens.

The evidence also indicates that the use of bronze, when once discovered, spread rapidly, because we find the simplest and earliest forms scattered over the whole area, whereas if the process had been slow, the more useful and complex forms would have been developed before the use of metal reached our shores.

The impurities in the bronze indicate, as was shown in the last chapter, that the copper ore was not all derived from one locality ; and lastly, the discovery of moulds in Ireland, Scotland, England, Switzerland, Denmark, and elsewhere, proves that the art of casting in bronze was known and practised in many countries.

On the whole, then, though there is, I think, ample evidence to prove that the general use of bronze weapons and implements characterizes a well-marked epoch in history, it must also be admitted that we have still very much to learn in regard to this interesting phase in the development of European civilization, and the race by whom the knowledge of metals was introduced into our Continent.

The discoveries of bronze implements may be arranged under three heads :—

(1) Objects lost ;
(2) Objects buried with the dead ;
(3) Hoards ;

Of these three classes the third is the most important and instructive.

In Great Britain the objects found with burials are

comparatively few. In Europe, on the contrary, some of them were rich and important.

Hoards, again, may be divided into

(1) Treasures.
(2) Stocks-in-trade.

The greatest of all hoards is that discovered in 1877 by Signor Zannoni, who in excavating for a new sewer on behalf of the municipality of Bologna came across an immense vase of bronze containing no less than 14,800 objects in that metal, and 3 small pieces of iron.[1]

Chantre describes some fifty French hoards, and Evans gives a most interesting table of 110 found in Britain.

The late Sir John Evans in his masterly work on *The Bronze Age* divided it into three periods. Montelius now considers[2] that five can be satisfactorily distinguished. Types belonging to two periods are very seldom found together. Some cases, indeed, occur in which types of the first and second, or of the third and fourth periods occur together, but the first and third, or the second and fourth, are never, or scarcely ever, represented in the same find. The exceptions to this rule are very rare, which shows that the types were really successive.

Period 1

This might be termed the Copper Age, most of the metallic objects being of pure copper. Stone implements were still abundant, metal being rare. The axes of copper were simple and flat, without ridges or stops (figs. 4, 7). There were also daggers with a broad flat tang and generally without rivet holes. The objects of bronze were in fact copies of those of stone.

The metallic objects of this period consisted of—

(1) Small bronze blades.

It may be suggested that these were in many cases made specially for the use of the dead in the next world,

---

[1] Ridgeway, *Early Age of Greece*, p. 242. Miss Cameron, *Old Etruria*, p. 104.
[2] *Archæologia*, lxi. p. 97.

and that this may account for their small size and
flimsiness.

(2) Simple flat axes without flanges or a stop-ridge.

There are also rare objects of gold, amber, and jet.
The pottery belongs to the classes known as drinking-
cups (fig. 180) and food vessels (fig. 178).

Stonehenge probably belongs to this period.

Period 2

The metal characteristic of this period is a true bronze
containing often 10 per cent. of tin. Weapons and
implements of stone are much rarer. The axes are in
many cases still flat, but broader at the edge : many, however, are flanged, and the blade is not unfrequently ornamented with chevrons or spiral fluting, but there are still
none with stop-ridges or sockets. The flange is so great,
and at the same time so simple, an improvement, that
when it was once introduced it would soon supersede the
old flat blade.

The daggers are larger and often provided with bronze
rivets, and sometimes with small gold pins. There are
also halberds with the blade inserted at right angles into
the handle. Gold is more abundant, and there are some
beautiful neck ornaments or lunulæ.

Period 3

No stone weapons have been found in any burial or
any hoard belonging to this or the later periods.

The bronze axes are more elaborate, the flanges are
higher, and the edge often more expanding, sometimes
almost semilunar. Some of them have a loop, for attachment to the handle, on one or both sides. There are no
socketed axes, but on the other hand some of the daggers
have sockets, if these really belong to this period.

Several sickles have been found and may be referred
to this period.

The ornaments are richer and more elaborate. They comprise bracelets, " torques " (figs. 64, 70), and gold collars.

Some rich hoards belong to this period ; I may mention those of Grunty Fen, Cambridge ; Lovehayne, Devon ; Plymstock, Devon ; Arreton Down, Isle of Wight ; West Buckland, Somerset ; Edington Burtle, Somerset ; Hollingbury, Sussex ; Wrexham.

Period 4

The objects of bronze are again more varied and elaborate : the axes have stop-ridges and are often socketed ; the daggers are more elongated ; swords make their appearance, sometimes with bronze handles ; there are also socketed spear-heads, sometimes with loops at the side, or at the base of the blade ; torques, armlets, etc.

Period 5

Socketed and winged axes.
Socketed hammers.
Tanged chisels.
Gouges.
Socketed daggers.
Leaf-shaped swords, some with solid handles.
Trumpets.
Socketed spear-heads.
Horse-bits.
Bracelets and necklets of bronze or gold.
Razors.
Knives.

The gradual development of the axe thus shown is very interesting. Beginning with the flat simple form (figs. 4, 11), which is obviously a copy of the stone axe, we pass (2) to the form (figs. 13, 15, 17) with slight side flanges ; the next stage (3) is the addition of a stop-ridge (figs. 5, 8, 20), the next the invention of the socket, and, lastly, the addition of wings placed (figs. 6, 9, 16) near the top.

From the evidence given in Chapter I., it may be, I think, concluded that iron was beginning to be used in Britain about 1000 B.C.

As regards bronze, some articles of copper are said by M. de Morgan to have been in the tomb supposed to have been that of Menes, 4400 B.C. A bronze rod was found in the Pyramid of Mêdûm 3700 B.C.[1] The copper mines of Sinai were worked in the time of Seneferu, 3733 B.C.

Sir Arthur Evans assigns the date of 2500 B.C. to some of the copper objects from Knossos. Schliemann found copper objects in the lowest stratum of the first prehistoric city, 3000–2500 B.C. according to Dorpfeld. From Mesopotamia there is a small bronze figure bearing the name of King Gudea, 2500 B.C.,[2] and blocks of the metal were recorded by Thothmes III. as among the tribute received by him.

It is evident that none of these finds takes us back to the earliest use of copper, for they all indicate considerable knowledge and skill. We may then, I think, safely carry back the discovery of copper to about 5000 B.C.

It remains to consider how long a period we should allow for the knowledge of metal to spread from the Ægean to Great Britain.

The late Sir John Evans, in his work on the Bronze Age, estimated[3] the commencement of the Bronze Age in England at from 1400 to 1200 B.C. To quote other high authorities, Dr Sophus Müller suggests about 1200 B.C.; Abercromby, in his excellent work on Pottery, agrees with Sir J. Evans' chronology;[4] and Sir C. H. Read, 1800 B.C., "within a few centuries."[5] This, however, Evans regarded as a conservative estimate, and if he were writing now he would, I think, have carried it further back.

Though it may seem an extreme view to adopt, I am disposed to suggest that we must carry the knowledge of bronze in this country to an even more remote period. Montelius himself says[6] that "new finds will probably

---

[1] *British Museum Bronze Age Cat.*, p. 126.
[2] *British Museum Cat., Bronze Age*, p. 9.
[3] *Loc. cit.*, p. 473. [4] *Bronze Age Pottery*, p. 102.
[5] *British Museum Guide to the Bronze Age*, p. 26.
[6] *Archæologia*, lxi. p. 162.

give a still higher date for the earliest use of copper there,"
i.e. in Britain.

In the first place, I am impressed by the number of
copper and bronze objects found here and in Scandinavia,
and which seems to indicate a very long period.

Secondly, the gradual development of new forms and
ornaments must have taken very long. We can hardly,
I think, attribute less than say three hundred years to each
of Montelius' five periods.

In the third place, if the dates given for Egypt and
Greece are correct, even Montelius' earliest date assumes
that metal was used in the South two thousand years before
the knowledge reached Britain. I cannot think it could
have taken so long.

Coins were invented about 650 B.C., and our earliest
coins were struck in Kent about 200 B.C., *i.e.* after an
interval of under five hundred years.

Fourthly, the copper and early bronze objects found in
Britain belong to the earliest and simplest types. Now,
if the use of bronze had been known in Southern and
Eastern Europe two thousand years before it reached us, it
must have attained to a high stage. Our earliest specimens
would be socketed celts, leaf-shaped spear-heads, swords,
etc. As a matter of fact they are, as we have seen,
simple flat axes, evident copies of stone implements,
small bronze knife-blades, etc., evidently dating back to
quite archaic times. We cannot, then, surely allow more
than a thousand years, if so much, to have elapsed between
the discovery of copper in the East and its appearance on
our shores.

The tendency of recent researches has been to carry
back our dates, and, taking all the facts into consideration, it seems reasonable to estimate that the Bronze Age
in Northern Europe and Great Britain commenced about
2500 B.C.

CHAPTER IV

THE USE OF STONE IN ANCIENT TIMES

THE preceding chapters have been devoted to the Age of
Bronze. We must now pass on to still earlier times and
ruder races of men ; to a period which, for obvious reasons,
is called by archæologists the Stone Age.[1]

The Stone Age, however, falls naturally, as has been
already stated, into two great divisions :

First, that of the Drift, which I have proposed to
call the Palæolithic Period.

Secondly, the later Stone Age, for which I have suggested the term Neolithic, and in which the stone implements are more skilfully made, more varied in form, and
often polished. We will now consider this later period,
reserving the earlier for a subsequent chapter.

The immense number of stone implements which occur,
in all parts of the world, is sufficient evidence of the important part they played in ancient times. M. Herbst
has favoured me with the following list of the numbers
contained in the Copenhagen Museum :—

Flint axes and wedges	1070
Broad chisels	285
Hollow ditto	270
Narrow chisels	365
Hollow ditto	33

[1] For further information on the subject of this chapter, I may refer to
Sir John Evans' excellent work on *Ancient Stone Implements* ; to Sir
C. H. Read's *British Museum Guide to Stone Implements* ; and to M.
Delechette's *Archéologie Préhistorique.*

Poniard chisels	250
Lance-heads	656
Arrow-heads	171
Half-moon-shaped implements . .	205
Pierced axes and axe-hammers . .	746
Flint flakes	300
Sundries	489
	4840
Rough stone implements from the Kjök-kenmöddings	3678
Bone implements	171
Ditto from Kjökkenmöddings . .	109
	8798

These figures refer to the year 1864, and if duplicates and broken specimens were counted, M. Herbst thinks that the number would have been between 11,000 and 12,000. He has also had the kindness to estimate for me the numbers in private and provincial museums, and, on the whole, he believes we shall be within the mark if we consider that the Danish museums contain 30,000 stone implements, to which, moreover, must be added the rich stores then at Flensborg and Kiel, as well as the very numerous specimens with which the liberality of Danish archæologists has enriched other countries, for there is scarcely any important collection in Europe which does not possess some illustrations of the Danish stone implements.

The museum of the Royal Irish Academy includes (1865) 512 celts, more than 400 arrow-heads, and 50 spear-heads, besides 75 "scrapers," and numerous other objects of stone, such as flakes, slingstones, hammers, whetstones, querns, grain-crushers, etc. Again, the museum at Stockholm is estimated to contain between 15,000 and 16,000 specimens.

In addition to those cases in which large numbers of stone implements have been found on spots which were evidently the sites of dwellings or villages, there are many instances in which considerable numbers have been met with under circumstances which show that they were purposely deposited, either hidden away for future use, or perhaps, as Worsaae has maintained,[1] as offerings to the gods. Thus at Frederickville in Illinois, 3500 disks of flint were found at a depth of about five feet ranged carefully side by side ; in Ross County, Ohio, 4000 disks and pointed instruments of stone were found near some ancient mounds known as Clark's Work.

Yet the very existence of a Stone Age has till lately been denied by some eminent archæologists. Thus, Mr Wright, the learned Secretary of the Ethnological Society, while admitting that " there may have been a period when society was in so barbarous a state that sticks or stones were the only implements with which men knew how to furnish themselves," doubted "if the antiquary has yet found any evidence of such a period."

If we consider the difficulties of mining in early days, the rude implements with which men had then to work, their ignorance of the many ingenious methods by which the operations of modern miners are so much facilitated, and, finally, the difficulties of carriage either by land or water, it is obvious that bronze implements must always have been very expensive.

In addition, moreover, to the *a priori* probability, there is plenty of direct evidence that bronze and stone were in use at the same time. Thus Mr Bateman records thirty-seven instances of tumuli which contained objects of bronze, and in no less than twenty-nine of these stone implements also were found. At the time of the discovery of America, the Mexicans, though well acquainted with the use of bronze, still used flakes of obsidian for knives and razors, and even after the introduction of *iron*, stone was still used for various purposes.

There can no longer, however, be any doubt not only that there was a period " when society was in so barbarous a state that sticks or stones " (to which we must add horns

[1] *Mat. p. Serv.* 1882, p. 131.

and bones) " were the only implements with which men knew how to furnish themselves," but also that the antiquary has found " clear evidence of such a period."

Moreover, as already mentioned, the Stone Age falls into two distinct periods, the óldest of which, or Palæolithic, will be dealt with in subsequent chapters.

So far as the Neolithic, or more recent Stone Age, is concerned, our knowledge is derived principally from four sources, to the consideration of which I propose to devote four separate chapters : namely, the Tumuli, or ancient burial-mounds ; the lake-habitations of Switzerland ; the Kjökkenmöddings, or shell-mounds, of Denmark ; and the Bone-caves. There are, indeed, many other remains of great interest, such, for example, as the ancient fortifications, the " castles " and " camps " which crown so many of our hill-tops ; and the great lines of embankment, which cross so many of our uplands, such as Offa's Dyke and the Wans Dyke ; there are the so-called Druidical circles and the vestiges of ancient habitations ; the " Hut-circles," " Cloghauns," " Weems," " Pen-pits," " Picts' houses," etc. The majority of these belong, however, in all probability, and many of them certainly, to a later period ; and in the present state of our knowledge, we cannot say which, or how many, are referable to the Stone Age.

Flint was the material most commonly used, but every kind of stone, hard and tough enough for the purpose, was utilized during the Stone Age in the manufacture of implements. The magnificent collection of celts at Dublin has been specially studied, from a mineralogical point of view, by the Rev. S. Haughton, and the results are thus recorded by Wilde :[1]

" Of the better qualities of rock suited for celt-making, the type of the felspathic extreme of the series of trap rocks is the pure felstone, or petrosilex, . . . of a pale blueish or greyish green, except where the surface has been acted upon, and the average composition of which is 25 parts quartz and 75 felspar. Its physical characters

[1] *Catalogue of the Royal Irish Academy*, p. 72.

are absence of toughness, and the existence of a splintery conchoidal fracture almost as sharp as that of flint. . . . At the hornblendic extreme of the trap rocks we find the basalt, of which also celts were made ; tough and heavy, the siliceous varieties having a splintery fracture, but never affording so cutting an edge as the former. . . . Intermediate in character between these two rocks we find all the varieties of felstone, slate, and porphyry streaked with hornblende, from which the great majority of the foregoing implements have been made."

It is very remarkable how carefully the best kinds of stone were selected, even when very rare. Of this the most interesting example is afforded by the axes, etc., of jade or nephrite, of jadeite and of saussurite. These minerals are very distinct chemically, but so similar in appearance that they can only be distinguished by analysis. Objects made from them, though far from common, are not very rare. M. Fischer gives the following table :—

	France.	Germany.	Switzerland.
Jade or nephrite	0	3	1118
Jadeite	77	46	138
Chloromelanite	53	17	66

Till 1884, no European locality of jade or nephrite was known, and though it has now been discovered in Silesia, and some few other places, they are very rare, and have not been found anywhere near Brittany.

Beads of Baltic amber are scattered over Central Europe. The same may be said of obsidian, for which there are only one or two sources. Another interesting case is afforded by the Pressigny flint implements (see page 81).

Again, beads of Callais, another mineral not known to occur in Europe, have been found in the tumuli of Brittany and some other parts of France.

Other facts of a similar nature are on record. Thus Messrs Squier and Davis tell us that in the tumuli of the Mississippi valley we find "side by side, in the same mounds, native copper from Lake Superior, mica from

the Alleghanies, shells from the Gulf, and obsidian
(perhaps porphyry) from Mexico." Fair representations
of the sea-cow or manatee are found a thousand miles
from the shores inhabited by that animal, and shells of
the large tropical *Pyrula perversa* are met with in the
tumuli round the great lakes, two thousand miles from
home.

In Central America thousands of jadeite implements
occur, but no locality for native jadeite has yet been
discovered.[1]

On the whole, however, flint was the stone most
frequently used in Europe ; and it has had a much more
important influence on our civilization than is generally
supposed. Savages value it on account of its hardness
and mode of fracture, which is such that, with practice, a
good sound block can be chipped into almost any form
that may be required.

In many cases, blocks and pebbles of flint, picked up
on the surface of the ground, were used in the manufacture of implements ; but in others much labour was
spent in obtaining flint of good quality. A good
illustration of this is afforded by the so-called Grimes'
Graves, near Brandon, which have, by the kind permission of Mr Angerstein, been explored by Canon
Greenwell ;[2] who has shown them to be excavations made
in the chalk for the purpose of obtaining flint. They are
254 in number, varying in diameter from 20 to 60 feet,
placed irregularly, generally about 25 feet apart, and
occupying rather more than 20 acres. They have been
filled up, and are now indicated by shallow depressions,
but Canon Greenwell has proved that the pits originally
went down to a depth of about 40 feet, when they branch
out into passages, often communicating with one another.
On the east side is a mound, apparently consisting of
chalk taken from the first pit ; after which it would seem
that when a new pit was dug, most of the material was
thrown down the old shafts, which were thus filled in, to

---

[1] Wilson, *Prehistoric Art*, Smithsonian Institution, 1898, p. 459.
[2] *Trans. Ethn. Soc.*, 1870, p. 419.

within a few feet of the surface. As usual in the Upper Chalk, the flint is disposed in layers, which differ in quality, while maintaining the same character over considerable areas. It may be remarked that, as Sir W. Fowler has well pointed out,[1] Brandon, "though situated in a bleak and barren district, has evidently been a place of considerable resort from a very remote period—a circumstance which can only be attributed to the abundance and good quality of the flint found there." Palæolithic implements abound in the drift gravels ; the surface is strewn with flint flakes and fragments of flint implements, and at the present time it is the only place in England where gun-flints are still made. For this purpose, one particular layer of flint is found to be peculiarly well adapted, on account of its hardness and fineness of grain, while another layer, less suitable for gun-flints, is known as " wall-stone," being much used for building purposes. Now it is interesting to find that, even in very early times, the merits of the gun-flint layer were well known and appreciated ; for although there is abundance of flint on the surface, the ancient flint-men sank their shafts down past the layer of " wall-stone," which occurs at a depth of $19\frac{1}{2}$ feet, to the gun-flint layer, which at the spot in question is 39 feet deep, although about a mile to the south-west, where it is now worked, it is much nearer the surface.

At present the workmen excavate the chalk both above and below the layer of flint ; but in the old galleries, perhaps from the greater difficulty of raising the material, the chalk below the flint-bed was in no case removed. The implements used in making these excavations were deers' horns ; the brow tine being used as a pick, and the others removed. Thus treated, a deer's horn closely resembles in form a modern pick, but of course it is subject to rapid wear by use, which accounts for the large numbers of worn-out implements found by Canon Greenwell among the rubbish.

In one case the roof of a passage had given way. On

[1] *Trans. Ethn. Soc.*, 1870, p. 437.

removing the chalk which had fallen in, the end of the gallery came in view. The flint had been hollowed out in three places, and in front of two of these recesses, pointing towards the half-excavated stone, were two deer-horn picks, lying just as they had been left, still coated with chalk dust, on which was in one place plainly visible the print of the workman's hand. The tools had evidently been left at the close of a day's work ; during the night the gallery had fallen in, and they had never been recovered.

" It was a most impressive sight," says Canon Green-well, " and one never to be forgotten, to look, after a lapse, it may be, of three thousand years, upon a piece of work unfinished, with the tools of the workmen still lying where they had been placed so many centuries ago."

Deer-horn picks have been found in other localities, where chalk has been worked for flint, and also in the Cornish Tin Stream Works.[1] Near Spiennes also, in Belgium, there are extensive workings, consisting of a system of shafts and galleries, very like those of Grimes' Graves. These have been described by MM. Malaise, Briart, Cornet, and Houzeau de Lehaie.[2] Many tools of deers' horns have been obtained, but they are of a very different character, having been apparently used as hammers, the horn being cut off just above the brow tine, which served as a handle.

In addition to the deer-horn picks, a few adze-shaped tools of flint have been discovered in Grimes' Graves, and a basalt hatchet, in form resembling that represented in fig. 106, but with an oblique cutting edge, the marks of which were distinctly seen upon the sides of the gallery, showing that it had been used in excavating the chalk.

As already mentioned, it was important, in the manu-facture of flint implements, to have the flint of a good quality, free from cracks and flaws, and easily accessible. Hence, places which fulfilled these conditions were

---

[1] See, for instance, *Rep. of the Roy. Inst. of Cornwall*, 1871, p. xxii.
[2] *Mém. de la Soc. des Sciences, des Arts, etc., du Hainaut*, 1866-7.

specially frequented in ancient times, and whole districts
were supplied from these
favoured localities. One
of the most remarkable of
these manufactories is that
discovered by Dr Leveillé
at Pressigny-le-Grand, in
France, about half-way between Tours and Poitiers.
Here there is an abundance
of good flint of a honey
colour, and of even, though
coarse, texture. This flint
was largely used in ancient
times : the fields are covered
with nuclei, flakes, etc. ; and
implements made here, and
easily recognizable by the
peculiar colour, have been
found in various parts of
France, and even, it would
seem, in Belgium. I have
in my collection a block of
Pressigny flint, from which
a flake more than 12 inches
in length has been struck.
The large nuclei of this
form (fig. 85), which from
their shape are known as
"livres de beurre," have
excited a good deal of discussion. They are generally
from 8 to 13 inches in
length, shaped more or less
like a boat, with a broad
butt at one end, tapering
gradually to the other. The
form has been attained by

FIG. 85.—Nucleus from which long flakes
have been struck in Pressigny, France.
In my own collection. One-half actual
size.

a succession of lateral chips, at right angles to the longer axis, while generally one or more longitudinal flakes have also been removed.

Many of the flint flakes were certainly never intended

Fig. 86.—Flint core or nucleus, from which flakes have been struck, Jutland. One-half of the actual size. In my own collection.

Figs. 87, 88, 89.—Three views of a flint flake from the Kjökkenmödding at Fannerup, in Jutland, one-half of the actual size. *a* represents the bulb of percussion, which is also shown by the shading in fig. 87. In my own collection.

to serve as knives, but were worked up into saws, awls, or arrowheads. Savages use flint or chert in this manner, even at the present day ; and the Mexicans, in the time of Cortez, used precisely similar fragments of obsidian.

The operations of modern gun-flint makers give us a very clear insight into the mode of manufacture of ancient flint implements, and the process is one of considerable interest.

If we take a rounded hammer, and with it strike on a flat surface of flint, a conoidal fracture is produced, the size of which depends, in a great measure, on the form of the hammer. The surface of fracture is propagated downwards through the flint, in a diverging direction, and thus embraces a cone, the apex of which is at the point struck by the hammer, and which can afterwards be chipped out of the mass. Flint cones, formed in this way, may sometimes be found among heaps of stones broken up to mend the roads, and have doubtless often been mistaken for casts of fossil shells.

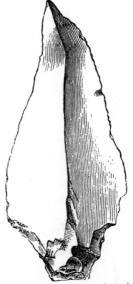

FIG. 90. — Arrow - shaped flake from Ireland. It is worked up at the butt end, as if intended for a handle.

If a blow is given, not on a flat surface, but at the angle of a more or less square flint, the fracture is at first semiconoidal or nearly so, but after expanding for a short distance, it becomes flat, and may be propagated through a length of as much as 13 inches, thus forming a blade-like flake (figs. 86-94), with a triangular cross section (fig. 95).

The consequence is, that a perfect flint flake will always have a small bulb, or projection (fig. 88, *a*), at the butt end, on the flat side ; this has been called the bulb, or cone, of percussion. After the four original angles of a square block have been thus flaked off, the eight new angles may be treated in a similar manner, and so on. Fig. 86 represents a block, or core, from which flakes have been struck off. A very long flake in my collection, from Fannerup in Jutland, is figured,

one-half of the natural size, in figs. 87-89. The bulb
is shown in figs. 88, *a*, and 89, and the flake has been
worked into a point at the end. The largest flake I am
acquainted with is described by M. de Caneto, in the
Revue de Gascoyne, for 1865. It was found in the
commune of Pauilhaic, and is 13½ inches in length.
Fig. 90 is an arrow-shaped flake, chipped away at the
base, apparently to adapt it to a handle or shaft.

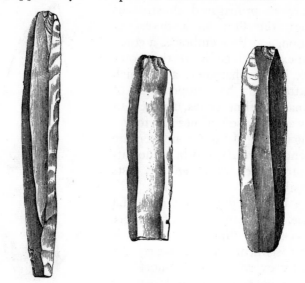

FIGS. 91, 92, 93.—Flakes from a Danish shell-mound, actual size.
In my own collection.

Figs. 91–94 represent small Danish flakes: forms
exactly similar may be found in any country where the
ancient inhabitants could obtain flint or obsidian. In
fig. 91 we see that another flake had been previously
taken from the same block. Figs. 91, 92 represent
flakes of which the points have been broken off, but we
see along their whole length the depression caused by
the previous removal of other flakes. The section of
such a flake is, therefore, not triangular, as in fig. 95, *a*,
but four-sided, as in fig. 95, *b*. Sometimes, though not
often, a wide flake is taken off in such a way as to over-

lap two previous flakes, as in the case of the one represented in fig. 94. In this instance, the section is
pentagonal ; the flat under-surface remaining always the
same, but the upper side showing four facets.

Easy as it may seem to make such flakes as these,
a little practice will convince anyone who attempts to do
so, that a certain knack is required ; and
a gun-flint maker at Brandon told me
that it took him two years to acquire the
art. It is also necessary to be careful in
selecting the flint. It is therefore evident
that these flakes, simple as they may
appear, are always the work of man.
To make one, the flint must be held
firmly, and then a considerable force
must be applied, either by pressure or
by blows, repeated three or four times, but at least
three, and given in certain slightly different directions,
with a certain definite force ; conditions which could
scarcely occur by accident ; so that a flint flake, simple as
it may seem to the untrained eye, is to the antiquary as

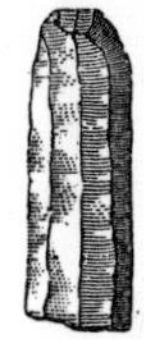

FIG. 94. — Minute
flint flake from
Denmark, actual
size. In my own
collection.

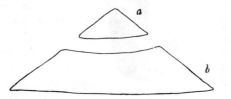

FIG. 95.—Sections of flakes. *a* is that of a simple triangular flake ; *b* is that of a
large flat flake split off the angle from which the smaller flake *a* had
been previously taken. Consequently the section is four-sided.

sure a trace of man as the footprint in the sand was to
Robinson Crusoe.

It is hardly necessary to say that flakes have a sharp
cutting edge on each side, and might therefore be at once
used as knives, as in fig. 96, which represents a North
American two-bladed knife : they are indeed so named by
some archæologists ; but it seems to me more convenient
to call them simply flakes, and to confine the name of

knife to implements more especially intended and adapted for cutting purposes. Fig. 98 represents an Australian flake, and fig. 97, one from the Cape of Good Hope. Figs. 101 and 102 represent a New Caledonian javelin, with an obsidian flake (fig. 101) for a head.

I give for comparison with the New Caledonian javelin a figure (fig. 99) of an Irish flake which I found some years ago on the shore of Loch Neagh, in Ireland. It will be seen that both are flat on one side, convex on the other, triangular in section, broad at the base, pointed at the tip, chipped up at the base so that they may be tied on to the shaft, and trimmed on one side near the tip, no doubt that they might fly straight.

Some of the old Spanish writers in Mexico give us a description of the manner in which the Aztecs obtained their obsidian flakes. Torquemada,[1] who is confirmed by Hernandez, tells us — I quote from Mr Tylor's *Anahuac*—" they had, and still have, workmen who make knives of a certain block stone or flint (obsidian), in this manner: one of these Indian workmen sits down upon the ground, and takes a piece of this black stone, which is like jet, and as hard as flint. . . . The piece they take is

Fig. 96. — North American two-bladed knife, made of two flakes.

Fig. 97.—Flake from the Cape of Good Hope, actual size. In my own collection.

Section

[1] Torquemada, *Monarquia Indiana*, Seville, 1615.

about eight inches long, or rather more, and as thick as one's leg, or rather less, and cylindrical ; they have a stick as large as the shaft of a lance, and three cubits or rather more in length, and at the end of it they fasten firmly another piece of wood, eight inches long, to give more weight to this part ;

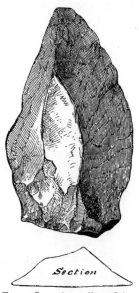

then pressing their naked feet together, they hold the stone as with a pair of pincers, or the vice of a carpenter's bench. They take the stick (which is cut off smooth at the end) with both hands, and set it well home against the edge

FIG. 98. — Australian flake. In my own collection. Actual size.

of the front of the stone, which also is cut smooth in that part ; and then they press it against their breast, and with the force of the pressure there flies off a knife, with its point and edge on one side, as neatly as if one were to make them of a turnip with a sharp knife, or of iron in the fire."

FIG. 99.—Flint flake from Loch Neagh, Ireland. In my own collection.

Thus it appears that the obsidian flakes were made, not by blows, but by strong pressure ; and the same is the case with the chert implements of the Esquimaux, according to the description given by Sir E. Belcher.[1] "Selecting," he says, "a log of wood in which a spoon-shaped cavity

[1] *Trans. of the Ethnological Soc.*, New Series, vol. i. p. 138.

B   C

was cut, they placed the splinter to be worked over it, and by pressing gently along the margin vertically, first on one side, then the other, as one would set a saw, they splintered off alternate fragments, until the object, thus properly out-

lined, presented the spear or arrow-head form, with two cutting serrated sides." A very similar account is also given by Lieutenant Beckwith of the method used by the North American Indians ;[1] among whom certain men devoted themselves specially to the manufacture of arrow-heads.[2]

Many of the ruder flint flakes were, no doubt, as Sir John Evans has suggested, used for strike o' lights.

Next to flint flakes, the axes, wedges, or celts are, perhaps, of most importance.

FIG. 100. — Polished stone gouge. Bergen Museum.

The largest and finest specimens are found in Denmark; one in my possession, of beautiful white flint, is 13 in. long, $1\frac{1}{2}$ in. thick, and $3\frac{1}{2}$ in. in breadth. The Seeland axes have very often, indeed generally, perpendicular sides ; in Jutland many have sloping sides ; this is also usually the case in other parts of North-Western Europe. Fig. 103, and a very large

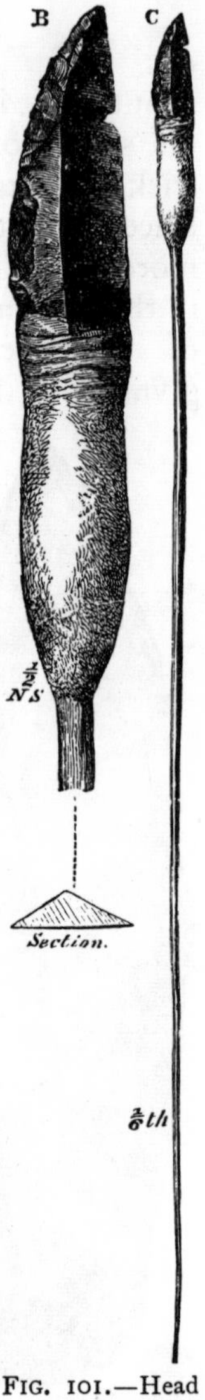

$\frac{2}{3}$ N.S.

Section.

$\frac{5}{6}$th

FIG. 101.—Head of New Caledonian javelin, one-half of actual size. In my own collection.

FIG. 102. — New Caledonian javelin, one-sixth actual size. In my own collection.

[1] *Report of the Explorations and Surveys of the Pacific Railroad,* 1855, vol. ii. p. 43.
[2] Bancroft, *Native Races of the Pacific States,* vol. i. p. 342.

specimen in fig. 104 was found in the same tumulus as the very fine stone chisel (fig. 105). The common Danish axe or wedge is figured in fig. 103. Figs. 106 and 107 represent forms which, though rare in Seeland, are common in other parts of Europe. Those found in Denmark are sometimes polished, but almost, if not quite as often, left rough. On the contrary, in other parts of North - Western Europe, the axes are usually ground to a more or less smooth surface. That some were held in the hand is evident, but that others were fixed in wooden handles is equally clear, in many specimens, from the presence of peculiar polished spaces, which have been produced by the friction of the wood. In almost all cases, the wooden handle has long perished, but there are one or two instances on record in which it has been preserved. Fig. 108 represents a stone hatchet, found some years ago, in the county of Monaghan; the handle was of pine, and was 13½ in. long. A somewhat similar specimen, found in Solway Moor, is preserved in the British Museum.

Fig. 109 represents another stone axe in its handle; this specimen was found at Concise,

FIG. 103.—Danish flint axe. In my own collection. One-third actual size.

on the Lake of Neufchâtel, and closely resembles the modern African axe (fig. 19). In the latter case, however, the blade is of iron. It will be observed that the Swiss specimen differs from the other two in having an intermediate piece of horn. These horn sockets are very numerous in some of the Swiss lake-villages.

To us, accustomed as we are to the use of metals, it seems difficult to believe that such rude implements were ever made use of ; we know, however, that many savages of the present day have no better tools. Yet, with axes such as these, generally with the assistance of fire, they will cut down large trees, and hollow them out into canoes. The piles used in the Swiss Stone Age lake-habitations were evidently, from the marks of the cuts on them, prepared with the help

Fig. 105.—Danish chisel. In my own collection. One-half actual size.

of stone axes ; and in Danish peat-bogs, several trees have been found with the marks of stone axes, and of fire, upon them, and in one or two

Fig. 104. — Danish flint axe. In my own collection. One-third actual size.

cases, stone celts have even been found lying at the side. In the excavations known as Grimes' Graves, again, as already mentioned (*ante*, p. 80), a basalt hatchet was found, which had evidently been used for excavating the gallery, as shown by the marks still distinctly visible on the walls.

One use of the North American tomahawk was to crush bones for the sake of the marrow ;[1] and no doubt the ancient stone implements also served the same purpose.

In many cases the axes themselves bear unmistakable marks of

FIG. 106.—Stone celt or hatchet. Formed of felstone, $5\frac{3}{4}$ inches long and 2 broad.

FIG. 107.—Stone celt or hatchet, actual size. Found in the riverShannon. One of the smallest yet found in Ireland.

FIG. 108.—Stone celt with a wooden handle, Monaghan, Ireland.

long continued use. For instance, the specimen represented in figs. 110, 111, has no doubt once been much longer, and had surfaces consisting of one continuous sweep. The edge, however, having been destroyed by use, it was again chipped sharp and repolished, the new surface meeting the old one at *a*. A second time the

[1] James' *Expedition to the Rocky Mountains*, vol. i. p. 193.

edge became destroyed, and the owner, as may be seen in fig. 111, has commenced the formation of a new one.

That they were also weapons of war is probable, not only on *a priori* grounds, but also because they have frequently been found in the graves of chiefs, associated with bronze daggers. About the year 1809, a large cairn in Kirkcudbrightshire, popularly supposed to be the tomb of a King Aldus M'Galdus, was removed by a farmer. "When the cairn had been removed, the workmen came to a stone coffin of very rude workmanship, and on removing the lid, they found the skeleton of a man of uncommon size. The bones were in such a state of decomposition that the ribs and vertebræ crumbled into dust on attempting to lift them. The remaining bones, being less decayed, were taken out, when it was discovered that one of the arms had been almost separated from the shoulder by the stroke of a stone axe, and that a fragment of the axe still remained in the bone. The axe was of greenstone, a material which does not occur in that part of Scotland. There were also found with this skeleton a ball of flint, about three inches in diameter, which was perfectly round and highly polished, and the head of an arrow, also flint, but not a particle of any metallic substance."[1]

FIG. 109.—Stone celt with wooden handle, one-third actual size. Found at Concise. From Desor.

We know also the North American stone axe or tomahawk served not merely as an implement, but also as a

---

[1] *New Statist. Acc., Kirkcudbrightshire*, vol. iv. p. 332. Quoted by Wilson, *Prehist. Ann. of Scotland*, 2nd edit., vol. i. p. 187.

weapon, being used both in the hand and also as a missile.[1]

Another class of stone hatchets are those which are pierced for the handle. From the nature of flint these were scarcely ever made of that material. There are, however, in Copenhagen, two such hatchets, in which advantage has been ingeniously taken of a natural hole in the flint. In many kinds of hard stone, however, it is

FIGS. 110, 111.—Danish axe, re-ground.   One-half actual size.
From my own collection.

quite possible to drill a hole by means of a cylinder of bone or horn, with a little sand and water ; yet it is very doubtful whether this class of implements truly belong to the Stone Age. The pierced axes are generally found in graves of the Bronze Period, and it is most probable that this mode of attaching the handle was used very rarely, if at all, until the discovery of metal had rendered the process more easy than could have been the case previously.

The "scrapers" (figs. 112, 113) are oblong stones

[1] Colden's *History of the Five Nations*, vol. i. p. 10.

rounded at one end, which is brought to a bevelled edge by a series of small blows. One side is flat, the other, or outer, one is more or less convex; sometimes they have a short handle, which gives them very much the appearance of a spoon. They have been found in England, France, Denmark, Ireland, Switzerland, and

FIG. 112.—Skin-scraper from Bourdeilles in the south of France, actual size. Found by me.

FIG. 113.—Ditto, under side.

other countries. They vary from one to four inches in length, and from half an inch to two inches in breadth. An Esquimaux scraper used in preparing skins is represented in figs. 114–116. These modern specimens are of exactly the same form as the old ones.

It is curious, that while these spoon-shaped scrapers are so common in Europe, they are very rare, if indeed they occur at all, in North America south of the Esquimaux region.

To the small, triangular "axes" (figs. 117–119), which are very characteristic of the Kjökkenmöddings, as well as of the coast-finds, I have applied the name by which they are usually known, but without wishing to prejudge the question as to their purpose. They are flat on one side, and more or less convex on the other ; rudely triangular or quadrangular in shape, with the cutting edge at the broader end ; and from $2\frac{1}{2}$ in. to $5\frac{1}{2}$ in. in length, with a breadth of $1\frac{1}{2}$ in. to $2\frac{1}{2}$ in. They are never ground, and the cutting edge, though not

FIGS. 114, 115. 116.—Skin-scraper used by the modern Esquimaux of the Polar basin, within Behring's Straits, actual size. It was fastened into a handle of fossil ivory. In the Christy Museum.

sharp, is very strong, as it is formed by a plane, meeting the flat side at a very obtuse angle. Professor Steenstrup doubts whether these curious and peculiar implements were ever intended for axes and regards them as having been, in all probability, mere weights for fishing-lines, in support of which view he figures some not, perhaps, very dissimilar stone objects, used for that purpose by the Esquimaux. The so-called edge, in his opinion, neither has nor could have been used for cutting, but is merely the result of that form which was found by the fishermen to be most convenient. He also calls attention to the polished facets on their surfaces, which he regards as affording strong support to his opinion.

It must be at once admitted that there are some of these "axes" which could never have been used for cutting, but these may be regarded as imperfect, and are certainly not to be taken as normal specimens. It is true that the two surfaces, constituting the edge, form a very obtuse angle with one another, but we must remember that if this detracts from the sharpness, it adds greatly to the strength. Moreover, the angle is almost exactly the

FIG. 117.—Flint axe from the shell-mound at Meilgaard, in Jutland, actual size. Upper surface.

FIG. 118.—Ditto, under surface.

FIG. 119.—Ditto, side view.

same as that which we find in the adze of the New Zealanders and other South Sea Islanders. Figs. 120–122 represent a recent adze, brought by the Rev. R. Taylor from New Zealand, and now in the British Museum, which very closely resembles the typical axes of the Kjökken-möddings. The edge, indeed, is polished, but is after all not smoother than the natural fracture of the flint. The projection on the under side of the Danish specimen (fig. 119) is accidental, and due to some peculiarity in the flint. This face is usually as flat in the Danish specimens

as in those from New Zealand. Axes of the same type
have been found by General Pitt Rivers in Wiltshire ;
they also occur in France, Egypt, and in the shell-mounds
of Japan.

The *chisels* (fig. 105) resemble the Danish axes in
having perpendicular sides, but they are narrower, and
are almost always ground to a smooth surface. Many of
them are slightly hollowed on one side, as in fig. 123.

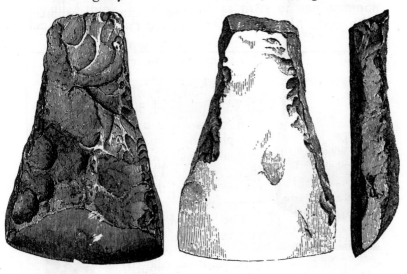

FIG. 120.—Modern New Zealand adze,   FIG. 121.—Ditto, under surface.   FIG. 122.—
actual size. Upper surface. In the   Ditto, side
British Museum.   view.

Certain flat, semicircular flint instruments are common
in Denmark and Scandinavia, but (with one exception)
rarely, if ever, found elsewhere. The convex edge was
fastened into a handle of wood, the marks of which are
still, in many cases, plainly visible. The other edge,
which is either straight or concave, is generally provided
with a number of teeth, giving it more or less resemblance
to a saw. In some cases it is so much worn away by
use, that the implement takes the form of a new moon
or of a boomerang. The edge is in many cases quite
polished, evidently by continuous friction against a soft

7

substance. I say a soft substance, because the polished part overlaps on both sides, and passes in between the teeth of the saw, which would not have been otherwise the case. It is probable that the semi-lunar instruments were fixed in wooden handles, and then used in cleaning skins. Similarly-shaped instruments are even now used as knives by the Esquimaux women, under the name of Ooloos. It might be convenient to apply this term to the ancient Danish specimens.

FIG. 123.—Hollow chisel from Denmark. In my own collection.

The so-called "awls" are rude pieces of flint, or flakes worked up at one place by a number of small chips to a point (fig. 195). Though not very sharp, they are pretty strong.

The *spear-heads* are very variable in size and form ; some of them are scarcely distinguishable from large arrow-heads ; others are much larger. Some are so rude that it is questionable whether they were finished, while others are marvellous specimens of ancient art. One in my possession is 12 in. in length, 1½ in. in breadth, and of wonderfully beautiful workmanship. It is one of six, found together in the chamber of a large tumulus in the island of Moen.

FIG. 124. — Flint dagger in the State Museum, Stockholm.

The *daggers* (figs. 124-128) are often marvels of skill in flint-chipping. The form so closely resembles that of metallic daggers, that some antiquaries are inclined to regard them as copies of bronze daggers, and therefore as not belonging to the Stone Age. The

localities in which they have been found do not, however, offer any support to this hypothesis. Another form
of flint weapon (fig. 129), which is common in Denmark, has a handle like that of the last form, but instead

of a blade, it ends in a point, and suggests the idea that if the tip of the
dagger had been accident-
ally broken off, or the
blade rendered narrow by
wear and tear, the rest of
the weapon might have
been worked up into a
poniard, and thus utilized.
In both these classes the
crimping along the edges
of the handle is very
curious.

The *sling-stones* are of
two kinds. The first are
merely rough pieces of
flint reduced by a few
blows of a hammer to a
convenient size and form.
But for the situations in
which they are found,
these might almost be re-
garded as natural frag-
ments. Professor Steen-
strup is now disposed to
think that many of them
were used as sink-stones
for nets, but that some

FIG. 126. — Flint
dagger in the
State Museum,
Stockholm.

FIG. 125. — Flint
dagger in the State
Museum, Stock-
holm.

have really served as sling-stones seems
to be indicated by their presence in the
Peat-mosses, which it is difficult to account for in any
other way. The other kind of sling-stones are round,
flattish flint disks, some of which are beautifully made.

The *oval tool-stones* (fig. 130), or " Tilhuggersteens " of
the northern antiquaries, are oval or egg-shaped stones,

more or less indented on one or both surfaces. Their use is not at present thoroughly understood.

Some antiquaries suppose that they were held between the finger and thumb, and used as hammers or chippers. If, however, a large series is obtained, it will be found that the depression varies greatly in depth, and that sometimes the stone is completely perforated, which favours the view of those who regard these implements as ring-stones for nets, or small hammer-heads. It is very doubtful whether these implements really belong to the Stone Age.

Other stones, in which the longer axis is encircled by a groove, appear to have been evidently intended as sink-stones for nets.

FIG. 127.—Danish dagger. In my own collection.

The *arrow-heads* may be divided into six varieties. Firstly, the *triangular* (fig. 131), which frequently had a notch on each side

FIG. 128.—Flint dagger, one-half of the actual size. This beautiful specimen was found in a large tumulus with a second imperfect dagger, a rude flint core, an imperfect crescent-shaped knife, one or two flakes, two amber beads, and some bits of pottery. Denmark. In my own collection.

to receive the string which attached it to the shaft ; secondly, that which is hollowed out or *indented* at the base, as in fig. 132 ; thirdly, the *stemmed* arrow, which has a tang or projection for sinking into the shaft ; fourthly, when the wings are prolonged on each side, this passes into the *barbed* arrow (fig. 133) ; fifthly, we have the *leaf-shaped* form, a beautiful example of which is represented in fig. 134. Lastly, there is a form resembling figs. 117–119, but in miniature. This form is not confined to Northern Europe, but occurs elsewhere, as for instance in Egypt, where one, still fixed to the shaft, has been discovered in a tomb.[1] True arrow-heads are generally about an inch in length, but they pass gradually into the javelin, and from that into the spear-head. The great similarity of arrow-heads, even from the most distant localities, may be seen in figs. 135, 136, and 137, which represent specimens from France, North America, and Tierra del Fuego respectively.

FIG. 130.—Oval tool-stone.

FIG. 131.—Triangular flint arrow-head, actual size.

FIG. 129. — Another form of flint dagger. Also from Denmark. In my own collection.

The different forms were perhaps in use in different tribes, but more probably they are due to the variety of purposes for which they were intended ; thus in North America the war arrows taper to the end, so that when the shaft is drawn out, the head remains in the wound ; while hunting arrows are expanded at

[1] Baye, *Pointes de flèche en Silex*, p. 139, 1874.

the end, so that the head is drawn out with the shaft. The Bygas, an aboriginal tribe of Central India, according to Forsyth, make the same distinction.[1]

FIG. 132.—Indented flint arrow - head, actual size.

Among other tribes, the lance-shaped arrows are used in hunting, barbed arrow-heads in war.[2] The Negritos of the Philippine Islands have three kinds of arrows. One, with a separate head-piece, for wild boars, one for birds. The use of the third is not stated. Every man carries one of each kind.[3] The manufacture of these arrows requires much time and skill : "Under the most favourable circum-

FIG. 133.—Barbed flint arrow-head, actual size.

stances," Messrs Blackmore and Dodge tell us, " the most skilful Indian work-man cannot hope to complete more than a single arrow in a hard day's work."[4]

There are various other kinds of flint im-plements such as ham-mers, saws (fig. 138), harpoons, etc., but— omitting for the pre-sent the earlier, or drift types—the above are the principal forms of stone weapons and implements.

FIG. 135.--French arrow-head, ac-tual size. In my own collection.

FIG. 134. — Leaf-shaped flint arrow-head, actual size. Showing the gradual passage into the spear-head.

Horns and bones, besides being em-ployed for handling the stone axes, were much used as the material of vari-ous simple implements, and those of the stag appear to

---

[1] *Highlands of Central India*, p. 361.
[2] Murray, *Travels in North America*, vòl. i. p. 385.
[3] Schadenberg, *Z. f. Ethn.*, 1880.
[4] *Hunting Grounds of the Great West*, Dodge and Blackmore, p. 349.

have been preferred, as being the hardest. The commonest
bone implement is the pin or awl (fig. 139) ; not much

less numerous are certain oblong chisel-
like implements (fig. 140), the use of which
it is not easy to determine. Ribs split
open, and pointed at one end, are sometimes found, and have been supposed by
some archæologists to have been used in
the manufacture of pottery ; others refer
them to a later period, and
think they were used in
preparing flax. Fish were
caught with bone harpoons
(figs. 141, 142). The latter
figure represents a bone
harpoon belonging to the
Reindeer Period, which will

FIG. 137.—Fuegian
arrow-head, ac-
tual size.

FIG. 136.—North-
American arrow-
head, actual size.
In my own col-
lection.

be described in the chapter on Caves.
Arrow-heads, spear-heads, and chisels,
also occur. Fig. 143 represents a North
American bone chisel used in dressing deer-
skins for taking off the hair. Pierced teeth
also were not unfrequently worn as amulets. Fragments of tissue made of flax have been met with in
some of the Swiss lake-dwell-
ings. Wool may also have
been used, and no doubt the
skins of animals.

Stone implements are fre-
quently found on the surface
of the ground, or are dug
up in agricultural and other

FIG. 138. — Stone saw in wooden
handle, Switzerland, one-half actual
size.

operations. But those found singly in this manner have
comparatively little scientific value : it is when they
occur in considerable numbers, and especially when
associated with other remains, that they serve to throw
much light on the manners and customs of ancient times.
As already mentioned, the tumuli, the lake habitations,
and the shell-mounds are specially valuable in this

respect, but I must also say a few words about the
" coast-finds " of the Danish antiquaries. " Coast-finds "

are discoveries of rude flint inplements,
which are found lying in large numbers
on certain spots along the whole line of
coast. Owing probably to the elevation
of the land which has taken place in
Jutland since the Stone Age, some of them
are now a considerable distance from the
present water-line. Some, on the other
hand, are at low levels ; one, for instance,
close to the railway-station at Korsör, is
exposed only at low tide, and others are
always covered. The " coast-finds," however, belong probably to
different classes. Thus,
one at Anholt was evidently
a workshop of flint implements, as is shown by the
character of the chips, and by
the discovery of more than
sixty flint cores. Those,
on the contrary, which, even
at the present day, are under

FIG. 139.—Bone
pin or awl from
Scotland, actual
size.

water, were probably so in
old times, and as there are
no traces of lake-habitations

FIG. 140. — Bone
chisel, actual size.
From Wangen,
on the Lake of
Constance. In
my own collec-
tion.

in Denmark, it has been supposed that
they were the places where the fishermen
used to drag their nets. It is still usual
to choose particular spots for this purpose, and it is evident that many of the
rude objects used in fishing, especially
of the stones employed as net-weights,
would there be lost. I am rather disposed to regard
them as camping stations. The objects discovered are
just what might have been expected under these circumstances. They consist of irregular flint chippings, net-
weights or sling-stones, flakes, scrapers, awls, and axes.

These six different classes of objects have been found in most, if not all, of the coast-finds, though in different proportions. To give an idea of the numbers in which they occur, I may mention that Professor Steenstrup and I gathered, in about an hour, at Froëlund, near Korsör, 141 flakes, 84 weights, 5 axes, 1 scraper, and about 150 flint chips ; while at a similar spot, near Aarhuus in Jutland, I myself picked up, in two hours and a half, 76 weights, 40 flakes, 39 scrapers, 17 awls, and a considerable number of flint chips.

In many instances, a layer of sand has accumulated over and thus protected the flint fragments. This was the case with both the above-mentioned coast-finds, one of which was exposed in draining the land, the other in a railway cutting. Some-times a change of conditions will remove the light sand, and leave the heavier stones, which again in other cases have lain apparently undis-turbed and exposed from the first; and in such instances the spots are sometimes so thickly strewn with white flints that they may be distin-guished by their colour, even at a considerable distance.

We could not expect to find similar coast-finds on our

FIG. 141.—Bone harpoon, actual size.

FIG. 142.—Ancient bone harpoon, actual size. Dor-dogne.

Southern and Eastern shores, because even in historical times the sea has encroached gently. "Flint-finds," however, resembling in many respects these Danish "coast-finds," are not unknown in this country, or on the Continent. They appear to indicate the position of

ancient villages ; and in some cases, as, for instance, those of Grimes' Graves and Pressigny, are evidently places selected for the manufacture of stone implements on account of the good quality of the flint. Nor are these discoveries confined to Europe. Mr Busk and Mr Langham Dale have met with a very similar assemblage of flakes, etc., on the Cape Flats, at the Cape of Good Hope.[1] I have myself found them in abundance on the high ground along the

Fig. 143.—Bone scraper, North America.

Nile valley.[2]

Throughout the whole of America, Australia, and Polynesia, indeed, stone implements were in use down to a comparatively modern period, and in many parts are so still. In Asia and Africa, on the contrary, as in Europe, stone implements have, for the most part, been long abandoned. Still there also, as, for instance, in Algeria, Egypt, Somaliland and at the Cape, in Palestine and Assyria, in India and Japan, stone implements have been discovered, showing that these countries, like Europe, have, undoubtedly, passed through an Age of Stone.

[1] *Trans. Ethn. Soc.*, 1869, p. 51. [2] *Jour. Anthrop. Institute*, 1871.

CHAPTER V

ALL over Europe, we might indeed say all over the world,
wherever they have not been destroyed by the plough

FIG. 144.—A tumulus of the Stone Age, at Röddinge in Denmark.
It contains two chambers.

or the hammer, we find relics of prehistoric times—
camps, fortifications, dykes, tumuli, menhirs or standing
stones, cromlechs or stone circles, dolmens [1] or stone

---

[1] In this country, it has become the custom to reverse these two names.
Cromlech, however, is derived from "crom," a circle, and "lech," stone ;

chambers, etc., many of which astonish us by their magnitude, so that of some of them we may almost say, with Sir Thomas Browne, that "these mountainous monuments may stand, and are like to have the same period with the earth"; while they all excite our interest by the antiquity of their origin, and the mystery by which they are surrounded.[1]

In our own island the smaller tumuli may be seen on almost every down; in the Orkneys alone it is estimated that more than 2000 still remain. On the Wiltshire Downs there are over 1000; in France there are 4000 dolmens, 6000[2] menhirs, and 450 stone circles; in Denmark they are even more abundant; they are found all over Europe, from the shores of the Atlantic to the Oural mountains; in Asia they are scattered over the great steppes, from the borders of Russia to the Pacific Ocean, and from the plains of Siberia to those of Hindostan; the entire plain of Jelalabad, says Masson, "is literally covered with tumuli and mounds."[3] In America we are told that they are to be numbered by thousands and tens of thousands; nor are they wanting

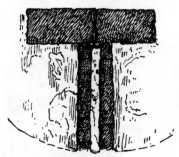

FIG. 145.—Ground plan of foregoing.

---

and dolmen from "daul," a table, and "maen," a stone. They should therefore, I consider, be used as in the text. I may add that "menhir," a standing stone, is derived from "maen," stone, and "hir," long.

[1] During the last fifteen years, several important contributions have been made to our knowledge of ancient British burial customs. I may refer especially to Gen. Pitt Rivers' researches among the *Antiquities of Wiltshire*; to Greenwell and Rolleston's *British Barrows*; Jewitt's *Grave Mounds, and their Contents*; Borlase's *Nenia Cornubiæ*; Warne's *Celtic Tumuli of Dorset*; and Borlase's *Dolmens of Ireland*. Fergusson's *Rude Stone Monuments*, also, though written in support of a theory which is, I think, erroneous, contains a valuable summary of our knowledge of megalithic monuments.

[2] Delechette, p. 431.

[3] *Journeys in Baloochistan, Afghanistan, etc.*, vol. ii. p. 164. See also p. 155, and vol. ii. pp. 111–113.

in Africa,[1] where the Pyramids themselves exhibit the most magnificent development of the same idea ; indeed

FIG. 146.—Stone circle, Denmark.

the whole world is studded with the burial-places of the dead. Many of them, indeed, are small, but some are

FIG. 147.—Dolmen, Denmark.

very large, such as, for instance, those of Odin, Thor, and Freya, at Upsala. Near Avebury, in Wiltshire, is (see p. 129) Silbury Hill, the greatest tumulus in Europe,

[1] See, for instance, *Livingstone's Miss. Travels*, pp. 219, 304.

having a height of one hundred and thirty feet, and covering five and a half acres.

The standing stones, or " menhirs," also were no doubt generally erected in memorial of some particular event, the majority being, in fact, the tombstones of Archaic times.

Fig. 148.—Brennanstown Dolmen, Co. Dublin. Photo by W. II. Matthews, F.R.S.A.I. Dimensions of covering-stone : length, 15¾ feet ; breadth, 15¼ ; the thickness varies from 3 feet at the east end to 5 feet at its west.

Tumuli were, as a rule, burial mounds, but sometimes memorials, as in Fiji.

In addition to these memorials of the past, ancient camps and fortifications crown many of our hills.

In parts of Scotland some of the old hill fortresses present the remarkable peculiarity, first noticed by Mr John Williams in 1777, of having been subjected to considerable heat. Until 1837 these vitrified forts were supposed to be peculiar to our island, but in that year Professor Zippe called attention to the existence of similar

FIG. 149.—Tumuli of Odin, Thor, and Freya at Upsala.

remains in Bohemia, and since that time vitrified forts have been discovered in various parts of France and Germany.[1]

FIG. 150.—The devil's arrows, Boroughbridge—Northern and Central menhirs.
Photo by W. H. Matthews, F.R.S.A.I.

Lastly, the country is intersected by great dykes, or lines of embankment—such, for instance, as the Wans

[1] References to the various memoirs in which these are described are given by Virchow, *Zeit. f. Ethnologie*, 1870, p. 258. See also papers by Mr Stuart and Dr Fodisch in the *Proc. Soc. Antiq. Scotland*, vol. viii.

Dyke, the Devil's Dyke at Newmarket, and Offa's Dyke, which runs from the Bristol Channel to the Dee, thus roughly dividing England from Wales—which were no doubt partly boundary-lines and partly fortifications, like the Roman Wall or the still more remarkable Wall of China.

The tumuli, menhirs, or standing stones, dolmens or stone chambers, stone circles, and stone rows or avenues, may all, I think, be considered as parts of one common plan. The great majority were tombs. In some cases

FIG. 151.—Kit's Coty House, near Maidstone.

the dead was buried in his actual house, the entrance of which was then closed. In others the tomb was a copy of the house. We may regard a perfect megalithic inter- ment as having consisted of a stone chamber, communi- cating with the outside by a passage, covered with a mound of earth, surrounded and supported at the circumference by a circle of stones, and in some cases surmounted by a stone pillar or "menhir." Sometimes, however, we find the central chamber standing alone, as at Kit's Coty House, near Maidstone, which may or may not have ever been covered by a mound ; sometimes—especially, of course, where stone was scarce—we find the earthen mound alone ; sometimes only the menhir. The celebrated

8

stone avenues of Carnac, in Brittany, and the stone rows of Avebury, may, I think, have been highly developed specimens of the entrance passage ; in Stonehenge, and many other instances, we have the stone circle.   In fact, these different parts of the perfect monument are found in every combination and in every degree of development, from the slight elevation, scarcely perceptible to the eye, excepting, perhaps, when it is thrown into relief by the slanting rays of the rising or setting sun, to the gigantic hill of Silbury ; from the small stone circle to the stupendous monuments of Stonehenge or Avebury.

Some of the oldest tumuli of Western Europe, as figs. 144-5,[1] contain a passage, formed by great blocks of stone, almost always opening (as do those of Brittany) towards the south or east—never to the north—and leading into a large central chamber, round which the dead sit.   At Godhavn, for instance, in the year 1830, a grave (if so it can be called) of this kind was opened, and numerous skeletons were found, sitting on a low seat round the walls, each with his weapons and ornaments by his side.   Now the dwellings used by Arctic nations—the " winter-houses " of the Esquimaux and Greenlanders, the " Yourts " of the Siberians—correspond closely with these " Ganggraben " or " Passage graves."   The Siberian Yourt, for instance, as described by Erman, consists of a central chamber, sunk a little in the ground, and, in the absence of great stones, formed of timber, while earth is heaped up on the roof and against the sides, reducing it to the form of a mound.   The opening is on the south, and a small hole for a window is sometimes left on the east side.   Instead of glass, a plate of ice is used ; it is at first a foot thick, and four or five generally last through the winter.   The fireplace is opposite the entrance ; and round the sides of the room, against the walls, " the floor is raised for a width of about six feet, and on this elevated part the inmates slept at night, and sat at work by day."

Captain Cook gives a very similar description of the winter habitations used by the Tschutski in the extreme

---

[1] M. Delechette gives a figure, *Man. d'Archéol.*, p. 381.

north-east of Asia.   They are, he says,[1] " exactly like a
vault, the floor of which is sunk a little below the surface
of the earth.   One of them, which I examined, was of an
oval form, about twenty feet long and twelve or more
high.   The framing was composed of wood, and the
ribs of whales, disposed in a judicious manner, and bound
together with smaller materials of the same sort.   Over
this framing is laid a covering of strong coarse grass, and
that, again, is covered with earth ; so that, on the outside,
the house looks like a little hillock supported by a wall

FIG. 152.—Summer and winter dwellings in Kamschatka.

of stone three or four feet high, which is built round the
two sides and one end."

" The Aleutian Islanders," says Mr Dall, " especially
in their winter villages, were used to construct large, half-
underground habitations, often of extraordinary size.
These were so arranged by internal partitions as to afford
shelter to even as many as one hundred families.   No
fires were built in the central undivided portion, which
was entered through a hole in the roof, provided with a
notched log by way of ladder.   In the small compartments
each family had its own oil lamp, which, with the closely
fitting door of skins, and the heat of numerous bodies in
a very small space, sufficed to keep them warm.   We

---

[1] *Voyages to the Pacific Ocean*, vol. ii. p. 450.   See also vol. iii. p. 374.

learn that the bodies, while being prepared for encasement, as above described, were sometimes kept in the compartment which they had occupied during life until ready for deposition elsewhere. We also know from early accounts, proved true by our own excavations, that the bodies of the dead, in the compressed position before mentioned, were sometimes placed in the compartment, laid on their sides, and covered with earth, with which the whole compartment was filled and then walled up. It is stated that others in the same yourt continued to occupy their several compartments after this as usual, a proceeding very different from that of the majority of the Innuit, who usually aban-

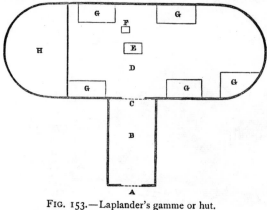

FIG. 153.—Laplander's gamme or hut.

don at once a house in which a death has occurred."[1]

Fig. 153 represents the plan of a Laplander's gamme, or hut, at Komagfiord, as given by Mr Brooke.[2] It was built of sods, supported by a rude framework, and the interstices were stuffed with moss. The greatest height was 6 ft., the breadth 14 ft., the whole length 30 ft. A is the door; B the passage, 3 ft. high, 6 ft. broad, and 12 ft. in length; C is the inner door, opening into the gamme, D; E the fireplace, composed of a few large stones to confine the wood-fire; F an opening in the roof to let out the smoke; G G are sleeping divisions, which serve also to support the roof; H is a portion fenced off for the sheep and goats. A comparison of this hut with

[1] Dall, *The Aleutian Islands.* Smithsonian Contributions, 1878.
[2] Brooke's *Travels in Lapland,* p. 318.

the corresponding plan of a tumulus (fig. 163, p. 163), will show how closely these dwellings appear to agree with the "Ganggraben" : indeed, it is possible that in some cases ruined dwellings of this kind have been mistaken for sepulchral tumuli ; [1] for some mounds have been examined which contained broken implements, pottery, ashes, etc., but no human bones ; in short, numerous indications of life, but no trace of death. We know, also, that several savage tribes have a superstitious reluctance to use anything which has belonged to a dead person, perhaps from fear of irritating his ghost ; in some cases this applies to his house, which is either deserted or used as a grave. Thus, some of the North American tribes, for instance, the Cherokees and Chichasaws, buried the dead under the couch on which he died.[2] The Indians of the Amazons also bury their dead under their houses, which, however, are not therefore abandoned by the living.

Among the New Zealanders, according to Mr Taylor, "when the owner died, and was buried in his house, it was left with all it contained ; the door was tied up and painted with ochre, to show it was made tapu, and then no one ever entered it again."[3] In many villages, he says, nearly half the houses belonged to the dead. The islanders of Torres Straits also used the ordinary huts as dead houses.[4]

Denham[5] tells us that in the great Central African kingdom of Bornou "every one is buried under the floor of his own house, without monument or memorial ; and among the commonalty the house continues occupied as usual, but among the great there is more refinement, and it is ever afterwards abandoned." The same is the case with the Dahomans, Yorubans, Fantees, and other African tribes.[6] Other races, as, for instance, some of the Tibeto-

---

[1] The so-called " Pond-barrows" perhaps belong to this class.
[2] Jones, *Antiquities of the Southern Indians*, p. 114.
[3] *New Zealand and its Inhabitants*, p. 101.
[4] M'Gillivray, *Voyage of the " Rattlesnake,"* vol. ii. p. 48.
[5] *Travels in Africa*, vol. iv. pp. 55–130
[6] Burton's *Mission to Dahome*, vol. ii. p. 2.

Burman[1] tribes and the natives of Madagascar,[2] erect miniature houses over graves.

Hut burial also occurs among several South American tribes.

It is still more significant that the Esquimaux themselves frequently leave the dead in the houses which they occupied when alive.[3] Nor can anyone compare the plan of a Scandinavian "passage grave," as, for instance, the one represented in fig. 163, with any drawing of an Esquimaux snow house, without being struck with the great similarity existing between them.

Under these circumstances we may consider these chamber graves as a copy, a development, or an adaptation, of the dwelling-house ; that the ancient inhabitants of Scandinavia, unable to imagine a future altogether different from the present, or a world quite unlike our own, showed their respect and affection for the dead by burying with them those things which in life they had valued most : with women, their ornaments ; with warriors, their weapons. They buried the house with its owner, and the grave was literally the dwelling of the dead. When a great man died, he was placed on his favourite seat, food and drink were arranged before him, his weapons were placed by his side, his house was closed, and the door covered up ; sometimes, however, to be opened again when his wife or children joined him in the land of spirits.

So, again, the tomb in the same way becomes a temple. The Khasias are a primitive people of India who even now construct monuments over the dead. They then proceed to offer food and drink to the deceased, and to implore their assistance. If after praying at a particular tomb they obtain their desires, they return again, and if success is repeated, this tomb gradually acquires a certain reputation, and the person buried in it becomes more or less a deity. When a considerable celebrity has thus

---

[1] M'Mahon, *Karens of the Golden Chersonese*, pp. 91, 318.
[2] Sibree, *Madagascar and its People*, pp. 166, 251.
[3] Ross' *Arctic Expedition*, 1829-1833, p. 290.

been acquired, other shrines would naturally be conse-
crated to him by those anxious for his assistance, and
these would be constructed on the model of the first. No
wonder, then, that it is impossible in all cases to distinguish the tomb from the temple.[1]

We will now briefly consider the different classes of
monuments.

Stone circles, or cromlechs, consist of rough upright
stones, arranged in a circle. The usual diameter is about
100 feet, but some are much larger, the principal circle
at Avebury, for instance, being 1200 feet across. The
stones are placed at equal distances, and the number of
them had probably some significance. "The two inner
circles at Abury, the lesser circle at Stennis, and one at
Stanton Drew, each consisted of twelve ; the outer circles
at Abury, the outer circles of uprights and transoms at
Stonehenge, the large circle at Stanton Drew, and the
circle at Arbor Low, each of thirty ; those of Rollrich and
Stennis, of sixty ; and the large enclosing circle of Abury,
of one hundred stones. Four circles at Boscawen, and
adjacent places in Cornwall, have each been formed of
nineteen stones."[2] Avebury and Stonehenge are the
most celebrated examples of stone circles, but they differ
from the usual type in several respects ; for instance, in
having the principal stones roughly hewn, and in the
presence of capstones.

Stone circles occur in various parts of the Continent,
but are less frequent than in our islands. Nor are they
by any means confined to Europe. The Todas of the
Neilgherry Hills have stone circles within which burial
ceremonies are performed, the ashes being placed under
one of the stones.[3] Throughout the Deccan are
numerous stone circles sacred to Vetal, whose worship
still holds its own against the Brahmanical innovations ;[4]
while Sir Bartle Frere, in his Introduction[5] to Miss

---

[1] Sir John Lubbock, Preface, p. 5, to *Our Ancient Monuments and the
Land Around Them*, by C. Ph. Kains-Jackson, 1880.
[2] Thurnam, *Crania Britannica*, Decade iv.
[3] Breeks, *Primitive Tribes of the Neilgherries*, pp. 24, 72.
[4] *Old Deccan Days*, p. x.   [5] *Loc. cit.*, p. x.

FIG. 154.—Stonehenge.

Frere's charming *Old Deccan Days*, tells us that in that part of India outside almost every village there is a circle of large stones sacred to Vetal. Stanley saw, a few miles to the north of Tyre, a circle of rough upright stones ; Mr Palmer, in his *Desert of the Exodus*, mentions the existence of "huge stone circles in the neighbourhood of Mount Sinai, some of them measuring 100 feet in diameter, having a cist in the centre covered with a heap of large boulders" ; and Kohen, a Jesuit missionary, has recently discovered in Arabia, near Khabb, in the district of Kasim, three large stone circles described as being extremely like Stonehenge, and consisting of very lofty trilithons.[1] Barth also describes and figures similar trilithons as occurring in Tripoli.[2] In this case the pillars are 10 feet high, and stand on a raised foundation.

Arctic travellers, also, mention stone circles and stone rows among the Esquimaux. These are, however, of a different character, being quite small, and probably are merely the lower part of habitations.

Lafitau figures an Indian (Virginian) temple consisting of a circle of upright stones, which, however, are carved at the top into rude representations of human faces.[3] Mr Squier mentions stone circles as occurring in Peru.[4]

As regards the period at, or purposes for, which the European stone circles were erected, history gives us no information.

Mr George Petrie, indeed, has pointed out several cases in which the Orkney circles were mentioned in old deeds, etc.[5] Thus, in 1349, William de Saint Michael was summoned to attend a court held "apud stantes lapides de Rane en le Garniach," to answer for his forcible detention of certain ecclesiastical property ; and in 1380, Alexander, Lord of Regality of Badenoch, and son of Robert II., held a court, "apud le standand stanys

---

[1] Bonstetten, *Sur les Dolmens*, p. 27.
[2] *Travels in Central Africa*, vol. i. pp. 58, 74.
[3] *Mœurs des Sauv. Amér.*, vol. ii. p. 135. I have given a copy in the *Origin of Civilization*, 2nd ed., p. 179.
[4] *Amer. Nat.*, vol. iv. p. 12.
[5] *Prehistoric Annals of Scotland*, 2nd ed., vol. i. p. 164.

de la Rathe de Kyngucy Estir," to inquire into the titles by which the Bishop of Moray held certain of his lands. Even so late as the year 1438, we find a notice that "John off Erwyne and Will Bernardson swor on the Hirdmane Stein before oure Lorde ye Erle off Orknay and the gentiless off the cuntre." It is obvious, however, that this comparatively recent use of the stone circles does not enable us to form any opinion as to the purpose for which they were originally intended.

It is perhaps more relevant to observe that both in the *Iliad* (B. xviii.) and *Odyssey* (B. viii.) assemblies of elders are mentioned as sitting in solemn conclave on stone seats arranged in circles. In the former case the seats are said to have been polished. None of our stone circles, however, appear to have been used for any such purpose. Some of them were certainly sepulchral ; and it seems probable that this was their original purpose ; but that, like other shrines, they were subsequently used as temples.

As regards stone pillars and tumuli, we are told, in Gen. xxxi., that "Jacob took a stone and set it up for a pillar " ; and in verse 51, "Laban said to Jacob, Behold this heap, and behold this pillar, which I have cast between me and thee. This heap is a witness, and this pillar is a witness, that I will not pass over this heap to thee, and that thou shalt not pass over this pillar to me, to do me harm," etc. At Mount Sinai, Moses erected twelve pillars.[1] And so, again, when the children of Israel had crossed over Jordan, Joshua took twelve stones and pitched them in Gilgal. "And he spake unto the children of Israel, saying, When your children shall ask their fathers in time to come, saying, What mean these stones ? then ye shall let your children know, saying, Israel came over this Jordan on dry land." [2]

Achan and his whole family were stoned with stones and burned with fire, after which we are told that Israel "raised over him a great heap of stones unto this day. So the Lord turned from the fierceness of his anger."

[1] Ex. xxiv. 4. [2] Joshua iv. 21, 22.

Again, the king of Ai was buried under a great heap of
stones ; and so also was Absalom, of whom likewise we
are told that he " reared up for himself a pillar, which is
in the King's Dale ; for he said, I have no son to keep
my name in remembrance ; and he called the pillar after
his own name, and it is called unto this day Absalom's
Place."

In one of the ancient Babylonian records, Izdubar is
recorded to have erected a memorial mound.[1]

According to Diodorus, Semiramis, the widow of
Ninus, buried her husband within the precincts of the
palace, and raised over him a great mound of earth.
Pausanias mentions that stones were collected together,
and heaped up over the tomb of Laius, the father of
Œdipus.   In the time of the Trojan war, Tydeus and
Lycus are mentioned as having been buried under two
earthen barrows.   " Hector's barrow was of stone and
earth.   Achilles erected a tumulus, upwards of an
hundred feet in diameter, over the remains of his friend
Patroclus.   The mound, supposed by Xenophon to
contain the remains of Alyattes, father of Crœsus, king
of Lydia, is of stone and earth, and more than a quarter
of a league in circumference.   The tradition that the
tumulus at Marathon is the tomb of the Greeks who fell
in that battle, has been confirmed by the recent discovery
in it of vases belonging to that period.   Alexander the
Great caused a tumulus to be heaped over his friend
Hephæstion, at the cost of 1200 talents, no mean sum
even for a conqueror like Alexander, it being £232,500
sterling."[2]   Virgil tells us that Dercennus, king of
Latium, was buried under an earthen mound ; and
according to the earliest historians, whose statements
are confirmed by the researches of archæologists, mound-
burial was practised in ancient times by the Scythians,
Greeks, Etruscans, Germans, and many other nations.
Silbury Hill near Avebury, the greatest tumulus in
Europe, is 130 feet high and covers 5½ acres.

[1] Le Normant, *Les Premières Civilizations*, vol. ii. p. 47.
[2] *Ten Years' Diggings in the Celtic and Saxon Gravehills*, p. v.

By far the greater number of the tumuli in Western Europe are entirely prehistoric, but there are some few of which the date and origin are known to us, such as the tumuli of Queen Thyra and King Gorm, who died about 950, at Jellinge, in Denmark.

The Mausoleum of Augustus was justly called by Tacitus a tumulus, since it was covered by an immense mound of earth. The tumulus from which Taplow takes its name, the Low or Mound on the Hill-top, was the burial-place of a Viking of about the seventh century.

There are, moreover, other cases in which tumuli are mentioned, though not in a manner which enables us to identify them with any of those now existing. Thus Gregory of Tours[1] has a quaint story to the effect that Macliav, flying from his brother Chanaon, took refuge with Chonomor, Count of the Bretons. Chanaon sent messengers to demand that Macliav should be given up to him, but Chonomor concealed him in a tomb, "rearing over him a tumulus in the usual manner, but leaving a small opening for the entrance of air" (componens desuper ex more tumulum, parvumque ei spiraculum reservans, unde halitum resumere posset). He then showed this tumulus to the messengers, and assured them that Macliav was buried in it.

The Codex Diplomaticus contains references to more than sixty barrows or lows, bearing the names of particular persons ; some of them, as, for instance, Wódne's Beorgh, or Woden's Barrow, are probably mythical, but there seems no reason to doubt that some—for instance, Alfrede's Beorh, Æthelwolde's Beorh, Cissan Beorh, Cwichelme's Hlœw, Oswolde's Hlœw, etc.—retain the name of the person really buried within.[2] It appears that in England the habit of burying under tumuli was finally abandoned during the tenth century.

The Danish Sagas also tell us that in the middle of the

---

[1] *Historia Francorum*, iv. 4.
[2] For an interesting memoir on notices of heathen interment in the Codex Diplomaticus, see Kemble, *Arch. Jour.*, vol. xiv. p. 119.

eighth century, Sigurd Ring, having conquered his uncle, King Harald Hildetand, in the battle of Braavalla, "washed the corpse, placed it on Harald's war-chariot, and buried it in a tumulus which he had formed for the purpose. Harald's horse also was slain and buried with him, with the saddle, so that Harald might either ride to Valhalla, or go in his chariot, as he preferred. Sigurd then gave a great feast, after which he recommended the chiefs present to throw their ornaments and arms into the tumulus in honour of Harald. Finally the tumulus was carefully closed."[1]

By far the greater number of these monuments, how-ever, are doubtless far older. Some, indeed, were ancient and mysterious even in the days of Homer. Thus, at the burial of Patroclus, when Nestor is pointing out to his son Antilochus the course for the chariot race, he says :—

> "Plain is the goal
> That now I tell thee of; nor canst thou miss it :
>
> .   .   .   .   .   .
>
> On either side
> Where narrowest is the way, and all the course
> Around is smooth, rise two white stones, set there
> To mark the tomb of some one long since dead,
> Or form a goal for men in ages past."[2]

It is very striking to find these menhirs mentioned in our earliest writings, as monuments of events even then already lost in the obscurity of the past.

Many of the very largest tumuli in Western Europe appear, from the nature of their contents, to have been constructed during the Stone Age. At first, indeed, it seems almost incredible that the immense tumuli of Brittany should have been erected by a people who possessed no metal. We must remember, however, that

---

[1] Engelhardt, *Guide Illustré du Musée des Antiquités du Nord à Copenhague*, 1868. See also Saxo Grammaticus, *His. Dan.*, l. x. ch. xii.

[2] *Iliad*, xxiii. 384. I have quoted from Mr Wright's translation, which, in this passage at least, is more faithful than any other with which I am acquainted.

some of the South Sea monuments were quite as considerable. Moreover, though hundreds of beautiful stone axes and ornaments have been found in the tumuli of Brittany, no weapons of metal have yet occurred in them. It has been supposed that the carvings on some of the stones could not have been cut without metal. Actual experiments, however, as Messrs Bertrand and de Mortillet have shown me, prove that the stone can be cut with flint, while bronze produces no effect on it. Sir James Y. Simpson also has shown that the engravings on the Scotch rocks, even those on granite, may have been carved with a flint tool.[1]

In this country we still habitually call the megalithic monuments " Druidical," but it is hardly necessary to mention that there is really no sufficient reason for connecting them with Druidical worship.

The greatest of all so-called Druidical monuments is the temple of Avebury, in Wiltshire. It is, indeed, much less known than Stonehenge ; and yet, though a ruder, it was a much grander temple. According to Aubrey, Avebury " did as much exceed Stonehenge as a cathedral does a parish church." When perfect, it consisted of an embankment and a circular ditch, containing an area of $28\frac{1}{2}$ acres ; inside the ditch was a circle of great stones, and within this, again, two smaller circles, formed by a double row of smaller stones, standing side by side. From the outer embankment started two long winding avenues of stones, one of which went in the direction of Beckhampton, and the other in that of Kennet, where it ended in another double circle. Stukely fancifully supposed that the idea of the whole was that of a snake transmitted through a circle ; the Kennet circle representing the head, the Beckhampton avenue the tail. Midway between the two avenues stood Silbury Hill, the largest artificial mound in Europe, measuring no less than 130 feet in height, and covering $5\frac{1}{2}$ acres. At one time it was no doubt even higher. From its position it appears to form part of the general plan, but

[1] *Proc. Soc. Antiq. Scotland,* vol. vi. 1867, p. 122.

though it has been twice examined, no primary interment
has been found in it.   On the whole, this appears to

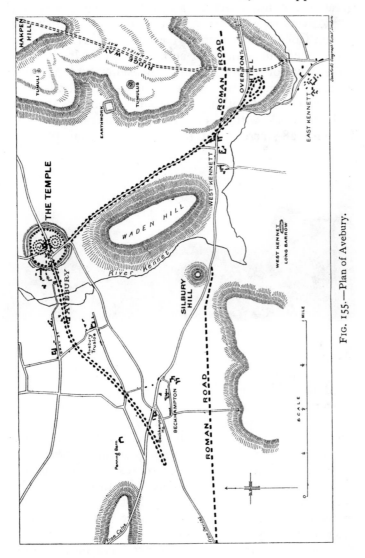

FIG. 155.—Plan of Avebury.

have been the finest megalithic ruin in Europe ; but, unfortunately for us, the pretty little village of Avebury,

like some beautiful parasite, has grown up at the expense,
and in the midst, of the ancient temple, and out of 650
great stones, not above 20 are still standing.

Excavations were made at Avebury by a British Association Committee of which I was a member. The work
was carried out under the supervision of Mr St George
Gray, Curator of the Taunton Museum, and has shown
what an immense undertaking it was, especially as the
constructors had nothing but stone implements and antler
picks to work with. The vallum as already mentioned
includes 28½ acres. At present the central plateau is

FIG. 156.—Avebury stones.

about 12 feet, and the crest of the vallum 31 feet above
the present level of the fosse, which however has gradually
filled in. The true bottom was 49·7 feet below the
crest of the vallum, and supposing this to have sunk
about 5 feet, the original depth of the fosse must have
been over 50 feet! The filling in may have been rapid
at first, but no doubt became gradually slower. The
fosse excavations so far made represent a length of 90
feet, and the objects found were very instructive. Near
the surface to a depth of 2 to 3 feet were fragments of
mediæval pottery; from 3·5 to 4·5 feet fragments of
Roman pottery and a brooch with the maker's name
"Aucissa," several of whose works have been found in
other parts of England. Nothing Roman was found
below this level, but only prehistoric pottery, flint chips,

scrapers, and a well-worked knife, antlers of red-deer and shoulder-blades, the horns having been used to dig out the chalk, and the shoulder-blades to shovel it up. The results therefore go far to confirm the view that Avebury belongs to the later Stone Age.

Mr Fergusson [1] has attempted to prove that both Stonehenge and Avebury belong to post-Roman times. "The Roman road," he says, "from Bath to Marlborough, either passes under Silbury Hill, or makes a sudden

FIG. 157.—Silbury Hill.

bend to get round it in a manner that no Roman road, in Britain at least, was ever known to do. . . . From a careful examination of all the circumstances of the case, the conclusion seems inevitable that Silbury Hill stands *on* the Roman road, and consequently must have been erected subsequently to the time of the Romans leaving the country."

Startled by this argument, and yet satisfied that there must be some error, I turned to the Ordnance map, and found, to my surprise, that the Roman road was distinctly laid down as passing, not under, but at the side of, Silbury Hill. Not content with this, I persuaded Pro-

[1] *Rude Stone Monuments.*

fessor Tyndall to visit the locality with me, and we convinced ourselves that upon this point the map was quite correct. The impression on our minds was that the Roman engineer, in constructing the road from Morgan's Hill, had taken Silbury Hill as a point to steer for, swerving only just before reaching it. Moreover, the map will show that not only this Roman road, but some others, in the same part of England, are less straight than is usually the case.

In order to set the point at rest, I caused excavations to be made, under the auspices of the Wiltshire Archæological Society, at the side of Silbury Hill. The ditches running along the Roman road could still be followed, and it is clear that the road swerved shortly before arriving at, and in order to avoid the tumulus. I quite agree, therefore, with old Stukely, that the Roman road curved abruptly southward to avoid Silbury Hill, and that "this shows Silbury Hill was ancienter than the Roman road."[1] How much more ancient it is impossible to say,[2] but some excavations made by Mr Pass in 1886[3] would seem to indicate that it cannot be later than the Bronze, if indeed it does not belong to the close of the Stone Age. Round the hill is an excavation from which the chalk, of which the hill is composed, was taken. The depression thus formed, though still well marked, is partly filled up with some 9 feet of white alluvial matter. Mr Pass sunk several shafts through this, and at the base of one of them he found several flakes and one well-marked flint implement. This may be either an unfinished arrow-head or a small cutting instrument.

As regards Stonehenge, we have, I think, satisfactory reasons for attributing it to the Bronze Age.

The account given by Giraldus Cambrensis, writing at

---

[1] Mr Blandford, who superintended the opening of the Hill in 1849, came also to the same conclusion. *Proc. Archæol. Inst.*, 1849, p. 303. See also the interesting memoir in the same volume, by the Rev. A. C. Smith.

[2] Stukely thinks it was founded in 1859 B.C., the year of the death of Sarah, Abraham's wife.

[3] *Journ. Wilts. Arch. and Nat. His. Soc.*, Aug. 1887.

the close of the 12th century, is clearly mythical. According to him, it was erected by Aurelius Ambrosius in memory of the British chieftains treacherously murdered by Hengist and the Saxons, about the year 460. "There was," he says, "in Ireland, in ancient times, a pile of stones worthy of admiration, called the Giant's Dance, because giants from the remotest part of Africa brought them into Ireland ; and in the plains of Kildare, not far from the castle of Naas, as well by force of art as strength, miraculously set them up ; and similar stones, erected in a like manner, are to be seen there at this day. These stones (according to the British history) Aurelius Ambrosius, king of the Britons, procured Merlin, by supernatural means, to bring from Ireland into Britain. And that he might leave some famous monument of so great a treason to future ages, in the same order and art as they stood formerly, set them up where the flower of the British nation fell by the cut-throat practice of the Saxons, and where, under the pretence of peace, the ill-secured youth of the kingdom, by murderous designs, were slain."[1]

This account is clearly mythical. The larger stones were evidently obtained in the neighbourhood, and are in fact "Sarcens," identical with those which occur in hundreds on Salisbury Plain. Moreover, the very name of Stonehenge, like those of Stanton Drew, Stennis, etc., seems to me a very strong argument against those who attribute these monuments to so recent an origin. Stanton Drew, for instance, is "The Stone Town of the Druids." How could it have been called so if it was erected in Saxon times ? Stonehenge is generally considered to mean the Hanging-stones, as indeed was long ago suggested by Wace, an Anglo-Norman poet, who says :

> Stanhengues ont nom en Englois
> Pieres pandues en Francois ;[2]

but it is surely more natural to derive the last syllable from the Anglo-Saxon word "ing," a field ; as we have

---

[1] Giraldus, *Topogr. of Ireland.*
[2] Wright's *Wanderings of an Antiquary*, p. 301.

Keston, originally Kyst-stan-ing, the field of stone coffins. What more natural than that a new race, finding this magnificent ruin standing in solitary grandeur on Salisbury Plain, and able to learn nothing of its origin, should call it simply the *place of stones* ? What more unnatural than that they should do so, if they knew the name of him in whose honour it was erected ? The plan also of Stonehenge seems to be a sufficient reason for not referring it to post-Roman times. It has, indeed, been urged that if Stonehenge had existed in the time of Cæsar, we should find it mentioned by ancient writers. Hecatæus, however, does allude to a magnificent circular temple in the island of the Hyperboreans, over against Celtica, and many archæologists have confidently assumed that this refers to Stonehenge. But why should we expect to find it described, if it was, as we suppose, even at that time a ruin, more perfect, no doubt, than at this day, but still a ruin ? The Caledonian Wall was a most important fortification constructed by the Romans themselves, and yet, as Dr Wilson tells us,[1] only one of the Roman historians makes the least allusion to its erection, nor is Avebury itself mentioned by any mediæval author.

It is evident that Stonehenge was at one time a spot of great sanctity. A glance at the Ordnance map will show that tumuli cluster in great numbers round and within sight of it ; within a radius of three miles, there are about three hundred burial mounds, while the rest of the country is comparatively free from them. If, then, we could determine the date of these tumuli, we should be justified, I think, in referring the Great Temple itself to the same period. Now, of these barrows, Sir Richard Colt Hoare examined a great number, 151 of which had not been previously opened. Of these the great majority contained interments by cremation, in the manner usual during the Bronze Age. Only two contained any iron weapons, and these were both secondary interments ; that is to say, the owners of the iron weapons were not the original occupiers of the tumuli. Of the other burial

[1] *Prehistoric Ann. of Scot.*, vol. ii. p. 39.

mounds, no less than 39 contained objects of bronze, and one of them, in which were found a spear-head and pin of bronze, was still more connected with the temple by the presence of fragments, not only of Sarcen stones, but also of the blue stones which form the inner circle at Stonehenge ; and which do not naturally occur in Wilt-shire. Stonehenge then may, I think, be regarded as a monument of the Bronze Age, though apparently it was not all erected at one time, the inner circle of small, unwrought, blue stones being probably older than the rest.[1]

Stonehenge points approximately to the rising of the sun on Midsummer Day, and visitors still go every year to watch the interesting spectacle of the sun rising over the so-called " Friar's Heel " (fig. 158).

An "avenue," as it is called, formed by two ancient earthen banks, which were formerly more marked than they are now, extends for a considerable distance in the direction of the rising sun. In Sir N. Lockyer's opinion the monument is a temple, was originally roofed in, "and the sun's first ray, suddenly admitted into the darkness, formed a fundamental part of the cultus." [2]

This was important, not only from a religious point of view, but as marking distinctly and officially the com-mencement of a new annual period, which was useful on various grounds and especially from an agricultural point of view.

The theory assumes that when the monument was

---

[1] Some archæologists, however, including the high authority of Mr Flinders Petrie, are of the opposite opinion. There are, in fact, four kinds of stones in Stonehenge. The great outer circle and the trilithons are " Sarcen " stones, that is to say, they are formed from the sandstone blocks of the neighbourhood. The majority of the small pillars forming the inner circle consist of an igneous rock known as Diabase, but four stones of this series are schistoid, and resemble some of the Silurian and Cambrian rocks of North Wales and Cumberland. Lastly, the so-called altar stone is grey sandstone, resembling some of the Devonian and Cambrian rocks. Maskelyne, *Wilts. Arch. Magazine*, Oct. 1877. It has been said that some Roman pottery was found under one of the trilithons at Stonehenge. Mr Cunnington, however, has pointed out that there is no authority for this statement. *Wilts. Arch. Mag.*, Dec. 1883.
[2] *Nature*, Nov. 1901.

erected the axis pointed exactly to the rising of the sun at Midsummer Day. This, however, does not now hold good, but Sir N. Lockyer on astronomical grounds concludes that this was the case in 1680 B.C., which accordingly

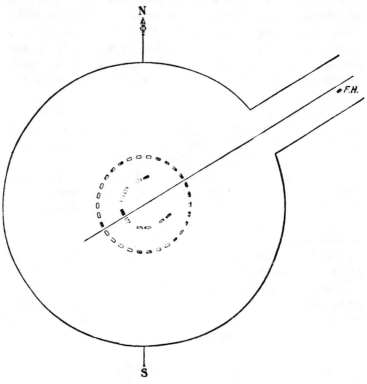

FIG. 158.—Plan of Stonehenge.

he considers to be the date of the monument, with a possible error of ±200 years.

But this was not the original monument. The socalled blue stones are considered by most, though not by all, archæologists to be much older, and Lockyer suggests for them a date of 2680 B.C. As regards Avebury, since the stones are all in their natural condition, while those of Stonehenge are roughly hewn, it seems reasonable to conclude that Avebury is the older of the two, and belongs either to the close of the Stone Age, or to the commencement of that of Bronze.

A complete burial-place may be described as a dolmen, covered by a tumulus, crowned by a menhir, surrounded by a stone circle, and led up to by a stone row. Often, however, we have only the tumulus, sometimes only the dolmen, and sometimes again only the stone circle.

The celebrated monument of Carnac (fig. 159), in Brittany, consists of eleven rows of unhewn stones, which differ greatly both in size and height, the largest being 22 feet above ground, while some are quite small. It appears that the avenues originally extended for several miles, but at present they are very imperfect, the stones having been cleared away in places for agricultural improvements. At present, therefore, there are several detached portions, which, however, have the same general direction, and appear to have been connected together.

They may, I think, be regarded as highly developed examples of the passage which leads to the central chamber in so many tumuli, or corresponds with the covered passage leading to the dwelling in arctic regions.

They appear to have always terminated in a circle, often, however, quite insignificant in comparison with the stone row.

Most of the great tumuli in Brittany probably belong to the Stone Age, and I am therefore disposed to regard the Carnac, and other rows of stones, as having been erected during the same period.

Megalithic erections, resembling those which are generally, but without sufficient reason, ascribed to the Druids, are found in very distant countries. In Moab, De Saulcy observed rude stone avenues, and other monuments, which he compares to Celtic dolmens. Lieut. Oliver, also, mentions that the Hovas of Madagascar to this day erect monoliths and stone tombs closely resembling those of Western Europe.[1] Mr Maurice[2] was, I believe, the first to point out, that in some parts of India

[1] *Trans. Ethn. Soc.*, 1870, p. 67. [2] *India Antiqua.*

FIG. 159.—Carnac, Brittany.

there are various monuments of stone, which, in the words of Colonel Yule, "recall strongly those mysterious, solitary, or clustered monuments of unknown origin, so long the puzzle and delight of antiquaries, which abound in our native country, and are seen here and there in all parts of Europe and Western Asia."[1] Mr Fergusson goes farther, and argues with great ingenuity that the "Buddhist architecture in India, as practised from the third century B.C. to seventh A.D., is essentially tumular, circular, and external, thus possessing the three great characteristics of all the so-called Druidical remains."[2] These resemblances, indeed, are too great to be accidental, and the differences represent, not so much a difference in style, as in civilization. " In the most celebrated example in India, that at Sanchee, the circle consists of roughly squared upright stone posts, joined at the top by an architrave of the same thickness as the posts, exactly as at Stonehenge ; the only difference being the insertion of three stone rails between each of the uprights, which is a masonic refinement hardly to be expected among the Celts." In India, then, the circles of stones seem generally to have surrounded tumuli ; but this is not always the case, and there are some "which apparently enclose nothing." Again, they are generally covered with sculpture ; but to this also there are exceptions, as, for instance, at Amravati, where there are numberless little circles of rude unhewn stone, identical with those in this country, but smaller.

In Europe we know that the stones of megalithic monuments are almost invariably uncarved.

There is indeed a dolmen, near Confolens in Charente, in which the upper stone is supported, not on rude stone blocks, but on four slender columns.[3] I agree, however, with M. Rochebrune, that the supports were probably carved at a period long subsequent to the erection of the

---

[1] *Jour. of the Asiat. Soc. of Bengal,* vol. xiii. p. 617. See also *Proc. Soc. Antiq. Scotland,* vol. i. p. 93. Babington, *Trans. Lit. Soc. Bombay,* 1823. Congreve, *Madras Jour. of Lit. and Science,* 1847. Yule, *Proc. Soc. Ant. Scotland,* vol. i. p. 93. Wise, ditto, p. 154. Hooker's *Himalayan Journals.* Taylor, *Trans. Roy. Irish Acad.,* vol. xxiv., etc.

[2] *Loc. cit.,* p. 212.   [3] *Statistique Monumentale de la Charente.*

monument.[1]   It is one of the many cases in which megalithic monuments have been "christianised." Many of
the French menhirs have had a cross fixed at the top, and
one is built into the wall of the cathedral at Mans.[2]   At
Stonehenge the stones are carefully hewn, but at this
stage the megalithic architecture in Western Europe seems
to have been replaced by a totally different style.   In
Algeria,[3] on the contrary, it advanced further ; we there
find tumuli of regular masonry and stone circles, in which
the floors are paved.   On the principal stones in one of the
stone circles are letters, the meaning of which, however,
is unknown.   In India it reached a still higher stage of
development, so that it requires an observant eye to
detect in the rude cromlechs, stone circles, and tumuli,
the prototypes of the highly decorated architecture of the
Buddhists.

It is a very remarkable fact, that even to the present
day, some of the hill tribes in India continue to erect
menhirs, cromlechs, and other combinations of gigantic
stones, sometimes singly, sometimes in rows, sometimes
in circles, in either case very closely resembling those
found in Western Europe.   Among the Khasias,[4] " the
funeral ceremonies are the only ones of any importance,
and are often conducted with barbaric pomp and expense ;
and rude stones of gigantic proportions are erected as
monuments, singly or in rows, circles, or supporting one
another like those of Stonehenge, which they rival in
dimensions and appearance."

Dalton[5] mentions several menhirs erected by the
present generation in memory of relatives who have
recently died.

An interesting account is given by Dr Inman, on the
authority of Mr Greey, of the mode in which these large

---

[1] *Mém. sur les Restes d'industrie appartenant aux temps primordiaux dans le Dép. de la Charente*, 1866.

[2] Delechette, *Archéol. Préhist.*, p. 440.

[3] *Recueil des Notices et Mémoires de la Société Archéologique de la Province de Constantine*, 1863, p. 214. See also Letourneux, *Ar. f. Anthropologie*, 1868, p. 307.

[4] Dr Hooker's *Himalayan Jour.*, vol. ii. p. 276. See also p. 320.

[5] *Ethnology of Bengal*, p. 203.

blocks of stone are moved. Two long horizontal poles are placed under the stone pillar, and firmly lashed to it, one at each end. At intervals of about three feet other poles were then fastened to the two first, parallel to the stone pillar, so that a large number of men could get a firm hand-hold. In this manner Mr Greey saw a stone about 30 feet long, 10 feet broad, and weighing about 24 tons, easily moved by about 600 men.[1]

The single pillars are sometimes tombstones, sometimes memorials of important events. Colonel Yule once asked a native if there were any tradition about one of these pillars, which is known as Mausmai, *i.e.* "the stone of the oath." "There was war," said the man, "between two villages, and when they made peace, and swore to it, they *erected this stone for a witness*."[2]

Sir Joseph Hooker[3] has called attention to the fact that the Khasian word for a stone, "Mau," as commonly occurs in the names of their villages and places, as that of Man, Maen, and Men, does in those of Brittany, Wales, Cornwall, etc. ; thus Mausmai signifies in Khasia the Stone of Oath,—Mamloo, the Stone of Salt,—Mouflong, the Grassy Stone,—just as in Wales, Penmaenmawr signifies the Hill of the Big Stone ; while a menhir is a standing stone, and a dolmen a table stone, etc. Those who believe that the use of metal was introduced into Europe by a race of Indo-European origin, will find in these facts an interesting confirmation of their opinion.

How closely these Indian dolmens resemble those of Europe may be seen by comparing figs. 160 and 161 with 147 and 148.

The Indian dolmens, as shown in the valuable memoirs by Colonel Meadows Taylor[4] (figs. 160, 161), may truly be said to be identical with those of Western Europe. He examined a very considerable number, having obtained particulars of no less than 2129 dolmens in the district of

---

[1] *Proceedings Lit. and Philos. Soc. of Liverpool,* vol. xxx. p. 108.
[2] *Proc. Soc. Antiq. Scotland,* vol. i. p. 93.
[3] *Address to the British Association,* 1868, p. 7.
[4] *Trans. R. Irish Academy,* vol. xxiv. p. 329. See also Col. Forbes Leslie's valuable work, *The Early Races of Scotland.*

Bellary, in the Dekkan, and it is interesting that, as is
sometimes the case in Europe, more than 1100 had an

FIG. 160.—Indian Dolmen.   After Colonel Meadows Taylor.

opening in one of the side stones, perhaps in order to
introduce food, perhaps as an exit for the spirit of the
dead.   Montpérieux figures (pl. xxx.) a dolmen with a
similar hole, in his work on the Caucasus.

FIG. 161.—Indian Dolmen.   After Colonel Meadows Taylor.

Schoolcraft also mentions that in the United States the
Redskins very frequently left an opening in the grave
cover for the same purpose.[1]

---

[1] Schoolcraft's *Indian Tribes*, pt. i. p. 33.

Archæologists are divided as to whether dolmens were in all cases originally covered over with earth. Mr Fergusson denies this, while it has been ably maintained by Mr Lukis. It must, I think, be admitted that some of the cases relied on by Mr Fergusson must be abandoned; nevertheless, I am disposed to believe that in some instances the dolmen was left uncovered.

The majority of these dolmens were no doubt sepulchral. Some, however, were very probably shrines, erected in honour of a god, not of a man. Mr Walhouse, in an interesting paper on non-sepulchral rude stone monuments,[1] describes a dolmen consisting of back and side slabs set on edge, observed by him on the table-land of Mysore, and which was a temple to Hanumân, containing a rude image of the god, with a few flowers strewn before it. Subsequently he found these temple dolmens in common use by the Malayâlies, a Tamil race inhabiting the Shiarâi Hills.

We must not, however, attribute too much importance to the similarity existing between the megalithic erections in various parts of the world. Give any child a box of bricks, and it will immediately build dolmens, cromlechs, and "trilithons," like those of Stonehenge, so that the construction of these remarkable monuments may be regarded as another illustration of the curious similarity existing between the child and the savage.

Tumuli or barrows are much more numerous and more widely distributed than stone circles. No doubt the great majority of them are burial mounds, but some also were erected as memorials, like the "heap of witness" erected by Laban and Jacob, or the mound heaped up by the Ten Thousand in their celebrated retreat, when they obtained their first view of the sea.

The tumuli were generally constructed of materials found on the spot, the cists, however, and chambers, when present, being often built of slabs brought from a distance. Generally the earth, etc., is heaped up without any order, having been, at any rate in many cases, dug with deer's-

[1] *Jour. Anthr. Inst.*, Aug. 1877.

horn picks, and carried to the mound perhaps in baskets. In other cases the materials are arranged in more or less regular layers.

The size of the tumulus may be taken as a rough indication of the estimation in which the deceased was held, as James[1] also tells us was the case among the North American Indians. The Scotch Highlanders[2] have a complimentary proverb, " Curri mi clach er du cuirn," *i.e.* " I will add a stone to your cairn " ; and I am informed by Mr R. Gray that the custom still exists in the Hebrides, as it does among various savage and semi-savage races.

The remark made by Schoolcraft as regards the American Indians is applicable to many savage tribes. " Nothing that the dead possessed was deemed too valuable to be interred with the body.   The most costly dress, arms, ornaments, and implements, are deposited in the grave " ; which is " placed in the choicest scenic situations —on some crowning hill or gentle eminence in a secluded valley."   And the North American Indians are said, even until within the last few years, to have long cherished a friendly feeling for the French, because, in the time of their supremacy, they had at least this one great merit, that they never disturbed the resting-places of the dead.

Coffins do not appear to have been used in ancient times.   Canon Greenwell has sometimes found traces of decayed wood, and in one case the side of a grave showed the impression of a rough board.   Such burials, I believe, generally belong to the Bronze Age.   A good example is that of Gristhorpe, near Scarborough, described by Prof. Williamson, which, among other relics, contained a small bronze dagger.   The majority of tumuli are mere heaps of earth, or of stones, covering the bones or ashes of the dead ; in many cases, however, the mound contains a cist of stones, evidently intended to protect the remains of the deceased, while in other cases the dead man was buried in a dolmen, more or less resembling those represented in figs. 146–148, and the whole was then covered over.   Such

[1] *Expedition to the Rocky Mountains*, vol. ii. p. 2.
[2] Wilson, *Prehistoric Annals of Scotland*, vol. i. p. 86, 2nd ed.

dolmens, either covered or uncovered, occur, as already mentioned, in Northern Africa and in India. Some archæologists have considered that all dolmens were originally covered with earth or stones, but I think the evidence shows that some at least were intentionally left exposed.

It is just possible that the comparative rarity of chambered tumuli in England and France may be connected with the greater mildness of the climate, which did not necessitate the use of underground "winter-houses"; or it may be an indication of a difference in race. Further investigations will, doubtless, decide this point. In the meantime we must remember that the so-called "Picts-houses" are abundant in the northern parts of Great Britain. These curious dwellings are "scarcely distinguishable from the larger tumuli; but on digging into the green mound, it is found to cover a series of large chambers, built generally with stones of considerable size, and converging towards the centre, where an opening appears to have been left for light and ventilation. These differ little from many of the subterranean weems, excepting that they are erected on the natural surface of the soil, and have been buried by means of an artificial mound heaped over them."[1]

According to Mr Bateman, who has recorded the systematic opening of more than four hundred tumuli (a very large proportion of which were investigated in his presence), and whose opinion is therefore of great value, the leading feature of these ancient British sepulchral mounds is, that they enclose either an artless stone vault, or chamber, or a stone chest, otherwise called a Kistvaen, built with more or less care; and, in other cases, a grave cut out more or less below the natural surface and lined, if need be, with stone slabs, in which the body was placed in a perfect state, or reduced to ashes by fire."[2]

The "long barrows" are rarer; they resemble, in

[1] Wilson, *loc. cit.*, vol. i. p. 161.
[2] Bateman, *Ten Years' Diggings*, p. 11.

some respects, the Scandinavian "Ganggraben," and, like them, in districts where large blocks of stones occur, contain megalithic chambers, in which the dead were buried and not burnt. No trace of metal has yet been found in this class of tumulus ; which therefore probably belongs to the Stone Age. The skulls found in these tumuli are long and narrow skulls, which have received from Dr Wilson the name of " Kumbecephalic," or boat-shaped skulls, resembling the one in fig. 162, which was obtained by Mr Bateman from the tumulus known as

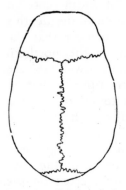

FIG. 162.—Kumbecephalic skull from Derbyshire. After Bateman.

"Longlow," near Watton, in Derbyshire. This tumulus contained the remains of thirteen individuals, who had been buried in the usual contracted position. They were contained in a cist composed of large stones, and were accompanied with several worked flints, including three carefully made arrow-heads. Long skulls are comparatively rare in the round tumuli of England, while, on the contrary, no round skulls have yet been met with in the long tumuli, at any rate in Wiltshire and Gloucestershire : so that the evidence appears to support Dr Thurnam's aphorism, long barrows, long skulls ; round barrows, round skulls.[1] This conclusion rests on the measurements of 137 skulls, 70 from round barrows and 67 from long ones, and it must be observed that these are not selected specimens, but, so far as the long-barrow skulls are concerned, comprise the whole number which we possess in a sufficiently perfect condition ; while, as regards the 70 from round tumuli, Dr Thurnam has taken the whole number (41) contained in the Bateman collection, those described in the *Crania Britannica*, and all those in his own collection. It is important to observe, therefore, that in neither case has any selection been made which could influence the re-

[1] *Mem. Anthropological Soc.*, vol. i.

sults. Now if we class those skulls in which the relation
of the breadth to the length is less than 73 to 100 as
long heads, or Dolichocephalic, those in which it is from
74–79 to 100 as medium heads, and those in which the
proportion is 80 or more than 80 to 100 as short heads,
or Brachycephalic, we shall have the following result :—

	Total number of skulls.	Dolicho-cephalic 63–73.	Ortho-cephalic 74–79.	Brachy-cephalic 80–89.
Long barrows .	67	55	12	0
Round barrows .	70	0	26	44

Thus there is not a single long head among the 70
specimens from round barrows, nor a single round head
among the 67 specimens from long barrows. So remarkable a distinction certainly appears to imply a difference
of race.

The more recent researches of Canon Greenwell and
Dr Rolleston confirm these views. They have never
found a round skull in a long barrow. On the other hand,
although Dr Thurnam found no long skulls in round
barrows, yet, unless the long-headed race were entirely
destroyed by the men with round heads, we should
naturally expect that, though the round heads would
preponderate in the later round barrows, still skulls of
the earlier long-headed race would sometimes occur ; and
this we find is really the case. The women at any rate
of the earlier race were probably not wholly exterminated.

Dr Thurnam is disposed to refer the Dolichocephalic
people to the Neolithic Age, the Brachycephalic to that
of Bronze.

It seems to me that both existed during the Neolithic
Period. Many, if not most, of the round barrows are
certainly referable to this phase in our history.

As yet, no bone belonging to any of the extinct
mammalia has been found in a tumulus. Even the reindeer, so far as our present evidence goes, is entirely
wanting. Again, the stone implements, as already
mentioned, are of a character very different from those

used by Palæolithic men. It is therefore not surprising to find that the skulls which have been obtained from tumuli attributed to the Stone Age, indicate that Europe was, even at that period, already inhabited by more than one race of men.

On the Continent, as in England, some are brachycephalic, or short-headed, and so far resemble those of the Lapps, while others are dolichocephalic, or long-headed[1] (fig. 162). Virchow[2] has published a memoir on the skulls obtained from Danish tumuli, and contained in the Copenhagen Museum. Omitting fragmentary specimens, and those belonging to young persons, he has examined 41 skulls referred to the Stone Age, 3 to the Bronze Age, and 5 to the Iron Age, and compared them with the specimens of Lapp (6), Greenland (5), and Finn (3) skulls contained in the same collection. On the whole, these Stone Age skulls are orthocephalic, inclining to brachycephalism ; the Bronze Age and Iron Age specimens are dolichocephalic, but it must be remarked that it would not be safe to draw any definite conclusion from so small a number of specimens ; and that even if the Bronze Age indicates the immigration of a new race into Western Europe, they would probably not exterminate the earlier inhabitants, but would at any rate spare the young women, so that, until we have a considerable body of evidence, it would be very unsafe to speculate on the character of the population during the Bronze Age.

The Lapps and Finns are brachycephalic ; but Virchow observes that if in this respect the skulls of the latter resemble the type of the Danish Stone Age, they differ greatly in height and breadth, so that no ethnic affinity can be predicated between them.

In some cases the skulls obtained from one and the same buried mound differ from one another very considerably. Thus among those found in the great tumulus at Borreby, in Denmark, the breadth, taking the length

---

[1] Nilsson's *Stone Age*, English ed., p. 121.
[2] *Ar. für Anthropologie*, 1870, p. 55.

at 100, varied from 71·8 to 85·7, or no less than 14 per cent.[1]

The care with which the dead were interred, and the custom of burying implements with them, may fairly be regarded as indicating the existence of a belief in the immortality of the soul, and in a material existence after death.

The objects buried with the dead are sometimes numerous, and always interesting. In a large tumulus near Everley, a deposit of burnt bones was "surrounded by a circular wreath of horns of the red-deer"; whilst at a higher level, though three feet from the summit, was the skeleton of a small dog, the "attendant in the chase, and perhaps the victim in death," of the hunter, whose exquisitely chipped arrow-heads, five in number, were deposited with his ashes.[2]

But it is very far from being "constantly" the case that the dead were so well supplied with what we call the necessaries of life; indeed, it is the exception and not the rule. Thus, out of more than 250 interments described by Sir R. Colt Hoare in the first volume of his great work on *Ancient Wiltshire*, only 18 had any implements of stone, only 31 of bone, 67 of bronze, and 11 of iron; and while pottery was present in 107, more than 60 of these contained only sepulchral urns, intended to receive the ashes of the dead, and certainly never meant to hold food. So far, however, as stone implements are concerned, Sir R. C. Hoare appears to have overlooked the ruder instruments and weapons. I will, therefore, rely principally on the evidence afforded by the researches of Mr Bateman and Canon Greenwell.

Although a large number of the interments described by Mr Bateman had been already examined, there were 297 which had not been already disturbed, and though he carefully mentions even the rudest bit of chipped flint, no less than 100 of these were without any implement at all, either of stone or metal, and the drinking-vessels and food-vases were only about 40 in number. Moreover,

[1] Busk, *Vogt's Lectures on Man*, p. 384.   [2] *Archæologia*, xliii. p. 536.

lest it should be supposed that these ill-provided interments were those of poor persons or enemies, we will
leave all these out of consideration. This we can easily
do. We may be sure that these tumuli, which must
have required much labour, were only raised in honour
of the rich or great ; though they may have served, and,
no doubt, often did serve afterwards, as burial-places for
the poor. But it is almost always easy to distinguish the
primary interment ; for though there are some few cases
in which the original occupant has been ignominiously
ejected from his grave to make room for a successor,
these instances are rare, and can generally be detected,
while the secondary interments are usually situated either
above the first or on the sides of the tumulus. The
same feeling which made our ancestors prefer to bury
their dead in a pre-existing tumulus, generally prevented
them from desecrating the earlier interments.

In the following tables, then, I have recorded the
primary interments only ; the first column contains the
name of the tumulus, the succeeding nine indicate the
disposition of the corpse, and the articles found therewith,
while the last is reserved for any special remarks. Out
of 139 interments examined by Mr Bateman, only 105
had any implements or weapons, and only 35 were
accompanied by any pottery that can have held either
food or drink. Moreover, if we examine the nature
of the implements which were deposited with the dead,
we shall find that they are far from representing complete
sets of tools or ornaments. The rarity of bronze in
tombs is, perhaps, not surprising ; but to men so practised
as our predecessors, it must have been an easy matter to
make a rude arrow-head, or a flint flake. Yet some of
the corpses are accompanied by but one single arrow-
head, others by a small flint flake ; some, again, by a
single scraper. Such isolated objects may in many cases
have been dropped accidentally. It must also be observed
that many of the stone objects found by Mr Bateman
are much ruder than might be supposed from the names
he has given them.

In the table (p. 154) with which Canon Greenwell has been so good as to furnish me, and which shows the primary deposits in 102 tumuli examined by him, it will be observed that only 30 contained any implement, the other 72 being altogether bare.[1] They were always buried in a contracted position,[2] or burnt, and there is not a single case in which the corpse was deposited in that extended position which seems to us so natural.

Thus, then, there seems to have been no intention of depositing with each corpse a complete set of implements. The barrow on Cronkstone Hill, for instance, contained the skeleton of a man, with whom had been buried the burnt bones of someone, probably a slave, or, perhaps, a wife, who had been sacrificed at his grave, and yet the only implement found with him was a "circular instrument," probably a flint scraper or a sling-stone. Again, the mound known as "Cow Low" contained only a bone pin. The affectionate relatives who heaped up this tumulus would certainly not have sent their dead sister into the new world with nothing but a bone pin, if they had thought that the things they buried with her could be of any use. Even the great tumulus at Arbor Low contained only a bone pin, a piece of iron pyrites, a kidney-shaped instrument of flint, and two vases. It would be easy to multiply illustrations, and it is, I think, sufficiently evident that the articles found in the graves cannot seriously be considered as affording any evidence of a definite and general belief in a future state of existence, or as having been intended for the use of the dead in the new world to which they were going. Moreover, there is a well-marked speciality in each case, which seems to show that the presence of these rude implements, far from being the result of a national belief, are simply the touching evidence of individual affection.

[1] Canon Greenwell's subsequent researches have tended to confirm this. Out of 379 burials, 63 only had implements of stone, 16 of bronze, and 4 of bone.

[2] The custom of burying the dead in a contracted position was very widely extended. In the Neolithic interments of Egypt the corpse was always in this attitude.

PRIMARY INTERMENTS.

BATEMAN'S VESTIGES OF THE ANTIQUITIES OF DERBYSHIRE.

	CORPSE				OBJECTS OF					CIST.	REMARKS.
	CONTRACTED.	BURNT.	EXTENDED.	POSITION UNCERTAIN.	STONE.	BONE.	BRONZE.	IRON.*	POTTERY.		
1 Gib Hill					Arrow-head and celt						Large tumulus, 18 ft. high. Pieces of burnt flint. Iron fibula near the surface.
2 Middleton Moor					Circular instrument					Cist	Two skeletons.
3 Lark's Low						Pin		Arrow-head		Cist	
4 Bee Low									Fragments	Cist	
5 Liff's					Two arrow-heads, two chisels, 2 spear-heads, 2 knives, etc.	Hammer of horn			Incense cup	Cist	Three bits of red ochre.
6 Brassington Moor					Lance-head and two circular instruments				Fragments	Cist	
7 Elk Low					Lance-head and three other instruments					Cist	Saudstone polisher. With burnt human bones.
8 Cross Low					Bit of a celt and of a chipped flint				Sepulchral urn	Cist	With burnt bones of two children and a horse's tooth.
9 Sliper Low									Drinking cup	Cist	Child.
10 Cross Low										Cist	With burnt human bones, and the skeleton of a child. Tumulus only about 18 in. high.
11 Green Low					Dagger, 3 arrow-heads, etc.	Three instruments			Drinking cup	Cist	With the remains of an infant. Piece of iron pyrites.
12 Sheldon					Flint chippings				Sepulchral urn		Piece of spherical iron pyrites.
13 Arbor Low					Kidney-shaped instrument	Pin			Two urns	Cist	
14 New Inns										Cist	Very small and low barrow.
15 The Low							Dagger			Cist	
16 Net Low					Two rude instruments		Dagger & 2 pins				Two ornaments of Kimmeridge coal. and fragments of calcined flint.
17 Wetton					One instrument				Urn	Cist	Burnt human bones.
18 Bostern					Two rude instruments					Cist	Small barrow.
19 Harthill Moor									Pieces	Cist	
20 Castern										Cist	Small barrow.
21 Moot Low					Spear-head		Box, etc.	Knives			Glass beads, silver needle.
22 Gratton Hill					Six rude instruments					Cist	Horses' teeth.
23 Bassett Wood									Fragments	Cist	This was a large barrow.
24 Ilam										Cist	Skeleton of a dog. Large barrow.
25 Ilam							Pin			Cist	Head of a bull. Large barrow.
26 Ilam									Fragments	Cist	Small barrow.

* It is probable that several of the tumuli which contained iron belonged to the Anglo-Saxon period.

No.	Name		Implement	Other object	Dagger	Knife/misc	Pottery	Type	Remarks
27	Welton	..	Rude instrument	Hammer & spear?	..	..	..	Cist	Skeleton of large dimensions.
28	Lid Low	..	..	..	..	..	..	Cist	With burnt human bones. Horses' teeth.
29	Casterne	..	Small instrument	..	..	..	Urn	Cist	Probably a female.
30	Buxton	..	Two instruments	..	Dagger	..	Drinking cup	Cist	Two skeletons.
31	Cow Low	..	..	Pin	..	..	..	..	
32	Dowe Lowe	..	Flint instrument	..	Dagger	..	..	Cist	Small piece of burnt flint.
33	Slip Low	..	Two arrow-heads	..	..	..	..	Cist	
34	Narrow Dale Hill	..	..	..	..	..	Sepulchral urn	Cist	
35	Middleton	..	Spear-head and circular-ended instrument	..	..	..	..	..	
36	Flaxdale	..	..	..	..	..	Sepulchral urn	Cist	Many pieces of flint.
37	Bruncliff	..	Part of a knife	..	..	Knife	Vessel	Cist	Burnt animal bones.
38	Monyash	..	..	..	..	..	..	..	
39	Gotam	..	Spear-head	Pin	..	..	..	Cist	

BATEMAN'S "TEN YEARS' DIGGINGS."

No.	Name		Implement	Other object	Dagger	Knife/misc	Pottery	Type	Remarks
1	Parcelly Hay	..	Three chipped flints	Beads	..	..	..	Cist	Animal's bones. Shreds of a drinking-cup.
2	Middleton Moor	..	..	..	..	..	..	Cist	Cow's tooth. Jet and bone necklace.
3	Sharpe Low	..	..	..	..	..	..	Cist	Evidently a female, with a child.
4	Dovedale	..	..	..	..	..	Vase	..	Tumulus about 2 ft. high. Fragments of pottery found in mound.
5	Ecton	..	Spear-head	Pin	..	..	..	Cist	With the unburnt skeleton of a child.
6	Shuttlestone	..	Circular flint	..	Celt and dagger	..	..	Cist	Bead of jet.
7	Booth Low	..	Chippings	..	..	..	..	..	Tumulus 8 ft. high.
8	Low Beut	..	Three spear-heads, etc.	Oval piece of stag's horn	..	..	..	..	Secondary } The former on the natural surface, the two latter under it.
9	" "	..	..	..	..	..	..	Cist	Secondary } it.
10	" "	..	..	..	..	..	..	Cist	Jet bead }
11	Dowel	..	Two flints, one an arrow-head	..	..	..	..	Cist	Jet stud.
12	End Low	..	Spear-head	..	Dagger	..	..	Cist	Chippings of flint. }
13	Moneystones	..	Spear-head	..	..	..	..	..	
14	" "	..	Spear-head	..	..	..	..	..	Female, with the skeleton of an infant. Stag's horn.
15	Blake Low	..	..	..	..	..	Drinking cup	..	
16	Rusden Low	..	One broken instrument	..	..	..	..	Cist	With the skeleton of a child.
17	Borthor Low	..	Arrow-head	..	..	..	Two vases	Cist	Female, with the skeleton of an infant.
18	Over Haddon	..	{ One or two rude instruments }	..	..	..	Drinking cup	..	
19	" "	..		..	..	..	..	..	One male and two females. Many jet ornaments.
20	" "	..		..	..	..	..	Cist	
21	" "	..		..	..	..	..	..	With a second slender skeleton. Large tooth of some animal. Core of a cow's horn. Large barrow.
22	Vincent Knoll	..		..	..	..	..	Cist	
23	Chelmorton	..	..	..	..	..	..	Cist	Saxon.
24	Nether Low	..	..	..	..	..	..	Cist	Saxon.
25	Hurdlow	..	Dagger and spear-head	..	Pins & box	Several things	..		
26	Minning Low	..	..	..	..	..	Bits of 3 vessels (Wheelmade)	..	One brass coin of the lower empire.

	CORPSE				OBJECTS OF					CIST	REMARKS
	CONTRACTED	BURNT	EXTENDED	POSITION UNCERTAIN	STONE	BONE	BRONZE	IRON	POTTERY		
27 Minning Low					Some good flints	Implement	Dagger			Cist	The grave contained three skeletons of men, besides other animals' bones.
28 Ballidon Moor					One poor flint only		Awl			Cist	
29 Hill Head					Thin instrument						
30 Vincent Knoll					Good instrument, etc.			Sword, etc.		Cist	Probably a late interment. Small barrow.
31 Brushfield										Cist	Or sepulchral chamber.
32 Taddington										Cist	In gravel.
33 Stakor							Twopieces		Drinking cup	Cist	
34 HobHurst'sHouse					Rude instrument					Cist	
35 Bole Hill								Pin			
36 Foremark								Bit			
37 ,,											
38 ,,											Perhaps Saxon.
39 ,,											
40 ,,											
41 Smerrill					Flake and Knife	Bone netting rule			Drinking cup	Cist	Primary, but not sole. Female.
42 ,,					Dagger, spear, etc.					Cist	
43 Chelmorton								Knives, etc.			
44 Haddon Field					Arrow-head, etc.	Mesh rule	Awl		Drinking cup	Cist	Two skeletons. Bit of pottery.
45 Throwley					Spear-head					Cist	
46 Mare Hill					Arrow-head					Cist	
47 Deepdale					Arrow-head		Dagger		Drinking cup		
48 Mouse Low					Spear-head and 4 arrows	Two implements					
49 Thorncliff					A neat instrument	Several implements	Dagger			Cist	Two skeletons. Bit of pottery.
50 Stanton					A few mean implements	Several implements				Cist	
51 Ribden Low					Several implements					Cist	With burnt bones.
52 Throwley					Two pointed flints	Rude implements	Pin		Incense cup	Cist	With burnt bones.
53 Lomberlow					Spear-head					Cist	With burnt human bones
54 Gateham					Chipped instrument						
55 Bunster					Arrow-head				Sepulchral urn		
56 Grublow					Two arrow-heads						
57 Throwley					Spear-head and basaltic axe	Several implements	Awl		Sepulchral urn, upright		With burnt human bones
58 Blore					Arrow-head	Pin	Bits				Some instruments of flint found in the earth above the interment. Part of a vase.
59 Wetton					Two neat pointed instruments	Pin				Cist	
60 Warslow					Three instruments						Two skeletons of young men.
61 ,,					Spear-head and oval instrument						
62 Scrip Low					Broken instrument						Surrounded by sandstones. Two small pieces of pottery.
63 Lady Low							Dagger				

No. & Locality	Implements / Flints	Weapons, etc.	Other objects	Vessel	Cist	Remarks
64 Ecton Hill	Round flint					Surrounded by six other contracted skeletons, which were accompanied by three rude flints.
65 Castern	Several instruments					Burnt human bones.
66 Elkstone	A few instruments	Armilla, Awl			Cist	Cist not entirely excavated. Tumulus only one foot high.
67 "						Arrow-head, etc., found in the tumulus.
68 Calton Moor	Two instruments		Two combs			Twenty-eight convex objects of bone, like button moulds.
69 Ecton Hill						
70 Cold Eaton			Fragments		Cist	
71 Wyaston			Beads			Saxon lady, ring and earring of silver, brooch and necklace of amber, porcelain, and glass. Only the teeth remaining.
72 Pickering	Arrow-head	Pin		Vase	Cist	
73 Saintoft				Incense cup	Cist	
74 Cawthorn Camps	Spear-head	Dagger			Cist	Two skeletons.
75				Vase	Cist	
76 Gindle Tap	Two instruments			Sepulchral urn		
77 Pickering	Several instruments			Drinking cup with handle		
78	Several instruments, including a spear-head			Thick vessel	Cist	With the skeleton of an infant.
79 "	Two lance-heads and one round-ended			Vase	Cist	
80 "	Spear-head			Vase	Cist	Bits of an urn.
81 "	Spear-head			Vessel	Cist	
82 "					Cist	
84 "	Lance and arrow-head			Vase	Cist	
85 "	Spear-head and spear-head				Cist	Jawbone of a sheep.
86 "	Lance, arrow-head, and circular instrument			Vase	Cist	
87	Two indifferent instruments			Incense cup	Cist	Head of a goat.
88 "	Spear-head, arrow-head, and hammer				Cist	
89 "	Two spears and round-ended instrument					
90	Spear-head, etc.			Incense cup	Cist	
91	Arrow-head and rough instruments	Dagger, Graver		Sepulchral urn	Cist	Two small balls of stone.
92 "	Cutting instruments			Vase	Cist	
93 "	Three poor flints				Cist	
94	Twenty-one implements			Vase	Cist	
95 Allerston Warren	Four instruments			Incense cup	Cist	
96 Pickering	Five flints			Vase	Cist	
97	Knife			Incense cup	Cist	
98 Allerston Warren	Spear-head			Incense cup, Very pretty vase	Cist	Mound not originally sepulchral.
99 Gib Hill	Round instrument		Many things			Saxon; hair only remaining; leather drinking cup.
100 Gib Hill						With burnt bones, apparently deposited at the same time.
101 Benty Grange						
102 Cronkstone	Circular instrument				Cist	

CONTENTS OF TUMULI EXAMINED BY THE REV. CANON GREENWELL.

	CORPSE		OBJECTS OF					GRAVE OR CIST	REMARKS
	BURNT	CONTRACTED	STONE	BONE	BRONZE	IRON	POTTERY		
NORTH RIDING.									
1 Egton Moor, I...		..	..	..	..	..	Food vessel	..	The deposit of bones three feet above the natural surface.
2 „ II...		..	..	..	..	..	..	..	The deposit of bones four feet above the natural surface.
3 Hambleton		..	..	..	..	..	..		Upon the natural surface.
4 Grimston Moor, I.		..	..	..	..	..	Cinerary urn	Shallow grave	
5 „ II.		..	..	..	..	..	Incense cup	Shallow grave	
6 „ III.		..	..	..	..	..	Food vessel	Shallow grave	
7 Castle Howard, I.		..	..	..	..	..	..		
8 „ II.		..	..	..	..	..	..		Deposit of bones upon the natural surface.
9 „ III.		..	..	..	..	..	Small urn	Shallow grave	Deposit of bones upon the natural surface.
10 „ IV.		..	..	..	..	..	Incense cup	Shallow grave	
11 „ V.		..	..	..	..	..	Cinerary urn	Shallow grave	Upon the natural surface.
12 „ VI.		..	..	..	..	..	..	Shallow grave	
13 „ VII.		..	..	..	..	..	Incense cup	Shallow grave	
14 „ VIII.		..	..	..	..	..	2 incense cups	Shallow grave	
15 „ IX.		..	..	..	..	..	Incense cup	Shallow grave	
16 „ X.		..	Round scraper of flint, unburnt	..	..	..	..	Shallow grave	
17 Wykeham Moor, I.		..	Two pieces of flint, burnt	..	..	..	Small urn		Deposit of bones upon the natural surface.
18 „ II.		..	..	..	..	..	Small urn	Shallow grave	Square trench around the base of the barrow.
19 „ III.		..	Large flint knife	..	..	..	..	..	On the natural surface.
20 „ IV.		..	Piece of flint, burnt	..	Dagger	..	2 cinerary urns, one covered by a third urn	..	The urns on the natural surface, and surrounded by a circle of stones, set on edge, four feet in diameter.
21 „ V.		..	Piece of flint, burnt	..	..	..	Cinerary urn, with a smaller one within it	Shallow grave	
22 „ VI.		..	Four pieces of flint, burnt	..	..	..	..	Shallow grave	On the natural surface.
23 „ VII.		..	Javelin head, burnt	..	..	..	Cinerary urn	..	
24 „ VIII.		..	Piece of flint, burnt	..	..	..	..	..	On the natural surface.
EAST RIDING.									
25 Kirby Underdale		..	..	..	..	..	..	Deep grave	Two shoulder blades of a boar in the grave.

No.	Locality	Flint implements	Bone implements	Awls	Pottery	Grave	Remarks
26	Langton Wold	Flint flake	...	...	...	...	A man on the natural surface, and, close to him, a woman; she had a jet bead, a piece of deer's tooth, pierced, a nerita pierced, a vertebra of a fish, and three cowries, at her waist.
27	Duggleby Wold	...	Two implements, one like the bow of a drill	Three awls	...	...	Body on the natural surface.
28	Heslerton Wold	...	...	...	...	...	A child about three years old.
29	Sherburn Wold, I.	...	...	...	Food vessel	Grave	On the natural surface.
30	„ II.	...	...	...	Food vessel	Deep grave	In this mound were the remains of a man and a woman, overlying a deposit of burnt bones. Probably a man, his wife and slave.
31	„ III.	Javelin head, burnt	...	...	Food vessel	Deep grave	
32	„ IV.	...	...	...	...	Shallow grave	
33	„ V.	Scraper and 5 chippings	...	...	...	Shallow grave	On the natural surface.
34	„ VI.	...	...	...	Urn	Shallow grave	In the grave was the body of a child touching the other body.
35	Potter "Brompton" Wold I.	Perforated axe, burnt	...	...	...	Deep grave	In the grave some broken human bones, and some potsherds.
36	„ II.	...	...	...	...	Shallow grave	A man of middle age, at the east end, and at the west a young man.
37	„ III.	Arrow point of flint, barbed	...	...	Food vessel	Deep grave	The urn laid on its side upon the bones.
38	„ IV.	...	Pin, burnt	...	Urn	Shallow grave	Behind the head was the body of a very young child.
39	„ V.	...	Pin	...	...	Shallow grave	
40	„ VI.	Long flint knife in the grave, but not with either the unburnt or burnt body	...	Flat piece	...	Shallow grave	In the grave were the scattered remains of three bodies, and several fragments of a "drinking cup," and two feet above the bodies were the bones of a burnt body.
41	„ VII.	...	...	...	...	Deep grave	
42	Ganton Wold, I.	...	...	...	Urn	...	On the natural surface.
43	„ II.	...	...	...	...	Shallow grave	Five bodies were laid close together, and evidently buried at the same time.
44	„ III.	Oval scraper	...	...	Food vessel	Deep grave	On the natural surface.
45	„ IV.	...	...	...	...	Deep grave	The body had been laid upon a wooden platform, which rested upon stakes.
46	„ V.	...	Pin	...	...	Shallow grave	
47	„ VI.	Oval scraper, burnt	...	...	...	Deep grave	
48	„ VII.	...	...	...	...	Shallow grave	On the natural surface.
49	„ VIII.	...	...	...	...	...	
50	Willerby Wold, I.	...	...	...	Food vessel	Deep grave	
51	„ II.	2 knives and 4 flint chips	...	...	...	Deep grave	In the grave the scattered bones of a body.
52	„ III.	...	...	...	Food vessel	Deep grave	On the natural surface.
53	„ IV.	...	...	...	...	Shallow grave	
54	„ V.	...	...	...	Drinking cup	Deep grave	
55	„ VI.	...	...	...	...	...	A woman. At the other end of the grave was a man and three children, the bones of whom had been displaced and relaid in a sort of rude order.

	CORPSE		OBJECTS OF					GRAVE OR CIST	REMARKS
	CONTRACTED	BURNT	STONE	BONE	BRONZE	IRON	POTTERY		
56 Rudston ..	..	..	..	Club made from the antler of a red deer	..	..	Drinking cup ..	Grave ..	In the grave were the remains of a disturbed body.
57 Butterwick .. I.	..	..	Knife	..	..	..	..	Deep grave ..	Five large jet, and one stone, button.
58 ,, II.	..	..	..	..	Dagger, axe & drill	..	Cinerary urn	Grave	On the natural surface.
59 Weaverthorpe, I.	..	..	..	..	Awl	..	Food vessel	Grave	A body cut through in making the grave.
60 ,, II.	..	..	Large flake	..	..	..	..	Deep grave ..	On the natural surface.
61 ,, III.	..	..	Knife and large flake	..	..	..	..	Deep grave	On the natural surface.
62 ,, IV.	..	..	..	..	..	..	Drinking cup ..	Shallow grave	Above the grave were three heads without lower jaws, carefully deposited in the form of Y.
63 ,, V.	..	..	..	..	..	..	..		
64 ,, VI.	..	..	Oval scraper or knife	..	..	..	..	Deep grave ..	Some disturbed bones of a child in the grave.
65 ,, VII.	..	..	..	Two tines of a red deer's antler, cut off	..	..	..	Grave ..	
66 ,, VIII.	..	..	..	..	..	..	Urn	Very shallow grave	Necklace of jet beads, 119 flat circular disks, and a triangular central pendant.
67 ,, IX.	..	..	..	..	Armlet, fibula	Tongue of fibula replacing the broken bronze tongue	..	Very shallow grave	On the natural surface.
68 ,, X.	..	..	..	..	..	..	..	Very shallow grave	Necklace of blue glass beads, with a zigzag pattern in white.
69 ,, XI.	..	..	..	..	Armlet ..	..	..	Very shallow grave	Nos. 66–69, a small group; 66, 67, women; 68, 69, men. The armlets of "late Keltic type," and, like the necklace, similar to those found at Arras.
70 ,, XII.	..	..	..	..	..	..	..	Very shallow grave	
71 ,, XIII.	..	..	..	..	..	..	..	Very shallow grave	
72 ,, XIV.	..	..	..	..	..	..	..	Grave	In the grave some burnt bones and unburnt bones of a child, all scattered, and several pieces of a "drinking cup." The two bodies were placed facing each other, and in a reverse position. The urn was between them.
73 ,, XV.	..	..	..	Hammer of red deer horn	..	..	Urn ..	Shallow grave	On the natural surface.
74 ,, XVI.	..	..	Perforated axe, a round scraper of flint, and a flake	..	..	..	..	Deep grave ..	Man: in the grave, some bones of a disturbed body.
75 ,, XVII.	..	..	Two flint chippings	..	2 earrings	..	..	Deep grave ..	Woman. The two graves joined by an opening two feet wide.

No. & Site	Implement	Pin	Vessel	Grave	Remarks
76 Weaverthorpe, XVIII.	Javelin head		Urn	Deep grave	On the natural surface. Urn laid upon the bones.
77 Enthorpe, I.			Urn		On the natural surface. Urn laid upon the bones.
78 ,, II.			Two urns		Just above natural surface. Urns amongst the bones.
79 ,, III.			Urn		Three feet above the natural surface.
80 ,, IV.				Deep grave	
81 ,, V.				Grave	
82 ,, VI.			Cinerary urn	Shallow grave	
83 Gardham, I.				Shallow grave	
84 ,, II.				Shallow grave	
85 Asby ,, III.				Shallow grave	
86 ,, IV.					
WEST RIDING.					
87 Ferrybridge		Pin	Drinking cup	Grave	Below the natural surface.
CUMBERLAND.					
88 Castle Carrock, I.	Long and narrow knife, unburnt		Drinking cup	Cist	
89 ,, II.				Shallow grave	
WESTMORELAND.					
90 Moor Divock			Food vessel	Grave	Stone circle round the base of the cairn.
91 Kirby Stephen, I.			Incense cup	Shallow grave	On the natural surface.
92 ,, II.				Grave	
93 ,, III.					
94 WarcoP ..					On the natural surface.
95 Asby ..				Shallow grave	Stone circle round the base of cairn.
NORTHUMBER- LAND.					
96 Ford, I. ..			Food vessel	Cist	A very young child. Stone circle round the base of the barrow.
97 ,, II.	Fragment of flint, burnt	Fragment of Pin pin	Cinerary urn		Four jet beads. Deposit of bones on surface.
98 ,, III.			Cinerary urn		On the natural surface.
99 ,, IV.	Pointed oval knife (?) unburnt			Grave	
100 Chatton ..	Arrow-point, burnt		Food vessel	Grave	
101 Old Bewick, I.				Cist	Below the natural surface. Stone circle round base of cairn.
102 ,, II.	Knife			Cist	Below the natural surface. Stone circle round base of cairn.
103 Chollerton				Cist	On the natural surface.

In some cases, however, the facts certainly seem to indicate a belief that the dead could carry their wealth with them to another world. For instance, Canon Greenwell found in one barrow[1] no less than 79 saws, 17 scrapers, 3 leaf-shaped arrow-points, 2 pointed tools (probably for boring), several flint articles of uncertain purpose, a hammer-stone, and a piece of a greenstone axe. Many of the saws were very delicately serrated, some along both edges, and showing by the glaze upon the edge that they had been in use. The number of saws in this case far exceeded the aggregate of those obtained from all the barrows he had opened ; and though, as he says, " it is by no means easy to give any reasonable explanation of the phenomenon," I would venture to suggest that they were regarded as wealth ; in fact as a form of money, which would enable their owner to purchase what he might require.

In some few cases, again, small models of weapons have been found, in lieu of the weapons themselves. In modern Esquimaux graves, small models of kajaks, spears, etc., are sometimes buried, and a similar fact has been observed in Egyptian tombs. Mr Franks informs me that much of the jewellery found in Etruscan tombs is so thin that it can scarcely have been intended for wear during life. In Japan those who are entitled to wear swords during life have wooden ones placed in their graves, as insignia of rank ; and it has long been the custom in China to bury paper cuttings, or drawings, of horses, money, etc., under the belief that the objects so represented will be actually possessed by the deceased.[2]

We must always bear in mind that the ancient tumuli do not all belong to one period, nor to one race of men. No tumuli belonging to the Palæolithic Period have yet been discovered, but this mode of burial appears to have existed in Northern and Western Europe from the Neolithic, or second Stone Period, down to the introduction of Christianity. Indeed it was the examination of

---

[1] *British Barrows*, p. 262.
[2] See, for instance, *Marco Polo's Travels*, Edinburgh, 1846, pp. 248–260.

the tumuli which first induced Sir R. Colt Hoare, and other archæologists, to adopt for Northern Europe the division into three great periods.

So far, however, as the barrows themselves are concerned (though the passage-graves and long barrows seem always to belong to the Stone Age), we are not acquainted with any external differences by which the tumuli of the Stone, Bronze, and Iron Ages can, with certainty, be distinguished from one another. The contents of the graves are more instructive, though it would of course be unsafe to conclude that a given tumulus belongs to the Stone Age, because it contained one or two implements made of that material. We know that stone was extensively used throughout the Bronze Age ; and, indeed, out of 37 tumuli in which Mr Bateman found objects made of bronze, no less than 29 contained also stone implements, many of which, moreover, were extremely rude.

Evidently, therefore, the mere presence of a few implements of stone is in itself no sufficient reason for referring any given interment to the Stone Age. The following tabular statement of 297 interments, recorded by Mr Bateman, will, I think, be found interesting :—

Implements.	Corpse.				Total.
	Contracted, i.e. in a sitting posture.	Burnt.	Extended.	Position uncertain.	
None . . .	27	63	3	7	100
Stone . . .	53	48	2	31	134
Bronze . . .	15	10	5	7	37
Iron . . .	2	3	14	7	26
Total . .	97	124	24	52	297

These interments are all from the counties of Derby, Stafford, and York. In his work on ancient Wiltshire, Sir R. C. Hoare records the examination of 267 interments, which may be tabulated in a similar manner, as follows :—

| Implements. | Corpse. | | | | Total. |
	Con-tracted.	Burnt.	Ex-tended.	Position Un-certain.	
None . . .	9	160	3	12	184
Stone . . .	2	5	1	1	9
Bronze . . .	4	49	2	8	63
Iron . . .	—	—	7	4	11
Total . .	15	214	13	25	267

We see that in these tables nearly all the cases of bronze were interments in which the body was contracted, preceded by cremation, and the same is the case in the Yorkshire tumuli examined by Canon Greenwell. As regards the Salisbury Plain tumuli, I am disposed to regard the great majority as belonging to the Bronze Age. No less than 270 cluster round Stonehenge, and it seems most probable that the dead were brought from a distance to lie near the great temple. In this case the great majority of the tumuli belong, therefore, to one period, that, namely, at which the temple was held sacred. Some few, indeed, may be referable to earlier or later times, but as out of 152 of these interments which were examined by Sir R. C. Hoare, no less than 39 contained objects of bronze, I am disposed to regard the whole group as belonging to the Bronze Period. Now in these 152 cases the corpse was contracted in 4 only, and extended in 3. In 16 the disposition of the corpse was not ascertained, and in no less than 129 it had been burnt.

If we combine the observations of Sir R. C. Hoare and Mr Bateman, we shall obtain the following table :—

| Implements. | Corpse. | | | | Total. |
	Con-tracted.	Burnt.	Ex-tended.	Position Un-certain.	
None . . .	36	223	6	19	284
Stone . . .	55	53	3	32	143
Bronze . . .	19	59	7	15	100
Iron . . .	2	3	21	11	37
Total . .	112	338	37	77	564

Some few of these interments were no doubt Anglo-Saxon ; if these had been eliminated the argument would have appeared still stronger ; but taking them as they are, out of 37 graves containing iron weapons or implements, the corpse was certainly extended in 21 cases, and probably so in several others ; while, out of no less than 527 cases in which iron was not present, the corpse was extended only in 16, the proportion being at least $\frac{7}{12}$ths in one case, and only $\frac{1}{33}$rd in the other. On the whole we may certainly conclude that this mode of burial was introduced at about the same period as the use of iron.

As regards the habit of burning the dead, the evidence is less conclusive. Out of 100 cases, indeed, of graves characterized by the presence of bronze, the corpse appears to have been buried in a contracted posture 19 times only; in an extended position, only 7 times. It would seem, therefore, that during the Bronze Age the dead were generally burnt. It is also true that there are many cases in which interments by cremation, if I may use such an expression, contain no weapons or objects of bronze. We know, however, that this metal must always have been expensive, and it is not unreasonable to suppose that many, at any rate, of these interments may belong to the Bronze Age, although no objects of metal occurred in them.

There can be no doubt that in the Neolithic Stone Age it was usual to bury the corpse in a sitting or contracted posture ; and, indeed, it appears probable, although far from being satisfactorily established, that in Western Europe this attitude generally indicates an interment of the Stone Age ; while those cases in which the skeleton was extended may be referred, with little hesitation, to the Age of Iron. At the same time we must remember that in Anglo-Saxon times the dead were burned by some tribes, and buried by others, and there may well have been differences during the Stone Age also between different tribes.

But although the presence of a few flint flakes, or other stone implements, is certainly no sufficient reason for referring any given tumulus to the Stone Age, the case is different where a large number of objects have been found together; for instance, I have in my collection a group of stone implements consisting of 14 beautifully made axes, wedges, chisels, spear-heads, etc., and more than 60 capital flakes, which were all found together in one of the large Danish sepulchral chambers, on the Island of Möen, and have been described by M. Boye.[1] The tumulus had a circumference of 140 ells, and a height of about 8 ells. It is probable that it had been surrounded by a circle of stones, for M. Jensen, the owner, remembered that, many years before, the northern side had been surrounded by a row of stones standing close together. None of them, however, at present remain. Unfortunately M. Boye was not present when they began to remove the tumulus; still he thinks that the account given to him may be relied on with safety. M. Jensen began to dig on the east side of the tumulus, and the first thing which he came to was a jar, which he unfortunately broke. It contained burnt bones and a bronze pin, the head of which was ornamented with concentric lines. Towards the S.S.E. was found a cist, about an ell long, and formed of flat stones. In it were burnt bones, a bent knife, and a pair of pincers two inches in length; both these objects were of bronze. Not far from this cist was another urn, containing burnt bones, with several objects of bronze, namely, a knife four inches in length, part of a small symbolical sword, and two fragments of an awl. It is evident that these three interments belonged to the Bronze Age, and also that they were secondary, that is to say, that they belonged to a later date than the original sepulchral chamber, over which the tumulus had been made.

The sepulchral chamber itself (fig. 163) lay north and south, was of an oval form, about eight and a half ells in length, and twenty and a half in circumference, and about two and a half in height. The walls consisted of twelve

[1] *Annaler for Nordisk Oldkyndighed og Historie*, 1858, p. 202.

very large, unhewn stones, which, however, did not in most cases touch one another, but left intervals which were filled up by smaller stones. The roof was formed by five great blocks, the spaces between them being filled up by smaller ones. The passage, which was on the east side, was five ells long and one ell broad, and was formed by eleven side stones and three roof stones. At the place (*a*) was, on each side, a smaller stone, which in conjunction with another on the floor between them, formed a sort of threshold, probably indicating the place where the door stood. Similar traces of a doorway have been found in other Danish tumuli, and may, perhaps, be taken as evidence that the mounds had been used previously as houses ; at the

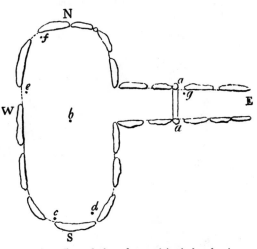

Fig. 163.—Ground plan of a sepulchral chamber in a large tumulus on the Island of Möen.

time of the interment the construction of a door would have been simply purposeless, the passage leading to it being filled up with rubbish. The chamber was filled up with mould to within half an ell of the roof. About the middle, not far from the bottom, a skeleton, perhaps of a sacrificed slave, was extended (at *b*), with the head towards the north. On the south side (at *c* and *d*) occurred two crania, each of which lay on a quantity of bones, indicating that the corpses had been buried in a sitting posture. At (*e*) was a similar skeleton, close to which were three amber beads, a beautiful flint axe, which did not seem to have been ever used, a small unfinished chisel, and some fragments of pottery, ornamented with points and lines. At (*f*) was another skeleton, in a similar position, with a flint flake, an amber bead, and some fragments of pottery. Figs. 164, 165 represent one of the skulls from this stone chamber. Several other skeletons were found sitting round the side walls, but they had unluckily been removed and thrown away before the arrival of M. Boye. With them were at least twenty different jars or urns, all of them inverted, and prettily decorated with points and lines.

Besides these objects, the earth in the chamber contained 5 flint spear-heads, a fragment of a flint spear which

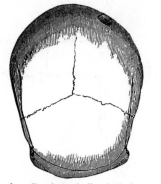

Fig. 164.—Brachycephalic skull from the same tumulus, one-quarter of the natural size.

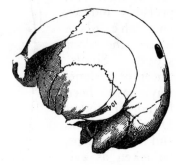

Fig. 165.—Ditto, side view.

had been broken and worked up again, 2 small flint chisels, 53 flint flakes, varying from three to five and a half inches in length ; 19 perfect, and 31 broken, amber beads, of which the greater number were hammer-like, the rest tubular or ring-shaped. The passage was filled up by earth, mixed with fragments of pottery, and small stones. About the middle was a skeleton, with the head towards the east, at the side of which were five flakes and an amber bead. Close to the feet was a jar, unornamented, and much ruder than those found in the chamber itself. Not the smallest fragment of metal was found either in the chamber or in the passage.

Again, as a second case of the same sort, I may mention the Long Barrow (fig. 166) near West Kennet, in Wiltshire, described by Dr Thurnam.[1] The tumulus in this case is 336 feet in length, 40 feet wide at the west end, and 75 feet at the east, with a height of 8 feet. The walls of the chamber are formed by six great blocks of stone, and it opens into a passage, so that the ground

FIG. 166.—Interior of the sepulchral chamber in the Long Barrow near West Kennet.[2]

plan very closely resembles that of the tumulus just described, and, in fact, of the " Passage graves " generally. The chamber and entrance were nearly filled with chalk rubble, containing also bones of animals, flint implements (figs. 167–170), and fragments of pottery. In the chamber were four skeletons, two of which appear to

---

[1] *Archæologia*, vol. xxxviii. p. 405.
[2] Figs. 166–176 are from *Archæologia*, vol. xxxviii.

have been buried in a sitting posture. In different parts
of the chamber were

found nearly 300
flakes, 3 or 4 flint
cores, a whetstone, a
scraper, part of a bone
pin, a bead of Kim-
meridge shale, and
several heaps of frag-
ments of pottery (figs.

FIGS. 167, 168.—Flint scrapers from Long
Barrow, two-thirds of the actual size.

171–176) belonging
apparently to no less

than 50 different vessels, and all made
by hand, with one doubtful exception.
No trace of metal was discovered. The
two pieces figs. 175, 176 were found
apart from the rest, and may, perhaps,
be of later origin.

The large
tumuli of Brit-
tany, most of
which have re-
cently been
opened, have
afforded several
other instances of
the same kind.

FIG. 169.—Flint flake
from the same, two-
thirds of the actual
size.

FIG. 170. — Flint implement
from the same, two-thirds
of the actual size.

Thus the great Mont St Michel, at
Carnac, which is no less than 380
feet in length, and 190 feet broad,
with an average height of 33 feet,
was found to contain a square
chamber, in which were 11 beautiful jade celts, 2 large rough celts,
and 26 small fibrolite celts, besides
110 beads, mostly of callais, and some fragments of flint.[1]

[1] *Rapport à M. le Préfet du Morbihan sur les fouilles du Mont
St Michel*, par M. Réné Galles, 1862. Beads of callais have also been
found in the south of France and in Portugal. Cartailhac, *Ages Préhist.
de l'Espagne et du Portugal*, pp. 130–132.

Again, the chamber in the tumulus called Manné-er-H'roek contained 103 stone axes, 3 flint flakes, and 50 beads of callais, jasper, quartz, and agate, but neither of these great tumuli con-

tained a trace of metal.[1]

Other similar cases might be mentioned,[2] in which tumuli of large size, covering a sepulchral chamber, constructed with great labour, and evidently intended for a person or persons of high rank, have contained numerous objects of stone and pottery, without a trace of metal.

FIG. 171.—Fragment of pottery from the same, two-thirds of the actual size.

It appears reasonable to conclude that these interments belong to the ante-metallic period ; especially when, as in the first-mentioned case, we find several secondary inter-

FIG. 172.—Fragment of pottery from the same, actual size.

ments, plainly belonging to a later age, and although presenting no such indications of high rank, still accompanied by objects of bronze.

It may seem at first sight very improbable that works so considerable should have been undertaken and carried out by nations entirely ignorant of metal. The burial mound of Oberea, in Otaheiti, was nevertheless 267 feet long, 87 feet wide, and 44 feet in height. And in treating of modern savages, I shall hereafter have occasion to notice other instances quite as extraordinary.

---

[1] *Manné-er-H'roeck* : *Rapport à la Sociéte Polymathique*, par M. Lefèbvre et M. Réné Galles, 1863.
[2] See, for instance, Lukis, *Archæologia*, vol. xxxv. p. 247.

The practice of burying in old tumuli, which continued even down to the times of Charlemagne,[1] has led to some confusion, because objects of very different date are thus liable to be described as coming from one grave ; yet, on the other hand, it is very instructive, as there are several cases on record, besides the one above mentioned, of interments characterized by bronze being found above, and being, therefore, evidently subsequent to others, accompanied by stone only.[2]

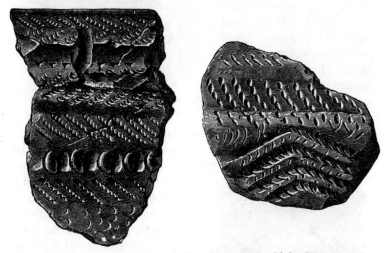

FIGS. 173, 174.—Fragments of pottery from the same, two-thirds of the actual size.

On the whole, however, though it is evident that the objects most frequently buried with the dead would be those most generally used by the living, and though the prevalence of stone implements proves the important part played by stone in ancient times, and goes far to justify the belief in a Stone Age ; still, the evidence to be brought forward on this point in the following chapters will, probably, to many minds seem more satisfactory ; and, at

[1] One of his regulations ran as follows :—" Jubemus ut corpora Christianorum Saxonorum ad cemeteria ecclesiæ deferantur, et non ad tumulus paganorum."
[2] See, for instance, Von Sacken, *Leitfaden zur Kunde des heidnischen Alterthums*, p. 15.

any rate, we must admit that in the present state of our knowledge, there are comparatively few interments which we could, with confidence, refer to the Neolithic Stone Age, however firmly we may believe that a great many of them must belong to it.

Mr Bateman[1] has proposed to range the pottery found in ancient British tumuli under four different heads, namely : (1) Urns ; (2) Incense Cups ; (3) Food Vases ; (4) Drinking Cups. The urns generally accompany interments by cremation, and have either contained or been inverted

FIG. 175.—Fragment of pottery from the same, two-thirds of the actual size.

over burnt human bones. They are generally of large size, "from 10 to 16 inches high, with a deep border, more or less decorated by impressions of twisted thongs,

and incised patterns in which the chevron or herring-bone constantly recurs in various combinations, occasionally relieved by circular punctures, or assuming a reticulated appearance. They are all made by hand, no trace of the potter's wheel being ever found on them. They almost invariably have an overhanging rim. The material of which they are formed is

FIG. 176.—Fragment of pottery, actual size.

clay mixed with pebbles, and some of them have been described as "sun-dried." This, however, appears to be altogether a mistake, arising from the imperfect manner in which they were burnt. In colour, they

---

[1] *Ten Years' Diggings in Celtic and Saxon Gravehills.* The pottery of the Stone Age has recently been well described by the Hon. J. Abercromby in a special work.

are generally brown or burnt umber outside and black inside. Fig. 177 represents a specimen from Flaxdale Barrow, in Derbyshire.

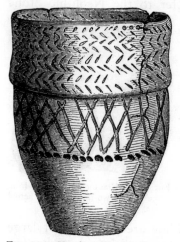

Secondly, the "incense cups," so called by Sir R. Colt Hoare. They differ very much in shape, and are seldom more than 3 inches high. When decorated the patterns are the same as those on the urns, and are usually on the under surface, but they are often left plain. They are often pierced. "Incense cups" have been found throughout Great Britain, and also in Ireland. Their use seems to me still very doubtful. They have in

FIG. 177.—Urn from Flaxdale Barrow. The original is 14 inches in height.

several cases been found with bronze. "The third division includes vessels of every style of ornament, from the rudest to the most elaborate, but nearly alike in size, and more difficult to assign to a determinate period than any other, from the fact of a coarse and a well-finished one having several times been found in com-pany." The woodcuts (figs.

FIGS. 178, 179.—Vases from Arbor Low, in Derbyshire.

178, 179) represent two vessels found in a barrow on the circle at Arbor Low, in Derbyshire.

Fourthly, "The drinking cups (fig. 180) are generally from six and a half to nine inches high, of a tall shape, contracted in the middle, globular below, and expanding at the mouth : they are carefully formed by hand, of fine clay, tempered with sharp sand, and well-baked ; the walls are thin, averaging about three-eighth of an inch, light brown outside, and grey within." They have not yet been found in Ireland. They are generally much ornamented, and usually accompany well-made flint implements and unburnt bodies. Mr Bateman considered that the greater number belong to the ante-metallic period, but they have so often been found in association with bronze, that I think we may safely refer them to the Bronze Age.

FIG. 180.—Drinking cup from Green Low.

The Domestic Pottery of the period is not so well known to us, but some has been found in caves, and on the site of ancient dwelling-places. It is formed of the same material as that found in the tumuli, but is of different and plainer forms, and generally entirely without ornament. The pottery of the pre-Roman tumuli is very distinctive, and differs in material, form, colour, and mode of decoration, both from that of the Roman and of the Anglo-Saxon periods. It is, I believe I may say invariably, hand-made ; and is never artificially coloured.

Numerous as are the varieties of pottery found in ante-Roman tumuli, they appear (so far, at any rate, as those discovered by Mr Bateman are concerned) to have been all made by hand, without any assistance from the potter's wheel ; they are formed of clay tempered with sand, and often containing small pebbles ; they very rarely have handles, and spouts seem to have been unknown ; the ornaments consist of straight lines, dots, or marks, as if a cord had been impressed on the soft clay ; circular or curved lines are rare, nor is there the slightest attempt to copy any animal or plant. In some cases it is obvious that woven fabrics have been impressed on the clay while still soft, and we thus obtain proof of the existence of prehistoric textile fabrics, the actual specimens of which have long ceased to exist.[1]

As a general rule the megalithic monuments are constructed of rough stones neither hewn nor ornamented. Lately, however, many instances of engravings have been observed. In the north of England and in Scotland these generally take the form of cups, spirals, circles with a dot in the middle, or incomplete circles with a dot in the middle, or incomplete circles with a line running from the centre through the interval, as in fig. 181.[2] We have as yet no satisfactory clue to the meaning of these engravings, many of which have been figured by Mr Tate and Sir J. Y. Simpson. They occur in evident association with ancient oppida and fortifications, as well as on menhirs, and on the stones composing dolmens and cromlechs. Fig. 181 represents a characteristic group on a rock at Auchnabreach in Argyllshire. The surface of the rock is well adapted to receive such sculpturings, having been smoothed and prepared by glacial action.

Similar sculpturings have been found in Ireland, where also the great tumuli on the Boyne afford instances of more elaborate ornamentation. The great stone at the entrance of New Grange, for instance, is covered with double spirals, and those forming the central chamber are also covered with circles, spirals, and other patterns, one of the most remarkable being that of a so-called fern leaf, which occurs also in Brittany and in the so-called temple of Hagiar Kem, in Malta. Mr Conwell has recently discovered an extensive series of interesting sepulchral sculptures in the county of Meath. With the exception

[1] See, for instance, Holmes, *Rep. of U.S. Bur. of Ethnology*, 1881.
[2] See Tate on *The Sculptured Rocks of Northumberland*, 1865; Sir J. Y. Simpson on "Ancient Sculpturings of Cups and Concentric Rings, etc.," *Proc. S. of Antiquaries of Scotland*, vol. vi., 1867. The monuments described by Mr Stuart, in his great work on *The Sculptured Stones of Scotland*, belong to a much later period, and scarcely fall within the scope of the present work. For rock carvings in Spain, see Don M. de Góngora y Martinez, *Antigüedades Prehistóricas de Andalucia*.

of the "fern leaf," all these archaic sculpturings in Great Britain are mere geometrical figures. The same figures also occur in Brittany, accompanied, however, by frequent representations of stone axes, both with and without handles.

The rock sculptures of Scandinavia present a still further advance, many of them being rude representations

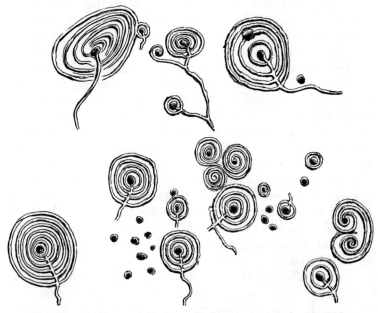

FIG. 181.—Sculptures on the Lower Rock at Auchnabreach, Argyllshire.
After Sir J. Y. Simpson.

of boats, much like those on some of the bronze knives (figs. 45–46).

The most remarkable monument of this kind, however, is that of Kivik in Scania, close to the shore of the Baltic.

Cup markings also occur among the Kumaon Hills in Hindostan. Mr Rivett Carnac has suggested that they are connected with Lingam worship ; the central mark representing the Lingam, the circle the Yoni. The rich, he supposes, put up a monument, the poor merely carved the symbol.

Crooke[1] mentions that "in almost every Panjab village may be seen small platforms with rows of little hemispherical depressions, into which milk and Ganges water are poured, and by which lamps are lit, and Bráhmans fed to conciliate the Dead"; "while the careful mother will always dedicate a rupee to him, and hang it round her child's neck till he grows up." Mr Ibbetson[2] suggests that this may have been the origin of the mysterious so-called "cup-marks." Montelius informs us[3] that in out-of-the-way parts of Sweden offerings to the Spirit are made in these cup-markings, even at the present day.

The remains of other mammals found with ancient human relics have acquired increased interest, since the admirable researches of the Danish and Swiss zoologico-archæologists, and especially of Steenstrup and Rütimeyer, by whose skilful cross-examination much valuable and unexpected evidence has been elicited from materials of most unpromising appearance. Unfortunately the non-human remains found in tumuli are usually in a very fragmentary condition. No remains of any extinct animal have as yet been found in the tumuli of Western Europe. Even the reindeer is altogether absent. The deer and ox are most frequent. The latter was certainly domesticated in Switzerland as early as the Neolithic period. Whether this was the case in Northern Europe, though probable, is still uncertain. Some archæologists believe the dog to have been at that period the only animal domesticated; others, on the contrary, consider the cow, sheep, pig, and goat, if not the horse, to have been at that early period domesticated in the North. In the contents of British barrows, bones of these animals have been frequently observed; and it would appear from the researches of Canon Greenwell that most of them belonged to domesticated animals.[4]

Remains of the horse are very rare in English barrows,

---

[1] *An Introduction to the Popular Religion and Folk-lore of Northern India*, by W. Crooke, B.A. (1894).
[2] Ibbetson, *Rep. on the Karnal Dis.*, ch. ix.
[3] *The Civilization of Sweden in Heathen Times*, p. 36.
[4] Greenwell, *British Barrows*.

and I know no well-authenticated case of their occurrence in a long barrow. I have thought, therefore, that it might be of interest to point out the class of graves in which bones or teeth of horses were found. In Mr Bateman's valuable works there are, altogether, 28 cases ; but of these, 9 were in tumuli which had been previously opened, and in one case no body was found. Of the remaining 18, 5 were tumuli containing iron, and 7 were accompanied with bronze. In one more case, that of the "Liffs," it is doubtful whether the barrow had not been disturbed. Of the remaining 6 tumuli, 2 contained beautiful drinking vessels, of a very well-marked type, certainly in use during the Bronze Age, if not peculiar to it ; and in both these instances, as well as in a third, the interment was accompanied by burnt human bones, suggestive of dreadful rites. Even, however, if these cases cannot be referred to the Bronze Age, we still see that out of the 297 interments only 63 contained metal, or about 21 per cent. ; while out of the 18 cases of horses' remains, 12, or about 66 per cent., certainly belong to the metallic period. Canon Greenwell also found the bones of the horse only in 3 or 4 interments, all apparently of the Bronze Age or later. This seems to be *primâ facie* evidence that the horse was very rare, if not altogether unknown, in England during the Stone Age. Both the horse and bull appear to have been sacrified at graves during later times, and probably formed part of the funeral feast. The teeth of oxen are so common in tumuli, that they are even said by Mr Bateman to be " uniformly found with the more ancient interments."

The very frequent presence of the bones of quadrupeds in tumuli appears to show that sepulchral feasts were generally held in honour of the dead, and the numerous cases in which interments were accompanied by burnt human bones tend to prove the prevalence of still more dreadful customs, and that not only horses[1] and dogs,

---

[1] Even so lately as in 1871, Frederick Casimir was laid in his grave with his slaughtered horse. *Horæ ferales*, p. 66.

but slaves also, were frequently sacrificed at their masters' graves ; it is not improbable that wives often were burnt with their husbands, as in India, and among many savage tribes. For instance, among the Fijis it is usual on the death of a chief to sacrifice a certain number of slaves, whose bodies " are called ' grass ' for bedding " the grave.[1] " It is probable," says Mr Bateman, " that the critical examination of all deposits of burnt bones would lead to much curious information respecting the statistics of suttee and infanticide, both which abominations we are unwillingly compelled, by accumulated evidence, to believe were practised in pagan Britain."

But it was not only human beings and animals who were sacrificed at the grave in order that their ghosts might accompany their masters to the land of spirits. The implements and weapons found in graves have in many cases been intentionally broken, and I have elsewhere suggested that this was done in order to kill them. Herodotus in an interesting passage [2] tells us that Melissa, wife of Periander, complained of cold in the other world, as she was naked, having no clothes, because none had been burnt at her burial.

From the numerous cases in which the bones of an infant and a woman have been found together in one grave, it would seem that if any woman died in childbirth, or while nursing, the baby was buried alive with her, as is still the practice among some Esquimaux families. It is, however, an interesting fact, and throws some light on the social relations of the times, that there are several cases in which a barrow even of considerable size has been erected over the remains of an infant—the favourite child, we may suppose, of some powerful chief.

No traces of Corn have yet been met with in any of our Neolithic barrows.

These conclusions, however, cannot be extended to Europe. In Switzerland, for instance, as far as our

---

[1] *Manners and Customs of the Feegees*, by T. Williams, 1860, vol. i. p. 189.
[2] *Terpsichore*, v. 92.

present evidence goes, though it is far from being so full as that derived from English sources, the introduction of bronze does not appear to have been accompanied by any change of race. In Scandinavia, again, we have two classes of barrows corresponding to those of this country. But though the Scandinavian long barrows so remarkably resemble those of England, they were erected by a very different race ; that of the English long barrows being long-headed, while the constructors of the Scandinavian chambered barrows were, on the contrary, almost always round-headed. It is curious that in certain barrows no trace of a burial has been found. Some archæologists suppose that in these cases the body was buried without any vase, ornament, or implement, and that it has wholly disappeared. I should, however, rather be disposed to regard them as memorial barrows. The common people were interred without barrows

On the whole, then, the tumuli of Northern Europe appear to range in point of time from the Neolithic down to post-Roman times. Since, however, they never contain remains of the extinct mammalia, nor even of the reindeer, and as no implements of the Palæolithic type have ever been discovered in them, we cannot refer any of them to the earlier Stone Age. So far as England is concerned, the ante-Roman barrows appear to fall into two great groups—the long barrows and the round barrows. The long barrows are apparently the earlier and belong exclusively to the Stone Age, as they also do in Scandinavia. They contain no metal, little pottery, and were constructed by a long-headed race. Professor Rolleston has called attention to the remarkable character afforded by the lower jaw ; the tumid horizontal segment corresponding to its molar teeth, the wide ramus, short coronoid process, feeble chin, and rounded, often inwardly bent, angle. It is true that similar lower jaws occur among the Bushmen, Tasmanians, Melanesians, and other low races, but Professor Rolleston affirms [1] that amongst Esquimaux only do we find such jaws combined with the

[1] Greenwell and Rolleston, *British Barrows*, p. 718.

widely open orbit and vertically elongated nasal cavity so characteristic of the long barrow race.

The round barrows belong in many cases to the Bronze Age. The presence of metal, the forms of some of the stone implements, as, for instance, the tanged arrow-heads and the pierced stone axes, as well as the character of the pottery, justify the conclusion that they belong to a later period than the long barrows—one, moreover, at which Britain was occupied by a round-headed race, among whom lived, however, probably in a subordinate position, representatives of the earlier long-headed people.

I would particularly urge on those who may in future open barrows—

(1) To record the sex of the person buried; this is more satisfactorily to be determined from the form of the pelvis than from the skull. In this manner we may hope to determine the relative position, and the separate occupation (if any) of the two sexes.

(2) To observe the state of the teeth, from which we may derive information as to the nature of the food.

(3) To preserve carefully any bones of quadrupeds that may be present, in order to ascertain the species, and, in the case of the ox and hog, to determine, if possible, whether they belong to wild or domesticated individuals.

We may fairly hope that when thoroughly questioned the barrows will not only answer many of these interesting questions, but that they will also tell us many things which it would never occur to us to ask. It is evident, at least, that when a sufficient number shall have been examined, we shall know much more than we do yet about the social and domestic life of those early ages ; we shall know whether during the Stone Age they had domestic animals in the North, as would appear to have been the case in Switzerland ; we shall know in part what kind of clothes they wore, and by the remains found with female skeletons we shall even be able to ascertain, in some measure, the position occupied by woman with reference to man.

If, however, we are to acquire all the information that

can be derived from the burial mounds, it must be done quickly. Every year many are destroyed, and Avebury itself, the grandest of megalithic monuments, was sacrificed for a paltry profit of a few pounds.

Moreover, as population increases, and land grows more valuable, these ancient monuments become more and more liable to mutilation and destruction. Since the first edition of this work was published, an Act of Parliament has been passed for their protection, and an inspector has been appointed. This is so far satisfactory. Unfortunately, however, the powers given under the Act are far from sufficient.[1] I have suggested that we might justly insist on the preservation of these national monuments, and that if their owners do not care to preserve them, the nation should have the option of purchase at a fair price. It is surely not only our right, but our duty, to protect them. These monuments are national heirlooms ; they do not belong to any one generation. They were erected by our forefathers, and we are bound to preserve them for those who will come after us.

---

[1] These have been strengthened by subsequent legislation.

CHAPTER VI

In consequence of the extraordinary dryness and cold of the weather during the winter months of 1853, the rivers of Switzerland did not receive their usual supplies, and the water in the lakes fell much below its ordinary level, so that, in some places, a broad strand was left uncovered along the margin, while in others shallow banks were converted into islands. The water level of this season was, indeed, the lowest upon record. The lowest level marked on the so-called stone of Stäfa was that of 1674; but in 1854 the water sank a foot lower still.

In a small bay between Ober Meilen and Dollikon, on the Lake of Zurich, the inhabitants had taken advantage of the lowness of the water to increase their gardens, by building a wall along the new water-line, and slightly raising the level of the piece thus reclaimed by mud dredged from the lake. In the course of this dredging they found great numbers of piles, of deer-horns, and also some implements. M. Aeppli was the first to observe these specimens of human workmanship, which he justly supposed might throw some light on the history and condition of the early inhabitants of the Swiss valleys. He at once, therefore, called the attention of Dr Keller to them, and that eminent antiquary soon satisfied himself as to their true nature, and proved that the early inhabitants of Switzerland constructed some, at least, of their dwellings above the surface of the water, and that they must have lived in a manner very similar to that of the Pæonians, thus described by Herodotus[1]:—

[1] *Terpsichore*, v. 14.

"Their dwellings," he says, "are contrived after this manner : planks fitted on lofty piles are placed in the middle of the lake, with a narrow entrance from the mainland by a single bridge. These piles that support the planks all the citizens anciently placed there at the public charge ; but afterwards they established a law to the following effect : whenever a man marries, for each wife he sinks three piles, bringing wood from a mountain called Orbelus ; but every man has several wives. They live in the following manner : every man has a hut on the planks, in which he dwells, with a trap-door closely fitted in the planks, and leading down to the lake. They tie the young children with a cord round the foot, fearing lest they should fall into the lake beneath. To their horses and beasts of burden they give fish for fodder ; of which there is such an abundance that when a man has opened his trap-door, he lets down an empty basket by a cord into the lake, and, after waiting a short time, draws it up full of fish."

At the Newcastle meeting of the British Association in 1863, Lord Lovaine described a lake-dwelling observed by him in the south of Scotland ; and in the *Natural History Review* for July 1863, I had already mentioned one in the North, which, however, had not at that time been thoroughly examined. Sir Charles Bunbury has recorded (*Quarterly Journal of the Geological Society*, vol. xii., 1856) some similar remains found near Thetford, which have been described at greater length by Mr Alfred Newton in an interesting paper "On the Zoology of Ancient Europe."[1] A lake-village has been discovered near Glastonbury, and is being carefully excavated by Dr Bulleid. In his fifth memoir on the Pfahlbauten,[2] Dr Keller has described a lake-dwelling at Peschiera, on the L. di Garda ; and we are indebted to MM. B. Gastaldi,[3]

---

[1] See also Munro, *Ancient Scottish Lake Dwellings* ; and *The Lake Dwellings oj Europe*.

[2] *Mittheilungen der antiquarischen Gesellschaft in Zurich*, 1863.

[3] *Nuovi Cenni sugli oggetti di alta Antichità trovati nelle Torbiere e nelle Marniere dell' Italia*. See also Stoppani, "Prima ricerca di Abitazioni lacustri nei Laghi di Lombardia," *Atti della Soc. Italiani di Scienze Naturali*, 1863, vol. v. p. 154.

P. Strobel, and L. Pigorini, for a description of ruins
of a similar nature which have been found in Northern
Italy. Dr Lisch has described several pile-dwellings
in Mecklenburg, and M. Boucher de Perthes, in his
celebrated work, *Antiquités Celtiques et Antédiluviennes*,
mentions certain remains found in the peat near Abbeville, which appear to have been the ruins of lake-
dwellings ; an observation which is of special interest,
as an additional argument for referring the Swiss lake-

Fig. 182.—Modern lake-dwellings in the Celebes.   After Sarasin.

dwellings to the period of the peat in the Somme
valley, and therefore to an epoch long subsequent to that
of the drift hatchets. This inference is entirely in accordance with the conclusions derived from the study of the
stone implements themselves.

But it is not necessary to go back to prehistoric times ;
nor need we appeal to doubtful history or ancient remains
for evidence of the curious habit of water-dwelling.
Many savage or semi-savage tribes live in the same
manner, even at the present day. I have been informed
by a friend who lives at Salonica that the fishermen of
Lake Prasias still inhabit wooden cottages built over the

water, as in the time of Herodotus. The city of
Tcherkask also is partly built over the Don. Some of
the Garos and Bogshas of Upper India, the Kanikars of
Southern India, the pastoral tribes in parts of Sinde,
dwell in habitations elevated 8 or 10 feet from the
ground, to avoid the damp and the insects occasioned by
it.[1] Similar dwellings are extensively used in the northern
parts of South America ; Venezuela, indeed, having been
so called because the houses resemble those of Venice
in being constructed over water. But it is in the East
Indies that this habit prevails most extensively. The
city of Borneo is altogether built upon piles, and similar
constructions have been described by various travellers
in New Guinea, Celebes, Solo, Ceram, Mindanao, the
Caroline Islands, on the Gold Coast, and elsewhere.
Dampier long ago mentioned similar dwellings constructed
over the water ; and Dumont d'Urville,[2] quoted by
M. Troyon, tells us that " Jadis toute la ville de Tondano
était construite sur le lac, et l'on ne communiquait d'une
maison à une autre qu'en bateau." The Bishop of
Labuan thus describes the dwellings of the Dyaks :
" They are built along the river-side, on an elevated
platform 20 or 30 feet high, in a long row ; or rather it
is a whole village in one row of some hundreds of feet
long. The platforms are first framed with beams, and
then crossed with laths about 2 inches wide and 2 inches
apart, and in this way are well ventilated ; and nothing
remains on the floors, but all the refuse falls through and
goes below."[3]

In Ireland a number of more or less artificial islands
called "Crannoges"[4] (fig. 183) are known historically to
have been used as strongholds by the petty chiefs. They
are composed of earth and stones, strengthened by piles,
and have supplied the Irish archæologists with numerous
weapons, implements, and bones. From the crannoge

[1] Burnes' *Travels into Bokhara*, vol. iii. p. 90.
[2] *Voyage de " l'Astrolabe*," vol. v. p. 635.
[3] *Trans. of the Ethnol. Soc.*, New Series, vol. ii. p. 28.
[4] See Wilde's *Catalogue*, vol. i. p. 220.

at Dunshaughlin, indeed, more than one hundred and
fifty cart-loads of bones were obtained and used as
manure !   These lake-dwellings of Ireland, however,
are referable to a much later period than those of
Switzerland, and are frequently mentioned in early
history.   Thus, according to Shirley, " One Thomas
Phettiplace, in his answer to an inquiry from the Government, as to what castles or forts O'Neill hath, and of
what strength they be, states (May 15, 1567) : ' For
castles, I think it be not unknown to your honours, he
trusteth no point thereunto for his safety, as appeareth
by the raising of the strongest castles of all his countreys,

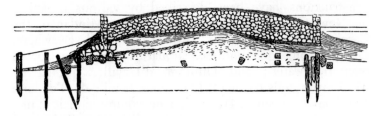

FIG. 183.—Crannoge in Ardakillin Lough, near Stokestown, county of Ros-
common. It is constructed of stones and oak piling. The top line shows
the former highest water level ; the second, that of the ordinary winter flood ;
the third, the summer level.

and that fortification which he only dependeth upon is
in sartin ffreshwater loghos in his country, which from the
sea there come neither ship nor boat to approach them :
it is thought that there in the said fortified islands lyeth
all his plate, which is much, and money, prisoners, and
gages : which islands hath in wars to fore been attempted,
and now of late again by the Lord Deputy there, Sir
Harry Sydney, which for want of means for safe conducts
upon the water it hath not prevailed.' "
    Again, the map of the escheated territories, made for
the Government, A.D. 1591, by Francis Jobson, or the
Platt of the County of Monaghan, contains rough sketches
of the dwellings of the petty chiefs of Monaghan,
which " are in all cases surrounded by water."   In
the *Annals of the Four Masters*, and other records of
early Irish history, we meet with numerous instances in

which the crannoges are mentioned, in some of which
their position has not preserved them from robbery and
destruction ; and we need not, therefore, be surprised to
find that many of the Swiss Pfahlbauten appear to have
been destroyed by fire.

Not only in the Lake of Zurich, but also in Lakes of
Constance, Geneva, Neufchâtel, Bienne, Morat, Sempach,
in fact in most of the large Swiss lakes, as well as in several
of the smaller ones (Inkwyl, Pfeffikon, Moosseedorf,
Luissel, etc.), similar lake-habitations have been discovered. In the larger lakes, indeed, not one, but many
of these settlements existed ; thus, there are already on
record, in Lake Bienne, twenty ; in the Lake of Geneva,
twenty-four ; in the Lake of Constance, thirty-two ; in
the Lake of Neufchâtel, as many as forty-nine ; on the
whole more than two hundred ; and many others, doubtless, remain to be discovered. Of those already known,
some belong to the Iron Age, some few even to Roman
times ; but the greater number appear to be divided in
almost equal proportions between the Age of Stone and
that of Bronze.

Though the architecture of this period was probably
simple, still the weight to be sustained on the wooden
platforms must have been considerable ; many of the
piles are either bent or broken ; and to prevent their
sinking too deeply into the soft mud, they were sometimes driven through boards which rested on the bottom.

The dwellings of the Gauls are described as having
been circular huts, built of wood and lined with mud.
The interstices appear to have been filled with moss or
clay. Some of the huts on the pile-works were probably
of a similar nature. This is not a mere hypothesis, but
many fragments of the clay used for the lining have been
discovered. Their preservation is evidently due to the
building having been destroyed by fire, which has hardened
the clay, and enabled it to resist the action of the water.
These fragments bear, on one side, the marks of inter-
laced branches, while on the other, which apparently
formed the inner wall of the cabin, they are quite smooth.

The huts, like those in the British lake-village of Glastonbury, were circular, and from ten to fifteen feet in diameter. It would be most interesting if we could construct a retrospective census for these early periods, and M. Troyon has made an attempt to do so. The settlement at Morges, which is one of the largest in the Lake of Geneva, is 1200 feet long and 150 broad, giving a surface of 180,000 square feet. Allowing the huts to have been fifteen feet in diameter, and supposing that they occupied half the surface, leaving the rest for gangways, he estimates the number of cabins at 311; and supposing again that, on an average, each was inhabited by four persons, he obtains for the whole a population of 1244. Starting from the same data, he assumes for the Lake of Neufchâtel a population of about 5000. Sixty-eight villages belonging to the Bronze Age are supposed to have contained 42,500 persons; while for the preceding epoch, by the same process of reasoning, he estimates the population at 31,875.

I am not, however, inclined to attribute much value to the estimates of population based on the extent of the platforms. M. Troyon himself admits that his " chiffres sont peut-être un peu élevés, en égard aux habitations sur terre ferme, dont il ne peut être question dans ce calcul, et vu qu'on est encore bien loin de connaître tous les points des lacs qui ont été occupés," and indeed, in Switzerland, since his book was written, the number of lake-villages discovered has already been more than doubled. Moreover, M. Troyon assumes that the lake-villages of the Bronze Age were contemporaneous, and that the same was the case with those belonging to the Stone Age. This also I should be disposed to question; both these periods, but especially the Stone Age, in all probability extended over a long series of years; and though in these matters it is of course necessary to speak with much caution, still if we are to make any assumption in the case, it would seem safer to suppose that in each period some of the villages had perished or been forsaken before others were built.

We might feel surprised that a people so uncivilized should have constructed their houses with immense labour on the water, when it would seem so much more easy to have built them on dry land. But we have already seen how, even in historical times, such dwellings have served as simple and yet valuable fortifications. Still, though it is evident that the security thus given would amply compensate for much extra labour, it remains difficult to understand in what manner the piles were driven into the ground.

In many cases, indeed, settlements of the Stone Age are characterized by what are called "steinbergs," that is to say, artificial heaps of stones, etc., evidently brought by the natives to serve as a support to the piles. A boat laden with stones, apparently for this purpose, was some years ago discovered in the Lake of Neufchâtel. In fact, it was in some places easier to raise the bottom round the piles than to drive the piles into the bottom. On the other hand, some of these constructions, as, for instance, those at Inkwyl and Wauwyl, described respectively by M. Morlot and Col. Suter, more closely resemble the Irish crannoge. We see, therefore, that, as Dr Keller says, the lake-dwellers followed two different systems in the construction of their dwellings, which he distinguishes as "Pfahlbauten," or pile-buildings, and "Packwerkbauten," or crannoges : in the first of which the platforms were simply supported on piles ; in the second of which the support consisted not of piles only, but of a solid mass of mud, stones, etc., with layers of horizontal and perpendicular stakes, the latter serving less as a support than to bind the mass firmly together. It is evident that the "Packwerkbau" is a simpler and ruder affair than the "Pfahlbau," in which no small skill must have been required to connect the perpendicular and horizontal piles firmly together. Still the "Packwerkbauten" were not suitable for the larger lakes, as during storms they would have been injured by the waves, which passed harmlessly through the open work of the "Pfahlbauten." We find, therefore, that while the former method of construction prevailed only in small lakes or morasses, the latter was adopted in the larger lakes, and even sometimes, possibly, *on dry land* ; a custom which, however singular, exists at the present day, as, for instance, in the island of Borneo, and even in Switzerland itself.

The antiquities found in the small Swiss lakes and peat-bogs are more or less covered by a thick layer of peat, which perhaps at some future date will give us a clue to their age. On the contrary, in the large lakes no peat grows. At the entrance of the rivers, indeed, much mud and gravel is of course accumulated ; the Lake of Geneva, for instance, once no doubt extended for a considerable distance up the valley of the Rhône. But the gravel and mud brought down by that river are deposited, as everyone knows, near its entrance into the lake, and the water of the lake is elsewhere beautifully clear and pure.

The lake itself is very deep, in parts as much as nine hundred and eighty feet ; and the banks are somewhat steep, but round the margin there is, in most places, a fringe of shallow water, due, probably, to the erosive action of the waves, and known to the fishermen as the "blancfond," because the lake is there of a pale greyish hue, when contrasted with the bright blue of the central deeper water. It is on this "blancfond," and at a depth of sometimes as much as fifteen feet, that the Pfahlbauten were generally constructed. On calm days, when the surface of the water is unruffled, the piles are plainly visible. Few of them now project more than two feet from the bottom ; eaten away by the incessant action of the water, some of them "n'apparaissent plus que comme aiguilles," which finally also disappear, and leave only a black disk at the surface of the mud. This, however, is the case principally in the lake-villages of the Stone Age.

The more complete destruction of the piles belonging to the earlier period depends not only on their greater age, but on their occurrence in shallower water. The action of the waves being greatest near the surface, and diminishing gradually downwards, not only are those piles which occupy the deeper parts least liable to destruction, but in each the erosion takes place gradually from above, so that the upper end of the piles is often more regularly pointed even than the lower. Lying among them are fragments of bone, horn, pottery, and sometimes objects of bronze. Most of these are embedded in the mud, or hidden under the stones, but others lie on the bottom yet uninjured ; so that when, for the first time, I saw them through the transparent water, a momentary feeling of doubt as to their age rose in my mind. So fresh are they and at first sight so unaltered, they look as if they were only things of yesterday, and it seems hard to believe that they can have remained there for centuries. The explanation of the difficulty is, however, to be found in the fact that the action of the most violent storms reaches only to a small depth. Except, therefore, near the mouths of rivers, or where there is much vegetation, which in the large lakes is rarely the case, the deposition of mud at depths greater than four feet is an extremely slow process, and objects which fall to the bottom in such situations will neither be covered over nor carried away. " J'ai pêché," says M. Troyon, " sur l'emplacement en face du Moulin de Bevaix, les fragments d'un grand vase qui gisaient à peu de distance les uns des autres, et que j'ai pu réunir de manière à les remontre complètement. A la Tongue, près d'Hermance, j'ai trouvé les deux fragments d'un anneau support, distants de quelques pieds, qui, en les raprochant ne laissent aucun interstice." The upper parts of the objects also, which are bathed by the water, are generally covered by a layer of carbonate of lime, while the lower part which has sunk into the mud is quite unaltered. M. Troyon once obtained at Cortaillod a pair of bracelets in one haul of the dredge—the first, which had been visible from the boat, was greenish and covered with incrustation ; the second, which had been in the mud immediately below, was as fresh as if it had only just been made.

As piles of the Bronze Age are sometimes found at a

depth of as much as fifteen feet, and as it is manifest that buildings cannot have been constructed over water much deeper than this, it is evident that the Swiss lakes cannot then have stood at a much higher level than at present. This conclusion is confirmed by the position of Roman remains at Thonon, on the Lake of Geneva, and we thus obtain satisfactory evidence that the height of the Swiss lakes must have remained almost unaltered for a very long period.

In the large lakes the passing traveller may readily mark the number and general distribution of the piles ; he may determine the area which they occupy, and pick up fragments of bone and pottery ; but, on the whole, the peat-mosses are more instructive. In them we not only obtain evidence as to the size, form, and construction of the huts, but implements of wood, specimens of fruit, nuts, grain, and even fragments of clothing, none of which can be preserved in the open water of the large lakes.

After having chosen a favourable situation, the first step in the construction of the lake-habitations was to obtain the necessary timber. To cut down a tree with a stone hatchet must have been no slight undertaking. It is, indeed, most probable that use was made of fire, in the same manner as is done by existing savages in felling trees and making canoes. Burning the wood and then scraping away the charred portion renders the task far more easy, and the men of the Stone Period appear to have avoided the use of large trees, except in making their canoes. Their piles were embedded in the mud from one to five feet, and must also have projected from four to six feet above the water level, which cannot have been very different from what it is at present. They must, therefore, have had a length of from fifteen to thirty feet, and they were from three to nine inches in diameter. The pointed extremity which entered into the mud still bears the marks of the fire and the rude cuts made by the stone hatchets. The piles belonging to the Bronze Period, being prepared with metal axes, were much more regularly pointed, and the differences between the two have been ingeniously compared to those shown by lead pencils well and badly cut. Moreover, the cuts made by the ordinary Swiss stone axe (fig. 185) are more or less concave, whereas those made with metal are flat. To drag the piles to the lake, and fix them firmly, must also have required much labour, especially when their number is considered. At Wangen alone M. Lohle has calculated that 50,000 piles were used; but we must remember that these were probably not all planted at one time nor by one generation. Wangen, indeed, was certainly not built in a day, but was, no doubt, gradually enlarged as the population increased. Herodotus informs us that the Pæonians made the first platform at the public expense, but that, subsequently, at every marriage (and polygamy was permitted), the bridegroom was expected to add a certain number of piles to the common support. Fig. 184 represents a section taken at Robenhausen, and shows two series of piles, one over the other. The layer of ashes appears to indicate that the settlement was burnt down, and subsequently rebuilt.

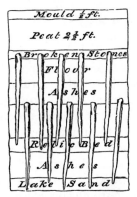

FIG. 184.—Section of the lake-dwelling at Niederwyl.

The pile-works of subsequent periods differ little from those of the Stone Age, so far at least as can be judged by the parts remaining, but the piles are less decayed, and project above the mud farther than is the case with those of the preceding epoch.

Through the kindness of Colonel Suter, I had an opportunity of examining the construction of the lake-dwelling at Wauwyl, near Zofingen, in the canton of Lucerne. This apparently belonged to the Stone Age, no trace of metal having yet been discovered in it. It is situated in a peat moss, which was evidently at one time the bed of a shallow lake. By the gradual growth of peat, however, the level has been raised several feet, and the plain has recently been drained. We were assisted by six labourers, who dug out the peat, which we then carefully examined. I mention this because the difference in the objects collected from different Pfahlbauten may probably be, in part at least, accounted for by the different ways in which the search has been made. The peat at Wauwyl varies in thickness from 3 to 10 feet, and rests on a white bed consisting of broken fresh-water shells. This stratum, though only a few inches thick, is found in the old beds of many small lakes, and is frequently mentioned by the Swiss archæologists under the name of "weissgrund." It must not, however, be confounded with the "blancfond" of the larger lakes. The piles go through the peat and the "weissgrund" into the solid ground below. It is not easy to obtain them whole, because the lower portions are much altered by time, and so thoroughly saturated by water that they are quite soft. Colonel Suter, however, extracted two of them ; one was 14 feet 6 inches in length, of which 4 feet was in the peat, and the remaining 10 feet 6 inches in the sand beneath ; the other was only 8 feet 6 inches long, 4 feet of which was in the peat, the other 4 feet 6 inches in the solid ground. The piles vary from 3 to 5 inches in diameter, and are always round, never having been squared. The lower part is very badly cut, so that it is difficult to understand how they can have been forced to so great a depth into the ground.

In most of the Pfahlbauten the piles are scattered, more or less irregularly, over the whole extent of the settlement : at Wauwyl this is not the case, but they enclose, as it were, four quadrangular areas, the interiors of which are occupied by several platforms one over the other, the interstices being filled up by branches, leaves, and peat. The objects of antiquity are not scattered throughout the peat, but lie either on the layer of broken shells, which formed the then bottom of the lake, or in the lower part of the peat. It is, therefore, evident that almost the whole, if not the whole, of the peat has grown since the time at which this interesting ruin was inhabited. The upper part had, however, been removed before our arrival, so that the "Culturgeschicht," the layer containing the objects of antiquity, was exposed ready for examination in the manner already described.

Some of the piles still stood two or three feet above the level of the peat, but the greater number were broken off lower down. We stood on one of the upper platforms, which seems to have been the floor on which the huts were erected, and the beams of which are still perfectly preserved. It was at first a question in what manner the platforms at this place were supported; whether they lay like a raft on the surface of the water, rising and sinking with it;[1] or whether they were fixed, and rested on a sort of artificial island, formed by the clay, branches, etc., which now occupy the interspaces between the different platforms. Subsequent observations, however, confirmed as they have been by discoveries elsewhere, as, for instance, at Inkwyl and Niederwyl, have decided the question in favour of the latter hypothesis.

During my visit at Wauwyl we obtained 4 small stone axes, 1 arrow-head, 4 flint flakes, 15 rude stone hammers, 8 whetstones, 33 slingstones, 8 instruments of bone, and 2 of wood, besides numerous bones, and a great quantity of broken pottery. Colonel Suter regarded this as a fair average day's work. Altogether about 500 instruments of stone and bone had been discovered at Wauwyl; at Moosseedorf more than 3300; at Wangen no less than 5800, while M. Troyon estimated that those at Concise must have amounted to 25,000, and these numbers have since been largely increased.

The axe was pre-eminently *the* implement of antiquity. It was used in war and in the chase, as well as for domestic purposes, and great numbers have been found, especially at Wangen (Lake of Constance) and Concise (Lake of Neufchâtel). With a few exceptions, they are small, especially when compared with the magnificent specimens

---

[1] Dwellings of this character occur in the East and in South America. See, for instance, Anderson's *Mission to Sumatra*, p. 395; Squier, *American Naturalist*, vol. iv. p. 18.

from Denmark ; in length they varied from 1 to 6 inches, while the cutting edge had generally a width of from 15 to 20 lines. Flint was sometimes used, and nephrite or jade in a few cases, but serpentine and diorite were the principal materials. Most of the larger settlements were evidently manufacturing places, and many spoilt pieces and half-finished specimens have been found. After having chosen a stone, the first step was to reduce it by

blows with a hammer to a suitable size. Then grooves were made artificially, which must have been a very tedious and difficult operation, when flint knives, sand, and water were the only available instruments. Having carried the grooves to the required depth, the projecting portions were removed by a skilful blow with a hammer, and the implement was then sharpened and polished on blocks of sandstone.

The axes appear to have been fastened into the handles by means of bitumen, obtained probably either from the Val de Travers near Neufchâtel or from the Perte du Rhône.

FIG. 185.—Swiss axe of serpentine, actual size. From Wangen, on the Lake of Constance. In my own collection.

The stone knives may be considered as of two sorts. Some differ from the axes principally in having their width greater than their length. In other cases flint flakes were set in wooden handles, and fastened, like the axes, by means of bitumen. Saws also (fig. 138) were made in a similar manner, but with their edges somewhat rudely dentated ; we do not find in Switzerland any of the semi-lunar stone implements which are frequent in Denmark. The arrow-heads were made of flint, or in some cases of rock-crystal, and were of the usual forms. Spindle-whorls of rude earthenware (fig. 186) were abundant in some of the lake-villages even of the Stone Age. The presence of these whorls indicates a knowledge of weaving, which indeed is proved by even more conclusive evidence. At Locray, a spindle-whorl was found actually attached to the spindle, which had thread still wound round it. There are also found rounded stones, pierced with one or sometimes two holes. The use of these is uncertain, but they may perhaps have been used to sink fishing-lines.

FIG. 186.—Spindle whorl, actual size. From Wangen, on the Lake of Constance. In my own collection.

The flint flakes offer no peculiarities ; the Swiss specimens are, however, of small size. Corn-crushers, which are round balls of hard stone, two or three inches in diameter, occur even in the villages of the Stone Age.

The list of objects hitherto found at Wauwyl is as follows :—

Stone axes, principally of serpentine 43
Small flint arrow-heads . . 36
Flint flakes 200
Corn-crushers . . . . 16 ⎫
Rude stones, used as hammers, common (say) . . . 20 ⎬ Not all collected.
Whetstones . . . . 26 ⎪
Slingstones, etc. . . . 85 ⎭

In all about . . . . 426 articles of stone.

The flint, of which the flakes and arrow-heads were formed, must have come from a distance, and the best pieces in all probability were obtained from France. Visits may have been made to the French quarries, just as Catlin tells us that the American tribes, from far and near, visited the red pipestone quarry of Coteau des

Prairies. A few fragments of Mediterranean coral have been found at Concise, and of Baltic amber at Meilen. Some archæologists have argued from these facts that there must have been a certain amount of commerce even in the Stone Age. As, however, both these settlements appear to have belonged to the transitional period between the Age of Stone and that of Bronze, it would be safer to refer both the amber and the coral to the later period.

Like other savages, the lake-dwellers made the most of any animal they could catch. They ate the flesh, used

FIG. 187.—Piece of pottery, showing the impressions of the finger-tip, and the marks of the nail, actual size. Lake of Zurich.

the skin for clothing, picked every fragment of marrow out of the bones, and then, in many cases, fashioned the bones themselves into weapons. The larger and more compact ones, as well as horns of the deer, served as hammers, and were used as handles for hatchets. In some cases, pieces of bone were worked to an edge, but they are neither hard nor sharp enough to cut well. Bone awls are numerous, and may have been used in preparing skins for clothes. Fig. 140 represents a chisel or scraper of bone, from Wangen. One purpose for which these were used was no doubt to scrape off the hair in dressing skins.

A few objects made of wood have also been found at Wauwyl and elsewhere ; but these, even if originally

numerous, would be difficult to distinguish from the
surrounding peat, especially as this contains so many
branches of trees and other fragments of wood ; and it
would also be very difficult to extract them entire.
Perhaps, therefore, implements of wood may have been
much more varied and common than the collections
would appear to indicate. Tinder has been found in
several of the lake-villages, and was no doubt used in
obtaining fire.

The pottery of the Stone Age presents nearly the same
characters in all the settlements. Very rude and coarse,
it is generally found in broken pieces, and comparatively
few entire vessels have been obtained. There is no
evidence that the potter's wheel was known, and the
baking is very imperfect, having apparently taken place
in an open fire. The material is also very rude, and
generally contains numerous grains of quartz. The form
is frequently cylindrical, but several of the jars are
rounded at the base, and without feet. A curious
character is the frequent presence of a row of depressions
which do not completely penetrate the thickness of the
vessel ; but the commonest decorations are simple lines
or furrows, made sometimes by a sharp instrument,
sometimes by the finger-nail (see fig. 187), and occasionally produced by pressing a cord on the soft clay.
Curved lines are rare ; no representation of any animal
has yet been met with ; and the vase found at Wangen,
a restored figure of which has been given both by Dr
Keller and by M. Troyon, is almost the only instance in
which any attempt has been made to represent a plant.
In this case the design is even ruder than might be
inferred from the above-mentioned figures.[1] In some of
the Bronze Age villages rings of pottery are found,
which were evidently intended to serve as supports for
these earthenware tumblers, but none of them have yet
been met with in any of the Stone Age villages. Possibly
the earthenware during the Stone Age rested on the soft

[1] In Lee's second edition of Keller's *Lake Dwellings*, pl. xv., a figure is
given of the actual fragments.

earth, and tables were only introduced in the Bronze Age, when by means of metallic implements it became so much easier to cut wood, and particularly to make boards. Many of the vessels had small projections, which were pierced in such a manner that strings might be passed through them, and which may, therefore, have served for suspension. Some of the vessels, also, are pierced by small holes at different levels ; it has been

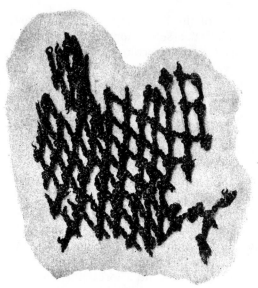

FIG. 188.—Net fragment from Robenhausen.

suggested that these may have been used in the preparation of curds, the small holes being intended to permit the escape of the milk. The ornaments on the pottery belonging to this age are of a very rude and simple character. Sometimes a row of knobs runs round the vase, just below the lip ; this style of ornamentation is common on the pottery found by M. Gilliéron at the Pont de Thièle.

Although there can be no doubt that the skins of animals supplied the ancient lakemen with their principal articles of clothing, still in several of the settlements, and especially at Wangen and Robenhausen, both of which belong to the Stone Age, pieces of rude fabric (figs. 188–191) have been found in some abundance. They consist either of flax fibres or straw. The presence of spindle-whorls has been already mentioned.

For our knowledge of the animal remains from the pile-works we are principally indebted to Professor Rütimeyer. The bones are in a very fragmentary condition, and have been broken open for the sake of the

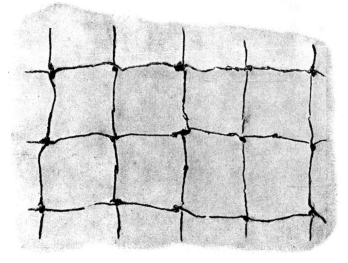

Fig. 189.—Net fragment from Robenhausen.

marrow. There is also the same absence of certain bones and parts of bones, so that it is impossible to reconstruct a perfect skeleton even of the commonest animal.

The total number of species amounts to about 70, of which 10 are fishes, 4 reptiles, 26 birds, and the remainder quadrupeds. Of the latter, 6 species may be considered as having been domesticated ; namely, the dog, pig, horse, goat, sheep, and at least two varieties of oxen. The bones very seldom occur in a natural condition ; but those of domestic and wild animals are mixed together, and the state in which they are found, the marks of knives upon them, and their having been almost always broken open for the sake of their marrow, are all evidences of human interference.

Two species, the one wild, the other domestic, are especially numerous—the stag and the ox. Indeed, the remains of these two equal those of all the others together. It is, however, an interesting fact, that in the older settlements, as at Moosseedorf, Wauwyl, and Roben-

FIG. 190.—Piece of tissue from Robenhausen.

hausen, the stag exceeds the ox in the number of specimens indicated, while the reverse is the case in the more modern settlements of the western lakes, as, for instance, those at Wangen and Meilen.

Next to these in order of abundance is the hog. Less numerous again, and generally represented by single specimens where the preceding occur in numbers, are the roe, the goat, and the sheep, which latter is most abundant in the later settlements. With these rank the fox and the marten. Foxes are occasionally eaten by the Esquimaux.[1] Captain Lyon seems to have taken rather a

[1] Crantz, *History of Greenland*, vol. i. p. 73.

fancy to them,[1] and Franklin assures us that fat fox is better than lean venison.[2] They also appear, whether from choice or necessity, to have been eaten during the Stone Period. This conclusion is derived from the fact

FIG. 191.—Piece of tissue from Robenhausen.

that the bones often present the marks of knives, and have been opened for the sake of the marrow. While, however, the fox is very frequent in the pile-works of the Stone Epoch, it has not yet been found in any settlement belonging to the Bronze Period. Oddly enough, the dog

[1] Lyon's *Journal*, p. 77. [2] Franklin, vol. iii. pp. 219-239.

is rarer than the fox, at least as far as the observations yet go, in the lake-dwellings of the Stone Period, though more common than the horse ; and of other species but few specimens have been met with, though in some localities the beaver, the badger, and the hedgehog appear in some numbers.   The bear and the wolf, as well as the urus, the bison, and the elk, seem to have occasionally been captured ; it is probable that the latter species were taken in concealed pits.

From the small lake at Moosseedorf, M. Rütimeyer has identified the following list :—Of the dog, 3 specimens ; fox, 4 specimens ; beaver, 5 specimens ; roe, 6 specimens ; goat and sheep, 10 specimens ; cow, 16 specimens ; hog, 20 specimens ; stag, 20 specimens.   It is certainly very striking to find two wild species represented by the greatest number of specimens, and particularly so, since this is no exceptional case ; but the whole sum of the wild exceeds that of the domesticated individuals, a result, moreover, which holds good in other settlements of this epoch.   Not only does this indicate a great antiquity, but also that the population must have been sometimes subjected to great privations, partly from the unavoidable uncertainty of supplies so obtained, partly because it is improbable that foxes would have been eaten except under the pressure of hunger.

The bones of the stag and the wild boar often indicate animals of an unusual magnitude, while, on the other hand, the fox appears to have been somewhat smaller than at present.   The dogs varied less than they do now ; in fact they all belong to one variety, which was of middle size, and appears to have resembled our present beagles. (M. Rütimeyer describes it as " resembling the Jagdhund " and the " Wachtelhund.")   The sheep of the Stone Period differed from the ordinary form in its small size, fine legs, and short goat-like horns ; particulars in which it is nearly resembled by some northern and mountain varieties at the present day, as, for instance, by the small sheep of the Shetlands, Orkneys, Welsh hills, and parts of the Alps.   At Wauwyl, however, M. Rütimeyer found traces of an individual, with large horns.   Our knowledge of the wild species of sheep is so deficient, that M. Rütimeyer does not venture to express any opinion concerning the origin of the domestic varieties, but his present impression is that they will eventually be traced up to several wild races.

LIST OF SPECIES.	Moosseedorf.	Wauwyl.	Robenhausen.	Wangen.	Meilen.	Concise.	Bienne.
1 Ursus Arctos	2	2	2	2	...	2	2
2 Meles vulgaris	2	2	3	...	1	3	2
3 Mustela Foina	2	3	3	2	...	1	2
4 ., Martes . .	2	3	3	2	1	2	...
5 „ Putorius . . .	2	2	1	...	...	1	...
6 „ Erminea . .	...	2	...	...	...	...	...
7 „ Lutra vulgaris . .	1	1	2	...	...	...	...
8 Canis Lupus	...	1	1	1	1	1	1
9 „ familiaris (palustris) .	2	2	2	3	3	3	3
10 „ Vulpes	3	3	3	2	2	2	2
11 Felis Catus (ferus) . .	2	2	1	...	...	...	...
12 Erinaceus europæus . . .	1	1	3	2	...	...	...
13 Castor Fiber . . .	3	2	3	2	...	2	2
14 Sciurus europæus . . .	2	2	2	2	...	...	...
15 Mus sylvaticus	...	...	2	...	...	...	...
16 Lepus timidus	1	...	1	1	...	...	...
17 Sus Scrofa ferus . . .	3	2	4	2	2	2	2
18 „ Palustris	5	5	5	5	5	5	5
19 „ Scrofa domesticus . .	...	1	...	...	...	2	2
20 Equus Caballus	1	2	2	2	1	2	3
21 E. Asinus	...	1	...	...	...	...	1
22 Cervus Alces	1	1	2	...	2	1	1
23 „ Elaphus . .	5	5	5	5	5	5	5
24 „ Capreolus . .	4	2	4	2	2	3	2
25 Capra Ibex	...	...	...	...	1	...	...
26 „ Hircus	2	2	2	2	...	2	34
27 Ovis Aries	2	2	2	2	1	3	34
28 Antilope rupicapra . . .	...	...	1	...	...	...	...
29 Bos primigenius . . .	2	2	3	1	...	2	...
30 „ Bison	1	1	4	?	...	...	1
31 „ Taurus primigenius . .	2	?	5	?	2	5	2
32 „ Taurus brachyceros . .	5	5	2	5	5	2	5
33 „ Taurus frontosus . .	...	1	...	...	...	2	2

In his first memoir, Professor Rütimeyer gives an interesting table, which, with some additions which I owe to his kind courtesy, is here subjoined, the relative frequency being indicated by numerals :

1 denotes a single individual ;
2 indicates that the remains of several individuals
    have been met with ;
3 the species which are common ;
4 those which are very common ; and lastly,
5 those which are present in great number.

The almost entire absence of the hare is perhaps owing to the curious prejudice which was and is entertained by many races against the flesh of this animal. It was never eaten by the ancient Britons, and is avoided by the Lapps at the present day. According to Burton,[1] the Somal Arabs will not touch it, and M. Schlegel also states that the prejudice against it existed among the ancient Chinese.[2] The Namaquas (S. Africa) do not eat it for fear of becoming timid. In confirmation of this, it may be mentioned that it was, among the Hottentots, forbidden to men, but permitted to women.[3] It was regarded as unclean by the Jews, being erroneously supposed to chew the cud. According to Crantz, the Greenlanders,[4] if in want, will eat foxes rather than hares, nor do its remains occur in the Danish shell-mounds. It appears, however, to have been eaten in Palæolithic times.[5]

The birds which have been discovered are :—

Aquila fulva. The golden eagle. At Robenhausen.
Aquila haliætus. A single bone found at Moosseedorf
    is rather doubtfully referred to this species by
    M. Rütimeyer.
Falco milvus. Robenhausen.
Falco palumbarius. Wauwyl, Moosseedorf.
Falco nisus. Moosseedorf.
Falco Buteo. Moosseedorf, Robenhausen.

[1] *First Footsteps*, p. 155.
[2] *Notes and Queries*, on China, Japan, Hong-kong, May 1868.
[3] Le Vaillant, *Voyages dans l'Afrique*, vol. iv. p. 187.
[4] *History of Greenland*, p. 73.
[5] Boyd Dawkins, *Geol. Jour.*, 1876, p. 247.

Strix aluco. Concise.
Strix otus. Moosseedorf.
Strix bubo. Wangen.
Sturnus vulgaris. Robenhausen.
Corvus corone.   „
Corvus corax.   „
Cinclus aquaticus.   „
Columba palumbus.   „   Moosseedorf.
Tetrao bonasia.   „
Tetrao lagopus. Moosseedorf.
Ciconia alba. Not unfrequent at Moosseedorf and
    Robenhausen.
Ardea cinerea. Robenhausen.
Grus cinerea.   „
Fulica atra.   „
Larus. Two sp.   „
Mergus.
Mergus merganser. Bienne.
Cygnus olor. Robenhausen.
Anser segetum.   „
Anas boschas. Robenhausen, Moosseedorf, Wauwyl.
Anas querquedula.   „   „
Podiceps minor. Robenhausen.

The reptiles and fishes are represented by about ten of our commonest species.

The common mouse and our two house-rats, as well as the domestic cat, are absent from the lake-habitations of Switzerland, as also from the Kjökkenmöddings of Denmark ; the same is the case with the common fowl, which seems, moreover, to have been unknown to Homer and Hesiod ; Professor Rütimeyer attributes to a later period a single bone of the latter bird which was found at Morges, a settlement belonging to the Bronze Period.

The earliest remains of the ass mentioned by Professor Rütimeyer are those found at Chavannes and Noville, which, however, were not connected with Pfahlbauten, and belonged to post-Roman times. In the Bible, the ass is first mentioned in the time of Abraham, who had "sheep, and oxen, and he-asses, and men-servants, and maid-servants, and she-asses, and camels."[1] It will be observed that in this enumeration no mention is made of horses. Laban, again, had sheep, and goats, and cattle, and camels, and asses, but apparently no horses. Again, the present which Jacob sent to Esau consisted of 200 she-goats and 20 he-goats, 200 ewes and 20 rams, 30 milch camels with their colts, 40 kine and 10 bulls, 20 she-asses and 10 foals.[2] Indeed, no mention whatever is made of horses until the children of Israel went into Egypt ; and from the copious and interesting details of their pastoral life, we may feel sure that horses would have been alluded to if the Hebrews had possessed them. As regards Egypt, the horse is not represented in any of the monuments anterior to the eighteenth dynasty, after which, however, it appears to have become abundant in that country.

As regards the Swiss lake-villages, it is singular that though remains of the horse have been found in all the pile-works, they are so rare that their presence may almost be considered accidental : thus, Wangen has only produced a single tooth ; Moosseedorf, a metatarsal bone, which has been polished on one side ; Robenhausen, a single os naviculare tarsi ; and Wauwyl, only a few bones, which may all have belonged to a single individual. On the other hand, when we come to the Bronze Period, we find at Nidau numerous bones of this species ; so that, as far as these slight indications go, the horse, even if present in the Stone Age, seems to have been rarer than at subsequent periods. All the remains of this animal belonged apparently to the domestic horse (*Equus caballus*), while those which occur in the Drift gravel beds and in caves fall into two well-marked races, named by Professor Owen *E. fossilis* and *E. spelæus*.

"The genealogy of the domestic hog," says Mr Boyd Dawkins,[3] "has been ascertained by MM. Rütimeyer,

---

[1] Gen. xii. 16.   [2] Gen. xxxiii. 14.
[3] *Palæontographical Soc.*, 1878, vol. xxxii. p. 13.

Nathusius, and Schütz, with great accuracy, and Dr Darwin has summed up the evidence with judicial impartiality.[1] It is traced, by these observers, to two distinct strains, the one being the wild boar, which is found throughout the temperate and hot regions of Europe, Asia, and in North Africa ; and (the other) that which is termed by Nathusius the *Sus Indica,* of Pallas, and which is known commonly as the small, short-legged, and short-headed pig of Siam and China."

M. Rütimeyer, in a letter with which he has favoured me, says he is now convinced that the *Sus palustris* " was imported from the East, and stands in nearest relation to *Sus vittatus* of East Asia, the stock from which all Asiatic, most African and Southern European (Roman and Greek) races are derived," the Northern European race being, on the contrary, derived from the wild boar.

Our domestic hog first makes its appearance in the later pile-works. Professor Rütimeyer does not, however, believe that it was tamed by the inhabitants of Switzerland, but is rather disposed to look upon it as having been introduced during the Bronze Age, and the more so as he also finds at Concise traces of a variety of the ox (*B. trochoceros*) which does not occur in the earlier pile-works.

The discovery of dung among the remains of the Pfahlbauten sufficiently proves that the lake-dwellers had domestic animals, but there are also other indications from which we may draw the same conclusion.

In endeavouring to ascertain whether any given bones belonged to a wild or domesticated animal, we must be guided by the following considerations : the number of individuals represented ; the relative proportions of young and old ; the absence or presence of very old individuals, at least in the case of species that serve for food ; the traces of long, though indirect, selection, in diminishing the size of any natural weapons which might be injurious to man ; the direct action of man during the life of the animal ; and, finally, the texture and condition of the bones.

[1] *Variations under Domestication,* vol. i. ch. i.

Applying these considerations to the *Sus palustris* from Moosseedorf, Professor Rütimeyer concludes that there is no evidence that any of them belonged to domesticated specimens.

Professor Rütimeyer has also paid great attention to the texture and condition of the bones themselves, and believes that he can, in many cases, from these alone distinguish the species, and even determine whether the bone belonged to a wild or a domesticated animal.

In wild animals the bones are of a firmer and closer

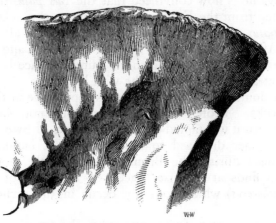

FIG. 192.—Portion of the vertebra of a cow.

texture ; there is an indescribable, but to the accustomed eye very characteristic, sculpturing of the external surface, produced by the sharper and more numerous impressions of vessels, and the greater roughness of the surfaces for the attachment of muscles. There is also an exaggeration of all projections and ridges, and a diminution of all indifferent surfaces. The contrast thus produced will be seen from figs. 192 and 193, the first of which represents a portion of a vertebra belonging to a domestic cow, the second the corresponding surface of the same bone from the bison. In considering the remains of oxen, these distinctions have proved of the greatest importance. By their assistance Professor Rütimeyer has convinced himself that, besides the two wild species of bos, namely, the urus (*B. primigenius*) and the aurochs (*B. bison* or *Bison europæus*), four principal races of domestic oxen occur in the lake-villages.[1]

The first of these, the *Primigenius* race, closely resembles the urus or *Bos primigenius*, and was no doubt descended from it. It occurs in all the earlier pile-works, and in the present day is best represented by the great oxen of Friesland, Jutland, and Holstein.

The second, or *Trochoceros* race, has not hitherto been

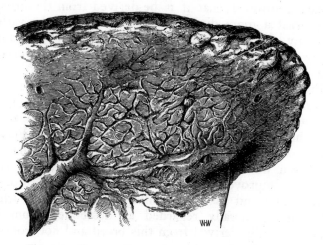

FIG. 193.—Corresponding portion of the vertebra of a bison.

found in any of the Stone Age villages. Rütimeyer regards it as scarcely distinguishable from the urus, and observes that its peculiarities are principally, though not exclusively, developed in the female sex.

The third, or *Frontosus* race, occurs but sparingly in the older Pfahlbauten ; becomes more frequent in the Bronze Age villages, and prevails at the present day in northern Switzerland. Professor Rütimeyer considers this variety also to be derived from the urus, and remarks that while the wild cattle of Chillingham are true to the *Primigenius* form, some of the Lyme Park cattle approach

[1] *Ar. für Anthropologie*, 1866, p. 219.

to the *Frontosus* type. He has, however, never seen a skull of this type belonging to an undoubtedly wild animal.

The fourth is the *Longifrons* or *Brachyceros* race. The name Brachyceros, by which it was at first known, must be abandoned, having been previously applied by Dr Gray to an African ox. This variety is extremely abundant in all the Pfahlbauten. Professor Rütimeyer regards it as descended, not from the urus, but from a second and smaller species, perhaps from the *Bos indicus*. He remarks, however, that if it be derived from the urus, it is at least a more distinct, and must be an older variety than any of the preceding. Professor Rütimeyer admits that we have no evidence that *B. longifrons* ever existed in a wild state in Central Europe.

Professor M'Kenny Hughes[1] considers that the bison became extinct in Britain before the Neolithic Period, and that none of our domestic breeds can be traced to it : that the urus was domesticated in the Neolithic Period, but became extinct before the Roman period : that the shorthorn was the characteristic ox of the Bronze Age, but was improved in Roman times by cattle brought from Italy : and that the Chillingham wild cattle, which have been generally regarded as descended from the urus, are really derived from this breed and not from the urus.

M. de Quatrefages[2] considers all our domestic oxen to be descendants of the urus ; while Mr Darwin[3] regards *B. longifrons* and *B. frontosus* as the modern representatives of wild ancestors, specifically distinct from *B. primigenius* ; and concludes therefore that our "domestic cattle are almost certainly the descendants of more than one wild form."

Mr Boyd Dawkins[4] has shown that, as far as this country is concerned, we have no conclusive evidence of

---

[1] *Archæologia*, 1898.
[2] *Rev. des Cours Scientifiques*, 1868, p. 563.
[3] *Animals and Plants under Domestication*, vol. i. p. 81.
[4] Boyd Dawkins, *Geol. Jour.*, 1867, p. 182.

more than two species of wild oxen, namely, the urus and the bison. The smaller varieties appear to have been introduced as domesticated animals, and probably do not go back beyond the Neolithic Period. According to Nilsson, on the contrary, both the *B. frontosus* and *B. longifrons* inhabited Sweden as wild races.[1] My own impression is that the urus was domesticated in Europe ; but also that some at least of the early settlers brought domestic cattle with them, which may very probably have belonged to a distinct wild race. Further evidence, however, is much needed on this interesting subject.

Making allowance then for the marine animals, such as seals, fish, oysters, cockles, whelks, etc., which we could not expect to find so far away from the sea, the fauna indicated by the remains found in the Swiss lakes agrees remarkably with that which characterizes the Danish Kjökkenmöddings, so far as wild animals are concerned, and belongs evidently to a far later age than that of the celebrated stone hatchets, which were first made known to us by the genius and perseverance of M. Boucher de Perthes.

Instead of the elephant and rhinoceros, we find in the Neolithic or second Stone Period—in that, namely, of the Kjökkenmöddings and "Pfahlbauten"—the urus and bison, the elk and the red deer, already installed as monarchs of the forest. Even the reindeer is altogether absent. The red deer, on the contrary, and the boar, appear to have been very frequent, and to have formed a most important article of food for the lake-dwellers. The urus, or great fossil ox, is now altogether extinct, at least as a wild species.[2] It is mentioned by Cæsar, who describes it as being little smaller than an elephant. (Hi sunt magnitudine paulo infra elephantos specie et colore et figura tauri.) According to Herberstein, it still

---

[1] *Ann. and Mag. of Nat. Hist.*, 1849, pp. 349–351.
[2] Professor Rütimeyer, as I have already mentioned, considers that the celebrated wild cattle of Tankerville Park are unmistakable, though dwarfish, descendants of the *B. primigenius*.

existed in Germany during the sixteenth century, soon after which, however, it must have become extinct.

The aurochs, or European bison, seems to have disappeared from Western Europe at about the same period as the urus. There is no historical record of its existence in England or Scandinavia. In Switzerland we cannot trace it later than the tenth century ; but it is mentioned in the *Niebelungen Lied*, of the twelfth century, as occurring in the Forest of Worms ; and in Prussia the last was killed in the year 1775. At one period, indeed, it appears to have inhabited almost the whole of Europe, much of Asia, and part even of America ; but at present it is confined in Europe to the imperial forests in Lithuania, where it is preserved by the Emperor of Russia ; while, according to Nordmann and Von Baer, it still exists in some parts of Western Asia.

We have no notice of the existence of the elk in Switzerland during the historical period, but it is mentioned by Cæsar as existing in the great Hercynian forest ; and even in the twelfth century it was to be met with in Sclavonia and Hungary, according to Albertus Magnus and Gesner. In Saxony, the death of the last elk is recorded as having occurred in 1746. At present it inhabits Prussia and Lithuania, Finland and Russia, Scandinavia and Siberia, as far as the shores of the Amoor.

The ibex survived in the Swiss Alps somewhat longer than the elk. It has lingered longest in the West. In Glarus the last one perished in 1550, though near Chiavenna it existed until the commencement of the seventeenth century, and in the Tyrol until the second half of the eighteenth ; while a few still exist in the neighbourhood of Mount Iséran, where they are protected by the King of Italy.

The extermination of the bear, like that of the ibex, seems to have begun in the East, and is not yet complete, since this animal still occurs in the Jura and the Grisons, whence it occasionally visits the Valais and the south-eastern parts of Switzerland.[1] The fox, the otter, and

[1] It is probably now (1913) extinct in Switzerland.

the different species of weasel, are still the common carnivora of Switzerland, and the wild cat, badger, and wolf still occur in the Jura and the Alps, the latter in cold winters venturing even into the plains. The beaver, on the contrary, has at last disappeared from Switzerland. It has long been very rare, but some survived until the beginning of the present century in Lucerne and Valais. A few still exist in France near the mouth of the Rhône. Red deer were abundant in the Jura and the Black Forest in the twelfth and thirteenth centuries, though they do not appear to have been so large as those which lived in earlier times. The last was shot in the canton of Basle, at the close of the eighteenth century, while in western Switzerland and Valais they lingered somewhat longer. The roe-deer still occurs in some places.

It appears, therefore, that the animals of the Swiss pile-works belong to the fauna which has occupied Europe from the commencement of the Palæolithic Period down to the present time.

While, however, we must regard the fauna of the Stone Age as belonging to the same great zoological epoch as that of the river drift gravels on the one hand, and the present time on the other, we cannot forget that the immense period which has elapsed since the end of the tertiary period has produced great changes in the fauna of Europe. In this post-tertiary era the pile-works occupy, so to say, the middle position. Distinguished from the present fauna of Switzerland by the possession of the urus, the bison, the elk, the stag, and the wild boar, as well as by the more general distribution of the beaver, the bear, the ibex, etc., their fauna differs from that of the drift gravels in the absence of the mammoth, the rhinoceros, the musk ox, the cave hyæna, and the reindeer.

Professor Rütimeyer thinks that from similar considerations alone, even if we had no other evidence, we might carry this division farther ; and if we take the settlements at Moosseedorf, Wauwyl, Robenhausen, and Nidau, which have been the most carefully studied in this respect, it certainly appears that the three former, which belong to the Stone Age, offer a marked contrast to the latter, which is the locality whence the largest number of bronze objects has as yet been obtained.

It is of course unnecessary to point out the interest and importance of such a distinction, which accords so well with that indicated by the study of the weapons and the state of preservation of the piles. Thus, the urus has only occurred at Moosseedorf, Wauwyl, Robenhausen, Wangen, and Concise ; the aurochs only at Moosseedorf, Wauwyl, and Robenhausen ; the bear only at Moosseedorf, Wauwyl, Robenhausen, Wangen, and Concise. A glance at the table given at page 203 will show that several other species have as yet only occurred at Moosseedorf and Robenhausen ; a fact, however, which indicates, perhaps, rather the richness than the antiquity of these localities. Possibly we may consider the presence of these larger species as an indication of their greater abundance in the oldest period ; but we must not forget that not only the bear and the elk, but also the aurochs and the urus, appear at a comparatively late period. On the other hand, the abundance of wild animals, and the fact that at Moosseedorf and Wauwyl the fox was more abundant than the dog, while elsewhere the reverse is the case, certainly speak in favour of the greater antiquity of these two settlements.

The evidence derived from the distribution of the domestic animals is more satisfactory. The sheep occurs even at Moosseedorf, though not so numerous as at Nidau. On the other hand, the horse is frequent at Nidau, while at Moosseedorf only a single bone of this animal was discovered, in a different condition from that of the other bones, and probably more recent. Finally, the domestic hog of the present race is absent from all the pile-works of the Stone Period, excepting the one at Wauwyl ; and becomes frequent only at Nidau. The following table shows the proportions of wild and tame animals at Wauwyl and Moosseedorf, as representing the Age of Stone ; and at Nidau, as perhaps the best illustra-

tion of that of Bronze. 1 represents a single individual ;
2, several ; 3, the species which are common ; 4, those
which are very common ; and 5, those which are present
in large numbers.

Wild Animals.	Wauwyl.	Moosseedorf.	Nidau.
Brown Bear . . .	2	2	...
Badger. . . .	2	2	...
Marten	3	2	...
Pine Marten . .	3	2	...
Polecat. . . .	2	2	...
Wolf	1	...	...
Fox	3	3	...
Wild Cat . . .	2	2	...
Beaver	2	3	...
Elk	1	1	1
Urus	...	1	...
Bison	1	1	...
Stag	5	5	5
Roe Deer . . .	2	4	...
Wild Boar . . .	2	3	...
Marsh Boar [1] . .	5	5	3
Domestic Animals.			
Domestic Boar . .	?1	...	3
Horse	2	?1	3
Ox	5	5	5
Goat	2	2	3
Sheep	1	2	4
Dog	2	2	3

If succeeding investigations confirm the conclusions
thus indicated, we may infer that the domestic animals,
which were comparatively rare in the Stone Period,
became more frequent after the introduction of bronze ;
a change which indicates and perhaps produced an alteration of habits on the part of the inhabitants.

Rare, indeed, as they may have been, oxen, horses,
sheep, and goats could not be successfully kept through
the winter in the climate of Switzerland without store of
provisions and some sort of shelter. A pastoral people,

[1] Considered by Professor Rütimeyer to have been at first wild, but
domesticated at Nidau, and in the later Pfahlbauten.

therefore, must have reached a higher grade than a mere nation of hunters. We know, moreover, in another way, that at this period agriculture was not entirely unknown. This is proved in the most unexpected manner, by the discovery of carbonized cereals at various points. Wheat is most common, having been discovered at Meilen, Moosseedorf, and Wangen. At the latter place, indeed, many bushels of it were found, the grains being united in large thick lumps. In other cases the grains are free, and without chaff, resembling our present wheat in size and form, while more rarely they are still in the ear. Ears of the *Hordeum hexastichon* L. (the six-rowed barley) are somewhat numerous. This species differs from the *H. vulgare* L. in the number of rows, and in the smaller size of the grains. According to De Candolle, it was the species generally cultivated by the ancient Greeks, Romans, and Egyptians. In the ears from Wangen, each row has generally ten or eleven grains, which, however, are smaller and shorter than those now grown.

Three varieties of wheat were cultivated by the lake-dwellers, who also possessed two kinds of barley, and two of millet. Of these the most ancient and most important were the small six-rowed barley and small "Lake-dwellers" wheat. The discovery of Egyptian wheat (*Triticum turgidum*) at Wangen and Robenhausen is particularly interesting. Oats were cultivated during the Bronze Age, but are absent from all the Stone Age villages. Rye also was unknown.

Wheat and millet only seem to have been used for making bread. Professor Heer thinks the barley was probably roasted. In six-rowed barley the husks adhere very closely to the grain, and it would have been difficult to separate them ; when roasted, however, they could be easily detached from one another.

Still more unexpected was the discovery of bread, or rather cakes, for their texture is so solid that leaven appears not to have been used. They were flat and round, from an inch to fifteen lines in thickness, and, to judge from one specimen, had a diameter of four or five inches. In other cases the grains seem to have been roasted, coarsely ground between stones, and then either stored up in large earthenware pots, or eaten after being slightly moistened. Grain treated in a similar manner is even now eaten in Germany and Switzerland. In what way the ground was prepared for the cultivation of corn we know not, as no implements have as yet been discovered which can with certainty be regarded as agricultural.

Carbonized apples have been found at Wangen, sometimes whole, sometimes cut into two, or more rarely into four pieces, and evidently dried and put aside for winter use. They have occurred not only at Wangen, but also at Robenhausen in Lake Pfeffikon, and at Concise in Lake Neufchâtel. They are small, and resemble generally those which still grow wild in the Swiss forests ; at Robenhausen, however, specimens have occurred which are of larger size and were probably cultivated. No trace of the walnut, the cherry, or the damson has yet been met with, but stones of the wild plum and the *Prunus padus* have been found. Seeds of the vine, raspberry, and blackberry, and shells of the hazel-nut and beech-nut occur plentifully in the mud, but those of the strawberry are rare. Peas have been found at Moosseedorf, but beans do not appear until the Bronze Age.

From all this, therefore, it is evident that the nourishment of the dwellers in the pile-works consisted of corn and wild fruits, of fish, and the flesh of wild and domestic animals. Milk also was doubtless an important article of their diet.

Altogether 115 species of plants have been determined. The wild species are almost entirely the same as those now living ; the *Silene cretica*, however, a South European weed, which was doubtless introduced originally and accidentally with the cereals, and which has been found at Robenhausen, does not now inhabit Switzerland ; and the *Trapa natans*, which was used as food by the inhabitants of Moosseedorf and Robenhausen, was supposed to be extinct in Switzerland, but is now known to occur in one locality.

I subjoin a table which I have compiled from Dr Heer's memoir, and which shows the more interesting species and varieties.

	Stone Age.		Transition.		Bronze Age.	
	Wangen.	Moosseedorf.	Robenhausen.	Montelier.	Parma.	Peter's Island.
1. Hordeum (barley) hexastichon sanctum	...	...	*	...	...	...
2. Hordeum hexastichon densum	...	...	*	*	*	...
3. Hordeum distichum	*	...	...	...	...	...
4. Triticum (wheat) vulgare antiquorum	*	*	*	...	...	*
5. Triticum vulgare compactum muticum	*	...	*	*	*	*
6. Triticum turgidum (Egyptian wheat)	*	...	*	*	...	...
7. Triticum spelta	...	...	...	...	...	*
8. „ dicoccum	*	...	...	...	...	...
9. „ monococcum	*1	...	...	...	...	...
10. Secale cereale	...	...	...	...	...	...
11. Avena sativa (oats)	...	...	...	*	...	*
12. Panicum miliaceum	*	...	...	*	...	...
13. Setaria italica	...	...	*	*	...	...
14. Silene cretica	...	...	*	...	...	...
15. Centaurea cyanus (cornflower)	...	...	*	...	...	...
16. Pastinaca sativa	...	*	...	...	...	...
17 Faba vulgaris	...	...	...	*	*	*
18. Pisum sativum	...	*	...	...	...	*
19. Ervum lens	...	...	...	...	...	*
20. Pyrus malus (small crab-apple)	*	*	*	...	...	...
21. Trapa natans	...	*	...	...	...	...
22. Linum angustifolium (flax)	*	*	*	...	...	...

Neither hemp, oats, nor rye have yet been found. Small pieces of twine and bits of matting made of flax may have been part of some article of clothing. For

1 Only one ear, subsequently lost.

this purpose also there can be little doubt that the skins of animals were used. Fragments of leather have been met with, and some of the stone implements seem well adapted to assist in their preparation, while the bone pins, and needles made from the teeth of boars, may have served to fasten them together.

Dr Heer, from whose very interesting memoir [1] the above facts are borrowed, calls particular attention to the fact that, while the remains of wild species found in the Pfahlbauten agree in the most minute particulars with those still living in Switzerland, the cultivated plants, on the contrary, differ from all existing varieties, and invariably have smaller seeds or fruits. Man has evidently in the course of time effected considerable improvements. It is also very interesting to observe how the evidence derived from the Swiss lake-dwellings agrees with that contained in the most ancient writings which we possess. Thus flax is mentioned in the Pentateuch and in Homer ; it was also largely used by the ancient Egyptians, while hemp seems to have been unknown until a later period. So also wheat and barley, but neither oats nor rye,[2] are mentioned in Exodus or by Homer. Even in the time of David, when Barzillai the Gileadite [3] " brought beds, and basins, and earthen vessels, and wheat, and barley, and flour, and parched corn, and beans, and lentiles, and parched pulse, and honey, and butter, and sheep, and cheese of kine," it will be observed that neither oats nor rye are mentioned. Flax also is alluded to nine times in the Old Testament, and linen thirteen times, but hemp not once.

To what race of men the Swiss lake-dwellings are ascribable we have as yet no direct evidence. Human bones are very rare in the pile-works, and may probably be referred to accidents, especially as we find that those of children are most numerous. M. Desor, indeed, states that not a single human skeleton has yet been found in

---

[1] *Die Pflanzen der Pfahlbauten.*

[2] According to the best Hebrew scholars, the word translated " rye" in Exodus ix. 32 really means " spelt."

[3] 2 Sam. xvii. 28.

any of the stations belonging to the Stone Age ; and Dr Keller, in his fifth report, informs us that all the lake-villages taken together have not yet produced more than half a dozen. One mature skull from Meilen has been described by Professor His, who considers that it does not differ much from the present Swiss type. While his work was in the press, Professor Rütimeyer received from Colonel Schwab four more skulls, two of which were obtained at Nidau, one at Sutz, and one at Biel. Another skull shown to me by Professor Desor, and found at Auvernier, completes the number mentioned by Dr Keller. All these settlements, however, appear to have belonged to the Bronze Age, nor has it yet been possible certainly to refer any of the ancient tumuli found in Switzerland to the earlier period.

Passing now to the lake-habitations belonging to the Bronze Age, we find that they are less generally distributed than those of the earlier period. They have as yet been found principally on the Lakes of Geneva, Luissel, Neufchâtel, Morat, Bienne, and Sempach ; scarcely any in eastern Switzerland. One settlement of the Bronze Age has been found on the Lake of Constance ; but as the question now stands, pile-works of the Metallic Period are almost peculiar to western and central Switzerland. The constructions of the Bronze Age are more solidly built, but do not otherwise appear to have differed materially from those of the Stone Age. They are often, however, situated farther from the land and in deeper water, partly no doubt on account of the greater skill in working timber, but partly also, perhaps, because more protection was needed as the means of attack were improved. The principal objects of bronze are swords, daggers, axes, spear-heads, knives, fish-hooks, sickles, pins, rings, and bracelets. The number of these articles which have been discovered is already very great, the collection of Colonel Schwab alone containing no less than 4346 objects of metal. They are classified in the table in p. 16, which gives an idea of the relative proportions in which they occur.

Many of them are really beautiful, and as bronze must have been at that early period of considerable value, it is difficult to understand how so many can have been left uncared for and forgotten, along the shallow margins of the Swiss lakes. " Il est évident," says Professor Desor, " que ce ne sont pas de rebuts qui se seraient perdus, sans qu'on s'en inquiétât. Ils ne sont pas tombés à l'eau par hasard, non plus que cette quantité de vases qui sont accumulés sur certain points, ni les jattes à provisions qu'on retire intactes." On the whole he is inclined to think that in some of these cases at least we have " de simples magasins destinés aux ustensiles et aux provisions, et qui auraient été détruits par l'incendie, comme semble l'indiquer la trace du feu que montrent fréquemment les poutres aussi bien que les vases en terre. On expliquerait ainsi comment il se fait que les objets en bronze sont presque tous neufs, que les vases sont entiers et réunis sur un seul point." Colonel Schwab, however, than whom no man has had more experience in such matters, while agreeing that comparatively little is ever found except in such lake-villages as show traces of fire, expresses himself decidedly, and I think with reason, against the " bazaar " theory.

It has been suggested that the early inhabitants of Switzerland may have worshipped the lakes, and that the beautiful bracelets, etc., may have been offerings to the gods. It appears from ancient writers that among the Gauls, Germans, and other nations, many lakes were regarded as sacred. According to Cicero,[1] Justin,[2] and Strabo,[3] there was a lake near Toulouse in which the neighbouring tribes used to deposit offerings of gold and silver. Tacitus, Pliny, and Virgil also mention the existence of sacred lakes. Even so late as the sixth century, Gregory of Tours tells us (*De Glor. Confes.*, chap. ii.) that on Mount Helanus there was a lake which was the object of popular worship. Every year the inhabitants of the neighbourhood brought to it offerings of clothes, skins, cheese, cakes, etc. Traces of a similar

[1] *De Nat. Deor.*, lib. iii. xxx.   [2] *Just.*, xxxii. iii.   [3] *Geog.*, vol. iv.

superstition may still be found lingering in the remote parts of Scotland and Ireland ; in the former country I have myself seen a sacred spring surrounded by the offerings of the neighbouring peasantry, who seemed to consider pence and halfpence as the most appropriate and agreeable sacrifice to the Spirit of the Waters. Neither the coarse, broken pottery, the castaway fragments of bones, nor the traces of habitations, can, however, be accounted for in this manner.[1]

The pottery of the Bronze Period is more varied and more skilfully made than that of the Stone Age, but the potter's wheel does not seem to have been in use. Rings of earthenware are common, and appear to have been used as supports for the round-bottomed vases. The ornaments are of the same general character as those on the objects of bronze. Many of the large urns appear to have been used as store-places for the grain, etc., which was collected during the summer for winter's use. In the absence, perhaps, of boxes and cupboards, even ornaments and instruments seem to have been kept in large jars. Some beautiful bracelets were found with several sickles in a jar at Cortaillod. Pieces of pottery, distorted by fire, during the process of baking, have, according to M. Troyon, been found in many of the lake-villages ; whence he concludes that the pottery was manufactured on the spot.

Colonel Schwab has found at Nidau more than twenty crescents made of earthenware, with the convex side flattened, to serve as a foot. They are compressed at the sides, sometimes plain, sometimes ornamented, from 10 to 12 inches wide, and 6 to 8 in height. Dr Keller was at first inclined to regard them as emblems of moon worship, but it is more probable that they were pillows.[2] Though this seems at first very unlikely, and they must, one would think, have been very uncomfortable, still we know that several barbarous races at the present day use

[1] See also Wylie, "On Lake-dwellings of the Early Periods," *Archæol.*, vol. xxxviii. p. 181.
[2] Vogt's *Lectures on Man*, p. 368.

wooden pillows or neck-rests of the same kind, as, for instance, the Fijians, who, having enormous heads of hair, sacrifice comfort to vanity, and use a mere wooden bar as a pillow. The very long bronze pins found with these "crescents" indicate that during the Bronze Age the hair was worn very long and was carefully arranged.

M. Troyon is of opinion that the inhabitants of Switzerland during the Bronze Age were of a different race from those who had lived there during the earlier period, and he agrees with some of the Scandinavian archæologists in regarding them as the true "Celts," and in attributing to them the habit of burning their dead. It would be very desirable to have some statistics, in order that we might appreciate the value of the evidence to be derived from the ancient Swiss burials. M. Troyon relies on the fact that many of the lake-villages were destroyed by fire, and that when, as appears to have been the case at several places, they were rebuilt during the Bronze Age, this was done, not exactly on the same spot, but farther away from the bank. Dr Keller, on the other hand, considers that the primitive population did not differ, either in disposition (*Anlage*), mode of life, or industry, from that which was acquainted with the use of bronze ; and that the whole phenomena of the lake-villages, from their commencement to their conclusion, indicate clearly a gradual and peaceable development. The number of instances in which lake-villages had been destroyed by fire has been, he considers, exaggerated. Of the settlements on the Lakes of Bienne and Neufchâtel, amounting in all to more than seventy, only a quarter have, according to Colonel Schwab, shown any traces of combustion ; a proportion which is, perhaps, not greater than might have been expected, remembering that the huts were built of wood, and in all probability covered by thatch. Moreover, if these conflagrations had resulted from the attacks of enemies, we ought surely to have found numerous remains of the slain, whereas all the lake-villages together have not as yet supplied us with the remains of more than half a dozen human skeletons.

It must, I think, be confessed that the arguments used by M. Troyon fail to prove that the introduction of bronze was accompanied by an entire change of population. However this may be, I have in a previous chapter (ch. iii.) given my reasons for believing that the use of bronze in Europe was introduced by a race coming from the East.

Towards the close of the Bronze Age the lake-villages appear to have gradually become less numerous. During the Stone Age they were spread over the whole country. Bronze Age settlements are very rare in the east of Switzerland, and the Iron Age is represented only on the Lakes of Bienne and Neufchâtel. In these settlements not only has a new substance made its appearance, but the forms of the implements are different. We have, indeed, copies of the bronze axes made in iron, just as we found before that some of the earlier bronze celts resembled the stone axes in form ; but these are exceptional cases. The swords have larger handles, and are more richly ornamented ; the knives have straight edges ; the sickles are larger ; the pottery is more skilfully made, and is of the kind generally known as Roman ; coins occur, the personal ornaments are more varied, and glass for the first time makes its appearance. Bronze also is present ; but in the first place it is no longer used for weapons, and in the second it is worked in a different manner, being hammered,[1] while, as already mentioned, all the objects of the Bronze Age are cast.

A field of battle at Tiefenau, near Berne (see p. 10), is remarkable for the great number of iron weapons and implements which have been found on it. Pieces of chariots, about a hundred swords, fragments of coat of mail, lance-heads, rings, fibulæ, ornaments, utensils, pieces of pottery and of glass, accompanied by more than thirty Gaulish and Massaliote coins of a date anterior to our era, enable us to refer this battle-field to the Roman period. About forty Roman coins have also been found at the small island on the Lake of Bienne.

[1] See Desor, *Les Constructions lacustres du Lac de Neuchâtel*, p. 27.

After this period we find no more evidences of lake-habitations on a large scale. Here and there, indeed, a few fishermen may have lingered on the half-destroyed platforms, but the wants and habits of the people had changed, and the age of the Swiss pile-works was at an end.

We have, however, traced them through the Ages of Stone and Bronze down to the beginning of the Iron Period. We have seen evidences of a gradual progress in civilization, and improvement in the arts, an increase in the number of domestic animals, and proofs at last of the existence of an extended commerce. We found the country inhabited only by rude savages, and we leave it the seat of a powerful nation. Changes so important as these are not effected in a day; the progress of the human mind is but slow; and the gradual additions to human knowledge and power, like the rings in trees, enable us to form some idea how distant must be the date of their commencement. So varied, however, are the conditions of the human mind, so much are all nations affected by the influence of others, that when we attempt to express our impressions, so to say, in terms of years, we are baffled by the complexity of the problem.

Some attempts have, indeed, been made to obtain a more definite chronology, and they have been alluded to in an earlier chapter. Though we must not conceal from ourselves the imperfection of the archæological record, still we need not despair of eventually obtaining some approximate chronology. Our knowledge of primitive antiquity has made an enormous stride in the last ten years, and we may fairly look forward with hope to the future.

The Swiss archæologists are continuing their labours, and they may rest assured that we in England watch with interest the result of their investigations. Few things, indeed, can be more interesting than the spectacle of an ancient and long-forgotten people thus rising, as it were, from the waters of oblivion, to take that place which properly belongs to it in the history of the human race.

CHAPTER VII

THE DANISH KJÖKKENMÖDDINGS OR SHELL-MOUNDS

Denmark occupies a larger space in the history than on the map of Europe ; the nation is greater than the country. With the growth of physical power in surrounding populations, she has lost much of her influence in political councils, and has been recently deprived of a great part of her ancient possessions ; but the Danes of to-day are no unworthy representatives of their ancestors. Many a larger nation might envy them the position they hold in science and art, and few have contributed more to the progress of human knowledge. Copenhagen may well be proud both of her museums and of her professors, and I would especially point to the celebrated Museum of Northern Antiquities, as being most characteristic and unique.

For the formation of such a collection Denmark offers great opportunities. The whole country appears to have been, at one time, thickly studded with tumuli ; where the land has not been brought into cultivation, many of them are often in sight at once, and even in the more fertile and thickly populated parts, the plough is often diverted from its course by one of these ancient burial-places. Fortunately, the stones of which they are constructed are so large and so hard, that their destruction and removal is a laborious and expensive undertaking. While, however, on the one hand, land grows gradually more valuable, and the stones themselves are more and more coveted for building or other purposes, on the other, the conservative traditions, the feeling of superstitious reverence for the dead, which have so long protected them from desecration, is gradually becoming weaker ; and it is estimated that not a day passes without witnessing the destruction of one or more of these tumuli, and the loss of some, perhaps almost irrecoverable, link in the history of the human race.

Many of these barrows, indeed, contain in themselves a small collection of antiquities, and the whole country may even be considered as a museum on a great scale. The peat bogs, which occupy so large an area, may almost be said to swarm with antiquities, and Professor Steen-strup estimates that, on an average, every column of peat three feet square contains some specimen of ancient work-manship. All these advantages and opportunities, how-ever, might have been thrown away but for the genius and perseverance of Professor Thomsen, who may fairly be said to have created the Museum over which he so long and so worthily presided.

In addition to the objects collected from the tumuli and the peat bogs, and to those which have been found from time to time scattered at random in the soil, the Museum of Northern Antiquities contains an immense collection of specimens from some very interesting shell-mounds, which are known in Denmark under the name of " Kjökkenmöddings," and were long supposed to be raised beaches, like those which are found at so many points along our own shores. True raised beaches, however, necessarily contain a variety of species ; the individuals are of different ages, and the shells are, of course, mixed with a considerable quantity of sand and gravel. But it was observed, in the first instance, I believe, by Professor Steenstrup, that in these supposed beaches, the shells belonged entirely to full-grown, or to nearly full-grown individuals ; that they consisted of four species which do not live together, nor require the same conditions, and would not, therefore, be found together alone in a natural deposit ; and, thirdly, that the stratum contained scarcely any gravel, but consisted almost entirely of shells.

The discovery of rude flint implements, and of bones

still bearing the marks of knives, confirmed the supposition that these beds were not natural formations, and it subsequently became evident that they were, in fact, the sites of ancient villages ; the primitive population having lived on the shore and fed principally on shell-fish, but partly also on the proceeds of the chase. In many places hearths were discovered consisting of flat stones, arranged in such a manner as to form small platforms, and bearing all the marks of fire. The shells and bones not available for food gradually accumulated round the tents and huts, until they formed deposits generally from 3 to 5 feet, but sometimes as much as 10 feet in thickness, and in some cases more than 300 yards in length, with a breadth of from 100 to 200 feet. The name Kjökkenmödding, applied to these mounds, is derived from *Kjökken*, "kitchen," and *mödding* (corresponding to our local word "midding"), a "refuse heap," and it was, of course, evident that a careful examination of these accumulations would throw much light on the manners and civilization of the then population.

Under these circumstances a Committee was formed, consisting of Professor Steenstrup, the celebrated author of the treatise *On the Alternation of Generations*, Professor Forchhammer, the father of Danish geology, and Professor Worsaae, the well-known archæologist ; a happy combination, promising the best results to biology, geology, and archæology. Much was naturally expected from the labours of such a triumvirate, and the most sanguine hopes have been fulfilled. More than fifty of the deposits have been carefully examined, many thousand specimens have been collected, ticketed, and deposited in the Museum at Copenhagen, and the general results have been embodied in six Reports, presented to the Academy of Sciences at Copenhagen.[1]

It is from these Reports, and from the excellent Memoir by M. Morlot, that the following information has principally been derived. Being, however, anxious to

---

[1] *Untersögelser i geologisk-antiquarisk Retning,* af G. Forchhammer, J. Steenstrup, og J. Worsaae. M. Morlot also has published an excellent abstract of the Reports in the *Mém. de la Société Vaudoise,* t. vi., 1860.

present to my readers a complete and accurate account of the interesting shell-mounds, 1 have more than once visited Denmark ; first in 1861, with Professor Busk, and again in the summer of 1863. On both these occasions, through the kindness of Professor Thomsen and Herr K. Herbst, every facility has been afforded me of examining the large collections made in different Kjökkenmöddings, in addition to which I had the great advantage of visiting several of the shell-mounds under the guidance of Professor Steenstrup himself—especially one at Havelse in 1861, and those at Meilgaard and Fannerup in 1863.

Mr Busk and I also visited by ourselves one at Bilidt, on the Isefjord, close to Fredericksund ; but this is one of the places at which it would seem that the inhabitants cooked their dinners actually on the shore itself, so that the shells and bones are much mixed up with sand and gravel ; and we were not very successful in our search for flint implements. At Havelse, on the contrary, the settlement was on rather higher ground, and, though close to the shore, beyond the reach of the waves ; the shells and bones are, therefore, almost unmixed with extraneous substances. At this place the Kjökken-mödding is of small extent, and is in the form of an irregular ring, enclosing a space on which the ancient dwelling or dwellings probably stood. In other cases, where the deposit is of greater extent, as, for instance, in the celebrated shell-mound at Meilgaard, the surface is undulating, the greater thickness of the shelly stratum in some places apparently indicating the arrangement of the dwellings. When the shell-mound at Havelse was previously visited by Professor Steenstrup, the shells were being removed to serve as manure, and the mound, presenting a perpendicular section, was in a very favour-able condition for examination. The small pits thus formed had, however, been filled in, so that we were obliged to make a fresh excavation. In two or three hours we obtained about a hundred fragments of bone, many rude flakes, slingstones, and flint fragments, together with nine rude axes of the ordinary "shell-mound" type (figs. 117-119).

Our visit to Meilgaard in 1863 was even more successful. This, which is one of the largest and most interesting shell-mounds hitherto discovered, is situated not far from the sea-coast, near Grenaa in North-East Jutland, in a beautiful beech-forest called "Aigt," or "Aglskov," on the property of M. Olsen, who, with a praiseworthy devotion to science, has given orders that the Kjökken-mödding should not be destroyed, although the materials of which it consists are well adapted for the improvement of the soil, and for other purposes, to which, indeed, they had already been in part applied before the true nature of the deposit was discovered. Arriving at his house, without invitation or notice, we were received by M. Olsen and his family with kindness and hospitality. M. Olsen immediately sent two workmen to clear away the rubbish which had fallen in since the last archæo-logical visit, so that when we reached the spot we found a fresh wall of the shell-mound ready for examination. In the middle, this Kjökkenmödding has a thickness of about ten feet, from which, however, it slopes away in all directions ; round the principal mound are several smaller ones, of the same nature. Over the shells a thin layer of mould has formed itself, on which trees grow. A good section of such a Kjökkenmödding can hardly fail to strike with astonishment anyone who sees it for the first time, and it is difficult to convey in words an exact idea of the appearance which it presents. The whole thickness consists of shells, oysters being at Meilgaard by far the most numerous, with here and there a few bones, and still more rarely stone implements or fragments of pottery. Excepting just at the top and bottom, the mass is quite unmixed with sand and gravel ; and, in fact, contains *nothing* but what has been in some way or other subservient to the use of man. The only exceptions which I could see were a few, very few, rough flint pebbles, which were probably dredged up with the oysters. While we were in this neighbourhood, we visited another Kjökkenmödding at Fannerup on the Kolindsund, which was even in historical times an arm of the sea, but is now a fresh-water lake. Other similar deposits have been discovered at various points along the Danish coast. Generally it is evident that deposits of this nature were scattered here and there over the whole shore, but that they were never formed inland. The whole country was more intersected by fjords during the Stone Period even than it is now. Under these circumstances it is evident that a nation which subsisted principally on marine mollusca would never form any large inland settlements. In some instances, indeed, Kjökkenmöddings have been found as far as eight miles from the present coast, but in these cases there is good reason for supposing that the land has encroached on the sea. On the other hand, in those parts where Kjökkenmöddings do not occur, their absence is no doubt occasioned by the waves having to a certain extent eaten away the shore ; an explanation which accounts for their being so much more frequent on the borders of the inland fjords than on the coast itself ; and which seems to deprive us of all hope of finding any similar remains on our eastern and south-eastern shores. Shell-mounds, although probably belonging to a later date, have, however, actually been found on our coasts. They were observed by Dr Gordon, of Birnie, on the shores of the Moray Firth. I have had the advantage of visiting these shell-mounds with him. The largest of the Scotch Kjökkenmöddings is on Loch Spynie. We did not find any imple-

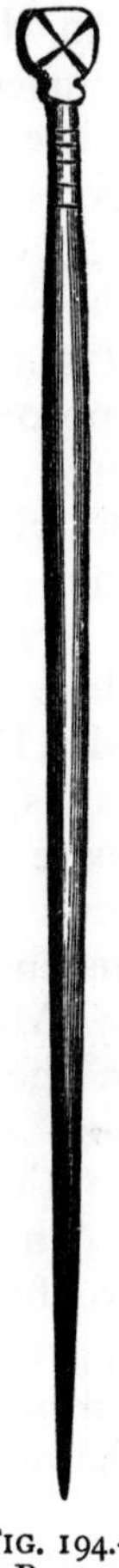

FIG. 194.— Bronze pin, actual size.

ments or pottery in it, although we searched for several hours ; but a labourer, who had been employed in carting it away for manure, had previously found some fragments of rude pottery and a bronze pin (fig. 194). Loch Spynie has been partially drained, and is shut out

from the sea by a great accumulation of shingle, so that
the water is now perfectly fresh. From ancient records
it appears that the shingle barrier was probably completed
and the lake shut out from the sea in the thirteenth and
fourteenth centuries. On the other hand, I have submitted the bronze pin figured here to Mr Franks, who
gives it as his opinion that it is probably not older than
800 or 900 A.D. If, therefore, it really belongs to the
shell-mound, and there seems no reason to doubt the
statement of the man who found it, we thus get an
approximate date for the accumulation of the mound
itself. Mr Pengelly and Mr Spence Bate have recently
described some shell-mounds in Cornwall and Devonshire, and similar shell-mounds have also been found
at various places on the Irish coast. At St Valéry,
close to the mouth of the Somme, Sir John Evans,
Mr Prestwich, and I found a large accumulation of
shells, from which I obtained several flint flakes, and
some pieces of rude pottery. Similar remains have
been observed in various parts of the world, as, for
instance, in Australia by Dampier,[1] in Tierra del Fuego
by Mr Darwin,[2] in the Malay Peninsula by Mr Earle,[3]
in the Andaman Islands by Dr Stolickza,[4] in Japan,[5] in
both North[6] and South America,[7] in Tasmania, and in
South Africa.

The fact that the majority of the Danish shell-mounds
are found at a height of only a few feet above the sea
appears to prove that there has been no considerable
subsidence of the land since their formation, while, on
the other hand, it clearly shows that there can have been
no elevation. In certain cases, however, where the shore
is steep, they have been found at a considerable height.
It might indeed be supposed that where, as at Bilidt, the

[1] Pinkerton's *Travels*, vol. ii. p. 473.   [2] *Journal*, p. 234.
[3] *Ethnological Soc. Trans.*, New Series, vol. ii. p. 119.
[4] *Proc. As. Soc. Bengal*, Jan. 1870.
[5] Morse, *Mem. of Univ. of Tokio*, vol. i.
[6] H. Wyman, *The American Naturalist*, vol. ii., Nos. 8, 9, and 11 ;
Foster, *Prehistoric Races of the United States*, p. 156.
[7] Brett's *Indian Tribes of Guiana* ; Agassiz, *Journey in Brazil*.

materials of the Kjökkenmödding were rudely inter-
stratified with sand and gravel, the land must have sunk ;
but if for any length of time such a deposit was subjected
to the action of the waves, all traces of it would be
obliterated, and it is, therefore, probable that an explanation is rather to be found in the fact that the action of
waves and storms may have been greater at that time
than it is now.   At present the tides only affect the
Kattegat to the extent of about a foot and a half, and the
configuration of the land protects it very much from the
action of the winds.   On the other hand, the tides on the
west coast of Jutland rise about nine feet, and the winds
have been known to produce differences of level amounting
to twenty-nine feet ; and as we know that Jutland was
anciently an archipelago, and the Baltic was more open to
the German Ocean than it is now, we can easily understand that the fluctuations of level may have been greater,
and we can thus explain how the waves may have risen
over the Kjökkenmödding at Bilidt (which is after all not
much more than ten feet above the water), without
resorting to the hypothesis of a subsidence and subsequent
elevation of the coast.

In the lake-habitations of the Stone Age in Switzerland,
grains of wheat and barley, and even pieces of bread, or
rather biscuit, have been found.   It does not, however,
appear that the men of the Kjökkenmöddings had any
knowledge of agriculture, no traces of grain of any sort
having been hitherto discovered.   The only vegetable
remains found in them have been burnt pieces of wood,
and some charred substance, referred by M. Forchhammer
to the *Zostera marina,* a sea-plant, which was, perhaps, used
in the production of salt.

The four species which are the most abundant in the
shell-mounds are :—

> The oyster (*Ostrea edulis,* L.),
> The cockle (*Cardium edule,* L.),
> The mussel (*Mytilus edulis,* L.), and
> The periwinkle (*Littorina littorea,* L.),

all four of which are still used as food for man. Other species occur more rarely, namely,—

Nassa reticulata, L.
Buccinum undatum, L.
Venus pullastra, Mont.
Helix nemoralis, Müll.
Venus aurea, Gm.
Trigonella plana, Da. C.
Littorina obtusata, L.
Helix strigella, Müll., and
Carocolla lapicida, L.

It is remarkable that the specimens of the first seven species are well developed, and decidedly larger than any now found in the neighbourhood.   This is especially the case with the *Cardium edule* and *Littorina littorea*, while the oyster has entirely disappeared, and even in the Kattegat itself occurs only in a few places ; a result which may, perhaps, be partly owing to the quantities caught by fishermen.   Some oysters were, however, still living in the Isefjord at the beginning of this century, and their destruction cannot be altogether ascribed to the fishermen, as great numbers of dead shells are still present ; but in this case it is attributed to the abundance of starfishes, which are very destructive to oysters.   On the whole, their disappearance, especially when taken in connection with the dwarf size of the other species, is evidently attributable in a great measure to the smaller proportion of salt in the water.

Of Crustacea, only a few fragments of crabs have hitherto been found.   The remains of vertebrata are very numerous and extremely interesting.   In order to form an idea of the number of bones, and of the relative proportions belonging to different animals, Professor Steenstrup dug out from three different parts of the shell-mound at Havelse, square pillars with sides three feet in length, and carefully collected the bones therein contained.   In the first pillar he found 175 bones of mammals and 35 of birds ; in the second pillar he found 121 of mammals and 9 of birds ; in the third, 309 of mammals and 10 of birds.   The pillars, however, were not exactly comparable, because their cubic contents depended on the thickness of the shell-mound at the place where they were taken, and varied between 17 and 20 cubic feet.   On the whole, Professor Steenstrup estimates that there were from 10 to 12 bones in each cubic foot.   It will be seen, therefore, that the number of bones is very great.   Indeed, from the mound at Havelse alone the Committee obtained in one summer 3500 bones of mammals and more than 200 of birds, besides many hundred of fishes, which latter, indeed, are almost innumerable.   The most common species are—

> *Clupea harengus*, L. (the herring),
> *Gadus callarias*, L. (the dorse),
> *Pleuronectes limanda*, L. (the dab), and
> *Muræna anguilla*, L. (the eel).

The remains of birds are highly interesting and instructive.   The domestic fowl (*Gallus domesticus*) is entirely absent.   The two domestic swallows of Denmark (*Hirundo rustica* and *H. urbica*), the sparrow, and the stork, are also missing.   On the other hand, fine specimens of the capercailzie (*Tetrao urogallus*), which feeds principally on the buds of the pine, show that, as we know already from the remains found in the peat, the country was at one time covered with pine forests.   Aquatic birds, however, are the most frequent, especially several species of ducks and geese.   The wild swan (*Cygnus musicus*), which only visits Denmark in winter, is also frequently found ; but perhaps the most interesting of the birds whose remains have been identified, is the Great Auk (*Alca impennis*, L.), a species which is now almost, if not altogether, extinct.

Of mammalia, by far the most common are—

> The stag (*Cervus elephus*, L.),
> The roe-deer (*Cervus capreolus*, L.), and
> The wild boar (*Sus scrofa*, L.).

Indeed, Professor Steenstrup estimates that these three species form ninety-seven per cent. of the whole ; the others are—

> The urus (*Bos urus*, L.)
> The dog (*Canis familiaris*, L.)
> The fox (*Canis vulpes*, L.)
> The wolf (*Canis lupus*, L.)
> The marten (*Martes sp.*)
> The otter (*Lutra vulgaris*, Exl.)
> The porpoise (*Delphinus phocæna*, L.)
> The seal (*Phoca sp.*)
> The water-rat (*Hypudæus amphibius*, L., and *Hypudæus agrestis*, L.)
> The beaver (*Castor fiber*, L.)
> The lynx (*Felis lynx*, L.)
> The wild cat (*Felis catus*, L.)
> The hedgehog (*Erinaceus europæus*, L.)
> The bear (*Ursus arctos*, L.)
> The mouse (*Mus flavicollis*, Mel.).

There are also traces of a smaller species of ox. The Lithuanian aurochs (*Bison europæus*) has been found, though rarely, in the peat bogs, but not yet in the Kjökkenmöddings. The musk ox (*Ovibus moschatus*) and the domestic ox (*Bos taurus*), as well as the reindeer, the elk, the hare, the sheep, and the domestic hog, are all absent.[1]

Professor Steenstrup does not agree with Professor Rütimeyer that the domestic hog of ancient Europe was directly derived from the wild boar, but rather that it was introduced from the east ; and the skulls which he showed me in support of this belief certainly exhibited very great differences between the two races. The sheep, the horse, and the reindeer are entirely absent ; the domestic cat was not known in Europe until about the

---

[1] It is a curious fact that, as Professor Steenstrup informs me, the bones from the Kjökkenmöddings of Jutland indicate, as a general rule, larger and more powerful animals than those of the islands.

ninth century ; and the bones of the urus are probably those of wild specimens ; so that the dog [1] appears to have been the only domestic animal of the period ; and though it may fairly be asked whether the bones may not have belonged to a race of wild dogs, the question admits of a satisfactory answer.

Among the remains of birds, the long bones, which form about one-fifth of the skeleton, are, in the Kjökkenmöddings, about twenty times as numerous as the others, and are almost always imperfect, the shaft only remaining. In the same manner it would be impossible to reconstruct a perfect skeleton of the quadrupeds, certain bones and parts of bones being always absent. In the case of the ox, for instance, the missing parts are the heads of the long bones (though while the shaft only of the femur is found, in the humerus one end is generally perfect), the backbone except the first two vertebræ, the spinous processes, and often the ribs, and the bones of the skull except the lower jaw and the portion round the eyes. It occurred to Professor Steenstrup that these curious results might, perhaps, be referred to dogs ; and, on trying the experiment, he ascertained that the bones which are absent from the Kjökkenmöddings are precisely those which dogs eat, and those which are present are the parts which are hard and solid and do not contain much nourishment. Professor Steenstrup has since published a diagram of a skeleton, tinted in such a manner as to show at a glance which of the bones occur in the Kjökkenmöddings, and points out that it coincides exactly with one given by M. Flourens to illustrate those portions of the skeleton which are first formed. Although a glance at the longitudinal section of a long bone, as, for instance, of a femur, and a comparison of the open cancelled tissue of the two ends with the solid, close texture of the shaft, at once justifies and accounts for the selection made by the dogs, it is interesting thus to

---

[1] From the marks of knives on the bones, it seems evident that the dog was then, as it is still among several savage tribes, an article of food.

ascertain that their predilections were the same in primæval times as at present. Moreover, we may in this manner explain the prevalence of some bones in fossil strata. I have already mentioned that of the skull ; the hard parts round the eye and the lower jaw are the only parts left ; now the preponderance of *lower jaws* in a fossil state is well known.

Dr Falconer indeed has pointed out " that in the smaller mammalia, unless the bone be complete, and supposing it to be a long bone, with both its articular surfaces perfect, it is almost hopeless, or, at any rate, very discouraging, to attempt to make out the creature that yielded it ; whereas the smallest fragment of a jaw, with a minute tooth in it, speaks volumes of evidence at the first glance." " This," he suggests, " is one great reason why we hear so much of jaw remains, and so little of other bones." No doubt it is so ; but these observations, made by Professor Steenstrup, afford a further explanation of the fact, and it is to be regretted that the parts of the long bones which are most important to the palæontologist are also those which are preferred by beasts of prey.

In every case the bones which contained marrow are split open in the manner best adapted for its extraction ; this peculiarity, which is in itself satisfactory proof of the presence of man, has not yet been observed in bones from the true tertiary strata.

The Kjökkenmöddings were not mere summer quarters ; the ancient fishermen resided on these spots for at least two-thirds, if not the whole of the year. This we learn from an examination of the bones of the wild animals, as it is often possible to determine, within very narrow limits, the time of year at which they are killed. For instance, the remains of the wild swan (*Cygnus musicus*) are very common, and this bird is only a winter visitor, leaving the Danish coast in March, and returning in November. It might naturally have been hoped that the remains of young birds would have supplied evidence as to the spring and early summer, but unfortunately, as has been already explained, no such bones are to be found. It is therefore fortunate that among the mammalia two periodical phenomena occur ; namely, the shedding and reproduction of stags' antlers, which, with slight variations according to age, have a fixed season ; and, secondly, the birth and growth of the young. These and similar phenomena render it highly probable that the " mound-builders " resided on the Danish coast all the year round, though I am disposed to think that, like the Fuegians, who lead, even now, a very similar life, they frequently moved from spot to spot. This appears to me to be indicated not only by the condition of the deserted hearths, but by the colour of the flint flakes, etc. ; for while many of these retain the usual dull bluish black colour which is characteristic of newly-broken flints, and which remains unaltered as long as they are surrounded by carbonate of lime, others are whitened, as is usual with those which have been exposed for any length of time. Perhaps, therefore, these were lying on the surface during some period of desertion, and covered over only when the place was again inhabited.

FIG. 195.—Flint awl from Denmark, actual size.

The flint implements found in the Kjökkenmöddings resemble those which are characteristic of the " coast-finds." They may be classed as flakes (figs. 86–99) ; " shell-mound " axes, which, as we have already observed, present a peculiar form (figs. 117–119) ; awls (fig. 195), slingstones or net-weights, and rude lance-heads (figs. 196, 197). With these occur other forms, which, though very rude, are evidently artificial, such as fig. 198, which appears to have been a kind of axe, and others of which the sharp edges were evidently used for cutting purposes.

In the two days which we spent at Meilgaard, we found the following objects:—

"Shell-mound" axes	19
Flint flakes . .	139
Bone pins, etc.. .	6
Horns . . .	6
Pottery, only . .	4 pieces
Stone hammer . .	1
Slingstones, about .	20
	195

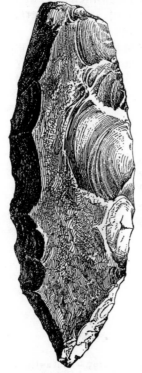

FIG. 196.—Lance-head (?) from Denmark, actual size.

Of the three "pillars" of material just alluded to (p. 234), the first contained seven flint flakes, two axes, one worked piece of horn, three worked pieces of bone, and some pottery; in the second were sixteen flint flakes, one axe, and seven slingstones; in the third, four flint flakes, two flint axes, and a pointed bone. In short, without appearing to be richer than other Kjökkenmöddings, Meilgaard and Havelse have each produced already more than a thousand of these rude relics, though but a small portion of the mound has in either case been hitherto removed. We need not, therefore, wonder at the number of axes found in the valley of the Somme, where so much larger a mass of material has been examined.

No polished axes have yet been found in the Kjökkenmöddings; but a fragment of one which was discovered at Havelse, and which had been worked up into a scraper, may indicate that they were not altogether unknown, though it would not be safe to decide from a single specimen. A very few carefully formed weapons have been found, but the implements generally are very rude, and of the same types as those which have been already described as characteristic of the "Coast-finds." Small pieces of very coarse pottery have also been discovered, and many of the bones from the Kjökkenmöddings bear evident marks of a sharp instrument ; several of the pieces found by us were in this condition, and had been fashioned into rude pins.

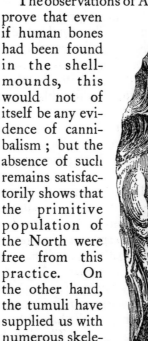

The observations of Arctic travellers prove that even if human bones had been found in the shell-mounds, this would not of itself be any evidence of cannibalism ; but the absence of such remains satisfactorily shows that the primitive population of the North were free from this practice. On the other hand, the tumuli have supplied us with numerous skeletons which probably belong to the

FIG. 197.—Lance-head (?) from Denmark, actual size.

FIG. 198.—Rude flint axe from Denmark, actual size.

Stone Age. The skulls are very round, and in many respects resemble those of the Lapps, but have a more projecting ridge over the eye. One curious peculiarity is, that their front teeth do not overlap as ours do, but meet one another, as do those of the Greenlanders of the present day. This perhaps is due to the manner of eating, rather than any indication of race.

Much as still remains to be made out respecting the men of the Stone Period, the facts already ascertained, like a few strokes by a clever draughtsman, supply us with the elements of an outline sketch. Carrying our imagination back into the past, we see before us on the low shores of the Danish Archipelago a race of small men, with heavy overhanging brows, round heads, and faces probably much like those of the present Laplanders. As they must evidently have had some protection from the weather, it is most probable that they lived in tents made of skins. The total absence of metal in the Kjökkenmöddings indicates that they had not yet any weapons except those made of wood, stone, horn, and bone. Their principal food must have consisted of shell-fish, but they were able to catch fish, and often varied their diet by game caught in hunting. It is evident that marrow was considered a great delicacy, for every single bone which contained any was split open in the manner best adapted to extract the precious morsel.

We have already seen that the mound-builders were regular settlers, and not mere summer visitors ; and on the whole they seem to have lived in very much the same manner as the Tierra del Fuegians, who dwell on the coast, feed principally on shell-fish, and have the dog as their only domestic animal. A good account of them is given in Darwin's *Journal* (p. 234), from which I extract the following passages, which give us a vivid and probably correct idea of what might have been seen on the Danish shores, long, long ago. " The inhabitants, living chiefly upon shell-fish, are obliged constantly to change their place of residence ; but they return at intervals to the same spots, as is evident from the pile of old shells, which must often amount to some tons in weight. These heaps can be distinguished at a long distance by the bright green colour of certain plants which invariably grow on them. . . . The Fuegian wigwam resembles, in size and dimensions, a haycock. It merely consists of a few broken branches stuck in the ground, and very imperfectly thatched on one side with a few tufts of grass and rushes. The whole cannot be so much as the work of an hour, and it is only used for a few days. . . . At a subsequent period, the *Beagle* anchored for a couple of days under Wollaston Island, which is a short way to the northward. While going on shore, we pulled alongside a canoe with six Fuegians. These were the most abject and miserable creatures I anywhere beheld. On the east coast, the natives, as we have seen, have guanoco cloaks, and on the west, they possess sealskins. Amongst the central tribes the men generally possess an otter-skin, or some small scrap about as large as a pocket-handkerchief, which is barely sufficient to cover their backs as low down as their loins. It is laced across the breast by strings, and according as the wind blows, it is shifted from side to side. But these Fuegians in the canoe were quite naked, and even one full-grown woman was absolutely so. It was raining heavily, and the fresh water, together with the spray, trickled down her body. . . . These poor wretches were stunted in their growth, their hideous faces bedaubed with white paint, their skins filthy and greasy, their hair entangled, their voices discordant, their gestures violent and without dignity. Viewing such men, one can hardly make oneself believe they are fellow-creatures and inhabitants of the same world. . . . At night, five or six human beings, naked and scarcely protected from the wind and rain of this tempestuous climate, sleep on the wet ground coiled up like animals. Whenever it is low water, they must rise to pick shell-fish from the rocks ; and the women, winter and summer, either dive to collect sea eggs, or sit patiently in their canoes, and, with a baited hair line, jerk out small fish. If a seal is killed, or the floating carcase of a putrid whale discovered, it is a feast ; such miserable food is assisted by a few tasteless berries and fungi. Nor are they exempt from famine, and, as a consequence, cannibalism accompanied by parricide." In this latter respect, however, the advantage appears to be all on the side of the ancients, against whom we have no evidence of cannibalism.

If the absence of cereal remains justifies us, as it appears to do, in concluding that they had no knowledge of agriculture, they must certainly have sometimes suffered from periods of great scarcity, indications of which may, perhaps, be seen in the bones of the fox, wolf, and other carnivora, which would hardly have been eaten from choice ; on the other hand, they were blessed in the ignorance of spirituous liquors, and saved thereby from what is at present the greatest scourge of Northern Europe.

The shell-mounds and coast-finds, according to Professor Worsaae, are characterized by rough flint implements (figs. 117–119, 195–198), and are the remains of a much ruder and more barbarous people than that which constructed the large Stone Age tumuli, and made the beautiful weapons, etc., found in them. He does not altogether deny that a few well-worked implements, and fragments of such, have been found in the Kjökkenmöddings, but he considers that some of these at least may be altogether more recent than the shell-mounds in which they are reported to have been found, and, at any rate, that their presence is altogether exceptional. At Meilgaard, for instance, the researches undertaken under the superintendence of the late king in June, 1861, produced more than five hundred flint flakes and other rude implements, but not a single specimen with a trace of polishing, or in any way resembling the flint implements found in the tumuli. On the other hand, these rude implements are said to be wanting in the tumuli, where they are replaced by instruments of a different character and more skilful workmanship. Moreover, while it is admitted on all hands that the shell-mound makers had no domestic animal but the dog, and no knowledge of agriculture, Professor Worsaae considers that during the later Stone Age the inhabitants of Denmark certainly possessed tame cattle and horses, and had in all probability some knowledge of agriculture.

Professor Steenstrup is of an entirely different opinion, and considers that the Kjökkenmöddings and Stone Age tumuli were contemporaneous. He denies altogether that remains of tame oxen or horses have been found in tumuli of the Stone Age, except in a very few instances, and in these he maintains that the fragments which have occurred are evidently not coeval with the mounds themselves, and that in all probability they have been introduced by foxes. He admits that the stone implements from the shell-mounds and coast-finds are altogether different from, and much ruder than, those from the tumuli ; he considers the two classes as representing, not two different degrees, but two different phases of one single condition of civilization. The tumuli are the burial-places of chiefs, the Kjökkenmöddings are the refuse heaps of fishermen. The first contained all that skill could contrive, affection offer, or wealth command ; the second, those things only which art could not make available, which were thrown away as useless, or accidentally lost. In order, therefore, to compare these two classes of objects, we must take, not the ordinary rude specimens which are so numerous in the shell-mounds, but the few better-made implements which, fortunately for science and for us, were lost among the oyster-shells, or which had been broken, and therefore thrown away. These, though few in number, are, in Professor Steenstrup's opinion, quite as numerous as could have been expected under the circumstances. Moreover, the long flint flakes, which are so common in the Kjökkenmöddings, are sufficient evidence that great skill in the treatment of flint had already been attained. Some of the flakes found in the Kjökkenmöddings are equal to any from the tumuli ; several of those which we found at Meilgaard were more than 5, and one was more than 6 inches in length ; while I have in my possession a giant flake from Fannerup (figs. 87–89), given to me by Professor Steenstrup, which has a length of $8\frac{3}{4}$ inches. As regards the rude, more or less triangular "axes" (figs. 117–119) which are so characteristic of the Kjökkenmöddings and coast-finds, Professor Steenstrup, as we have already seen, declines to compare them with the polished axes of the tumuli, because in his opinion they were not intended for the same purposes. In addition to the direct evidence derived from the discovery of some few well-made flint axes of the tumulus type, Professor Steenstrup relies much on the indirect evidence derivable from the other contents of the shell-mounds. Thus the frequent remains of large and full-grown animals—for instance, of the seal and the wild ox—are in his opinion sufficient evidence that the shell-mound builders must have had weapons more useful and destructive than any which Professor Worsaae will concede to them ; moreover, he considers that many of the cuts which are so common on the bones found in the shell-heaps must have been made by polished implements, and are too smooth to be the marks of flint flakes, according to the suggestion of Professor Worsaae. Finally, Professor Steenstrup, though not attributing so much weight as Professor Worsaae to the absence of the ruder implements from the tumuli, even if this had been the case, disputes the fact on the ground that these implements would not until recently have been recognized and collected, and that they have, in fact, been found whenever they were looked for.

After having carefully considered the evidence on both sides, I find myself, as might naturally be expected, unable altogether to agree with either.

The small rude axes seem to me even less well adapted to the purpose suggested by Professor Steenstrup, than to those which have generally been attributed to them. There are, no doubt, some which could never have been used for cutting, but these may have been failures, owing to some want of skill on the part of the manufacturer, or some flaw in the flint itself. Others appear to me, as to Professor Worsaae, serviceable, though rude ; and well adapted for some purpose (possibly for oyster dredging or chopping wood) which required a strong rather than a sharp edge. They also very closely resemble in form some of the adzes used by the South Sea Islanders, one of which I have figured for comparison (see fig. 120). They seem to me, however, as to Professor Steenstrup, to differ in character from the well-made and generally polished axes, and not to be ruder implements of the same type. Although the carefully formed knives, axes, lance-heads, etc., would not be likely to abound in the Kjökkenmöddings, any more than works of art or objects of value in modern dust-heaps ; still I confess I should have expected that fragments of these instruments, recognizable to us, though useless to their original owners, would have been more numerous than, in reality, they appear to be.

In addition to the 500 rude implements described by Professor Worsaae as having been found at Meilgaard during the king's visit, I myself obtained 140 flint flakes, with about 50 other implements, in the visit to this celebrated locality which I made some years ago under the guidance of Professor Steenstrup. To these, again, must be added many which had previously been collected by M. Olsen, and the members of the Kjökkenmödding Committee ; and yet among so large a number of instruments of various kinds there is only one which in any respect resembles the well-worked implements of the tumuli. So, again, at Havelse only a single fragment of polished axe has been found among more than a thousand objects of the ruder kind. It might, however, fairly be urged that in such a comparison neither the flakes nor " slingstones " ought to be brought into consideration in this case ; and if we were to count the axes only, the numbers would be greatly diminished.

Moreover, the alleged absence of rude implements in the Stone Age barrows has been satisfactorily explained by Professor Steenstrup. In this country it might be argued, from the statements of so intelligent an antiquary as Sir R. Colt Hoare, that rude implements were never, or very rarely, found in tumuli ; but the more recent researches of Mr Bateman, Canon Greenwell, and other archæologists, have shown that this is very far from being the case, and have made it evident that the ruder implements of stone were overlooked by the earlier archæologists. In the tumuli examined by Mr Bateman, he obtained many flint flakes, etc., quite as rude as those which are found in the shell-mounds. So far as I am aware, however, none of the small triangular axes, which are so characteristic of the shell-mounds, have yet been met with in the tumuli. Nor, on the other hand, has a single specimen resembling those which are characteristic of the Palæolithic Age yet been found in the shell-mounds.

Finally, we have, I think, no conclusive evidence of the remains of domestic animals (other than the dog) in Stone Age tumuli.

On the whole, the evidence appears to show that the Danish shell-mounds represent a definite period in the history of that country, and are probably referable to the early part of the Neolithic Age, when the art of polishing flint implements was known, but before it had reached its greatest development.

It is, however, as yet, impossible to affix even an approximate date in years to the formation of the Kjökken-möddings. Their accumulation, indeed, must evidently have occupied a considerable period, and it is of course highly probable that some are much older than others. They must all, however, be of very considerable antiquity. We know that the country has long been covered by beech forests, and yet it appears that during the Bronze Age beeches were absent, or only represented by stragglers, while the whole country was covered with oaks. This change implies a great lapse of time, even if we suppose that but a few generations of oaks succeeded one another. We know also that the oaks had been preceded by pines, and that the country was inhabited even then.

Again, the immense number of objects belonging to the Bronze Age, which have been already found in Denmark, and the great number of tumuli, appear to justify the Danish archæologists in assigning to this period a great lapse of time. This argument applies with peculiar force to the remains of the Stone Period : for a country, the inhabitants of which live by hunting and fishing, can never be thickly populated ; and, on the whole, the conclusion is forced upon us, that the country must have been inhabited for a lengthened period, although none of the Danish remains yet discovered belong to a time as ancient as some of those which have been found in other parts of Europe, and which will be described in subsequent chapters.

CHAPTER VIII

OUR knowledge of North American archæology is derived mainly from the valuable researches of Mr Caleb Atwater, contained in the first volume of the *Archæologia Americana*, and from four excellent memoirs published under the auspices of the Smithsonian Institution :— (1) *Ancient Monuments of the Mississippi Valley, comprising the Results of extensive Original Surveys and Explorations*, by E. G. Squier, A.M., and E. H. Davis, M.D. (2) *Aboriginal Monuments of the State of New York, comprising the Results of Original Surveys and Explorations, with an illustrative Appendix*, by E. G. Squier, A.M. (3) *The Antiquities of Wisconsin*, as surveyed and described by J. A. Lapham. (4) *The Archæology of the United States, or Sketches, Historical and Biographical, of the Progress of Information and Opinion respecting Vestiges of Antiquity in the United States*, by Samuel F. Haven. Nor must I omit to mention Schoolcraft's *History, Condition, and Prospects of the Indian Tribes of the United States*.[1]

The antiquities fall into two great divisions : implements (including ornaments) and earthworks. The earthworks have been again divided by the American archæologists into six classes :—(1) Defensive enclosures ; (2) Sacred and miscellaneous enclosures ; (3) Sepulchral mounds ; (4) Temple mounds ; (5) " Animal " mounds ; and (6) Miscellaneous mounds. These classes 1 shall

---

[1] Among more recent works on the subject, I may specially refer to Bancroft's *Native Races of the Pacific States* ; Jones's *Antiquities of the Southern Indians* ; Foster's *Prehistoric Races of the United States* ; Abbott's *Stone Age in New Jersey.*

treat separately, and we can then better consider the
" mound-builders " themselves.

The simple weapons of bone and stone, found in
America, closely resemble those which occur in other
countries. The flakes, hatchets, axes, arrow-heads, and
bone implements are, for instance, very similar to those
which occur in the Swiss lakes, if only we make allowance for the differences of material. In
addition to the simple forms, which may
almost be said to be ubiquitous, there are
some, however, which are more complicated. The perforated axes found in
Europe are generally considered to belong to the Metallic Age ; but as far as
America is concerned, we have not yet
any evidence as to the relative antiquity
of the perforated and imperforated types.

At the time of the discovery of America,
iron was absolutely unknown to the natives,
with the exception, perhaps, of a tribe near
the mouth of the La Plata, who had arrows
tipped with this metal, which they are
supposed to have obtained from masses
of native iron. The powerful nations of
Central America were, however, in an Age
of Bronze, while the North Americans
were in a condition of which we find in
Europe but scanty traces—namely, in an

FIG. 199.—Copper
arrow or spear-
head, Cincin-
nati, one-third
actual size.

Age of Copper. Silver is the only other metal which
has been found in the ancient tumuli, and that but in
very small quantities. It occurs sparingly in a native
form with the copper of Lake Superior, whence, in all
probability, it was derived. It does not appear to have
been ever smelted. From the large quantity of galena
which is found in the mounds, Messrs Squier and Davis
are disposed to think that lead must have been used to
a certain extent by the North American tribes ; the metal
itself, however, has not, I believe, yet been found.

Copper, on the other hand, both wrought and unwrought, occurs frequently in the tumuli. It is interesting to observe that the copper arrow- or spear-heads (fig. 199) resemble the American type of stone arrowheads. The axes have a striking resemblance to those simple European forms which contain the minimum quantity of tin, and as in them the socket, when there is one, is made by flattening the copper and turning over the edge (fig. 200); and some of the Mexican paintings give us interesting evidence as to the manner i. which they were handled and used. These, however, were of bronze, and had, therefore, been fused; but the Indian axes, which are of pure metallic copper, appear in all cases to have been worked in a cold state, which is remarkable, because, as Messrs Squier and Davis have pointed out, "the fires upon the altar were sufficiently intense to melt down the copper implements and ornaments deposited upon them. The hint thus afforded does not seem to have been seized upon." Mr Perkins, indeed, who has devoted much attention to these implements, is of opinion that some of them were cast; and this view has also been adopted by Mr Foster and Professor Butler. Sir John Evans has also called attention to a passage in which De Champlain, the founder of Quebec, tells us that in 1610 he met a party of Algonquins, one of whom met him on his barque, and, after conversation, "tira d'une sac une pièce de

FIG. 200.—Copper lance-head, Ontonagon, one-third actual size.

cuivre de la longueur d'un pied qu'il me donna, lequel
estoit fort beau et bien franc, me donnant à entendre
qu'il en avoit en quantité là où il l'avoit pris, qui c'etoit
sur le bort d'une rivière proche d'une grand lac et qu'ils le
prenoient par morceaux, et le faisant fondre le mettoient
en lames, et avec des pierres le rendoient uny." [1] Mr
Foster gives a plate [2] showing what he considers to
be the mark left by the line of junction between the
two halves of the mould. Dr Schmidt [3] has, however,
given strong reasons for doubting this conclusion, and
certainly the marks shown on the above-mentioned
figures have rather the appearance of weathering. On
the whole, though it would seem that they sometimes at
any rate softened the metal by heat, we have not, I think,
at present any sufficient evidence that the Redskins were
acquainted with the art of casting. This is the more
surprising, because, as Schoolcraft [4] tells us, "in almost
all the works lately opened there are heaps of coals and
ashes, showing that fire had much to do with their
operations." Thus, though they were acquainted with
metal, they did not know how to use it; and, as Professor
Dana has well observed in a letter with which he has
favoured me, they may in one sense be said to have been
in an Age of Stone, since they used the copper, not as
metal, but as stone. This intermediate condition between
an Age of Stone and one of Metal is most interesting.

In the neighbourhood of Lake Superior, and in some
other still more northern localities, copper is found
native in large quantities, and the Indians had therefore
nothing to do but to break off pieces, and hammer them
into the required shape. Hearne's celebrated journey to
the mouth of the Coppermine River, under the auspices
of the Hudson's Bay Company, was undertaken in order
to examine the locality whence the natives of that district
obtained the metal. In this case it occurred in lumps
actually on the surface, and the Indians seem to have

---

[1] *Les Voyages du Sieur de Champlain*, Paris, 1613.
[2] *Prehistoric Races of the United States*, p. 259.
[3] *Ar. für Anthropologie*, 1878, p. 65.   [4] *Indian Tribes*, p. 97.

picked up what they could, without attempting anything that could be called mining. Round Lake Superior, however, the case is very different. A short account of the ancient copper mines is given by Messrs Squier and Davis in the work already so often cited, by Mr Squier in *The Aboriginal Monuments of the State of New York*, by Mr Lapham,[1] and by Mr Schoolcraft;[2] while the same subject is treated at considerable length by Professor Wilson.

The works appear to have been first discovered in 1847 by Mr Knapp, the agent of the Minnesota Mining Company. His observations have "brought to light ancient excavations of great extent, frequently from twenty-five to thirty feet deep, and scattered over an area of several miles. He counted 395 annular rings on a hemlock-tree which grew on one of the mounds of earth thrown out of an ancient mine. Mr Foster also notes the great size and age of a pine stump, which must have grown, flourished, and died since the works were deserted ; and Mr C. Whittesley not only refers to living trees upwards of three hundred years old, now flourishing in the gathered soil of the abandoned trenches, but adds, 'On the same spot there are the decayed trunks of a preceding generation or generations of trees that have arrived at maturity, and fallen down from old age.' According to the same writer, in a communication made to the American Association, at the Montreal meeting in 1857, these ancient works extend over a tract from 100 to 150 miles in length, along the southern shore of the lake."

Wooden implements are so perishable that we could not expect many of them to have been found. Two or three wooden bowls, a trough, and some shovels with long handles, are all that appear to be recorded.

It has often been stated that the Indians possessed some method, at present unknown, by which they were enabled to harden the copper. This however, seems to be an error. Some copper implements, which Mr Wilson

[1] *L.c.*, p. 74.   [2] *L.c.*, p. 95.

submitted to Professor Crofts, were found to be no harder than the native copper from Lake Superior. "The structure of the metal was also highly laminated, as if the instrument had been brought to its present shape by hammering out a solid mass of copper."

Before the introduction of metallic vessels, the art of the potter was more important even than it is at present. Accordingly, the sites of all ancient habitations are generally marked by numerous fragments of pottery ; this is as true of the ancient Indian settlements, as of the Celtic towns of England, or the lake-villages of Switzerland. These fragments, however, would generally be those of rude household vessels, and it is principally from the tumuli that we obtain those better-made urns and cups from which the state of the art may fairly be inferred.

In North America the art of the potter attained to a considerable degree of perfection ; some of the vases found in the tumuli are said to rival, "in elegance of model, delicacy, and finish," the best Peruvian specimens. The material used is a fine clay : in the more delicate specimens, pure ; in the coarser ones, mixed with pounded quartz. The art of glazing and the use of the potter's wheel appear not to have been known, though that "simple approximation to a potter's wheel may have existed," which consists of "a stick of wood grasped in the hand by the middle, and turned round inside a wall of clay, formed by the other hand, or by another workman."[1]

Among the most characteristic specimens of ancient American pottery are the pipes. Some of these are simple bowls, not unlike a common every-day pipe, from which they differ in having generally no stem, the mouth having apparently been applied direct to the bowl. Many are highly ornamented, others are spirited representations of monsters or of animals, such as the beaver, otter, wild cat, elk, bear, wolf, panther, racoon, opossum, squirrel, manatee, eagle, hawk, heron, owl, buzzard,

[1] Squier and Davis, *l.c.*, p. 195.

raven, swallow, parroquet, duck, grouse, and many others. The most interesting of these, perhaps, is the manatee or lamantin, of which seven representations have been found in the mounds of Ohio. These are no mere rude sculptures, about which there might easily be a mistake, but we are assured that "the truncated head, thick semicircular snout, peculiar nostrils, tumid, furrowed upper lip, singular feet or fins, and remarkable moustaches, are all distinctly marked, and render the recognition of the animal complete."[1] This curious animal is not at present found nearer than the shores of Florida, a thousand miles away.

FIG. 201.—Heron pipe, carved in porphyry.

The ornaments which have been found in the mounds consist of beads, shells, necklaces, pendants, plates of mica, bracelets, gorgets, etc. The number of beads is sometimes quite surprising. Thus the celebrated Grave Creek mound contained between three and four thousand shell-beads, besides about two hundred and fifty ornaments of mica, several bracelets of copper, and various articles carved in stone. The beads are generally made of shell, but are sometimes cut out of bone or teeth; in form they are generally round or oblong; sometimes the shell of the Unio is cut and strung so as to "exhibit the convex surface and pearly nacre of the shell." The necklaces are often made of beads or shells, but sometimes of teeth. The ornaments of mica are thin plates of various forms, each of which has a small hole. The bracelets are of copper, and generally encircle the arms of the skeletons, besides being frequent on the "altars." They are simple rings "hammered out with more or less skill, and so bent that the ends approach, or lap over, each other." The so-called "gorgets" are thin plates of copper, always

[1] Squier and Davis, *l.c.*, p. 252.

with two holes, and probably, therefore, worn as badges of authority.

The earthworks are most abundant in the central parts of the United States. They decrease in number as we approach the Atlantic, and are very scarce in British America and on the west of the Rocky Mountains.

The works belonging to this class " usually occupy strong natural positions," and as a fair specimen of them we may take the Bourneville Enclosure in Ross County, Ohio, which consists of a wall of stone, which is carried round the hill a little below the brow ; but at some places it rises, so as to cut off the narrow spurs, and extends across the neck that connects the hill with the range beyond. It must not, however, be understood that anything like a true wall now exists ; the present appearance is rather what might have been " expected from the falling outwards of a wall of stones, placed, as this was, upon the declivity of a hill." Where it is most distinct it is from 15 to 20 feet wide, by 3 or 4 in height. The area thus enclosed is about 140 acres, and the wall is 2¼ miles in length. The stones themselves vary much in size, and Messrs Squier and Davis suggest that the wall may originally have been about 8 feet high, with an equal base. At present, trees of the largest size are growing upon it. On a similar work known as " Fort Hill," Highland County, Ohio (fig. 202), Messrs Squier and Davis found a splendid chestnut tree, which they suppose to be six hundred years old. " If," they say, " to this we add the probable period intervening from the time of the building of this work to its abandonment, and the subsequent period up to its invasion by the forest, we are led irresistibly to the conclusion that it has an antiquity of at least one thousand years. But when we notice, all around us, the crumbling trunks of trees, half hidden in the accumulating soil, we are induced to fix on an antiquity still more remote."

The enclosure known as " Clark's Work," in Ross County, Ohio, is one of the largest and most interesting. It consists of a parallelogram, 2800 feet by 1800, and enclosing about 111 acres. To the right of this, the principal work is a *perfect square*, containing an area of about 16 acres. Each side is 850 feet in length, and in the middle of each is a gateway 30 feet wide, covered by a small mound. Within the area of the great work are several smaller mounds and enclosures, and it is estimated that not less than three millions of cubic feet of earth were used in this great undertaking. Yet from the

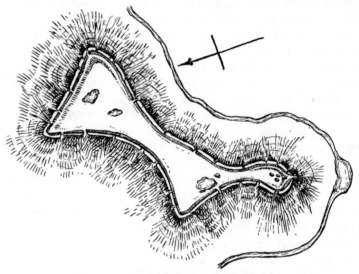

Fig. 202.—Fort Hill, Highland County, Ohio.

peculiarly mottled character of the earth forming these mounds, it would appear to have been brought in bags or small parcels. It has also been observed that water is almost invariably found within or close to these enclosures.

It is remarkable that there is not a single case in which counter-works occur near any of the ancient North American fortifications. It is probable, therefore, that the warfare of the mound-builders, like that of the more modern Red Indians, consisted, not of persevering sieges, but of sudden attacks and surprises.

If the purpose for which the works belonging to the first class were erected is very evident, the same cannot be said for those which we have now to mention. These differ from the preceding in their small size, from the ditch being inside the embankment, and from their position, which is often completely commanded by neighbouring heights.

Dr Wilson (vol. i. p. 324) follows Sir R. C. Hoare in considering the position of the ditch as being a distinguishing mark between military and religious works. Catlin, however, tells us that in a Mandan village, which he describes, the ditch was on the inner side of the embankment, and the warriors were thus sheltered while they shot their arrows through the stockade. We see, therefore, that in America, at least, this is no certain guide.

While, however, the defensive earthworks occupy hilltops and other situations most easy to defend, the so-called sacred enclosures are generally found on " the broad and level river bottoms, seldom occurring upon the table-lands or where the surface of the ground is undulating or broken." They are usually square or circular in form ; a circular enclosure being often combined with one or two squares. Occasionally they are isolated, but more frequently in groups. The greater number of the circles are of small size, with a nearly uniform diameter of 250 or 300 feet, and the ditch is invariably inside the wall. Some of the circles, however, are larger, enclosing 50 acres or more. The squares or other rectangular works never have a ditch, and the earth of which they are composed appears to have been taken up evenly from the surface, or from large pits in the neighbourhood. They vary much in size ; five or six of them, however, are " exact squares, each side measuring 1080 feet—a coincidence which could not possibly be accidental, and which must possess some significance." The circles also, in spite of their great size, are so nearly round, that the American archæologists consider themselves justified in concluding that the mound-builders must have had some standard of measurement, and some means of determining angles.

The most remarkable group is that near Newark, in the
Scioto Valley, which covers an area of four square miles !
(fig. 203). A plan of these gigantic works is given by
Messrs Squier and Davis, and another, from a later
survey, by Mr Wilson. They consist of an octagon, with
an area of 50, a square occupying 20 acres, and two large
circles occupying respectively 30 and 20 acres. From
the octagon an avenue formed by parallel walls extends
southwards for 2½ miles ; there are two other avenues

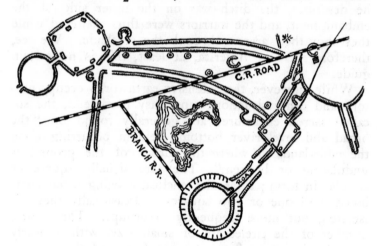

FIG. 203.—Village enclosures near Newark, Ohio.

which are rather more than a mile in length, one of
them connecting the octagon with the square.

Besides these, there are various other embankments
and small circles, the greater number about 80 feet in
diameter, but some few much larger. The walls of these
small circles, as well as those of the avenues and of the
irregular portions of the works generally, are very slight,
and for the most part about 4 feet in height. The other
embankments are much more considerable ; the walls
of the large circle are even now 12 feet high, with a
base of 50 feet, and an interior ditch 7 feet deep and
35 in width. At the gateway, however, they are still
more imposing ; the walls being 16 feet high, and the

ditch 13 feet deep. The whole area is covered with "gigantic trees of a primitive forest"; and, say Messrs Squier and Davis, "in entering the ancient avenue for the first time, the visitor does not fail to experience a sensation of awe, such as he might feel in passing the portals of an Egyptian temple, or gazing upon the silent ruins of Petra of the Desert."

The city of Circleville takes its name from one of these embankments, which, however, is no more remarkable than many others. It consists of a square and a circle, touching one another; the sides of the square being about 900 feet in length, and the circle a little more than 1000 feet in diameter. The square had eight doorways, one at each angle, and one in the middle of each side, every doorway being protected by a mound. The circle was peculiar in having a double embankment. This work, alas! has been entirely destroyed; and many others have also disappeared, or are being gradually obliterated by the plough. Under these circumstances, we read with pleasure that "the Directors of the Ohio Land Company, when they took possession of the country at the mouth of the Muskingum River, in 1788, adopted immediate measures for the preservation of these monuments. To their credit be it said, one of their earliest official acts was the passage of a resolution, which is entered upon the *Journal* of their proceedings, reserving the two truncated pyramids and the great mound, with a few acres attached to each, as public squares." Such enlightened conduct deserves the thanks of archæologists.

Another group of earthworks in Wisconsin is interesting as presenting a resemblance to a fortified town. It was situated on the west branch of Rock River, discovered in 1836 by N. F. Hyer, Esq., who surveyed them roughly, and published a brief description, with a figure, in the *Milwaukee Advertiser*. The most complete description is contained in Mr Lapham's *Antiquities of Wisconsin*.[1] The name "Aztalan" was given to this place by Mr Hyer, because the Aztecs had a tradition that they originally

[1] P. 41.

came from a country to the north, which they called Aztalan. It is said to be derived from two Mexican words, Atl, "water," and An, "near." "The main feature of these works is an enclosure of earth (not brick, as has been erroneously stated), extending around three sides of an irregular parallelogram"; the river "forming the fourth side on the east. The space thus enclosed contains $17\frac{2}{3}$ acres. The corners are not rectangular, and the embankment or ridge is not straight." "The ridge forming the enclosure is 631 feet long at the north end, 1419 feet long on the west side, and 700 feet on the south side; making a total length of wall of 2750 feet. The ridge or wall is about 22 feet wide, and from 1 to 5 feet in height. The wall of earth is enlarged on the outside, at nearly regular distances, by mounds of the same material. They vary from 61 to 95 feet apart, the mean distance being 82 feet. Near the south-west angle are two outworks, constructed in the same manner as the main embankment."

In many places the earth forming the walls appears to have been burnt. "Irregular masses of hard reddish clay, full of cavities, bear distinct impressions of straw, or rather wild hay, with which they had been mixed before burning." "This is the only foundation for calling these 'brick walls.' The 'bricks' were never made into any regular form, and it is even doubtful whether the burning did not take place in the wall after it was built." These walls must therefore present some faint resemblance to the celebrated vitrified forts of Scotland. Some of the mounds or buttresses, though forming part of an enclosure, were also used for sepulchral purposes, as was proved by their containing skeletons in a sitting posture, with fragments of pottery. The highest point inside the enclosure is at the south-west corner, and is "occupied by a square truncated mound, which . . . presents the appearance of a pyramid, rising by successive steps like the gigantic structures of Mexico." "At the north-west angle of the enclosure is another rectangular, truncated, pyramidal elevation, of sixty-five feet level area at the top, with remains of its graded way, or sloping ascent, at the south-west corner, leading also towards a ridge that extends in the direction of the river."

Within the enclosure are some ridges about two feet high, and connected with them are several rings, or circles, which are supposed to be the remains of mud houses. "Nearly the whole interior of the enclosure appears to have been either excavated or thrown up into mounds and ridges ; the pits and irregular excavations being quite numerous over much of the space not occupied by mounds."

The last Indian occupants of this interesting locality had no tradition as to the history or the purpose of these earthworks.

Among the Northern tribes of existing Indians, there do not appear to be any earthworks corresponding to these so-called sacred enclosures. "No sooner, however, do we pass to the southward, and arrive among the Creeks, Natchez, and affiliated Floridian tribes, than we discover traces of structures which, if they do not entirely correspond with the regular earthworks of the West, nevertheless seem to be somewhat analogous to them."[1] These tribes, indeed, appear to have been more civilized than those of the North, since they were agricultural in their habits, lived in considerable towns, and had a systematized religion, so that, in fact, they must have occupied a position intermediate, as well economically as geographically, between the powerful monarchies of Central America and the hunting tribes of the North. The "structures" to which Mr Squier alludes are described by him, both in his *Second Memoir* and also in the *Ancient Monuments of the Mississippi Valley* (p. 120). The "Chunk Yards," now or lately in use among the Creeks, and which have only recently been abandoned among the Cherokees, are rectangular areas, generally occupying the centre of the town, closed at the sides, but with an opening at each end. They are sometimes from 600 to 900 feet in length, being largest in the older towns.

[1] Squier, *loc. cit.*, p. 136.

The area is levelled and slightly sunk, being surrounded by a low bank formed of the earth thus obtained. In the centre is a low mound, on which stands the Chunk Pole, to the top of which is some object which serves as a mark to shoot at. Near each corner, at one end, is a small pole, about twelve feet high ; these are called the "slave posts," because in the "good old times" captives condemned to the torture were fastened to them. The name "Chunk Yard" seems to be derived from an Indian game called "Chunke," which was played in them. At one end of, and just outside, this area stands generally a circular eminence, with a flat top, upon which is elevated the Great Council House. At the other end is a flat-topped, square eminence, about as high as the circular one just mentioned ; "upon this stands the public square."

These and other accounts given by early travellers among the Indians throw much light on the circular and square enclosures, some of which, though classed by Messrs Squier and Davies under this head, seem to me to be the slight fortifications which surrounded villages, and were undoubtedly crowned by stockades. We have already seen that the position of the ditch is no conclusive argument against this view ; nor does the position of the works seem conclusive, if we suppose that they were intended less to stand a regular siege than to guard against a sudden attack.

The *Sepulchral Mounds* are very numerous in the central parts of the United States. "To say that they are innumerable, in the ordinary sense of the term, would be no exaggeration. They may literally be numbered by thousands and tens of thousands." They are usually from six to eight feet in height ; generally stand outside the enclosures ; are often isolated, but often also in groups ; they are usually round, but sometimes elliptical or pear-shaped. They cover generally a single interment, often of burnt bones. Occasionally there is a stone cist, but urn burial also prevailed to a considerable extent, especially in the South. The corpse, if not burnt, was generally buried in a contracted position. Implements both of stone and metal occur frequently; but while personal ornaments, such as bracelets, perforated plates of copper, beads of bone, shell or metal, and similar objects, are very common, weapons are but rarely found; a fact which, in the opinion of Dr Wilson, "indicates a totally different condition of society and mode of thought" from those of the present Indian.

No remains of the mastodon, or indeed of any extinct animals, have been found in any of the American burial mounds.

Some of the tumuli contain great quantities of human remains. This was long supposed to be the case with the great Grave Creek Mound, which indeed was positively stated by Atwater[1] to be full of human remains. This has turned out to be an error, but the statement is not the less true as regards other mounds. In conjunction with them may be mentioned the "bone pits," many of which are described by Mr Squier. "One of these pits," he says, "discovered some years ago in the town of Cambria, Niagara County, was estimated to contain the bones of several thousand individuals. Another which I visited in the town of Clarence, Erie County, contained not less than four hundred skeletons." A tumulus described by Mr Jefferson in his *Notes on Virginia* was estimated to contain the skeletons of a thousand individuals, but in this case the number was perhaps exaggerated.

The description given by various old writers of the solemn "Festival of the Dead" satisfactorily explains these large collections of bones. It seems that every eight or ten years the Indians used to meet at some place previously chosen, that they dug up their dead, collected the bones together, and laid them in one common burial-place, depositing with them fine skins and other valuable articles. Several of these ossuaries are described by Schoolcraft.[2]

Another class of mounds, called by Messrs Squier and

[1] See also Lapham, *loc. cit.*, p. 80.　　　　[2] *Loc. cit.*, p. 102.

Davis *Temple Mounds*, are pyramidal structures, truncated, and generally having graded avenues to their tops. In some instances they are terraced, or have successive stages. But whatever their form, whether round, oval, octangular, square, or oblong, they have invariably flat or level tops, of greater or lesser area. These mounds much resemble the Teocallis of Mexico, and had probably a similar origin. They are rare in the North, though examples occur even as far as Lake Superior, but become more and more numerous as we pass down the Mississippi, and especially on approaching the Gulf, where they constitute the most numerous and important portion of the ancient remains. Some of the largest, however, are situated in the North. One of the most remarkable is at Cahokia, in Illinois. This gigantic mound is stated to be 700 feet long, 500 feet wide at the base, and 90 feet in height. Its solid contents have been roughly estimated at 20,000,000 cubic feet.

Probably, however, these mounds were not used as temples only, but also as sites for dwellings, especially for those of the chiefs. We are told that among the Natchez Indians "the temples and the dwellings of the chiefs were raised upon mounds, and for every new chief a new mound and dwelling were constructed." Again, Garcilasso de la Vega, in his *History of Florida*, quoted by Mr Haven,[1] says, "The town and house of the Cacique of Osachile are similar to those of all other caciques in Florida, and, therefore, it seems best to give one description that will apply generally to all the capitals and all the houses of the chiefs in Florida. I say, then, that the Indians endeavour to place their towns upon elevated places ; but because such situations are rare in Florida, or that they find a difficulty in procuring suitable materials for building, they raise eminences in this manner. They choose a place, to which they bring a quantity of earth, which they elevate into a kind of platform 2 or 3 pikes in height (from 18 to 25 feet), of which the flat top is capable of holding ten or twelve,

[1] *Loc. cit.*, p. 57.

fifteen or twenty houses, to lodge the cacique, his family, and suite." [1]

Not the least remarkable of the American antiquities are the so-called *Animal Mounds*, which are principally, though not exclusively, found in Wisconsin. In this district " thousands of examples occur of gigantic basso-relievos of men, beasts, birds, and reptiles, all wrought with persevering labour on the surface of the soil," while enclosures and works of defence are almost entirely wanting, the "ancient city of Aztalan" being, as is supposed, the only example of the former class.

The *Animal Mounds* were discovered by Mr Lapham in 1836, and described in the newspapers of the day, but the first account of them in any scientific journal was that by Mr R. C. Taylor, in the *American Journal of Science and Art*, for April 1838. Messrs Squier and Davis devoted to them a part of their work on the *Ancient Monuments of the Mississippi Valley*; but the seventh volume of the Smithsonian Contributions contains the work, by Mr Lapham, which gives the most complete account of these interesting remains.

Mr Lapham adds a map, showing the distribution of these curious earthworks. They appear to be most numerous in the southern counties of Wisconsin ; and extend from the Mississippi to Lake Michigan, following generally the course of the river, and being especially numerous along the great Indian trail, or war-path, from Lake Michigan, near Milwaukee, to the Mississippi, above the Prairie du Chien. This, however, does not prove any connection between the present Indians and the mounds ; the same line has been adopted as the route of the United States' military road, and may have been in use for an indefinite period.

The mounds themselves not only represent animals, such as men, buffaloes, elks, bears, otters, wolves, racoons, birds, serpents, lizards, turtles, and frogs, but also some inanimate objects, if at least the American archæologists are right in regarding some of them as crosses, tobacco-pipes, etc.

[1] See also Schoolcraft, *loc. cit.*, vol. iii. p. 47.

Many of the representations are spirited and correct, but others, probably through the action of time, are less definite ; one, for instance, near the village of Muscoda, may be either "a bird, a bow and arrow, or the human figure." Their height varies from 1 to 4 feet, sometimes, however, rising to 6 feet ; and as a "regular elevation of six inches can be readily traced upon the level prairies " of the West, their outlines are generally distinctly defined where they occupy favourable positions. It is probable, however, that many of the details have disappeared under the action of rain and vegetation. At

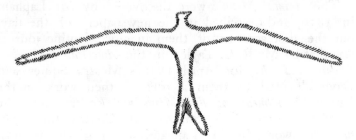

FIG. 204.—Plan ot an eagle mound, Honey Creek Mills, Wis.

present a "man" consists generally of a head and body, two long arms and two short legs, no other details being visible. The "birds" differ from the "men" principally in the absence of legs. The so-called "lizards," which are among the most common forms, have a head, two legs, and a long tail ; the side view being represented, as is, indeed, the case with most of the quadrupeds. One mound has been supposed to represent a mastodon, but the similarity is, I think, far from conclusive.[1]

One remarkable group in Dale County, close to the great Indian war-path, consists of a man with extended arms, seven more or less elongated mounds, one tumulus, and six quadrupeds. The length of the human figure is 125 feet, and it is 140 feet from the extremity of one arm to that of the other. The quadrupeds vary from 90 to 126 feet in length.

[1] M'Lean, *The Mound-builders.*

At Waukesha are a number of mounds, tumuli, and animals, including several " lizards," a very fine " bird," and a magnificent " turtle." " This, when first observed, was a very fine specimen of the art of mound-building, with its graceful curves, the feet projecting back and forward, and the tail, with its gradual slope, so acutely pointed, that it was impossible to ascertain precisely where it terminated. The body was 56 feet in length, and the tail 250 ; the height 6 feet." This group of mounds is now, alas, covered with buildings : " A dwelling-house stands on the body of the turtle, and a Catholic church is built upon the tail."

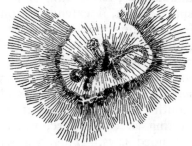

FIG. 205.—Alligator mound, Granville, Ohio.

" But," says Mr Lapham, " the most remarkable collection of lizards and turtles yet discovered is on the school section about a mile and a half south-east from the village of Pewaukee. This consists of seven turtles, two lizards, four oblong mounds, and one of the remarkable excavations before alluded to. One of the turtle mounds, partially obliterated by the road, has a length of 450 feet, being nearly double the usual dimensions. Three of them are remarkable for their curved tails, a feature here first observed."

In several places a curious variation occurs. The animals, with the usual form and size, are represented, not in relief, but intaglio ; not by a mound, but by an excavation.

The *Animal Mounds* which have been observed out of Wisconsin differ in many respects from the ordinary type. Near Granville, in Ohio, on a higher spur of land, is an earthwork, known in the neighbourhood as the " Alligator " (fig. 205). It has a head and body, four sprawling legs, and a curled tail. The total length is 250 feet, the breadth of the body 40 feet, and the length of the legs 36 feet. "The head, shoulders, and rump are more elevated than the other parts of the body, an attempt having evidently been made to preserve the proportions of the object copied." The average height is 4 feet, at the shoulders 6 feet. Even more remarkable is the great serpent in Adams County, Ohio. It is situated on a high spur of land which rises 150 feet above Brush Creek. "Conforming to the curve of the hill, and occupying its very summit, is the serpent, its head resting near the point, and its body winding back for 700 feet, in graceful undulations, terminating in a triple coil at the tail. The entire length, if extended, would be not less than 1000 feet. The work is clearly and boldly defined, the embankment being upwards of 5 feet in height, by 30 feet base at the centre of the body, but diminishing somewhat toward the head and tail. The neck of the serpent is stretched out, and slightly curved, and its mouth is opened wide, as if in the act of swallowing or ejecting an oval figure, which rests partially within the distended jaws. This oval is formed by an embankment of earth, without any perceptible opening, 4 feet in height, and is perfectly regular in outline, its transverse and conjugate diameters being 160 and 80 feet respectively."

When, why, or by whom these remarkable works were erected, as yet we know not. The Indian tribes, though they look upon them with reverence, have thrown no light upon their origin. Nor do the contents of the mounds themselves assist us in this inquiry. Several of them have been opened, and, in making the streets of Milwaukie, many of the mounds have been entirely removed ; but the only result has been to show that they are not sepulchral, and that, excepting by accident, they contain no implements or ornaments.

Under these circumstances speculation would be useless ; we can but wait, and hope that time and perseverance may solve the problem, and explain the nature of these remarkable and mysterious monuments.

There is one class of objects which I have not yet

mentioned, and which yet ought not to be left entirely unnoticed.

The most remarkable of these is the celebrated Dighton Rock, on the east bank of the Taunton River. Its history, and the various conclusions which have been derived from it, are very amusingly given by Dr Wilson.[1] In 1783, the Rev. Ezra Stiles, D.D., President of Yale College, appealed to this rock, inscribed, as he believed, with Phœnician characters, for a proof that the Indians were descended from Canaan, and were therefore accursed. Count de Gebelin regarded the inscription as Carthaginian. In the eighth volume of the *Archæologia*, Colonel Vallency endeavours to prove that it is Siberian; while certain Danish antiquaries regard it as Runic, and thought that they could read the name "Thorfinn," "with an exact, though by no means so manifest, enumeration of the associates who, according to the Saga, accompanied Karlsefne's expedition to Vinland, in A.D. 1007." Finally, Mr Schoolcraft submitted a copy of it to Chingwauk, an intelligent Indian chief, who "interpreted it as the record of an Indian triumph over some rival native tribe," but without offering any opinion as to its antiquity.

In the "Grave Creek Mound" is said to have been found a small oval disk of white sandstone, on which were engraved twenty-two letters. I mention it because it has been the subject of much discussion, but it is now generally admitted to be a fraud. It is inscribed with Hebrew characters, but the forger has copied the modern instead of the ancient forms of the letters.

One or two other equally unsatisfactory cases are upon record, but upon the whole we may safely assert that there is no reason to suppose that the nations of America had developed for themselves anything corresponding to an alphabet. The art of picture-writing, which they shared with the Aztecs and the Quipa of the Peruvians, was supplemented among the North American Indians by the "wampum." This curious substitute for writing consisted of variously-coloured beads, generally worked

---

[1] *Prehistoric Man*, vol. ii. p. 172.

upon leather. One very interesting example is the belt
of wampum " delivered by the Lenni Lenape Sachems to
the founder of Pennsylvania, at the Great Treaty, under
the elm-tree at Shachamox in 1682." It is still preserved in the collection of the Historical Society at
Philadelphia, and consists of "eighteen strings of
wampum formed of white and violet beads worked upon
leather thongs," the whole forming a belt 28 inches long
and 2½ broad. "On this, five patterns are worked in
violet beads on a white ground, and in the centre Penn
is represented taking the hand of the Indian Sachem."
The numerous beads found in some of the tumuli were
perhaps in a similar manner intended to commemorate
the actions and virtues of the dead.

Just as the wigwam of the recent Mandan consisted of
an outer layer of earth supported on a wooden framework, so also, in the ancient sepulchral tumuli, the body
was protected only by beams and planks ; when therefore
these latter decayed, the earth sank in and crushed the
skeleton within. Partly from this cause, and partly from
the habit of burying in ancient tumuli, which makes it
sometimes difficult to distinguish the primary from
secondary interments, it happens that from so many
thousand tumuli we have very few well-preserved skulls
which indisputably belong to the ancient race. These
are decidedly brachycephalic ; but it is evident that we
must not attempt to build much upon so slight a basis.

No proof of a knowledge of letters, no trace of a burnt
brick, have yet been discovered ; and so far as we may
judge from their arms, ornaments, and pottery, the
mound-builders closely resembled the more advanced
of the recent Indian tribes, and the earthworks agree in
form with, if they differ in magnitude from those still, or
until lately, in use. Yet this very magnitude is sufficient to
show that, at some early period, the great river valleys of
the United States must have been more densely populated
than they were when first discovered by Europeans.
The immense number of small earthworks, and the
mounds, "which may be counted by thousands and tens

of thousands," might indeed be supposed to indicate either a long time or a great population ; but in other cases we have no such alternative. The Newark constructions ; the mound near Florence in Alabama, which is 45 feet in height by 440 feet in circumference at the base, with a level area at the summit of 150 feet in circumference ; the still greater mound on the Etowah river, also in Alabama, which has a height of more than 75 feet, with a circumference of 1200 feet at the base, and 140 at the summit ; the embankments at the mouth of the Scioto river, which are estimated to be twenty miles in length ; the great mound at Selserstown, Mississippi, which covers six acres of ground ; and the truncated pyramid at Cahokia, to which we have already alluded : these works, and many others which might have been quoted, indicate a population both large and stationary ; for which hunting cannot have supplied enough food, as it has been estimated that in a forest country each hunter requires an area of not less than 50,000 acres for his support ; and which must, therefore, have derived its support, in a great measure, from agriculture. "There is not," say Messrs Squier and Davis, "and there was not in the sixteenth century, a single tribe of Indians (north of the semi-civilized nations) between the Atlantic and the Pacific, which had means of subsistence sufficient to enable them to apply, for such purposes, the unproductive labour necessary for the work ; nor was there any in such a social state as to compel the labour of the people to be thus applied." We know also that many, if not most of the Indian tribes, at that time still cultivated the ground to a certain extent, and there is some evidence that, even within historic times, this was more the case than at present. Thus De Nonville estimates the amount of Indian corn destroyed by him in four Seneca villages at 1,200,000 quarters.

In many places, moreover, the ground is covered with small mammillary elevations, which are known as Indian corn-hills. "They are without order of arrangement, being scattered over the ground with the greatest irregularity. That these hillocks were formed in the manner indicated by their name, is inferred from the present custom of the Indians. The corn is planted in the same spot each successive year, and the soil is gradually brought up to the size of a little hill by the annual additions." But Mr Lapham has also found traces of an earlier and more systematic cultivation. These consist "of low parallel ridges, as if corn had been planted in drills. They average four feet in width, twenty-five of them having been counted in the space of a hundred feet; and the depth of the walk between them is about six inches. These appearances, which are here denominated 'ancient garden-beds,' indicate an earlier and more perfect system of cultivation than that which now prevails; for the present Indians do not appear to possess the ideas of taste and order necessary to enable them to arrange objects in consecutive rows. Traces of this kind of cultivation, though not very abundant, are found in several other parts of the State (Wisconsin). The garden-beds are of various sizes, covering, generally, from twenty to one hundred acres, though some are much larger. As a general fact, they exist in the richest soil, as it is found in the prairies and bun oak plains. In the latter case, trees of the largest kind are scattered over them."

In the *Ancient Monuments of the Mississippi Valley*, it is stated that no earthwork has ever been found on the first or lowest terrace of any of the great rivers, and that "this observation is confirmed by all who have given attention to the subject." If true, this would indeed have indicated a great antiquity, but in his subsequent work Mr Squier informs us that "they occur indiscriminately upon the first and upon the superior terraces, as also upon the islands of the lakes and rivers." Messrs Squier and Davis [1] are of opinion that the decayed state of the skeletons found in the mounds may enable us to form "some approximate estimate of their remote antiquity," especially when we consider that the earth round

[1] *Loc. cit.*, p. 168.

them "is wonderfully compact and dry, and that the conditions for their preservation are exceedingly favourable." "In the barrows of the ancient Britons," they add, "entire well-preserved skeletons are found, although possessing an undoubted antiquity of at least eighteen hundred years." Dr Wilson[1] also relies much on this fact, which, in his opinion, "furnishes a stronger evidence of their great antiquity than any of the proofs that have been derived either from the age of a subsequent forest growth, or the changes wrought on the river terraces where they most abound." It is true that the bones in Stone Age graves are often extremely well preserved ; but it is equally true that those in Saxon barrows have in many cases entirely perished. In fact, the condition of ancient bones depends so much on the circumstances in which they have been placed, that we must not attribute much importance to this argument.

The evidence derived from the forests is more to be relied on. Thus Captain Peck[2] observed near the Ontonagon river, and at a depth of twenty-five feet, some stone mauls and other implements in contact with a vein of copper. Above these was the fallen trunk of a large cedar, and "over all grew a hemlock-tree, the roots of which spread entirely above the fallen tree," . . . and indicated, in his estimation, a growth of not less than three centuries, to which must then be added the age of the cedar, which indicates a still "longer succession of centuries, subsequent to that protracted period during which the deserted trench was slowly filled up with accumulations of many winters."

The late President Harrison, in an address to the Historical Society of Ohio, made some interesting remarks on this subject, which are quoted by Messrs Squier and Davis.[3] "The process," he says, "by which nature restores the forest to its original state, after being once cleared, is extremely slow. The rich lands of the west are, indeed, soon covered again, but the character of the

---

[1] *Loc. cit.*, vol. i. p. 359.
[2] Wilson, *loc. cit.*, vol. i. p. 256.   [3] *Loc. cit.*, p. 306.

growth is entirely different, and continues so for a long period. In several places upon the Ohio, and upon the farm which I occupy, clearings were made in the first settlement of the country, and subsequently abandoned and suffered to grow up. Some of these new forests are now of fifty years' growth, but they have made so little progress towards attaining the appearance of the immediately contiguous forest, as to induce any man of reflection to determine that at least ten times fifty years must elapse before their complete assimilation be effected. We find in the ancient works all that variety of trees which give such unrivalled beauty to our forests, in natural proportions. The first growth of the same kind of land, once cleared and then abandoned to nature, on the contrary, is nearly homogeneous, often stinted to one or two, at most three kinds of timber. If the ground has been cultivated, the yellow locust will quickly spring up ; if not cultivated, the black and white walnut will be the prevailing growth. . . . Of what immense age, then, must be the works so often referred to, covered as they are by at least the second growth, after the primitive forest state was regained ! " [1]

We obtain another indication of antiquity in the " garden-beds," which we have already described. This system of cultivation has long been replaced by the irregular " corn-hills " ; and yet, according to Mr Lapham,[2] the garden-beds are much more recent than some of the mounds, across which they sometimes extend in the same manner as over the adjoining grounds. If, therefore, these mounds belong to the same area as those which are covered with wood, we get thus indications of three periods : the first, that of the mounds themselves ; the second, that of the garden-beds ; and the third, that of the forests.

But American agriculture was not imported from abroad ; it resulted from, and in return rendered possible, the gradual development of American semi-civilization. This is proved by the fact that the grains of the Old

[1] See also *Arch. Amer.*, vol. i. p. 306.   [2] *Loc. cit.*, p. 19.

World were entirely absent, and that American agriculture was founded on the maize, an American plant. Thus, therefore, we appear to have indications of four long periods :

(1) That in which, from an original barbarism, the American tribes developed a knowledge of agriculture and a power of combination.

(2) That in which for the first time mounds were erected, and other great works undertaken.

(3) The age of the " garden-beds," which occupy some at least of the mounds. Hence it is probable that these particular " garden-beds " were not in use until after the mounds had lost their sacred character in the eyes of the occupants of the soil ; for it can hardly be supposed that works executed with so much care would be thus desecrated by their builders.

(4) The period in which man relapsed into partial barbarism, and the spots which had been first forest, then, perhaps, sacred monuments, and thirdly, cultivated ground, relapsed into forest once more.

But even if we attribute to these changes all the importance which has ever been claimed for them, they will not require an antiquity of more than three thousand years. I do not, of course, deny that the period may have been, and in all probability was, very much greater. There are, moreover, other observations, which appear to indicate a very much higher antiquity.

Dr A. C. Koch[1] records the case of a mastodon found in Gasconade County, Missouri, which had apparently been stoned to death by the Indians, and then partially consumed by fire.

The same writer mentions a second case in which several stone arrow-heads were found mingled with the bones of a mastodon. These statements, however, are not generally accepted by geologists, and the evidence in support of them is, to say the least, very doubtful.

In the valley of the Mississippi, Dr Dickeson, of Natchez, found the os innominatum of a man with some bones of

[1] Trans. of the Academy of Science of St Louis, 1857, p. 61.

the *Mastodon ohioticus*, which had fallen from the side of a cliff undermined by a rivulet. This case, however, is also open to doubt, and Sir C. Lyell was of opinion that this bone might have been derived from one of the Indian graves, which are very numerous in this locality. Dr Usher, on the contrary,[1] regards it as "an undoubted fossil," belonging to the same period as the remains of the mastodon with which it was discovered. Count Pourtalis records the discovery of some human bones in a calcareous conglomerate, estimated by Agassiz to be ten thousand years old, though it must be added that this calculation has been disputed by the Count himself.

The so-called "Calaveras" skull was found in the county so named by Mr Mattison, who assures us that he took it with his own hands from a bed of gravel 130 feet from the surface and under four layers of lava. The antiquity of this skull has been much questioned, but Mr Whitney seems to feel no doubt on the subject. He maintains[2] that the chemical condition proves that it is of considerable antiquity and not a mere modern skull, as some have supposed. Of course if it really belonged to the bed in which Mr Mattison supposes that it was found, it must be of great antiquity, but we do not know enough of the locality to be able to form even a vague idea of its age. Dr Wright believes it to be genuine, and mentions the occurrence of a stone mortar in the same gravel bed. This discovery, however, suggests doubt as to its great antiquity.[3]

Dr Douler obtained from an excavation near New Orleans some charcoal and a human skeleton, to which he was inclined to attribute an antiquity of no less than fifty thousand years. The plain on which the city of New Orleans is built, and which rises only about ten feet above the sea-level, consists of alluvial soil, which has been proved by borings to have a depth of more than five hundred feet, and which contains several successive

---

[1] Dr Usher, in Nott and Gliddon's *Types of Mankind*, p. 344.
[2] Whitney, *Auriferous Gravels of the Sierra Nevada*, p. 271.
[3] Wright, *Man and the Glacial Period.*

layers of cypresses. The river banks show similar remains of ancient forests, and Messrs Dickeson and Brown have found remains of no less than ten cypress forests at different levels below the present surface. These trees are not unfrequently as much as ten feet in diameter, and there are from 95 to 120 rings in an inch. The human skeleton above referred to was found at a depth of sixteen feet, and beneath the roots of a cypress-tree belonging to the fourth forest level below the surface.[1] Dr Andrews, indeed, in a letter cited by Mr Southall,[2] questions this calculation. He maintains that the accretion of river mud in the region of the lower Mississippi is very rapid, and points out as a proof of this that trunks of trees may be seen standing in the banks of the river, showing that the accretion must have been rapid enough to cover them before they had had time to decay. Whether, however, we accept Dr Douler's calculation or not, it is obvious that, if the statements are trustworthy, this skeleton certainly must carry back the existence of man in America to a very distant period.

In another case a piece of a wicker basket is said to have been found in Louisiana,[3] in association with elephants' remains. Lastly, implements curiously resembling the Palæolithic implements of Western Europe, have been found by Mr Jones at a depth of nine feet in the gravel of the Chattahoochee valley,[4] and by Mr Abbott in the drift gravels of New Jersey.[5]

On the whole, then, the evidence certainly seems to indicate that man has inhabited America for a considerable period, and it is even probable, though there may not as yet be any absolute proof, that he co-existed there with the mammoth and mastodon.

[1] Dr Usher, in Nott and Gliddon's *Types of Mankind*, p. 338.
[2] *Recent Origin of Man*, p. 472.
[3] Desnoyers, *Cong. Int. d'Anthropologie*, p. 98
[4] Jones, *Ant. of the Southern Indians*, p. 294.
[5] *Rep. of the Peabody Museum*, 1878.

CHAPTER IX

In addition to those still existing, the fauna of Northern Europe during the Palæolithic Period comprised several species of mammalia which have either become entirely extinct, or very much restricted in their geographical distribution, since the appearance of man in Europe. The principal of these are—

> *Ursus spelæus* (the cave-bear).
> *Ursus priscus.*
> *Hyæna spelæa* (the cave-hyæna).
> *Felis spelæa* (the cave-lion).
> *Elephas primigenius* (the mammoth).
> *Elephas antiquus.*
> *Rhinoceros tichorhinus* (the hairy rhinoceros).
> *Rhinoceros leptorhinus*, Cuv.
> *Rhinoceros hemitæchus.*
> *Hippopotamus major* (the hippopotamus).
> *Ovibos moschatus* (the musk ox).
> *Megaceros hibernicus* (the Irish elk).
> *Equus fossilis* (the wild horse).
> *Gulo luscus* (the glutton).
> *Cervus tarandus* (the reindeer).
> *Bison europæus* (the aurochs).
> *Bos primigenius* (the urus).

Besides many smaller, but very interesting, species.

The first ten of these have been regarded, until lately, as altogether extinct, but recent researches have induced many naturalists to regard some of them as the direct ancestors of species still existing in other parts of the world, so that the Irish elk, the elephants, and the three species of rhinoceros are perhaps the only ones which have left no descendants. Most of the smaller species now inhabiting Europe already existed in quaternary times, from which we may conclude that the changes which have taken place were due to a gradual change of circumstances, rather than to any sudden cataclysm, or general destruction of life ; it is also very improbable that the extinction of the different species was simultaneous ; and,

FIG. 206.—Painting on the roof of the cave of Altamira, Santander, Spain. After H. Breuil.

acting on this idea, M. Lartet has attempted[1] to construct a palæontological chronology.

He considered that we may establish four divisions, namely, the age of the cave-bear, of the mammoth and rhinoceros, of the reindeer, and of the aurochs. It is evident, I think, that the appearance of these mammalia in Europe was not simultaneous, and that their disappearance has been successive. The evidence is very strong that in Central and Western Europe the aurochs survived the reindeer, and that the reindeer, on the other hand, lived on to a later period than the mammoth or the woolly-haired rhinoceros. But the chronological dis-

[1] *Ann. des Sci. Nat.*, 1861, p. 217.

tinction between these two species and the cave-bear does not appear to be so well established. Admitting that the cave-bear has not yet been found in the river gravels of the Somme valley, we must remember that the animal was essentially a cave-dweller, and that its absence is, perhaps, to be attributed rather to the absence of caves than to the extinction of the species. Moreover, the bones found in the gravel are very much broken, and are seldom in such a condition as to enable the palæontologist to distinguish the remains of *U. spelæus* from those of other large bears.

There is as yet no evidence that the cave-bear existed in Europe before the commencement of the quaternary period, when it appears to have been abundant in Central Europe and in the southern parts of Russia. It has not yet been found in Siberia,[1] it is doubtful whether it has been discovered north of the Baltic, nor has it yet been found in Spain or in Ireland. In Italy, on the contrary, it has been met with, and in one instance apparently in association with a polished stone implement, and even pottery.[2] M. Regnoli has been so good as to forward me a cast of the specimen on which this statement rests ; it belongs to the cave-bear, but I can hardly regard it as being undoubtedly contemporaneous with the pottery and stone axe which were found near it. In Northern Europe no such case has yet been met with, but it is of course possible that in Italy the cave-bear may have survived to a more recent period than in the region north of the Alps. No trace of it has yet been found by Mr Busk and Dr Falconer among the numerous remains from Gibraltar, nor has it yet been met with in Siberia.

The late Dr Falconer referred to this species the leg bones of a bear found in Brixham Cave, above a flint implement. Mr Busk, however, who has carefully examined these bones, and detached them more completely from the matrix in which they were imbedded than was

---

[1] Brandt, *Bull. de l'Acad. Imp. de St Pétersbourg*, 1870, vol. vii. pt. 3.
[2] *Richerche Paleoetnologiche nelle Alpi Apuane*, Nota del Dott. C. Regnoli.

the case when they were examined by Dr Falconer, is of opinion that there is no sufficient reason for referring them to *Ursus spelæus* rather than to one of the other large species of fossil bear.

It has been stated that remains of the cave-bear have occurred in the river gravels at Ilford and Gray's Thurrocks. In the opinion, however, both of Mr Busk and Mr Boyd Dawkins, we have no clear case of the remains of this species being found in river-drift gravels. In fact, as materials for comparison have increased, it has proved more and more difficult to separate *Ursus spelæus* from other large species of bear. The jaws and teeth are characteristic, but the other portions of the skeleton are scarcely distinguishable, especially when they are so much fractured, as is generally the case with those found in gravel deposits.

Vogt, indeed, has expressed the opinion that every gradation may be traced between this species and our common brown bear (*Ursus Arctos*), and Brandt leans to the same opinion.[1] Mr Boyd Dawkins also says that "those who have compared the French, German, and British specimens gradually realize the fact that the fossil remains of the bears form a graduated series, in which all the variations that at first sight appear specific vanish away."[2] Whether, however, the cave-bear will eventually be regarded as belonging to the same species as the brown bear or not, it will still remain a well-characterized variety, and one which has never yet been certainly met with in the peat mosses, in the tumuli of Western Europe, in the Danish shell-mounds, the Swiss lake-villages, or, in short, associated with Neolithic remains.

Mr Busk, whose views have more recently been supported by Dr Leith Adams and Mr Boyd Dawkins, has made the interesting observation that some remains of bear found in our British caves and gravels are identical with the corresponding bones of *U. Ferox*, or grizzly bear of the Rocky Mountains.

---

[1] *Zoogeographische und Palæontologische Beiträge*, 1867, p. 220.
[2] *Pleistocene Mammalia*, Palæontographical Soc., vol. xviii. p. xxii.

The *cave-hyæna*, like the preceding species, is in Europe characteristic of the Palæolithic Age ; by some authorities it is now regarded as scarcely distinguishable from the *Hyæna crocuta*, or spotted hyæna of Southern Africa.

Felis spelæa, the *cave-lion* (fig. 207), attained a somewhat larger size than the lion of the present day, and possessed in an exaggerated degree the characters by which that species is distinguishable from the tiger.   It has hitherto been regarded as a distinct species, but Messrs Dawkins

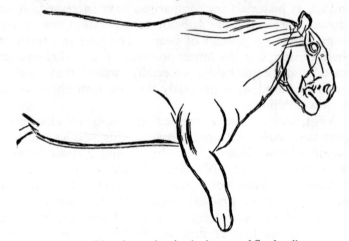

FIG. 207.—Lion, from a drawing in the cave of Combarelles.
After A. Breuil.

and Sanford now consider[1] it as only a large variety of the lion.   It has not yet been found in Scotland, Ireland, Scandinavia, Denmark, or Prussia.   It occurs, however, in France, Germany, Italy, and Sicily.   As long ago as 1672, Dr John Hains figured a bone of this species from the Carpathians, an observation of considerable interest, as it carries the area of the. *F. spelæa* so near to the mountains of Thessaly, where, as Herodotus tells us, the camels attached to the army of Xerxes were attacked by lions.[2]   Messrs Boyd Dawkins and Sanford refer also

[1] Palæontological Soc., vol. for 1868, p. 149.
[2] See also Mr Newton's interesting memoir, *On the Zoology of Ancient Europe*, Cam. Phil. Soc., March, 1862.

to the same species the remains found at Natchez, in Mississippi, which were described by Dr Leidy as a new species under the name of *Felis atrox*. The characters, however, which induced Dr Leidy to regard his specimens as distinct, are met with in some of the bones of *F. spelæa* from the Mendip Hills. If this opinion be correct, *F. spelæa* must have stretched eastwards across Russia and Siberia, where no remains of it have yet been observed. Inasmuch, however, as the mammoth, the musk ox, the reindeer, the bison, the elk, the horse, the wolf,—in short, many of our most characteristic quaternary mammalia— occur also in America, it seems *a priori* rather probable than otherwise that Messrs Dawkins and Sanford are correct in regarding *F. atrox* of that continent as specifically identical with the *F. spelæa* of Europe.

Remains of a second large species of *Felis*, considered to be identical with the leopard, have been discovered in the bone-caves of England, France, Germany, Belgium, Italy, and Spain ; and the lynx has been found by Dr Ransom in a Derbyshire cave.

The *Mammoth*, or *Elephas primigenius* (figs. 208, 225), had very extensive geographical range. Its remains are found in North America, but not east of the Rocky Mountains nor south of Columbia River ; in the old continent, from the farthest extremity of Siberia to the extreme west of Europe, occurring, though rarely, even in Ireland ; it crossed the Alps, and established itself in Italy as far southward as Rome, but it has not yet been discovered in Naples, in any of the Mediterranean islands, or in Scandinavia. In Spain and Denmark it occurs, but is very rare.

In the extreme north, on the contrary, remains of this species are remarkably abundant. Kotzebue was struck by this in Escholtz Bay (N.-W. America), and his remarks have been fully confirmed by Beechey.[1] The islands of Lachowski and New Siberia are said to contain innumerable bones of extinct animals, and particularly of the mammoth ; from them and from other parts of Siberia

[1] *Narrative of a Voyage to the Pacific*, vol. i. p. 257.

so much fossil ivory is obtained that it forms a regular article of commerce. Nor have skeletons alone been discovered. In 1799 a Tungusian hunter discovered the body of a mammoth embedded in a cliff of frozen soil, where it remained for several years. In 1806 it was visited by Mr Adams, who found it partly devoured by wolves and other wild animals, and partly removed by the Yakuts, who used it as food for their dogs. Fortunately,

FIG. 208.—Mammoth, from a drawing in the cave of Font-de-Gaume. After A. Breuil.

however, a considerable portion of the animal still remained. The skin was dark grey, covered with reddish wool, mixed with long black bristles, somewhat thicker than horsehair. Another frozen mammoth was discovered in 1846, besides several other well-preserved portions, and it was probably from earlier finds of a similar nature that the Siberian tribes began to regard the mammoth as a gigantic burrowing animal. It is hardly necessary to observe that the state of preservation in which mammoths have been found is no evidence of recent existence, for when once enveloped in frozen soil they might remain unchanged for an indefinite period.

The best authorities consider that the mammoth and the woolly-haired rhinoceros lived in Siberia before, as well as during the glacial period, and though as regards Europe the evidence is not so conclusive, it appears probable that they also existed in Europe in pre-glacial times. It is probable that during the severer portions of the period they retreated south, and advanced northward again during the milder inter-glacial period. Whatever doubt, however, there may be as to the date at which this species made its appearance in Europe, we can no longer hesitate to believe that our ancestors, or at least our pre-

Fig. 209.—Molar tooth of *E. antiquus,* one-third actual size.

decessors, co-existed in England with the mammoth, which they no doubt hunted, as the wildest tribes of Africa and India do now.

The only other species of elephant which inhabited Northern Europe during the quaternary period was the nearly allied *Elephas antiquus,* remains of which have been found in English caves and river gravels, though, on the whole, it had a more southerly range than the mammoth. It is generally associated with *Rhinoceros leptorhinus,* Cuv., while, on the contrary, the mammoth and *R. tichorhinus* usually occur together.

In Southern Europe unmistakable remains of the existing African elephant have been met with.

Fig. 209 represents a molar tooth of *E. antiquus,* and fig. 210 one belonging to *E. primigenius*; it will at once be seen that the plates are much narrower in the latter than in the former.

At least three species of rhinoceros inhabited Europe during the quaternary period ; on this all are agreed, but, unfortunately, the nomenclature is involved in very considerable confusion. *R. leptorhinus* was originally so named by Cuvier in 1812, from a drawing of a specimen found in the Val d'Arno, and in which the bony septum between the nostrils was represented as deficient. In 1835, M. de Christol stated that he had examined the specimen in question, that the drawing was incorrect, and the name consequently inapplicable. Subsequently, however, Dr Falconer visited Italy and satisfied himself that after all the original drawing was correct, and that therefore Cuvier's name must be restored. In the meantime Professor Owen had unfortunately described another

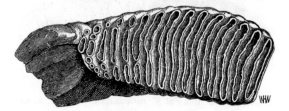

Fig. 210.—Molar tooth of the mammoth, one-third actual size.

species of rhinoceros found at Clacton as *R. leptorhinus*, which name must of course be abandoned if Cuvier's name is permitted to stand. Hence Dr Falconer proposed to call this latter species *R. hemitæchus*. It is necessary therefore to bear in mind that the *R. leptorhinus* of Owen is not the *R. leptorhinus* of Cuvier, but that it is the *R. hemitæchus* of Falconer, while M. Lartet maintains that it is identical with the *R. Merkii* of Kaup. On the other hand, M. de Christol, in 1835, described a rhinoceros, which undoubtedly wanted the nasal septum, and believing himself to have proved that the figure on which Cuvier based his description of *R. leptorhinus* was incorrect, he named this species *R. megarhinus*. Hence Cuvier's *R. leptorhinus* is identical with De Christol's *R. megarhinus*. The third species is the *R. tichorhinus* (fig. 211) of Cuv., a name which has been generally adopted,

although Blumenbach had previously proposed that of
R. antiquitatis.

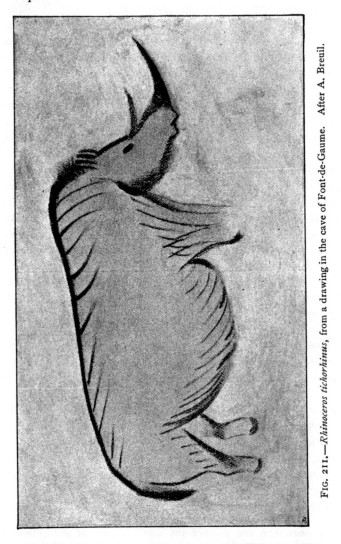

FIG. 211.—*Rhinoceros tichorhinus,* from a drawing in the cave of Font-de-Gaume.   After A. Breuil.

Mr Boyd Dawkins considers that there is still some
doubt about the real character of the specimen on which
Cuvier founded his *R. leptorhinus,* and consequently adopts

the following nomenclature : *R. megarhinus,* De Christol ; *R. leptorhinus,* Owen ; and *R. tichorhinus,* Cuvier. M. Lartet uses the names *R. leptorhinus,* Cuv. ; *R. Merkii,* Kaup ; and *R. tichorhinus,* Cuvier. These differences of opinion, however, relate merely to the nomenclature, and do not touch the existence of the species themselves. The first two belonged to the pre-glacial as well as to the post-glacial period. The woolly-haired, two-horned, smooth-skinned *R. tichorhinus,* on the contrary, which appears to have been the commonest in post-glacial times, has not yet been proved to have existed in Europe in the period before the glacial epoch. The two other species also have a more southerly range, having been found in Italy and Spain, while *R. tichorhinus,* though it has been met with from the extreme north of Siberia,[1] throughout Central Europe and England, does not appear to have crossed either the Alps or the Pyrenees. It is somewhat remarkable that no remains of rhinoceros have yet been discovered in Sicily, Malta, Scotland, Ireland,[2] or America,[3] in all of which countries the elephant has been met with. On the other hand, a single tooth has, according to Brandt, been found in Scandinavia, where no remains of elephant have yet been discovered.

The *Musk-ox,* or rather *Musk-sheep,* is at present confined to the northern part of Arctic America. Its remains, however, occur in Siberia ; and in 1856 Mr Kingsley and I were so fortunate as to obtain a portion of a skull from the large gravel-pit near Maidenhead Station. Since then I have met with it again at Greenstreet Green, near Bromley, in Kent ; it has also been found in the gravel of the Avon, near Bath, in that of the Severn, near Gloucester, and at Crayford. It has since been found, though rarely, in France and Germany.

The *Hippopotamus,* though hitherto regarded as a distinct

---

[1] In more than one instance the actual carcase of this animal has been found preserved like the mammoth, by being imbedded in frozen soil.

[2] Lartet, " Note sur deux têtes de Carnassiers Fossiles," *Ann. d. Sci. Nat.,* Ser. 5, vol. viii.

[3] D'Archiac, *Leçons sur le Faune Quaternaire,* p. 196.

species from the *H. amphibius* of Africa, was, if not identical with, at any rate very closely allied to it. Some palæontologists believe that, like the mammoth and the *R. tichorhinus*, it was covered with hair ; we have, however, no distinct evidence in support of this view. It may, moreover, be remarked, though too much importance must not be attached to the observation, that our ancient hippopotamus has been less frequently found in association with these two species, than with *E. antiquus* and *R. hemitæchus*, Falc. (*leptorhinus*, Owen), which, as just mentioned, have a more southerly range. Thus, in this country, it has only been found in four bone-caves, those of Durdham Down, Kirkdale, Kent's Hole Cavern, and Ravenscliff in Gower, and in the two former it was associated with *E. antiquus* and *R. hemitæchus*. In the river gravels its remains are found at Grays and Ilford, associated with the *R. tichorhinus*, *R. leptorhinus*, and *R. hemitæchus* ; at Walton and Folkestone, with *Elephas antiquus* ; at Peckham, with *E. antiquus*, and *E. primigenius* ; at Bedford, with *E. antiquus*, the tichorhine rhinoceros, and the reindeer ; and at Barton, with the mammoth and *R. hemitæchus*.[1]

The magnificent Irish elk, or *Megaceros hibernicus*, which attained a height of more than ten feet, with antlers measuring eleven feet from tip to tip, may perhaps have lived to a somewhat more recent period, but appears to have had a much more restricted range. Its remains have been found in Sweden, in Germany, in France as far as the Pyrenees, and in Central Italy. It seems, however, to have been most abundant in the British Isles, and especially in Ireland. It is reported to have been frequently found in peat-bogs, but Professor Owen believes that, in reality, the bones generally occur in the lacustrine shell marl, which underlies the peat or bog earth.[2]

In the *Niebelungen Lied* of the twelfth century, a

---

[1] *The British Pleistocene Mammalia*, Palæontological Soc., 1866, p. xxviii.

[2] Owen, *loc. cit.*, p. 465.

mysterious animal is mentioned under the name of schelch :

> " After this he straightway slew a bison and an elk,
> Of the strong uri four, and one fierce schelch."

It has been supposed by some writers that the schelch was, in fact, the *Megaceros hibernicus*. There is, however, no sufficient reason for this hypothesis, and we must

FIG. 212.—Deer, from a drawing in the cave of Altamira.   After A. Breuil.

remember that the same poem, as Dr Buckland has pointed out, contains allusions to giants, dwarfs, pigmies, and fire-dragons. Neither Cæsar nor Tacitus mentions the Irish elk, and they would surely not have omitted such a remarkable animal, if it had been known to them.

No remains of the Irish elk have yet been found in association with bronze, nor indeed am I aware of any which can be referred to the later Stone or Neolithic Age.

These twelve species, then, are especially characteristic of the river-drift deposits. Most of them occur also in the loëss of the Rhine and its principal tributaries, but, except perhaps the last, they have not yet been met with in the peat-bogs. They never occur in the Kjökken-möddings, the lake-habitations, or tumuli ; nor are there any traditions in Western Europe which can be regarded as indicating, even in the most obscure manner, any recollection of these gigantic mammalia.

Another remarkable group of animals invaded Europe soon after the glacial period, from the dry steppes of Central Asia. Amongst these were the Saiga Antelope (*A. saiga*), the *Lagopus fusillus*, the Common Hamster (*Cricetus vulgaris*), the Small Hamster (*C. phæus*), the Steppe Marmot (*Arctomys bobac*), the *Spermophilus rufescens*, *Alactaga jaculus*, and *Arvicola gregaris* (*Kriz. Mit. Anthr. Ges. Wien*, 1898, p. 8). These have been supposed to indicate the prevalence of a very dry period. Of fourteen special " Tundra " species, twelve have been found in Western Europe. Is it not possible, however, that they happened to be amongst the first arrivals on the return of a milder period, and were not able to maintain themselves in the struggle for existence ?

The *Wild Horses* (fig. 213 and Plate) which in ancient times inhabited Europe differed somewhat from our present breed, and have been described as separate races by Professor Owen, under the names of *Equus fossilis* and *Equus spelæus*. The latter is the race which was largely used for food by the ancient inhabitants of the Bruniquel Cave in Dordogne.[1] It was rather small in size, but appears to have resembled the true horse more than the ass. Some naturalists have, indeed, been disposed to believe that Europe contained two wild species of the genus *Equus* during quaternary times. This opinion, however, seems to depend on difference of size rather than of form, and we know that the varieties of the horse differ considerably in magnitude. At Solutré the wild horse seems to have been the principal article of food, and it is estimated that the deposit must have contained the remains of 100,000 animals.

[1] Owen, *Philosophical Transactions*, 1869, p. 535. See also Rütimeyer *Beiträge zur Kenntniss der fossilen Pferden.*

Ekkehard, in the *Benedictiones ad mensas Ekkehardi monachi Sangallensis,* mentions "ferales equi" as existing in the eleventh century in Switzerland. Lucas David also (*Reuss. Chronik.,* Bd. ii. s. 121) alludes to the wild horse as existing in 1240 in Russia. Even at the beginning of the seventeenth century, Herberstein expressly says, "Feras habet Lithuania, præter eas, quæ in Germania referuntur, bisontes, uros, alces, *equos sylvestres,*" etc.

Perhaps, however, these mediæval wild horses were

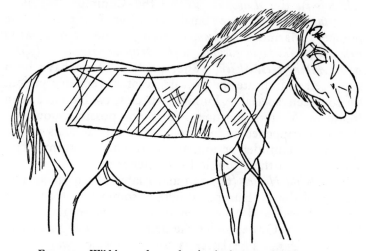

FIG. 213.—Wild horse, from a drawing in the cave of Combarelles.
After A. Breuil.

merely tame ones which had escaped and bred in the extensive forests of Central Europe. Indeed, the history of the horse in Europe seems to have been much the same as in America. In the one country as in the other, wild horses were at one time frequent, and their remains are abundant. The Spanish conquerors, however, found no trace or tradition of the horse at the time of the discovery of America ; and so also in the Danish shell-mounds, and at the earlier Swiss lake-villages, the horse was either unknown, or at least extremely rare. Gradually it seems to have become again abundant, both in a domesticated and a wild condition ; until at length, as population increased, the wild horse finally disappeared in Europe, as he seems destined ere long to do in America.[1]

The *Reindeer* (figs. 214, 224) still exists in Northern Europe, in Siberia, and in North America, where it has been found as far north as man has yet penetrated. Even so recently as the time of Pallas it might still be met with on the wooded summits of the Oural Mountains, as far south as the Caucasus. In Western Europe it is now an extinct species, though it was at one time abundant in

FIG. 214.—Reindeer, from a painting in the cave of Font-de-Gaume (Dordogne). After A. Breuil.

England and France, whence, however, it is unnecessary to say, it has long disappeared. M. Lartet found no traces of it in any of the Spanish caves examined by him ; Ponzi mentions it, though apparently with some little doubt, as occurring among the animal remains collected by M. Regnoli, at Cantalupo, near Rome ; but its existence south of the Alps seems still doubtful.[2]

At the present day the reindeer, like the Laplander, is gradually retiring northwards, unable to resist the pressure

[1] See, for further particulars, Brandt, *Zoographische und Palæonto-logische Beiträge*, p. 176.
[2] *Rapporto sugli Studi e sulle Scoperte Paleoetnologiche nel Bacino della Campagna Romana*, Roma, 1867.

of advancing civilization. Even within the last ten years a few families of Lapps might still be found in the neighbourhood of Nystuen, on the summit of the Fillefjeld, and some other places in the south of Norway, but none are now to be found on this side of the Namsen river. The reindeer, in a wild state, indeed, even at the present day, is generally distributed, though in small numbers, over the highest and wildest of the Norwegian fjelds, protected, however, by stringent game laws, but for which it would probably have ere now ceased to exist.

On the other hand, this species must have been at one time very abundant in Great Britain, no fewer than a thousand horns having been found by Colonel Wood in some of the Gower caves on the Welsh coast.

As far as we can judge from the present evidence, the first appearance of the reindeer in Europe coincided with that of the mammoth, and took place at a later period than that of the cave-bear or Irish elk. It is generally found wherever the mammoth and woolly-haired rhinoceros occur ; but, on the other hand, as its remains are abundant in some of the bone-caves in which the gigantic Pachyderms are wanting, it is probable that it survived to a still later period. The reindeer has not, however, been found in the Kjökkenmöddings of Denmark, nor in any of the tumuli of England, France, or Germany. It is also wanting in the Swiss lake-villages, although we know that it was at one time an inhabitant of Switzerland, bones of it having been found in a cave at L'Echelle, between the Great and Little Salève, near Geneva, where they were mixed with worked flints, ashes, and remains of the ox and horse.

As might naturally have been expected, remains of the reindeer occur in the peat mosses of Sweden, as well as in those of Scotland and England. It is not, however, represented on any of the ancient British or Gallic coins. Cæsar, indeed, mentions it as existing in the great Hercynian forest ; but his description is both imperfect and incorrect. He seems to have heard of it only at second-hand, and never to have met with anybody who had actually seen one. It does not appear to have been ever exhibited in the Roman circus.

Buffon stated on the authority of Gaston, Comte de Foix, that in his time (1331 to 1390) the reindeer still lived in the south of France. Cuvier, however, by examining an ancient manuscript, sent by Gaston himself to Philippe le Hardi, showed that, though his expression is a little ambiguous, he probably intended to say exactly the reverse, his words being—

" J'en ay veu en Nourvegne et Xuedene et en ha oultre mer, mes en Romain pays en ay je peu veu." [1] /

Remains of the reindeer have been found in Scotland in beds of marl and till, and also, though very rarely, in peat.[2] Hibbert,[3] Brandt,[4] Boyd Dawkins, J. A. Smith, and other good authorities, consider that it survived in the extreme north down to the twelfth century ; relying on the statement of Torfæus, that the Norwegians used to make incursions from the Orkneys into Caithness for the purpose of hunting reindeer (*hreina*) and other game.[5]

While, however, fully admitting the high authority of Torfæus, I cannot regard a casual statement of this character as conclusively deciding the question, and I may add that Sir G. Dasent, who was so great an authority on all questions connected with Scandinavian literature, was convinced that the reindeer was extinct in Scotland at the period in question. It may also be remarked that several attempts which have been made to introduce the reindeer into Scotland have completely failed, the animals dying without any very apparent reason, while, on the contrary, in Iceland they have become numerous. I admit that these experiments are far from conclusive ; but, on the other hand, in Scandinavia the deer are said to be larger in the northern districts than in the southern, while the Spitzbergen specimens are the finest of all.

---

[1] *Recherches sur les Ossements Fossiles*, vol. vi. p. 125.
[2] See Dawkins, *Popular Science Review*, Jan. 1868 ; Smith, *Proc. Soc. Ant. Scot.*, 1869, p. 186.
[3] *Edinburgh Journal of Sci.*, 1831.
[4] *Zoögeogr. und Palæont. Beiträge*, 1867, pp. 62, 256.
[5] *Rerum Orcadensium His.*, i. 36.

If, indeed, Torfæus had distinctly stated that the reindeer existed in northern Scotland during the twelfth century, the state of the case would have been very different ; the passage referred to, however, could hardly be accepted as conclusive by itself, especially as long as no traces of reindeer had been found among the ancient ruins which abound in that district. On the other hand, Dr J. A. Smith has carefully examined the horns and bones found in the ruins of the curious towers known as " Brochs," or " Burghs," and has shown that some of them certainly belonged to the reindeer.[1] Thus fragments of reindeer's horns have been collected by Mr Joass among the ruins of the Cill-Trölla Broch, on the farm of Kintradwell, near Brora, on the sea-coast of Sutherlandshire. Dr Smith, on carefully examining the remains of deer obtained by Mr Laing at Keiss, in Caithness, finds that they do not all belong, as at first supposed, to the red deer, but that some of them were those of the reindeer. Lastly, remains of this species have been collected by Mr Anderson in the ruins of the Yarhouse Broch, in the same county. It is indeed more than probable that in other cases remains of the reindeer have been incorrectly ascribed to the red deer.

We do not, unfortunately, know the date at which these Burghs or Brochs were first constructed, but it is on record that some of them were in use down to the twelfth century (see *ante*, p. 62).

No doubt these observations tend to support the inference derived from the statement of Torfæus, and though I am not entirely convinced, it must be admitted that there are strong grounds for believing that the reindeer survived in northern Scotland down to a comparatively recent period, if not so late as the time mentioned by Torfæus.

The true *Arctic Fox* has also been found in English bone-caves, as well as in those of Central Europe. Indeed, in the Kessorloch cave in Switzerland, out of 150 lower jaws of foxes, only 2 belonged to our Common Fox,

---

[1] *Proc. Soc. Antiq.*, 1868, vol. viii. p. 186.

66 to the Arctic Fox (*Canis lagopus*), and the remainder to the Red Fox of North America.[1] In the same cave the Common Hare was represented by two individuals only, while of the Alpine Hare not less than 250 individuals were indicated by the remains.

The *Glutton*, of North Europe, which is the wolverine of the North American fur-hunters, has been found in several of the English bone-caves, as well as in the

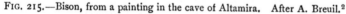

FIG. 215.—Bison, from a painting in the cave of Altamira. After A. Breuil.[2]

Norfolk "Forest-beds,"[3] and is abundant in those of Belgium.

The *Aurochs*, or European bison (see Frontispiece and figs. 215, 216), appears to have been abundant in Western Europe. It has been found in Scotland, England, France, Germany, Denmark, Sweden, Poland, and Italy, as well as in Russia. Its remains occur in the river-drift gravels, the bone-caves, the lake-villages of Switzerland, and in the peat-bogs, though none have yet been found in the shell-mounds of Denmark, nor, so

[1] *Merk. Mitt. der Ant. Ges. in Zurich*, 1875; Rütimeyer, *Die Veränd. der Thierwelt in der Schweiz seit Anwesenheit der Menschen.*
[2] *Anthropologie*, vol. xv.
[3] Newton, *Quart. Journ. Geol. Soc.*, 1880.

far as I am aware, in any of our British peat-bogs or tumuli. M. Lartet thinks that it is represented on a coin of the Santones, which was shown to him by M. de Saulcy. It is stated by Pliny and Seneca to have existed in their time, with the urus, in the great forests of Germany. Though not mentioned by Cæsar, it is alluded to in the *Niebelungen Lied*, and is said to have existed in Prussia down to the year 1775. According to Nordmann and Von Baer, it still survives in some parts of Western Asia.

The bison is also preserved by the Emperor of Russia

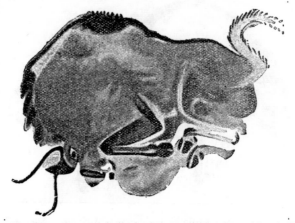

FIG. 216.—Bison, from a painting in the cave of Altamira.   After A. Breuil.[1]

in the imperial forests of Lithuania, where, however, its existence seems to be very precarious. In 1830 the herd numbered 711 head, of which, during the Polish revolution in 1831, 115 were killed. From that time they gradually increased until 1857, when the numbers were 1898, but during the late Polish rebellion they fell to 874. Since 1863 no numbers have been given.

According to Rütimeyer, than whom it is impossible to cite a greater authority on such a question, our ancient bison (*B. priscus*) was specifically identical with the existing American bison. Every stage, however, between the fossil form and the existing European aurochs can be

[1] *Anthropologie*, vol. xv.

traced, so that it is impossible to separate the two, an opinion in which Brandt also coincides. It would appear, moreover, that the American form of bison is more archaic than that of Europe.

Allen regards the gigantic *Bos latifrons*, which had immense horns spreading from ten to twelve feet, as the parent form, passing through *B. priscus* into the present European, and through *B. bonasus* into the American bison.[1] We have here, therefore, a clear case in which two now distinct species are connected by the evidence of fossil remains.

The urus, or *Bos primigenius*, did not extend its range to America, nor, so far as I am aware, have its remains yet been met with in North-Eastern Asia. They occur, however, throughout Europe—in England, Scotland, Denmark, and the south of Sweden, in France and Germany. Across the Alps and Pyrenees, it occurs in Italy and Spain, and even, according to M. Gervais, in Northern Africa. In the museum at Lund is a skeleton belonging to this species, in which one of the vertebræ still shows traces of a wound, made, in the opinion of Professor Nilsson, by a flint arrow. Bones of this species have also been met with in ancient tumuli, as well as in the lake-habitations, and in the Kjökkenmöddings.

Cæsar particularly mentions the urus as occurring in the Hercynian forest : it is alluded to in the *Niebelungen Lied*, and, according to Herberstein, it existed in Germany down to the sixteenth century. In England, wild bulls are mentioned by Fitz-Stephen, in his *Life of Becket*, as occurring near London as late as the twelfth century. It does not seem certain, however, that these were uri. The celebrated wild cattle of Chillingham, and some of our domestic breeds, are generally regarded by palæontologists as being descended from the ancient urus, but this is denied by others, who consider that the Chillingham cattle are descended from the imported Shorthorn breed (see *ante*, p. 210).

Mr Dawkins is of opinion that *Machairodus latidens*,

---

[1] *The American Bisons*, p. 35.

one of the most remarkable of the Pliocene carnivora, survived to post-glacial times.   It was found by MacEnery in Kent's Hole, but was apparently very rare, and our committee only found a single tooth in the subsequent examination of that interesting cavern.   Nor has it occurred in any other of our bone-caves or river gravels with remains of post-glacial mammalia.   The *Norway Elk*, which is identical with the American moose, was also an inhabitant of this country, but has long become extinct here, as, indeed, throughout Western Europe.   Even in Prussia it is said that there are only about 226 remaining.[1] The lemming has been discovered by Dr Blackmore in the river gravels at Fisherton, near Salisbury ; and the lagomys, or tailless hare, a genus now confined to the Himalayas, Siberia, and the colder regions of North America, has been identified by Professor Owen among the bones from Kent's Cavern, and by Dr Falconer among those from the Brixham Cave.   Among other northern and eastern forms may be also mentioned a species allied to Dipus, *Alactaga jaculus*, and a small mouse, *Arvicola gregaris*.[2] Another glacial genus, that of the marmots, is represented by two species, one of them very closely resembling that now living in Siberia.   These later species, together with the Saiga antelope, indicate the existence, during part of the period, of a dry and cold interval with a climate resembling the Siberian tundras.   Lastly, it may be observed that remains of the great snowy owl (*Strix nivea*) and of the willow grouse (*Tetrao albus*) are met with in abundance in most of the caves of the south-west of France.

The river gravels contain also 36 species of shell-fish, of which 34 at present live in Sweden,[3] and 29 in Lombardy.   These latter, however, are principally species having a very wide range, and we shall see still more clearly that the leaning of the molluscan fauna is towards

[1] See *Report from Her Majesty's Representatives abroad, on the Laws and Regulations relating to Game, presented to Parliament,* 1871.
[2] *Arch. f. Anthropologie,* 1876, p. 162.
[3] *Proc. Roy. Soc.,* 1862, p. 44.

the north, if we remember that out of 77 Finland species, 31 have been found in the upper level gravels, while of 193 Lombard species, only 29 have as yet occurred.

A very interesting point connected with this quaternary fauna is the manner in which it connects together species now quite distinct.   Opponents of Mr Darwin's theory often ask for the links connecting any two species.   In fact, however, every species is a link between other allied forms.   Of course, indeed, as long as any varieties remain undescribed there will be intervals—indicating, however, gaps not in nature, but in our knowledge.   Moreover, it is admitted by everyone that there are variable species, that is to say, species which present two or more extreme forms, with intermediate gradations.   Now we may fairly ask those who assert that no two species are connected by links, how they would separate the instances of variable animals (which they admit to occur) from the case which they say does not exist.   If we were to obtain to-morrow all the links between any two species which are now considered distinct, no one can deny that the two would at once be united, and would hereafter appear in our classifications as one variable species.   In fact, therefore, they first unite into one species all these forms, however different, between which a complete series is known, and then argue in favour of the permanence of species because no two of them are united by intermediate links.

Moreover, if species were in reality unconnected by common ancestors, then it would necessarily follow that, as our knowledge of any group increased, the separations between the different species would become more and more unmistakable.   On the contrary, however, it is a well-known fact that the difficult genera become still more difficult as they are more profoundly studied.   If, indeed, we consider existing forms only, no doubt the distinctions between the greater number of species are well-marked, nor does anyone expect to find a living series of links between them.   The intermediate forms lived in tertiary and quaternary times. Thus directly we commence to study the extinct forms, all the convenient lines of separation gradually thin out. For instance, the larger species of mammalia are at present in most cases well marked, but it becomes much more difficult satisfactorily to distinguish them from one another when we consider fossil specimens as well as recent ones. To take only two cases from the group of quaternary mammalia, we have seen that, according to Rütimeyer, the European and American bisons, which are now quite distinct, are connected by the *Bison priscus*, while between our brown bear and the grizzly bear of the Rocky Mountains a series of links has been discovered among the abundant remains in the bone-caves.

Great as is the interest attaching to the existence of man at a period so much more ancient than that hitherto assigned to him, there is something which, to many minds, will appear even more fascinating, in the presence of such a fauna as that which I have thus briefly indicated. For it must be regarded as a well-ascertained fact that, even during the human period, the pleasant and sunny valleys of England and of France have been inhabited by the gigantic Irish elk, two species of elephant, and three of rhinoceros, together with the reindeer, a large bear closely resembling the grizzly bear of the Rocky Mountains, a bison scarcely distinguishable from that of the American Prairies, the musk-ox of Arctic America, the lemming of the Siberian steppes, the lion of the Tropics, the hyæna of the Cape, and a hippopotamus closely resembling that of the great African rivers.

Influenced mainly by the presence of the great pachyderms, and particularly by that of the hippopotamus, M. d'Archaic was disposed to consider that the climate of the quaternary period was warmer than ours,[1] while M. Lartet[2] suggests that we may have had a climate like that of Chili, where, as Mr Darwin had pointed out, glaciers actually come down to the sea-level in latitudes

[1] *Leçons sur la Faune Quaternaire*, pp. 15, 16.
[2] Lartet, *Ann. des Sc. Nat.*, 1867, p. 37.

corresponding with that of our south coast and the northern provinces of France.

In other respects, however, the fauna of the quaternary deposits indicates a more severe climate. The presence of the reindeer and musk ox, the lemming and the marmot, corroborated, as we shall see in the next chapter, by physical evidence, leaves little doubt on this subject. Moreover, we must remember that the tichorhine rhinoceros and the mammoth were not only well provided against cold, but in some cases were enveloped in the ice and frozen mud of the Siberian rivers so soon after death that the flesh had not had time to decay. Much weight is also to be attributed, I think, to the presence of smaller quadrupeds, as, for instance, of the lemming and lagomys.

Yet it cannot be denied that some of the species, and particularly the hippopotamus, indicate a warmer climate. Even if protected by fur, as Sir J. Prestwich supposes, this animal could never live in a country where the rivers were frozen every winter. To meet this difficulty, a suggestion has been thrown out that it may have made annual migrations. In the Gulf of Penas, on the west coast of South America, lat. 47° S., Mr Darwin has pointed out that glaciers now " descend to the sea within less than nine degrees of latitude from where palms grow, less than two and a half from arborescent grasses, less than two from orchideous parasites, and within a single degree of tree-ferns." [1] The reindeer in America makes, we know, very extensive annual migrations, but a heavy animal like the hippopotamus could hardly do so. I am, therefore, rather disposed to believe that the presence of the hippopotamus, the *E. antiquus*, and *R. leptorhinus* indicates that the climate of the quaternary period was not uniformly severe, but contained at least one interval of exceptional mildness.

The late M. Morlot, well known as an excellent and careful observer, was, I believe, the first to point out that, in Switzerland, there was evidence of three periods of great extension of the glaciers, separated by epochs of

[1] *Researches in Geology and Natural History*, p. 285.

comparative warmth. And in Great Britain also there is strong geological evidence of the existence of several such warm interglacial periods.[1]

We shall also see presently that if the cold of the glacial epoch was due to the astronomical causes pointed out by M. Adhémar and Mr Croll, the period of extreme cold must have been followed by one of unusual warmth, or rather there must have been several oscillations of climate from unusual heat to extreme cold.

I am disposed then, on the whole, to consider that the quaternary fauna consists of two different groups, belonging to different periods and to (at least) two different conditions of climate, one warmer than the present, the other colder. The whole subject, however, while of great interest, is also one of extreme difficulty, and I shall return to it more at length in a subsequent chapter. On many points we must be contented to suspend our judgment, but we may at least regard it as proved that, since the appearance of man, there have been great changes in the fauna of Western Europe, which then contained several important species, either now altogether extinct, or existing only in distant parts of the world.

[1] Geikie, *The Great Ice Age* ; Croll, *Climate and Time*.

CHAPTER X

PRIMEVAL MAN

It would be quite impossible, within the limits of a single chapter, to describe all the caves in which human remains have been found in association with, and apparently belonging to, the same period as those of the extinct mammalia. I will only call attention to a few of those which have been most thoroughly examined, and by the researches in which the conclusions appear to be satisfactorily established.

It is unnecessary to observe that a great number of caves present evidence of having been occupied during times long subsequent to those which we are now considering ; but for the Neolithic Age, as well as for all later periods, we have, as has been already mentioned, other sources of information, and more satisfactory evidence than any which can be derived from the examination of caves.

Some writers, indeed, have gone so far as to question altogether the value of what may be called cave evidence. They have suggested that the bones of extinct animals may have lain in the caves for ages before the appearance of man ; that relics of the human period may have been introduced subsequently ; and that remains belonging to very different periods may have been mixed together. This was, for instance, the conclusion arrived at by M. Desnoyers, even so recently as the year 1845, in his article on Bone-caves.[1] Unless this argument admitted

---

[1] " Recherches Géologiques et Historiques sur les Cavernes, particulièrement sur les cavernes à ossements," *Dictionnaire Universel d'Histoire Naturelle.*

of a satisfactory answer, it must be conceded that the evidence derivable from cave contents would always be liable to grave suspicion. I trust, however, to be able to show that this is not the case.

As long ago as the year 1828, MM. Tournal and Christol in the south of France had found fragments of pottery and human bones and teeth intermingled with remains of extinct animals ; and M. Tournal distinctly expressed the opinion that these had certainly not been washed in by any diluvial catastrophe, but must have been introduced gradually. The presence of pottery, however, throws much doubt on the supposed antiquity of these remains.

A few years later, in 1833 and 1834, Dr Schmerling[1] published an account of his researches in some caves near Liége in Belgium. In four or five of these he found human bones, and in all of them rude implements, principally flint flakes, were discovered, scattered in such a manner among the remains of the mammoth, *Rhinoceros tichorhinus*, cave-hyæna, and cave-bear, that Dr Schmerling referred them to the same period. One feels a natural surprise that such animals as these should ever have been natives of England and France, ever have wandered about among our woods or along our streams ; but when it was also suggested that they were contemporary with man, surprise was succeeded by incredulity. Yet these cave researches appear to have been conducted with care, and the principal results have been confirmed by more recent discoveries.

The hesitation, however, with which the statements of Dr Schmerling were received by scientific men arose, no doubt, partly from the fact that some of the fossil remains discovered by him were certainly referred to wrong species, and partly because, with reference to several of the extinct species, and especially to the mammoth, he expressed the opinion that the remains had been brought from a distance, and had very likely been washed out of some earlier bed.

[1] *Recherches sur les Ossements Fossiles découverts dans les Cavernes de la Province de Liége*, par le Dr P. C. Schmerling.

Even, therefore, though Dr Schmerling might be quite right in his conclusion that the human remains had been "enfouis dans ces cavernes à la même époque, et par conséquent par les mêmes causes qui y ont entraîné une masse d'ossements de différentes espèces éteintes," still it would not necessarily follow that man had *lived* at the same period as these extinct species.

Careful explorations of the Belgian caves were subsequently made, under the auspices of the Government, by M. E. Dupont.[1]   These caverns belong principally to the so-called Reindeer Period, and the flint implements are never ground.   Thus out of 30,000 worked flints found in the cavern of Chaleux, and 1200 in those of Furfooz, not one presents a trace of grinding.   Some of these flint flakes, etc., appear to consist of Pressigny (Touraine) flint, and, in the opinion of Dr Dupont, as well as of M. de Mortillet, must have come from that distant locality.   In this cavern the humerus of an elephant was discovered, but in M. Dupont's opinion, founded on the state of the bone, it belonged to an earlier period than the other remains.   Human bones have been found in several of these caverns.   The Trou du Frontal contained bones belonging to no less than thirteen individuals. They had probably been buried in the cave, the entrance to which seemed to have been purposely closed by a large block of stone.   When discovered they were in great confusion, having, in the opinion of MM. Dupont and Van Beneden, been disturbed and rearranged by water. The form of the cavern, and the fact that the opening was in great measure closed by the above-mentioned stone, seem to me to speak strongly against this suggestion, and I should rather regard the disturbance of the bones as due to foxes and badgers.   The Trou de la Naulette contained a very remarkable lower jaw, of which M. Dupont says that "regardé dans la face interne, elle offre une telle proclivité d'arrière en avant de la partie symphysaire qu'on est porté à y voir un prognatisme tout animal.

---

[1] *Notices Préliminaires sur les Fouilles exécutées sous les auspices du Gouvernement Belge dans les Cavernes de la Belgique*, 1867.

Les apophyses géni ne sont pas indiquées ; les fossettes latérales sont très-prononcées, et le rebord mentonnier est reduit à son minimum. Les alvéoles des canines, bien que très-rapprochées des alvéoles des incisives, et des molaires, nous rappellent la disposition qu'on observe sur la mâchoire du singe. En effet, l'alvéole qui logeait la canine est fort vaste et bombée à la face externe. Ce qui semble plus étrange encore, c'est que les trois alvéoles des grosses molaires présentent absolument l'ordre typique du maxillaire simien par l'augmentation progressive des alvéoles de la première à la deuxième et à la troisième molaire."

The celebrated cavern of Kent's Hole, near Torquay, was examined by Mr MacEnery as long ago as 1825. He did not, however, publish his notes on the subject, and they remained in manuscript until 1859, when Mr Vivian succeeded in obtaining them. Mr MacEnery found human bones, flint flakes, etc., but all either on the surface or in disturbed soil, so that on the whole he regarded them, though apparently with much doubt, as posterior to the remains of the cave-bear, hyæna, etc.

In the year 1840, Mr Godwin-Austen communicated to the Geological Society a memoir on the Geology of the south-east of Devonshire,[1] and in his description of Kent's Hole he says, that "human remains and works of art, such as arrow-heads and knives of flint, occur in all parts of the cave, and throughout the entire thickness of the clay : and no distinction founded on condition, distribution, or relative position, can be observed, whereby the human can be separated from the other reliquiæ," which included bones of the "elephant, rhinoceros, ox, deer, horse, bear, hyæna, and a feline animal of large size." The value, he truly adds, "of such a statement must rest on the care with which a collector may have explored. I must therefore state that my own researches were constantly conducted in parts of the cave which had never been disturbed, and in every instance the bones were procured

[1] *Transactions of the Geol. Soc.*, Ser. 2, vol. vi. p. 433.

from beneath a thick covering of stalagmite ; so far, then, the bones and works of man must have been introduced into the cave before the flooring of stalagmite had been formed." Notwithstanding the high authority of Mr Godwin-Austen, these statements attracted little attention ; and the very similar assertions made by Mr Vivian, in a paper read before the Geological Society, were considered so improbable that the memoir containing them was not published.

They have, however, been completely confirmed by the systematic examination which was instituted by the British Association. Worked flints were found less abundantly in the lower layers than near the surface, but several were discovered under circumstances which left no doubt that they were deposited at the same time as the bones of the large mammalia. The researches were carried on by a Committee, consisting of Sir C. Lyell, Mr Busk, Sir J. Evans, Professor Phillips, Mr Vivian, Mr Pengelly, and myself, and the work was under the more immediate superintendence of Mr Pengelly and Mr Vivian.

In May 1858, Dr Falconer called the attention of the Geological Society to a newly-discovered cave at Brixham, near Torquay, and a Committee was appointed to assist him in examining it. Grants of money were obtained for the same object from the Royal Society and Miss Burdett Coutts. In addition to Dr Falconer, Mr Busk, Sir J. Evans, Mr Pengelly, Sir J. Prestwich, and Professor Ramsay were entrusted with the investigations. In September 1858 a preliminary notice was published by the Geological Society, but the General Report is contained in the *Philosophical Transactions* for 1874.

The deposits in the cave were, in descending order—

(1) Stalagmite of irregular thickness.
(2) Ochreous cave-earth with limestone breccia.
(3) Ochreous cave-earth with comminuted shale.
(4) Rounded gravel.

The organic remains belonged chiefly to the following species :—

(1) *Elephas primigenius.*
(2) *Rhinoceros tichorhinus.* Teeth in considerable numbers and an astragalus.
(3) *Bos primigenius.*
(4) *Bos.*
(5) *Equus caballus.*
(6) *Cervus tarandus.* The reindeer—skull and horns.
(7) *Cervus elaphus.* Horns.
(8) *C. capreolus.*
(9) *Ursus spelæus*—the cave-bear. Lower jaws, teeth, etc.
(10) *U. ferox.*
(11) *U. arctos.*
(12) *Hyæna spelæa.* Lower jaws, teeth, fragments of skulls, and other bones.
(13) *Felis spelæa.*
(14) *Lagomys.*

Several flint flakes were also found indiscriminately mixed with these bones, and, according to all appearance, of the same antiquity. They occurred at various depths, from ten inches to eleven feet, and some of them were in the gravel, below the whole of the ochreous cave-earth.

Again, in the grotto of Maccagnone, in Sicily, Dr Falconer found human traces, consisting of ashes and rude flint implements, in a breccia containing bones of the *Elephas antiquus*, of the hyæna, of a large *Ursus*, of a *Felis* (probably *F. spelæa*), and especially with large numbers of bones belonging to the hippopotamus. The "ceneri impastati," or concrete of ashes, had at one time filled the cavern, and a large piece of bone breccia was still cemented to the roof, but owing to some change in the drainage the greater part had been washed out again. The presence of the hippopotamus sufficiently proves that the geographical conditions of the country must have been very different from what they are now ; but I

cannot do better than quote Dr Falconer's own summary
of his observations in this case :

" The vast number of *Hippopotami* implied that the
physical condition of the country must have been greatly
different, at no very distant geological period, from what
obtains now. He considered that all deposits *above* the
bone breccia had been accumulated up to the roof by
materials washed in from above, through sinuous crevices
or flues in the limestone, and that the uppermost layer,
consisting of the breccia of shells, bone-splinters, siliceous
objects, burnt clay, bits of charcoal, and hyæna coprolites,
had been cemented to the roof by stalagmitic infiltration.
The entire condition of the large fragile *Helices* proved
that the effect had been produced by the tranquil agency
of water, as distinct from any tumultuous action. There
was nothing to indicate that the different objects in the
roof breccia were other than of contemporaneous origin : subsequently a great physical alteration in the contour, altering
the flow of superficial water and of the subterranean
springs, changed all the conditions previously existing,
and emptied out the whole of the loose incoherent contents,
leaving only the portions agglutinated to the roof. The
wreck of these ejecta was visible in the patches of ' ceneri
impastati,' containing fossil bones, below the mouth of
the cavern. That a long period must have operated in
the extinction of the hyæna, cave-lion, and other fossil
species is certain, but no index remains for its measurement. The author would call the careful attention of
cautious geologists to the inferences—that the Maccagnone
Cave was filled up to the roof within the human period,
so that a thick layer of bone splinters, teeth, landshells,
hyænas' coprolites, and human objects, was agglutinated
to the roof by the filtration of water holding lime in
solution ; that subsequently, and within the human
period, such a great amount of change took place in the
physical configuration of the district as to have caused
the cave to be washed out and emptied of its contents,
excepting the patches of material cemented to the roof,
and since coated with additional stalagmite."

Similar proofs of great and recent geographical changes have been afforded by the examination of certain Spanish caves. The Rock of Gibraltar abounds in caverns containing human remains, with stone, bone, and bronze implements, mixed with those of domesticated animals, such as the goat and ox. In the bone breccia from the Genista Cave and fissure, Mr Busk and Dr Falconer have discovered *Hyæna crocuta*, an existing African species, the leopard, lynx, serval and Barbary stag, together with *Rh. hemitæchus* and a species of ibex. But, although it is more than probable, it does not appear to be proved, that man co-existed with these animals on the Rock of Gibraltar. Among some bones found in another cave near Madrid, M. Lartet has discovered molars of the existing African elephant.

M. Lartet[1] has also described with his usual ability an interesting grotto, or small cave, which was discovered some years ago at Aurignac, in the south of France. A peasant named Bonnemaison, seeing a rabbit run into a hole on a steep slope, put his hand in, and to his surprise pulled out a human bone. Curiosity urged him to explore farther, and on removing a quantity of rubbish, he found a large block of stone, which almost closed up the entrance to a small chamber, in which were no less than seventeen human skeletons. Unfortunately for science, the Mayor of Aurignac, hearing of these discoveries, collected the human bones, had them reburied, and when M. Lartet some years afterwards explored the cavern, they could not be found again.

After carefully examining the locality, M. Lartet came to the conclusion that this small cavern had been used as a burial-place, and from the remains of bones broken for marrow, and marks of fire immediately outside the cave, he inferred that funeral feasts had been held there.

The following is the list of species determined by

[1] *Ann. des Sc. Nat.*, 1861, p. 177.

M. Lartet, together with the approximate number of individuals belonging to each :—

Number of individuals.

(1) Cave bear (*Ursus spelæus*) . . 5— 6
(2) Brown bear (*U. arctos ?*) . . 1
(3) Badger (*Meles taxus*) . . . 1— 2
(4) Polecat (*Putorius vulgaris*) . . 1
(5) Cave lion (*Felis spelæa*) . . 1
(6) Wild cat (*F. catus*) . . . 1
(7) Hyæna (*Hyæna spelæa*) . . 5— 6
(8) Wolf (*Canis lupus*) . . . 3
(9) Fox (*C. vulpes*) . . . . 18—20
(10) Mammoth (*Elephas primigenius*).
Two molars and an astragalus.
(11) Rhinoceros (*Rhinoceros tichorhinus*) . 1
(12) Horse (*Equus caballus*) . . . 12—15
(13) Ass ?[1] (*E. asinus*). . . . 1
(14) Boar (*Sus scrofa*). Two incisors.
(15) Stag (*Cervus elaphus*) . . . 1
(16) Irish elk (*Megaceros hibernicus*) . 1
(17) Roe (*C. capreolus*) . . . 3— 4
(18) Reindeer (*C. tarandus*) . . . 10—12
(19) Aurochs (*Bison europæus*) . . 12—15

Some of these were found in the grotto, others outside ; the latter had been gnawed by some large carnivorous animal, no doubt the hyæna, coprolites of which were found among the ashes. On the other hand, the bones inside the cave were untouched, from which M. Lartet concludes that after the funeral feasts, hyænas came and devoured all that had been left by the men, but that they could not effect an entrance into the cave on account of the large block of stone by which the entrance was closed, and which was actually found in its place by Bonnemaison.

In addition to the hyæna, the animals occurring in this list, and yet no longer existing, or known historically to

---

[1] This is, I presume, a small variety of horse, and not the true ass. The query is in the original.

have existed in France, are the reindeer, cave-bear, rhinoceros, cave-lion, Irish elk, and mammoth. The contemporaneity of the reindeer with man is very evident ; all the bones are broken for marrow, and many bear the marks of knives, besides which, the greater number of the bone implements are made out of the bones or horns of this species. That the rhinoceros also was contemporaneous with man is inferred by M. Lartet, firstly, on chemical grounds, the bones of this species, as well as those of the reindeer, aurochs, etc., having retained the same amount of nitrogen as the human bones from the same locality ; and secondly, because the bones appear to have been broken by man, and in some cases are marked by knives. Moreover, he has ingeniously pointed out that these bones must have belonged to an individual recently killed, because, after having been broken by man, they were gnawed by the hyænas, which would not have been the case if they had not been fresh and still full of their natural juices.

The elephant was represented only by some detached plates of molars and a calcaneum. This latter was the *only* gnawed bone found in the interior of the grotto. He is of opinion that these plates were purposely separated, and the calcaneum appears to have been placed in the vault at the time of the last interments ; but there is no evidence that it was then in a fresh condition. Indeed, the fact of its being gnawed seems rather to point the other way.

Remains of the *Ursus spelæus* (cave-bear) were much more abundant, and some of them were found in the grotto. In one case a whole limb appears to have been buried with the flesh on, as the different bones were all found together. It is well known that food and drink were in ancient times frequently buried with the dead, and M. Lartet thinks that we may account in this manner for the bones of quadrupeds found in the grotto at Aurignac.

I have given the particulars of this case at length, because, if the evidence was well established, we should here have an instance of a sepulture belonging to the period at which the cave-bear, the reindeer, the Irish elk, the woolly-haired rhinoceros, and probably the mammoth, still lived in the south of France. It is, however, much to be regretted that M. Lartet was not present when the place was first examined ; and, under all the circumstances, we cannot, I think, feel satisfied that the human remains found in this cave were coeval with those of the extinct mammalia.

Another remarkable case is that of the Hyæna-den at Wokey Hole, near Wells, which has been ably explored and described by Mr Boyd Dawkins.[1] In this instance the cave was filled with débris up to the very roof, and it appears that the accumulation of material was partly due to the disintegration of the dolomitic conglomerate forming the roof and walls of the cavern, and partly to the sediment washed in gradually by rain and small streams. It is evident that the bones and stones were not brought into the cave by the action of water ; firstly, because none of the bones are at all rolled ; secondly, because, though several rude flint implements were found in the cave, *only one single unworked* flint was met with ; and thirdly, because, in some cases, fragments of the same bone have been found close together, while, if they had been brought from a distance, it is almost incredible that they should have been again deposited close to one another. Again, there are several layers—one over the other—of *album græcum*, that is to say, the excrement of hyænas, each of which indicates, of course, an old floor, and a separate period of occupation ; so that the presence of, at least, one such floor above some of the flint implements, proves two things : firstly, that the hyænas which produced the *album græcum* occupied the cave after the savages who used the flint instruments ; and, secondly, that these implements have not been disturbed by water since the period of the hyæna.

During the last years of his life, Mr Christy examined and described, in conjunction with M. Lartet, with great

[1] *Quart. Journ. Geol. Soc.*, May 1862, p. 115.

care a number of small caves and rock-shelters in the Dordogne, some of which had already attracted the attention of archæologists.[1] These caves are particularly interesting, because, so far at least as we can judge from the present state of the evidence, the remains found in them belong to M. Lartet's Reindeer Period, and tend, therefore, to connect the later Stone or Neolithic Age with the period of the river-drifts and the great extinct mammalia ; representing a period about which we had previously very little information. Those which have been most carefully examined are ten in number, viz. Laugerie, La Madelaine, Les Eyzies, La Gorge d'Enfer, Le Moustier, Liveyre, Pey de l'Azé, Combe-Granal, and Badegoule, most of which I have myself had the advantage of visiting. Some of these, as, for instance, Les Eyzies and Le Moustier, are at a considerable height above the stream, but others—as those at La Madelaine and Laugerie—are little above the present flood-line, showing, therefore, that the level of the river is now nearly the same as it was at the period during which these caves were inhabited.

The rivers of the Dordogne run in deep valleys cut through calcareous strata ; and while the sides of the valleys in chalk districts are generally sloping, in this case, owing probably to the hardness of the rock, they are often vertical. Small caves and grottos frequently occur ; besides which, as the different strata possess unequal power of resistance against atmospheric influences, the face of the rock is, as it were, scooped out in many places, and thus " rock-shelters " are produced. In very ancient times these caves and rock-shelters were inhabited by men, who have left behind them abundant evidences of their presence. But as civilization advanced, Man, no longer content with the natural but inconvenient abode thus offered to him, excavated chambers for himself, and in places the whole face of the rock is honeycombed with doors and windows leading into suites of rooms,

---

[1] *De l'Origine et de l'Enfance des Arts en Perigord*, par M. l'Abbé Audierne.

often in tiers one over another, so as to suggest the idea of a French "Petra." Down to a comparatively recent period, as, for instance, in the troublous times of the Middle Ages, many of these, no doubt, served as very efficient fortifications, and even now some of them are still in use as storehouses, and for other purposes, as at Brantôme, where there is an old chapel cut in the solid rock. Apart from the scientific interest, it was impossible not to enjoy the beauty of the scene which passed before our eyes as we dropped down the Vezére. As the river visited sometimes one side of its valley, sometimes the other, so we had at one moment rich meadowlands on each side, or found ourselves close to the perpendicular and almost overhanging cliff. Here and there we came upon some picturesque old castle, and though the trees were not in full leaf, the rocks were in many places green with box and ivy and evergreen oak, which harmonized well with the rich yellow brown of the stone itself.

But to return to the bone-caves. Remains of the cave-bear have been found at the Pey de l'Azé, of the cave-hyæna at Le Moustier, and separated plates of elephant molars have occurred at Le Moustier and at Laugerie, accompanied at the latter place by a piece of a pelvis. As regards the two first species, MM. Christy and Lartet regard them as probably belonging to an earlier period than the human remains found in the same caves. The presence of the pelvis has been regarded as an evidence of the contemporaneity of the mammoth with the reindeer hunters of Laugerie, and it is certainly difficult to see why they should have brought a fossil-bone into their cave, more especially as the bones of elephants, from the looseness of their texture, are not well adapted for implements.

As regards the *Felis spelæa*, a metacarpal bone belonging probably to this species, and bearing marks of knives, was found in the cave of Les Eyzies.

Still, so far as the positive zoological evidence is concerned, the antiquity of the human remains found in these grottos rests mainly on the presence of the reindeer, as regards which the evidence is conclusive. The bones of this species are all broken open for the marrow ; many of them bear the marks of knives, and at Les Eyzies a vertebra was found which had been pierced by a flint flake. MM. Christy and Lartet are quite satisfied that this bone must have been fresh when it was thus transfixed. Moreover, as we shall presently see, there is still more conclusive evidence that man and the reindeer were contemporaneous in this locality.

But in its negative aspect, the zoological evidence is also very instructive. No remains have been found which, in the opinion of MM. Christy and Lartet, can be referred to domestic animals. It is true that bones of the ox and horse occur, but there is no evidence that they belonged to domesticated individuals. Remains of the boar are very rare, and if these animals had been domesticated we might have expected to find them in greater abundance. The sheep and goat are entirely wanting, and, what is still more remarkable, even the dog appears to be absent. At the same time, the bones of the horse and reindeer, especially of the latter, are very numerous ; but MM. Christy and Lartet do not think that they were domesticated. On the other hand, M. Rütimeyer seems to be of a different opinion.[1] Of the bones from the cave of Veyrier he has drawn out the following list : Ptarmigan 31 individuals, reindeer 18, ibex 6, horse 5, stag 4, mountain hare 4, marmot 4, chamois 1, wolf 1, bear 1, ox 1, fox 1, stork 1. He points out that this is decidedly an Alpine fauna, and he asks why, if the reindeer were wild, they did not retire into the high Alps with the bear, the ibex, and the chamois ? The condition of the bones, and especially of the horns, will enable us some day to answer this question, but we have at present no case in which the reindeer and the horse are held in domestication together by the same race, and we must be satisfied to wait for further evidence before the question can be decided.

In the collections made by MM. Christy and Lartet, as

[1] *Revue Savoisienne*, 25th April 1868.

well as that of M. Le Vicomte de Lastic from Bruniquel, a very large proportion of the animal remains consists of teeth, lower jaws, and horns. Other bones do indeed occur, but they form a small fraction of the whole. Yet we cannot attribute this to the presence of dogs, partly because no remains of this species have yet been discovered, partly because the bones which remain have not been gnawed, but principally because dogs eat only certain bones and parts of bones, as a general rule selecting the spongy portions, and rejecting the solid shafts.

Sir F. Galton has pointed out that some of the savage tribes of Africa, not content with the flesh of the animals which they kill, pound up also the bones in mortars, and then suck out the animal juices contained in them. So also, according to Leems, the Danish Laplanders used to break up with a mallet all the bones which contained any fat or marrow, and then boil them until all the fat was extracted.[1] The Esquimaux also mash up the bones for the sake of the marrow contained in them.[2] Some of the ancient stone hammers and mortars were no doubt used for this purpose, and the proportions of the different bones afford us, I think, indirect evidence that a similar custom prevailed among the ancient inhabitants of southern France.

Passing on now to the flint implements found in these caves, we must first call attention to their marvellous abundance. Without any exaggeration they may be said to be innumerable. Of course this adds greatly to the value of the conclusions ; nor need it surprise us, because flint is so brittle, that implements made of it must have been easily broken, and, in that case, the fragments would be thrown away as useless ; especially in a chalk district where the supply of flint would, of course, be practically inexhaustible. Many implements, no doubt, would be left unfinished, having been rendered useless, either by some misdirected blow, or some flaw

[1] *Account of Danish Lapland*, by Leems, Copenhagen, 1767 ; translated in Pinkerton's *Voyages*, vol. i. p. 396.
[2] Hall, *Life with the Esquimaux*, vol. ii. pp. 147, 176.

in the flint. Moreover, we should naturally expect that, in a bone-breccia of this nature, the flint implements would be relatively more abundant than in a Kjökkenmödding. Each oyster furnishes but a single mouthful, so that the edible portions evidently form a greater proportion of the whole in the mammalia than in the mollusca. The Kjökkenmöddings, therefore, would grow, *cæteris paribus*, more rapidly than the bone-breccia ; and supposing the flint implements to be equally numerous in both cases, they would, of course, be more sparingly distributed in the former than in the latter.

The principal objects of stone found in the bone-caves which we are now considering are flakes, both simple and worked, scrapers, cores, awls, lance-heads, cutters, hammers, and mortar-stones.

The simple and worked flakes are, of course, very numerous, but they do not call for any special observations. They present the usual varieties of size and form.

Though less numerous than the flakes, the scrapers[1] are still very abundant. On the whole, they seem to me longer and narrower than the usual Danish type. Some of them were probably intended to be used in the hand, as both ends are fashioned for scraping. They may be called double-scrapers. Others were apparently fixed in handles, as the end opposite to the scraper is broken, sometimes on one side, sometimes on both, so as to form a tapering extremity, which may have been fixed in a handle either of wood, bone, or horn. Many of the flakes are also nipped off at one end, in the same manner. Perhaps, as no trace of such a handle has yet been discovered by MM. Christy and Lartet, wood was the material used for this purpose.

Of course, where there was a manufactory of flint flakes, the cores or nuclei, from which they were struck, must also be present. I was, however, astonished at the number of them in these caves ; during my short visit, I myself picked out more than ninety.

Awls and saws are very much less frequent, but some

[1] See *ante*, pp. 94, 95.

few good specimens have been found. At some of the stations, curious flat implements (fig. 217) are met with. From the constancy of their form, which, moreover, is somewhat peculiar, we may safely infer that they were applied to some definite purpose. For hammers, the reindeer hunters seem to have used round stones, a good many of which occur in the caves, and which bear unmistakable marks of the purpose to which they were applied. Some of them, however, may have served also as heaters. The North American Indians, the Esquimaux, and some other savages, having no pottery, but only wooden vessels, which could not be put on the fire, used to heat stones, and then place them in the water which they wished to boil. Many of the stones found in these caverns appear to have been used in this manner, firstly from their position on the lower terraces, and secondly from the character of the implements.

FIG. 217.—Flat stone implement of uncertain use, actual size.

These, the commonest sorts of flint implements, are found indiscriminately in all the grottos, but there are some other types which appear to be less generally distributed. Thus, at Laugerie and Badegoule, fragments of leaf-shaped lance-heads, almost as well worked as some of those from Denmark, are far from uncommon. If, therefore, we were to attempt any classification of the grottos, according to the periods of their occupation, we might be disposed to refer these to a somewhat later period than most of the others. On the contrary, to judge from the flint implements, the station at Le Moustier would be the most ancient. Though it would perhaps be premature to attempt any such classification, there can be no doubt that Le Moustier presents some types not yet found in the other caves, and resembling in certain respects those of the drift.

One of these peculiar forms has one side left unchipped, and apparently intended to be held in the hand, while the other has a cutting edge, produced by a number of small blows.   Some of these instruments are of large size, and they are supposed by MM. Christy and Lartet to have been used for cutting wood, and perhaps also the large bones of mammalia. Another very interesting type is figured in figs. 218-220. This specimen is worked on both sides, but more frequently one of them is left flat. MM. Christy and Lartet regard this type as identical with the " lance-head " implements found in the drift. I cannot altogether agree with them in this comparison.   Not only are the Le Moustier specimens smaller, but the workmanship is different, being much less bold. Moreover, the flat surface (fig. 218, A) is no individual peculiarity.   It is very frequently, not to say generally, present, and occurs also on the similar implement found by Mr Boyd Dawkins in the Hyæna-den at Wokey Hole, and figured by him in the *Geological Journal*, May 1862, No. 70, p. 119.   This very interesting type seems rather to be derived from the " cutters " above described, at the same time its resemblance to the drift forms is certainly great.   MM. Christy and Lartet, indeed, call the implements of this type " lance-heads " ; but it may well be doubted whether they were intended for use in this manner, though there

FIG. 218.—Stone implement, resembling in some respects those characteristic of the drift gravels, actual size.

are other specimens at Le Moustier which have all the appearance of having been intended for this purpose. On the whole, then, although these Le Moustier types are of great interest, we must pause before we regard them as belonging to the drift forms. No polished implements have yet been found in any of these caverns.

The station at Moustier has not as yet produced any implements made of bone, but a good many have been obtained from the other caves. " They consist of square chisel-shaped implements ; round, sharply-pointed, awl-like tools, some of which also may have served as the spike of a fish-hook ; harpoon-shaped lance-heads ; plain or barbed arrow-heads with many and double barbs, cut with wonderful vigour ; and lastly, eyed needles of compact bone finely pointed, polished, and drilled with round eyes, so small and regular that some of the most

FIG. 219.—Fig. 218, seen from the side.

FIG. 220.—Fig. 218, seen from the other side.

assured and acute believers in all the other findings might well doubt whether they could indeed have been drilled with stone, until their repetition by the hand of that practical and conscientious observer, Monsieur Lartet, by the very stone implements found with them, has dispelled their honest doubts."[1] Moreover, we must remember that the New Zealanders were able with their stone tools to drill holes even through glass.[2] No pottery has yet been found in these caves. It is doubtful whether the bow was in use, but it is interesting that they seem to have invented the throwing-stick.

So far, then (with the exception, perhaps, of the well-worked lance-heads of Laugerie and Badegoule), all the evidence we have yet obtained from these caves points to a very primitive period, earlier even than that of the first Swiss lake-villages, or Danish shell-mounds.

But there is one class of objects in these caves which, taken alone, might have led us to a very different conclusion. No representation, however rude, of any animal has yet been found in any of the Danish shell-mounds, or the Stone Age lake-villages. Even on objects of the Bronze Age they are so rare that it is doubtful whether a single well-authenticated instance could be produced. Yet in these archaic bone-caves, many very fair sketches have been found, scratched on bone or stone with a sharp point, probably of a flint implement. In some cases there is even an attempt at shading. In the *Annales des Sciences Naturelles*,[3] M. Lartet had already made known to us some rude drawings found in the cave of Savigné, and in his last memoir he has described and figured some more objects of a similar character.

In the Dordogne caves also, several of these remark-

FIG. 221.—A cylindrical piece of reindeer horn, on which are engraved two outlines of fishes, one on each side.

---

[1] Christy, *Trans. Ethn. Soc.*, New Series, vol. iii.
[2] Cook's *First Voyage*, p. 464.
[3] *Ann. des Sc. Nat.*, 1861, vol. xv.

able drawings have been discovered, under circumstances
which seem to guarantee their authenticity. Fig. 221
represents a cylindrical piece of reindeer's horn, found at
La Madelaine, and on
which are carved two
outlines of fishes, one
on each side. Fig.
222 is the piece of
the palm of a rein-
deer's horn, on which
is represented the
head and chest of an
ibex. Fig. 223 repre-
sents a very curious
group, consisting of
a snake, or rather eel,
a human figure, and
two horses' heads.

FIG. 222.—Piece of the palm of a reindeer's
antler, on which is engraved the head and neck
of an ibex.

Fig. 224 is a spirited group of rein-
deer, and fig. 225 is considered to represent a mammoth ;
it was found at La Madelaine, and the engraving was for
some time unnoticed, as it is rather faint and obscured by
numerous scratches. It is on a piece of mammoth's tusk,
and indications of long hair will readily be perceived.

FIG. 223.—Group of figures.

In one case there is an unmistakable representation of
a glove, or rather gauntlet. Another interesting specimen
is a poniard cut out of a reindeer's horn (fig. 226).
The horns are thrown back on the neck, the forelegs are
doubled up under the belly, and the hindlegs are stretched
out along the blade. Unfortunately, the poniard seems
to have been thrown away before it was quite finished,
but several of the details indicate that the animal was

intended for a reindeer. Messrs Dawkins and Miall have also found an engraving of a horse on a bone from the Caves of Creswell Crags. Many other specimens have since been discovered. In a cave at Combarelles, near Tayac, MM. Capitan and Breuil found 64 figures of entire animals and 43 heads (see figs. 207, 213) : equine 23, bovine 3, bisons 2, reindeer 3, mammoths 14, ibex 3, *Antilope saiga*, 4.[1] Besides these primitive sculptures and engravings coloured pictures have been found. The

FIG. 224.—Group of reindeer.

first were discovered by M. de Sautuola in the cave of Altamira near Santander (Spain) in 1875 (see figs. 206, 212, and Plates). Some years later M. Rivière found others in the cave of La Mouthe, M. Daleau in the Gironde, and M. Moissan in the classical locality of Les Eyzies. MM. Capitan and Breuil have more recently discovered a long series in the cave of Font-de-Gaume. Some of the horses have drawings on them which almost seem to represent coverings and halters, and to indicate that they were domesticated.[2] Although it is natural to feel some surprise at finding these works of art, still there

---

[1] "Gravures paléo. de la Grotte des Combarelles," *Bull. Soc. Anthr.*, Paris, 1902.

[2] *Rev. de l'École d'Anthropologie*, 1902, p. 39.

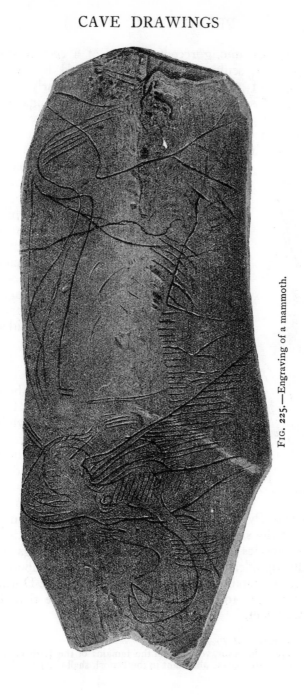

FIG. 225.—Engraving of a mammoth.

are instances among recent savages of a certain skill in drawing and sculpture being accompanied by an entire ignorance of metallurgy. This is particularly the case with the Esquimaux, some of whose drawings will be reproduced in a future chapter. M. Delechette gives[1] a list of twenty French and Spanish caves on the walls of which drawings occur.

FIG. 226.—Poniard of reindeer horn.

In considering the probable condition of these ancient cave-men, we must give them full credit for their love of art, such as it was ; while, on the other hand, the want of metal, of polished flint implements, and even of pottery,[2] the ignorance of agriculture, and the apparent absence of all domestic animals, including even the dog, certainly imply a very low state of civilization and a very considerable antiquity.

There is also evidence that a considerable change of climate must have taken place. The reindeer is the most abundant animal, and evidently formed the principal article of food ; while we know that this species is now confined to Arctic climates, and could not exist in the south of France. Again, the ibex and the chamois, both of which are now restricted to the snowy summits of the Alps and Pyrenees, and a species of spermophilus, also point to the same conclusion. The presence of the two former species in some of the Swiss lake-dwellings is not equally significant, because they are in the neighbourhood of high mountains, while the highest hills of the Dordogne do not reach to an altitude of much more than eight hundred feet.

---

[1] *Man. d'Archéol. Préhist.*, p. 241.
[2] Pottery is, however, very rare in the remains of the Irish crannoges, and is not by any means abundant in the Danish shell-mounds.

Another very interesting species determined by M. Lartet is the *Antilope Saïgo* of Pallas, which now abounds on the steppes of North-Eastern Europe and Western Asia, in the plains of the Dnieper and the Volga, round the shores of the Caspian, and as far as the Altai Mountains. Mr Christy tells us that the northern plains of Poland, and the valley of the Dnieper, are the southern limits of this species at the present day.

Again, the accumulation of animal remains in these caves is itself, as Mr Christy has ingeniously suggested, a good evidence of change in the climate. We know that the Esquimaux at present allow a similar deposit to take place in their dwellings, but this can only be done in Arctic regions ; in such a climate as that now existing in the south of France, such an accumulation would, except of course in the depth of winter, soon become intolerably offensive.

So far, then, as the present evidence relating to the Dordogne Caves is concerned, it appears to indicate a race of men living almost as some of the Esquimaux do now, and as the Laplanders did a few hundred years ago ; and a period intermediate between that of the polished stone implements and of the great extinct mammalia ; apparently also somewhat more ancient than that of the shell-mound builders of Denmark. The cases in which the remains of cave-men have been found in association with those of the cave-tiger, the cave-bear, the cave-hyæna, and the mammoth, are, I think, conclusive evidence that they must be referred to the same period.

As regards the earliest races of men themselves, we have, unfortunately, but very little information. For, although fragmentary human bones have been frequently found, there are, as yet, very few cases on record in which skulls have been obtained in such a condition as to allow of restoration, or of which the age is incontestable. For instance, remains of man, though rare in the loëss, have been described by Ami Boué, Faudel, Crahay, Wurmbrand, Ecker, and others ; but, as the latter has himself suggested,[1] from the composition of loëss, and from the habit of making underground chambers in it, which make

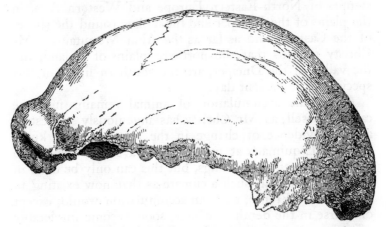

FIG. 227.—The Neanderthal skull, seen from the side, one-half natural size.

excellent cellars, and even dwellings—so to say, cave-dwellings—it is difficult to satisfy oneself that the remains are clearly contemporaneous with the deposit of the loëss.

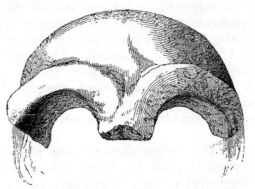

FIG. 228.—Ditto, seen from the front.

The earliest remains of man found in Northern Europe belong to three well-marked types, the Neanderthal, Cromagnon, and Chancelade types. A skull of the Nean-

<hr />

[1] *Archiv für Anthropologie*, 1875, p. 99.

derthal type was acquired in 1700, by Duke Eberhard of
Würtemberg, from Cannstatt, near Stuttgart, but not
described until the year 1835. The skulls of this type
are narrow and low, with very large frontal ridges. To
it belongs the celebrated skull (figs. 227–229) found in a
limestone cave in the Neanderthal, near Hochdal, between
Düsseldorf and Elberfeld. This remarkable specimen was

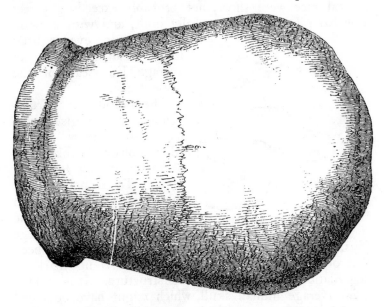

FIG. 229.—-The Neanderthal skull, seen from above, one-half natural size.

first described by Schaafhausen,[1] and "under whatever
aspect," says Prof. Huxley,[2] "we view this cranium,
whether we regard its vertical depression, the enormous
thickness of its supraciliary ridges, its sloping occiput,
or its long and straight squamosal suture, we meet
with ape-like characters, stamping it as the most pithe-
coid of human crania yet discovered." The shape of
this skull is so remarkable, that as long as it stood
alone considerable doubt was naturally felt whether, in the

[1] Muller's *Archiv*, 1858 ; *Nat. Hist. Rev.*, 1861.
[2] *Loc. cit.*, p. 156.

words of Busk, it represented "an individual peculiarity or a typical character." Subsequently, however, two other skulls, almost identical in form, have been discovered in the talus at the outside of a cave at Spy, in Belgium (fig. 230). These skulls, though not entirely, were more complete, and were associated with other bones, indicating a short, robust, prognathous race.[1] The Neanderthal race were short, not probably exceeding 5 feet 4 inches ; but very powerfully built, and with a brain as large as, or even a little larger than, that of an average European of the present day.

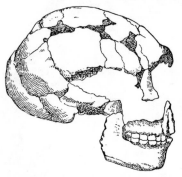

FIG. 230.—The Spy skull.

The second, the "Cromagnon" or "Engis" type, has also narrow skulls, which, however, unlike those of the preceding type, are high. To it belongs the celebrated skull, discovered by Dr Schmerling in the cave of Engis, near Liége (figs. 231–232). As regards form, it might have been that of a modern European. "There is no mark of degradation about any part of its structure. It is, in fact, a fair average human skull, which might have belonged to a philosopher, or might have contained the thoughtless brains of a savage."[2] To the same type belong the skulls found at Cromagnon, in the Dordogne.[3] It was a tall race, in some cases attaining, or even exceeding, six feet.

Several other skulls, more or less imperfect, of this type have since been discovered, amongst which may be specially mentioned a woman's skull from a Gibraltar cave, a skeleton found at La Chapelle in the Corrèze (fig. 233), two in the Dordogne, and a skull from Salley Hill, near Northfleet.

[1] Poydt and Lohert, *Ann. Soc. Biol. Belgique,* 1886.
[2] Huxley, *Man's Place in Nature,* p. 156.
[3] *Reliquiæ Aquitanicæ,* part vi.

The third, or Chancelade, race is represented by one

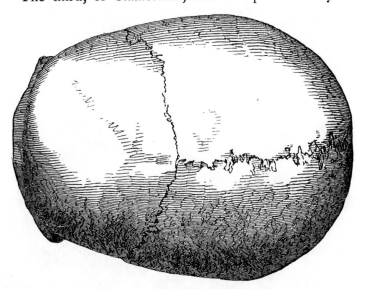

FIG. 231.—The Engis skull, seen from above.

well-preserved skull (fig. 234), described by M. Testut.[1]
It belonged to a man about five feet high, who Prof. Sollas,

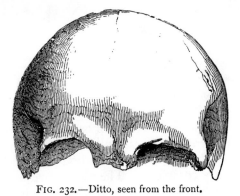

FIG. 232.—Ditto, seen from the front.

President of the Geological Society, in his annual address
for 1909, says "was beyond doubt an Eskimo." That

[1] *Bull. Soc. Anthrop.*, Lyon, vol. viii., 1889.

the Esquimaux once extended to Western Europe I quite believe. We find not only the animals with which they are even now associated, but implements closely resembling, it might almost be said identical with, those which they still use.

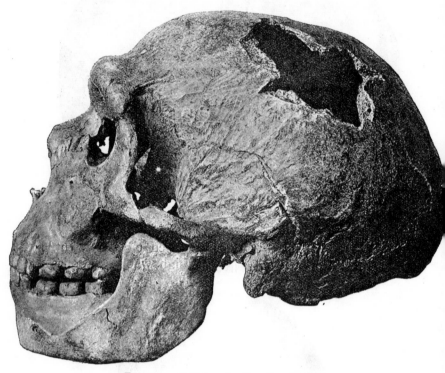

FIG. 233.—Skull from La Chapelle aux Saints.

The remains of a fourth race have been discovered in the caves at Mentone, so carefully examined by the Prince of Monaco. Remains of sixteen bodies were found, two of them nearly complete. The skulls are of a distinctly Negroid type.[1] No remains of this race have yet been found in Northern Europe.

They have been described by M. Verneau, and, in

[1] Verneau, *Les Grottes de Grimaldi,* 1906

M. Piette's opinion, belonged to a race resembling the present Bushmen or Hottentots.

These four races of men, while presenting certain ape-like characters, and, in the Neanderthal race at any rate, a very savage and brutal aspect, have large brains, and are unmistakably human. This cannot be said for the skull, or rather skull-top, discovered about twenty years ago by Dr Dubois in Java, at a depth of thirty feet, in gravel, which may be either pliocene or pleistocene. The skull is so low and flat as much to resemble, though much larger than, that of an existing Gibbon. The brain represented about 900 units, the average for the Gorilla being about 500, for the Australian 1200, and the European 1500. There has been much difference of opinion among anatomists as to whether it was that of a man or a monkey, and having had, through the courtesy of Dr Dubois, an opportunity of carefully examining it, I feel much doubt whether it should be described as that of a large Gibbon, or as belonging to a man of a very small and distinct race.

FIG. 234.—Skull from Chancelade (Dordogne).

But the most ape-like of all, except of course the *Pithecanthropus* of Java (fig. 235), are the remains recently discovered by Mr Dawson at Piltdown near Uckfield in Sussex. The lower jaw, if found by itself, would certainly have been referred to an anthropoid ape, though the teeth are decidedly human. The skull is of great thickness, and happily well enough preserved to permit of a cast showing the brain, which is of so lowly a type that Prof. Elliot Smith doubts whether the creature possessed the power of articulate speech. Though more a man than a monkey, both he and Dr A. S. Woodward consider it to be not only a different species, but even to differ generically.

All the remains which can be regarded as certainly

palæolithic are long-headed, or dolichocephalic. The short-headed race has not been proved to have reached Western Europe till the Neolithic Period. Some archæologists, indeed, are disposed to consider that the advent of this race coincides with the commencement of the Neolithic Period.

Even, however, in Palæolithic times, Europe appears

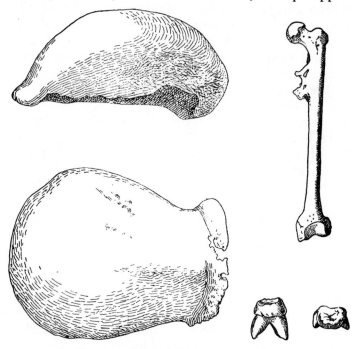

FIG. 235.—Bones of *Pithecanthropus erectus*.

to have been already occupied by more than one race of man. Under these circumstances, great as is undoubtedly the antiquity of these remains, they do not in any way represent the earliest men, but there must have been another, and perhaps still longer period, in which these varieties were gradually developed ; and Prof. Huxley was of opinion that " they indicate an epoch more distant from the age of the *Elephas primigenius* than that is from us."

If space permitted, I would gladly have referred to other cave explorations ; to those, for instance, of Dr Regnoli and others in Italy, of the Marquis de Vibraye, M. Garrigou, M. Bourguignet, M. Filhol, and many other archæologists in the south of France, where these researches have been prosecuted with great energy and success.   In our own country, Mr Boyd Dawkins has published an excellent work on the subject,[1] and it is impossible in the limits of a single chapter to do justice to these and other observers.

I trust, then, that the evidence brought forward in this chapter has been sufficient to prove that the presence in bone-caves of ancient implements and human remains, associated with those of extinct mammalia, is no rare or exceptional phenomenon.   Nor, if we look at the question from a scientific point of view, is there anything in this that ought to excite our astonishment.   Since the period at which these caves were filled up, the changes which have taken place have resulted rather in the extinction than in the creation of species.   The stag, the horse, the boar, the dog, in short, all our existing forms of mammalia, were already in existence ; and there would have been in reality more just cause for surprise if man alone had been unrepresented.

[1] *Cave-Hunting.*

CHAPTER XI

WHILE we have been straining our eyes to the East, and eagerly watching excavations in Egypt and Assyria, suddenly a new light has arisen in the midst of us ; and the oldest relics of man yet discovered have occurred, not among the ruins of Nineveh or Heliopolis, not on the sandy plains of the Nile or the Euphrates, but in the pleasant valleys of England and France, along the banks of the Seine and the Somme, the Thames and the Waveney.

So unexpected were these discoveries, so irreconcilable with even the greatest antiquity until lately assigned to the human race, that they were long regarded with neglect and suspicion. M. Boucher de Perthes, to whom we are principally indebted for this great step in the history of mankind, observed, as long ago as the year 1841, in some sand containing mammalian remains, at Menchecourt, near Abbeville, a flint, rudely fashioned into a cutting instrument. In the following years other weapons were found under similar circumstances, and especially during the formation of the Champ de Mars at Abbeville, where a large quantity of gravel was moved and many of the so-called "hatchets" were discovered. In the year 1846, M. Boucher de Perthes published his first work on the subject, entitled *De l'Industrie Primitive, ou les Arts et leur Origine*. In this he announced that he had found human implements in beds unmistakably belonging to the Age of the Drift. In his *Antiquités Celtiques et Antédiluviennes* (1847), he also gave numerous illustrations of these stone weapons, but unfortunately the figures were rude, and did but scanty justice to the originals. For seven years M. Boucher de Perthes made few converts; he was looked upon as an enthusiast, almost as a madman. At length, in 1853, Dr Rigollot, till then sceptical, examined for himself the drift-beds at the now celebrated St Acheul near Amiens, found several weapons, and believed. Still the new creed met with but little favour; prophets are proverbially without honour in their own country, and M. Boucher de Perthes was no exception to the rule. At last, however, the tide turned in his favour. In 1859 Dr Falconer examined his collection, and on his return to England called the attention of English geologists, and especially of Sir J. Prestwich, and of Sir John Evans, to the importance of his discoveries.

My first visit to the Somme valley was made in company with Sir John Evans, Mr Busk, Sir D. Galton, and Sir J. Prestwich in 1860, and I communicated the results to the *Natural History Review*, in an article "On the Evidence of the Antiquity of Man afforded by the Physical Structure of the Somme Valley." [1] I have seen no reason to modify the general conclusions contained in that article, of which, indeed, this chapter is in the main a reprint.

We examined carefully not only the flint weapons, but also the beds in which they were found. For such an investigation, indeed, our two countrymen were especially qualified: Sir J. Prestwich, from his long study and profound knowledge of the tertiary and quaternary strata; and Sir J. Evans, from his intimate acquaintance with the stone implements belonging to what we must now consider as the second, or at least the more recent, Stone Period. On our return to England, Sir J. Prestwich communicated the results of his visit to the Royal Society, [2] while Sir J. Evans described the implements themselves in the *Transactions of the Society of Antiquaries.* [3]

---

[1] *Natural History Review*, 1862, pp. 244–269.
[2] "On the Occurrence of Flint Implements associated with the Remains of Extinct Species, in Beds of a late Geological Period," *Phil. Trans.*, 1860.
[3] "Flint Implements in the Drift," *Archæologia*, 1860–62.

This important discovery is due to M. Boucher de
Perthes. There has, however, long been in the British
Museum a similar stone weapon, described as follows :—
" No. 246. A British weapon, *found with elephant's tooth*,
opposite to Black Mary's, near Grayes inn lane. Conyers."
It has a large black flint, shaped into the figure of a

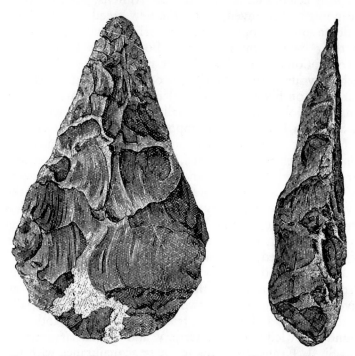

FIG. 236.—Rude flint implement from the drift   FIG. 237.—Ditto, side
gravel at Hoxne, one-half actual size.   view.

spear's point. Sir J. Evans tells us, moreover (*loc. cit.*,
p. 22), that a rude engraving of it illustrates a letter on
the " Antiquities of London," by Mr Bagford, dated 1715,
printed in Hearne's edition of *Leland's Collectanea*, vol. i.
6, p. lxiii. From his account it seems to have been
found with a *skeleton* of an elephant, in the presence of
Mr Conyers. This most interesting weapon agrees exactly
with some of those found in the valley of the Somme.

Sir J. Evans, on his return from Abbeville, observed in the museum belonging to the Society of Antiquaries some specimens exactly like those in the collection of M. Boucher de Perthes. On examination, it proved that they had been presented by Mr Frere, who found them with bones of extinct animals in a gravel-pit at Hoxne in Suffolk, and had well described and figured them in the *Archæologia* for the year 1800. This communication is of so much interest that I have thought it desirable to reproduce his figures (figs. 236–237, 239–240).

Excavations undertaken at Hoxne under the auspices of the British Association[1] have shown that the brick earth containing the palæolithic implements lie over glacial boulder clay. Mr

FIG. 238.—Stone implement, Madras.

Clement Reid has shown that similar relations also occur in the Hitchin valley.[2]

Again, in 1835, Mr Whitburn, of Godalming,[3] while examining the gravel pits between Guildford and Godalming, remarked a peculiar flint, which he carried away, and has since preserved in his collection. It

[1] *Report*, 1896.   [2] *Geol. Mag.*, 1897.
[3] Prestwich, *Jour. Geol. Soc.*, August 1861.

belongs to the "drift" type, but is very rude. Thus, this peculiar type of flint implement has been actually

FIG. 239.—Palæolithic implement.   FIG. 240.—The same, side view.

found in association with the bones of the mammoth on various occasions during nearly a hundred and fifty years ! While, however, these instances remarkably corroborate the statements made by M. Boucher de

Perthes, they in no way detract from the credit due to that gentleman.

In addition to the above-mentioned, similar hatchets have been found in various other localities, as for instance by Mr Warren, at Icklingham; by Mr Leech, near Herne Bay; by Sir John Evans himself at Abbot's Langley and elsewhere; by Mr Norman at Greenstreet Green in Kent; by Messrs Whitaker and Hughes, near Dartford; in fact, similar discoveries have been made in most of our south-eastern counties.

FIG. 241.—Reconstructed flint, Thames valley.

Mr Spurrell actually found near Crayford in Kent the spot where some of these ancient men had been making their implements. It was on the bank of the Thames, and, probably by some flood, had been covered over with loam, which had then accumulated to some depth without disturbing the flakes and chips. The illustration (fig. 242) shows the chalk cliff, the brick earth and the floor on which the flakes were lying. By great patience he found some that fitted, and he was even able to reconstruct the original flint. Fig. 241, from the *Journal of the Geological Society*,[1] shows one of these reconstructed flints. One of

---

[1] *Geol. Soc.*, 1880.

the pieces has J. L. on it. Mr Spurrell has found all the rest, and the day I was with him I found this flake, which completes the specimen.

In the gravel near Bedford, again, associated with the remains of the mammoth, rhinoceros, hippopotamus, ox, horse, and deer, Mr Wyatt[1] has found flint implements resembling both of the two principal types found at Abbeville and Amiens. This case is interesting, because it shows that the drift flint hatchets are subsequent to the boulder clay ; the Bedford valley being cut through hills capped by a deposit of that period.

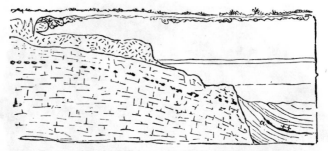

FIG. 242.—Section of Bank of Thames near Dartford, where fig. 241 was found.

Prestwich, however, tells us that " the great masses of gravel in the neighbourhood of Mildenhall and Lackenheath, also containing flint implements, . . . seem to me to be part of the phenomena connected with the passage of the great Ice-sheet over the Eastern Counties, and on that score pre-glacial."[2] Mr Harrison of Ightham in Kent has also discovered palæolithic implements in the high level plateau gravels near Sevenoaks, which have no reference to the present lines of river drainage, but must have been deposited by water running several hundred feet above the level of the present rivers.

The number of localities on the Continent in which stone implements have been obtained from beds of the quaternary period has also largely increased.

---

[1] *Flint Implements in the Drift*, by J. Wyatt. Bedfordshire Architectural and Archæological Society, 1862.

[2] *Quart. Jour. Geol. Soc.*, 1887, p. 406.

Palæolithic implements have not yet, so far as I am aware, been found in Scandinavia, or in England north of Saltley in Warwickshire (where a specimen was discovered by Mr Landon) and Bridlington in Yorkshire. It has been supposed, and seems probable, that this is due to the glacial conditions then prevailing in the north ; but it must be remembered that flint is scarce in the north, and the river gravels have not been so thoroughly searched as those further south.

Stone implements, more or less resembling those characteristic of the Palæolithic Age, have also been found in other parts of the world, as, for instance, in Assyria, Algeria, and Hindostan. I myself found some in the Egyptian Desert near Thebes in 1872. The Indian specimens were first described by Mr Bruce Foote[1] : they were found in the Madras and North

FIG. 243.—Stone implement from Madras.

Arcot districts, and are of quartzite, and in several cases were found by Messrs Foote and King *in situ* at depths of from three to ten feet. The specimens figured (figs. 238, 243) will show how closely they resemble our European specimens, and it is interesting that, in the

[1] *On the Occurrence of Stone Implements in Lateritic Formations in Various Parts of the Madras and North Arcot Districts*, by R. Bruce Foote.

words of Mr Foote, "the area, over which the lateritic formations were spread, has undergone, as already stated,

FIG. 244.—Palæolithic flint implement.

great changes since their deposition. A great part of the formation has been removed by denudation, and deep valleys cut into them, now occupied by the alluvium of various rivers."[1] Unfortunately, no bones have yet been found in these beds. Worked agates have also been found in the deposits of the Nerbudda, and in the bonebeds of the upper Godavery, "which are, there is little doubt, the same age as those of the Nerbudda, which contain *Elephas insignis*, *E. Namadacus*, *Hippopotamus palæindicus*, *Bos palæindicus*, and *B. Namadicus*."[2]

The implements found in the river gravel may be divided into several categories :—

(1) Hammers.

(2) Flakes. Figs. 86–98. These have been described on page 82. They commenced at the earliest period and came down to Roman times, so that though certain proofs of intention, they do not characterize any particular period.

(3) Scrapers. See p. 94. Almost the same may be said of these.

(4) Implements worked to a cutting edge at one side.

[1] *Loc. cit.*, p. 28.
[2] Blandford, *Geol. Magazine*, February 1866.

(5) Implements which, for want of a better name, we may call axes. They are left rough at one end, and are worked up to an edge at the other (fig. 245) being evidently intended to be held in the hand : or (fig. 244) they may be slightly worked at the butt end, so as to afford a better grip.

(6) Similar implements (figs. 247–249), worked down at the butt end, evidently in order that they might be invested in a handle. The free end is sometimes broad (figs. 244, 245), sometimes brought to a point (figs. 246, 249). Fig. 246 is from St Acheul ; fig. 249 represents a magnificent specimen from the valley of the Axe kindly presented to me by Mr Rolls.

(7) Flat ovoid implements (fig. 247), worked to an edge all round.

(8) The same with worked twist in the centre (fig. 248). These are so numerous, and the twist is so marked, that it cannot be accidental.

(9) Shaft-scrapers. These seem to have been used in the preparation of the shafts for javelins.

The specimens found in the Somme valley are, as I shall endeavour to show, connected with the present river system, and the same was the case with those first discovered in England. Further researches, however, have brought to light cases in which flint implements have been found in beds of gravel having no relation to the existing river systems. Mr Flower has called attention to several of these in our eastern counties, and I have had the advantage of visiting them with him. The Shrub Hill gravel-bed, for instance, is a low mound of gravel of about fifteen feet thick, rising in the middle of the fen near Ely, and surrounded on all sides by a low flat district. Mr Skertchly also has found flint implements in beds which he considers to be pre-glacial, but the evidence does not seem to be quite conclusive.

Some of the Hampshire specimens also have been found *in situ*, in a mass of drift gravel which covers the tertiary beds, and is intersected by all the streams which now run into the Southampton Water. This bed of gravel, moreover, is not confined to the mainland, but caps also the Foreland Cliffs on the east of the Isle of Wight, where an oval flint implement has recently been discovered by Mr T. Codrington. As Sir J. Evans has pointed out, we seem in this discovery to have clear evidence that man existed in this country before the Southampton Water was formed, or the Isle of Wight was separated from the mainland, and we may therefore regard these implements as among the most striking proofs of Man's Antiquity, which they carry back to a period far more ancient than that which had previously been assigned to him.

FIG. 245.—Palæolithic flint implement.

So great is the antiquity indicated by these stone implements, so improbable did it seem that man was a contemporary of the mammoth, the woolly-haired rhinoceros, etc., that we cannot wonder that the statement by Mr Frere has been distrusted for more than half a century; that the weapon found by Mr Conyers has lain unnoticed for more than double that time; that the discoveries by M. Boucher de Perthes have been ignored for fifteen years; that the numerous cases in which caves have contained the remains of men together with those of extinct animals have been suppressed or explained away: these facts show how deeply rooted was the conviction that man belonged altogether to a more recent order of things; and whatever other accusation may be brought against them, geologists can at least not be said to have hastily accepted the theory of the co-existence of the human race with the now extinct *Pachydermata* of Western Europe.

Although, however, geologists are now almost unanimous as to the great antiquity of these curious weapons, still it is not necessary that they should be received as judges ; I only propose to summon them as witnesses.

The questions to be decided may be stated as follows :—

1st. Are the so-called flint implements of human workmanship ?

2ndly. Are the flint implements of the same age as the beds in which they are found, and the bones of the extinct animals with which they occur ?

3rdly. What are the conditions under which these beds were deposited ?   And how far are we justified in imputing to them a great antiquity ?

To the first two of these questions an affirmative answer would be given by every geologist.   " For more than twenty years," says Prof. Ramsay, " I have daily handled stones, whether fashioned by nature or art, and the flint hatchets

Fig. 246.—Palæolithic implement. One-half actual size.

of Amiens and Abbeville seem to me as clearly works of art as any Sheffield whittle." [1]   But best of all, an hour or two spent in examining the forms of ordinary flint gravel, would, I am sure, convince any man that these stones, rude though they be, were undeniably fashioned by the hand of man.

The stone implements of some modern savages are

[1] *Athenæum*, July 16, 1859.

quite as rude, and some even ruder, as, for instance, those of the Tasmanians, which were only flaked on one side and were held in the hand, not fixed into any handle.[1]

Still it might be supposed that they were forgeries made by ingenious workmen to entrap unwary geologists. They have, however, been actually found by Messrs Boucher de Perthes, Henslow, Christy, Flower, Wyatt, Evans, myself, and others (I might now say many others),

FIGS. 247, 248.—Palæolithic implements.   One-half actual size.

under circumstances which preclude all idea of deception. One seen, though not found, by himself *in situ*, is thus described by Sir J. Prestwich : " It was lying flat in the gravel at a depth of seventeen feet from the original surface and six and a half feet from the chalk.   One side slightly projected.   The gravel around was undisturbed, and presented its usual perpendicular face.   I carefully examined the specimen, and saw no reason to doubt that it was in its natural position, for the gravel is generally so loose, that a blow with a pick disturbs and brings it

[1] H. Ling Roth, *The Tasmanians*, pp. 156–8.

down for some way round ; and the matrix is too little adhesive to admit of its being built up again as before with the same materials. . . . I found also afterwards, on taking out the flint, that it was the thinnest side which projected, the other side being less finished and much thicker."[1] But evidence of this nature, though interesting, is unnecessary ; *the flints speak for themselves.* Many of them are more or less rolled or worn at the edges. Those which have lain in siliceous or chalky sands are more or less polished, and have a beautiful glossiness of surface, very unlike that of a newly broken flint. In ochreous sand, especially if argillaceous, they are stained yellow, whilst in ferruginous sands and clays they assume

FIG. 249.—Another specimen. One-half actual size.

a brown colour, and in some beds they become white and porcellaneous. In many cases, moreover, they have encrustations of carbonate of lime and small dendritic

[1] *Phil. Trans.*, 1860, p. 292.

markings. The freshly-broken chalk flints, on the contrary, are of a dull black or leaden colour ; they vary a little in darkness but not in colour, and do not present white or yellow facings ; moreover, the new surfaces are dead, and want the glossiness of those which have been exposed. It is almost unnecessary to say that they have no dendritic markings, nor are they encrusted by carbonate of lime.

Now the forgeries—for there *are* forgeries—differ from the genuine implements by just those characteristics which distinguish newly-broken flints from those which have lain long in sand or gravel, or exposed to atmospheric agencies. They are black, never white or yellow ; their surfaces are not glossy, but dull and lustreless, and they have no dendritic markings or encrustations. Nor would it be possible for an ingenious rogue to deceive us by taking a stained flint and fashioning it into a hatchet, because the discoloration of the flint is quite superficial, seldom more than a quarter of an inch in thickness, and follows the outline of the present surface, showing that the change of colour was subsequent to the manufacture ; while if such a flint were tampered with, the fraud would be easily detected, as each blow would remove part of the outer coating, and expose the black flint inside (p. 83).

Moreover, it must be remembered, that when M. Boucher de Perthes' work was published, the weapons therein described were totally unlike any of those familiar to archæologists. Since that time, however, not only have similar implements been found in England, France, and other countries, but, as already mentioned, it has since come to light that similar weapons were in two cases actually described and figured in England many years ago, and that in both these instances they were found in association with the bones of extinct animals. On this point, therefore, no evidence could be more conclusive.

We may, then, pass on to the second subject, and consider whether the flint implements are as old as the beds in which they occur, and as the remains of extinct mammalia with which they are associated.

It has been suggested by some writers, that though they are really found in the mammaliferous gravel, they may be comparatively recent, and belong really to the Neolithic or later Stone Age, but have gradually sunk down from above by their own weight, or perhaps have been buried in artificial excavations.   There are, however, no cracks or fissures by which the hatchets could have reached their present positions, and the strata are too compact and immovable to admit of any such insinuation from the surface.   Nor could any ancient excavations have been made and filled in again without leaving evident traces of the change.   Moreover, we may in this case also appeal to the flint implements themselves, which, as we have already seen, agree in colour and appearance with the gravel in which they occur ; it is, therefore, only reasonable to infer that they have been subjected to the same influer.ces.   Moreover, if they belonged to the later Stone Period, and had found their way by any accident into these gravels, then they ought to correspond with the other flint implements of the Stone Period. But this is not the case.   The flakes, indeed, offer no peculiarities of form.   Similar splinters of flint, or obsidian, have been used in the absence of metal by savage tribes in almost all ages and all countries.   In the southeast of England the other implements, on the contrary, are very characteristic.   They are almost always made of flint, whereas many other minerals, such, for instance, as serpentine, jade, clayslate, etc., were used in the later Stone Age.   Their forms are also peculiar.   They present many differences, but may be classed, as already mentioned, under a few types.   Those with a heavy butt at one end, and a point at the other, are regarded by Sir John Evans[1] as having served as spear or lance heads.   He treats as a mere variety of this type those implements in which the cutting end is rounded off but not pointed.   Some of these, however, were evidently intended to be held in the

[1] *Loc. cit.*, 1860, p. 11.

hand, and probably served a different purpose ; they may, I think, fairly be considered as a fourth type, though it must be confessed that all these types run into one another, and in any large collection many intermediate forms may be found. The smaller end is, in all cases, the one adapted for cutting, while the reverse is almost invariably the case in the oval celts of the Neolithic Stone Age (figs. 106 and 107).

Again, the flint implements of the drift are never polished or ground, but are always left rough. Many thousands have now been found in the drift gravels of England and France, and of this large number there is not one which shows a trace of polishing or grinding ; while we know that the reverse was almost always the case with the celts of the later Stone Period. It is true that the latter is not an invariable rule ; thus, in Denmark there are two forms of so-called "axes" which are left rough—namely, the small triangular axes of the Kjökkenmöddings (figs. 117–119) which are invariably so, and the large square-sided axes with which this is often the case. But, though rough, these two forms of implements resemble in no other way those which are found in the drift, and could not for a moment be mistaken for them. It is not going too far to say that there is not a single well-authenticated instance of a "celt" being found in the drift, or of an implement of the drift type being discovered either in a tumulus or associated with remains of the later Stone Age.

It is useless to speculate upon the use made of these rude yet venerable weapons. Almost as well might we ask, to what use could they *not* be applied ? Numerous and specialized as are our modern instruments, who could describe the exact use of a knife ? But the primitive savage had no such choice of weapons ; we see before us perhaps the whole contents of his workshop ; and with these implements, rude as they seem to us, he cut down trees, scooped them out into canoes, grubbed up roots, attacked his enemies,[1] killed and cut up his food,

---

[1] Some savages even now fight with stones, which they simply hold in their hands.

made holes through the ice in winter, prepared fire-wood, etc.

The almost entire absence of human bones, which has appeared to some so inexplicable as to throw a doubt on the whole question, is, on consideration, less extraordinary than it might at first sight appear to be. If, for instance, we turn to other remains of human settlements, we shall find a repetition of the same phenomenon. Thus in the Danish shell-mounds where worked flints are by far more plentiful than in the St Acheul gravel, human bones are of the greatest rarity, only one piece in fact having ever been found. At that period, as in the Drift Age, mankind lived by hunting and fishing, and could not, therefore, be very numerous. In the era, however, of the Swiss lake - habitations, the case was different. M. Troyon estimates the population of the "Pfahlbauten" during the Stone Age at about 32,000 ; in the Bronze Era, 42,000. On these calculations, indeed, even their ingenious author would not probably place much reliance ; still the number of the lake-villages already known is very considerable ; in four of the Swiss lakes only, more than seventy have been discovered, and some of them were of great extent : Wangen, for instance, being, according to M. Lohle, supported on more than 50,000 piles. Yet, if we exclude a few bones of children, human remains have been obtained from these settlements in six cases only. The number of flint implements obtained hitherto from the drift of the Somme valley probably does not much exceed 5000[1] ; the settlement at Concise alone (Lake of Neufchâtel) has supplied about 24,000, and yet has not produced a single human skeleton.[2] Probably this absence of bones is in part attributable to the habit of burying or burning ; the instinct of man has long been in most cases to bury his dead out of sight. Still, so far as the drift of St Acheul is concerned, the

---

[1] One of the tumuli in the Mississippi valley is estimated to have alone contained nearly four thousand stone implements. This, however, is a very exceptional case.

[2] *Rapport à la Commission des Musées*, October, 1861, p. 16.

difficulty will altogether disappear, if we remember that *no trace has ever yet been found of any animal as small as a man.* Even of the elephant and rhinoceros, the ox, horse, and stag,[1] only the larger and more solid bones remain ; every vestige of the smaller ones has perished. No one supposes that this scanty list fairly represents the mammalian fauna of this time and place. When we find at St Acheul the remains of the wolf, boar, roedeer, badger, and other animals which existed during the Drift Period, then, and not till then, we may perhaps begin to wonder at the entire absence of human skeletons.

We must also remember that when man lived on the produce of the chase, there must have been a very large number of wild animals to each hunter. Among the Laplanders, 100 reindeer is the smallest number on which a man can subsist, and no one is considered rich who does not possess at least from 300 to 500. But these are domesticated, and a large supply of nourishment is derived from their milk. In the case of wild animals, we may safely assume that a much larger number would be necessary. The Hudson's Bay territory is said to comprise about 900,000,000 acres. The number of Indians was estimated at 139,000. Allowing one wild animal to each twenty acres, this would give about 300 animals to each Indian ; and, if we consider the greater longevity of man, we must multiply this by six, or even more.

Or, again, we may attempt to form an estimate in the following manner. The number of skins received by the

---

[1] The bones of the stag owe their preservation perhaps to another cause. Professor Rütimeyer tells us that among the bones from the Pfahlbauten none are in better condition than those of the stag : this is the consequence, he says, of their " dichten Gefüge, ihrer Härte und Sprödigkeit, so wie der grossen Fettlosigkeit," peculiarities which recommended them so strongly to the men of the Stone Age, that they used them in preference to all others, nay, almost exclusively, in the manufacture of those instruments which could be made of bone (*Fauna der Pfahlbauten*, p. 12). How common the bones of the stag are in quaternary strata geologists know, and we have here perhaps an explanation of the fact. The antler of the reindeer is also preferred at the present day by the Esquimaux in the manufacture of their stone weapons. (Sir E. Belcher, *Trans. Ethn. Soc.*, vol. i. p. 139.)

Hudson's Bay Company in 1866 amounted to 1,250,000, made up as follows :—

Beaver	144,744
Fox	32,982
Lynx	68,040
Marten	92,373
Mink	73,149
Musquash . . .	608,396
Otter	14,376
Rabbit	105,909
Bear	6,457
Racoon	24,860
Wolf	7,429
Sundries	63,950
	———1,242,765

The number of Indians is estimated at 139,000, and Hearne states that every one requires at least twenty deerskins for clothes, without counting those required for tent-cloths, bags, etc. ; this therefore would give us 139,000 × 20 . . .   2,780,000
But the deerskins are fit for clothes only during two months in the year, and as it will be observed that the majority of the animals enumerated above are not fit for food, others must have been killed in sufficient quantities to serve as food for ten months. Assuming that an Indian requires one every month, which is probably well within the mark, we shall again require 139,000 × 10 (the number of months), . . .   1,390,000

Making, therefore, a total of . . 5,412,765

And even if we assume that one animal only out of twenty is killed by the Indians, which is probably much too large a proportion, we shall have 108,000,000 to 139,000 Indians, or about 750 animals to each man ; besides which, a further allowance must be made as before on account of man's greater longevity. Dr Rae, who has had so much experience in these matters, has been good enough to look over the above calculation, which he considers fairly estimated, but it has, of course, no pretensions to accuracy.

Lastly, it may be observed that man is less likely to be drowned by sudden river floods, than is the case with other land mammalia ;[1] and on the whole, therefore, it is natural that the bones of animals would be far more common in these gravels than those of man.

It must not, however, be supposed that the latter are altogether absent. Without relying on the human lower jaw, stated to have been found in the pit at Moulinquignon, and about which there has been much discussion and difference of opinion, I may instance the discovery of human remains by M. Bertrand,[2] at Clichy, in the valley of the Seine. Among these bones, about the authenticity and antiquity of which there seems to be no doubt, was a skull which has been examined by M. Lartet, and which is decidedly dolichocephalic.

We have as yet but partly answered the second of the two questions with which we started. Even admitting that the flint hatchets are coeval with the gravel in which they occur, it remains to be shown that the bones of the extinct animals belong also to the same period. This was at first doubted by some geologists, who suggested that they might have been washed out of earlier strata.

If, however, these bones belonged to a period earlier than that of the gravel, where, we may ask, are the remains of the animals which did exist at that time ? Moreover, the bones, though sometimes much worn and broken, are at others, and even, according to Sir J. Prestwich, "as a general rule,[3] either not rolled at all, or are slightly so." Secondly, these species, and particularly the mammoth and the woolly-haired rhinoceros, are the characteristic and commonest species of these beds, not only in the valley of the Somme, but in all the drift gravels of England and

[1] See, for instances, Bakie, *Exploring Voyage up the Kwora*, p. 315.
[2] *Les Mondes*, 1869, p. 64.   [3] *Phil. Trans., loc. cit.*, p. 300.

France ; while, if they belonged in reality to an earlier period, they would not occur so constantly, and they would be accompanied by other species characteristic of earlier times.

Thirdly, the materials forming the drift gravels of the Somme valley have all been obtained from the present area of drainage, and there are in this district no older beds from which the remains of these extinct mammalia could possibly have been derived. There are, indeed, outliers of tertiary strata, but the mammalian remains found in those beds belong to other, and much more ancient, species.

Fourthly, as regards the rhinoceros, we have the express testimony of M. Baillon, that on one occasion all the bones of a hind-leg were found in their natural positions at Menchecourt, near Abbeville, while the rest of the skeleton was found at a little distance. In this case, therefore, the animal most have been entombed before the ligaments had decayed away.

M. Casciano de Prado has made a very similar discovery in Spain, not far from Madrid. There the section was as follows : first, vegetable soil ; then about twenty-five feet of sand and pebbles, under which was a layer of sandy loam, in which, during the year 1850, a complete skeleton of the mammoth was discovered. Underneath this stratum was about ten feet of coarse gravel, in which some flint axes, very closely resembling those of Amiens, have been discovered.

Finally, as regards the rhinoceros, M. Lartet assures us [1] that some of the bones bear the marks of flint implements ; nay, more than this, he has even satisfied himself, " by comparative trials on homologous portions of existing animals, that incisions, presenting such appearances, could only be made in fresh bones, still retaining their cartilage."

There is, then, no more reason for believing that the bones of these extinct mammalia were washed out of earlier strata into the drift gravels, than for attributing

[1] *Geological Journ.*, vol. xvi. p. 471.

such an origin to the implements themselves ; and we may, I think, regard it as well established, that the mammoth and woolly-haired rhinoceros, as well as the other above-mentioned mammalia, co-existed with the savages who used the rude "drift hatchets," at the time when the gravels of the Somme were being deposited.

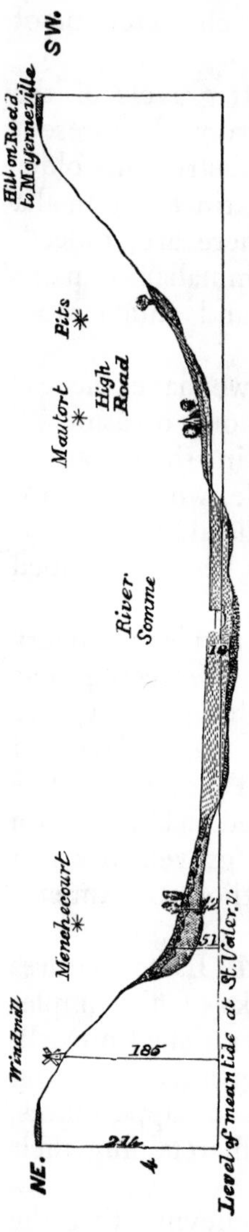

The second of the three questions with which we started (p. 351) may therefore be answered in the affirmative.

Must we, then, carry man back far into the past, or may we bring the extinct animals down to comparatively recent times ? The absence of all tradition of the elephant and rhinoceros in Europe carries us back far indeed in years, but a little way only, when measured by geological standards, and we must therefore solve this question by examining the drift gravels themselves, the materials of which they are composed, and the positions which they so occupy, as to determine, if possible, the conditions under which they were deposited, and the lapse of time which they indicate.

Fig. 250 gives a section across the valley of the Somme at Abbeville, taken from the memoir in the *Philosophical Transactions*,[1] by Sir J. Prestwich, who has long studied the quaternary beds, and has done more than any other man to render them intelligible. We should find almost

FIG. 250.—Section across the Valley of the Somme at Abbeville. The proportion of the length is reduced to one-third.

[1] *Phil. Trans.*, 1860.

the same arrangement and position of the different beds not only at St Acheul, but elsewhere along the valley of the Somme, wherever the higher beds of gravel have not been removed by subsequent action of the river. Even at St Valéry, at the present mouth of the river, I found a bed of gravel at a considerable height above the level of the sea. This would seem to show that at the period of these high-level gravels, the English Channel was narrower than it is at present, as indeed we know to have been the case down to historical times. So early as 1605, our countryman, Verstegan, pointed out that the waves and tides were eating away our coasts. Sir C. Lyell [1] gives much information on this subject, and it appears, for instance, that, even so lately as the reign of Queen Elizabeth, the town of Brighton occupied the site of the present pier.

The difference between the height of the high-level gravels and the river increases from the source to the sea. For instance, in the Seine valley at the boundaries of La Brie and Champagne it is nothing ; at Paris, 34 metres ; at the sea, 50 or 60.[2]

Sir J. Prestwich has pointed out[3] that a section, similar to that of the Somme, is presented by various rivers—the Lark, Waveney, Ouse, etc., while it is well shown also along the banks of the Seine. Indeed it holds good of most of our rivers, that along the sides of their valleys are patches of old gravels left by the stream at various heights, before they had excavated the channels to their present depth. Sir J. Prestwich considers that the beds of sand and gravel can generally be divided into two more or less distinct series, one continuous along the bottom of the valleys, and rising little above the water level— these he calls the low-level gravels ; the other, which he terms the upper or high-level gravels, occurring in detached masses at an elevation of from fifty to two hundred feet above the valley. Those of the Somme seem to me, on the contrary, only the two extremes of a

---

[1] See *Principles of Geology*, p. 315.
[2] Belgrand, *Bassin Parisien*, p. 90.   [3] *Phil. Trans.*, 1864.

single series, once continuous, but now generally presenting numerous interruptions. A more magnified view of
the strata at St Acheul, near Amiens, is shown in
fig. 251. The upper layer of vegetable soil having been
removed, we have—

(1) A bed of brick earth (*a*), from 4 to 5 feet in thickness, and containing a few angular flints.

(2) Below this is a thin layer of angular gravel (*b*), 1 to
2 feet in thickness.

(3) Still lower is a bed of sandy marl (*c*), 5 to 6 feet
thick, with land and freshwater shells, which, though
very delicate, are in most cases perfect.

FIG. 251.—Section of St Acheul, near Amiens.

(4) At the bottom of all these, and immediately overlying the chalk, is the bed of partially rounded gravel (*d*)
in which principally the flint implements are found.
This layer also contains many well-rolled tertiary
pebbles.

In the early Christian period this spot was used as a
cemetery : the graves generally descend into the marly
sand, and their limits are very distinctly marked, as in
fig. 251 ; an important fact, as showing that the rest of
the strata have lain undisturbed for fifteen hundred years.
Some of the coffins were of hard chalk (fig. 251, *e*), some
of wood, in which latter case the nails and clamps only
remain, every particle of wood having perished, without
leaving even a stain behind. Passing down the hill
towards the river, all these strata are seen to die out, and
we find ourselves on the bare chalk ; but again at a lower

level occurs another bed of gravel, resembling the first, and capped also by the bed of brick earth which is known as loëss. This lower bed of gravel is known as the lower-level gravel, a somewhat misleading term, as it is of course more recent.

These strata, therefore, are our witnesses ; but of what ? Are they older than the valley, or the valley than they ? Are they the result of causes still in operation, or the offspring of cataclysms now happily at an end ?

If we can show that the present river, somewhat swollen perhaps, owing to the greater extension of forests in ancient times, and by an alteration of climate, has excavated the present valley, and produced the strata above numerated ; then " the suggestion of an antiquity for the human family so remote as is here implied, in the length of ages required by the gentle rivers and small streams of eastern France to erode its whole plain to the depths at which they now flow, acquires, it must be confessed, a fascinating grandeur, when by similitude of feature and geology, we extend the hypothesis to the whole north-west frontiers of the continent, and assume that, from the estuary of the Seine to the eastern shores of the Baltic, every internal feature of valley, dale, and ravine— in short, the entire intaglio of the surface—has been moulded by running waters, since the advent of the human race."[1]

But, on the other hand, it has been maintained that the pliant facts may be read as " expressions of violent and sudden mutations, only compatible with altogether briefer periods." The argument of the Paroxysmist would probably be something like the following :—

" Assuming the pre-existing *relief*, or excavation rather, of the surface to have approximated to that now prevailing, he will account for the gravel by supposing a sudden rocking movement of the lands and the bottom of the sea of the nature of an earthquake, or a succession of them, to have launched a portion of the temporarily uplifted waters upon the surface of the land."

[1] *Blackwood's Magazine*, October, 1860.

Let us, then, examine the strata, and see whether the evidence they give is in reality so confused and contradictory.

Taking the section at St Acheul and commencing at the bottom, we have first of all the partially rounded high-level gravel, throughout which, and especially at the lower part, the flint implements occur.

These beds but rarely contain vegetable remains. Large pieces of the oak, yew, and fir have, however, been determined at Hoxne. The mammalia, also, are but few; the mammoth, the *Elephas antiquus*, with species of *Bos*, *Cervus*, and *Equus*, are the only ones which have yet occurred at St Acheul, though beds of the same age in other parts of England and France have added the *Rhinoceros tichorhinus*, the reindeer, and several other species. The mollusca are more numerous; they have been identified by Mr J. G. Jeffreys, who finds in the upper-level gravel thirty-six species, all of them land or freshwater forms, and all belonging to existing species. It is hardly necessary to add that these shells are not found in the coarse gravel, but only here and there, where quieter conditions, indicated by a seam of finer materials, have preserved them from destruction. Here, therefore, we have a conclusive answer to the suggestion that the gravel may have been heaped up to its present height by a sudden irruption of the sea. In that case we should find some marine remains; but as we do not, as all the fossils belong to animals which live on the land, or inhabit fresh waters, it is at once evident that this stratum, not being sub-aerial, must be a freshwater deposit; and as the most delicate shells are entire, it is equally evident that they were deposited in tranquil water, and not by a cataclysm.

But the gravel itself tells us even more than this : the river Somme flows through a country in which there are no rocks older than the chalk, and the gravel in its valley consists entirely of chalk flints and tertiary débris.[1] The Seine, on the other hand, receives tributaries which drain

[1] Buteux, *loc. cit.*, p. 98.

other formations. In the valley of the Yonne we find fragments of the crystalline rocks brought from the Morvan.[1] The Aube runs through cretaceous and Jurassic strata, and the gravels along its valley are entirely composed of materials derived from these formations. The valley of the Oise is in this respect particularly instructive : " De Maquenoise à Hirson[2] la vallée ne présente que des fragments plus ou moins roulés des roches de transition que traverse le cours de la rivière. En descendant à Etréaupont, on y trouve des calcaires jurassiques et des silex de la craie, formations qui ont succédé aux roches anciennes. A Guise, le dépôt erratique . . . est composé de quartzites et de schistes de transition de quelques grès plus récents, de silex de la craie, et surtout de quartz laiteux, dont le volume varie depuis celui de la tête jusqu'à celui de grains de sable. . . . Au delà les fragments de roches anciennes diminuent graduellement en volume et en nombre." At Paris the granitic débris brought down by the Yonne forms a notable proportion of the gravel ; and at Précy, near Creil, on the Oise, the fragments of the ancient rocks are abundant ; but lower down the Seine, at Mantes, they are smaller and less numerous, while at Rouen and Pont de l'Arche I found none, though a longer search would doubtless have shown fragments of them. This case of the Oise is, however, interesting, not only on account of the valuable evidence contained in the above quotation, but because, though the river flows, as a glance at the map will show, immediately across and at right angles to the Somme, yet none of the ancient rocks which form the valley of the Oise have supplied any débris to the valley of the Somme : and this, though the two rivers are at one point within six miles of one another, and separated by a ridge only eighty feet in height.

The same division occurs between the Seine and the Loire : " Bien que la ligne de partage des eaux de la Loire et de la Seine, entre St Amand (Nièvre) et Artenay, au nord d'Orléans, soit à peine sensible, aucun débris de

---

[1] D'Archiac, *Progrès de la Géologie*, p. 163. [2] *Ibid., loc. cit.*, p. 155.

roches venant du centre de la France, par la vallée de la Loire n'est passé dans le bassin de la Seine."[1]

In the Vivarais near Auvergne, "Les dépôts diluviens sont composés des mêmes roches que celles que les rivières actuelles entraînent dans les vallées, et sont les débris des seules montagnes de la Lozin, du Tanargue et du Mézène, qui entourent le bassin du Vivarais."[2]

Again :

"Le diluvium des vallées de l'Aisne et de l'Aire ne renferme que les débris plus ou moins roulés des terrains que ces rivières coupent dans leur cours."[3]

The same thing holds good in various English rivers. The conclusion deduced by M. D'Archiac from the consideration of these observations, and specially from those concerning the valley of the Seine, is, "Que les courants diluviens ne venaient point d'une direction unique, mais qu'ils convergaient des bords du bassin vers son centre, suivant les dépressions préexistantes, et *que leur élévation ou leur force de transport ne suffisait pas pour faire passer les débris qu'ils charriaient d'une de ces vallées dans l'autre.*"[4]

Considering, however, all these facts, remembering that the constituents of these river-drift gravels are, in all cases, derived from beds now *in situ* along the valley, that they have not only followed the lines of these valleys, but have done so in the direction of the present waterflow, and without in any case passing across from one river system to another, it seems quite unnecessary to call in the assistance of diluvial waves, or indeed any other agency than that of the rivers themselves.

There are, however, certain facts in the case which were long regarded by most geologists as fatal to this hypothesis, and which prevented M. D'Archiac, as well as the French geologists generally, from adopting an explanation apparently so simple and so obvious. These difficulties appear to have been twofold, or at least the two principal were firstly, the large sandstone blocks which are scattered throughout the river gravels of

[1] *Loc. cit.*, p. 164.
[2] *Loc. cit.*, p. 160.
[3] *Malbos. Bull. Geo.*, vol. iii. p. 631.
[4] *Loc. cit.*, p. 163.

northern and central France ; and secondly, the height
at which the upper-level gravels stand above the present
water-line. We will consider these two objections
separately.

It must be admitted that the presence of the sandstone
blocks in the gravels appears at first sight to be irreconcilable with our hypothesis. In some places they occur
frequently, and are of considerable size ; the largest I
have myself seen is represented in the section, fig. 252,
taken close to the railway-station at Joinville. It was
8 ft. 6 in. in length, with a width of 2 ft. 8 in., and a
thickness of 3 ft. 4 in.

Even when we re-
member that at the
time of its deposition
the valley was not
excavated to its pre-
sent depth, we must
still feel that a body
of water with power
to move such masses
as these must have
been very different
from any floods now

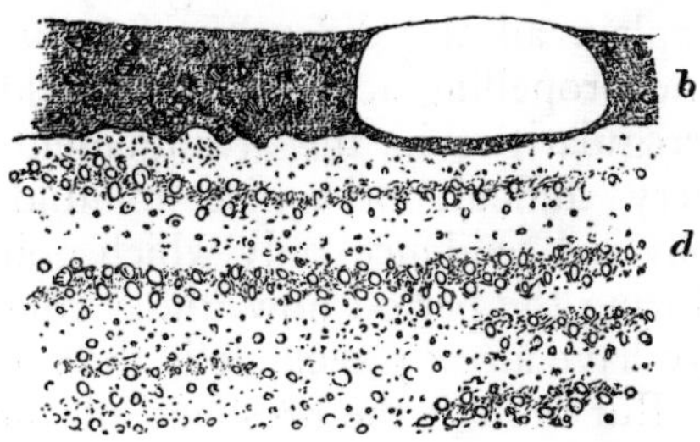

FIG. 252.—Section taken in a pit close to the
Joinville station.
b, Red angular gravel, containing a very large
sandstone block ; d, Grey subangular gravel.

occurring in those valleys, and might fairly deserve the
name of a cataclysm. But whence could we obtain
so great a quantity of water ? We have already seen
that the gravel of the Oise, though so near, is entirely
unlike that of the Somme ; while that of the Seine, again,
is quite different from that of any of the neighbouring
rivers. These rivers, therefore, cannot have drained a
larger area than at present ; the river systems must have
been the same as now. Nor would the supposition,
after all, account for the phenomena. We should but
fall from Scylla into Charybdis. Around the blocks we
see no evidence of violent action ; in the section at
Joinville, the grey sub-angular gravel passed under the
large block above-mentioned, with scarcely any traces of
disturbance. But a flood which could bring down so

great a mass would certainly have swept away the comparatively light and movable gravel below. We cannot, therefore, account for the phenomena by violent aqueous action, because a flood which would deposit the sandstone blocks would remove the underlying gravel, and a flood which would deposit the gravel would not move the blocks. The *deus ex machinâ* has not only been called in most unnecessarily, but, when examined, turns out to be but an idol after all.

Driven, then, to seek some other explanation of the difficulty, Sir J. Prestwich falls back on that of floating ice. Here we have an agency which would satisfactorily explain all the difficulties of the case. The "packing" and propelling action of ice would also account for some irregularities in the arrangement of the beds, which are very difficult otherwise to understand. Nor is it the physical evidence only which points to an arctic climate during the period now under consideration; the fauna, as we have already seen, tells the same tale.

But though the presence of the sandstone blocks and the occasional contortions of the strata are in perfect accordance with the view that the gravels have been deposited by the rivers, our second difficulty still remains —namely, the height at which the upper-level gravels stand above the present water-line. We cannot wonder that these beds were so long attributed to violent cataclysms.

M. Boucher de Perthes was always of this opinion. "Ce coquillage," he says, "cet éléphant, cette hache, ou la main qui la fabriqua, furent donc témoins du cataclysme qui donna à notre pays sa configuration présente." [1]

M. C. D'Orbigny, observing that the fossils found in these quaternary beds are all either of land or freshwater animals, wisely dismisses the theory of any marine action, but he expresses himself as follows :—" En effet l'opinion de la plupart des géologues est que les cataclysmes diluviens ont eu pour causes prédominantes de fortes

[1] *Mém. Soc. d'Em. d'Abbeville*, 1861, p. 475.

oscillations de l'écorce terrestre, des soulèvement de montagnes au milieu de l'océan, d'où seraient résultées de grandes érosions. Par conséquent les puissants courants d'eau marine, auxquels on attribue ces érosions diluviennes, auraient dû laisser sur les continents des traces authentiques de leur passage, tels que de nombreux débris de coquilles, de poissons et autres animaux marins analogues à ceux qui vivent actuellement dans la mer. Or, ainsi que M. Cordier l'a fait remarker depuis long-temps à sons cours de géologie, rien de semblable n'a été constaté. Sur tous les points du globe où l'on a étudié les dépôts diluviens, on a reconnu que, sauf quelques rares exceptions très contestables il n'existe dans ces dépôts aucun fossil marin : ou bien ce sont des fossiles arrachés aux terrains préexistants, dont la dénudation a fourni les matériaux qui composent le diluvium. En sorte que les dépôts diluviens semblent avoir eu pour cause des phénomènes météorologiques, et paraissent être le résultat d'immenses inondations *d'eau douce* et non d'eau marine, qui, se précipitant des points élevés vers la mer, auraient dénudé une grande partie de la surface du sol, balayé la généralité des êtres organisés et pour ainsi dire nivelé, coordonné les bassins hydrographiques actuels."[1]

Such cataclysms, however, as those thus suggested by M. D'Orbigny, and many other French geologists, even if admitted, would not account for the results before us. We have seen that the transport of materials has not followed any single direction, but has in all cases followed the lines of the present valleys, and the direction of the present water-flow ; that the rocks of one valley are never transported into another ; that the condition of the loëss is irreconcilable with a great rush of water ; while, finally, the perfect preservation of many of the most delicate shells is clear proof that the phenomena are not due to violent or cataclysmic action.

We must, moreover, bear in mind that the gravels and

[1] C. D'Orbigny, *Bull. Géo.*, 2nd series, V. xvii. p. 6. See also D'Archiac, *loc. cit. passim.*

sands are themselves both the proof and the results of an immense denudation. In a chalk country, such as that through which the Somme flows, each cubic foot of flint, gravel, or sand represents the removal of, at the very least, twenty cubic feet of chalk, all of which, as we have already seen, must have been removed from the present area of drainage. In considering, therefore, the formation of these upper and older gravels, we must not picture to ourselves the original valley as it now is, but must, in imagination, restore all that immense mass of chalk which has been destroyed in the formation of the gravels and sands. This is no mere hypothesis, since the mass of sand and gravel cannot have been produced without an immense removal of the chalk. On the whole, then, we may safely conclude that the upper-level gravels were deposited by the existing river, before it had excavated the valley to its present depth, and when consequently it ran at a level considerably higher than the present.

Far, therefore, from requiring an immense flood of water, two hundred feet in depth, the accumulation of the gravel may have been effected by an annual volume of water, differing little from that of the present river.

A given quantity of water will, however, produce very different effects, according to the rapidity with which it flows. "We learn from observation that a velocity of three inches per second at the bottom will just begin to work upon fine clay fit for pottery, and, however firm and compact it may be, it will tear it up. Yet no beds are more stable than clay when the velocities do not exceed this ; for the water even takes away the impalpable particles of the superficial clay, leaving the particles of sand sticking by their lower half in the rest of the clay, which they now protect, making a very permanent bottom, if the stream does not bring down gravel or coarse sand, which will rub off this very thin crust, and allow another layer to be worn off. A velocity of 6 inches will lift fine sand, 8 inches will lift sand as coarse as linseed, 12 inches will sweep along fine gravel, 24 inches will roll along rounded pebbles an inch in diameter, and it requires 3 feet per second at the bottom to sweep along shivery angular stones of the size of an egg."[1]

If, therefore, we are justified in assuming a colder climate than that now existing, we should much increase the erosive action of the river, not only because the rains would fall on a frozen surface, but because the rainfall of the winter months would accumulate on the high grounds in the form of ice and snow, and would every spring produce floods much greater than any which now occur.[2]

Moreover, as Sir J. Evans has well pointed out, in ancient times, and before the river valleys were excavated to their present depths, the chalk might have been saturated with water to a greater height than at present, and this also would have rendered floods more frequent and more severe than at present.

Returning to the fig. given on p. 364, we now come to the light-coloured marl (fig. 251, *c*). Sir J. Prestwich described it as follows : Of white siliceous sand and light-coloured marl, mixed with fine chalk grit, a few large sub-angular flints, and an occasional sandstone block, irregular patches of flint gravel, bedding waved and contorted, here and there layers with diagonal seams, a few ochreous bands, portions concreted. Sand and fresh-water shells common, some mammalian remains.

In the pits at Amiens this bed is generally distinct from the underlying gravels, owing perhaps to the upper portion of the gravel having been removed ; but in several places (Précy, Ivry, Bicêtre, etc.) this section is complete, the coarser gravel below becoming finer and finer, and at length passing above into siliceous sand. These sections evidently indicate a gradual loss of power in the water at these particular spots ; rapid enough at first to bring down large pebbles, its force became less and less, until at length it was only able to carry fine sand. This, therefore, appears to indicate a slight change in the course of the river, and gradual excavation of the valley, which,

---

[1] *Cyc. Brit.*, article " Rivers," p. 274.
[2] See Murchison's *Geology of Russia and the Ural Mountains*, p. 572.

by supplying the floods with a lower bed, left the waters at this height with a gradually diminishing force and velocity.

The upper part of the section of St Acheul consists of brick earth (fig. 251, *a*), passing below into angular gravel, while between this and the underlying sandy marl is sometimes a small layer of darker brick earth. These beds, however, vary much even in adjoining sections. Taken as a whole, they may be regarded as the representatives of that remarkable loamy deposit which is found overlying the gravels in all these valleys of northern France, and which, as the celebrated "loëss" of the Rhine, attains in some places a thickness of three hundred feet. The greatest development of it which I have seen in the north of France was in a pit in the Rue de la Chevalerie, near Ivry, where it was twenty-two feet thick ; some of this, however, may have been reconstructed loëss brought down by rain from the higher ground in the immediate neighbourhood. Assuming that this loëss is composed of fine particles deposited from standing or slowly-moving waters, we might be disposed to wonder at not finding in it any traces of vegetable remains. We know, however, from the arrangement of the nails and hasps, that in some of the St Acheul tombs wooden coffins were used, while the size of the nails shows that the planks must have been tolerably thick ; yet every trace of wood has been removed, and not even a stain is left to indicate its presence. We need not, therefore, wonder at the absence of vegetable remains in the drift.

Such is a general account of those gravel-pits which lie at a height of from eighty to one hundred and fifty feet above the present water-level of the valleys, and which, along the Somme, are found in some places even at a height of two hundred feet.

Sir J. Prestwich gives the following table of the mammalia. To this list we may add the lemming, the *Myodes torquatus*, and the musk-ox, which has been found at two spots in the Thames valley, as well as at Chauny on the Oise.

	BEDFORD. Great Northern Railway, or Summerhouse Hill.	ABBE-VILLE. Menchecourt.	AMIENS. St Roch.	PARIS. Grenelle, Ivry, Clichy, or the Rue de Reuily.
Elephas primigenius, *Blum.*	*	*	*	*
—— antiquus, *Falc..* .	*s	...	*	*c
Rhinoceros tichorhinus, *Cuv.*	*r	*	*	*
—— megarhinos, *Christol.* .	*r	...	...	* ?g
Ursus spelæus, *Blum.* .	*s	*	...	...
Hyæna spelæa, *Gold.* .	...	*	...	* ?g
Felis spelæa, *Gold.* .	...	*	...	*
Bos primigenius, *Boj.* .	* ?	*	*	*
Bison priscus, *Boj.* .	*r	*	...	*c
Equus (possibly two species)	*	*	*	*
Cervus euryceros, *Aldr.* .	*r	...	...	...
—— elaphus, *Linn.* .	*	*	*	*
—— tarandus, *Linn.* .	*	*	...	*c
Hippopotamus major, *Nesti*	*	...	*	*g
Sus	*r	...	...	*

Let us now visit some of the pits at the lower levels. At about thirty feet lower, as for instance at Menchecourt, near Abbeville, and at St Roch near Amiens, where the gravel slopes from a height of sixty feet down to the present bottom of the valley, we find almost a repetition of the same succession ; coarse sub-angular gravel below, finer materials above. So similar, indeed, are these beds to those already described, that it will be unnecessary for me to give any special description of them.

It is possible that when the fauna and flora of the upper and lower level gravels shall have been more thoroughly investigated, they may be found to be almost identical. At present, however, the species obtained from the lower-level gravels are more numerous than those from the upper levels.

The mollusca are 52 in number, of which 42 now live in Sweden, 37 in Finland, and 38 in Lombardy. Bearing in mind that Lombardy is much richer than Finland in mollusca, this assemblage has rather a northern aspect.

In such a group of species as this, the hippopotamus seems singularly out of place, and in the preceding chapter I have discussed the conclusions which are, I think, to be drawn from its presence : taking the fauna as a whole, however, and looking more especially to such animals as the musk-ox, the reindeer, the lemming, the *Myodes torquatus*, the Siberian mammoth, and its faithful companion, the woolly-haired rhinoceros, we have clear evidence of a climate unlike that now prevailing in Western Europe.

The valley was once considerably deeper than at present and is partly filled up by a bed of gravel, covered by silt and peat, which latter is in some places more than thirty or even forty feet thick, and is extensively worked for fuel. These strata have afforded to the antiquaries of the neighbourhood, and especially to M. Boucher de Perthes, a rich harvest of interesting relics belonging to various periods. The depth at which these objects are found has been carefully noted by M. Boucher de Perthes.

"Prenant," he says, "pour terme moyen du sol de la vallée, une hauteur de 2 mètres audessus du niveau de la Somme, c'est à 30 à 40 centimètres de la surface qu'on rencontre le plus abondamment les traces du moyen-âge. Cinquante centimètres plus bas, on commence à trouver des débris romains puis gallo-romains. On continue à suivre ces derniers pendant un mètre, c'est à dire jusqu'au niveau de la Somme. Après eux, viennent les vestiges gaulois purs qui descendent sans interruption jusqu'à près de 2 mètres audessous de ce niveau, preuve de la longue habitation de ces peuples dans la vallée. C'est à un mètre plus bas, ou à 4 mètres environ audessous de ce même niveau, qu'on arrive au centre du sol que nous avons nommé Celtique, celui que foulèrent les Gaulois primitives ou les peuples qui les précédèrent" ; and which belonged, therefore, to the Neolithic Period. It is, however, hardly necessary to add that these thicknesses are only given by M. Boucher de Perthes "comme terme approximatif" ; and in other localities no doubt the growth was more rapid. Mr Southall[1] gives instances of more rapid accumulation ; nevertheless, without attaching too much importance to M. Boucher de Perthes' calculation, it is obvious that the formation of so great

[1] *Recent Origin of Man*, pp. 270, 467.

a mass of peat must have required a considerable lapse of time.

The *Antiquités Celtiques* was published several years before the Swiss archæologists had made us acquainted with the nature of the lake-dwellings ; but, from some indications given by M. Boucher de Perthes, it would appear that there must have been, at one time, lake-habitations in the neighbourhood of Abbeville. He found considerable platforms of wood, with large quantities of bones, stone implements, and handles closely resembling those which come from the Swiss lake-villages.

These weapons cannot for an instant be confounded with the ruder ones from the drift-gravel. They are ground to a smooth surface and a cutting edge, while those of the more ancient types are merely chipped, not one of the many hundreds already found having shown the slightest trace of grinding. Yet though the former belong to the Stone Age, to a time so remote that the use of metal was apparently still unknown in Western Europe, they are separated from the earlier weapons of the upper-level drift by the whole period necessary for the excavation of the Somme valley, to a depth of more than one hundred feet and its refilling by some twenty or thirty feet of peat.

If, therefore, we get no definite date for the arrival of man in these countries, we can at least form a vivid idea of his antiquity. He must have seen the Somme running at a height of about a hundred feet above its present level. It is, indeed, probable that he dates back in northern France almost, if not quite, as far as some of the rivers themselves. The fauna of the country was unlike what it is now. Along the banks of the rivers ranged a savage race of hunters and fishermen, and in the forests wandered the mammoth, the two-horned woolly rhinoceros, a species of lion, the musk-ox, the reindeer, and the urus.

Yet the geography of France cannot have been very different from what it is at present. The present rivers ran in their present directions, and the sea even then lay between the Somme and the Adour, though the channel was not so wide as it is now.

Gradually the river deepened its valley; ineffective, or even perhaps constructive, in autumn and winter, the melting of the snows turned it every spring into a roaring torrent. These floods were perhaps more destructive to animals even than man himself; while, however rude they may have been, our predecessors can hardly be supposed to have been incapable of foreseeing and consequently escaping the danger.

While the water had sufficient force to deposit coarse gravel at any given level, at a still higher one it would part with finer particles, and would thus form the loëss, which at the same time would here and there receive angular flints and shells brought down from the hills in a more or less transverse direction by the rivulets after heavy rains.

Sir J. Prestwich regards the difference of level between the upper gravels and the loëss as "a measure of the floods of that period." If the gravel-beds were complete, this would no doubt be the case; but it seems to me that the upper-level gravels are mere fragments of an originally almost continuous deposit, and under such circumstances the present cannot be taken as evidence of the original difference.

As the valley became deeper and deeper, the gravel would be deposited at lower and lower levels, the loëss always following it;[1] thus we must not consider the loëss as a distinct bed, but as one which was being formed during the same time, though never at the same place, as the beds of gravel. In fig. 253 I have given a diagram, the better to illustrate my meaning; the loëss is indicated by letters with a dash and is dotted, while the gravels are represented as rudely stratified. In this case I suppose the river to have run originally on the level (1), and to have deposited the gravel (*a*) and the loëss (*a'*); after a certain amount of erosion, which would reduce the level

[1] See Sir J. Prestwich's paper read before the Royal Society, June 19, 1862.

to (2), the gravel would be spread out at (*b*), and loëss at (*b'*). Similarly the loëss (*c'*) would be contemporaneous with the gravel (*c*).

Thus, while in each pit the lower beds would of course be the oldest, still the upper-level gravels as a whole would be the most ancient, and the beds lying in the lower parts of the valley the most modern.

For convenience, I have represented the sides of the valley as forming a series of terraces ; and though this is not actually the case, there are places in which such terraces do occur.

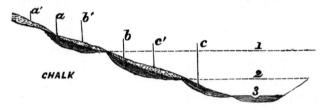

Fig. 253.—Diagram to illustrate deposit of loëss and gravel.
a', Loëss corresponding to and contemporaneous with the gravel *a* ; *b'*, Loëss corresponding to and contemporaneous with the gravel *b* ; *c'*, Loëss corresponding to and contemporaneous with the gravel *c*. 1, Level of valley at period *a* ; 2, Level of valley at period *b* ; 3, Level of valley at present.

The valley of the Somme is comparatively straight, but within it the river winds considerably, and when in one of its curves the current crosses " its general line of descent, it eats out a curve on the opposite bank, or in the side of the hills bounding the valley, from which curve it is turned back again at an equal angle, so that it recrosses the ·line of descent, and gradually hollows out another curve lower down in the opposite bank," till the whole sides of the valley, or river-bed, " present a succession of salient and retiring angles." [1]   During these wanderings from one side of the valley to the other, the river continually undermines and removes the gravels which at an earlier period it had deposited. Thus the upper-level gravels are now only to be found here and there, as it were, in patches, while in many parts they

[1] Lyell's *Principles*, p. 206.

have altogether disappeared ; as, for instance, on the right side of the valley between Amiens and Pont Rémy, where hardly a trace of the high-level gravels is to be seen.

The neighbouring shores of England and France show various traces of a slight and recent elevation of the land. Raised beaches have been observed at an elevation of from five to ten feet at various points along the coast of Sussex and the Pas de Calais. Marine shells also occur at Abbeville about twenty-five feet above the sea-level,[1] and no doubt this change of level has had an important bearing on the excavation of the valley.

Mr A. Tylor,[2] in a recent memoir, agrees with me that the upper-level and lower-level gravels are merely the extremes of a series, seldom complete, but generally imperfect, sometimes in one part, sometimes in another. But he also maintains that the surface of the chalk in the valley of the Somme had assumed its present form prior to the deposition of any of the gravel or loëss now existing in it. As, however, he admits that the materials forming this gravel and loëss are derived exclusively from the area drained by the Somme and its tributaries, he involves himself in a double difficulty. In the first place he maintains that the materials, by the removal of which the valley was formed, were swept completely out of the valley, which, considering its length, depth, and narrowness, appears to be impossible ; and in the second place, the admission that the gravel and sand consist of flint débris brought down by the Somme and its tributaries is fatal to his argument, since you cannot remove matter from one place to another without affecting the configuration of the surface in both. In admitting, then, that " the gravel in the valley of the Somme at Amiens is partly derived from débris brought down by the river Somme, and by the two rivers, the Celle and the Arve, and partly consists of material from the adjoining higher grounds,

---

[1] The higher-level gravels in some places fringe the coast at an elevation of as much as one hundred feet ; this phenomenon, however, I should be disposed to refer partly to an encroachment of the sea on the land, and the consequent intersection of the old river-beds at a higher level.

[2] *Geol. Journal*, vol. xxiv. p. 105.

washed in by land-floods,"[1] Mr Tylor virtually adopts
the explanation of the phenomena given in this work,
since the formation or removal of this gravel necessarily
involved an alteration of the surface and a deepening of
the valley.

When, finally, the excavation of the valley was completed, the climate had gradually become more like our
own, and either from this change, or rather perhaps
yielding to the irresistible power of man, the great *Pachydermata* became extinct.   Under the altered conditions
of level, the river, unable to carry out to sea the finer
particles brought down from the higher levels, deposited
them in the valley, and thus raised somewhat its general
level, checking the velocity of the stream, and producing
extensive marshes, in which a thick deposit of peat was
gradually formed.   We have, unfortunately, no trustworthy means of estimating the rate of formation of this
substance, which indeed varies considerably, according to
the conditions of the case ; but on any supposition the
production of a mass in some places more than thirty feet
in thickness must have required a very considerable
period.   Yet it is in these beds that we find the remains
of the Neolithic or later Stone Period.   From the tombs
at St Acheul, from the Roman remains found in the
superficial layers of the peat, at about the present level
of the river, we know that fifteen hundred years have
produced scarcely any change in the configuration of the
valley.   In the peat, and at a depth of about fifteen feet
in the alluvium at Abbeville, are the remains of the
Neolithic Period, which we have ample reason for believing, from the researches in Denmark, Switzerland, and
other countries, to be of no slight antiquity.   Yet all
these are subsequent to the excavation of the valley.
What date, then, are we to ascribe to the men who lived
when the Somme was but beginning its great task ?   No
one can properly appreciate the lapse of time indicated,
who has not stood on the heights of Liercourt, Picquigny,
or on one of the other points overlooking the valley of

[1] *Loc. cit.*, p. 105.

the Somme ; or I may add, on the summit of one of our English Chalk hills, as for instance on Well Hill above Chelsfield, or on the ridge of the escarpment in Kent, overlooking the valleys of the Darent or the Medway ; nor I am sure, could any geologist return from such a visit without an overpowering sense of the changes which have taken place, and the length of time which must have elapsed since the first appearance of man in Western Europe.

CHAPTER XII

ALTHOUGH the facts recorded in the preceding chapters have been for the most part discovered within a comparatively recent period, it is by no means merely of late years, or among archæologists only, that the difficulties in Archbishop Usher's chronology have been felt to be insuperable. Historians, philologists, and physiologists have alike admitted that the short period allowed could hardly be reconciled with the history of some Eastern nations; that it did not leave room for the development either of the different languages, or (assuming the unity of the human race) for the important physical peculiarities by which the various races of men are distinguished.

Thus, Dr Prichard says : "Many writers who have been by no means inclined to raise objections against the authority of the Sacred Scriptures, and in particular Michaelis, have felt themselves embarrassed by the shortness of the interval between the Noachic Deluge and the period at which the records of various nations commence, or the earliest date to which their historical memorials lead us back. The extravagant claims to a remote and almost fathomless antiquity, made by the fabulists of many nations, have vanished before the touch of accurate criticism ; but after abstracting all that is apparently mythological from the early traditions of the Indians, Egyptians, and some other nations, the probable history of some of them seems still to reach up to a period too remote to be reconciled with the short chronology of

Usher and Petavius. This has been so universally felt by all those writers who have entered on the investigation of primeval history that it is superfluous to dwell upon the subject." [1]

Baron Bunsen, one of the ablest among those who regard the various forms of language as having had a common origin, is forced to claim for the human race an antiquity of at least twenty thousand years. Again, the ingenious author of *The Genesis of the Earth and of Man* [2] says truly that " one of the greatest of the difficulties that beset us when we endeavour to account for the commonly supposed descent of all mankind from a single pair, . . . lies in the fact of our finding, upon Egyptian monuments, mostly of the thirteenth, fourteenth, and fifteenth centuries before the Christian era, representations of individuals of numerous nations, African, Asiatic, and European, differing in physical characteristics as widely as any equal number of nations of the present age that could be grouped together ; among these being Negroes, of the true Negritian stamp, depicted with a fidelity, as to colour and features, hardly to be surpassed by an accomplished modern artist. That such diversities had been produced by natural means in the interval between that remote age and the time of Noah, probably no one versed in the sciences of anatomy and physiology will consider credible " ; and he concludes, therefore, that the human race cannot have been derived from a single pair. For, just as the philological difficulties will not, of course, affect those who accept literally the account given in our English version of the miraculous creation of languages at the Tower of Babel, so in the same way " the shortness of the period allowed by the received chronology, for the development of those physical varieties which distinguish the different races of men," [3] though felt as " one of the greatest difficulties connected with the opinion that all mankind are descended from one primitive stock," will

---

[1] Prichard, *Researches into the Physical Hist. of Mankind*, vol. v. p. 553.
[2] *Loc. cit.*, p. 117.   [3] Prichard, *loc. cit.*, p. 552.

not affect those who believe in the existence of separate species of men.

The study of language, again, clearly proves the great antiquity of man. Four thousand years ago the Assyrians, as proved by their inscriptions, spoke a tongue in many respects less archaic than that of Central Arabia is now ; and when we consider that it was descended from a parent source which has produced all the other Semitic languages, that this again was probably related to Libyan and Egyptian, and that still further back lie the ages in which inarticulate cries were gradually moulded into true language, we must feel that linguistic researches point most strongly in the same direction.[1]

Professor Huxley has also deduced a very interesting argument from the geographical distribution of the races of men. He divides mankind into four groups, the Australoid, Negroid, Mongoloid, and Xanthochroid. The latter are the fair, light-haired, blue-eyed people who occupy a large part of Europe ; the Mongoloid are the Tartar, American, and Polynesian races ; the Negroid are the Negroes, Hottentots, and Negritos ; and the Australoid type contains all the inhabitants of Australia, and the native races of the Deccan, with whom he also associates the ancient Egyptians. Whatever difference of opinion may exist among ethnologists about the other three divisions, still as to the Negroid race most are agreed, and this is the one to which I now wish to call attention. The geographical distribution of the Xanthochroid and Mongoloid races presents no difficulty, nor will I here discuss that of the Australoid group. But I entirely agree with Professor Huxley that the present position of the Negro race cannot be explained excepting on the hypothesis that since the appearance of that race immense geographical changes have taken place,—that continent has become ocean, and sea, land. The negroes are essentially a non-navigating race ; they build no ships, and even the canoes of the Fijians are evidently copied from those of the Polynesians. Now what is the

[1] See Sayce, *Int. to the Sci. of Lang.*, vol. ii. p. 319.

geographical distribution of the race ? They occupy all Africa south of the Sahara, which neither they nor the rest of the true African fauna have ever crossed ; and though they do not occur in Arabia, Persia, Hindostan, Siam, or China, we find them in Madagascar, and in the Andaman Islands,—not in Java, Sumatra, or Borneo, but in the Malay peninsula, in the Philippines, New Guinea, the New Hebrides, New Caledonia, the Fiji Islands, and in Tasmania.

This remarkable distribution is perhaps most easily explicable on the hypothesis that since the Negroid race came into existence, there must have been an immense tract of land or a chain of islands stretching from the eastern coast of Africa right across the Indian Ocean, and secondly, that the sea then occupied the area of the present great desert. In whatever manner, however, these facts are to be explained, they certainly indicate that the Negro race is of very great antiquity.

I have often been much struck, when standing at the feet of glaciers, by the great size of the terminal moraines, and the length of time which must have been required for their formation. Let us take as an instance the Nigard glacier in the Justedal, on the Sognefjord. The Norwegian glaciers no doubt covered formerly a much larger area than that which they now occupy. They retreated as the cold diminished ; but we have already seen that man was present in Western Europe when the general temperature was several degrees at least lower than it is at present ; and we shall probably, therefore, be within the mark if we suppose that the glacier at Justedal has retreated at least a mile up the valley since the period of the river-drift gravels, and the entrance of man into Europe. Now the terminal moraine of the glacier covers the whole of this space with great blocks of stones, thousands and hundreds of thousands in number, and yet, although all these have probably been brought down in the human period, I could only see a few blocks on the lower end of the glacier itself.

As far as Denmark is concerned we must, for the

present, rely principally on the double change which has taken place in the prevalent vegetation. Beech forests are now the pride of the country, and, as far as tradition goes, they have always been so. But, as is shown by the peat-bogs, this is a mistake. The large peat-mosses do not help us very much in this matter, but there are in many of the forests small and deep depressions, filled with peat, and called skov-mose. These, as might naturally be expected, contain many trees which grew on their edges, and at length fell into them. At the bottom is usually an amorphous peat, above is a layer of pines— a tree which does not now grow naturally in Denmark. Higher up the pines disappear, and are replaced by oaks and white birches, neither of which are now common in Denmark ; while the upper layer consists principally of the *Betula verrucosa,* and corresponds to the present, which we may call the Beech Period. Professor Steenstrup has found stone implements among the stems of the pines ; and as the capercailzie, which feeds on the young shoots of the pine, has been found in the Kjökkenmöddings, it seems likely, to say the least, that these shell-mounds belong to the Pine Period, and that the three great stages of civilization correspond in some measure to these three periods of arborescent vegetation. For one species of tree thus to displace another, and in its turn to be supplanted by a third, would evidently require a great, though at present we have no means of measuring how great, lapse of time.

Turning now from Denmark to Switzerland, there are two cases in which a more definite estimate has been attempted. We must not, indeed, place too much reliance on them as yet, but if many calculations made on different data shall agree in the main, we may at length come to some approximate conclusion.

The first of these calculations we owe to M. Morlot. The torrent of the Tinière, at the point where it falls into the Lake of Geneva, near Villeneuve, has gradually built up a cone of gravel and alluvium. In the formation of the railway this cone has been bisected for a length of

1000 feet, and to a depth, in the central part, of about 32 feet 6 inches above the level of the railway. The section of the cone thus obtained shows a very regular structure, which proves that its formation was gradual. It is composed of the same materials (sand, gravel, and large blocks) as those which are even now brought down by the stream. The amount of detritus does, indeed, differ considerably from year to year, but in the long-run the differences compensate for one another, so that, when considering long periods, and the structure of the whole mass, the influences of the temporary variations, which arise from meteorological causes, altogether disappear, and need not, therefore, be taken into account. Documents preserved in the archives of Villeneuve show that in the year 1710 the stream was dammed up, and its course a little altered, which makes the present cone slightly irregular. That the change was not of any great antiquity is also shown by the fact that on the side where the cone was protected by the dykes, the vegetable soil, where it has been affected by cultivation, does not exceed two or three inches in thickness. On the side thus protected by the dykes, the railway cutting has exposed three layers of vegetable soil, each of which must, at one time, have formed the surface of the cone. They are regularly intercalated among the gravel, and parallel to one another, as well as to the present surface of the cone, which itself follows a very regular curve. The first of these ancient surfaces was traced on the south side of the cone, over a surface of 15,000 square feet : it had a thickness of 4 to 6 inches, and occurred at a depth of about 4 feet (1·14 metres measured to the base of the layer) below the present surface of the cone. This layer, which belonged to the Roman period, contained tiles and a Roman coin.

The second layer was traced over a surface of 25,000 square feet ; it was 6 inches in thickness, and lay at a depth of about 10 feet (2·97 metres) including the thickness of the layer. In it have been found several fragments of unglazed pottery, and a pair of tweezers in bronze. The third layer has been followed for 3500 square feet ;

it was 6 or 7 inches in thickness, and lay at a depth of 19 feet (5·69 metres) below the present surface : in it were found some fragments of very rude pottery, some pieces of charcoal, some broken bones, and a human skeleton with a small, round, and very thick skull. Fragments of charcoal were even found a foot deeper, and it is also worthy of notice that no trace of tiles was found below the upper layer of earth.

Towards the centre of the cone the three layers disappear, since at this part the torrent has most force, and has deposited the coarsest materials, even some blocks as much as three feet in diameter. The farther we go from this central region, the smaller are the materials deposited, and the more easily might a layer of earth, formed since the last great inundations, be covered over by fresh deposits. Thus, at a depth of ten feet, in the gravel on the south of the cone, at a part where the layer of earth belonging to the Bronze Age had already disappeared, two unrolled bronze implements were discovered. They had probably been retained by their weight, when the earth which once covered them was washed away by the torrent. After disappearing towards the centre of the cone, the three layers reappear on the north side, at a slightly greater depth, but with the same regularity and the same relative position. The layer of the Stone Age was but slightly interrupted, while that of the Bronze Era was easily distinguishable by its peculiar character and colour.

It must be confessed that the starting-point of this argument, viz., the so-called " Roman " layer, is far from being satisfactorily determined. It is quite possible that tiles were used in Switzerland before the " Roman " period ; it is probable that they continued in use to a later period. The coin found in the " Roman " layer was so much worn as to be undeterminable ; it had, therefore, probably been long in use. M. Uhlmann has also argued [1] that the bones found in the lower layer are not such as we should expect to find in a Stone Age

[1] *Ueber Thierreste und Gebisstheil gefunden in den Schuttablagerungen der Tinière*, Bern, 1868.

deposit, since they are not so much discoloured as those from the Stone Age Pfahlbauten, and all belong to domestic animals. Only fourteen determinable fragments, however, were found, and of these several probably belonged to a single individual. Moreover, the condition of bones from a peat-moss cannot fairly be compared with those which had been lying in a material such as that forming the cone of the Tinière.

M. Morlot did not disguise from himself that there were certain elements of doubt in the case, but on the whole it seemed to him that the phenomena were so regular and so well marked that he was justified in applying to them a calculation with some little confidence of at least approximate accuracy. Making some allowances ; for instance, admitting three hundred years instead of one hundred and fifty, for the period since the embankment, and taking the Roman period as representing an antiquity of from sixteen to eighteen centuries, he obtains for the Age of Bronze an antiquity of from 2900 years to 4200 years, for that of the Stone Period from 4700 to 7000 years, and for the whole cone an age of from 7400 to 11,000 years. M. Morlot thought that we should be most nearly correct in deducting two hundred years only for the action of the dykes, and in attributing to the Roman layer an antiquity of sixteen centuries, that is to say, in referring it to the middle of the third century. This would give an antiquity of 3800 years for the Bronze Age, and 6400 years for that of Stone ; and, on the whole, he is inclined to suppose for the former an antiquity of from 3000 to 4000 years, and for the latter of from 5000 to 7000 years.

Not less ingenious is the attempt which has been made by M. Gilliéron,[1] Professor at the college of Neuveville, to obtain a date for the lake-habitation at the Pont de Thièle. This stream connects the lakes of Neufchâtel and Bienne. During the first part of its course the valley is narrow, and the bridge, close to which the lake-dwelling

[1] *Notice sur les Habitations Lacustres du Pont de Thièle*, Porrentruy, 1862.

has been discovered, is situated at the narrowest spot. A little further down the valley suddenly expands, and from this point remains of the same width until it joins the Lake of Bienne. It is evident that the valley, as far as the bridge over the Thièle, was once occupied by the lake, which has gradually been silted up by the action of forces still in operation ; and if we could ascertain how long it would have taken to effect this change, we should then know approximately the date of the remains found at the Pont de Thièle, which are evidently those of a lake-dwelling. The Abbey of St Jean, which stands in this valley, about 375 metres from the present shore of the lake, was founded, according to ancient documents, between the years 1090 and 1106, and is therefore about 750 years old. It is possible that the abbey may not have been built exactly on the then edge of the lake ; but even if this were the case, the gain of land will only have been 375 metres in 750 years. Professor Gilliéron does not compare with this the whole space between the convent and the lake-dwelling, because in the narrower part of the valley, in which the latter is situated, the gain may have been more rapid ; but if we only go to the point at which the basin contracts, we shall have a distance of 3000 metres, which would, upon these data, indicate a minimum antiquity of 6750 years. This calculation assumes that the shape of the bottom of the valley was originally uniform. M. Morlot agrees with Professor Gilliéron in believing that this was the case, and from the general configuration of the valley it seems to me also to be a reasonable supposition. Moreover, the soundings taken by M. Hisely in the Lake of Bienne show that the variations in depth are but of slight importance. We must not, indeed, attach too much importance to these two calculations ; but they appear to indicate that at least 6000 or 7000 years ago Switzerland was already inhabited by men who used polished stone implements ; but how long they had been there, or how many centuries elapsed before the discovery of metal, we have as yet no evidence to show.

These figures only, however, give us a minimum, and a much greater antiquity was obtained by Mr Horner as the result of his Egyptian researches, which were undertaken at the joint expense of the Royal Society and the Egyptian Government. Every year the Nile, during its periodical overflow, deposits a certain amount of fine mud, and even as long ago as the time of Herodotus it was inferred that Egypt had been formerly an arm of the sea, filled up gradually and converted into dry land by the mud brought down from the upper country.

In the great work on Egypt which we owe to the French philosophers who accompanied Napoleon's expedition to that country, an attempt was made to estimate the secular elevation thus produced, and it was assumed to be five inches in a century. This general average was consistent, however, with great differences at different parts, and Mr Horner, therefore, did not consider himself justified in applying this estimate to particular cases, even if he had been satisfied with the evidence on which it rested. He preferred to examine the accumulation which had taken place round monuments of known age, and selected two—namely, the obelisk at Heliopolis and the statue of Rameses II. in Memphis. The obelisk was "erected 2300 years B.C., and adding 1850, the year when the observation was made (June 1851, *i.e.* before the inundation of that year), we have 4150 years in which the eleven feet of sediment were deposited, which is at the rate of 3·18 inches in a century."[1] But Mr Horner himself admits that "entire reliance cannot be placed on this conclusion, principally because it is possible that the site originally chosen for the temple and city of Heliopolis was a portion of land somewhat raised above the level of the rest of the desert." He relies, therefore, principally on the evidence supplied by the colossal statue in Memphis. In this case the present surface is 10 feet 6¾ inches above the base of the platform on which the statue stood. Assuming that the platform was sunk 14¾ inches below the surface of the ground at the time it was laid, we have

[1] Horner, *Phil. Trans.*, 1858, p. 73.

a depth of sediment from the present surface to that level of 9 feet 4 inches. Rameses reigned between 1394 and 1328 B.C., which would give an antiquity of 3215 years, and consequently a mean increase of $3\frac{1}{2}$ inches in a century. Having thus obtained an approximate measure of the rate of deposit in that part of the Nile valley, Mr Horner dug several pits to a considerable depth, and in one of them, close to the statue and at the depth of 39 feet, a piece of pottery was found, which upon the above data would indicate an antiquity of about 13,000 years.

In many other excavations pieces of pottery and other indications of man were found at even greater depths, but it must be confessed that there are several reasons which render the calculations somewhat doubtful. For instance, it is impossible to ascertain how far the pedestal of the statue was inserted into the ground ; Mr Horner has allowed $14\frac{3}{4}$ inches, but if it was deeper, the rate of deposition would be diminished and the age increased. On the other hand, if the statue was on raised ground, of course the reverse would be the case.

It has also been argued that the ancient Egyptians were in the habit of making embankments round the areas on which they erected temples, statues, etc., so as to keep out the waters of the Nile.

" Whenever, then," says Sir Charles Lyell, " the waters at length break into such depressions, they must at first carry with them into the enclosure much mud washed from the steep surrounding banks, so that a greater quantity would be deposited in a few years than, perhaps, in as many centuries on the great plain outside the depressed area, where no such disturbing causes intervened." This objection is, however, untenable, because the rapidity of deposition will be in proportion to the previous retardation, and will only tend to bring the depressed area up to the general level. Supposing, for instance, that the monument of Rameses, erected on the flat plain of Memphis 3200 years ago, was protected by embankments for the first 2000 years, and that during that time the plain outside was gradually raised 5 feet

10 inches, being at the rate of $3\frac{1}{2}$ inches in a century :
when the embankment gave way the space enclosed would
soon be filled up to the general level, and a thickness of
5 feet 10 inches might be deposited in a few years : still
this exceptionally rapid accumulation would only be the
complement of the exceptional want of deposit which had
preceded it ; and, consequently, when the level of the
surrounding plain had been attained, then, although the
mud covering the base of the statue may have been
altogether deposited in the last few hundred years, *i.e.*
since the embankments have been neglected, the thickness
of the deposit will still be a measure of the general
elevation which has taken place on the surrounding plain
since the erection of the monument.

Even if the embankments had remained intact to this
day, and the monument stood now in the hollow thus
produced, Mr Horner's argument would not be invali-
dated, but rather confirmed. The depth of the hollow
would give us a measure of the deposit which had taken
place since the erection of the monument, or rather since
the formation of the embankment. If, however, the
monument had been erected in an area already depressed
by the action of still older embankments, the calculation
would be vitiated, but in this case the rate of deposition
would appear to be more than it really is, and the true
age consequently would be even greater than the above
estimate. Much credit is due to the Egyptian Government for the liberal manner in which they assisted Mr
Horner and the Royal Society in this investigation.

I have already mentioned the evidence on which
M. Morlot has endeavoured to estimate the age of the
Cone de la Tinière, and which gave about 6000 years
for the lower layer of vegetable soil, and 10,000 years
for the whole of the existing cone. But above this
existing cone is another, which was formed when the
lake stood at a higher level than at present, and which
M. Morlot refers to the period of the river-drift gravels.
This drift-age cone is about twelve times as large as
that now forming, and would appear, therefore, on the

same data, to indicate an antiquity of more than 100,000 years.

In his *Travels in North America*, Sir C. Lyell has endeavoured to estimate the age of the Mississippi delta in the following manner :—" Dr Riddle," he says, " communicated to me, at New Orleans, the result of a series of experiments which he had made to ascertain the proportion of sediment contained in the waters of the Mississippi. He concluded that the mean annual amount of solid matter was to the water as $\frac{1}{1245}$ in weight, or about $\frac{1}{3000}$ in volume. Since that period he has made another series of experiments, and his tables show that the quantity of mud held in suspension increases regularly with the increased height and velocity of the stream. On the whole, comparing the flood season with that of clearest water, his experiments, continued down to 1849, give an average annual quantity of solid matter somewhat less than his first estimate, but not varying materially from it. From these observations, and those of Dr Carpenter and Mr Forskey (an eminent engineer, to whom I have before alluded), on the average width, depth, and velocity of the Mississippi, the mean annual discharge of water and sediment were deduced. I then assumed 528 feet, or the tenth of a mile, as the probable thickness of the deposit of mud and sand in the delta ; founding my conjecture chiefly on the depth of the Gulf of Mexico between the southern point of Florida and the Balize, which equals on an average one hundred fathoms, and partly on some borings six hundred feet deep, in the delta near Lake Pontchartrain, north of New Orleans, in which the bottom of the alluvial matter is said not to have been reached. The area of the delta being about 13,600 square statute miles, and the quantity of solid matter annually brought down the river 3,702,758,400 cubic feet, it must have taken 67,000 years for the formation of the whole ; and if the alluvial matter of the plain above be 264 feet deep, or half that of the delta, it must have required 33,500 more years for its accumulation, even if its area be estimated only as equal to that of the delta, whereas it is, in fact, larger."

Moreover, as Sir Charles has himself pointed out, a very large proportion of the mud brought down by the river is not deposited in the delta, but is carried out into the gulf. In the *Antiquity of Man*[1] he refers to the above-given calculation, and admits that the discharge of water seems to have been much underrated by the earlier experiments. Messrs Humphrey and Abbot, who have recently surveyed the delta, also remark that " the river pushes along its bottom into the gulf a certain quantity of sand and gravel, which would," they suppose, "augment the volume of solid matter by about one-tenth." This, of course, would greatly diminish the time required ; but, taking into consideration the quantity of mud which is carried out to sea, and which was not allowed for in the previous calculation, Sir Charles Lyell still regards 100,000 years as a moderate estimate ; and he considers that " the alluvium of the Somme containing flint implements and the remains of the mammoth and hyæna," is not less ancient.

Attempts have also been made to calculate the time required to excavate the ravine between the present Niagara Falls and Queenstown, which has been estimated at about 35,000 years ;[2] others, however, make it much less.

Again, whatever cause or causes may have produced the great change which has taken place in the climate of Western Europe, there can be little doubt that this change indicates a very considerable lapse of time. We are indebted to Mr Hopkins for a very interesting memoir on this subject. Among the possible causes of change he discusses—

Firstly. A variation in the intensity of solar radiation.

To this theory Mr Hopkins sees no *a priori* objection ; but he does not feel disposed to attach much weight to

---

[1] Appendix to third edition, p. 16. See also *Geological Journal*, 1869, vol. xxv. p. 11.

[2] Geikie, *Phys. Geog.*, p. 280.

it, because it is "a mere hypothesis framed to account for a single and limited class of facts, and unsupported by the testimony of any other class of allied but independent phenomena."

It is, moreover, open to the objections stated with great force by Professor Tyndall,[1] who argues that the ancient glaciers indicate the action of heat as much as of cold. "Cold," he says, "will not produce glaciers. You may have the bitterest north-east winds here in London throughout the winter, without a single flake of snow. Cold must have the fitting object to operate upon, and this object—the aqueous vapour of the air—is the direct product of heat. Let us put this glacier question in another form : the latent heat of aqueous vapour, at the temperature of its production in the tropics, is about 1000° Fahr., for the latent heat augments as the temperature of evaporation descends. A pound of water thus vaporized at the equator, has absorbed one thousand times the quantity of heat which would raise a pound of the liquid one degree in temperature. . . . It is perfectly manifest that by weakening the sun's action, either through a defect of emission, or by the steeping of the entire solar system in space of a low temperature, we should be cutting off the glaciers at their source."

Secondly. Admitting the proper motion of the sun, it has been suggested that we may have recently passed from a colder into a warmer region of space.

I must refer to Mr Hopkins' memoir for his objections to this suggestion ; they certainly appear to "render the theory utterly inapplicable to the explanation of the changes of temperature at the more recent geological epochs."

This hypothesis, moreover, is liable to the same fatal objection as the first. To produce snow requires both heat and cold ; the first to evaporate, the second to condense. In fact, what we require is a greater contrast between the temperature of the tropics and that of our latitudes ; so that, paradoxical as it may appear, the

[1] *Heat considered as a Mode of Motion*, p. 192.

primary cause of the "glacial" epoch may be, after all, an elevation of temperature in the tropics, causing a greater amount of evaporation in the equatorial regions, and consequently a greater supply of the raw material of snow in the temperate regions during the winter months.

Thirdly. An alteration in the earth's axis.

The possibility of such a change has been denied by many astronomers. My father, the late Sir J. W. Lubbock, has, on the contrary, maintained[1] that this would necessarily follow from upheavals and depressions of the earth's surface if only they were of sufficient magnitude. The same view has recently been taken by other mathematicians, and among geologists by Dr Duncan and M. Carret. Sir John Evans has made the ingenious suggestion that the solid external crust of the earth may have slid over its fluid or semi-fluid nucleus. On the other hand, Sir George Darwin, who has recently dealt with the subject,[2] concludes that, while theoretically such a change may have taken place, the amount could not have been sufficient to cause any considerable change of climate in a recent geological period. The subject is one of extreme difficulty ; but it is at any rate clear that this suggestion, like the preceding, presupposes immense geographical changes, which would therefore necessarily imply an enormous lapse of time.

Fourthly. Mr Hopkins inclines to find the true solution of the difficulty in the supposition that the Gulf Stream did not at this period warm the shores of Europe. "A depression of 2000 feet would," he says, "convert the Mississippi into a great arm of the sea, of which the present Gulf of Mexico would form the southern extremity, and which would communicate at its northern extremity with the waters occupying the . . . great valley now occupied by the chain of lakes." In this case the Gulf Stream would no longer be deflected by the American coasts, but would pass directly up this channel into the Arctic Sea ; and as a very great ocean current

[1] *Geol. Journ.*, vol. v. p. 4.   [2] *Phil. Trans.*, vol. clxvii.

must have its counter current, it is probable that there would be a flow of cold water from the North between the coasts of Norway and Greenland. The absence of the Gulf Stream would probably lower the January temperature of Western Europe ten degrees, while the presence of a cold current from the North might make a further difference of about three or four degrees[1]—an alteration of the climate which would apparently be sufficient to account for all the phenomena. This theory Mr Hopkins considers as no mere hypothesis, but as necessarily following from the submergence of North America, which has been inferred from evidence of a different nature.

In this case, of course, the periods of great cold in Europe and in America must have been successive, and not synchronous; and it may also be observed that in this suggested deflection of the Gulf Stream, Mr Hopkins was contemplating a period anterior to that of the present rivers. For if we are to adopt this solution of the difficulty, an immense time would be required. If, when the gravels and loëss of the Somme and the Seine were being deposited, the Gulf Stream was passing up what is now the valley of the Mississippi, then it follows that the formation of the loëss in the valley and its delta—an accumulation which Sir C. Lyell has shown to require a period of about 100,000 years—would be subsequent to the excavation of the Somme valley, and to the presence of man in Western Europe.

The deflection of the Gulf Stream from our coasts might, however, be owing to another cause, namely, a subsidence of the Isthmus of Panama; in support of which suggestion may be mentioned the remarkable fact recently observed by Dr Günther, that out of 173 tropical marine fish, no less than 57, or 30 per cent., occur on both sides of the isthmus—in both the Atlantic and the Pacific.[2]

Mr Croll has pointed out that at present the " S.E. trade winds of the Atlantic blow with greater force than

---

[1] Hopkins, *loc. cit.*, p. 85.   [2] *Trans. Zool. Soc.*, vol. vi. p. 397.

the N.E. trades, and the consequence is that the S.E.
trades sometimes extend to 10° or 15° N. lat., whereas
the N.E. trades seldom blow south of the equator. But
during the glacial epoch the very reverse must have
occurred. Hence the great equatorial current of the
Atlantic must during that period have been driven considerably south of its present position." [1]   Even at present,
while the greater part of the water enters the Gulf of
Mexico, one portion is deflected southwards, which in the
case mentioned above would happen to the greater
portion, if not the whole.

Under existing circumstances, the southern division is
comparatively small ; by far the larger portion of the
great equatorial current turns northwards, and warms the
northern hemisphere, so that the comparatively high
temperature of the Northern Atlantic is in some measure
due to heat derived from the southern hemisphere. In
a subsequent memoir,[2] Mr Croll has made some interesting calculations with reference to the great effect produced
by the Gulf Stream on the present climate of Europe.
He estimates that it conveys as much heat as is received
from the sun by 3,121,870 square miles of the equator :
nearly as much as is received from the sun by the entire
Arctic regions, the proportions being as 15 to 18.   Our
present climate is 12° higher than the normal due to its
latitude, but Mr Croll points out that this is by no means
to be considered as measuring the effect of the Gulf Stream.
The temperature of the whole hemisphere is raised by
the equatorial currents, and the 12° "only represent the
number of degrees that the mean normal temperature of
our island stands above what is called the normal temperature of the latitude."

Professor Spencer has recently given some reasons for
believing in the existence of an Antillean continent at a
recent geological period.   This would have affected our
climate considerably.   It would not indeed necessarily
have directed the Gulf Stream from our shores ; but as

---

[1] Croll, *Philosophical Magazine*, Aug. 1864.
[2] *Loc. cit.*, Feb. and Oct. 1870.

the water could not have made its long journey round the Gulf of Mexico, it could not have been so long exposed to a tropical sun, and could not have attained so high a temperature.

There is yet another cause to which the present mild temperature of Europe is partly due, and which must not be altogether neglected. At the period under consideration, indeed, the geography of Western Europe must have been very nearly what it is now. There is, however, good reason for considering that the Desert of Sahara then formed part of the Atlantic Ocean. Mr Tristram has called attention to cliffs, ancient sea-beaches, and lines of terraces along the northern margin of the desert, and the common cockle is still found living in some of the salt lakes. Mr Tristram also discovered a species of *Haligenes*, which inhabits the Gulf of Guinea, in a salt lake in lat. 32° N. and long. 7° E., separated, therefore, from its present marine habitat by the whole extent of the great Desert. Moreover, as we have already seen, the present geographical distribution of animals can only be explained on the hypothesis that the existing fauna, including man, occupied Africa long before the Sahara became dry land.

Mr Croll has shown in the memoir already cited, that currents of warm water produce a far greater effect upon climate than aerial currents of equal volume and temperature; yet it is evident that such a change would have a great effect on the climate of Europe. At present we receive from the South hot dry winds, which warm us both directly and also indirectly by melting the snow and ice on our mountain-tops. If the Sahara was a sea, the "Fohn," instead of being a burning, dry wind, which strips the snow off the Alps, both by melting and evaporation, would be a moist, damp wind, and when it reached the mountains would produce dense clouds and thick fogs, which would prevent the sun's rays from warming the earth or melting the glaciers. So that to the barren desert of the Sahara, which we are apt to look upon as a useless waste, we are in reality much indebted for the fertility and civilization of Europe. It is true that the effect of a water area in the Sahara would not be so great as might at first sight be supposed, because the prevalent winds would carry the moisture mainly to Eastern Europe and Western Asia. If, however, these regions thus became damper, our east winds would be less dry and cold than is now the case.

M. Adhémar[1] has suggested a mode of accounting for the cold of the glacial epoch, which, if the true one, would give us means of calculating its antiquity. If the plane of the equator coincided exactly with that of the ecliptic, *i.e.* with that of the earth's orbit, then it is evident that every day would be followed by a night of equal length. In consequence, however, of the obliquity of the ecliptic, there are only two days in the year when this is actually the case, namely, the 20th of March and the 23rd September. Thus our year is divided into four well-marked periods. "Winter" begins on the 22nd December, which is the shortest day of the year, and continues until the 20th March, which is called the spring equinox, because on it the · day and night are of equal lengths. "Spring" commences on the 20th March and continues till the 21st June, during which time the days continue to elongate at the expense of the night.

From the 21st June, however, which is the first day of "Summer," the days begin to shorten, until, on the 23rd of September, day and night are again equal, and we have the autumn equinox.

Autumn commences on the 23rd September, and the days continue to diminish till the 22nd December, which is the shortest day, and after which they begin to lengthen.

At present, then, the northern hemisphere enjoys in each year seven days more of spring and summer than of autumn and winter ; while, on the other hand, the southern hemisphere has seven days more of autumn and winter than of spring and summer. This inequality

---

[1] *Revolutions de la Mer*, J. Adhémar, Paris.

of the seasons is due to the greater rapidity with which the earth moves when it is in perihelion, or nearest the sun, as is the case on the 31st December.

The perihelion has not always been, nor will it always continue to be, at the same time of year as at present. On the contrary, a constant though slow movement is continually taking place : the time of perihelion takes place in each year a little later than the preceding, so that perihelion, which now happens on the 31st December, will in the lapse of time fall on the 1st of January, then on the 2nd, and so on. The interval between the times at which perihelion occurs on the same day of the year is about 21,000 years. At some future day, about 5000 years hence, the perihelion will occur on the 20th March, and in about 21,000 years it will again be on the 31st December. The aphelion changes of course in the same way, and consequently the northern and southern hemispheres alternately enjoy a preponderance of summer. The year 1248 A.D. was that in which the first day of winter corresponded with the passage of the earth into perihelion, and consequently was the period when the balance of summer in favour of the northern hemisphere was greatest. Up to that date the duration of summer was increasing ; it is now, and has been for six hundred and thirty years, gradually diminishing.

Astronomers have not, however, generally considered that these changes, or even those which affect the excentricity of our orbit, would produce any material difference between the climates of the two hemispheres, because, whatever the excentricity of our orbit may be, the two hemispheres must receive exactly the same amounts of heat, " the proximity of the sun in perigee, or its distance in apogee, exactly compensating the effect of its swifter or slower motion " ; in other words, the southern hemisphere has a shorter summer than ours because it is nearer the sun, and for the same reason it receives in a given time more heat, so that the two differences neutralize one another.

M. Adhémar points out that the temperature of each

hemisphere does not depend on the quantity of heat received from the sun, but on the difference between the amount received and the amount radiated away into space ; in other words, on the quantity retained. If, he says, in illustration, you burn a given quantity of wood in two identical rooms, and then open the windows in one and not in the other, you will soon have a difference of temperature, though the supply of the heat has been the same in both.[1]

Now, our northern hemisphere has $186 \times 24 = 4464$ hours of day in the year, and $179 \times 24 = 4296$ hours of night, while the southern hemisphere has 4464 hours of night, and only 4296 of day. We may admit that the southern hemisphere will receive as much heat from the sun in its 4296 hours of day as we do in our 4464 ; but it is evident that it will retain less, because it will have 168 hours more of night, during which radiation will be going on. Though, therefore, the heat received by the two hemispheres will be equal, the temperature of the two will not, M. Adhémar maintains, be by any means the same ; and though at first this difference may be slight, it will in its nature be to a certain extent cumulative.

Mr Croll, however, was of opinion that this difference can, after all, produce little or no effect on climate. However this may be, it is evident that, on account of the much greater accumulation of ice, the southern hemisphere is colder than the northern ; and it is also clear that this very fact tends to aggravate the difference to which it is due.

Moreover, M. Adhémar affirms that the immense cupola of ice which is known to exist round the South Pole must affect the centre of gravity of the earth, and consequently attract the ocean southwards. In this manner, indeed, he attempts to explain the remarkable preponderance of land in the north, and of sea in the southern hemisphere. A glance at the map will show this difference, but the following table makes it more

[1] *Revolutions de la Mer*, p. 344.

apparent. Taking each parallel as unity, the proportion of sea is as follows :—

60° North .	. 0·353	15° South .	. 0·786
50° ,,	. 0·407	20° ,,	. 0·777
40° ,,	. 0·527	30° ,,	. 0·791
30° ,,	. 0·536	40° ,,	. 0·951
20° ,,	. 0·677	50° ,,	. 0·972
10° ,,	. 0·710	60° ,,	. 1·000
0° ,,	. 0·771		

Certainly a progressive increase of sea, which is so remarkably regular, can hardly be the result of accident.[1]

M. Adhémar maintains that this is due to the alteration of the centre of gravity of the earth, caused by the great southern cupola of ice ; and consequently that 11,120 years ago (*i.e.* 10,500 years before 1248), when the northern hemisphere was at its coldest, the northern glacier consequently at its maximum, and the southern at its minimum, the preponderance of water would have been in the northern hemisphere, and the submersion of the lower lands of Europe and America may have been due to an alteration, not in the level of the land, but in that of the sea. He conceives that when the increasing cupola counterbalances the decreasing one, there is a sudden transfer of the centre of gravity of the earth from one side of the centre of the solid part to the other, and consequently a rush of water, or deluge, alternately from north to south and from south to north, occurring every 10,500 years. It seems to me, however, that the alterations of the ice cupolas would be too slow, and consequently the change in the centre of gravity too gradual, to cause any sudden rush or deluge of water from one pole to the other.

According to this theory, the year 1248 was that in which our northern hemisphere was at its period of greatest heat, the southern at that of greatest cold ; and as 630 years have since elapsed, we might expect to find some evidence of subsequent change.

[1] I have elsewhere (*Nature*, 1887, and *Journal Geogr. Society*, 1895) attempted to show that this may explain the remarkable predominance of land pointing southwards.

As regards the southern hemisphere, M. Adhémar points out that the great southern glacier has considerably retreated since the time of Captain Cook, but it is in the northern hemisphere that he finds the greatest evidence of alteration. He dwells much on the increase, during the last few centuries, of the ice in Greenland, and points out that the cultivation of the vine does not now extend so far northwards as was once the case. M. Adhémar, then, considers that the last epoch of greatest cold must have been 11,120 years ago, since which time the climate of our hemisphere gradually improved up to the year 1248, when it was most genial, and after which it has, in his opinion, gradually commenced again to deteriorate. Sir Charles Lyell,[1] however, does not think that this change, " which could hardly produce more than a difference of half a degree Fahrenheit between the cold of the present winter and that of 1248, would be appreciable." He considered that the whole effect which can be produced by secular astronomical changes must "always be very subordinate to the influence of geographical conditions."[2]

Sir John Herschel[3] also " was very far from supposing it competent " to account for so great an alteration. Moreover, it is remarkable as showing how far we are from possessing the data necessary for any satisfactory conclusions, that while, as we have seen, M. Adhémar regards the enormous cupola of ice at the South Pole as the reason for the almost entire absence of land at that pole, Sir C. Lyell, on the other hand, states as a fact that the chief cause of the intense cold of high southern latitudes is " the vast height and extent of the Antarctic continent," the very existence of which is denied by, and is indeed incompatible with, the theory of M. Adhémar, while it is necessary to that of Sir C. Lyell.

Although, then, there can be no doubt that astronomical changes would, to a certain extent, affect our climate in the manner indicated by M. Adhémar, those best qualified to form an opinion do not consider that the

[1] *Principles of Geology*, 1867, vol. i. p. 278.   [2] *Ibid.*, vol. i. p. 243.
[3] *Outlines of Astronomy*, 1858, p. 235.

cause assigned by him would by itself be sufficient to account for changes so great as those which have taken place. The effect produced increases, however, with the excentricity of the earth's orbit. The form of this orbit is always altering ; as it approaches to a circle, the effect produced by precession and change of position of perihelion diminishes, while on the other hand it increases as the orbit elongates. At present the excentricity of our orbit is only 0·0168—that is to say, the orbit is nearly circular ; but there have been periods when it was much more elongated, and when consequently the extremes of temperature dependent on precession and the position of perihelion must also have been much greater.

Mr Croll and Mr Stone have calculated the excentricity for the last million years, and Mr John Carrick Moore has worked out the effect upon our climate, assuming other things to remain unchanged, in the four last columns of the following table, which is given by Sir C. Lyell in the last edition of the *Principles of Geology*.[1]

Mr Croll[2] does not indeed consider that an increase in the excentricity would directly alter the relative temperature of the two hemispheres, though it would bring about a condition of things that would have this effect. The mid-winter temperature of one hemisphere would be greatly lowered, the consequence of which would be that all the moisture would take the form of snow instead of rain, which would be the more important because the winter would be longer. The heat of the summer would be insufficient to melt the snow, which consequently would accumulate year by year. On the opposite hemisphere the reverse would be the case, and comparatively little snow would fall. The difference of temperature thus produced would cause the aerial currents, and especially the trade winds on the colder hemisphere, to be much stronger than those on the other ;

[1] *Loc. cit.*, vol. i. p. 293.
[2] *Climate and Time*, p. 228. See also Sir R. Ball, *The Cause of an Ice Age*. I ought to add that the argument has been disputed—as, for instance, by Mr Culverwell—but not I think disproved.

they would, therefore, blow across the equator, and, by impelling the equatorial waters towards the hemisphere which was already the warmer of the two, would raise its temperature still further.

TABLE SHOWING THE VARIATIONS IN THE EXCENTRICITY OF THE EARTH'S ORBIT FOR A MILLION YEARS BEFORE A.D. 1800, AND SOME OF THE CLIMATAL EFFECTS OF SUCH VARIATIONS.

		1	2	3	4	5	6
		Number of years before A.D. 1800.	Excentricity of orbit.	Difference of distance in millions of miles.	Number of winter days in excess.	Mean of hottest month in lat. of London.	Mean of coldest month in lat. of London.
		1,000,000	·0151	2¾	7·3	13° F.	21° F.
D		950,000	·0517	9¼	25·1	109°	3°
		900,000	·0102	1¼	4·9	80°	23°
C	{ a	850,000	·0747	13⅛	36·4	126°	7°
	b	800,000	·0132	2¼	6·4	82°	22°
	c	750,000	·0575	10½	27·8	113°	0°6
		700,000	·0220	4	10·2	87°	17°
		650,000	·0226	4	11	88°	16°
		600,000	·0417	7½	20·3	101°9	7°9
		550,000	·0166	3	8	84°	20°
		500,000	·0388	7	18·8	99°	9°
		450,000	·0308	5½	15	94°	13°
		400,000	·0170	3	8·2	84°	20°
		350,000	·0195	3½	9·5	86°	18°
		300,000	·0424	7¾	20·6	102°	7°
		250,000	·0258	4½	12·5	99°	15°
B	{ a	210,000	·0575	10½	27·8	113°	0°7
	b	200,000	·0567	10¼	27·7	113°	1°9
		150,000	·0332	6	16·1	95°	12°
A		100,000	·0473	8½	23	105°	5°
		50,000	·0131	2¼	6·3	82°	22°
		0	·0168	3	8·1	84°	20°

EXPLANATION OF THE TABLE.

COLUMN 1.—Division of a million years preceding 1800 into twenty equal parts.

COLUMN 2.—Computed by Mr James Croll, by aid of Leverrier's formula, gives the excentricity of the earth's orbit, in parts of a unit equal to the mean distance, or half the longer diameter of the ellipse.

COLUMN 3.—Which, together with the three following columns, has been computed by Mr John Carrick Moore, gives in millions of miles the difference between the greatest and least distances of the earth from the sun, during the excentricities given in Column 2.

COLUMN 4.—Gives the number of days by which winter, occurring in aphelion, is longer than the summer in perihelion.

COLUMN 5.—Gives the mean temperature of the hottest summer month in the latitude of London when the summer occurs in perihelion.

COLUMN 6.—Gives the mean temperature of the coldest winter month in the latitude of London when the winter occurs in aphelion.

The table shows that there are four periods, marked A, B, C, and D, in which there has been a large excentricity and an extreme climate. The periods marked A and B, says Sir Charles Lyell, " would not, I conceive, be sufficiently distant from our era to afford time for that series of glacial and post-glacial events which we can prove to have happened since the epoch of the greatest cold. These events relate to changes in the level of the land in opposite directions, as well as the excavation of valleys, and variations in the range and distribution of aquatic and terrestrial animals, all of which take place at so slow a rate that 200,000 years would not be sufficient to allow of the series of changes with which we are acquainted. I cannot but think, therefore, that if the date of the most intense glacial cold can be arrived at by aid of a very large excentricity, it would be a more probable conjecture to assign C than B as the period in question ; in other words, to regard the glacial epoch as representing a period 800,000 years ago."

In differing from such a great authority as Sir C. Lyell, I do so with great diffidence, but I confess that I should be disposed rather to assign the glacial era to the periods A and B, than to either C or D.[1]

It seems to me unlikely that the present fauna of Europe should have continued to exist, almost without alteration, for so long a period as 800,000 years, and the " variations in the range and distribution of aquatic and terrestrial animals," might, I think, have occurred in even less than 200,000 years under the great changes in climate which have taken place.

Professor Heim has made an interesting calculation as to the annual denudation in the Reuss valley. He estimates the yearly rainfall in the area drained by that river at 1,070,000,000 cubic metres, and the outflow of the river into the Lake of Lucerne at 750,000,000. The daily discharge of sand he calculates as about 150,000 cubic metres, to which he adds a quarter for finely divided matter. This would be equal to about 1000 waggon-

---

[1] Mr Croll has also expressed this opinion, *Phil. Mag.*, 1868, p. 367.

loads a day. According to his calculation, then, the average annual removal from each square kilometre of surface would be 242 cubic metres.

From the amount of material removed, he calculates the ages of the terraces as follows :—

The first or oldest . .	1,150,000 years.
The second . . .	330,000 „
The third	130,000 „
The fourth . . .	23,000 „

From the commencement of the excavation of the valleys to the present there would, he estimates, be required at the present rate of erosion a period of 3,750,000 years.

The *Geological Magazine* for June 1868 contains an interesting paper by Mr (now Sir Archibald) Geikie, " On Denudation now in Progress," in which he discusses the general effect produced by rivers excavating valleys and lowering the general level of the country. " For it is clear that if a river carries so many millions of cubic feet of sediment every year into the sea, the area of the country drained by it must have lost the quantity of solid material, and if we could restore the sediment so as to spread it over the basin, the layer so laid down would represent the fraction of a foot by which the basin had been lowered during a year." From observations made on the Mississippi, Ganges, Rhone, Danube, and other great rivers, Geikie estimates the annual loss at $\frac{1}{6000}$ of a foot. But he points out that this would not be uniform. The plains and watersheds would lose little, the slopes and valleys much. " There can be no doubt," he says, " that the erosion of the slopes and water-courses is very much greater than that of the more level grounds. Let it be assumed that the waste is nine times greater in the one case than in the other (in all likelihood it is more) : in other words, that while the plains and table-lands have been having one foot worn off their surface, the declivities and river-courses have lost nine feet. Let it be further assumed that one-tenth part of the surface of a country is occupied by its water-courses and glens, while the remaining nine-tenths are covered by the plains, wide valleys, or flat grounds. Now, according to the foregoing data, the mean annual quantity of detritus carried to the sea is equal to the yearly loss of $\frac{1}{6000}$ of a foot from the general surface of the country. The valleys, therefore, are lowered by $\frac{1}{1200}$ of a foot, and the more open and flat land by $\frac{1}{10800}$ of a foot."

Geikie calculates in this manner that Europe would disappear in little more than 4,000,000 of years. I cannot altogether accept this conclusion, for when a river has less than a given amount of fall, it ceases to excavate. Thus the effect of the Nile is to raise, not to lower, the level of Egypt, and most of our large rivers near their mouths act in a somewhat similar manner. As regards the higher districts, however, his data are perhaps not far wrong, and if we apply them to the valley of the Somme, where the excavation is about 200 feet in depth, they would indicate an antiquity for the Palæolithic Epoch of from 100,000 to 240,000 years, which, though arrived at from perfectly different data, agrees with the periods A and B in the calculation made by Messrs Croll and Stone.

In addition to the causes already alluded to, there is at least one other astronomical phenomenon—namely, the change in the obliquity of the ecliptic, which must be taken into account in considering the effects which cosmical causes may, or must, have exercised on climate. The whole question then is one, not only of extreme interest, but also of very great difficulty, and we are not, I think, at present in a position to estimate with confidence the effects on climate which may have been produced by these various causes.

Several other points connected with the glacial period receive a natural explanation from the suggestions of M. Adhémar and Mr Croll. Thus M. Morlôt[1] some years ago pointed out that there are in Switzerland

[1] *Bull. de la Soc. Vaudoise des Sciences Naturelles*, March 1854; *Bibl. Universelle de Genève*, May 1858.

evidences of several periods of cold, during what is called the glacial epoch, separated by an interval of mildness.

Of this the most striking instance is afforded by the Dürnten beds, where a layer of coal or lignite no less than twelve feet thick, lies between two glacial deposits. Again, Mr Croll gives[1] particulars of 250 borings through the surface deposits of the mining districts in Scotland. Of these, 25 showed two distinct boulder clay beds, 26 three, 1 four, 2 five, and 1 as many as six, with stratified beds of sand and gravel between. In England it is generally stated that there are two beds of boulder clay separated by one of sand and gravel. These may, however, not really correspond. There may have been several layers, of which, however, not more than two are shown in any single section. The beds of clay would indicate glacial conditions, the sand and gravel being deposited during the milder interglacial periods.[2]

There is still much difference of opinion whether M. Adhémar is right in attributing the preponderance of ocean in the southern hemisphere to the influence of the great Antarctic glacier. There can, however, be no doubt that an accumulation of snow and ice at one pole would, by affecting the position of the centre of gravity of the earth, attract the waters towards that pole. Mr Croll calculates that a diminution of 470 feet in the thickness of the Antarctic glacier would raise the sea-level at the North Pole 26 feet 5 inches, and 25 feet at the latitude of Glasgow. A mile of ice removed in the same way would produce a change of 280 feet. Mr Adhémar dwells on various considerations which induce him to attribute a very great thickness to the great southern glacier, and consequently he considers that the alterations of sea-level which would result from the alternate preponderance of ice in the Arctic and Antarctic regions,

---

[1] *Climate and Time*, p. 254.
[2] Mr Skertchly also considers that he has found a clear case, near Brandon, in which palæolithic brick earth underlies boulder clay. Other geologists, however, have contested his interpretation of the fact.

would account for the various alterations in the distribution of land and water. That there have been elevations and depressions of the land itself is sufficiently evident from other considerations ; and it is impossible to deny that the cause pointed out by M. Adhémar may have produced the relative elevation of the sea, as proved by the various raised beaches which fringe our shores, and the depression on the other hand indicated by the submerged forests, observed at so many points.

The former would indicate the periods of cold ; the latter, those of heat. The present condition of our rivers will also thus be simply explained. It is obvious that they have excavated their own valleys. At present, however, they are most of them filling up the lower parts of the excavation, as, for instance, we have seen to be the case with the Somme.

Moreover, the bottom of these valleys is in most cases lower than the present sea-level, which cannot have been the case at the time when they were excavated. It is evident, then, that the excavation must have been finished at the time when the land was at a higher relative level than at present.

Again, it will be remembered that side by side with the remains of Arctic animals, have been found others indicating a warm climate, such, for instance, as the hippopotamus. This fact, which has always hitherto been felt as a difficulty, is at once explained by Mr Croll's suggestion ; for when the excentricity was at a high value, we should have a change every ten or twelve thousand years from a high to a low temperature, and *vice versâ*. But a period of ten thousand years, long as it may appear to us, is very little from a geological point of view ; and we can thus understand how the remains of the hippopotamus and the musk-ox come to be found together in England and France. The very same astronomical conditions which fitted our valleys for the one, would at an interval of ten thousand years render them suitable for the other. In this case, palæolithic man would date back to the warmer interglacial times, which perhaps may explain the absence of any human remains of this period in Scandinavia and Germany.

Another consideration which tends to throw light on the glacial period, is the existence of submarine river valleys on the bed of the Atlantic. It has long been known that the Western European rivers—and the same applies to the eastern rivers of North America—can be traced out to sea, and the subject has recently been studied by Professor Hull.

The following figure shows the "continental shelf," the submerged river channel, and the profound depths

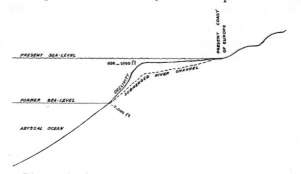

FIG. 254.—Diagram showing present and former sea-levels, the continental shelf, and the submerged river valley, as shown by the Admiralty soundings.

of the Atlantic. Professor Hull, to whom I have submitted the diagram, has passed it, but would have made the elevation even greater, say 7000 to 8000 feet.

For some hundred miles west of Ireland and the west of Europe the sea is very shallow, reaching a depth of 100 fathoms only. It then drops rapidly to the abysses of the ocean, 2000 to 4000 fathoms. Now, Professor Hull has shown by setting out the Admiralty Charts that the valleys of the ancient rivers which drained the English Channel and the Irish Sea, when they were dry land, the Loire, the Gironde, the Adour, the Tagus, the Congo, etc., can be traced out to sea, gradually deepening, and on approaching the edge of the continental shelf rapidly descending so as to form a gorge no less than some 6000 feet in depth. Of course rivers cannot excav-

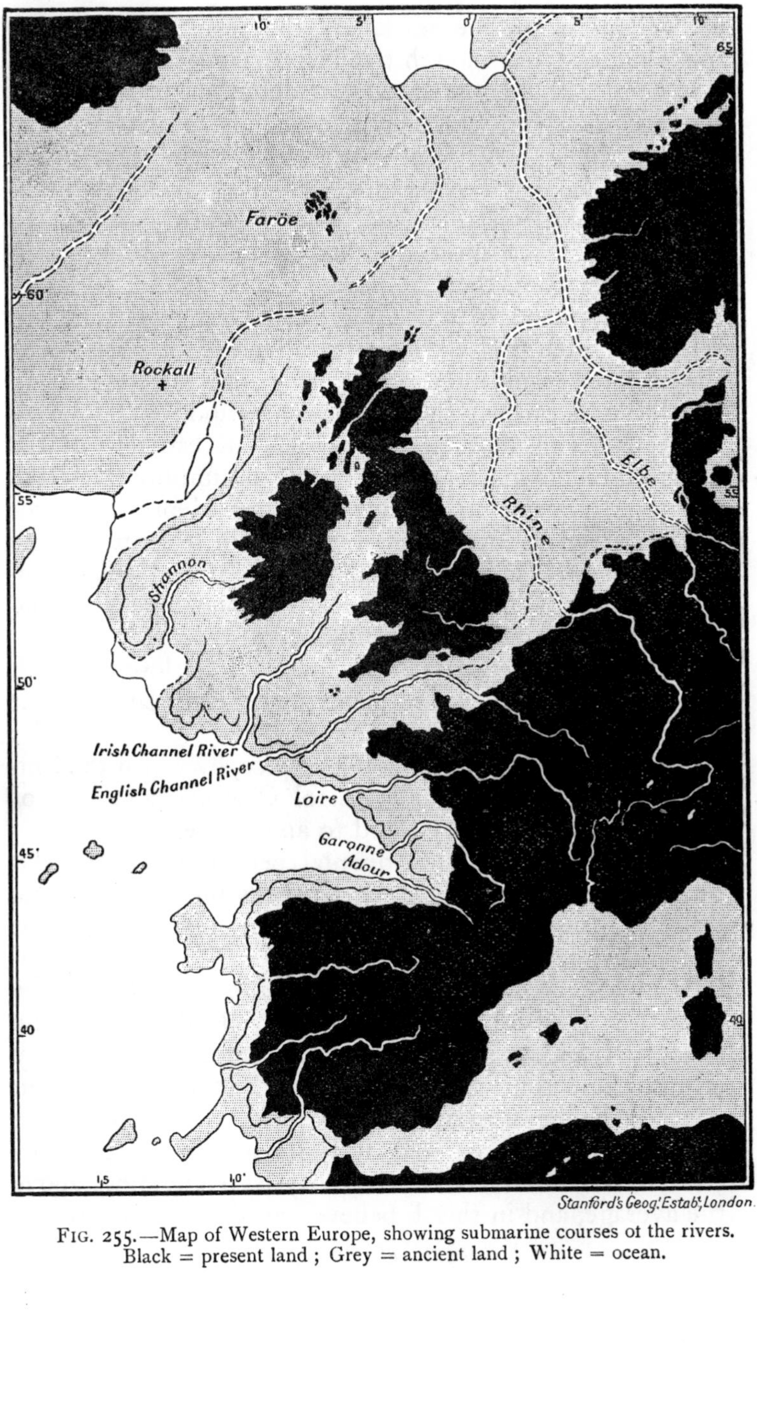

FIG. 255.—Map of Western Europe, showing submarine courses of the rivers.
Black = present land ; Grey = ancient land ; White = ocean.

ate valleys below the sea-level: the result would be to make deltas ; and though this is prevented in tidal seas, which accounts for the absence of deltas at the mouths of the Atlantic rivers, still they tend slowly to obliterate the ancient valleys, and raise the level of the sea bottom. The existence of river valleys attaining such depths as 6000 feet implies, therefore, that Western Europe and Eastern America must at that time have stood 6000 feet higher than they do now. This would certainly involve a period of cold, but there seems no sufficient reason to refer this elevation to Pliocene or Pleistocene times, and I think most geologists would carry it back to the Miocene or even the Oligocene Period.

Sir C. Lyell attempted[1] to form an estimate of the duration of the glacial epoch, on the assumption that the different movements of elevation and depression proceeded at an average rate of $2\frac{1}{2}$ feet in a century. As the simplest " series of changes in physical geography which can possibly account for the phenomena of the glacial period," he gave the following :—

" First, a continental period, towards the close of which the forest of Cromer flourished ; when the land was at least 500 feet above its present level."

" Secondly, a period of submergence, by which the land north of the Thames and Bristol Channel, and that of Ireland was gradually reduced to an archipelago."

" Thirdly, a second continental period, when the bed of the glacial sea, with its marine shells and erratic blocks, was laid dry, and when the quantity of land equalled that of the first period."

It is evident that such changes as these would require a great lapse of time. Sir Charles Lyell admits that the average change of $2\frac{1}{2}$ feet in a century is a purely arbitrary and conjectural rate, and that there are cases in which a change of as much as six feet in a century appears to have taken place : still, it is in his opinion probable that the rate assumed in a century is, if anything, above the average, and in this I believe most geologists would

[1] *Antiquity of Man*, pp. 282, 285.

be disposed to agree with him.   On this hypothesis he
estimates that the whole series of changes would have
required some 220,000 years.

To most geologists these figures, large as they are, will
have no appearance of improbability.   Prestwich indeed
was disposed to consider that the whole glacial period
need not have occupied more than 20,000 years.   This
is also the opinion of Mr Wright.[1]   The facts, however,
mentioned above seem to me incompatible with so short
a period.   In fact all the evidence of geology seems to
me to indicate an antiquity of which we are but beginning
to form a dim idea.   Take, for instance, one single
formation—our well-known chalk.   This consists entirely
of shells and fragments of shells deposited at the bottom
of an ancient sea, far away from any continent.   Such a
process as this must be very slow : we should certainly
be well within the mark if we were to assume a rate of
deposition of an inch in a century.   Now the chalk is
nearly two thousand feet in thickness, and would have
required therefore more than, in round numbers, 2,000,000
years for its formation.   The fossiliferous beds of Great
Britain, as a whole, are more than seventy thousand feet
in thickness ; and many which with us measure only a
few inches, on the Continent expand into strata of immense depth ; while others of great importance elsewhere
are wholly wanting with us ; for it is evident that during
all the different periods in which Great Britain has been
dry land, strata have been forming (as is, for example,
the case now) elsewhere, and not with us.   Moreover, we
must remember that many of the strata now existing have
been formed at the expense of older ones ; thus all the
flint gravels in the south-east of England have been produced by the destruction of chalk.   This, again, is a very
slow process.   It has been estimated that a cliff 500 feet
high will be worn away at the rate of an inch in a
century.   This may seem a low rate ; but we must bear
in mind that along any line of coast there are comparatively few points which are suffering at one time, and

[1] *Man and the Glacial Period*, p. 364.

that even on those, when a fall of cliff has taken place, the fragments serve as a protection to the coast until they have been gradually removed by the waves. Looking at the evidence as a whole, we can hardly, I think, estimate at less than 100,000,000 years the time which must have elapsed since the commencement of life on our planet.

There can be no doubt about the interest of these calculations, and they have also the great merit of giving some definiteness to our ideas. We must not, however, attribute to them a value which has been distinctly disclaimed even by their authors. Moreover, we must remember that these estimates are brought forward not as a proof, but as a measure, of antiquity. Our belief in the antiquity of man rests not on any isolated calculations, but on the changes which have taken place since his appearance : changes in the geography, in the fauna, and in the climate of Europe. Valleys have been deepened, widened, and partially filled up again ; caves through which subterranean rivers once ran are now left dry ; even the configuration of land has been materially altered, and Africa finally separated from Europe.

Our climate has greatly changed for the better, and with it the fauna has materially altered. In some cases— for instance, in that of the hippopotamus and of the African elephant—we may probably look to the diminution of food and the presence of man as the main cause of their disappearance ; the extinction of the mammoth, the *Elephas antiquus*, and the *Rhinoceros tichorhinus* may possibly be due to the same influences ; but the retreat of the reindeer and the musk-ox are probably in great measure owing to the change of climate. These and similar facts, though they afford us no means of measurement, impress us with a vague and overpowering sense of antiquity. All geologists, indeed, are now prepared to admit that man has existed on our earth for a much longer period than was until recently supposed to have been the case.

But it may be doubted whether even geologists yet realize the great antiquity of our race.

" When speculations on the long series of events which occurred in the glacial and post-glacial periods are indulged in," says Sir C. Lyell,[1] " the imagination is apt to take alarm at the immensity of the time required to interpret the monuments of these ages, all referable to the era of existing species. In order to abridge the number of centuries which would otherwise be indispensable, a disposition is shown by many to magnify the rate of change in prehistoric times, by investing the causes which have modified the animate and the inanimate world with extraordinary and excessive energy. . . . We of the living generation, when called upon to make grants of thousands of centuries, in order to explain the events of what is called the modern period, shrink naturally at first from making what seems so lavish an expenditure of past time."

That palæolithic implements belong to a period of great cold, *i.e.* to the glacial period, seems indicated by the fact that they have not yet been found in the areas occupied by the deposits of the late glacial epoch. If a map be constructed showing the regions occupied by the deposits of the glacial epoch, the morainic débris, diluvial gravels, and boulder clay, on the one hand, and the palæolithic implements on the other, it would be seen at a glance that the former end when the latter begin.

The period thus indicated must certainly have been of very long duration. Lartet, as we have seen (*ante*, p. 281), suggested a division into four periods : those of the (1) Cave Bear, (2) Mammoth and *Rhinoceros tichorhinus*, (3) the Reindeer, and (4) the Aurochs.

M. de Mortillet has suggested a division into five periods, founded on the character of the implements, and named after typical localities, viz : (1) Chelléenne, (2) Acheuléenne, (3) Moustérienne, (4) Solutréenne, and (5) Magdalénienne. The first is characterized by axes boldly worked ; the second by the " Langues de Chat " of St Acheul (figs. 244–248) ; those most characteristic of the Moustérien are generally worked only on one side ; those

---

[1] *Address to the Brit. Ass.*, 1864, p. 21, Bath.

of Solutré are leaf-like lance-heads beautifully worked ; the Magdalénienne is remarkable for the number and variety of bone implements.

Messrs Penck and Brückner consider that there were four main periods of great cold separated by milder intervals. As to this authorities are not altogether agreed, and no doubt there were numerous changes ; but the evidence seems very strong that there were four main oscillations,[1] and Sir C. H. Read, in his excellent *British Museum Guide to the Stone Age*, gives the following table :—

TABLE SHOWING SUCCESSION OF GLACIATIONS AND THE PALÆOLITHIC INDUSTRIES, ACCORDING TO THE AUTHORITIES NAMED.

Professors Penck and Brückner.	Professor James Geikie.	Professor Penck and Dr Rutot.	Dr Obermaier.	Professor Boule.
Postglacial, with oscillations.	Upper Turbarian Upper Forestian Lower Turbarian Lower Forestian	Madeleine	Madeleine Solutré	Madeleine. Solutré.
Würm (4th glacial).	Mecklenburgian . . (Depositing purple boulder clay.)	Madeleine	Moustier	Moustier. (3rd glacial.)
3rd inter-glacial.	Neudeckian . . . (Beds between chalky and purple boulder clays.)	Solutré	St Acheul (cool) Chelles (warm)	Chelles. (2nd in-terglacial.)
Riss (3rd glacial).	Polandian . . . . (Depositing the upper boulder clay.)	Moustier	3rd glacial	2nd glacial.
2nd inter-glacial.	Helvetian . . . . (Represented in part by middle glacial beds.)	Chelles	2nd inter-glacial	1st inter-glacial.
Mindel (2nd glacial).	Saxonian . . . . (Severe, Cromer till and contorted beds.)	...	2nd glacial	1st glacial. (Pliocene.)
1st inter-glacial.	Norfolkian . . . (Cromer forest bed, pre-glacial in Britain.)	...	1st inter-glacial	
Günz (1st glacial).	Scanian . . . . (Not in Britain.)	Pliocene	1st glacial	

Guide to the Antiquities of the Stone Age (*British Museum*), 1911, p. 11.

That man existed in Western Europe during the period of the mammoth and the *Rhinoceros tichorhinus* no

[1] M. Obermaier has come to the same conclusion as regards the Pyrenees.

longer, I think, admits of a doubt ; and as regards Pliocene times the existence of man, or of some semi-human
ancestors of ours, seems also to be well established.

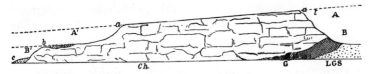

FIG. 256.—Section of North Downs, showing relative positions of
plateau and river drift.

a, Red clay drift, 5 to 20 feet thick, with unrolled flints from chalk, overlying
thin patches of lower Eocene and Pliocene beds. On the surface are found
eoliths, and fragments of chert and ragstone from the lower greensand
outcrop. *t*, Position of Pliocene beds.
b, High-level river gravel, about 100 ft. above the Thames.
c, Low-level river gravel and loam, sloping down to the Thames.
Ch, chalk. *G*, Upper greensand and gault. *L.G.S.*, Lower greensand.
AA', Major valleys of glacial period.
BB', Later valleys.

Mr Benjamin Harrison has found on the summit of
the Kentish Downs near Ightham a certain number of
palæolithic implements belonging to the well-known types,

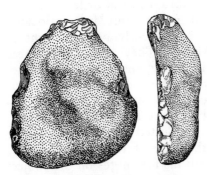

FIG. 257.—Eolith with edge-chipping,   FIG. 258.—Beak-shaped
      Kent plateau.   eolith, Kent plateau.[1]

and a much larger number of very rude specimens
(figs. 257 and 258), so rude indeed that their claim to
classification as worked implements has been, and is,
disputed by some high authorities. Many of them are,

[1] *Guide to the Antiquities of the Stone Age (British Museum)*, 1911,
pp. 14–15.

however, as it seems to me, undoubtedly worked. They have been termed " Eolithic " ; but if the term is intended to imply antiquity, it must of course include the more elaborately worked and typical palæolithic implements which occur with them. They are found in a peculiar brown gravel deposited by a stream or streams which ran at a much higher level than, and had no relation to, the existing rivers as shown in fig. 256. Similar implements have been found in Wilts and Herts by Mr Kendall, and in several other southern counties, and in Belgium by M. Rutot.

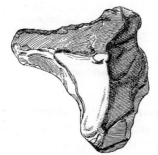

FIG. 259.—Eolithic double scraper, Kent plateau.

The Tasmanians used stone implements quite as rudely worked in various ways—for instance, in preparing spears, and in scraping the skin, especially that of the feet.

Mr Worthington Smith has found palæolithic implements on an old floor covered over with contorted glacial drift.

A remarkable series of rough, but unquestionably worked flint implements has recently been brought to light by Mr J. Reid Moir.[1] They were found near Ipswich, resting on London Clay, and Messrs Whitaker and Marr, after careful examination of the locality, tell us that in their opinion the bed in which they occur is the undisturbed base of the Red Crag, resting on London Clay. Similar specimens had been collected by Mr W. G. Clarke as long ago as 1905, at the base of the Norwich Crag ; but he says, " It was not till his first notes on the subject appeared that the possibility of my specimens being Pre-Crag occurred to me with any force." The specimens are also ably described by Sir E. Ray Lankester in his memoir mentioned below. The most characteristic are a

[1] See his letter to the *Times*, October 17, 1910 ; a paper in the *Transactions of the Prehistoric Society of East Anglia* ; the report of a committee of the same Society, 1911; a report by Mr Whitaker and Dr Marr ; and a paper by Sir E. Ray Lankester in the *Phil. Trans.* for November 1911.

very peculiar "eagle's beak" or "rostro-carinate" type, which had not been previously described. Besides Mr Clarke's specimens, there is one in Sir John Evans' collection, now in Sir Arthur Evans' possession, and some have been found by Mr Heron-Allen in a gravel of undetermined age at Selsea Mill in Sussex.

The existence of man in Pliocene times seems therefore now to be satisfactorily established.

M. Desnoyers[1] has called attention to some marks noticed by him on bones found in the Upper Pliocene beds of St Prest, and belonging to the *Elephas meridionalis*, *Rhinoceros leptorhinus*, *Hippopotamus major*, several species of deer (including the gigantic *Megaceros carnutorum*, Laugel), and two species of *Bos*, which he considers to be of human origin.

Among the bones of the deer were several crania, all of which have been broken in one way, namely, by a violent blow given on the skull between, and at the base of, the horns. M. Steenstrup has noticed fractures of this kind in other less ancient skulls of ruminants, and at the present day some of the modern tribes treat the skulls of ruminants in the same manner. Through the courtesy of M. Desnoyers, I have had the opportunity of examining some of the scratched bones from St Prest. The markings fully bear out the description given by him, and some of them at least appear to me to be probably of human origin ; at the same time, and in the present state of our knowledge, I am not prepared to say that there is no other manner in which they might have been produced. At the same place, that indefatigable archæologist, M. l'Abbé Bourgeois, has more recently discovered worked flints, including flakes, awls, and scrapers ; but unfortunately there is some doubt as to the stratigraphical relations of the bed in which they occurred.[2] Moreover, some authorities consider these beds to be inter-glacial. In the inter-glacial coal-beds of Dürnten already alluded to (*ante*, p. 412), Professor Rütimeyer

---

[1] *Comptes Rendus*, June 8, 1863.
[2] *Mat. pour l'Histoire de l'Homme*, 1867, p. 17 ; ditto, 1873, p. 14.

has found a fragment apparently of rough basket or wattle work. The interpretation in this case again has been questioned, but Professor Schwendener, who has recently examined the specimens with great care, is decidedly of opinion that it is of human workmanship.

At the meeting in Spezzia of the " Société Italienne des Sciences Naturelles," Professor G. Ramorino exhibited some bones of Pliocene Age, said to bear marks of knives.[1]

M. Capellini also described certain bones supposed to belong to the same geological period, which, in his opinion, bear marks of flint knives. Sir J. Evans, however, has suggested that these marks may have been made by the teeth of fishes.[2]

The existence of man during the period of the Crag has been supposed to be indicated by the fact that some of the sharks' teeth, so abundant in these deposits, are perforated in a manner which at first sight certainly resembles that in which we find similar teeth pierced by savages at the present day. Mr Charlesworth, while carefully abstaining from the expression of any opinion, exhibited several such specimens at a recent meeting of the Anthropological Institute. It has, however, I think, been shown that these perforations are probably the work of boring parasites.[3]

Dr Dubois has discovered in Java,[4] in a layer apparently of Pliocene Age, to judge from the other mammalian remains, the upper part of the skull, a thigh bone and two teeth of an animal about as large as a chimpanzee (fig. 235), which he regards as having been intermediate between man and the anthropoid apes, and there is this strong support of his view that while the remains, in the opinion of some eminent authorities, are those of an anthropoid ape allied to the existing Gibbons, others are equally convinced that they are those of a low type of man. Through the kindness of Dr Dubois I have had the

---

[1] *Loc. cit.*, vol. ii. p. 41.   [2] *Congrès Int. d'Anth.*, 1876, p. 46.
[3] Hughes, "Man in the Crag," *Geol. Mag.*, vol. ix., June 1872.
[4] *Pithecanthropus erectus*, Batavia, 1894. See also C. R., 3me *Cong. Int. de Zool*, Leyde, 1896.

opportunity of examining these interesting remains. It is greatly to be regretted that they are not more complete, but they certainly belonged either to a very large Gibbon or a very small man.

Dr Noetling, of the Geological Survey of India, has also recorded unquestionable flint flakes found in Burma with remains of *Rhinoceros perimensis*, and *Hippotherium* (Hipparion) *antelopinum*, in strata considered to belong to the Pliocene Period.[1]

Of course, for the believers in evolution man must have had a precursor in Miocene times ; but no mammalian species goes so far back in time. It is therefore extremely improbable that man in the strict sense should then have existed, but it would seem that his predecessors of that period were sufficiently advanced to make use of rude stone implements. M. Bourgeois has found in the Calcaire de Beauce, near Pontlevoy, many flints which have been subjected to the action of heat, and others which he considers to show marks of human workmanship. On the age of the deposit there is still some difference of opinion, and the action of fire, though it points strongly to, does not absolutely prove, the presence of man. These interesting specimens were found in a stratum which contains the remains of acerotherium, an extinct animal allied to the rhinoceros, and beneath a bed which contains the mastodon, dinotherium, and rhinoceros. I had the advantage of visiting Pontlevoy with Sir J. Evans and examining the specimens. They are certainly very rude, but the action of fire could not be doubted.

In the *Matériaux pour l'Histoire de l'Homme* for 1870[2] is a figure of a flint flake found by M. Tardy in the Miocene beds of Aurillac (Auvergne), together with the remains of *Dinotherium giganteum* and *Machairodus latidens*. I have not visited the locality, and cannot express any opinion as to the age of the bed in which this interesting specimen was discovered, but from the figure given

---

[1] *Records of the Geol. Survey of India*, vol. xxvii., 1894.
[2] *Loc. cit.*, p. 93.

there can be no reasonable doubt that it is of human workmanship. This has been confirmed by M. Rames and by Mr Westlake, who devoted several years to the locality, and Sir E. Ray Lankester considers that the age is definitely fixed, as the layer is covered by a lava flow of ascertained Upper Miocene Age. M. Delaunay also has called attention to a rib, found by him at Pouancé (Maine et Loire), and belonging to a well-known Miocene species, the *Halitherium fossile* ;[1] this bears certain marks which closely resemble those which might have been made by flint implements. M. Hamy gives a good figure of this interesting specimen.

The worker of these flints would probably have differed so much from existing men that he would be regarded as belonging to a different species, and would be one of the " missing links."

No living species of land mammal has yet been found in the Miocene strata. It is true that by the exercise of his brains man is more able to render himself independent of external conditions than other animals ; cold, for instance, leading to warmer clothes in the one, to more fur in the other ; still, judging from the analogy of other species, I am disposed to think that in the Miocene Period man was probably represented by anthropoid apes, more nearly resembling us than do any of the existing quadrumana. We need not, however, expect necessarily to find the proofs in Europe ; our nearest relatives in the animal kingdom are confined to hot, almost to tropical climates ; and though we know that during parts of the Miocene Period the climate of Europe was warmer than at present, so that monkeys lived much north of their present limits, still it is in the warmer regions of the earth that we may reasonably find the earliest traces of the human race.

[1] *Précis de Paléontologie Humaine*, p. 58.

CHAPTER XIII

MODERN SAVAGES

ALTHOUGH our knowledge of ancient times has of late years greatly increased, it is still very imperfect, and we cannot afford to neglect any possible source of information. It is evident that history cannot throw much light on the early condition of man, because the discovery—or, to speak more correctly, the use—of metal has in all cases preceded that of writing. Even as regards the Age of Bronze, we derive little information from history ; and although, as we have seen, the Age of Stone is vaguely alluded to in the earliest European writers, their statements have generally been looked upon as imaginative rather than historical, and contain, indeed, little more than the bare statement that there was a time when metal was unknown.

Nor will tradition supply the place of history. At best it is untrustworthy and short-lived. Thus in 1770 the New Zealanders had no recollection of Tasman's visit.[1] Yet this took place in 1643, less than one hundred and thirty years before, and must have been to them an event of the greatest possible importance and interest. In the same way the North American Indians soon lost all tradition of De Soto's expedition, although " by its striking incidents it was so well suited to impress the Indian mind." [2]

Even as regards events which are contemporary, or

[1] Cook's First Voyage round the World, Hawkesworth's *Voyages*, vol. ii. p. 388.
[2] Schoolcraft's *Indian Tribes*, vol. ii. p. 12.

nearly so, we find that the accounts given by savages become rapidly distorted. Thus Nilsson[1] quotes the account given by Mackenzie, that the Esquimaux described the English to him as being giants, with wings, who could kill with a glance of their eye, and swallow a whole beaver at a mouthful. So also Colonel Dalton tells us that "though the Kols have known the English for little more than half a century, they assign to them a most honourable place in their genesis. The Assam Abors and Garrows do the same."[2]

The Bungogees and Pankhos (hill tribes of Chittagong) believe that their ancestors came out of a cave in the earth under the guidance of a chief named Tlandrokpah, who was so powerful that he married the daughter of the Deity, to whom he presented his gun. "You can still hear the gun : the thunder is the sound of it."[3] In this case the mention of the gun shows that the tradition must be of modern origin. Again, Speke says : "I found that the Waganda have the same absurd notion here as the Wanyambo have in Karagüé, of Kamrisi's supernatural power in being able to divide the waters of the Nile in the same manner as Moses did the Red Sea."[4]

Mansfield Parkyns relates how it is firmly believed in the remote parts of Abyssinia, that the German missionaries had, "in the course of only a few days, perforated a tunnel all the way (from Adowa) to Massowa, on the coast of the Red Sea, a distance of above a hundred and fifty miles, whence they were to obtain large supplies of arms, ammunition, etc."[5]

Sir S. Baker[6] also, in his *Nile Tributaries*, says : "The conversation of the Arabs is in the exact style of the

[1] *The Stone Age*, English edition, p. 209.

[2] *Trans. Ethn. Soc.*, New Ser., vol. vi. p. 38. See also Lichtenstein's *Travels*, vol. i. p. 290; James' *Expedition to the Rocky Mountains*, vol. iii. p. 247 ; and Campbell, *Trans. Ethn. Soc.*, 1870, p. 335.

[3] Capt. Lewin, *The Hill Tribes of Chittagong*, Calcutta, 1869, p. 95. See also Lichtenstein's *Travels*, vol. i. p. 290.

[4] Speke, p. 438, also p. 504.   [5] *Life in Abyssinia*, p. 151.

[6] *Loc. cit.*, pp. 129, 130.

Old Testament. The name of God is coupled with every trifling incident in life, and they believe in the continual action of Divine special interference. Should a famine afflict the country, it is expressed in the stern language of the Bible, ' The Lord has sent a grievous famine upon the land ' ; or, ' The Lord called for a famine, and it came upon the land.' Should their cattle fall sick, it is considered to be an affliction by Divine command ; or should the flocks prosper and multiply particularly during one season, the prosperity is attributed to special interference. Nothing can happen in the usual routine of daily life without a direct connection with the hand of God, in the Arab's belief.

" This striking similarity to the description of the Old Testament is exceedingly interesting to a traveller when residing among these curious and original people. With the Bible in one hand, and these unchanged tribes before the eyes, there is a thrilling illustration of the sacred record : the past becomes the present, the veil of three thousand years is raised, and the living picture is a witness to the exactness of the historical description. At the same time, there is a light thrown upon many obscure passages in the Old Testament by the experience of the present customs and figures of speech of the Arabs, which are precisely those that were practised at the periods described. I do not attempt to enter upon a theological treatise, therefore it is unnecessary to allude specially to these particular points. The sudden and desolating arrival of a flight of locusts, the plague, or any other unforeseen calamity, is attributed to the anger of God, and is believed to be an infliction of punishment upon the people thus visited, precisely as the plagues of Egypt were specially inflicted upon Pharaoh and the Egyptians. Should the present history of the country be written by an Arab scribe, the style of the description would be purely that of the Old Testament, and the various calamities or the good fortunes that have in the course of nature befallen both the tribes and individuals, would be recounted either as special visitations of Divine wrath, or blessings for good deeds performed. If in a dream a particular course of action is suggested, the Arab believes that God has *spoken* and directed him. The Arab scribe or historian would describe the event as the ' *voice* of the Lord ' (Kallam el Allah) having spoken unto the person ; or, that God appeared to him in a dream and ' *said.*' Thus, much allowance would be necessary on the part of a European reader for the figurative ideas and expressions of the people."

Although, then, traditions and myths are of great importance, and indirectly throw much light on the condition of man in ancient times, we must not expect to learn much directly from them. At any rate, as regards the Stone Age in Europe both history and tradition are silent, and here, as in all long-civilized countries, stone weapons and arrow-heads are regarded as thunderbolts or " elfin " arrows.

Deprived, therefore, as regards this period, of any assistance from history, but relieved at the same time from the embarrassing interference of tradition, the archæologist is free to follow the methods which have been so successfully pursued in geology—the rude bone and stone implements of bygone ages being to the one what the remains of extinct animals are to the other. The analogy may be pursued even farther than this. Many mammalia which are extinct in Europe have representatives still living in other countries. Much light is thrown on our fossil pachyderms, for instance, by the species which still inhabit some parts of Asia and Africa ; the secondary marsupials are illustrated by their existing representatives in Australia and South America ; and in the same manner, if we wish clearly to understand the antiquities of Europe, we must compare them with the rude implements and weapons still, or until lately, used by the savage races in other parts of the world. In fact, the Van Diemaner and South American are to the antiquary what the opossum and the sloth are to the geologist.

A certain space, therefore, devoted to the consideration

of the modern savages will not be out of place in this work ; and though it would require volumes to do justice to the subject, still it may be possible to bring together a certain number of facts which will throw light on the ancient remains found in Europe, and on the condition of the early races which inhabited our continent. In order, however, to limit the subject as much as possible, I propose, with one exception, to describe only the "non-metallic savages" (if such an expression may be permitted), and even of these, only some of the most instructive, or of those which have been most carefully observed by travellers.

It used to be a common opinion that savages are, as a general rule, only the miserable remnants of nations once more civilized ; but although there are some well-established cases of national decay, there is no scientific evidence which would justify us in asserting that this applies to savages in general. No doubt there are instances in which nations once progressive have not only ceased to advance in civilization, but have even fallen back. Still, if we compare the accounts of early travellers with the state of things now existing, we shall find no evidence of any general degradation. The Australians, Bushmen, and Fuegians lived when first observed almost exactly as they do now. In some savage tribes we even find traces of improvement ; the Bachapins, when visited by Burchell, had just introduced the art of working in iron ; the largest erection in Tahiti was constructed by the generation living at the time of Captain Cook's visit, and the practice of cannibalism had been recently abandoned ;[1] the largest Mexican temple was built only six years before the discovery of America ; in the north of Australia, M'Gillivray tells us that the rude bark canoes which were formerly in general use have been quite superseded by those dug out of the trunk of a tree ; again, outriggers are said to have been recently adopted by the Andaman Islanders ; and if certain races, as, for instance, some of the American tribes,

---

[1] Forster, *Observations made during a Voyage round the World*, p. 327. See also Ellis, *Polynesian Researches*, vol. ii. p. 29.

have fallen back, this has, I think, been due less to any inherent tendency than to the injurious effect of European influence. Moreover, if the Cape of Good Hope, Australia, New Zealand, etc., had ever been inhabited by a race of men more advanced than those whom we are in the habit of regarding as the aborigines, some evidence of this would surely have remained ; and this not being the case, none of our travellers having observed any ruins or other traces of a more advanced civilization, there does not appear to be any sufficient reason for supposing that the present savage races are at all inferior to the ancestors from whom they are descended.

The Hottentots

Speaking generally, we may say that the use of metal has been long known throughout Europe, Asia, and Africa ; while in America, in Australia, and in the Oceanic Islands, all implements and weapons were, until within the last three hundred years, made of wood, bone, stone, or other similar materials.

The semi-civilized nations of Central America formed, indeed, a striking exception to the rule, since they were acquainted with the use of bronze. The North American Indians also had copper hatchets, but these were simply hammered into shape, without the assistance of heat. Here, therefore, we seem to get a glimpse of the manner in which our ancestors may have acquired the knowledge of metal. No doubt the possession of iron generally marks a great advance in civilization ; still, the process is very gradual, and there are some nations, which, though provided with metal implements, are nevertheless but little removed from a state of barbarism.

The Hottentots, who were not only acquainted with the use, but even with the manufacture of iron, and who possessed large numbers of sheep and cattle, were yet in many respects among the most disgusting of savages. Even Kolben, who generally takes a favourable view of them, admits that they are, in his opinion, the filthiest people in the world.[1] We might go farther and say the filthiest animals ; I think no species of mammal could be fairly compared with them in this respect. Animals, indeed, for the most part keep themselves beautifully clean. But this is not the case with man. Clothes introduce an element of dirt, the use of grease for the skin and hair accumulates dust, and the construction of permanent huts leads to an accumulation of filth. Thus the Hottentots were covered with grease, their clothes were never washed, and their hair was loaded "from day to day with such a quantity of soot and fat, and it gathers so much dust and other filth which they leave to clot and harden in it, for they never cleanse it, that it looks like a crust or cap of black mortar."[2] They wore a skin over the back, fastened in front. They carried this as long as they lived, and were buried in it when they died. Their only other garment was a square piece of skin, tied round the waist by a string, and left to hang down in front. In winter, however, they sometimes used a cap. For ornaments they wore rings of iron, copper, ivory, or leather. The last had the advantage of serving for food in bad times.

Their huts were generally oval, about fourteen feet by ten in diameter, and seldom more than four or five in height. They were made of sticks and mats. The sticks were fastened into the ground at both ends, or, if not long enough, two were placed opposite to one another, and secured together at the top. One end of the hut was left open to form the door. The mats were made of bulrushes and flags dried in the sun, and so closely fitted together that only the heaviest rain could penetrate them.[3] "With respect to household furniture," says Thunberg,[4] "they have little or none. The same dress that covers a part of their body by day, serves them also for bedding at night." Their victuals are boiled in leathern sacks and

---

[1] Kolben's *History of the Cape of Good Hope*, vol. i. p. 47.
[2] Kolben, *loc. cit.*, p. 188.
[3] Thunberg in Pinkerton's *Travels*, vol. xvi. p. 33 ; Kolben, *loc. cit.*, p. 221 ; Sparrman, vol. i. p. 195.
[4] Page 141.

water, by means of heated stones, but sometimes in earthen pots.[1] Milk is kept in leathern sacs, bladders of animals, and baskets made of platted rushes, perfectly watertight. These, a tobacco pouch of skin, a tobacco pipe of stone or wood, and their weapons, constitute the whole catalogue of their effects. According to Kolben, they sometimes broiled their meat, sometimes boiled it in blood, to which they often added milk ; " this they look on as a glorious dish." They were, however, both filthy and careless about their cookery, and the meat was often eaten half putrid, and more than half raw.[2]

Their weapons consisted of bows and poisoned arrows, spears, javelins or assegais, stones, and darting-sticks or " kirris," about three feet long and an inch thick. With these weapons they were very skilful, and feared not to attack the elephant, the rhinoceros, or even the lion. Large animals were also sometimes killed in pitfalls, from six to eight feet deep, and about four feet in diameter. They fixed a strong pointed stake in the middle. " Into this hole an elephant falling with his fore-feet (it is not of dimensions to receive his whole body), he is pierced in the neck and breast with the stake and there held securely,"[3] for the more he struggled the farther he penetrated. They caught fish both with hooks and in nets. They also ate wild fruits and roots of various kinds, which, however, they did not take the trouble to cultivate.

For domestic animals the Hottentots had oxen, sheep, and dogs. It might have naturally been supposed that oxen were used in the same manner all over the world. They seem evidently adapted either for draught or for food. With the dog the case is different ; we ourselves use him in various ways, and one feels therefore the less surprise at the different services which he performs for different races of savages. But even with regard to cattle

---

[1] This, however, they appear to have learnt from the Europeans.
[2] Thunberg, p. 141 ; Kolben, p. 283; Harris, *Wild Sports of Africa*, p. 142.
[3] Kolben, p. 250.

the same was the case : besides what we may call their normal uses, the Veddahs, or wild inhabitants of Ceylon, used oxen in hunting ; and the Hottentots trained some to serve as what we may call sheep-oxen, or cow-oxen— that is to say, to guard and manage the flocks and herds —and others as war-oxen, a function which might have been considered as opposed to the whole character of the beast, but in which, nevertheless, they appear to have been very useful.

The Hottentots of late years not only used iron weapons, but even made such for themselves. The ore was smelted in the following manner :[1] "They make a hole in a raised ground, large enough to contain a good quantity of ironstones, which are found here and there in plenty in the Hottentot countries. In this hole they melt out the iron from the ore. About a foot and a half from this hole, upon the descent, they make another, something less. This is the receiver of the melted iron, which runs into it by a narrow channel they cut from one hole to the other. Before they put the ironstones into the hole where the iron is to be smelted out of them, they make a fire in the hole, quite up to the mouth of it, in order to make the earth about it thoroughly hot. When they suppose the earth about it is well heated, they fill the hole almost up with ironstones. They then make a large fire over the stones, which they supply from time to time with fuel, till the iron is melted and all of it is run into the receiver. As soon as the iron in the receiver is cold, they take it out, and break it to pieces with stones. These pieces the Hottentots, as they have occasion, heat in other fires, and with stones beat 'em out and shape 'em to weapons. They rarely make anything else of iron."

The Hottentot customs, some of which are extremely curious, are fully described by Thunberg,[2] Kolben,[3] Cook,[4] Sparrman,[5] and other travellers. Whether the

---

[1] Kolben, *loc. cit.*, p. 239.
[2] *Loc. cit.*, pp. 141, 142.
[3] Pp. 113, 115, 118, 121, 153, 252.
[4] Hawkesworth's *Voyages*, vol. iii. p. 791.
[5] Vol. i. p. 357.

Hottentots can be said to have had any religion,[1] depends upon the exact meaning we attach to the word. Though they seem to have had some notion of a Deity, even Kolben admits that they had not "any institution of worship." Le Vaillant expressly declares that the Hottentots had no religion. Some of the older writers, indeed, consider certain dances as being religious ceremonies. This was stoutly denied by the natives themselves,[2] in spite of which Kolben assures us that they *were* "acts of religion," adding candidly, "let the Hottentots say what they will." They are very fond of smoking, and are great drunkards. It is only fair to say that Kolben gives them a good character for integrity, chastity, fidelity, and liberality, assuring us that they "are certainly the most friendly, the most liberal, and the most benevolent people to one another that ever appeared upon earth."[3] Other travellers also speak of them in very high terms.[4] At the same time it is difficult to see how these statements can be reconciled with the admitted fact that, as soon as any man or woman is so enfeebled by old age that he or she is unable to work, and can "no longer"—I am quoting from Kolben himself—"be of any manner of service in anything, they are thrust out of the society and confined to a solitary hut at a considerable distance from the kraal, there, with a small stock of provisions placed within their reach, but without any one to comfort or assist 'em, to die either of age or hunger, or be devoured by some wild beast."[5] This, it must be remembered, was no exceptional atrocity, but a general custom, and applied to the rich as well as the poor, for if an old man had property it was taken away from him. Infanticide, again, was very common among them, and was not

---

[1] Thunberg, *loc. cit.*, p. 141, etc. ; Kolben, pp. 37, 93, etc. Beeckman thought they had no religion at all. Pinkerton's *Voyages*, vol. ii. p. 153 ; so also Harris, *Wild Sports of Africa*, p. 160 ; Sparrman, vol. i. p. 207.

[2] Sparrman, vol. i. p. 212 ; Kolben, *loc. cit.*   [3] *Loc. cit.*, p. 331.

[4] See, for instance, Philips' *South Africa*, pp. 4, 5, 6.

[5] *Loc. cit.*, p. 321.

regarded as a crime. Girls were generally the victims ; and, if a woman had twins, the ugliest of them was almost always exposed or buried alive. This was done with the consent of "the whole kraal, which generally allows it without taking much pains to look into it."[1] The poverty and the hardships which they had to undergo may perhaps plead as some excuse for these two unnatural customs.

The Bushmen resembled the Hottentots in many things, but were even less civilized. They had no knowledge of metallurgy, no domestic animals, and no canoes. They frequently stole the cattle of their more advanced neighbours, but always killed and ate them as quickly as possible. Their principal weapons were bows and poisoned arrows. Lichtenstein asserts that they had no names,[2] but this was probably an error. Bleek regards them as the lowest of human races, and Haeckel even goes so far as to assert that they seem "to the unprejudiced comparative student of nature, to manifest a closer connection with the gorilla and chimpanzee than with a Kant or a Goethe."[3]

The Veddahs

The Veddahs, or wild tribes who inhabit the interior of Ceylon, have been described by Knox,[4] Tennent,[5] and Bailey.[6] They live in huts very rudely formed of boughs and bark, and cultivate small patches of chena, but subsist principally on honey and the produce of the chase. Their weapons consist of axes and bows and arrows. With the latter they are not very skilful, as they pursue only the larger game, and the art of hunting consists in creeping close up to their prey and taking it unawares. They are very good deer-

---

[1] *Loc. cit.*, p. 144.   [2] *Travels in Southern Africa*, vol. i. p. 192.
[3] *On the Origin of Language*, by W. H. J. Bleek, edited by Dr E. Haeckel, pp. 4, 5.
[4] *An Historical Relation of Ceylon*, 1681.   [5] *Ceylon.*
[6] *Transactions of the Ethnological Society*, New Series, vol. ii. p. 278. See also Davy's *Ceylon.*

stalkers, and, besides excellent dogs, have also hunting buffaloes. These are so trained that they are easily guided by a string tied round the horn, and are used at night. The buffalo feeds, the man crouches behind him, and thus, unseen and unsuspected, steals upon his prey.

They have no pottery, and their cookery is very primitive. They wear scarcely any clothes, nothing in fact but a scrap of dirty rag, supported in front by a string tied round the waist. Perhaps the women's cloth is a trifle larger than the men's, but that appears to be the only difference. They are very dirty and very small ; the ordinary height of the men being from four feet six to five feet one, and of the women from four feet four to four feet eight. Mr Bailey thinks that it would be impossible to conceive more barbarous specimens of the human race. Davy even asserts that they have no names, and do not bury the dead.

They have, however, one remarkable peculiarity which it would be unfair to omit. They are kind, affectionate, and constant to their wives ; abhor polygamy, and have a proverb that " Death alone can separate husband and wife." In this they are very unlike their more civilized neighbours.[1] An intelligent Kandyan chief, with whom Mr Bailey visited these Veddahs, was " perfectly scandalized at the utter barbarism of living only with one wife, and never parting until separated by death." It was, he said, "just like the wanderoos" (monkeys). Even in their marriage relations, however, the Veddahs cannot altogether be commended, as it is—or was until lately—very usual with them for a man to marry his younger sister. This is the more remarkable, as marriage with an elder sister seemed to them as horrible as it does to us.

Messrs Sarasin in their work on the Veddahs regard them as being certainly Dravidian, and not Aryan—*i.e.* as a remnant of the pre-Aryan population of India.

[1] It is only fair to add that the Kandyans are said to have much improved in this respect of late years.

The Andaman Islanders

The Mincopies, or inhabitants of the Andaman Islands, have been described by Dr Mouatt,[1] Sir E. Belcher,[2] Mr Day,[3] Mr Man, and Professor Owen,[4] who considers that they "are, perhaps, the most primitive, or lowest in the scale of civilization of the human race." Their huts consist of four posts, the two front ones six to eight feet high, the back ones only one or two feet. They are open at the sides, and covered with a roof of bamboo, or a few palm-leaves bound tightly together. The Mincopies live chiefly on fruit, mangroves, and shell-fish. Sometimes, however, they kill the small pigs which run wild in the jungle.

They have single-tree canoes, hollowed out with a p-shaped axe, assisted probably by the action of fire. They are acquainted with the use of outriggers, which, however, appear to have been of recent introduction, as they are not alluded to by the earlier writers.[5] Their arrows and spears are now generally tipped with iron and glass, which they obtain from wrecks, and which have to a great extent replaced bone. Their harpoons, like those of so many other savages, have a movable head, and a long cord by which this may be held when fixed in the victim.[6] They are very skilful with the bow, and " make practice at forty or fifty yards with unerring certainty,"[7] though their arrows have no feathers. Their nets are made with great ingenuity and neatness. They now make some rough pottery, but generally use either shells or pieces of bamboo to hold water. They kill fish by harpoons, or with small hand-nets take any that are left by the tide, and it is even said that they are able to dive and catch them with their hands.[8]

[1] *Adventures and Researches among the Andaman Islanders.*
[2] Belcher, *Trans. Ethn. Soc.*, New Series, vol. v. p. 40.
[3] *Proc. Asiat. Soc. of Bengal*, 1870.
[4] *Transactions of the Ethnological Society*, New Series, vol. ii. p. 34.
[5] Mouatt, *loc. cit.*, p. 317.   [6] *Loc. cit.*, p. 326.
[7] Belcher, *Trans. Ethn. Society*, New Series, vol. v. p. 49.
[8] Mouatt, *loc. cit.*, pp. 310, 333.

They cover themselves with mud, and also tattoo, but wear no clothes. They count only up to two. According to Man,[1] they have "no forms of worship or religious rites." They believe, however, in the existence of a "spirit" whom they call Puluga. They suppose that he created everything, except the evil spirits. He is regarded as omniscient "while it is day." He lives in a large store-house, and eats and drinks. He "has no authority over the evil spirits," and under these circumstances, though Mr Man speaks of him as the "Supreme Being," he cannot be so termed in the usual sense. After death, the corpse is buried in a sitting posture. When it is supposed to be entirely decayed, the skeleton is dug up, and each of the relations appropriates a bone. In the case of a married man, the widow takes the skull and wears it suspended by a cord round her neck.[2] It forms a very convenient box for small articles. Marriage, however, only lasts, at least in some tribes, until the child is born and weaned, when, according to Lieutenant St John, as quoted by Sir E. Belcher, the man and woman generally separate, each seeking a new partner.[3]

They have no dogs, nor indeed any domestic animals.

The Australians

Throughout the whole continent of Australia the aborigines were remarkably similar in physical appearance, in character, and in general habits. They were, in some respects, scarcely, if at all, farther advanced than those of the Andaman Islands. The "houses" observed by Captain Cook "at Botany Bay, where they were best, were just high enough for a man to sit upright in, but not large enough for him to extend himself in his whole length in any direction ; they were built with pliable rods about as thick as a man's finger, in the form of an oven, by sticking the two ends into the ground, and then covering them with palm-leaves and broad pieces of bark ;

---

[1] *Journal Anthr. Institute*, v. 12, p. 156.
[2] *Loc. cit.*, p. 327 ; Belcher, *loc. cit.*, p. 43.   [3] *Loc. cit.*, p. 45.

the door is nothing but a large hole at one end." Eyre also gives a very similar description of those observed by him.[1] Further north, where the climate was warmer, the dwellings were even less substantial, and being comparatively open on one side, scarcely deserve even the name of huts, and were little more than a protection against the wind. Finally, the natives observed by Dampier near C. Levéque, on the north-west coast, seem to have had no houses at all. Round their dwelling-places Captain Cook observed " vast heaps of shells, the fish of which we suppose had been their food."[2] Sir G. Grey also describes similar shell-mounds,[3] some of which covered quite half an acre, and were as much as ten feet high. They seem to have been first noticed by Dampier.[4]

The food of the Australian savages differs much in different parts of the continent. Speaking generally, it may be said to consist of various roots, fruits, fungi, shell-fish, frogs, snakes, honey, grubs, moths, birds, birds' eggs, fish, turtles, dog, kangaroo, and sometimes of seal and whale.[5] The kangaroo, however, forms only an occasional luxury ; nor are the natives, so far as I am aware, able to kill whales for themselves, but when one is washed on shore it is a real godsend to them. Fires are immediately lit to give notice of the joyful event. Then they rub themselves all over with blubber, and anoint their favourite wives in the same way ; after which they cut down through the blubber to the beef, which they sometimes eat raw and sometimes broil on pointed sticks. As other natives arrive, they " fairly eat their way into the whale, and you see them climbing in and about the stinking carcase, choosing titbits." For days " they remain by the carcase, rubbed from head to foot with stinking blubber, gorged to repletion with putrid

---

[1] *Discoveries in Central Australia*, vol. ii. p. 300.
[2] *First Voyage*, vol. iii. p. 598.
[3] *Loc. cit.*, vol. i. p. 110. See also King's *Australia*, vol. i. p. 87.
[4] Pinkerton's *Voyages*, vol. ii. p. 473.
[5] Grey's *Explorations in North-West and Western Australia*, p. 263 ; Eyre, vol. ii. p. 251 ; M'Gillivray's *Voyage of H.M.S. " Rattlesnake,"* vol. i. p. 148.

meat—out of temper from indigestion, and therefore engaged in constant frays—suffering from a cutaneous disorder by high feeding—and altogether a disgusting spectacle. There is no sight in the world," Sir G. Grey adds, "more revolting than to see a young and gracefully formed native girl stepping out of the carcase of a putrid whale." The Australians also mash up bones and suck out the fat contained in them. Like other savages, they are excessively fond of fatty substances.

In a cave on the north-eastern coast, Mr Cunningham observed certain "tolerable figures of sharks, porpoises, turtles, lizards, trepang, starfish, clubs, canoes, water-gourds, and some quadrupeds which were probably intended to represent kangaroos and dogs." The natives round Sydney also frequently drew upon the rocks "various figures of fish, clubs, swords, animals, and branches of trees, not contemptibly represented." [1] Most of the tribes, on the contrary, were very deficient in art, and, according to Mr Oldfield, are " quite unable to realize the most vivid artistic representations. On being shown a large coloured engraving of an aboriginal New Hollander, one declared it to be a ship, another a kangaroo, and so on; not one of a dozen identifying the portrait as having any connection with himself." [2] It is not, however, quite clear to me that they were not poking fun at Mr Oldfield.

On the north-eastern coasts they use canoes made from the trunks of trees, each canoe being formed from a single trunk, probably hollowed by fire. " They are about fourteen feet long, and being very narrow, are fitted with an outrigger." [3] Farther south the canoes were nothing but a piece of bark, tied together at the ends and kept open in the middle by small bows of wood. The western tribes had no canoes,[4] owing, according to King,[5] to the

---

[1] King, vol. ii. p. 26; Grey, vol. i. p. 259; Collins, p. 381.
[2] Oldfield, "On the Aborigines of Australia," *Transactions of the Ethnological Society*, New Series, vol. iii.
[3] Freycinet, *Voyage autour du Monde*, vol. ii. p. 705; Jukes, *Voyage of H.M.S. "Fly,"* ii. 243.
[4] *Cook's First Voyage*, vol. iii. p. 643.
[5] *Loc. cit.*, vol. i. pp. 38, 43, 49; vol. ii. pp. 66, 69.

absence of large timber.[1] Instead of a boat they used a
log of wood, on which they sat astride, with a bit of bark
in each hand, which served as a paddle. Some tribes
fasten four or five mangrove stems together so as to make
a small float or raft. The natives observed by Dampier
were even worse off in this respect ; they had " no boats,
canoes, or bark logs." Yet they dwelt on the shore,
lived principally on fish, and swam about from island to
island. The Western Australians, according to Jukes,
had neither boats nor rafts, " and the islands close to the
mainland had never been visited by them previously to
the founding of our colonies." So also some of the
tribes near Sydney are said to have been unable to swim.[2]
The absence of canoes is very remarkable in a people
whose habits were so littoral, and whose food was derived
mainly from the sea.

The implements of the Australians are very simple.
They have no knowledge of pottery, and carry water in
skins or in vessels made of bark. They are quite
ignorant of warm water, which strikes them with great
amazement.[3] Some of them carry "a small bag, about the
size of a moderate cabbage-net, which is made by laying
threads loop within loop, somewhat in the manner of
knitting used by our ladies to make purses. This bag
the man carries loose upon his back by a small string,
which passes over his head ; it generally contains a lump
or two of paint and resin, some fish-hooks and lines, a
shell or two, out of which their hooks are made, a few
points of darts, and their usual ornaments, which includes
the whole worldly treasure of the richest man among
them."

A very similar inventory is given by Sir G. Grey, who
adds, however, a flat stone to pound roots with.[4] They
have also stone hatchets, hammers, knives, pieces of flint,
and sticks to dig up roots. The hammer is used for

---

[1] In his view, however, of Careening Bay, the country appears to be
well wooded.
[2] *Voyage of the " Novara,"* English Trans., vol. iii. p. 36.
[3] D'Urville, vol. i. p. 461.   [4] *Loc. cit.,* p. 266.

killing seals or other animals, and for breaking open shell-fish. The handle is from twelve to fifteen inches long, pointed at one end, and having on each side at the other a hard stone attached to the handle by a mass of gum. The knives (fig. 260, which represents a specimen presented to me by A. W. Franks, Esq.) have a similar handle, and at the end a few splinters of quartz or flint, arranged in a row and fastened into a slit with gum in the same manner.

The natives of Botany Bay had fish-hooks, but no nets : on the contrary, Sir G. Grey, in describing those of Western Australia, mentions nets, but not hooks ; Eyre also states that hooks were unknown in South Australia, while nets were used in hunting and as bags ; Taplin says that the Narinyeri had neither nets nor hooks ; the natives of the North-west also, according to Dampier, had " no instruments to catch great fish." Those seen by King were also without hooks or nets.[1] Throughout the continent they were ignorant both of slings and bows and arrows. On the other hand, they had spears, clubs (fig. 261), shields, and two very peculiar instruments, namely, the throwing-stick (fig. 262), and the boomerang (fig. 263). The spear is their principal weapon. These are about ten feet long, and very slender, made of cane or wood, tapering to a point, which is barbed. They are light, and one would scarcely be inclined

FIG. 260.—Australian knife.

FIG. 261.—Australian club, one-fifth of the actual size.

[1] *Loc. cit.*, vol. ii. p. 137.

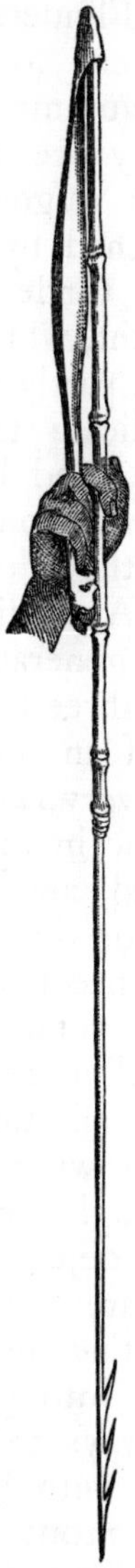

to believe that they could be darted with any force ; this, however, is affected by the aid of the wummera, a straight flat stick, three feet in length, terminating in a socket of bone or hide into which the end of the spear is fixed. The throwing-stick or wummera is only used in three localities, viz. by the Australians, in the country of the Corribas and Purus on the Upper Amazon, and the Esquimaux. It is grasped in the right hand by three fingers (fig. 262), the spear lying between the forefinger and the thumb. Previous to throwing it, a tremulous or vibratory motion is given to it, which is supposed to add to the accuracy of the aim ; in projecting the spear, the wummeru is retained in the hand, and the use of this simple contrivance adds greatly to the projectile force given to the spear. They are well practised in the use of these weapons.[1] Indeed, Sir G. Grey tells us that he has often seen them kill a

FIG. 263.—Australian boomerang, one-sixth of the actual size.

FIG. 262. — Australian spear and spear-caster.

pigeon with a spear at a distance of thirty yards ; and Captain Cook says that "at a distance of fifty yards these Indians were more sure of their mark than we could be with a single bullet."[2] The "wummera" seems to have been used by almost all the

[1] *United States Explor. Exped.*, vol. i. p. 191. [2] Cook, *loc. cit.*, p. 642.

Australian tribes.   It was, however, according to Flinders,[1] unknown at King George's Sound.   The very long Australian spears are not thrown with the wummera, but by the strength of the arm alone.   They are of several kinds : those used for striking turtle or dugong have a movable, barbed blade, which is attached by a string to the butt-end of the spear ; when the turtle is struck, the shaft becomes detached from the point, which remains fixed in the body, while the shaft serves partly to impede motions, and partly as a float to indicate the position of the turtle.[2]   A similar weapon is used by the Esquimaux, the Mincopies, the Fuegians, some Brazilian Indians, and other savages.   But the most extraordinary weapon, and one quite peculiar to Australia, is the boomerang.   This is a curved stick, generally rounded on one side, flatter on the other, about three feet long and two inches wide, by three-quarters of an inch thick.   At first sight it looks something like a very rude wooden sword.   It is used both in the chase and in war. " It is grasped at one end in the right hand, and is thrown sickle-wise, either upwards into the air, or downwards so as to strike the ground at some distance from the thrower.   In the first case it flies with a rotatory motion, as its shape would indicate ; after ascending to a great height in the air, it suddenly returns in an elliptical orbit to a spot near its starting-point.   On throwing it downwards on the ground, it rebounds in a straight line, pursuing a ricochet motion until it strikes the object at which it is thrown.   Birds and small animals are killed with it, and it is also used in killing ducks.   The most singular curve described by it is when thrown into the air above the angle of 45° ; its flight is always then backwards, and the native who throws it stands with his back, instead of his face, to the object he is desirous of hitting."[3]   Mr Merry, a gentleman who resided for

---

[1] *Voy. to Terra Australis*, vol. ii. p. 66.
[2] Hawkesworth's *Voyages*, vol. iii. p. 636.   See also Eyre, vol. ii. p. 305 ; M'Gillivray, vol. i. p. 147.
[3] *United States Explor. Exped., loc. cit.*

some time in Australia, informs me that on one occasion, in order to test the skill with which the boomerang could be thrown, he offered a reward of sixpence for every time the boomerang was made to return to the spot from which it was thrown. He drew a circle of five or six feet on the sand, and although the boomerang was thrown with much force, the native succeeded in making it fall within the circle five times out of twelve. Eyre also says that this weapon is particularly useful in war, "as it is almost impossible, even when it is seen in the air, to tell which way it will go, or where descend. I once nearly had my arm broken by a wangno, whilst standing within a yard of the native who threw it, and looking out purposely for it."[1] Mr Oldfield,[2] on the contrary, speaks much less favourably of the boomerang. It is, he says, but little used in war ; nor do the natives "ever attempt to kill a solitary bird or beast by means of" it. On the other hand, in swampy localities, where waterfowl "congregate largely, the boomerang is of essential use ; for a great number of them being simultaneously hurled into a large flock of waterfowl, ensures the capture of considerable numbers." According to M'Gillivray, the boomerang is unknown on the north coast from Cape York to Port Essington.[3] Mr W. D. Campbell has suggested that the idea of the boomerang was given by the leaf of the "Blue Gum," Eucalyptus, which is very similar in form.

The Australians obtain fire by rubbing together two pieces of wood. This process, however, being one of considerable labour, particularly in damp weather, great care is taken to prevent the fire, when once lighted, from becoming extinguished. For this reason they often carry with them a cone of banksia, which burns slowly, like amadou.[4]

Mr Stuart informs me that some of the northern tribes

---

[1] *Loc. cit.*, vol. ii. p. 308.
[2] *Trans. Ethn. Soc.*, New Series, vol. iii. p. 264.
[3] *Voyage of the "Rattlesnake,"* vol. i. p. 92.
[4] D'Urville, vol. i. p. 194.

had no means of relighting their fires, but if they ever became simultaneously extinguished, used to go to a neighbouring tribe for a fresh light. So also, according to M. Angas, some of the western tribes "have no means of kindling fire. They say that it formerly came down from the north," and if it happens to go out they procure it again from some neighbouring encampment.[1]

According to Captain Cook, the Australians had " no idea of traffic, nor," he says, " could we communicate any to them : they received the things which we gave them, but never appeared to understand our signs when we required a return. The same indifference, which prevented them from buying what we had, prevented them also from attempting to steal : if they had coveted more, they would have been less honest." [2] In other parts, however, they are more advanced in this respect. Various kinds of pigments, feathers, shells, implements, and especially flints, are the principal articles of barter.

The Australians observed by Cook, Dampier, and Flinders, were entirely destitute of clothing, and their principal ornament consisted of a bone, five or six inches long, and half an inch thick, thrust through the cartilage of the nose. They did not tattoo. On the north-west coast, King observed some of the natives with a very peculiar decoration. At every three inches between the upper part of the chest and the navel, the body was scarified in horizontal bands, the cicatrices of which were at least an inch in diameter, and raised half an inch from the body.[3] Some of them fastened to their hair by means of gum, teeth of kangaroos or of men, dogs' tails, fish-bones, bits of wood, and other objects which they regarded as ornamental. Sometimes they wore pieces of opossum or kangaroo skin—not for decency, but for warmth, and, while hunting, as a protection from thorns. According to D'Urville, however, the natives of New South Wales did not think it decent that young children should go quite naked.[4] M'Gillivray also mentions a very similar

---

[1] *Savage Life and Scenes*, vol. i. p. 112. [2] *Loc. cit.*, p. 635.
[3] *Loc. cit.*, p. 42. [4] *Voyage de " l'Astralobe,"* vol. i. p. 471.

idea at Moreton Bay. In many parts of Australia the natives also paint themselves, red and white being the favourite, or at least the commonest, colours. The red is laid on in broad patches, the white generally in stripes or spots, a circle often being drawn round each eye. Some tribes, but not all, tattoo themselves on the back and breast in rows, rings, and semicircles. Among the females on the Murray, the only ceremony of importance with which Eyre was acquainted, was that of scarring the back. Eyre indeed calls it tattooing, but " crimping " would, I think, be a more correct expression. It takes place at the age of puberty, and is extremely painful. The young woman kneels down and places her head between the knees of a strong old woman, and the operator, who is always a man, cuts the back with a piece of shell or flint in rows of long, deep gashes from left to right quite across the back, and completely up to the shoulders. The whole scene is most revolting : the blood gushes out in torrents, and saturates the ground, while the cries of the poor victim gradually rise into screams of agony. Still the girls submit voluntarily, as a well-carved back is much admired. The lads also generally have to undergo a ceremony of initiation before they are permitted to rank as men. This sometimes consists in circumcision,[1] sometimes in another almost incredible ceremonial,[2] or frequently in punching out one of the front teeth. Other tribes have peculiar and distinctive incisions, such as scars running across the chest, circles on the shoulders, or various combinations of small dots.

The severe sufferings they inflict on themselves are very remarkable. In the Adelaide district, according to Mr Moorhouse, there are five distinct stages of initiation, before the native is admitted to all the privileges of a man. Their rules and ceremonies are very elaborate, and are conducted by the elder men, but they cannot be said to have any form of government, nor have any distinctions of rank, or recognised chiefs, ever been found amongst them.

[1] Eyre, vol. ii. p. 332.
[2] *Finditur usque ad urethram a parte inferâ penis.*

The children have a game with string something like our cat's-cradle, but their principal amusements consist in learning to hunt, fish, etc.   The elder people are fond of dances, which may be divided into war-dances, hunting-dances, and love-dances—the two latter being most common.   These generally take place when tribes meet, and are held at night.   Their songs are rude, with simple and generally extempore words.

They have no systematized religion, nor any worship or prayer ; but most of them have an indistinct dread of evil beings, which, though mysterious, cannot, I think, be said to be regarded as supernatural.   They all have a great fear of the dark, and of witchcraft.   In fact, they believe that no one ever dies a natural death.

Captain Wilkes[1] describes an Australian funeral as follows.   Almost immediately after death the corpse was arranged in a sitting posture, the knees bent up close to the body, the head pressed forwards, and the whole body closely tied up in a blanket.   An oval grave was then dug, about six feet long, three wide, and five deep.   At the bottom was a bed of leaves, covered with an opossum-skin cloak, and with a stuffed bag of kangaroo-skin for a pillow ; on this the body was laid with its implements and weapons.   Above the corpse were strewn leaves and branches, and the hole was then filled up with stones.   Finally, the earth which had been removed was put over the whole, making a mound eight or nine feet high.   According to D'Urville, the natives of New South Wales bury the young, and burn the old.[2]   Other tribes dispose of their dead in other ways ; but none of them were addicted to cannibalism as a matter of habit or choice, although they were not unfrequently driven to it by the scarcity of other food, and sometimes ate portions of enemies whom they had slain.

No single fact, perhaps, gives us a more vivid idea of the low condition of these miserable savages than the observation that they have no numerals enabling them to count their own fingers—not even those of one hand.

[1] *L.c.*, vol. ii. p. 195 ; Fitzroy, *l.c.*, vol. ii. p. 628.   [2] Vol. i p. 472.

Mr Crawfurd[1] has examined the numerals of thirty Australian languages, " and in no instance do they appear to go beyond the number four." Mr Scott Nind, indeed, has given an account of the Australians of King George's Sound, to which a vocabulary is annexed, containing the numerals, which are made to reach the number five. The term for this last unit, however, turns out to be only the word " many." In fact, the word " five " is used by them to express the idea of a great number, just as a " thousand " sometimes is by us.

Their language, moreover, contains " no generic terms, as tree, fish, birds, etc., but only specific ones, as applied to each particular variety."[2]

Though they are apparently fond of their children, even Eyre admits that there is little affection between husband and wife. " After a long absence," he says, " I have seen natives upon their return go to their camp, exhibiting the most stoical indifference, never take the least notice of their wives, but sit down, and act and look as if they had never been out of the encampment."[3] Women, in fact, are regarded as mere property. " No one," says Eyre, " ever attempts to take the part of a female."[4] Beauty only makes matters worse. " The early life," says Sir G. Grey, " of a young woman at all celebrated for beauty is generally one continued series of captivity to different masters, of ghastly wounds, rapid flights, and bad treatment from other females "[5] jealous of her superior attractions. Few women in Australia, it is said, live to thirty. Yet with all this lawlessness and tyranny, marriage is regulated by certain very curious prohibitions. Thus a man may steal another man's wife if he can ; but, as already mentioned, he may not under any circumstances marry a woman of the same clan, even though not related in the remotest degree. There are certain great families, such as the Ballaroke, Tdondarup, Ngotak, Nagarnook, Nogonyuk, Mongalmy, and Narrangur, which occur over

---

[1] *Transactions of Ethn. Soc.*, New Series, vol. ii. p. 84.
[2] Eyre, vol. ii. p. 392.   [3] *L.c.*, pp. 2, 215, also p. 320.
[4] *L.c.*, vol. ii. p. 387.   [5] *L.c.*, vol. ii. p. 249.

a great portion of the continent, and within which marriage is not permitted.[1] Every tribe is divided into clans, and no man may marry a woman belonging to his own clan. On the other hand, in one sense every man is regarded as a husband of every woman belonging to any clan into which he may legally marry. These "communal marriages," however, as I have elsewhere proposed to call them, are often more or less theoretical, and a man has also his own special wife or wives, but even as regards them other men have certain curiously regulated rights.[2] There are many other cases of prohibitions ; "indeed," says Mr Lang,[3] "instead of enjoying perfect personal freedom, as it would at first appear, they are governed by a code of rules and a set of customs which form one of the most cruel tyrannies that has ever, perhaps, existed on the face of the earth, subjecting not only the will, but the property and life of the weak to the dominion of the strong. The whole tendency of the system is to give everything to the strong and old, to the prejudice of the weak and young, and more particularly to the detriment of the women. They have rules by which the best food, the best pieces, the best animals, etc., are prohibited to the women and young men, and reserved for the old. The women are generally appropriated to the old and powerful, some of whom possess from four to seven wives ; while wives are altogether denied to young men, unless they have sisters to give in exchange, and are strong and courageous enough to prevent their sisters from being taken without exchange." They have also very long and elaborate ceremonies.[4]

The Tasmanians

The inhabitants of Van Diemen's Land belonged to quite a different race, but were just as wretched as those

[1] Eyre, vol. ii. p. 329. For further particulars, see my *Origin of Civilisation.*
[2] Spencer and Gillen, *Native Tribes of Central Australia*, p. 62.
[3] *The Aborigines of Australia*, G. S. Lang, p. 7.
[4] Spencer and Gillen, *Native Tribes of Central Australia*, p. 272.

of Australia. According to Captain Cook's account, they had no houses, no clothes, no canoes, no instrument to catch large fish, no nets, no hooks; they lived on mussels, cockles, and periwinkles, and their only weapon was a straight pole, sharpened at one end.[1] Mr Dove informs us that they are entirely without any "moral views and impressions." Indeed, he scarcely appears to regard them as rational beings.[2] Milligan states that they believed in the existence of a number of mischievous spirits who lived in caverns, or the dark recesses of the forest; and that after death their spirits went to England.

Dr Nixon, the first Bishop of Tasmania, made careful inquiries on the subject, and came to the conclusion that "No trace can be found of the existence of any religious usage, or even sentiment among them."[3] Like the Australians, they have no means of expressing abstract ideas; they have not even a word for a "tree." Although fire was well known to them, some tribes, at least, appear to have been ignorant whence it was originally obtained, or how, if extinguished, it could be relighted. "In all their wanderings," says Mr Dove, "they were particularly careful to bear in their hands the materials for kindling a fire. Their memory supplies them with no instances of a period in which they were obliged to draw on their inventive powers for the means of resuscitating an element so essential to their health and comfort as flame. How it came originally into their possession is unknown.

FIG. 264.—Tasmanian firesticks, one-third actual size.

1 *Third Voyage*, vol. i. p. 100.
2 *Tasmanian Jour. of Nat. Sci.*, vol. i. p. 249.
3 See also Bonwick, *Daily Life of the Tasmanians*, p. 166; H. Ling Roth, *The Tasmanians*, p. 66.

Whether it may be viewed as a gift of nature, or the product of art and sagacity, they cannot recollect a period when it was a desideratum. . . . It was the part of the females especially to carry a firebrand in their hands, which was studiously refreshed from time to time as it became dull and evanescent."[1]   Fig. 264 represents a pair of Tasmanian firesticks, presented to me by Mr Robinson.   The Tasmanians did not use either the boomerang or the throwing-stick.[2]

Fiji Islanders

The islands of the Pacific contain two very distinct races of men—the Negrito and the Polynesian. My space does not permit me to enter into the interesting question of their relationships and affinities.

The Fijians belong to the former category, though probably with some infusion of Polynesian blood, and in many respects resemble Negroes. They are darker than the Polynesians. The jaws are larger, and the hair, though not exactly woolly, is frizzled. They are a powerful race, but not so graceful as the Polynesians. Their language is, however, more Polynesian than Negrito. Their institutions, customs, and manners were partly Polynesian, partly Negrito.[3] It is remarkable that they did not use the consonants "b," "d," or "g," without placing "m" or "n" before them, as for instance, Mbau, Nduandua, Ngata. It is well known how frequent these sounds are in Negro names.

The food of the Fiji Islanders consisted of fish, turtle, shellfish, crabs, human flesh whenever it could be obtained, taro, yams, mandrai, bananas, and cocoa-nuts ; in addition to which the higher classes occasionally indulged in pigs and fowls. They drank *ava* habitually, and at all their ceremonies.

Their weapons consisted of spears, slings, clubs, bows

---

[1] *Tasmanian Journal of Nat. Sci.*, vol. i. p. 250.
[2] Bonwick, *Daily Life of the Tasmanians*, p. 43.
[3] Latham, *Varieties of Man*, p. 226.

and arrows. The spears were from ten to fifteen feet long, and were generally made of cocoa-nut wood ; the end was pointed and charred ; sometimes, though not often, a sharp bone was used for the point. They had several kinds of clubs, all made of ironwood. That most esteemed was about three feet long, with a heavy knob at the end. Another kind was somewhat shovel-shaped, and might rather be called a short sword. The *ula* was a short heavy club, about eighteen inches long, with a large and heavy knob. It was used as a missile, and the natives threw it with great accuracy and force. These were their principal weapons, the bows and arrows being weak and light. They were, however, used in war, as well as in killing fish. The fortified towns of the Fijians had an earthen "rampart, about six feet thick, faced with large stones, surmounted by a reed fence of cocoa-nut trunks, and surrounded by a muddy moat." [1]

Their houses were oblong, from twenty to thirty feet long, and fifteen feet high. They were made of cocoa-nut wood and tree fern, and were sometimes very well built. They had two doorways on opposite sides, from three to four feet high and four feet wide. The sides were made of posts about three feet apart, and filled in with wicker work. The roof had a steep pitch ; the rafters were generally of palm wood, thatched with wild sugar-cane, under which they placed fern leaves. A mat served as a door, and a few flat stones near the middle of the house served as the fireplace. The houses were seldom divided by partitions, but the two ends were raised about a foot, and were covered with layers of mats on which the natives slept.

Their temples were pyramidal in form, and were often erected on terraced mounds, like those of Central America. [2] They also venerated certain upright stones, [3] resembling those which we call Druidical. "The Feegeeans," says Mr Hazlewood, "consider the gods as

---

[1] Williams, *Figi and the Figians*, vol. i. p. 48.
[2] B. Seemann, in the *Vacation Tourist* for 1861, p. 269.
[3] *Figi and the Figians*, vol. i. p. 220.

beings of like passions with themselves. They love and
hate ; they are proud and revengeful, and make war, and
kill and eat each other ; and are, in fact, savages and
cannibals like themselves." "Cruelty," says Captain
Erskine,[1] "a craving for blood, and especially for human
flesh as food, are characteristic of the gods." Yet the
Fijians looked upon the Samoans with horror, regarding
them as having no religion, because they had no belief
in any such deities, nor any of the sanguinary rites which
prevailed in other islands.

The Fiji canoes were large and well constructed. They
were generally double, of unequal size, the smaller one
serving as an outrigger. The larger ones were sometimes
more than a hundred feet in length. The two canoes
were connected by a platform, generally about fifteen feet
wide, and projecting two or three feet beyond the sides.
The bottom of each consisted of a single plank ; the sides
were fitted by dovetailing, and closely united by lashings
passed through flanges left on each of the pieces. The
joints were closed by the gum of the bread-fruit tree.
The sails were large and made of mats. The mast was
generally about half the length of the canoe, and the yard
and boom usually twice as long as the mast. Their
principal tool was an adze, formerly of stone, but now
generally of iron. For boring holes they used the long
spines of the echina, pointed bones, and, when they
could get them, nails. Small teeth, such as those of rats
and mice, were used for carving ; and their knives were
made of the outside of a piece of bamboo, shaped into
form while green. After being dried, it was charred,
and thus became very hard and sharp, so that it might
even be used in surgical operations. They differed from
the Polynesians in using earthenware pots for cooking.
These were graceful and well made, though the potter's-
wheel was unknown. The pottery was all made by
women. Their tools were very simple, consisting of a
small round flat stone to fashion the inside, and a flat
mallet or spatula for the surface, which they made almost

[1] *Journal of a Cruise in the Western Pacific*, p. 247.

as round as if it had been turned in a lathe. Forks appear to have been long in use among the Fijians ; a remarkable fact, if we remember that they were unknown in Northern Europe until the seventeenth century.

The Fijians have several kinds of games. They are fond of swinging, and of throwing stones or fruits at a mark. They have also a game resembling skittles. Their dances, like those of so many other nations, are anything but decorous. Their musical instruments are the conch-shell, the nose-flute, pipes, a Jew's-harp made of a strip of bamboo, and several sorts of drums. They are also fond of poetry.

Their agricultural implements have been described by Mr Williams. The digging-sticks are made of a young mangrove-tree. They are about the size of an ordinary hay-fork, and the lower end " is tapered off on one side, after the shape of a quill toothpick. In digging, this flattened side is kept downwards. When preparing a piece of ground for yams, a number of men are employed, divided into groups of three or four. Each man being furnished with a digging-stick, they drive them into the ground so as to enclose a circle of about two feet in diameter. When, by repeated strokes, the sticks reach the depth of eighteen inches, they are used as levers, and the mass of soil between them is thus loosened and raised." [1] The clods are then broken up by boys with short sticks. Weeding " is accomplished by means of a tool used like a Dutch hoe, the workman squatting so as bring the handle nearly level with the ground. The blade used formerly to be made of a bone from the back of a turtle, or a plate of tortoise-shell, or the valve of a large oyster, or large kind of pinna. In the Windward Islands they use a large dibble, eight feet long, about eighteen inches in circumference, and tapering to a point. They had also pruning knives of " tortoise-shell lashed to the end of a rod ten feet long. They are skilful in basket-making, and have good strong nets made of creepers or of sinnet.

[1] *Figi and the Figians*, vol. i. p. 63.

The women are kept in great subjection. "The men frequently tie them up and flog them. Like other property, wives might be sold at pleasure, and the usual price is a musket. Those who purchase them may do with them as they please, even to knocking them on the head." Erskine, however, gives a more satisfactory account of the position held by the women ; and it appears that they are on the whole more chaste than is the case in some of the other Pacific Islands, which is saying something for them, but certainly not much. Although so lax in some things, they were very strict in others, and it was thought improper in some of these islands for husband and wife to spend the night under the same roof.

Although but scantily clothed, the Fijians were very particular about their garments and their paint. They were specially proud of their hair, and if it was short they wore a wig as a substitute. Some of these wigs were most elaborate. The men wore " tapa," which is a kind of cloth obtained from the inner bark of the paper-mulberry, and made into a sash, from three to one hundred yards in length. Six or ten yards is, however, the usual quantity, and it is passed between the legs and round the waist.[1] The women are not permitted to use " tapa," and their dress is more scanty than that of the men, consisting, indeed, only of the " liku," a kind of band, made of the bark of the hibiscus, and fastened round the waist. It ends in a fringe, which is worn short by the girls, but longer after marriage. Nevertheless, though almost naked, the Fijians are said to have been very modest, and if anyone were found entirely without clothes, Captain Wilkes thinks that the offender would be immediately put to death.

Tattooing is confined to the women, who are ornamented in this manner on the fingers, the corners of the mouth, and, oddly enough, on those parts of the body which are covered by the " liku." The process is very painful, but submission to it is regarded as a religious

[1] *Figi and the Figians*, vol. i. p. 156.

duty,[1] any neglect of which will assuredly be punished after death.[2]

The graves of the common people are only marked by a few stones, but over those of chiefs they build small houses, from two to six feet high, or in some cases erect large cairns of stone ; these also are sometimes " set up to mark the spot where a man has died." [3] The body is buried in a sitting posture. The usual sign of mourning is to crop the hair or beard, or both. Very often, also, they burn the skin into blisters, and cut off the end-joints of the small toe and little finger.

Among the Fijians, parricide is not a crime but a custom. They believe that " as they die, such will be their condition in the next world." Moreover, the road to Mbulu is long and difficult. Hence it would be cruel to allow a beloved relative to become old and infirm. We are assured that so deeply rooted was this conviction, that as a matter of fact parents were generally killed by their children. Sometimes the aged people make up their minds that it is time to die ; sometimes it is the children who give notice to their parents that they are a burden to them. In either case, the friends and relatives are summoned, a consultation takes place, and a day is fixed for the ceremony, which commences with a great feast. The missionaries have often witnessed these horrible tragedies. On one occasion a young man invited Mr Hunt to attend his mother's funeral, which was just going to take place. Mr Hunt accepted the invitation ; but when the funeral procession started, he was surprised to see no corpse, and accordingly made inquiries, when the young savage " pointed out his mother,[4] who was walking along with them as gay and lively as any of them present, and apparently as much pleased. . . . He added that it was from love for his mother that he had done so ; that in consequence of the

---

[1] *Figi and the Figians*, vol. i. p. 160 ; Wilkes, *l.c.*, p. 355.
[2] *A Mission to Viti*, p. 112.
[3] *Figi and the Figians*, vol. i. p. 192.   [4] Wilkes, *l.c.*, p. 95.

same love, they were now going to bury her, and that none but themselves could or ought to do so sacred an office. . . . She was their mother, and they were her children, and *they ought* to put her to death." In such cases, the grave is dug about four feet deep, the relatives and friends begin their lamentations, take an affectionate parting, and bury the poor victim alive. It is surprising after this to hear that Mr Hunt regarded the Fijians as being kind and affectionate to their parents ; but in fact " they consider this custom so great a proof of affection, that none but children could be found to perform it." So general in fact was this custom, so powerful the influence which it had upon them, that in one town, containing several hundred inhabitants, Captain Wilkes did not see one man over forty years of age ; and, on asking for the old people, he was informed that they were all buried. Again, during the first year of Mr Hunt's residence at Somo-somo, there was only one instance of natural death, all the aged and diseased having been strangled or buried alive.

When a chief died, it was usual to " send with him " some of his women and some slaves. At the death of Ngavindi, Mr Calvert went to Mbau hoping " to prevent the strangling of women, but was too late. Three had been murdered. Thakombau proposed to strangle his sister, the chief wife of the deceased, as was the usual custom ; but the Lasakau people begged that she might be spared, and that her child might become their chief. Ngavindi's mother offered herself as a substitute, and was strangled. The dead chief lay in state, with a dead wife by his side, on a raised platform ; the corpse of his mother on a bier at his feet, and a murdered servant on a mat in the midst of the house. A large grave was dug in the foundation of a house near by, in which the servant was laid first, and upon her the other three corpses, wrapped and wound up together." [1] In these cases the wives generally die voluntarily, believing that thus only can they hope to go to heaven. Horrible as

[1] *Figi and the Figians*, vol. ii. p. 301.

are these facts, they at least show how strong must be the belief felt in a future state of existence.

Still, though we may allow the goodness of the motive to extenuate some of these atrocities, it must be allowed that human life was but little regarded in Fiji. Not only infanticide, but also human sacrifices, were very common, and, in fact, scarcely anything was undertaken without the latter. When the king launched a canoe, ten or more men were slaughtered on the deck, in order that it might be washed with human blood. But there is even worse to be told. The Fijians were most inveterate cannibals, and so fond were they of human flesh, that " the greatest praise they can bestow on any delicacy is to say that it is as tender as a dead man." Nay, they were even so fastidious as to dislike the taste of white men,[1] to prefer the flesh of women to that of men, and to consider the arm above the elbow and the thigh as the best joints ; and so greedy, that human flesh was reserved for the men, being considered too good to be wasted upon the women. When the king gave a feast, human flesh always formed one of the dishes, and though the bodies of enemies slain in battle were always eaten, they did not afford a sufficient supply, but slaves were fattened up for the market. Sometimes they roasted them alive and ate them at once, while at others they kept bodies until they were far gone in decay. Ra Undre-undre, Chief of Rakiraki, was said to have eaten nine hundred persons himself, permitting no one to share them with him.[2]

It was not from any want of food that the Fijians were cannibals. On one occasion they offered to the God of War " ten thousand yams (weighing from six to twelve pounds each), thirty turtles, forty roots of yaquona (some very large), many hundreds of native puddings (two tons), one hundred and fifty giant oysters, fifteen water-melons, cocoa-nuts, a large number of violet land-crabs, taro, and ripe bananas."[3] At a public feast Mr

---

[1] So also did the Australians, the Tongans, and the New Zealanders.
[2] *Figi and the Figians*, vol. i. p. 213.   [3] *Ibid.*, vol. i p. 44.

Williams once saw "two hundred men employed for nearly six hours in collecting and piling cooked food. There were six mounds of yams, taro, vakalolo, pigs, and turtles : these contained about fifty tons of cooked yams and taro, fifteen tons of sweet pudding, seventy turtles, five cartloads of yaquona, and about two hundred tons of uncooked yams. One pudding, at a Lakemba feast, measured twenty-one feet in circumference." Yet so habitual has cannibalism become, that they have no word for a corpse which does not include the idea of something edible. Human flesh is known as "puaka balava," or "long pig."[1] "On contemplating the character of this extraordinary people," says Erskine,[2] "the mind is struck with wonder and awe at the mixture of a complicated and carefully-conducted political system, highly finished manners, and ceremonious politeness, with a ferocity and practice of savage vices which is probably unparalleled in any other part of the world." "Murder," says Mr Williams, "is not an occasional thing in Figi, but habitual, systematic, and classed among ordinary transactions."[3] Elsewhere he tells us that no Fijian ever feels safe with a stranger at his heels,[4] and that to be "an acknowledged murderer is the object of the Figian's restless ambition."[5] On the island of Vanua Levu, even among the women, there were "few who had not in some way been murderers."[6] To this they are trained up from infancy. "One of the first lessons taught the infant is to strike its mother." At Somo-somo, Mr Williams saw mothers leading their children "to kick and tread upon the dead bodies of enemies."[7] No wonder that under these circumstances "a happy and united household is most rare." Indeed, it is nearly impossible, for by an arrangement which seems almost incredible,

[1] Erskine, *l.c.*, p. 260. Other mammalia, when introduced into the South Sea Islands, received names indicative of their similarity to this their principal quadruped : thus the horse was called the "man-carrying pig" in Tahiti ; the sheep was the "hog with teeth on its forehead" (Forster, *l.c.*, p. 384).

[2] Erskine, *l.c.*, p. 272.　　　[3] *Figi and the Figians*, vol. i. p. 134.
[4] *L.c.*, p. 133.　　　[5] *L.c.*, p. 112.
[6] *L.c.*, p. 180.　　　[7] *L.c.*, p. 177.

" brothers and sisters, first cousins, fathers and sons-in-law, mothers and daughters-in-law, and brothers and sisters-in-law, are severally forbidden to speak to each other, or to eat from the same dish." [1] Yet amid so much that is horrible, there is still something in the Fijian which redeems his character from utter atrocity. If he hates deeply, he also loves truly ; if his revenge never dies, his fidelity and loyalty are strong and enduring. Thakombau was a thorough Fijian. Almost to the last he opposed the missionaries. He was not only heathen, but anti-Christian. At length being converted, he called his people together, and, says Mr Calvert, " What a congregation he had !—husbands whose wives he had dishonoured ! widows whose husbands he had slain ! sisters whose relatives had been strangled by his orders ! relatives whose friends he had eaten ! and children, the descendants of those he had murdered, and who had vowed to avenge the wrongs inflicted on their fathers ! " [2] Yet even this man—an adulterer, a parricide, and a cannibal, whose hands were stained with a hundred murders—had still something noble and lovable about him ; so much so, indeed, that, in spite of his crimes, he secured the affection, the friendship, even the respect, of a man so excellent as Mr Calvert.

The Maories

The New Zealanders are the southernmost representatives of the great Polynesian family. Their principal food consisted of fern roots, which they scorched over the fire, and then beat with a stick, till the bark and dry outside fell off ; the remainder being a soft substance, rather clammy and sweet, not unpleasant to the taste, but mixed with numerous stringy fibres which are very disagreeable. [3] In the northern districts were large plantations of yams and sweet potatoes. They also cultivated gourds, which were used for vessels, as they had no pottery. Their only

---

[1] *Figi and the Figians*, vol. i., p. 136.   [2] *L.c.*, vol. ii. p. 357.
[3] Dieffenbach's *New Zealand*, vol. ii. p. 11.

instrument for tillage was " a long narrow stake sharpened
to an edge at one end, with a short piece fastened transversely at a little distance above it, for the convenience of
pressing it down with the foot." Their animal food
consisted principally of fish and shell-fish, and Captain
Cook observed large shell-mounds near their houses.
They sometimes also, though rarely, killed rails, penguins,
shags, and other birds. They obtained fire from two
pieces of wood in the usual manner.[1] A New Zealand
stone adze is represented in figs. 120–122.

The only quadrupeds in the islands were dogs and rats.
They had no hogs, and the dogs were kept entirely for
food. They were skilful in fishing, having excellent
lines, hooks made of bone and shell, and very large nets,
which were made of the leaves of the so-called New
Zealand flax, a plant allied to the Lilies, split into strips
of the proper breadth and tied together. In making the
lines the leaves are " scraped by a shell, which removes
the upper or green part, and leaves the strong white fibres,
that run longitudinally along the under side."[2] This
kind of cordage has even been preferred to that made of
European hemp.

Of these leaves also they made most of their clothes,
for, though acquainted with the manufacture of bark-cloth,
it was very scarce, and worn only as an ornament. The
leaves were split into three or four slips, which were
interwoven into a kind of stuff, something between
netting and cloth. Dog's wool was also used for the
same purpose.[3] The dress was alike in both sexes, and
consisted of two parts ; one piece of their rude cloth (if
so it may be called) was tied over the shoulders and
reached to the knees, being fastened in front by a piece of
string or a bone bodkin ; the other piece was wrapped
round the waist, and reached nearly to the ground. This
garment, however, was worn by the men only on particular occasions.

[1] D'Urville, vol. ii. p. 479.
[2] Fitzroy's *Voyage of the " Adventure" and " Beagle,"* vol. ii. p. 599.
[3] D'Urville, vol. ii. p. 500.

For ornament they wore combs of wood or bone, feathers, necklaces, bracelets, and anklets of bones and shells, and earrings of jade or albatross-down. Many of them had also small grotesque figures of jade, which were suspended from the neck, and were regarded as very precious. The New Zealanders were also tattooed with great dexterity and elegance ; not only on the body, but even on the face, the general effect of which was in many cases far from unpleasant. The process, however, was extremely painful, so much so, indeed, that it could not be supported all at once, but was sometimes spread over several months or even years. The lips and the corners of the eyes were the part that hurt most. To have shrunk from it would, however, have been a great disgrace.

Their houses were from eighteen to twenty feet long, eight or ten broad, and five or six high. The sides sloped quite down to the ground, differing in this respect from those of Tahiti, which are left open at the sides. This was done, however, not for the sake of privacy, but to keep out the wind and rain. The sides were made of sticks, closely thatched with grass and hay, and the door was at one end, just high enough to admit a man on all fours. Another hole served both for window and chimney. The roof was often carved, and they frequently attached to the end of the ridge pole a monstrous representation of the proprietor.[1]

The villages were all fortified. They chose the strongest natural situations, and surrounded the houses with a palisade about ten feet high. The weaker sides were also defended " by a double ditch, the innermost of which has a bank, and an additional palisade." The stakes were driven obliquely into the ground, so that they projected over the ditch, which " from the bottom to the top or crown of the bank is four-and-twenty feet. Close within the innermost palisade is a stage, twenty feet high, forty feet long, and six broad ; it is supported by strong posts, and is intended as a station for those who defend

[1] Dieffenbach, *l.c.*, p. 69.

the place, from which they may annoy the assailants by darts and stones, heaps of which lie ready for use. Another stage of the same kind commands the steep avenue from the back, and stands also within the palisade."[1] Within the palisades they had reduced the ground, " not to one level, but to several, rising in stages one above the other, like an amphitheatre, each of which is enclosed within its separate palisade." These different platforms communicated only by narrow passages, so that each one was capable of separate defence ; and they were provided with large stores of dried fish, fern-roots, etc. As the natives, when first discovered, had no bows and arrows, nor even slings, in fact, no " missile weapon except the lance, which was thrown by hand," such positions as these must have been almost impregnable. Their principal weapon was the patoo-patoo (fig. 265), which was fastened to the wrist by a strong strap, lest it should be wrenched from them. They had no defensive armour, but besides their weapons the chiefs carried a " staff of distinction."

FIG. 265.—New Zealand patoo-patoo, one-fourth of the actual size.

Their canoes were well built, and resembled those of the other islands. Many of them, however, were broad enough to sail without an outrigger. The two ends were often ingeniously carved.[2]

The dead were wrapped in native cloth, and either buried in a contracted posture or exposed for a while on small square platforms ; when the flesh had decayed away, the bones were washed, and finally deposited in a small covered box, which was generally elevated on a

[1] Cook's *First Voyage*, p. 343.　　　[2] Forster, *l.c.*, p. 326.

column in or near the village.[1] In some districts, however, they were usually thrown into the sea, except indeed
those that were killed in battle. These were generally eaten
by their enemies. None of the objects used by the dead
during his last illness were ever employed again ;[2] they
were generally broken and buried with the deceased. In
one case a moa's egg has been found in the hands of a
dead Maori, who was buried in the usual sitting posture.
The egg was perfect,[3] and may have been intended to
serve as food for the dead.

In the Taranaki district, according to Taylor, the natives
were buried in their houses, the door was tied up and
painted with ochre to show that it was " taboo." In
most of the Pahs or fortified villages half the houses
belonged to the dead, and these being never repaired
gave the village a very neglected appearance.[4]

Their principal musical instrument was the flute, of
which they had three or four varieties. D'Urville[5] also
observed among them a kind of lyre, with three or four
strings. They used large shells, too, as a kind of trumpet.
They were very fond of singing, of poetry, and of dances.
The latter were of two kinds, warlike and amorous.

In character the New Zealanders were proud, jealous,
irritable, cruel, and implacable ; but at the same time
sensible, generous, sincere, hospitable, and affectionate.
Like other Polynesians, the Maories were much given
to infanticide.[6] The girls before marriage were allowed
great freedom. When once married, however, the
women were faithful and affectionate to their husbands,
by whom, on the other hand, they were generally treated
with both kindness and respect. On the whole, it must
be admitted that the position of the women among the
New Zealanders was far from unsatisfactory. The
Maories were perpetually at war during life, and hoped
to continue so after death. Heaven they regarded as a

---

[1] Dieffenbach, *l.c.*, p. 63 ; Fitzroy, *l.c.*, p. 579.
[2] D'Urville, vol. ii. p. 536. [3] *Zoologist*, February, 1865, p. 9454.
[4] Taylor, *New Zealand and its Inhabitants*, p. 101.
[5] *L.c.*, vol. ii. p. 501. [6] Dieffenbach, *l.c.*, p. 16.

place where there would be continual feasts of fish and sweet potatoes ; where they would be always fighting, and always victorious. Whether they can be said to have had a religion or not depends upon the meaning we attach to the word. They believe in the survival of the soul, but not in the resurrection of the body—an article of faith which, as Mr Marsden tells us, the missionaries could not induce them to accept. They had no idea of an Almighty Deity. Speaking to Mr Taylor, Te Heuheu, chief of Taupo, ridiculed the idea. " Is there," he asked, " one maker of all things amongst you Europeans ? Is not one a carpenter, another a blacksmith, another a ship-builder, and another a house-builder ? So it was in the beginning ; one God made this, another that : Tane made trees, Ru mountains, Tangaroa fish, and so forth. Your religion is of to-day, ours from remote antiquity. Do not think, then, to destroy our ancient faith with your fresh-born religion." [1]

Their principal deity was known as the Atoua, who was a cruel cannibal like themselves. When anyone was ill, Atoua was supposed to be devouring his inside, and they endeavoured to frighten him away by curses and threats.[2] This we may regard as a kind of negative worship ; but on other occasions they certainly offered human and other sacrifices, in the vain hope of appeasing his wrath. They did not worship idols, but many of the priests seem to have really thought that they had been in actual communication with the Atoua ; and some of the early missionaries were inclined to believe that Satan might have been permitted to practise a deception upon them in order to strengthen his power ! However extraordinary this may appear, the same was the case in Tahiti. " In addition," says Mr Ellis, " to the firm belief which many who were sorcerers, or agents of the infernal powers, and others who were the victims of incantation, still maintain, some of the early missionaries are disposed to think this was the fact." [3] Even Mr

---

[1] Dieffenbach, *l.c.*, p. 13.   [2] *Missionary Register*, Nov. 1819.
[3] *Polynesian Researches*, vol. ii. p. 226.

Ellis himself was of the same opinion. With such low ideas of the Divinity, it is perhaps not surprising that some of the chiefs were looked upon as gods even during life. Watches and white men also were at first regarded as deities; the latter not, perhaps, unnaturally, their fire-arms being regarded as thunder and lightning.

The New Zealanders had but little regard for human life. Earle relates that a young chief named Atoi, who is described as having "a handsome open countenance," on one occasion recognized a pretty girl of about sixteen, who had been working for Mr Earle, and, claiming her as a runaway slave, took her back with him to his village, where he killed and ate her. The next day he showed Mr Earle "the post to which she had been tied, and laughed to think how he had cheated her." "For," said he, "I told her I only intended to give her a flogging; but I fired, and shot her through the heart." "Yet," adds Mr Earle, "I again affirm that he was not only a handsome young man, but mild and genteel in his demeanour, and a general favourite with us all." [1]

Although the New Zealanders were addicted to cannibalism, it was with them a very different habit from that of the Fijian. No doubt the Maori enjoyed his meals of human flesh. But the cannibalism of a New Zealander, though often a mere meal, was also sometimes a ceremony; in these cases the object was something very different from mere sensual gratification; it must be regarded as a part of his religion, as a sort of unholy sacrament. This is proved by the fact that after a battle, the bodies which they preferred were not those of plump young men or tender damsels, but of the most celebrated chiefs, however old and dry they might be. [2] In fact, they believed that it was not only the material substance which they thus appropriated, but also the spirit, the ability, and the glory of him whom they devoured. The greater the number of corpses they had eaten, the higher they thought would be their position in the world to come. The Fans of Central Africa are said to entertain a similar

[1] *Residences in New Zealand*, p. 117.   [2] D'Urville, vol. ii. p. 547.

idea. Under such a creed there is a certain dignity about the habit, which is, at any rate, far removed from the sensuality of ordinary cannibalism. To be eaten was, on the other hand, the greatest misfortune that could happen to a New Zealander, since he believed that the soul was thus destroyed as well as the body. The chief who could both kill and devour his enemy had nothing more to fear from him either in this world or the next; on the contrary, the strength, ability, and prestige against which he had had to contend were not only conquered, but, by this dreadful process, incorporated with and added to his own.

In other cases slaves were killed and eaten in honour of the gods. The New Zealanders declared that criminals alone were thus treated. The celebrated chief, E'hongui, maintained that the whole analogy of nature was in favour of cannibalism. He was surprised at the horror of it felt by D'Urville. Big fish, he said, eat little fish; insects devour insects; large birds feed upon small ones; it is in accordance with the whole analogy of nature that men should eat their enemies.[1]

Tahiti

Tahiti, the queen of islands, has excited the wonder and admiration of almost all those by whom it has been visited. In some respects the Tahitians were surpassed by other South Sea Islanders; the Fijians, for instance, being, as we have seen, acquainted with pottery; but on the whole they may be taken as representing the highest stage in civilization to which man has in any country raised himself before the discovery or introduction of metallic implements. It is not, indeed, at all probable that any inhabitants of the great continents were so far advanced in civilization during their Stone Age. Doubtless, the Society Islanders would not have remained without metal if the country had afforded them the means of obtaining it. On the other hand, the ancient

[1] D'Urville, vol. ii. p. 548.

inhabitants of Europe were confined to the use of stone weapons only until they became acquainted with the superiority of, and acquired the art of working in, copper, bronze, or iron ; and it is evident that a nation would in all probability discover the use of metal before attaining the highest pitch of civilization, which, without such aid, it would be possible for it to attain.

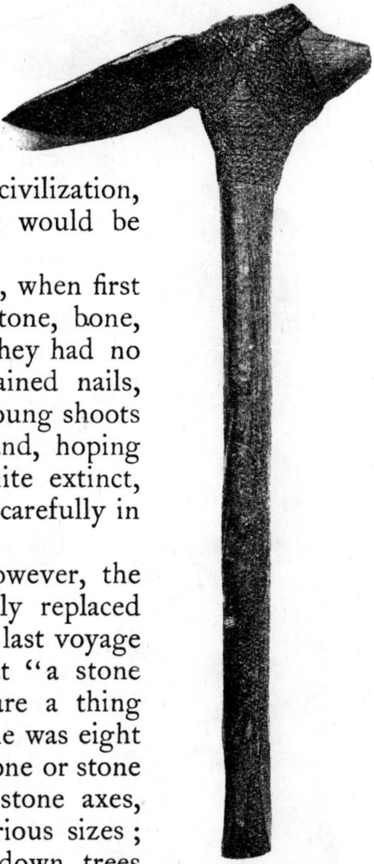

The tools of the Tahitians, when first discovered, were made of stone, bone, shell, or wood. Of metal they had no idea. When they first obtained nails, they mistook them for the young shoots of some very hard wood, and, hoping that life might not be quite extinct, planted a number of them carefully in their gardens.[1]

In a very short time, however, the earlier weapons were entirely replaced by those of iron ; and in his last voyage Captain Cook tells us[2] that "a stone hatchet is, at present, as rare a thing amongst them as an iron one was eight years ago ; and a chisel of bone or stone is not to be seen." The stone axes, or rather adzes, were of various sizes ; those intended for cutting down trees weighed six or seven pounds, the little ones, which were used for carving, only a few ounces. All of them required

FIG. 266.—Stone axe with wooden handle, one - fourth of the actual size.

continual sharpening, and a stone was always kept in readiness for this purpose. The natives were very skilful in the use of their adzes (fig. 266) ; nevertheless, to fell a tree was a work of several days. Some of the South

[1] Ellis, *Polynesian Researches*, p. 298.
[2] *Voyage to the Pacific Ocean*, vol. ii. p. 137.

Sea axes have beautifully carved handles, as in fig. 267,

representing a specimen in my own collection. These were axes of state. The chisels, or gouges, were of bone, generally that of a man's arm between the wrist and elbow. Pieces of coral were used as rasps, and splinters of bamboo for knives. For cultivating the ground they had instruments of hard wood, about five feet long, narrow, with sharp edges and pointed. These they used as spades or hoes.[1] They had fish-hooks (fig. 268) made of mother-of-pearl, and every fisherman made them for himself. They generally served for the double purpose of hook and bait. "The shell[2] is first cut into square pieces by the edge of another shell, and wrought into a form corresponding with the outline of the hook by pieces of coral, which are sufficiently rough to perform the office of a file ; a hole is then bored in the middle, the drill being a pointed stone ; this they fix into the end of a piece of bamboo, and turn it between the hands like a chocolate mill ; when the shell is perforated and the hole sufficiently wide, a small file of coral is introduced, by the appli-

FIG. 267.—South Sea axe of ceremony.

[1] Wilson, *Missionary Voyage to the South Pacific*, p. 245.
[2] Cook's *Voyage round the World*, vol. i. p. 483 ; vol. ii. p. 218.

cation of which the hook is in a short time completed, few costing the artificer more time than a quarter of an hour. From the bark of the Poerou, a species of Hibiscus, they made ropes and lines, from the thickness of an inch to the size of a small pack-thread ; with these they make nets for fishing." They had also a kind of seine net, made " of a coarse broad grass, the blades of which are like flags : these they twist and tie together in a loose manner, till the net, which is about as wide as a large sack, is from sixty to eighty fathoms long ; this they haul in shoal-smooth water, and its own weight keeps it so close to the ground that scarcely a single fish can escape." They also use certain leaves and fruit which, when thrown into the water, inebriate the fish to such a degree that they might be caught by the hands.[1] Their fishing-lines were made of the bark of the Erowa, a kind of nettle which grows in the mountains, and were described as " the best fishing-lines in the world," better even than our strongest silk lines. They also used the fibres of the cocoa-nut for mak-ing threads, with which they fastened together the various parts of their

FIG. 268.—South Sea fish-hook, one-half of the actual size.

canoes. They were very dexterous in making basket and wicker work, " of a thousand different patterns, many of them exceedingly neat" ; they also made many sorts of mats from rushes, grass, and bark, which were woven with great neatness and regularity, although en-tirely by hand and without any loom or machinery.[2] But their principal manufacture was a kind of cloth,

---

[1] Forster, *Observations made during a Voyage round the World*, p. 463 ; Ellis, vol. ii. p. 288.
[2] Ellis, vol. ii. pp. 179, 180.

made from bark, and of which there were three varieties, obtained either from the paper-mulberry, which was the best, the bread-fruit tree, or a kind of fig. This last, though less ornamental, was more useful than either of the others, because it resisted water, which they did not. All three kinds of cloth were made in the same way, the difference between them being only in the material. When the trees were of a proper size, that is to say, about six or eight feet high, and somewhat thicker than a man's thumb, they were pulled up and the roots and branches were cut off. The bark being slit up longitudinally, it peeled off readily, and was then soaked for some time in running water. After this, the green outside bark was carefully scraped off with a shell, and the strips were laid out in the evening to dry, being placed one by the side of another " till they are about a foot broad, and two or three layers are also laid one upon the other." By the morning a great part of the water had drained off or evaporated, and " the several fibres adhere together, so as that the whole may be raised from the ground in one piece." It was then placed on the smooth side of a long piece of wood, and beaten by the women-servants with a wooden instrument, shaped like a square razor-strap, and about a foot long. The four sides of this instrument were " marked lengthways with small grooves or furrows, of different degrees of fineness ; those on one side being of a width and depth sufficient to receive a small pack-thread, and the others finer in a regular gradation, so that the last are not more than equal to sewing silk." They beat the cloth first with the coarsest side, and afterwards with the others, ending with the finest : under this treatment it expanded greatly, and might be made almost as thin as a muslin. The different pieces of bark by this treatment were so closely fastened together that the cloth might be washed and wrung out without any fear of tearing ; but even if it were accidentally broken, it was repaired without difficulty, by pasting on a patch with a gluten prepared from the root of the pea : this was done so nicely that it could not be discovered.

This cloth was cool and agreeable to the touch, being even softer than our broadcloth. It is hardly necessary to say that the fineness was regulated according to the purpose for which it was intended. The first two kinds were easily bleached, and then dyed of various colours, generally red and yellow. Both of these were vegetable colours, and not very fast.

They had various strange and complicated dresses for great occasions, but their ordinary clothes were very simple, and consisted of two parts. One of them was a piece of cloth with a hole " in the middle to put the head through," and long enough to reach from the shoulder to the knee. The other was wrapped round the waist so as to hang down like a petticoat as low as the knee ; this was called the Parou. Frequently also they wore a piece of cloth tied round the head like a turban. The dress of the Queen is thus described by Ellis [1] : " She was attired in a light, loose, and flowing dress of beautifully white native cloth, tastefully fastened on the left shoulder, and reaching to the ankle ; her hair was rather lighter than that of the natives in general ; and on her head she wore a light and elegant native bonnet, of green and yellow cocoa-nut leaves ; each ear was perforated, and in the perforation two or three flowers of the fragrant Cape jessamine were inserted." The dress of the men was very similar, but instead of the petticoat they brought the cloth between the legs ; this was called the Maro. In hot weather,[2] and at noon, both sexes went almost naked, wearing only the cloth round the waist. Besides the turbans and head-dresses of leaves, they sometimes wore long plaits of human hair, which they wound about the head in such a manner as to produce a very pretty effect. They were very clean both in their persons and their clothes ; washing, as a rule, three times a day. Ornaments were worn by the men as much as by the women, and consisted of feathers, flowers, pieces of shells, and

---

[1] L.c., p. 148.
[2] The Sandwich Islanders had small square fans of mat or wicker-work, with handles of the same or of wood.

pearls.   Tattooing also was almost universal ; and a
person not properly tattooed would "be as much
reproached and shunned, as if with us he should go about
the streets naked." [1]   They anointed their heads frequently
with perfumed cocoa-nut oil, but had no combs, which in
so hot a country must have been much wanted.   Notwithstanding this, the hair of the grown-up people was
very neatly dressed.

Their houses were used principally as dormitories.
They were made of wood, and were generally about
twenty-four feet long, eleven wide, and nine feet high.
They had no side walls, but the roof reached to within
about three feet and a half of the ground.   Palm leaves
took the place of thatch, and the floor was generally
covered with soft hay.

The canoes resembled those of the Fijians, but are said
to have been scarcely so well built.   "To prepare the
planks was no easy task, but the great difficulty was to
fasten them together.   This was effected by strong thongs
of plaiting which are passed several times through holes
that are bored with a gouge or auger of bone." [2]   The
length of the canoes varied from ten up to ninety feet,
"but the breadth is by no means in proportion ; for those
of ten feet are about a foot wide, and those of more than
seventy are scarcely two." [3]   These larger ones were not,
however, used singly, but were fastened together side by
side, in the manner already described.   A canoe without
an outrigger seemed to them an impossibility. [4]   The
labour of constructing these canoes must have been
immense ; nevertheless, the South Sea Islanders possessed
large numbers of them.   On one occasion Captain Cook
saw more than three hundred in one place ; and, without
counting the smaller vessels, he estimated the whole
naval force of the Society Islands at 1700 war canoes,
manned by 68,000 men. [5]

---

[1] Wilson, *l.c.*, p. 355.
[2] Cook's *First Voyage*, p. 225 ; Forster, *l.c.*, p. 459.
[3] Cook's *First Voyage*, p. 221.   [4] Ellis, *l.c.*, vol. ii. p. 55.
[5] Cook's *Second Voyage*, vol. i. p. 349.

Their principal musical instrument was the drum ; it was made from a piece of solid wood, hollowed out, and covered over with shark's skin. They had also a kind of trumpet made of a large shell, with a hole at the small end, into which they fastened a bamboo cane about three feet long. Their flutes were of bamboo, and were blown with the nose. They had various kinds of games, some of which appear to have resembled our hockey and football. They were also very fond of dancing.

They were quite ignorant of pottery, but had large dishes made of polished wood. The shells of cocoa-nuts were used as water-bottles and cups. They were scraped thin, polished, often very ingeniously carved, and kept extremely clean. Generally the natives of Tahiti sat cross-legged on mats spread on the floor ; but the chiefs had often four-legged stools. Chairs and tables were unknown. They slept also on mats and used a wooden pillow, very much resembling a small stool. The upper side was carved like the seat of the stool, to admit the neck. Each house also contained a light post, planted in the floor, and with several projections, from which the various dishes, calabashes of water, baskets of food, etc., were hung.[1]

Their weapons were formidable, though simple. They consisted of slings, pikes headed with stone, and long clubs made of hard, heavy wood. With the first they were very skilful. Their slingstones were of two kinds, " either smooth, being polished by friction in the bed of a river, or sharp, angular, and rugged ; these were called *ofai ara*—faced or edged stones." [2] We have already mentioned (p. 99) that two sorts of slingstones, closely corresponding to these, were used by the ancient inhabitants of Europe. It would be interesting to know the relative advantage of the two classes, which surely cannot have been used for exactly the same purposes. They had also bows and arrows, which, however, were not sufficiently strong to be used in warfare. The bow-

[1] Ellis, *l.c.*, vol. ii. p. 184. [2] *Ibid.*, vol. ii. p. 49.

strings were made of Roava bark.[1] The Society Islanders
are said to have been cruel in war, but, according to
Captain Cook, "they are seldom disturbed by either
foreign or domestic troubles." Though not cowards,
they regard it as "much less disgraceful to run away
from an enemy with whole bones, than to fight and be
wounded."[2]

"Of tame animals they had only hogs, dogs, and
poultry;[3] neither was there a wild animal in the island,
except ducks, pigeons, parroquets, with a few other birds,
and rats, there being no other quadruped, nor any serpent."[4]
The dogs were kept entirely for food, and Captain Cook
assures us that "a South Sea dog was little inferior to an
English lamb; their excellence is probably owing to their
being kept up and fed wholly on vegetables." The
natives prefer dog to pork. From the sea they obtained
excellent fish and shell-fish. They had also bread-fruit,
bananas, plantains, yams, cocoa-nuts, potatoes, the sugar-
cane, a fruit not unlike an apple, and several other plants
which served for fruit, and required very little culture.
The bread-fruit tree supplied them with abundance of
fresh fruit for eight months, and during the other four
they used "mahie," which is a kind of sour paste, prepared
from the fermented ripe fruit. It is probable that nine-
tenths of their diet consisted of vegetable food; and the
common people scarcely ever tasted either pork or dog,
although the hogs appear to have been very abundant.

They obtained fire by friction. When the wood was
quite dry, the process did not take longer than two minutes,
but in wet weather it was very tedious. Having no
pottery, they did not boil their food. "It is impossible,"
says Wallis, "to describe the astonishment they expressed
when they saw the gunner, who, while he kept the market,
used to dine on shore, dress his pork and poultry by
boiling them in a pot; having, as I have before observed,

---

[1] Wilson, *l.c.*, p. 368.   [2] Wilson, p. 363.
[3] Wallis's *Voyage round the World*; Hawkesworth's *Voyages*, vol. i.
p. 482.
[4] Cook's *Voyage round the World*, p. 187.

no vessel that would bear the fire, they had no idea of hot water."[1] Captain Cook also expressly states that "they had but two ways of applying fire to dress their food, broiling and baking."[2] Mr Tylor, however, has pointed out[3] that they were acquainted with the use of boiling stones, and that they could not therefore have been entirely ignorant of hot water. In order to bake a hog, they made a small pit in the ground, which they paved with large stones, over which they then lighted a fire. When the stones were hot enough, they took out the embers, raked away the ashes, and covered the stones with green cocoa-nut leaves. The animal which was to be dressed, having been cleaned and prepared, was wrapped up in plantain leaves, and covered with the hot embers, on which again they placed bread-fruit and yams, which also were wrapped up in plantain leaves. Over these they spread the rest of the embers, and some hot stones, finally covering the whole with earth. The meat thus cooked is described as being tender and full of gravy ; in fact, both Wallis and Cook considered that it was "better in every respect than when it is dressed in any other way." For sauce they used salt water, without which no meal was ever eaten, and a kind of thick paste made from the kernels of cocoa-nuts. At their meals they drank either water or cocoa-nut juice. The Sandwich Islanders were very fond of salt meat, and had regular salt pans on the sea-shore.[4]

The only intoxicating liquor was the ava, an infusion made from the root, stalks, and leaves of a kind of pepper, which, however, fortunately for them, was entirely forbidden to the women, and seldom permitted to the lower classes. In some of the other islands this liquid is prepared in a disgusting manner. The roots were broken in pieces, cleaned, chewed, and then placed in a wooden bowl, mixed with a certain quantity of water, and stirred up with the hands. In Tahiti, however, the chewing was

[1] *L.c.*, vol. i. p. 484.   [2] *Second Voyage*, vol. ii. p. 197.
[3] *Early History of Mankind*, p. 266.
[4] Cook's *Third Voyage*, vol. iii. p. 151.

dispensed with. The wooden bowls out of which the chiefs drank their ava were often very fair specimens of carving. In the Sandwich Islands they are described as having been "usually about eight or ten inches in diameter, perfectly round, and beautifully polished. They are supported by three, and sometimes four, small human figures, in various attitudes. Some of them rest on the hands of their supporters, extended over the head; others on the head and hands; and some on the shoulders." These figures are said to have been "accurately proportioned and neatly finished, and even the anatomy of the muscles, in supporting the weight, well expressed." [1]

Sir J. Banks [2] gives an interesting description of the manner in which the chiefs dined. They had no table, and each person ate alone and in silence. Some leaves were spread on the ground to serve as a table-cloth, and a basket was set by the chief containing his provision, which, if fish or flesh, was ready dressed and wrapped in leaves. Two cocoa-nut shells were put by the side, one containing salt water and the other fresh. He first washed his hands and mouth thoroughly with the fresh water, and this he repeated almost continually through the meal. He then took part of his provision out of the basket, which generally consisted of a small fish or two, two or three bread-fruits, fourteen or fifteen ripe bananas, or six or seven apples. He began by eating some bread-fruit, at the same time breaking one of the fishes into the salt water. He then took up the bits of fish in his fingers, in such a manner as to get with it as much salt water as possible, and very frequently he took a mouthful of the salt water, either out of the cocoa-nut or in his hand. Sometimes, also, he drank the juice of a cocoa-nut. When he had finished his bread-fruit and fish, he began his plantains or apples, after which he ate some more bread-fruit, beaten into a sort of paste, and generally flavoured with banana or some other fruit. For a knife

---

[1] *Third Voyage*, vol. iii. p. 148.
[2] Cook's *First Voyage*, vol. ii. p. 200; *Journal*, p. 139.

he used either a shell or a piece of split bamboo, and in conclusion he again washed his hands and mouth. They were quite unacquainted with forks, and Captain Wallis[1] tells us that, during his visit, one of the natives who "tried to feed himself with that instrument, could not guide it, but by the mere force of habit his hand came to his mouth and the victuals at the end of the fork went away to his ear." Nor did they use plates. Poulaho, chief of the Friendly Islands, dining one day on board the ship, was so much struck by the pewter plates that Captain Cook gave him one. He did not, however, intend to employ it in the usual manner, but said that "whenever he should have occasion to visit any of the other islands, he would leave this plate behind him at Tongataboo, as a sort of representative in his absence."[2]

Captain Cook was much surprised to find that a people who were so sociable, and who enjoyed so much the society of women, never made their meals together. Even brothers and sisters had each their own basket, and when they wished to eat would go out, "sit down upon the ground, at two or three yards' distance from each other, and, turning their faces different ways, take their repast without interchanging a single word." They ate alone, they said, "because it was right," but why it was right they were unable to explain. We must, however, remember that these islanders were together much more than we are. We enjoy a sociable meal, because the nature of our occupations keeps us apart so much at other times; but among a people whose wants were supplied with so little exertion on their part, who were all day long together, and had no rooms into which they could retire and be alone, it must have been a great thing to have some way of escaping from their friends and being quiet without giving offence. As there were no stated times for meals, a man who wished to be alone need only to take out his basket of provisions, and he might be sure that he would not be disturbed. This

---

[1] *Voyage round the World*, p. 482.   [2] *Third Voyage*, vol. i. p. 326.

custom, therefore, seems to have been both ingenious and convenient.[1]

Although they usually went to bed soon after dark, still the natives of Tahiti were not entirely without candles, for which they used the " kernels of a kind of oily nut, which they stick one over another upon a skewer that is thrust through the middle of them." These candles burn a considerable time, and are said to have given a pretty good light. The Society Islanders had no knowledge of medicine as distinct from witchcraft ; but some wonderful stories are told of their skill in surgery.

The nostrils of the female infants were often pressed or spread out during infancy, because they looked on a flat nose as a mark of beauty. In the same way the boys sometimes had their forehead and the back of their head pressed upwards, so that the upper part of the skull appeared in the shape of a wedge. This was supposed to make them look more formidable in war.[2]

The dead were not buried at once, but were placed on a platform raised several feet above the ground, and neatly railed in with bamboo. The body was covered with a cloth, and sheltered by a roof. By the side were deposited the weapons of the deceased, and a supply of food and water. When the body had entirely decayed, the bones were collected, carefully cleaned and buried, according to the rank of the deceased, either within or without a " morai." [3] The largest morai seen by Captain Cook was the one prepared for Oamo and Oberea, who were the then reigning sovereigns. This was indeed the principal piece of architecture in the island, and is remarkable as showing what considerable works may be

[1] Since the above was written, I have met with the following passage in Burchell : " I had sufficient reason for admiring one of the customs of the Bachapins ; that, notwithstanding they never at any other time left me alone, they always retired the moment my dinner or breakfast was brought to me. This gave me a few moments' relief from the fatigue of incessant conversation."—*Travels in Southern Africa*, vol. ii. p. 408.

[2] *L.c.*, vol. i. p. 343.

[3] In some cases the head is not buried with the other bones, but is deposited in a kind of box.

undertaken by a people ignorant of the use of metal. "It was a pile of stonework, raised pyramidically upon an oblong base, or square, two hundred and sixty-seven feet long, and eighty-seven wide. It was built like the small pyramidal mounts upon which we sometimes fix the pillar of a sun-dial, where each side is a flight of steps ; the steps, however, at the sides, were broader than those at the ends, so that it terminated not in a square of the same figure with the base, but in a ridge, like the roof of a house : there were eleven of these steps, each of which was four feet high, so that the height of the pile was forty-four feet ; each step was formed of one course of white coral stone, which was neatly squared and polished ; the rest of the mass, for there was no hollow within, consisted of round pebbles, which, from the regularity of their figure, seemed to have been wrought."[1] A very similar account of this structure has been more recently given by Wilson,[2] who makes the size and height a little greater ; and when it is considered that this was raised without the assistance of iron tools to shape the stones, or of mortar to fasten them together, it is impossible not to be struck with admiration at the magnitude of the enterprise, and the skill with which it appears to have been carried out. It is, perhaps, the most important monument which is positively known to have been constructed with stone tools only, and renders it the less unlikely that some of the large tumuli and other ancient monuments of Europe may belong to the Stone Age. When a chief died, his relations and attendants cut and mangled themselves in a dreadful manner. They ran spears through their thighs, arms, and cheeks, and beat themselves about the head with clubs "till the blood ran down in streams." They also frequently cut off the little finger on these occasions ;

---

[1] Cook's *Voyage round the World*, vol. ii. p. 166. Similar but somewhat smaller morais were observed in the Sandwich Islands (*Third Voyage*, vol. iii. p. 6). In the Friendly Islands, D'Urville saw a similar mausoleum built with blocks of stone, some of which were twenty feet long, six or eight broad, and two in height. They were neatly squared. *L.c.*, vol. iv. p. 106.

[2] *L.c.*, p. 207.

a curious custom, which is common also in the Friendly Islands.

In Tiarrabou, Captain Cook saw a rude figure of a man, made of basket-work, and about seven feet high. This was intended as a representation of one of the inferior gods, but was said to be the only one on the island ; for the natives, when first discovered, though they worshipped numerous deities, to whom also human sacrifices were sometimes offered, yet were not idolators. At a later period, however, Ellis saw among them many rude idols.[1] Captain Cook found their religion, " like that of most other countries, involved in mystery, and perplexed with apparent inconsistencies." [2]   They believed in the survival of the soul, and in " two situations of different degrees of happiness, somewhat analogous to our heaven and hell " ; but, far from regarding them as places of reward and punishment, thought that the happiest lot was of course intended for the chiefs and superior classes, the other for the people of inferior rank.[3] Indeed, they did not suppose that their actions here in the least influenced their future state ; so that their religion did not act upon them by promises or threats, and their " expressions of adoration and reverence, whether by words or actions, arise only from a humble sense of their own inferiority, and the ineffable excellence of divine perfection."   However mistaken they may have been on many points, however wrong many of their customs doubtless appear to us, surely under such a creed as this, good actions become doubly virtuous, and virtue itself shines the brighter.

They had no laws, nor courts of justice. Personal security and the rights of private property were but little regarded among them. The chiefs and priests exercised an authority founded on fear and superstition. They were, in fact, governed by custom rather than by law, for which, indeed, they had no word in the

---

[1] Ellis, *l.c.*, vol. i. p. 526 ; Wilson, *l.c.*, p. 242.
[2] See also Forster, *l.c.*, p. 539.
[3] Cook's *First Voyage*, vol. ii. p. 239 ; Ellis, vol. i. p. 518.

language.[1] It is only fair to the chiefs to add that they
were above being idle, and thought it a disgrace if they
did not excel in all departments of labour.[2] In character the inhabitants of Tahiti, according to Captain Cook,
"were liberal, brave, open, and candid, without either suspicion or treachery, cruelty, or revenge."[3] They were
very anxious for education. The women were affectionate,
tender, and obedient ; the men mild, generous, slow to
take offence, and easily satisfied. Both sexes were very
healthy. " I never saw anyone," says Forster,[4] "of a
morose, peevish, discontented disposition in the whole
nation ; they all join to their cheerful temper a politeness
and elegance which is happily blended with the most
innocent simplicity of manners." Murders were very
rare among them ; and though much licence was permitted to the young women before marriage, the married
women, according to Captain Cook,[5] were as well behaved
" as in any other country whatever." They were very
thievish ; but we must consider the immense temptations
to which they were subjected, and the, to them, inestimable
value of the articles which they stole. Like other savages,
they resembled children in many respects : their sorrows
were transient, their passions suddenly and strongly
expressed. On one occasion, Oberea, the queen, who
was then about forty years old, took a particular fancy to
a large doll, which was accordingly presented to her.
Shortly afterwards they met Tootahah, one of the
principal chiefs, who became so jealous of Oberea's doll
that they were obliged to give him one also.

There are scarcely any nations, whether barbarous or
civilized, in which the relations of the two sexes are on
the whole satisfactory. Savages, almost without exception, treat their women as slaves, and civilized nations
too often avoid this error only to fall into others.

The inhabitants of Tahiti are said to have been
absolutely without any ideas of decency, or rather, as

---

[1] Ellis, *l.c.*, vol. ii. p. 437. [2] *Ibid.*, vol. ii. p. 178.
[3] *First Voyage*, vol. ii. p. 188. [4] *L.c.*, p. 582.
[5] *Voyage to the South Pole*, vol. i. p. 187.

Captain Cook puts it, perhaps more correctly, "of in-decency"—that is, at least, in our sense of the term. This no doubt arose in part from their large open houses, which were not divided into separate rooms. However this may be, where there was no sin they saw no shame, and it must be confessed that in many points their idea of sin was very different from ours. Before, however, we condemn them, let us remember that a dinner-party would have seemed as wrong to them as many of their customs do to us. If the freedom, both in language and in action, which they permitted to themselves seems to us in many respects objectionable, we must not forget that our ideas of delicacy shut out from general con-versation numerous subjects of great interest and im-portance, and throw round many matters of the utmost importance an air of mystery which is not without serious disadvantages.

A considerable number of the principal people of both sexes in Tahiti were formed into an association called the "Arreoy," all the members of which were regarded as being married to one another. If any of the women of the society had a child, it was almost invariably killed ; but if it was allowed to live, the father and mother were regarded as having definitely engaged themselves to one another, and were ejected from the association — the woman being known from that time as a "bearer of children," which was among this extraordinary people a term of reproach. The existence of such a society shows how fundamentally the idea of virtue may differ in different countries. Yet the married women were faith-ful to their husbands, and beautifully modest. It is impossible, indeed, to acquit even them of the charge of infanticide, for which we may find a cause, though not an excuse. I do not allude to the curious custom that a child, as soon as it was born, inherited the titles, rank, and property of its father, so that a man who was yester-day a chief might be thus at once reduced to the con-dition of a private person ; nor to the fact that any Arreoy who spared her infant was at once excluded from that society. We cannot suppose that such customs were without their effect; but a more powerful reason may perhaps be found in the fact that their numbers were already large, the means of subsistence limited, and that, as but few were carried off either by disease or in war, the population would soon have outgrown their supplies if some means were not taken to check the natural increase of numbers.[1] However this may be, infanticide appears to have been dreadfully prevalent amongst them. It has been estimated that two-thirds of the children were destroyed by their own parents,[2] and both Nott and Ellis agree that, during the whole of their residence in the island, until the adoption of Christianity, they did not know a single case of a mother who had not been guilty of this crime.

According to Wilson,[3] their language contained no word for " thanks," and even Cook admits that they had no respect for old age. Fitzroy goes still farther, and assures us that " they scrupled not to destroy their aged or sick—yes, even their parents, if disabled by age or sickness."[4] No such accusation is, however, brought against them by earlier writers, so that such actions are probably very rare, and the result, perhaps, as among the Fijians, of misdirected affection rather than of deliberate cruelty.

They had no money; and though it was easy to obtain the necessaries of life, to accumulate property was almost impossible. Again, the absence of spirituous liquors and the relations between the sexes (however unsatisfactory in some respects) took away from them some of the principal incentives to crime. On the whole, then, if we judge them by a South Sea standard, the natives of the Society Islands appear to have been very free from crime.

In spite of the differences which sometimes arose in consequence of their thievish disposition, and also perhaps

---

[1] See, for instance, Kotzebue's *New Voyage*, vol. i. p. 308.
[2] Ellis, vol. i. pp. 334, 336.   [3] *L.c.*, p. 365.
[4] *L.c.*, vol. ii. p. 551.

in great measure from their not being able perfectly to understand each other, Captain Cook and his officers lived with the natives "in the most cordial friendship," and took leave of them with great regret. Mr Ellis, on the contrary, assures us that "no portion of the human race was ever perhaps sunk lower in brutal licentiousness and moral degradation than this isolated people."[1] Such a statement is surely quite inconsistent with the account he gives of their anxiety to possess copies of the Bible when it was translated into their own language. "They were," he says, "deemed by them more precious than gold—yea, than much fine gold," and "became at once the constant companion of their possessors, and the source of their highest enjoyment."[2]

The inhabitants of the Friendly, or Tonga, and of the Sandwich Islands, are also very well described by Captain Cook, but they belonged to the same race as those of Tahiti and New Zealand, and resembled them in religion, language, canoes, houses, weapons, food, habits, etc. It is somewhat remarkable that the Sandwich Islanders, in many respects—as, for instance, in their dances, houses, tattooing, etc.—resembled the New Zealanders even more than their nearer neighbours in the Society and Friendly Islands. In the Friendly Islands Captain Cook observed a very singular luxury in which the chiefs indulged themselves. When one of them wished to go to sleep, two women came and sat by him "beating briskly on his body and legs with both fists, as on a drum, till he fell asleep, and continuing it the whole night, with some short intervals." When the chief is sound asleep they sometimes rest themselves a little, "but resume it if they observe any appearance of his waking."[3] A similar statement is made by Wilson in his *Missionary Voyage*.[4] In all the islands the chiefs appear to have been treated with respect, none the less profound because shown in ways which seem to us peculiar. One of them was to uncover the body from the waist, and it seems to have been a

---

[1] Ellis, *l.c.*, vol. ii. p. 25.
[3] *Third Voyage*, vol. i. p. 323.
[2] Ellis, vol. i. pp. 393-408.
[4] *L.c.*, p. 237.

matter of indifference, or rather of convenience, whether this was done upwards or downwards.[1] In the Friendly Islands it was accounted a striking mark of rudeness to speak to the king while standing up.

There was also a certain amount of commerce between the different islands. Bora-bora and Otahaw produced abundance of cocoanut oil, which was exchanged at Tahiti for cloth. The Low Islands, again, could not successfully grow the paper-mulberry; but they had a breed of dogs with long silky hair, which was much prized in the other islands.

[1] Cook's *First Voyage*, vol. ii. p. 125.

CHAPTER XIV

MODERN SAVAGES—*continued*

Esquimaux

THE Esquimaux, and the Esquimaux alone among savage races, occupy both the Old and the New World. They inhabit the shores of the Arctic Ocean from Siberia to Greenland ; and throughout this great extent of country the language, appearance, habits, occupations, and weapons of the natives are very similar, and it must be added that the latter are most ingenious. The language of the Innuit, or Esquimaux, is akin to that of the North American Indians in structure, while their appearance has a decided likeness, particularly about the eyes, to the Chinese and Tartars.

Their dwellings are of two kinds. The summer they pass in tents or wigwams, with the entrance to the south or south-east. In those observed by Captain Parry, the tent-poles were, in the absence of wood, formed of stags' horns, or bones lashed together. The lower borders of the skins were held down by large stones. These were sometimes built up into regular circles, eight or nine feet in diameter, and four or five feet high.[1] These circles were at first supposed to be the remains of winter-houses ; but it was subsequently ascertained that they were exclusively used for extending the skins of the summer-tents. Near these " hut circles " long rows of standing-stones were several times observed.[2] The winter-houses in the southern

---

[1] Parry's *Voyage*, 1821–23, pp. 17, 51.   [2] *L.c.*, pp. 62, 285, 363.

districts are constructed of earth or drift-timber, which is very abundant in some places. In the north, however, wood becomes extremely rare. The Esquimaux at the northern end of Baffin's Bay,[1] who had no wood, excepting twigs of a dwarfish heath, were so little acquainted with the nature of timber, that several of them successively seized on the spare top-mast of the *Isabella* evidently with the intention of stealing it, and quite unconscious of its weight. In the absence of wood, their houses were built of ice and snow ; those of ice are beautiful, and almost transparent, so that even at some little distance it is possible to see everything that takes place in them. They are, however, much colder than those of snow, which therefore are generally preferred. West of the Rocky Mountains the winter-houses were usually underground. They much resemble the tumuli of Northern Europe (see *ante*, p. 114). A Kamskatka-dale "yourt" is thus described by Captain Cook[2] : "An oblong square, of dimensions proportionate to the number of persons for whom it is intended (for it is proper to observe that several families live together in the same *jourt*), is dug into the earth to the depth of about six feet. Within this space strong posts, or wooden pillars, are fastened to the ground, at proper distances from each other, on which are extended the beams for the support of the roof, which is formed by joists resting on the ground with one end, and on the beams with the other. The interstices between the joists are filled up with a strong wicker-work, and the whole covered with turf ; so that a jourt has externally the appearance of a low round hillock. A hole is left in the centre, which serves for chimney, window, and entrance, and the inhabitants pass in and out by means of a strong pole (instead of a ladder) notched deep enough to afford a little holding for the toe," as in fig. 152 (p. 115). More often, however, the entrance consisted of a sunken passage, as also shown in fig. 152 or fig. 153 (pp. 115, 116).

---

[1] Ross, *Baffin's Bay*, p. 122.
[2] *Voyage to the Pacific Ocean*, vol. iii. p. 374. See also vol. iii. p. 450.

As a general rule, we may say that the western yourts are subterranean, while those of the tribes who live east of the Rocky Mountains are generally above-ground. The manner in which the Esquimaux construct their snow igloos has been well described by Captain Parry. They choose[1] a drift of hard and compact snow, and from this they cut oblong slabs six or seven inches thick and about two feet in length. With these they build a circular wall, inclining inwards so as to form a dome, which is sometimes as much as nine or ten feet high, and from eight to fifteen feet in diameter. A small door is then cut on the south side. It is about three feet high, two and a half wide at the bottom, and leads into a passage about ten feet long, and with a step in the middle, the half next the hut being lower than either the floor of the hut or the outer passage. For the admission of light a round hole is cut on one side of the roof, and a circular plate of ice, three or four inches thick and two feet in diameter, is let into it. If several families intend to live together, other chambers are constructed which open into the first, and then, after a quantity of snow has been shovelled up on the outside, the shell of the building is regarded as finished. The next thing is to raise a bank of snow two and a half feet high all round the interior of the building, except on the side next the door. This bank forms the bed. Over it is laid some gravel, upon that again paddles, tent-poles, pieces of whalebone, twigs of birch and of andromeda, etc., and finally a number of deer-skins, which form a soft and luxurious couch. They have no fireplace, properly so called, that is to say, no hearth, but each family has a separate lamp or shallow vessel generally made of *lapis ollaris* in which they burn seal's oil, with a wick made of dry moss.

Although they had no knowledge of pottery, Captain Cook saw at Oonalashka vessels "of a flat stone, with sides of clay, not unlike a standing pie."[2] We here obtain an idea of the manner in which the knowledge of

---

[1] Parry, *l.c.*, p. 500.
[2] *Voyage to the Pacific Ocean*, vol. ii. p. 510.

pottery may have been developed. After using clay to raise the sides of their stone vessels, it would naturally occur to them that the same substance would serve for the bottom also, and thus the use of stone might be replaced by a more convenient material.

The natives of the Lower Murray cook their food in a hollow in the ground, which they line with clay, and in other cases gourds and wooden vessels are coated with clay in order to enable them to stand heat. Thus we see three ways in which pottery may have been invented.

The snow-houses melt away every spring; but in some places the Esquimaux construct their dwellings on a similar plan, but with the bones of whales and walruses on a foundation of stones, and with a covering of earth. The snow-houses are of course pretty clean at first, but they gradually become very filthy. The bone huts are even dirtier, because more durable. "In every direction round the huts," says Captain Parry, "were lying innumerable bones of walruses and seals, together with skulls of dogs, bears, and foxes, on many of which a part of the putrid flesh still remaining sent forth the most offensive effluvia."[1] He even observed a number of human bones lying about among the rest.[2] The inside of the huts, "from their extreme closeness and accumulated filth, emitted an almost insupportable stench, to which an abundant supply of raw and half-putrid walrus flesh in no small degree contributed."[3]

On the north-western coast of America the natives find plenty of driftwood, and the floors of their yourts are, according to Belcher, made of split timber, nicely smoothed and carefully caulked with moss. Underneath is often a large store-room, for in summer they kill many reindeer, whales, walrus, seals, swans, ducks, etc., the greater part of which are laid by for winter use. One of these winter stores is thus expressively, though somewhat hastily, described by Sir E. Belcher:[4] "It was frozen into a

---

[1] Parry, *l.c.*, p. 280.
[2] See also Lyon's *Journal*, p. 236.   [3] Parry, *l.c.*, p. 358.
[4] *Trans. Ethn. Soc.*, New Series, vol. i. p. 132.

solid mass beneath, but loose from those on the surface, and seemed to be incorporated, by some unexplained process, into a *gelatinous snow*, which they scraped up easily with the hand and ate with satisfaction—fish oil predominating. It was not offensive nor putrid. How many years the lower mass may have remained there, I could not determine." He estimates the quantity of solid meat in this storehouse alone at 71,424 pounds. Sir John Ross also mentions[1] the large stores of food laid up by the Esquimaux of Boothia Felix during the summer for winter use. The habit does not, however, appear to be general among the Esquimaux, though they all of them make "caches" of meat under stone cairns.

Charlevoix derives the name "Esquimaux" from the Indian word *Eskimantsik*, which means "eaters of raw food," many of these northern tribes being in the habit of eating their meat uncooked. We must in justice to them remember that several of our Arctic expeditions have adopted the same custom, which seems indeed in those latitudes highly conducive to health.[2]

Their food, if cooked at all, is broiled or boiled. Their vessels being of stone or wood cannot, indeed, be put on the fire, but heated stones are thrown in until the water becomes hot enough, and the food is cooked. Of course, the result is a mess of soot, dirt, and ashes, which would, according to our ideas, be almost intolerable ; but if the stench of their houses does not take away a man's appetite nothing else would be likely to do so. They never wash their pots or kettles ; the dogs save them this trouble. Those who have arrived at a dim consciousness of their dirtiness do generally, but make matters worse, for if they wish to treat a guest "genteelly, they first lick the piece of meat he is to eat clean from the blood and scum it has contracted in the kettle, with their tongue ; and should anyone not kindly accept it, he

---

[1] *Narrative of a Second Voyage*, p. 251 ; and Appendix, p. 21. See also Hall's *Life with the Esquimaux*, vol. ii. p. 311 ; Kane's *Arctic Explorations*, vol. ii. p. 133.

[2] See, for instance, Kane's *Arctic Explorations*, vol. ii. p. 14.

would be looked upon as an unmannerly man for despising their civility."[1] The Esquimaux observed by Dr Rae at Repulse Bay were, however, much cleaner in their habits.

Their food consists principally of reindeer, musk-ox, walrus, seals, birds, and salmon. They will, however, eat any kind of animal food. They are very fond of fat and marrow, to get at which they pound the bones with a stone. The southern tribes get a few berries in summer, but those who live in the north have scarcely any vegetable food except that which they obtain in a half-digested form from the stomach of the reindeer, and this they regard as a great delicacy;[2] the northernmost of all, being unable to kill reindeer, are entirely deprived of vegetable food.

A feast among some of the more civilized Esquimaux of Greenland is thus described by Crantz:[3] "A factor being invited to a great entertainment with several topping Greenlanders, counted the following dishes: (1) Dried herrings; (2) Dried seal's flesh; (3) Boiled ditto; (4) Half-raw and rotten ditto, called Mikiak; (5) Boiled willocks; (6) A piece of a half-rotten whale's tail: this was the dainty dish or haunch of venison to which the guests were properly invited; (7) Dried salmon; (8) Dried reindeer venison; (9) A dessert of crowberries mixed with the chyle out of the maw of a reindeer; (10) The same, enriched with train oil.

Their drink consists of blood or water: during the greater part of the year they have considerable difficulty in obtaining sufficient water to satisfy their thirst, and it is much too precious to be used for washing. It may seem surprising that people who are surrounded by snow and ice should suffer from want of water, but the amount of heat required to melt snow is so great that a man without the means of obtaining fire might die of thirst in these Arctic regions as easily as in the sandy

[1] Crantz, p. 168; Parry, *Second Voyage*, p. 293; Lyon's *Journal*, p. 142.
[2] Ross, *Narrative of a Second Voyage*, p. 352.
[3] *History of Greenland*, vol. i. p. 172.

deserts of Africa. Any direct "resort to snow," says
Kane, "for the purpose of allaying thirst, was followed
by bloody lips and tongue ; it burnt like caustic." [1]
When the Esquimaux visited Captain Parry, they were
always anxious for water, which they drank in such
quantities "that it was impossible to furnish them with
half as much as they desired." [2]   In the extreme north,
one of the principal duties of the women in the winter is
to thaw snow over their lamps, feeding the wick with oil
if it does not rise well of its own accord ; [3] the natural heat
of the room is not sufficient to melt snow, as the temperature of the huts is always kept, if possible, below the
freezing-point.   In South Greenland, however, the huts
are built of turf, etc., and are very warm. [4]   But we must
remember that coolness, rather than heat, is required by
the Esquimaux who live in snow dwellings, because if
the temperature rises to thirty-two degrees, the continual
dripping from the roof produces extreme inconvenience,
and, in fact, the most unhealthy season is the spring,
when the weather is too warm for snow huts and too cold
for tents.   Thus, therefore, the Esquimaux, though living in a climate so extremely rigorous, would be debarred
from the use of fires by the very nature of their dwellings,
even if they were enabled to obtain the necessary materials.
They never, says Simpson, "seem to think of fire as a
means of imparting warmth " ; [5] their lamps are used for
cooking, for light, and for melting snow and drying
clothes, rather than to warm the air, [6] and as, nevertheless,
the body temperature of the Esquimaux is almost the
same as ours, it is evident that they must require a large
amount of animal food.   The quantity of meat which
they consume is indeed astonishing ; and it is worthy of
remark that, from the scarcity of wood in the far north,
they use the same substance for food and fuel ; the
calorific material being the same—namely, blubber—

---

[1] *Arctic Explorations*, vol. i. p. 190.　　[2] *L.c.*, p. 188.
[3] Osborn's *Arctic Journal*, p. 17.　　[4] Egede, *l.c.*, p. 116.
[5] *Discoveries in North America*, p. 346.
[6] Kane, *l.c.*, vol. ii. p. 202.

whether the heat is to be obtained by digestion or combustion ; whether the material is to be placed in a lamp
and burnt, or to be eaten. In summer, however, when
it is less necessary to keep down the general temperature,
they sometimes burn bones well
saturated with oil. For obtaining
fire the Esquimaux generally use
lumps of iron pyrites and quartz,
from which they strike sparks on
to moss which has been well dried
and rubbed between the hands.[1]
They are also acquainted with the
method of obtaining it by friction,[2] which is a slower and more
laborious process. It appears, however, to be the one generally pursued by the Greenland Esquimaux.[3]

It has been generally assumed
that man could scarcely live in
temperate climates, and certainly
not in the Arctic regions, without
the advantage of fire. From the
above facts, however, as well as
from others which will presently
be recorded, it may be doubted
whether this is really the case.
Esquimaux do not use fire to warm
their dwellings, and cookery is with
them a refinement. In fact, those
Esquimaux who live on reindeer
more than on seal, having little
blubber, make hardly any use of fire.

FIG. 269.—Esquimaux knife.

In the south the men have bows and arrows, harpoons,
spears, lines, fish-hooks, knives, snow-knives, ice-chisels,
snow-shovels, groovers, drill-bows, drills, etc. The women
have lamps and stone kettles, lamp moss, pieces of iron
pyrites, bone needles, pieces of sinew, scrapers (figs. 114–

[1] Kane, *l.c.*, vol. i. p. 379 ; Parry, *l.c.*, p. 504 ; Ross, *l.c.*, p. 513.
[2] Lyon's *Journal*, p. 290. [3] Egede, *l.c.*, p. 138.

116), horn spoons, sealskin vessels, pointed bones, marrow-spoons, and knives (figs. 269, 270). They have generally also, according to Dr Rae, a small piece of stone, bone, or ivory, about six inches long and half an inch thick ; this is used for arranging the wicks of the lamps.

Kane gives the following inventory of an Esquimaux hut visited by him : a sealskin cup, for gathering and holding water ; the shoulder-blade of a walrus, to serve as a lamp ; a large flat stone to support it; another large, thin flat stone to support the melting snow ; a lance-head, with a long coil of walrus line ; a stand for clothes ; and the clothes themselves completed the whole worldly goods of this poor family.[1] On their travelling expeditions, even less than this is necessary ; raw meat and a fur bag are all they require.

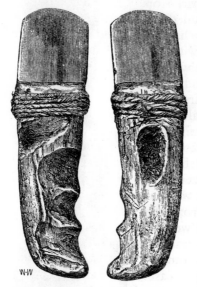

FIG. 270 *a, b.*—Esquimaux knife.

The implements of the Esquimaux are very ingenious. Besides knives resembling figs. 269, 270, the women use others of a semicircular form, and very similar to the curious semi-lunar knives which are so common in Denmark. They are, however, now made of metal, which the southern Esquimaux have been enabled to obtain, though in small quantities, from the Europeans. Some few of them also break off bits of meteoric iron, which they hammer to an end, and then fix in a handle of horn or bone. The arrow-heads are of several kinds and shapes. Those of stone (fig. 271) are made, not by blows, but by pressure, for which purpose they use the point of a rein-

[1] Kane's *Arctic Explorations*, vol. i. p. 381.

deer's horn, set in bone ; bone itself would not be tough enough. Other arrow-heads are of horn ; these often bear "owners' marks," as may be seen by fig. 2 (p. 13). The shafts of the arrows are short, straightened by steam, and provided with feathers at the butt end. These are fastened on by deer sinews. The bows are generally of wood, either made of one piece steamed into the right form, or of three parts most ingeniously fastened together, and strengthened by pieces of bone or sinew. When wood cannot be obtained, they use bone or horn. They do not appear to be particularly good shots : but Captain Parry[1] thinks that they would generally hit a deer from forty to forty-five yards, if the animal stood still.[2] Moreover, against large game they are, after all, not very effective. Sir J. C. Ross gives an interesting account of a musk-sheep hunt which he witnessed. At length becoming impatient, as the Esquimaux "continued to shoot without apparent effect, finding his opportunities for an aim with much difficulty, and losing much time afterwards in recovering his arrows, Sir James fired, and broke the animal's shoulder-blade, to the immense astonishment of his companion."[3]

FIG. 271.—Esquimaux arrow-head, actual size.

The spears (fig. 272) are made like the arrows, but are larger ; the heads also are frequently barbed, and in many cases fit loosely into the shaft, but are securely fastened to a long leathern thong, which is tied to the butt end of the spear. For throwing the harpoon they use a short handle or throwing-stick, about two feet long, narrow below, four inches wide above, and with a notch on each

---

[1] *L.c.*, p. 511.

[2] The Esquimaux of Greenland have long abandoned the bow and arrow, using guns obtained from the Danes. In many other respects also their ancient habits have been modified, and their condition greatly improved, by this intercourse.

[3] Sir J. Ross's *Arctic Expedition*, 1829–33, p. 350.

side for the thumb and forefinger. With these weapons they attack not only seals and walruses, but even whales. They strike the whale, if possible at the same time, with many harpoons, "to which bladders are hung, made of

FIG. 272.—Esquimaux spear-head, actual size.

great sealskins, several of which so encumber and stop the whale, that it cannot sink deep. When he is tired out, they despatch him quite with their little lances." Kane gives the figure of a lance, the blade of which closely resembles one of the longer "axes" from the Danish shell-mounds.[1]

The Esquimaux have three principal ways of killing seals. The commonest is with the harpoon and bladder. When an Esquimaux in his kayak "spies a seal, he tries to surprise it unawares, with the wind and sun in his back, that he may not be heard or seen by it. He tries to conceal himself behind a wave, and makes hastily but softly up to it till he comes within four, five, or six fathoms of it; meanwhile he takes the utmost care that the harpoon, line, and bladder lie in proper order."[2] As soon as the seal is struck, the point of the spear detaches itself from the shaft, and at the same moment the Esquimaux throws the large air-bladder on to the water. This is often dragged under water a little way, but it is so great an impediment, that the seal is soon obliged to come up. "The Greenlander hastens to the spot where he sees the bladder rise up, and smites the seal as soon as it appears" with the great lance or "angovigak." This is not barbed, and does not therefore remain in the seal's body, but can be used again and again until the animal is

[1] *Arctic Explorations*, vol. ii. p. 129.   [2] Crantz, p. 154.

exhausted. The second way is the "clapper-hunt." If the Esquimaux find, or can drive any seals into the creeks or inlets, they frighten them by shouting, clapping, and throwing stones every time they come up to breathe, until at last they are exhausted and easily killed. In winter, when the sea is frozen, the seals, which are obliged to come up from time to time for the sake of air, keep open certain breathing-holes for this purpose, and the Esquimaux, when he has found one of these, waits patiently till the seal makes its appearance, when he kills it instantly with his harpoon.

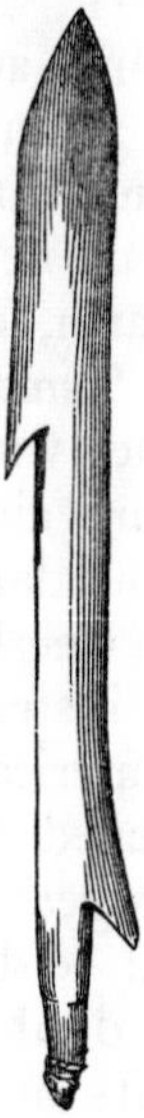

Fig. 274 represents a modern chert Esquimaux harpoon head found in the body of a whale. "While the Dundee whaling steamship *Eclipse*, commanded by Captain Milne, was fishing in Coutt's Inlet, Davis Straits, a large whale was harpooned and killed. While the animal was in process of dissection, one of the knives came in contact with some hard substance, betokening the presence of some foreign body, which proved to be the lance-head of chert, embedded in the blubber at a depth of about three inches from the surface. It measures $3\frac{13}{16}$ inches long, $2\frac{5}{16}$ inches greatest breadth of blade, $1\frac{1}{16}$ inches greatest width of haft, and in thickness about half an inch."

FIG. 273. — Esquimaux bone harpoon, one-third of the actual size.

FIG. 274.—Modern Esquimaux' chert harpoon.

The form of the implement is that of the "tobang" or harpoon formerly used by the Esquimaux of North-East America. At the present day, however, the harpoons are tipped with bone, and the use of chert has been abandoned. As the Esquimaux, however, only attack whales when young, this weapon may have been in the animal for many years.[1]

The Esquimaux are excellent deer-stalkers, and are much assisted by the skill with which they can imitate the cry of the reindeer. Fish are caught sometimes with the hook and line, sometimes by means of small nets when they come to the shore in shoals to spawn, or finally with the spear. The nets are made of " small hoops or rings of whalebone, firmly lashed together with rings of the same material." [2] The fishing-lines are also made of whalebone.[3] Salmon are sometimes so abundant that in Boothia Felix Sir John Ross bought a ton weight for a single knife. For killing birds they use an instrument in some respects like the "bolas" of South America: a number of stones or walrus teeth being fastened to short pieces of string, and all the strings then tied together at the other end.[4] The spears, which are intended to be thrown at birds or other small animals, have a double fork at the extremity, and three other barbed points near the middle. These diverge in different directions, so that if the end pair should miss, one of the central trio might strike the victim. Aquatic birds are also caught in whalebone nooses ; but the "moulting season is the great bird-harvest, as a few persons wading into the shallow lakes can soon tire out the birds and catch them by hand." [5]

The so-called " Arctic Highlanders," however, are said to have no means of killing the reindeer, though it abounds in their country ; nor have they the art of fishing, although, curiously enough, they catch large numbers of birds in small hand-nets. Seals, bears, walrus, and birds constitute almost the whole of their diet.[6] Neither the American

---

[1] *Proceedings of the Soc. Antiq. of Scot.*, vol. xxxi., 1896–7, p. 279.
[2] Parry, *l.c.*, p. 100.   [3] Egede, *l.c.*, p. 107.
[4] Simpson, *l.c.*, p. 156.   [5] Lyon's *Journal*, p. 338.
[6] Kane, *Arctic Explorations*, vol. ii. pp. 208, 210. See also Richardson's *Arctic Expedition*, vol. ii. p. 25 ; Simpson's *Discoveries in North America*, p. 347 ; Ross, *l.c.*, p. 585.

nor Greenland Esquimaux have succeeded in taming the reindeer. Dogs are their only domestic animals, and are sometimes used in hunting, but principally to draw the sledges.

The sledges vary much both in materials and form : according to Captain Lyon, the best are made of the jaw-bones of the whale, sawn to about two inches in thickness, and from six inches to a foot in depth. These are the runners, and are shod with a thin plank of the same material. The sides are connected by pieces of bone, horn, or wood, firmly lashed together. In Boothia Sir John Ross saw sledges in which the runners were made of salmon, packed into a cylinder, rolled up in skins, and frozen together. In spring the skins are made into bags, and the fish are eaten.[1] Altogether these sledges are well constructed, when it is considered with what simple tools they are made.

The dogs by which these sledges are drawn are by no means easy to manage. Each has a separate trace attached to the front of the sledge, passing between the legs, and fastened in front to a collar. The dogs there-fore are nearly abreast, and the traces are very liable to become entangled. The team is guided by throwing the lash of the whip on one side or the other, and repeating certain words. "Wooa," as among our carters, means "Stop."[2]

Their boats are also very ingeniously built, and are of two kinds : the kajak or men's boat, and the umiak or women's boat. The kajak is from eighteen to twenty feet long, eighteen inches broad in the middle, tapering to both ends, and scarcely a foot deep. It has no outriggers, and is therefore very difficult to sit in. It is quite covered over at the top, with the exception of a hole in the middle, into which the Esquimaux puts his legs. The boat therefore cannot fill with water, and even if it upsets, can be righted again by a sudden jerk of the oar, or rather

---

[1] *L.c.*, Appendix, p. 24.
[2] Parry's *Three Voyages for the Discovery of a N.W. Passage*, vol. iv. p. 310.

paddle. Indeed, a skilful Esquimaux will even turn somersaults in the water in his boat. In spite of this, they are frequently drowned : and, indeed, so dangerous is the navigation that they generally go in pairs, so as to assist one another on an emergency, for the skin sides of the kajak are very thin, and if they come in contact with any of the floating ice or drift-timber which abound in the Greenland seas, are liable to be torn open, in which case the unfortunate Esquimaux has little chance of saving himself. The umiak is much larger and has a flat bottom. It is made of slender laths, fastened together with whalebone, and covered over with sealskins. The Esquimaux observed by Ross, at the northern end of Baffin's Bay, were entirely without canoes, and were "ignorant, even traditionally, of the existence of a boat."[1] It is, as he justly observes, an extraordinary thing to find " a maritime and a fishing tribe unacquainted with any means of floating on the water"; but we must remember that they had no wood, and that there were only a few weeks in the year when the sea was unfrozen. No wonder that Ross's ships were mistaken for living creatures,[2] and that his boats excited the most unbounded astonishment and admiration. Kane also[3] confirms the absence of boats, but he adds "that the kayak *was* known to them traditionally."

In the preparation of skins the Esquimaux use certain stone instruments (figs. 114–116), which have frequently been overlooked on account of their simplicity, but which yet are interesting because they are exactly similar to certain ancient implements which are very common in various parts of Europe, and have been already described in page 94. The collection bequeathed by my lamented friend, Mr Christy, to the nation, and which is now in the British Museum, contains four of these skin-scrapers, three of which were obtained from the Esquimaux north of Behring Straits. These are set in fossil ivory. The fourth was found in a Greenland grave, probably not

[1] Ross, *Baffin's Bay*, p. 170.
[2] *L.c.*, p. 118.   [3] *Arctic Explorations*, vol. ii. pp. 135, 210.

older than the fifteenth century, and belonging to the
Stone Period which supervened when the intercourse
with Norway was suspended. Some archæologists had
considered that the "scrapers" were "probably knives,
the prolonged thick ends of which were intended for
handles, to be held between the finger and thumb, or
possibly for attachment to a short wooden shaft."[1] The
true nature and use of the ancient skin-scrapers has,
however, been entirely explained by these modern
specimens, with which they are absolutely identical.
The method of preparing skins is curious and ingenious,
but very disgusting.

The clothes of the Esquimaux are made from the skins
of reindeer, seals, and birds, sewn
together with sinews. For needles
they use bones either of birds or
fishes ; yet with these simple instruments they sew very strongly and well.
The outer dress of the men resembles
a short great-coat, with a hood that can

FIG. 275.—Esquimaux
cheek-stud of stone.

be pulled over the head if necessary, and which serves
as a substitute for a hat or cap. Their under-garments
or shirts are made of bird-skins with the feathers inwards ;
or of skins with the hair inside ; sometimes, however,
they wear in addition another shirt made of seal's entrails.
Their breeches, "of which in winter they also wear two
pair, and similarly disposed as to the fur,"[2] are either
of seal-skin or reindeer-skin, and their stockings of skins
from very young animals. The boots are of smooth
black dressed seal's leather, and sometimes when at sea
they wear a great overcoat of the same material. Their
clothes are generally very greasy and dirty, and swarm
with lice. The dress of the women does not differ much
from that of the men.

Among the western tribes the principal ornaments are
cheek-studs (fig. 275) or pieces of polished stone or bone,
which are worn in the lower lip or cheeks. The hole is
made in early infancy, and gradually enlarged by a series

---

[1] See *Archæologia*, vol. xxxviii. p. 415.　　[2] Parry, *l.c.*, p. 495.

of " guides." [1]   These " labrets," however, are not worn
by the eastern tribes. According to Richardson, they
are in use from Behring Straits to the Mackenzie River.[2]
They are worn exclusively by the men. The women
paint their eyebrows ; and tattoo the face, and especially
the chin, in blue lines.[3] The other ornaments consist of
strips of variously coloured fur, and fringes of pierced
teeth, generally those of the fox or wolf. Among the
Esquimaux visited by Captain Lyon, the ornaments were
all appropriated by the men.[4] Some of the families are
in the habit of tattooing themselves.

The men hunt and fish. They make the weapons and
implements, and prepare the woodwork of the boats.
The women [5] are the cooks, prepare the skins, and make
the clothes. They also repair the houses, tents, and
boats, the men doing only carpenter's work. Though
they do not appear to be harshly treated, still the women
have certainly " a hard and almost slavish life of it,"
although perhaps, after all, not more so than the men.

The Esquimaux are not altogether without music. They
have a kind of drum, and sing both alone and in chorus.
They are acquainted with several kinds of games,[6] both
of strength and skill, and are fond of dances, which are
often very indecent. One of their games resembled our
cat's-cradle,[7] and Kane saw the children in Smith's Sound
playing hockey on the ice. The Esquimaux have also a
great natural ability for drawing. In many cases they
have made rude maps for our officers, which have turned
out to be substantially correct. Many of their bone
implements are covered with sketches. Figs. 276–278
represent three bone drill-bows presented to the Ash-
molean Museum by Captain Beechey, and which I presume to be some of those which he obtained in Hotham
Inlet, Kotzebue Sound, and described in his *Voyage to*

---

[1] Vancouver's *Voyage*, vol. ii. p. 280 ; see also p. 408 ; Belcher, *l.c.*,
p. 141.
[2] *Arctic Expedition*, vol. i. p. 355.
[3] Beechey's *Voyage*, vol. i. p. 280.
[4] Lyon's *Journal*, p. 314.   [5] Crantz, p. 164.
[6] Egede, *l.c.*, p. 162.   [7] Hall, *l.c.*, vol. ii. p. 316.

the Pacific. In fig. 278 we see yourts, or winter-houses, in two cases, with dogs standing on them ; men armed with bows and arrows, and others dragging seals home over the ice, and one man about to spear a reindeer with a movable-headed harpoon. In fig. 277 are reindeer, geese, a baidar, or flat-bottomed boat, a tent, round which various articles of clothing are hung up to dry, a woman, apparently engaged in the preparation of food, and a hunting scene. A decoy, roughly representing the head and antlers of a reindeer, has been put up ; and a real reindeer, while unsuspiciously browsing close by, is about to be shot by an Esquimaux hunter. In fig. 276 are represented two animals, apparently intended for crocodiles ; the draughtsman must, I think, have seen drawings of this animal in some European vessel.

According to Crantz, the Greenland Esquimaux " have neither a religious nor an idolatrous worship, nor so much as any ceremonies to be perceived tending towards it." [1] This statement has been confirmed by many other observers.[2] Their burial ceremonies have, however, been supposed by some to indicate a belief in the resurrection. They generally bend the body into a sitting posture, bringing the knees up under the chin, and then wrap the corpse in one of

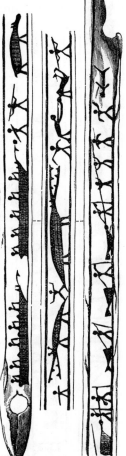

Fig. 276.—Drawings on Esquimaux bone implement.

[1] *L.c.*, p. 197.
[2] Graah's *Voyage to Greenland*, p. 123 ; Ross, *Baffin's Bay*, vol. i. p. 175 : *Voyage of Discovery*, p. 128 ; Parry, *l.c.*, p. 551 ; Richardson's *Arctic Expedition*, vol. ii. p. 44 ; Egede, *l.c.*, p. 183.

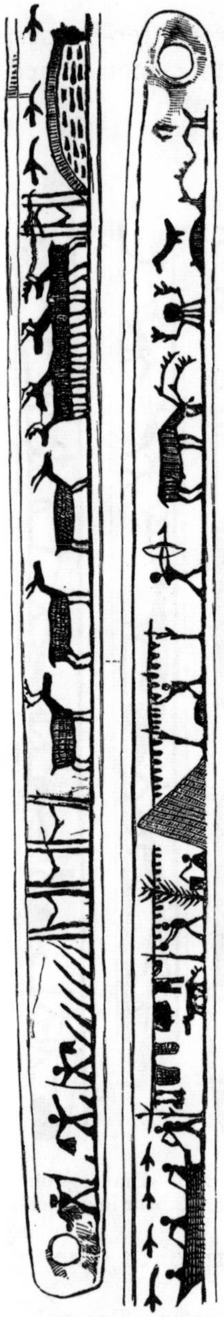

their best skins. For the grave they choose some high place, and over the corpse they make a heap of stones. Near the body some of them place the implements of the deceased, and even sometimes, if he was a man, his kajak ; believing, as it has been said, that they will be of use to him in the new world. Egede,[1] however, expressly denies that it is done with any such idea. This view is also confirmed by Hall, according to whom the Esquimaux have a superstitious objection to use, or even touch, anything which has been in a house containing a dead body.[2] It is, perhaps, the same idea which induces them to remove a corpse, not through the ordinary entrance, but by way of the window.[3] In other cases, when a person is evidently dying, they place by him everything which can soothe and comfort his last moments, and then leave the igloo, or house, which they close up, thus converting it into a tomb.[4] Crantz tells us that they "lay a dog's head by the grave of a child, for the soul of a dog can find its way anywhere, and will show the ignorant babe the way to the land of souls," and this is admitted by Egede. Moreover, the custom of occasionally burying models of implements, instead of the implements themselves, tends to the same conclusion.

Captain Cook saw burial-mounds of

Fig. 277. — Drawings on Esquimaux bone implement.

[1] *L.c.*, p. 151.
[2] *L.c.*, vol. i. p. 201, vol. ii. p. 221.
[3] Graah, *l.c.*, p. 128 ; Ross, *Arctic Expedition*, 1829–33, p. 290.
[4] Graah, *l.c.*, p. 126.

earth or stone at Oonalashka. One of the latter was
near the village, and he observed that,
in accordance with a custom which seems
to prevail all over the world, everyone
who passed threw a stone on it.[1] Infants,
if unfortunate enough to lose their
mothers, are always buried with them ;
and sickly aged people are sometimes
buried alive, as it is considered a kindness
to spare them the pain of a lingering
death. The Esquimaux observed by
Captain Parry had a superstitious idea
that any weight pressing upon the corpse
would give pain to the deceased.[2] Such
a belief would naturally give rise, in a
more favoured country, to vaulted tumuli ;
but in the extreme north, the only result
is that the dead bodies are but slightly
covered up, in consequence of which the
foxes and dogs frequently dig them up
and eat them. This the natives regard
with the utmost indifference ; they leave
the human bones lying about near the
huts, among those of animals which have
served for food : another reason for doubting whether their burial customs can be
regarded as satisfactory evidence of any
very definite and general belief in a resurrection, or whether the objects which
they bury with their friends are really
supposed to be of actual use to them.
On the whole, the burial customs of the
Esquimaux are very like those of which
we find evidence in the ancient tumuli of
Northern and Western Europe.

In character the Esquimaux are a
quiet, peaceable people. Those observed

[1] *Voyage to the Pacific Ocean*, vol. ii. p. 519.
[2] *L.c.*, pp. 395, 417, 550.

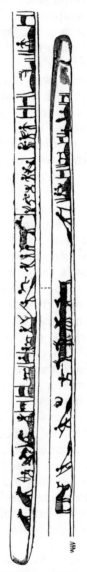

FIG. 278.—Drawings
on Esquimaux bone
implement.

by Ross, in Baffin's Bay, "could not be made to understand what was meant by war, nor had they any warlike weapons."[1] Like other savages, they resemble children in a great many respects. They are such bad arithmeticians that the "enumeration of ten is a labour, and of fifteen an impossibility with many of them."[2] Dr Rae, who was much attached to the Esquimaux, assures us that if a man is asked the number of his children, he is generally much puzzled. After counting some time on his fingers, he will probably consult his wife, and the two often differ, even though they may not have more than four or five.[3]

Amongst the Esquimaux both polygamy and polyandry appear to occur. A strong or skilful man has often more than one wife, a beautiful or clever woman in some cases more than one husband.[4] Again, the temporary loan of a wife is considered a mark of peculiar friendship ; in which, however, the advantage is not all on one side, as a large family, far from being any incumbrance, is among the Esquimaux a great advantage.[5] Apart, moreover, from these recognized customs, it does not appear that the Esquimaux set any very high value on the virtue of chastity.

They are excessively dirty. Considering the difficulty in obtaining enough water even to drink during the greater part of the year, we cannot, perhaps, wonder that they never dream of washing. Their word for dirt, *eberk*, conveys no idea of anything disagreeable or offensive ;[6] but, in justice to them, we must remember that the extreme cold, by preventing putrefaction, removes one of our principal inducements to cleanliness, and at the same time induces so great a scarcity of liquid water as to render washing almost an impossibility. Indeed, they often have difficulty in procuring enough even for drinking purposes.

---

[1] *L.c.*, p. 186. [2] Parry, *l.c.*, p. 251.
[3] See, for a curious instance of this, Graah, *l.c.*, p. 131.
[4] Ross, *l.c.*, p. 273. [5] *Ib.*, *l.c.*, p. 515.
[6] Kane, *Arctic Explorations*, vol. ii. p. 116.

As a general rule, it is impossible to put any dependence on their promises, not so much that they are intentionally deceitful as on account of the wavering and inconstant disposition which they possess in common with so many other savages. Among themselves a successful huntsman or fisherman is always ready to share his seal or walrus with his less fortunate neighbours ; but he expects, as a matter of course, that sufficient return will be made to him when an opportunity occurs. They give away nothing themselves without expecting to receive as much again, and, being unable to imagine any other line of conduct, are naturally very deficient in gratitude. Sir John Ross, however, and Dr Rae consider that the Esquimaux encountered by them were neither ungrateful nor particularly selfish. In other respects also these appear to have been very favourable specimens of the race. Though not cruel, the Esquimaux seem to be a somewhat heartless people. They do not, indeed, feel any actual pleasure in the infliction of pain, but they will take little trouble to remove or relieve suffering. They are also great thieves ; but, as Captain Parry truly observes,[1] we must "make due allowance for the degree of temptation to which they were daily exposed, amidst the boundless stores of wealth which our ships appear to them to furnish." According to Hall,[2] moreover, they are strictly honest among themselves, kind, generous, and trustworthy.

Parry thus describes them : " In the few opportunities we had of putting their hospitality to the test, we had every reason to be pleased with them. Both as to food and accommodation, the best they had were always at our service ; and their attention, both in kind and degree, was everything that hospitality and even good breeding could dictate. The kindly offices of drying and mending our clothes, cooking our provisions, and thawing snow for our drink, were performed by the women with an obliging cheerfulness which we shall not easily forget, and which commanded its due share of our admiration and esteem. While thus their guest, I have passed an

[1] *L.c.*, p. 522.   [2] *L.c.*, vol. ii. p. 312.

evening not only with comfort, but with extreme gratification ; for, with the women working and singing, their husbands quietly mending their lines, the children playing before the door, and the pot boiling over the blaze of a cheerful lamp, one might well forget for the time that an Esquimaux hut was the scene of this domestic comfort and tranquillity ; and I can safely affirm with Cartwright that, while thus lodged beneath their roof, I know no people whom I would more confidently trust, as respects either my person or my property, than the Esquimaux." [1]

Dr Rae has also a very high opinion of them, and they seem from all accounts to present the remarkable phenomenon of a really high state of morality without anything which can be called religion.

The North American Indians

The aboriginal, or at least the pre-Columbian, inhabitants of North America, fall naturally into three divisions : the Esquimaux in the extreme north, the Indian tribes in the centre, and the comparatively civilized Mexicans in the south. The central tribes, which occupied by far the greater extent of the continent, were again divided by the Rocky Mountains into two great groups, that on the western side being in much the most abject condition. Though no doubt there was and is an immense difference between different tribes—and particularly between the semi-agricultural nations of the west and the filthy barbarians of northern California—still, as Mr Schoolcraft, to whom we are indebted for an excellent work on the *History, Condition, and Prospects of the Indian Tribes*,[2] truly says, "their manners and customs, their opinions and mental habits, had, wherever they were inquired into, at the earliest dates, much in common. Their modes of war and worship, hunting and amusements were very similar. In the sacrifice of prisoners taken in war ; in

[1] Parry's *Three Voyages for the Discovery of a North-West Passage*, vol. v. p. 13.
[2] Published by authority of Congress, Philadelphia, 1853 ; see also Bancroft, *The Native Races of the Pacific States*.

the laws of retaliation ; in the sacred character attached
to public transactions solemnized by smoking the pipe ;
in the adoption of persons taken in war, in families ; in
the exhibition of dances on almost every occasion that
can enlist human sympathy ; in the meagre and inartificial
style of music ; in the totemic tie that binds relationships
together, and in the system of symbols and figures cut
and marked on their grave-posts, on trees, and sometimes
on rocks, there is a perfect identity of principles, arts,
and opinions. The mere act of wandering and petty
warfare kept them in a savage state, though they had
the element of civilization with them in the maize." [1]

As regards dress, many of the Indian chiefs had
magnificent dresses of skins and feathers. Some of the
tribes, indeed, wore no clothes ; but this was rarely the
case with the women, and even the men had generally
at least a loin-cloth. The amount of clothing, however,
depended very much on the temperature. In the plains
and forests of the tropical and southern latitudes, "the
Indian wears little or no clothing during a large part
of the year" ; but it is very different on the mountains
and in the north, where the common dress was the
breech-cloth and moccasins, with a buffalo-skin thrown
over the shoulders. The inhabitants of Vancouver's
Island had mats, made either of dog's-wool alone, or of
dog's-wool and goose-down together, or of threads
obtained from cedar-bark. They often wore " necklaces
of shells, claws, or wampum ; feathers on the head and
armlets, as well as ear and nose jewels." [2]   Many of
the Indian tribes are clean in their person, and frequently
use both the sweat-house and cold bath ; others are
described as repulsive in countenance and filthy both in
person and habit.

Among the western tribes tattooing is very general
with the women, though not carried to any great extent.

The eastern tribes do not generally disfigure themselves
artificially, except indeed by the use of paint ; but it is
very different in the west. The Sachet Indians of De

[1] *L.c.*, vol. ii. p. 47.   [2] Schoolcraft, vol. iii. p. 65.

Fuca's Straits wear pieces of bone or wood passed through the cartilage of the nose ; the Classet Indians cut their noses when they capture a whale ; among the Babines, who live north of Columbia River, the size of the under-lip is the standard of female beauty.[1] A hole is made in the under-lip of the infant, in which a small bone is inserted ; from time to time the bone is replaced by a larger one, until at last a piece of wood three inches long and an inch and a half wide is inserted in the orifice, which makes the lip protrude to a frightful extent. The process appears to be very painful.

Owing to the almost universal custom of fastening babies to a cradle-board, the American skulls are charac-terized by a flattened occiput. This peculiarity does not now occur in European heads, but it is found in many ancient skulls from various parts of the old continents, and indicates, as pointed out by Vesalius, Gosse, and Wilson, that the cradle-board, though long abandoned, was at one time used in Western Europe, as it is even now among the Indians of North America. The extra-ordinary practice of moulding the form of the head was common to several of the Indian tribes. It prevailed in Mexico and Peru, in the Carib Islands, and among the savage tribes of Oregon. Among the Natchez the de-formity is described by the historian of De Soto's expedi-tion as consisting of an upward elongation of the cranium, until it terminated in a point or edge. The Choctaws, though enemies of the Natchez, "improved" their heads in the same way. Their children were placed upon a board, and a bag of sand was laid upon the forehead, "which, by continual gentle compressure, gives the forehead somewhat the form of a brick from the temples upwards, and by these means they have high and lofty foreheads sloping off backwards."[2] The Waxsaws, Muscogees or Crees, Catawbas, and Altacapas, are described as having had a similar custom. It was, how-

---

[1] Kean's *Indians of North America*, p. 242 ; Vancouver, *l.c.*, vol. ii. pp. 280, 408.
[2] Schoolcraft, *l.c.*, vol. ii. p. 324.

ever, only the male infants which were treated in this manner. Among the Nootka-Columbians the practice of flattening the head was universal. The child was placed in a box or cradle lined with moss. The Newatees, a tribe residing on the north end of Vancouver's Island, forced the head into a conical shape by means of a cord of deer-skin padded with the inner bark of the cedar-tree. The cord, which is about as thick as a man's thumb, is wound round the infant's head, and gradually forces it to take the shape of a tapering cone.[1] Among the Peruvians the forehead was pressed downwards and backwards by tight bandages, of which there seem to have been generally two, leaving a space between them, and thus producing a well-marked ridge running transversely across the skull. Thus, while the forehead was prevented from rising and the sides of the head from expanding, the occipital region was allowed full freedom of growth, and the development of the brain was forced to take an unnatural direction. It is very remarkable that this unnatural process does not appear to have any prejudicial effect on the minds of the sufferers.[2]

Hearne states that the Northern Indians had no religion; even the celebrated " five nations " of Canada, according to Colden, had no religion, nor any word for God. Burnet[3] never found any semblance of worship among the Comanches. In the central parts of North America, however, the Indian tribes generally believed in the existence of a Great Spirit, and the survival of the soul ; but they seem to have had scarcely any religious observances, still less any edifices for sacred purposes. The Dacotahs never pray to the Creator ; if they wish for fine weather, they pray to the weather itself. They are said to have believed that the Great Spirit made all things except thunder and rice, but we are not told the reason for these two curious exceptions.

[1] Wilson on Physical Ethnology, *Smithsonian Report*, 1862, p. 288.
[2] Beecher's *Voyage round the Wold*, vol. i. p. 308 ; Wilson, *Smithsonian Report*, 1862, p. 287.
[3] Schoolcraft, vol. i. p. 237. See also Richardson's *Arctic Expedition*, vol. ii. p. 21.

The social position of the women seems to have been very degraded among the aboriginal tribes of North America. " Their wives, or dogs, as some of the Indians term them," were indeed well treated as long as they did all the work and there was plenty to eat ; but throughout the Continent, as indeed among all savages, the domestic drudgery falls to their lot, while the men hunt and make war ; though in justice to them we must remember that the former at least of these two occupations was of the greatest possible importance, and that upon it depended their principal means of subsistence. Polygamy generally prevailed ; the husband had absolute power over his wives, and the marriage lasted only as long as he pleased. Among some of the North Californian Indians it is not thought right to beat the wives, but the men " allow themselves the privilege of shooting such as they tired of."[1] Among the Dogribs and other northern tribes, the women are the property of the strongest. Everyone is considered to have both a legal and moral right to take the wife of any man weaker than he is. In fact, the men fight for the possession of the women, just like stags and the males of other wild beasts.[2] Lending wives is a frequent custom.[3]

" Imperturbability,[4] in all situations, is one of the most striking and general traits of the Indian character. To still his muscles to resist the expression of all emotion seems to be his great ambition ; and this is particularly observed on public occasions. Neither fear nor joy are permitted to break this trained equanimity." Even among relations " it is not customary to indulge in warm greetings. The pride and stoicism of the hunter and warrior forbid it. The pride of the wife, who has been made the creature of rough endurance, also forbids it."

But perhaps the most remarkable evidence of this is the fact that some of the American languages, and even

---

[1] Colonel M'Kee in Schoolcraft's *Indian Tribes*, vol. iii. p. 127.
[2] See Hearne's *Journey to the Copper-Mine River*, p. 104.
[3] Hearne, *l.c.*, p. 128 ; Carver's *Travels*, p. 131 ; James' *Expedition to the Rocky Mountains*, vol. i. p. 212.
[4] Schoolcraft, vol. iii. p. 58.

the Algonquin, although one of the richest, contained no word for "to love"; and when Eliot translated the Bible for them in 1661 he was obliged to coin one. He introduced the word "woman" to supply the want. Again, the Tinnè language[1] contains no word to express "dear" or "beloved." It is only fair to add that Kane found the Cree Indians *swearing* in French, having no oaths in their own language.[2] Mr Schoolcraft records, as an indication that they are in reality of affectionate disposition, that he "once saw a Fox Indian on the banks of the Mississippi, near whose wigwam I had, unnoticed to him, wandered, take up his male infant in his arms, and several times kiss it."[3] The special mention of this fact conveys a different impression from that which was intended. Nevertheless, among the better tribes many no doubt are capable of feeling strong affection, and there are even cases on record in which the father has redeemed his son from the stake, and actually been burnt in his stead.

Partly no doubt from the hatred produced by almost incessant wars, partly perhaps encouraged by the stoical disregard of pain which it was their pride to affect, the North American Indians were very cruel to captives taken in war. Scalping seems to have been an universal practice, and it is even said that the Sioux sometimes ate the hearts of their enemies, every one of the war-party getting a mouthful, if possible.

Infanticide was common in the north, but does not seem to have prevailed among the southern tribes to any great extent; and until the advent of Europeans they do not appear to have had any fermented liquors. The Sioux, Assiniboines and other tribes on the Missouri are said to have habitually abandoned those who from age or infirmities were unable to follow the hunting-camps. The same was frequently the case among the northern tribes.

Copper is found native in the northern districts, and

[1] Richardson's *Arctic Expedition*, vol. ii. p. 24.
[2] *L.c.*, p. 339.   [3] *L.c.*, vol. iii. p. 64.

even before the advent of the Europeans was used for hatchets, bracelets, etc   Nevertheless, it was used rather as a stone than as a metal ; that is to say, the Indians did not heat it and run it into moulds, or work it when hot, but simply took advantage of its malleability and hammered it into form, without the assistance of heat.   Metallic vessels were quite unknown to the aborigines of North America.

The implements of the Shoshonees, or Snake Indians, are described by Wyeth.   Their possessions were confined to " the pot, bow and arrow, knives, graining tools, awls, root-digger, fish-spears, nets, a kind of boat or raft, the pipe, mats for shelter, and implements to produce fire." [1]

The pot was made of " long tough roots, wound in plies around a centre, shortening the circumference of the outer plies so as to form a vessel in the shape of an inverted beehive."   They were so well made as to be quite water-tight, and though, of course, they could not be put on the fire, still they were used for boiling, in the manner already described as practised by other savages.   The Dacotahs are said to have sometimes boiled animals in their own skins, taking the skin off whole, suspending it at the four corners, and making use of boiling stones as usual.   They had also stone vessels, but these were rare, and probably used only as mortars.

Their bows are skilfully made of the horns of the mountain sheep and elk, or sometimes of wood.   " The string is of twisted sinew, and is used loose, and those using this bow require a guard to protect the hand which holds it."   The arrow is driven with such force that it will pass right through the body of a horse or buffalo.[2] Although on the whole far inferior to the rifle, still, in hunting, the bow has the one great advantage of silence. Among several of the tribes, arrow-making was a distinct profession.   The arrow-heads are of obsidian, about three-

[1] Schoolcraft, vol. i. p. 212.
[2] *Ibid.*, *l c.*, vol. iii. pp. 35, 46 ; Kane's *North American Indians*, p. 141 ; Catlin, *l.c.*, vol. i. p. 31, vol. ii. p. 212 ; M'Kean and Hall's *Indian Tribes*, vol. ii. p. 4.

fourths of an inch long and half an inch wide, and quite thin.   The base is expanded and is inserted into the split end of the shaft, being kept in its place by sinews.   The shaft is about two feet and a half long ; when intended for hunting it is expanded at the end, so that when it is drawn out of the wound the arrow-head is extracted also ; but the shafts of war-arrows taper to the end, so that when they are drawn out the head remains behind.   The sling does not appear to have been much used.

The knives are rudely made of obsidian, and are some-times fastened in handles of wood or horn.   The graining tools for preparing skins are sometimes of bone, some-times of obsidian.   Mr Wyeth does not describe their form.   Awls were made of bone, large thorns also being sometimes used for the purpose.   Root-diggers are either made of horns, or of crooked sticks pointed and hardened by fire.   " The fish-spear is a very simple and ingenious implement.   The head is of bone, to which a small strong line is attached near the middle, connecting it with the shaft about two feet from the point.   Near the forward end of this head there is a small hole, which enters it, ranging acutely towards the point of the head ; it is quite shallow.   In this hole the front end of the shaft is placed." The shaft is of light willow, and about ten feet long. When the fish is struck, the shaft is withdrawn, and the string at once pulls the bone end into a transverse posi-tion.   The fish-nets are made of bark, which gives a very strong line, and are of two kinds, the scoop and the seine.   They are, however, unknown among the northern tribes west of the Mackenzie.[1]   The boats of the Sho-shonees hardly deserve the name, and seem to be used only for crossing rivers.   They are about eight feet long, and made of reeds, but there is no attempt to make them water-tight.   Other tribes, however, have much better canoes, made either of bark or of a log hollowed out. The pipes are large, and the bowl is generally of fuller's-earth, or of soapstone.   The mats are about four feet

[1] Richardson's *Arctic Expedition*, vol. ii. p. 25.

long, are made of rushes, and are used either as beds, or in the construction of wigwams.

They obtain fire by rubbing a piece of wood in a hole. The Chippeways and Natchez tribes had an institution for keeping up a perpetual fire, certain persons being set aside and devoted to this occupation.

The Dacotahs used a drill bow (fig. 279) for the purpose of obtaining fire. This instrument, as shown in the accompanying figure, is a small

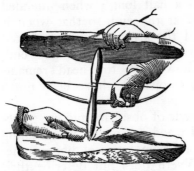

FIG. 279.—Dacotah fire drill bow.

stiff bow, the string of which forms a loop round the upright stick, and thus, when the bow is moved backwards and forwards, gives it a rotatory movement. The Iroquois had effected a still further improvement, and worked with an instrument (fig. 280) closely resembling that used in Western Europe, in Samoa,[1] and Ceylon,[2] to drill holes in earthenware and metal.

The use of the bow drill is very ancient. Ulysses used one to put out the eye of the unfortunate Cyclops. I myself, he says, twirled it round, while my companions pulled the "thong," and it requires no great stretch of the imagination

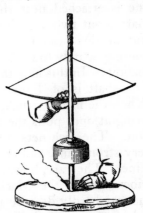

FIG. 280.—Iroquois fire pump drill.

to see the strap drill working until "the very roots of the eye hissed in the fire." The bow drill was used still earlier by the Egyptians—even in the fourth dynasty.

[1] Turner, *Nineteen Years in Polynesia*, p. 274.
[2] Davy's *Ceylon*, p. 263.

The huts or wigwams of the North American Indians are of two kinds, one for summer and the other for winter. The winter wigwam of the Dacotahs is thus described by Schoolcraft : " To erect one of them it is only necessary to cut a few saplings about fifteen feet in length, place the large ends on the ground in a circle, letting the tops meet, thus forming a cone. The buffalo skins, sewed together in the form of a cap, are then thrown over them and fastened together with a few splints. The fire is made on the ground in the centre of the wigwam, and the smoke escapes through an aperture at the top. These wigwams are warm and comfortable. The other kind of hut is made of bark, usually that of the elm." [1] The huts of the Mandans,[2] Minatarees, etc., were circular in form, and from forty to sixty feet in diameter. The earth was removed to a depth of about two feet. The framework was of timber, covered with willow boughs, but leaving a space in the middle to serve both as chimney and window. Over the woodwork was placed a thick layer of earth, and at the top of all some tough clay, which was impervious to water, and in time became quite hard, as in fine weather the tops of the huts were the common lounging-place for the whole tribe. Though these dwellings were sometimes kept very clean and tidy,[3] this was not always the case. Speaking of the Nootka Sound Indians, Captain Cook [4] says : " The nastiness and stench of their houses are, however, at least equal to the confusion. For, as they dry their fish within doors, they also gut them there, which, with their bones and fragments thrown down at meals, and the addition of other sorts of filth, lie everywhere in heaps, and are, I believe, never carried away till it becomes troublesome, from their size, to walk over them. In a word, their houses are as filthy as hog-sties : everything in and about them stinking of fish, train-oil, and smoke."

[1] *L.c.*, vol. ii. p. 191.
[2] This tribe, one of the most interesting, has been entirely swept away by the smallpox.
[3] Catlin's *American Indians*, vol. i. p. 82.
[4] *Third Voyage*, vol. ii. p. 316.

The Wallawalla Indians[1] of Columbia dig a circular hole in the ground about ten or twelve feet deep, and from forty to fifty feet in circumference, and cover it over with driftwood and mud. A hole is left on one side for a door, and a notched pole serves as a ladder. Here twelve or fifteen persons burrow through the winter, requiring very little fire, as they generally eat their salmon raw, and the place is warm from the numbers collected together and the absence of ventilation. In summer they use lodges made of rushes or mats spread on poles. This tribe lives principally on salmon, preferring it putrid.

South of the Gulf of St Lawrence and west of the Rocky Mountains almost all the tribes seem to have grown more or less maize. In the Carolinas and Virginia the Indians raised large quantities, and "all relied on it as one of their fixed means of subsistence."[2] The Delawares had extensive maize-fields at the time of the discovery of America. In 1527, De Vaca saw it in small quantities in Florida, and De Soto, twelve years later, found it abundant among the Muscogees, Choctaws, Chickasaws, and Cherokees. On one occasion his army marched through fields of it for a distance of two leagues. It is known to have been cultivated by the Iroquois in 1610, and, though only in small quantities, "by the hunter communities of the Ohio, the Wabagh, the Miami, and the Illinois," as well as by the natives along both banks of the Mississippi. The evidences of ancient agriculture have been already alluded to in the chapter on North American Archæology; the maize appears to have been the only plant actually under cultivation; but some of the tribes depended for their subsistence very much on roots, etc. The principal implement of agriculture seems to have been the hoe, for which they often used the shoulder-blade of the bison fixed into a handle of wood. Wild

---

[1] Kane's *North American Indians*, p. 272 ; *United States Exploring Expedition*, vol. iv. p. 452.

[2] Schoolcraft, *l.c.*, vol. i. p. 6. See also Richardson's *Arctic Expedition*, vol. ii. p. 51.

rice also grew abundantly in the shallow lakes and streams of Michigan, Wisconsin, Iowa, Minnesota, as well as in the upper valleys of the Mississippi and Missouri. It was gathered by the women, and formed one of their principal articles of food. They went into the rice-fields in canoes, and, bending the stalks in handfuls over the sides of the canoe, beat out the grain with paddles.

The North American Indians, however, depended mainly on the animal kingdom for their subsistence. They were essentially hunters and fishermen ; the buffalo, the deer, and the salmon supplying them with their principal articles of food. The buffaloes were sometimes driven into pounds, sometimes shot on the open prairie with bows and arrows. Fish were speared, caught in weirs, etc., or shot with the bow. The Macaws and Clallums on the Pacific coast sometimes even killed whales. For this purpose they use large barbed harpoons of bone, with a string, and a strong sealskin bag filled with air. This apparatus was used in the same manner as among the Esquimaux (*ante*, p. 500). Like all carnivorous animals, the Indians alternate between seasons of great plenty and extreme want. Usually game is abundant, and Noka, one of their most celebrated hunters, is said to have killed in one day sixteen elks, four buffaloes, five deer, three bears, a porcupine, and a lynx. This of course was a very exceptional case. Still there is generally some season of the year when they kill more game than is required for immediate consumption. In this case the surplus is dried and made into pemmican. In winter, however, they are often very short of provisions. Back gives a terrible picture of their sufferings in famine times ;[1] and Wyeth tells us that the Shoshonees "nearly starve to death annually, and in winter and spring are emaciated to the last degree ; the trappers used to think they all eventually died from starvation, as they became old and feeble."[2]

---

[1] *Arctic Land Expedition*, pp. 194–226. See also Richardson's *Arctic Expedition*, vol. ii. p. 96.
[2] Schoolcraft, vol. i. p. 216.

As might naturally be expected, the mode of burial varies much in different parts of North America. In Columbia, and among many of the Prairie tribes, the dead are generally sewn up in a skin or blanket, and placed either on the boughs of a tree or on a scaffold ; the personal property of each deceased individual being placed near the body.[1] In some cases the bodies were placed in canoes, and deposited among the branches of trees. Many of the Eastern races, as already mentioned (*ante*, p. 265), buried their dead under tumuli. Among the Clear Lake Indians, the Carriers, etc., it was usual to burn them, while in Florida they were interred in a sitting posture. Among other tribes the bones of the dead were collected every eight or ten years, and laid in one common burial-place. Here, therefore, we see that even among nearly allied races the burial customs differed considerably.

The Redskins are not altogether deficient in art, being able to make rude carvings, and to trace equally rude drawings on their wigwams, robes, etc. ; but about portraits they have some curious ideas. They think that an artist acquires some mysterious power over anyone whose likeness he may have taken ; and on one occasion, when annoyed by some Indians, Mr Kane got rid of them at once by threatening to draw anyone who remained. Not one ventured to do so. If the likeness is good, so much the worse ; it is, they fancy, half alive —at the expense of the sitter. So much life, they argue, could only be put in the picture by taking it away from the original. Again, they fancy that if the picture were injured, by some mysterious connection the original would suffer also. But perhaps the oddest notion of all is recorded by Catlin. He excited great commotion among the Sioux by drawing one of their great chiefs in profile. " Why was half his face left out ? " they asked ; " Mahtocheega was never ashamed to look a white man in the face." Mahtocheega himself does not seem to have taken any offence, but Shonka, The Dog, took

[1] *United States Exploring Expedition*, vol. iv. p. 389.

advantage of the idea to taunt him. "The Englishman knows," he said, "that you are but *half a man*; he has painted but one half of your face, and knows that the rest is good for nothing." This view of the case led to a fight, in which poor Mahtocheega was shot; and as ill-luck would have it, the bullet by which he was killed tore away just that part of the face which had been omitted in the drawing. This was very unfortunate for Mr Catlin, who had great difficulty in making his escape, and lived some months after in fear for his life; nor was the matter settled until both Shonka and his brother had been killed in revenge for the death of Mahtocheega.

Like so many other savage races, the North Americans are rapidly disappearing. Left to themselves they would perhaps have developed an indigenous civilization, but for ours they are unfit. Unable to compete with Europeans as equals, and too proud to work as inferiors, they have profited by intercourse with the superior race only where the paternal government of the Hudson's Bay Company has protected them both from the settlers and from themselves, has encouraged hunting, put an end to war, prevented the sale of spirits, and, in times of scarcity, provided food. Ere long almost the only remains of the Indian blood will, perhaps, be found in the territories of the Hudson's Bay Company.

The Paraguay Indians

The Indians of Paraguay have been described by Dobritzhoffer[1] and by Don Fêlix de Azara,[2] who lived a long time among them. He found them divided into several different nations or tribes, with at least forty distinct languages, and with different customs. Some of them lived by fishing, but the greater number depended for their subsistence on the wild horses and cattle, and must therefore have had different habits before the discovery of America by the Europeans. Their principal

---

[1] Dobritzhoffer, *History of the Abipones.*
[2] *Voyages dans l'Amérique Méridionale,* 1809.

arms were long spears, clubs, and bows and arrows. Some tribes, however, as, for instance, those of the Pampas, do not use bows and arrows, but prefer the bolas. In war, the Indians of Paraguay gave no quarter to men, but spared only the women and children.

Their houses, if we can call them so, were of the simplest character ; they cut three or four boughs, stuck the two ends into the ground, and threw over them a cow-skin. Their bed consisted of another skin ; they had no chairs or tables, or any kind of furniture. The men seldom wore any clothes ; the dress of the women consisted usually of a poncho, although among some of the tribes, as the Nalicuégas, even this was dispensed with. The art of washing seems to have been entirely unknown, though Azara admits that in very hot weather they used sometimes to bathe, rather, however, as it would appear, for coolness than for cleanliness. It is unnecessary, therefore, to say that they were excessively filthy. They had no domestic animals, nor any idea of agriculture. Their doctors had but one remedy, which they applied in all cases, and which had at least the great merit of being harmless — since it consisted in applying their lips to the seat of any pain, and sucking with all their force, in order to extract the evil.

Many of the tribes painted their bodies in various ways, and it was usual to pierce the under-lip and insert a piece of wood, about four or five inches long, which they never removed.

They had no regular form of government, nor, according to Azara, any ideas of religion. He makes this latter statement generally for all the Indians, and repeats it particularly for the following tribes — namely, the Charruas, Minuanas, Aucas, Guaranys, Guayanas, Nalicuégas, Guasarapos, Guatos, Ninaquiguilas, Guanas, Lenguas, Aguilots, Mocobys, Abipones, and Paraguas ; yet it appears from other passages that some at least of these tribes were believers in witchcraft and in mysterious evil beings.

Azara describes the language of the Guaranys as being

the most copious, and yet it was in many respects very deficient ; for instance, they could only count up to four, and had no words for the higher numbers, not even for five or six.   The marriage tie was little regarded among them ; they married when they liked, and separated again when they pleased.

Infanticide was, in several of the tribes, the rule, rather than the exception ; the women brought up but one child each, and as they spared only the one which they thought likely to be the last, it often happened that they were left without any at all.

The Patagonians

The inhabitants of the southern parts of South America, although they are divided into numerous different tribes, may be considered as falling into two great groups : the Patagonians, or Horse Indians, on the east, who have horses but no canoes ; and the Chonos and Fuegians, or Canoe Indians, who have canoes but no horses, and who inhabit the tempestuous islands on the south and west.

The Yacana-kunny, who inhabit the north-eastern part of Tierra del Fuego, are, properly speaking, not Fuegians, but Patagonians, and resemble them in colour, stature, and clothing, except the peculiar boots.   They live now pretty much as the mainlanders probably did before the introduction of horses, and feed principally on guanacoes, ostriches, birds, and seals, which they kill with dogs, bows and arrows, bolas, slings, lances, and clubs.[1]   The habits of the Patagonians must have been much altered by the introduction of the horse, but we can only deal with them as they now are.

The Horse and Canoe Indians offer a great contrast in point of size ; while the latter are short, ill-looking, and badly-proportioned, the former are considerably above the average height, and are described by early travellers as being truly gigantic.   They were first visited in 1519

[1] Fitzroy, l.c., vol. ii. p. 137.

by Magellan, who assures us that many of them were above seven feet (French) in height. In 1525 they were seen by Garcia de Loaisa, who mentions their great stature, but does not seem to have measured them. Similar statements were made by Cavendish, Knevett, Sibald de Veert, Van Noort, Spilbergen, and Lemaire; in fact, out of the fifteen first voyagers who passed through the Magellanic Straits, not fewer than nine attest the fact of the gigantic size of the Patagonians; in which they are confirmed by the testimony of several subsequent travellers, and especially of Falkner, who assures us that he saw many men who were over seven feet in height.

It is difficult altogether to reject these statements, and as they are certainly not applicable to the present race, it is possible that there may have been a change of size owing to the introduction and general use of the horse.

The huts, or "toldos," of the Patagonians are "rectangular in form, about ten or twelve feet long, ten deep, seven feet high in front, and six feet in the rear. The frame of the building is formed by poles stuck in the ground, having forked tops to hold cross pieces, on which are laid poles for rafters, to support the covering, which is made of skins of animals sewn together, so as to be almost impervious to rain or wind. The posts and rafters, which are not easily procured, are carried from place to place in all their travelling excursions. Having reached their bivouac, and marked out a place with due regard to shelter from the wind, they dig holes with a piece of pointed hard wood, to receive the posts: and all the frame and cover being ready, it takes but a short time to erect a dwelling." [1]

They have no pottery, and for carrying water the only vessels they use are bladders. Their dress consists principally of skins, sewn together with ostrich sinews, and often curiously painted on one side; but, according to Falkner, [2] some of the tribes "make or weave fine mantles of woollen yarn, beautifully dyed with many colours. They have also a small triangular apron, two

[1] Fitzroy, *l.c.*, vol. i. p. 93.　　　　[2] Falkner's *Patagonia*, p. 128.

corners of which are tied round the waist, while the third
passes between the legs and is fastened behind. When
on horseback they use a kind of poncho or mantle, with
a slit in the middle, through which they put their head.
For boots they wear the "skin of the thighs and legs of
mares and colts"; they clean the skins, and then, after
drying, soften with grease, and so put them on without
either shaping or sewing.[1] They make brushes of grass,
twigs, and rushes, and use the jaw of a porpoise for a
comb.[2] The women wear a mantle, fastened across the
breast by a wooden skewer, or pin, and tied round the
waist. They have also a kind of apron which reaches
down to their knees, but which only covers them in
front. Their boots are made in the same way as those of
the men. Like other savages, they are fond of beads,
feathers, and other ornaments. They also paint themselves
with red, black, and white, which, however, to European
eyes is anything but an improvement. Their defensive
armour consists of a helmet and a shield, both made of
thick hide, and strong enough to resist either arrows or
lances.

Bows and arrows have been abandoned by most of the
Patagonian tribes. Where used, the bows are small, and
the arrows, which are pointed with stone or bone, are said
to be sometimes poisoned. They have also clubs and
long cane lances, most of which are now tipped with iron.
But the weapons which are most characteristic of the
Patagonians, and which are indeed almost peculiar to
them, are the bolas,[3] of which there are two or three
sorts. That used in war is a single rounded stone or ball
of hardened clay, weighing about a pound, and fastened
to a short rope or sinew of skin. This they sometimes
throw at their adversary, rope and all, but generally they
prefer to strike at his head with it. For hunting they
use two similar stones fastened together by a rope, which

---

[1] When first visited they used the skin of the guanaco for this purpose,
and it was on account of these shoes that Magellan called them
"Patagonians."

[2] Fitzroy, vol. i. p. 75.   [3] Falkner, *l.c.*, p. 130.

is generally three or four yards long. One of the stones
they take in their hand, and then whirling the other
round their head, throw both at the object they wish to
entangle. Sometimes several balls are used, but two
appears to be the usual number. They do not try to
strike their victim with the balls themselves, but with the
rope, "and then of course the balls swing round in
different directions, and the thongs become so 'laid up,'
or twisted, that struggling only makes the captive more
secure." [1] It is said that a man on horseback can use
the "bolas" effectually at a distance of eighty yards. [2]
They also use the lasso.

On the coast their food consists principally of fish,
which they kill either by diving or striking them with
their darts. Guanacoes and ostriches they catch with the
bolas, and they also eat the horse, as well as various sorts
of small game, and at least two kinds of wild roots.
They have no fermented liquor, and the only prepared
drink which they use is a decoction of chalas and the
juice of berberries mixed with water.

The death of a native is attended with peculiar ceremonies. The bones, having been as much as possible
freed from the flesh, are hung "on high, upon canes or
twigs woven together, to dry and whiten with the sun
and rain." One of the most distinguished women is
chosen to perform the disgusting office of making the
skeleton, and, during the process, "the Indians, covered
with long mantles of skins, and their faces blackened with
soot, walk round the tent with long poles or lances in
their hands, singing in a mournful tone of voice and
striking the ground, to frighten away the Valichus or evil
beings. . . . The horses of the dead are killed, that
he may have wherewithal to ride upon in the Alhue
Mapu, or Country of the Dead." In about a year the
bones are "packed together in a hide, and placed upon
one of the deceased's favourite horses, kept alive for that
purpose," and in this manner the natives bear the relics,
sometimes to a very great distance, until they arrive at

[1] Fitzroy, *l.c.*, vol. ii. p. 148.   [2] Darwin's *Journal*, p. 129.

the proper burial-place, where the ancestors of the dead man are lying. The bones are arranged in their proper positions, and fastened by string. The skeleton is then placed, with others, in a square pit, clothed in the best robes, and adorned with beads, feathers, etc. The arms of the deceased are buried with him, and round the grave are ranged several dead horses, raised on their feet, and supported with sticks.[1] Sometimes a cairn of stones is raised over the grave.[2]

Falkner regarded the Patagonians as Polytheists, but we do not know much about their religion. According to the missionaries, neither the Patagonians nor the Araucanians had any ideas of prayer, or "any vestige of religious worship."[3]

The Fuegians

The inhabitants of Tierra del Fuego are even more degraded than those of the mainland : in fact, they have been regarded by many travellers as being the lowest of mankind.[4] Adolph Decker, who visited Polynesia and Australasia under Jaques le Hermite in 1624, describes them as "rather beasts than men ; for they tear human bodies to pieces, and eat the flesh raw and bloody as it is. There is not the least spark of religion or policy to be observed among them : on the contrary, they are in every respect brutal"—of which he proceeds to give evidence so convincing, that I refrain from quoting it.[5] "The men go altogether naked, and the women have only a bit of skin about their middles. . . . Their huts are made of trees, in the shape of tents, with a hole at the top to let out the smoke. Within they are sunk two or three feet under the earth ; and the mould is thrown upon the outside. Their fishing-tackle is very curious, and their stone hooks very nearly the same shape as ours. They

---

[1] Falkner's *Patagonia*, pp. 118, 119.   [2] Fitzroy, vol. ii. p. 158.
[3] *The Voice of Pity*, vol. ii. pp. 37, 95.
[4] Byron's *Voyage Round the World*, p. 80 ; Wallis's *Voyage Round the World*, p. 392 ; Cook's *Voyage to the South Pole*, vol. ii. p. 187 ; Darwin's *Journal*, p. 235.
[5] Callander's *Voyages*, vol. ii. p. 307.

are differently armed, some having bows, and arrows
headed with stone ; others have long javelins, pointed
with bone ; some, again, have great wooden clubs ; and
some have slings, with stone-knives, which are very
sharp." Their arrows are of hard wood, straight and well
polished. They are about two feet long, and are tipped
with a piece of agate, obsidian, or glass. The bows are
from three to four feet long, and quite plain. The
string is made of twisted sinews.

Forster[1] found them "remarkably stupid, being incapable of understanding any of our signs, which, however,
were very intelligible to the nations of the South Sea."
Wallis, in his *Voyage Round the World*,[2] describes them as
follows : "They were covered with seal-skins, which
stunk abominably, and some of them were eating the
rotten flesh and blubber raw, with a keen appetite and
great seeming satisfaction." And again he says : "Some
of our people, who were fishing with a hook and line,
gave one of them a fish, somewhat bigger than a herring,
alive, just as it came out of the water. The Indian took
it hastily, as a dog would take a bone, and instantly
killed it, by giving it a bite near the gills ; he then proceeded to eat it, beginning with the head, and going on
to the tail, without rejecting either the bones, fins, scales,
or entrails."[3] Their cookery is, if possible, still more
disgusting. Fitzroy tells us that it was "too offensive"
for description ; and the account given by Byron[4] entirely
confirms this statement.

The men, says Fitzroy,[5] "are low in stature, ill-
looking, and badly proportioned. Their colour is that of
very old mahogany—or rather between dark copper and
bronze. The trunk of the body is large, in proportion
to their cramped or rather crooked limbs. Their rough,
coarse, and extremely dirty black hair half hides, yet
heightens, a villainous expression of the worst description

---

[1] *L.c.*, p. 251.
[2] Hawkesworth's *Voyages, l.c.*, p. 403.   [3] *L.c.*, p. 403.
[4] Byron's *Loss of the "Wager,"* p. 132.
[5] *Voyages of the "Adventure" and "Beagle,"* vol. ii. p. 137.

of savage features. The hair of the women is longer,
less coarse, and certainly cleaner than that of the men.
It is combed with the jaw of a porpoise, but neither
plaited nor tied ; and none is cut away, excepting from
over their eyes. They are short, with bodies largely out
of proportion to their height ; their features, especially
those of the old, are scarcely less disagreeable than the
repulsive ones of the men. About four feet and some
inches is the stature of these she-Fuegians—by courtesy
called women. They never walk upright ; a stooping
posture and awkward movement is their natural gait.
They may be fit mates for such uncouth men, but to
civilized people their appearance is disgusting. . . .
The smoke of wood fires confined in small wigwams
hurts their eyes so much that they are red and watery :
the effects of their oiling or greasing themselves, and
then rubbing ochre, clay, or charcoal over their bodies ;
of their often feeding upon the most offensive substances,
sometimes in a state of putridity ; and of other vile
habits, may readily be imagined."[1] Their incisors are
worn flat,[2] like those of the Esquimaux and of many
ancient races.

"The men procure food of the larger kind, such as
seal, otter, porpoise, etc. ; they break or cut wood and
bark for fuel, as well as for building the wigwams or
canoes. They go out at night to get birds ; they train
the dogs, and of course undertake all hunting or warlike
excursions. The women nurse their children, attend the
fire (feeding it with dead wood rather than green, on
account of the smoke), make baskets and water-buckets,
fishing-lines and necklaces, go out to catch small fish in
their canoes, gather shell-fish, dive for sea-eggs, take care
of their canoes, upon ordinary occasions paddle their
masters about while they sit idle, and do any other
drudgery."[3]

"When there is time, the natives roast their shell-fish,
and half-roast any other food that is of a solid nature ;
but when in haste, they eat fish, as well as meat, in a raw

---

[1] *L.c.*, p. 139.   [2] Fitzroy, Appendix, p. 144.   [3] *Ibid.*, *l.c.*, p. 185.

state. . . . Both seals and porpoises are speared by them
from their canoes. When struck, the fish usually run
into the kelp, with the spear floating on the water, being
attached by a short line to a movable barb : and then
the men follow with their canoe, seize the spear, and tow
by it till the fish is dead. To them the taking of a seal
or a porpoise is a matter of as much consequence as the
capture of a whale is to our countrymen. On moonlight
nights birds are caught when roosting, not only by the
men, but by their dogs, which are sent out to seize them
while asleep upon the rocks or beach ; and so well are
these dogs trained, that they bring all they catch safely to
their masters, without making any noise, and then return
for another mouthful. Birds are also frequently killed
with arrows or by stones slung at them with unerring
aim. Eggs are largely sought for by the natives ; indeed,
I may say that they eat anything and everything that is
eatable, without being particular as to its state of fresh-
ness, or as to its having been near the fire." [1]

According to Byron, the dogs of the Chonos Indians
assist in killing fish as well as birds. They are, he says,
" cur-like looking animals, but very sagacious, and easily
trained to this business. . . . The net is held by two
Indians, who get into the water ; then the dogs, taking
a large compass, dive after the fish, and drive them into
the net ; but it is only in particular places that the fish
are taken in this manner." He adds, that the dogs
" enjoy it much, and express their eagerness by barking
every time they raise their heads above the water to
breathe." [2]

" In the winter, when the snow lies deep, the Tekeenica
hunt the guanaco, which then comes down from the
high lands to seek for pasture near the sea. The long
legs of the animal stick deeply into the snow and soft
boggy ground, disabling him from escape, while the
Fuegians and their dogs hem him in on every side, and

[1] Fitzroy, *l.c.*, p. 184.
[2] Byron's *Loss of the "Wager,"* in Kerr's *Voyages and Travels*, vol.
xvii. pp. 339, 368, 463.

quickly make him their prey. . . . At other times of the year they sometimes get them by lying in wait, and shooting them with arrows, or by getting into a tree near their track, and spearing them as they pass beneath the branches. Fig. 281 represents the head of a Fuegian harpoon, which closely resembles the ancient Danish specimen figured in fig. 141.

Of vegetable food they have very little : a few berries, cranberries, those which grow on the arbutus, and a kind of fungus which is found on the beech, being the only sorts used. The unfortunate Fuegians often suffer greatly from famine. Their principal food consists of limpets, mussels, and other shell-fish.

Admiral Fitzroy entertained no doubt that the Fuegians are cannibals. "Almost[1] always at war with adjoining tribes, they seldom meet but a hostile encounter is the result ; and then those who are vanquished and taken, if not already dead, are killed and eaten by the conquerors. Again, in severe winters, when they can obtain no other food, they take "the oldest woman of their party, hold her head over a thick smoke, made by burning green wood, and, pinching her throat, choke her. They then devour every particle of the flesh. When asked why they did not rather kill their dogs, they said, "Dog catch iappo," i.e. otters.

Like Decker, Admiral Fitzroy "never witnessed or heard of any act of a decidedly religious nature."[2] Still, it is said that some of the natives suppose that there is a powerful and mysterious being who resides in the woods. When a person dies, they carry the

FIG. 281. — Fuegian harpoon, one-half of the actual size.

[1] L.c., p. 183.
[2] See also Weddell, *Voyage to South Pole*, p. 179 ; *The Voice of Pity*, vol. vi. p. 92, etc.

body far into the woods,[1] "place it upon some broken boughs, or pieces of solid wood, and then pile a great quantity of branches over the corpse."

Their canoes are large pieces of bark sewn together. In the bottom they make a fireplace of clay, for they always keep fires alight, though with the help of iron pyrites they soon obtain sparks if any accident happens. The Chonos Indians, who in most respects resemble the Fuegians, have much better canoes. These are formed of planks, which are generally five in number, two on each side and one at the bottom. Along the edges of each are small holes about an inch apart. The planks are sewn together with woodbine, the holes being filled with a kind of bark beaten up until it resembles oakum. Byron truly observes that in the absence of metal, "the labour must be great of hacking a single plank out of a large tree with shells and flints, even though with the help of fire."

The Fuegians have no pottery, but, like the North American Indians, use vessels made of birch, or rather of beech-bark. On the east coast many of the natives possess guanaco-skins, and on the west some of them wear seal-skins. "Amongst the central tribes the men generally possess an otter-skin, or some small scrap about as large as a pocket-handkerchief, which is barely sufficient to cover their backs as low down as their loins. It is laced across the breast by strings, and according as the wind blows, it is shifted from side to side."[2] Many, however, even of the women, go absolutely without clothes. Yet, as Captain Cook quaintly expresses it, "although they are content to be naked, they are very ambitious to be fine," for which purpose they adorn themselves with streaks of red, black, and white ; and the men as well as the women wear bracelets and anklets of shell and bone. Sir J. D. Hooker informs us that at the extreme south of Tierra del Fuego, and in mid-winter, he has often seen the men lying asleep in their wigwams,

[1] *L.c.*, p. 181.
[2] Darwin's *Researches in Geology and Natural History*, p. 234.

without a scrap of clothing, and the women standing naked, and some with children at their breasts, in the water up to their middles, gathering limpets and other shell-fish, while the snow fell thickly on them and on their equally naked babies. It is remarkable that the Fuegians, like the Esquimaux, make so little use of fire ; they do not employ it to warm the air of their huts as we do, though sometimes as a luxury they take advantage of it to toast their hands or feet. Doubtless, however, if deprived of this source of warmth, they would die of starvation rather oftener than is now the case.

If not the lowest, the Fuegians certainly appear to be among the most miserable specimens of the human race. The conditions of their existence are very unfavourable, and their habits are of special interest from their similarity to those of the ancient Danish shell-mound builders, who, however, were in some respects rather more advanced, being acquainted with the art of making pottery.

CHAPTER XV

MODERN SAVAGES—*concluded*

In reading almost any account of savages, it is impossible not to admire the skill with which they use their weapons and implements, their ingenuity in hunting and fishing, and their close and accurate powers of observation. Some savages even recognize individuals by their footsteps. Thus Mr Laing mentions[1] that one day while travelling near Moreton Bay, in Australia, he pointed to a footstep, and asked whose it was. The guide " glanced at it, without stopping his horse, and at once answered, 'White fellow call him Tiger.'" This turned out to be correct, which was the more remarkable as the two men belonged to different tribes, and had not met for two years. Among the Arabs, Burckhardt asserts[2] that some men know every individual in the tribe by his footstep. "Besides this, every Arab knows the printed footsteps of his own camels, and of those belonging to his immediate neighbours. He knows by the depth or slightness of the impression whether a camel was pasturing, and therefore not carrying any load, or mounted by one person only, or heavily loaded."

Skyring[3] saw a Fuegian who " threw stones from each hand with astonishing force and precision. His first stone struck the master with much force, broke a powder-horn which hung round his neck, and nearly knocked him backwards." In his description of the Hottentots, Kolben says[4] that their dexterity in throwing the " hassa-

---

[1] *Aborigines of Australia*, p. 24.
[3] *Bedouins and Wahabys*, p. 374.
[2] Fitzroy, *l.c.*, vol. i. p. 398.
[4] Kolben, *l.c.*, vol. i. p. 243.

gaye and rackum-stick strikes every witness of it with
the highest admiration. . . . If a Hottentot, in the chase
of a hare, deer, or wild goat, comes but within thirty or
forty yards of the creature, away flies the rackum-stick
and down falls the creature, generally pierced quite
through the body." The death of Goliath is a well-
known instance of skill in the use of the sling ; and
we are told also that in the tribe of Benjamin there was
a corps of "seven hundred chosen men left-handed ;
every one could sling stones at an hair-breadth, and not
miss."[1]

Having few weapons, and those in constant use,
savages acquire a skill which seems almost marvellous.
I have seen the boomerang thrown with a force and skill
which I should have thought quite impossible. The
North American Indian will send an arrow right through
a horse or even a buffalo. The African savage will kill
the elephant, and the Chinook fears not to attack even
the whale. Sir G. Grey tells us that he has often seen
the Australians kill a pigeon with a spear at a distance of
thirty paces.[2] Speaking of the Chamisso Island Esquimaux, Beechey says that one day a Diver was swimming
at a distance of thirty yards from the beach, and a native was
offered a reward if he could shoot it. He immediately
frightened it so that it dived, and directly it reappeared,
he transfixed both eyes with an arrow.[3] Speaking of the
Australians, Mr Stanbridge asserts that "it is a favourite
feat on the Murray to dive into the river, spear in hand,
and come up with a fish upon it."[4] Woodes Rogers says
that the Californian Indians used to dive, and strike
the fish under water with wooden spears,[5] and Falkner[6]
tells us that some of the Patagonian tribes live chiefly on
fish, "which they catch *either* by *diving*, or striking them
with their darts." Tertre again says the same of the

[1] Judges xx. 16.   [2] Grey, *l.c.*, vol. ii. p. 285.
[3] Beechey's *Narrative*, vol. ii. p. 574.
[4] "On the Aborigines of Victoria," *Ethn. Trans.*, New Series, vol. i.
p. 293.
[5] Callander's *Voyages*, vol. iii. p. 331.
[6] *Patagonia*, p. 111.

Caribs,[1] and Wallace of the Brazilian Indians.[2] The
South Sea Islanders are particularly active in the water.
They dive after fish, which "takes refuge under the
coral rock ; thither the diver pursues him, and brings him
up with a finger in each eye."[3] They are even more
than a match for the shark, which they attack fearlessly
with a knife. If they are unarmed, "they all surround
him and force him ashore, if they can but once get him
into the surf ; but even if he escapes they continue their
bathing without the least fear.[4] Ellis more cautiously
says only, that "when armed they have sometimes been
known to attack a shark in the water."[5]

The Andaman Islanders also are said to dive and catch
fish under water ;[6] and Rutherford makes a similar statement as regards the New Zealanders. Dobritzhoffer tells
us that the Payajuas and Vilelas live principally on fish,
using a small net with which they dive, "and if they
spy any fish at the bottom, swim after it, catch it in the
net," and so bring it to shore.[7] The Esquimaux in his
kayak can actually turn somersaults in the water.

The Brazilian Indians kill turtles with bows and arrows ;
but if they aimed direct at the animal, the arrow would
glance off the smooth, hard shell ; therefore they shoot
up into the air, so that the arrow falls nearly vertically on
the shell, which it is thus enabled to penetrate.[8] What
an amount of practice must be required to obtain such
skill as this ! How true also must the weapons be !
Indeed, it is very evident that each distinct type of flint
implement must have been designed for some distinct
purpose. Thus the different forms of arrow-head, of
harpoon, or of stone axe, cannot have been intended to be
used in the same manner. Among the North American
Indians the arrows used in hunting were so made that
when the shaft was drawn out of the wound the head
came out also ; while in the war-arrows the shaft tapered

[1] *History of the Carriby Islands*, p. 305.
[2] *Travels on the Amazon*, p. 488. [3] Wilson, *l.c.*, p. 385.
[4] *L.c.*, p. 368. [5] *Polynesian Researches*, vol. i. p. 178.
[6] Mouatt, *l.c.*, pp. 310, 333. [7] *History of the Abipones*, vol. i. p. 343.
Wallace's *Amazon*, p. 466.

to the end, so that even when it was withdrawn the head of the arrow remained in the wound. Again, the different forms of harpoons are illustrated by the barbed and unbarbed lances of the Esquimaux (*ante*, figs. 272, 273). Unfortunately, however, we have but few details of this kind ; travellers have generally thought it unnecessary to observe or record these apparently unimportant details ; and that our knowledge of flint implements is most rudimentary, is well shown by the discussion between Professors Steenstrup and Worsaae, whether the so-called " axes " of the shell-mounds were really axes, or whether they were not rather used in fishing.

We may hope, however, that in future those who have the opportunity of observing stone implements among modern savages will give us more detailed information both as to the exact manner in which they are used, and also about the way in which they are made ; that they will collect not only the well-made weapons, but, also, and even more carefully, the ruder implements of every-day life.

Some archæologists have argued that the shell-mound builders of Denmark must have possessed more formidable weapons than any that have yet been found, because it was considered impossible that they could have killed large game, as, for instance, the bull and seal, with the simple weapons of bone and stone which alone have hitherto been discovered. Professor Worsaae [1] even went so far as to say : "Against birds and other small creatures these stone arrows might prove effectual, but against larger animals, such as the aurochs, the elk, the reindeer, the stag, and the wild boar, they were evidently insufficient ; particularly since these animals often become furious as soon as they are struck." I can, however, by no means agree with Professor Worsaae in this supposition ; we know, on the contrary, that modern savages are able to kill even the largest game with arrows and spears tipped with stone. Knives, again, of stone, are much more effective than might at first be expected,

---

[1] Page 18.

and many savage tribes readily cut flesh with pieces of shell or of hard wood.

The neatness with which the Hottentots, Esquimaux, North American Indians, etc., are able to sew, is very remarkable, although awls and sinews would in our hands be but poor substitutes for needles and thread. As already mentioned in p. 325, some cautious archæologists hesitated to refer the reindeer caves of the Dordogne to the Stone Age, on account of the bone needles and the works of art which are found in them. The eyes of the needles especially, they thought, could only be made with metallic implements. Professor Lartet ingeniously removed these doubts by making a similar needle for himself with the help of a flint; but he might have referred to the fact stated by Cook[1] in his first voyage, that the New Zealanders succeeded in drilling a hole through a piece of glass which he had given them, using for this purpose, as he supposed, a piece of jasper.

The Brazilians also use ornaments of imperfectly crystallized quartz, from four to eight inches long and about an inch in diameter. Hard as it is, they contrive to drill a hole at each end, using for that purpose the pointed leaf-shoot of the large wild plantain, with sand and water. The hole is generally transverse, but the ornaments of the chiefs are actually pierced lengthways. This, Mr Wallace thinks, must be a work of years.[2]

The works of art found in the Dordogne caves are little ruder than those of the Esquimaux or the North American Indians. In fact, the appreciation of art is to be regarded rather as an ethnological characteristic than as an indication of any particular stage in civilization. We see, again, that in many cases a certain knowledge of agriculture has preceded the use of metals; and the fortifications of New Zealand, as well as the large morais of the South Sea Islands, are arguments in favour of the theory which ascribes some of our camps, our great tumuli, and other Druidical remains, to the later part of

---

[1] Vol. iii. p. 464.   [2] *Travels on the Amazon*, p. 278.

the Stone Age. The great morai of Oberea, in Tahiti, has been already described (p. 482). Again, the celebrated statues of Easter Island are really colossal. One of them, which has fallen down, measures twenty-seven feet long, and others appear to be even larger. The houses of the Ladrone Islanders, also, are remarkable. The larger ones were supported on strong pyramids of stone. They were found in large numbers ; in one case they formed a stone row four hundred yards long. They were first described by Anson, who saw many which were thirteen feet in height ; while one of those seen by Freycinet measured as much as twenty feet. They were square at the base, and rested on the ground. On each pillar was a hemisphere, with the flat side upwards. The South Sea Islanders afford, indeed, wonderful instances of what can be accomplished with stone implements. Their houses are large and often well built, and their canoes have excited the wonder of all who have seen them.

Although, then, the use of stone as the principal material of implements and weapons may be regarded as characterizing an early stage in the development of civilization, still it is evident that this stage is itself susceptible of much subdivision. The Mincopie, or the Australian, for instance, is not to be compared for an instant with the semi-civilized native of the Society Islands. So also in the ancient Stone Age of Europe we find evidences of great difference. The savage inhabitants of the South French caves had, according to MM. Christy and Lartet, no domestic animals, and no knowledge of pottery or agriculture. The shell-mound builders of Denmark had the dog ; the Swiss lake-dwellers also possessed this animal, together with the ox, sheep, and pig, perhaps even the horse ; they had a certain knowledge of agriculture, and were acquainted with the art of weaving. Thus, then, even when we have satisfied ourselves that any given remains belong to the Stone Age, we are still but on the threshold of our inquiry.

Travellers and naturalists have differed a good deal
in opinion as to the race of savages which is entitled
to the unenviable reputation of being the lowest in
the scale of civilization. Cook, Darwin, Fitzroy, and
Wallis were decidedly in favour, if I may so say,
of the Fuegian; Burchell maintained that the Bushmen are the lowest; D'Urville voted for the Australians
and Tasmanians; Dampier thought the Australians
" the miserablest people in the world"; Forster said
that the people of Mallicollo " bordered the nearest
upon the tribe of monkeys"; Owen inclined to the
Andamaners; others have supported the North
American root - diggers; and one French writer
even insinuates that monkeys are more human than
Laplanders.

The civilization, moreover, of the Stone Age differs,
not only in degree, but also in kind, varying according to
the climate, vegetation, food, etc., from which it becomes
evident—at least to all those who believe in the unity of
the human race—that the present habits of savage races,
while throwing, no doubt, much light on those of our
earliest ancestors, are not to be regarded as representing
them exactly, because they have been to some extent
modified by external conditions, influenced by national
character, which, however, is after all but the result of
the external conditions which have acted on previous
generations.

If we take a few of the things which are most generally
useful in savage life, and at the same time most easily
obtainable, such, for instance, as slings, spear-casters,
pottery, bows and arrows, boomerangs, bolas, nets,
domestic animals, or a knowledge of agriculture, we
might, perhaps, have expected *a priori* that the acquisition
of them would have followed some regular succession.
That this, however, was not the case is shown by the
annexed table, which will, I think, be found interesting.
It gives some idea of the progress made by various
savage tribes at the time when they were first visited by
Europeans.

	Friendly Islanders.	Society Islanders.	Feegeeans.	New Zealanders.	North American Indians.		Esquimaux.		Australians.		Andamaners.	Hottentots.	Bushmen.	Fuegians.	Eastern Islanders.
					East.	West.	Northern.	Southern.	West.	North-East.					
Bows and Arrows...	Weak	Weak	Good	..	Good	Good	..	Good	..	..	Good	Weak	Weak	Weak	..
Slings.............	?	Yes	Yes	..	Yes	Yes	..	Yes	..	..	..	..	..	Yes	..
Throwing-sticks....	..	..	..	..	..	..	?	Yes	Yes	Yes	..	..	..	..	..
Boomerangs........	..	..	..	..	..	..	..	..	Yes	Yes	..	..	..	..	..
Bolas.............	..	..	..	..	..	..	?	Yes	..	..	..	..	..	..	..
Pottery...........	..	..	Yes	..	Yes	..	..	Good	..	..	..	Yes	..	..	Bad
Canoes............	Very good	Very good	Very good	Very good	Middling	Bad	..	..	Bad	..	Good	..	..	Bad	Bad
Agriculture........	Yes	Yes	Yes	Yes	Maize	..	..	..	..	..	..	..	..	..	..
Fortifications......	Yes	..	Yes	Many	..	..	..	..	..	..	..	..	..	..	..
Fish-hooks.........	Shell	Bone and shell	Bone and shell	Bone and shell	Yes	Yes	For bird catching	Bone	Neat	..	?	Iron	..	Stone	..
Nets..............	Yes	Large	Yes	Large	Yes	Yes	For draught	Small	Neat	..	Good	Yes	..	..	..
Dogs..............	..	For food	For food	For food	For hunting	For wool & hunting	..	For draught	For hunting	For hunting	..	For hunting	For hunting	For hunting	..
Hogs (Domestic)....	..	Many	Some	..	..	..	..	..	..	..	..	..	..	..	..

Some, no doubt, of the differences exhibited in this table may be easily accounted for. The frozen soil and arctic climate of the Esquimaux would not encourage, would not even permit, any agriculture. So, again, the absence of hogs in New Zealand, of dogs in the Friendly Isles, and of all mammalia in Easter Island, is probably due to the fact that the original colonists did not possess these animals, and that their isolated position prevented them afterwards from obtaining any. Moreover, we must remember that as a general rule the lowest savage can only use one or two weapons. He is limited to those which he can carry about with him, and naturally prefers those which are of most general utility.[1] We cannot, however, in this manner account for all the facts. In Columbia, Australia, the Cape of Good Hope, and elsewhere, agriculture was unknown before the advent of Europeans. Easter Island, on the contrary, contained large plantations of sweet potatoes, yams, plantains, sugar-canes, etc. Yet the Chinooks of Columbia had bows and arrows, fish-hooks, and nets ; the Australians had throwing-sticks, boomerangs, fish-hooks, and nets ; the Hottentots had bows and arrows, nets, fish-hooks, pottery, and at last even a certain knowledge of iron ; all of which seem to have been unknown to the Easter Islanders, though they would have been very useful, and, excepting the iron, might have been invented and used by them.

If the case of Easter Island stood alone, the absence of bows and arrows might, perhaps, be plausibly accounted for by the absence of game, the scarcity of birds, and the isolation of the little island, which rendered war almost impossible. But such an argument cannot be applied to other cases which are indicated in the table. Let us compare, for instance, the Atlantic tribes of North American Indians, the Australians, Bushmen, Kaffirs, New Zealanders, and Society Islanders. All these were constantly at war, and the three first lived very much on

[1] Weapons of war depending very much on the caprice of chiefs, are probably more liable to change than those used in hunting.

the produce of the chase.   They at least had therefore
similar wants.   Yet spears, and perhaps clubs, were the
only weapons which they had in common ; the North
Americans had good bows and arrows, the Society
Islanders and Bushmen had bad ones—in fact, those of
the former were so weak as to be useless in war ; the
Australians, Kaffirs, and New Zealanders had none.   On
the other hand, the Australians had the throwing-stick
and the boomerang ; the Society Islanders used slings ;
and the New Zealanders, besides very effective clubs, had
numerous and extensive fortifications.   It is certainly
most remarkable that tribes so warlike, and in many
respects so advanced, as the New Zealanders and Kaffirs,
should have been ignorant of bows and arrows, which
were used by many very low races, such as the Fuegians,
the Chinooks, the Andamaners, and Bushmen ; particularly
as it is impossible to doubt that the New Zealanders at
least would have found bows of great use, and that any
of their tribes, having invented them, would have had an
immense advantage in the "struggle for existence."
Other similar contrasts will strike anyone who examines
the table ; but perhaps it may be said that some of these
cases may be explained by the influence of more civilized
neighbours ; that the comparison above made, for
instance, might be regarded as unfair, because the New
Zealanders were an isolated race, while the Chinooks
might have derived their knowledge of bows and arrows
from the eastern tribes, and these again might have
acquired the art of making pottery from the semi-
civilized nations of the south.   No one can deny that
this may be true in some instances, because we know
that at the present day most savages possess hatchets,
knives, beads, etc., which they have received from
traders, and which they cannot yet manufacture for
themselves.

It is certainly possible that the Chinooks may have
derived their knowledge of the bow from their northern
neighbours ; but we can hardly suppose that they did so
from the Red Indian tribes to the east, because in that

case it is difficult to understand why they should not also
have learnt from these the much simpler, and almost
equally useful, art of making pottery.   Moreover, there
are some cases in which any such idea is absolutely out
of the question ; thus, the spear-caster is used by the
Esquimaux, the Australians, the New Caledonians, and
some Brazilian tribes ; the bolas by the Esquimaux and
the Patagonians ; the boomerang is peculiar to the
Australians.[1]   The "sumpitan," or blow-pipe of the
Malays, occurs again in the valley of the Amazon.
Again, different races of savages have but little peaceful
intercourse with one another.   They are almost always at
war.   If their habits are similar, they are deadly rivals,
fighting for the best hunting-grounds or fisheries ; if
their wants are different, they fight for slaves, for women,
for ornaments ; or if they do not care about any of these,
for the mere love of fighting, for scalps, heads, or some
other recognized emblems of glory.   In this condition of
society, each tribe lives in a state either of isolation from,
or enmity with, its neighbours.   *Delenda est Carthago* is
the universal motto, and savages can only live in peace
when they have a little world of their own.   Sometimes
a broad sea or a high range of mountains, at others a wide
" march " or neutral territory, supplies the necessary conditions and keeps them apart.   They meet only to fight,
and are therefore not likely to learn much from one
another.   Moreover, there are cases in which some tribes
have weapons which are quite unknown to their neighbours.   Thus, among the Brazilian tribes we find the
bow and arrow, the blow-pipe, the lasso, and the throwing-
stick.   The first is the most general ; but the Barbados
use only the blow-pipe, the Moxos have abandoned the
bow and arrow for the lasso, and the Purupurus are distinguished from all their neighbours by using, not bows
and arrows, but the " palheta," or throwing-stick.   Again,
the Kaffirs have not generally adopted the bows and

[1] The ancient Egyptians had, and the Negroes of Niam Niam have,
iron crescents resembling boomerangs, which are thrown in war. But
these do not appear to possess the peculiar properties of the boomerang.

arrows of the Bushmen ; the Esquimaux have not acquired the art of making pottery from the North American Indians, nor the southern Columbian tribes from the northern Mexicans.

Many, again, of the ruder arts, as, for instance, the manufacture of pottery and of bows, are so useful, and at the same time, however ingenious in idea, so simple in execution, as to render it highly improbable that they would ever be lost when they had once been acquired. Yet we have seen that the New Zealanders and Kaffirs had no bows, and that none of the Polynesians had any knowledge of pottery ; though it is evident from their skill in other manufactures, and their general state of civilization, that they would have found no difficulty in the matter if the manner had once occurred to them. Again, "bolas" are a most effectual weapon, and there is certainly no difficulty in making them, yet the knowledge of them appears to be confined to the Patagonians and the Esquimaux. The art of pottery, on the contrary, sometimes has been, I believe, communicated by one race to another. Nevertheless, there are cases, even among existing races,[1] in which we seem to find indications of an independent discovery ; at any rate, in which the art is in a rudimentary stage.

On the whole, then, from a review of these and other similar facts which might have been mentioned, it seems to me most probable that many of the simpler weapons, implements, etc., have been invented independently by various savage tribes, although there are no doubt also cases in which they have been borrowed by one tribe from another.

The contrary opinion has been adopted by many writers on account of the undeniable similarity existing between the weapons used by savages in very different parts of the world. But however paradoxical it may sound, though the implements and weapons of savages are remarkably similar, they are at the same time curiously different. No doubt the necessaries of life are simple and

---

[1] See, for instance, p. 493.

similar all over the world. The materials also with which man has to deal are very much alike ; wood, bone, and to a certain extent stone, have everywhere the same properties. The obsidian flakes of the Aztecs resemble the flint flakes of our ancestors, not so much because the ancient Briton resembled the Aztec, as because the fracture of flint is like that of obsidian. So also the pointed bones used as awls are necessarily similar all over the world. Similarity exists, in fact, rather in the raw material than in the manufactured article, and some even of the simplest implements of stone are very different among different races. The adze-like hatchets of the South Sea Islanders are unlike those of the Australians or ancient Britons ; the latter again differ very much from the type which is characteristic of the Drift or Palæolithic Period.

Again, the habits and customs of savages, while presenting many remarkable similarities, which, as it seems to me, go far to prove the unity of the human race, still differ greatly, and thus give strong evidence of independent development. Many, indeed, of those differences which must have struck anyone in reading the preceding part of the chapter, follow evidently and directly from the external conditions in which different races are placed. The habits of an Esquimaux and a Hottentot could not possibly be similar. But let us take some act which is common to many races, and is susceptible of being accomplished in several ways. For instance, most savages live in part on the flesh of birds ; how is this obtained ? Generally with bows and arrows ; but while the Australians catch birds with the hand, or kill them with the simple spear or the boomerang, the Fuegians have both the sling and the bow, while the Esquimaux use a complex spear with several points, or a projectile which consists of a number of walrus-teeth fastened together by short pieces of string, and thus forming a kind of bolas. The northern tribes visited by Kane practised a different method. They caught large numbers of birds, especially little auks, in small nets, resembling landing-nets, with long ivory handles. Yet this very people were entirely ignorant of fishing.[1]

Take, again, the use made of the dog. At first, probably, the dog and the man hunted together,[2] the cunning of the one supplemented the speed of the other, and they shared the produce of their joint exertions. Gradually mind asserted its pre-eminence over matter, and the man became master. Then the dog was employed in other ways, less congenial to his nature. The Esquimaux forced him to draw the sledge ; the Chinook kept him for the sake of his wool ; the South Sea Islanders, having no game, bred the dog for food ; the Chonos Indians taught him to fish ; where tribes became shepherds, their dogs became shepherds also ; finally, it is recorded by Pliny that in ancient times troops of dogs were trained to serve in war. Even the ox, though less versatile than the dog, has been used for the first and the last two of these purposes.

Again, in obtaining fire, two principal methods are followed ; some savages, as for instance the Aleutians and Fuegians, using percussion, while others, as the South Sea Islanders, rub one piece of wood against another. The Aleutians rub two pieces of quartz with sulphur, and then strike them together, catching the sparks on dry grass.[3] Opinions are divided whether we have any trustworthy record of a people without the means of obtaining fire. It has been already mentioned (pp. 448, 453) that some of the Australians and Tasmanians, though acquainted with fire, did not know how to obtain it. In his history of the Ladrone Islands, Father Gobien asserts that fire, " an element of such universal use, was utterly unknown to them, till Magellan, provoked by their repeated thefts, burned one of their villages. When they saw their wooden houses blazing, they first thought the fire a beast which fed upon wood,

---

[1] Kane, *Arctic Explorations*, vol. ii. pp. 203, 243.
[2] The low American Wood Indians, however, used the dog rather as a watch-dog than as a hound.
[3] Bancroft, *Nat. Races of the Pacific States*, vol. i. p. 91.

and some of them who came too near being burnt, the
rest stood afar off, lest they should be devoured, or
poisoned, by the violent breathings of this terrible animal."
The fact is not mentioned in the original account of
Magellan's *Voyage*. Freycinet believes that the assertion
of Father Gobien is entirely without foundation. The
language, he says, of the inhabitants contains words for
fire, burning charcoal, oven, grilling, boiling, etc. ; and
even before the advent of the Europeans, pottery[1] was
well known. It is difficult, however, to get over the
distinct assertion made by Gobien, which moreover derives
some support from similar statements made by other
travellers. Thus Alvaro de Saavedra states that the
inhabitants of certain small islands in the Pacific, which
he called " Los Jardines," but which cannot now be satisfactorily determined, stood in terror of fire, because they
had never seen it.[2] Again, Wilkes tells us[3] that on the
island of Fakaafo, which he calls " Bowditch," " there was
no sign of places for cooking, nor any appearance of fire."
The natives also were very much alarmed when they saw
sparks struck from flint and steel. Here, at least, we
might have thought was a case beyond question or suspicion ; the presence of fire could hardly have escaped
observation ; the marks it leaves are very conspicuous.
If we cannot depend on such a statement as this, made
by an officer in the United States Navy, in the official
report of an expedition sent out especially for scientific
purposes, we may well be disheartened, and lose confidence in ethnological investigations. Yet the assertions
of Wilkes *are* questioned, and with much appearance of
justice, by Mr Tylor.[4] In the *Ethnography of the
United States Exploring Expedition*, Hale gives a list
of Fakaafo words, in which we find *afi* for " fire." This
is evidently the same word as the New Zealand *ahi* ; but
as it denotes light and heat, as well as fire, we might
suppose that it thus found its way into the Fakaafo

[1] *L.c.*, vol. ii. p. 166.   [2] *Hakluyt Soc.*, 1862, p. 178.
[4] *United States Expl. Exped.*, vol. v. p. 18.
[3] *Early History of Mankind*, p. 230.

vocabulary. I should not, therefore, attribute to this argument quite so much force as does Mr Tylor. It is, however, evident that Captain Wilkes did not perceive the importance of the observation, or he would certainly have taken steps to determine the question ; and as Hale, in his special work on the Ethnology of the Expedition, does not say a word on the subject, it is clear he had no idea that the inhabitants of Fakaafo exhibited such an interesting peculiarity. The fact, if established, would be most important ; but it cannot be said to be satisfactorily proved that there is at present, or has been within historical times, any race of men entirely ignorant of fire. It is at least certain that as far back as the earliest Swiss lake-villages and Danish shell-mounds the use of fire was well known in Europe.

On the other hand, as already mentioned, some of the Tasmanian and Australian tribes, and of the Andaman Islanders, though well acquainted with the use of fire, know no way of kindling it. Consequently, they take great pains to keep it always burning, and, if by any mischance it should be extinguished, are obliged to get a fresh light from some neighbouring tribe.

There is, again, scarcely any conceivable way in which the dead could be disposed of which has not been adopted in some part of the world. Among some races the corpse is simply buried ; by others it is burned. Some of the North American Indians expose their dead on scaffolds in the branches of trees. Some tribes deposit them in sacred rivers ; others in the sea. Among the Sea Dyaks, the dead chief is placed in his war canoe, with his favourite weapons and principal property, and is thus turned adrift. Other tribes gave their dead to be food for wild beasts ; and others preferred to eat them themselves. Some Brazilian tribes *drink* the dead.[1] The Tarianas and Tucanos, and some other tribes, about a month after the funeral, disinter the corpse, which is then much decomposed, and put it in a great pan or oven over the fire, till all the volatile parts are driven off with a most

[1] Wallace, *Travels on the Amazon*, p. 498.

horrible odour, leaving only a black carbonaceous mass, which is pounded into a fine powder, and mixed in several large conches of caxiri ; this is drunk by the assembled company, under the full belief that the virtues of the deceased will thus be transmitted to the drinkers. The Cobeus also drink the ashes of the dead in the same manner.

Indeed, if there are two possible ways of doing a thing, we may be sure that some tribes will prefer one, and some the other. It seems natural to us that descent should go in the male line ; but there are very many races in which it is traced from the mother, not the father. The husband or father seems to us to be the natural head of the family ; in Tahiti the reverse is the case, and the son enters at once into the property and titles of his father, who then holds them only as a guardian or trustee ; so that among this extraordinary people, not the father, but the son, is in reality the head of the family. So also in Australia, the father is called after the son, not the son after the father. At Cape York and in the neighbouring islands the youngest son has a double share.[1] Among the New Zealanders, and various other races, including some districts in our own country, the *youngest* son succeeds to the property of the father.[2] Among the Wanyameuzi, property descends not to the legitimate, but to the illegitimate children.[3] There are many races in which those holding certain relationships are forbidden to talk to one another, an extraordinary superstition which, as we have seen (p. 463), reaches its climax among the Fijians.

It seems natural to us that after child-birth the woman should keep her bed, and that as far as possible the husband should relieve her for a time from the labours and cares of life. In this, at least, one might have thought that all nations would be alike. Yet it is not so. Among the Caribs the father, on the birth of a child, took to his

---

[1] M'Gillivray, *Voyage of H.M.S. " Rattlesnake,"* vol. ii. p. 28.
[2] *New Zealand and its Aborigines*, p. 26.
[3] Burton's *Lake Regions of Africa*, p. 198.

hammock, and placed himself in the hands of the doctor, the mother meanwhile going about her work as usual. A similar custom has been observed on the mainland of South America, among the Abipones, Mundrucus, Fuegians, etc. ; among the Arawaks of Surinam ; in the Chinese province of West Yunnan ; among the Dyaks of Borneo, and the Esquimaux of Greenland. It is mentioned by Xenophon as occurring in Asia Minor, and by Strabo among the Iberians ; is found even in the present day among the Basques, among whom we are told that in some of the valleys the " women rise immediately after child-birth, and attend to the duties of the household, while the husband goes to bed, taking the baby with him, and thus receives the neighbours' compliments." The same habit has been noticed also in the south of France ; according to Diodorus Siculus, it prevailed at his time in Corsica ; and finally, it "is said still to exist in some cantons of Bearn, where it is called *faire la couvade*."

Again, the love of life—the dread of death—are among the strongest of our feelings. " Everything that a man hath he will give in exchange for his life." This is true, but by no means universally so. According to Azara, the Indians of Paraguay have a great indifference to death ; and we have already seen that this is the case with the Fijians ; while Burton makes a similar statement as regards the Negroes of Dahomey. Among the Chinese it is said that a man condemned to death, if permitted to do so, may always secure a substitute on payment of a moderate sum of money ; and a coffin is regarded as a most appropriate present for an aged relative.

Again, the sounds of which language is constituted differ extremely in different parts of the world. The clicks of the Hottentots are a striking illustration of this. The Hurons did not use the labials ; the Indians of Port au Français in Columbia, acccording to M. de Lamanon,[1] make no use of the consonants b, f, x, j, d, p, or v. The

---

[1] *Voyage de la " Perouse*," vol. ii. p. 211.

Peruvian language wanted the letters *b*, *d*, *f*, *g*, *s*, and *x*.[1]
The Australians did not use the sound conveyed by our
letter *s*.[2] Many of the Negroes have no *r*. The Fijians
do not use the letter *c*, the Somo-Somo dialect has no *k*,
that of Rakiraki and other parts no *t*.[3] The Society
Islanders and Australians exclude both *s* and *c*.[4] In representing the New Zealand language, the missionaries
found themselves able to discard no less than thirteen
letters, namely *b*, *c*, *d*, *f*, *g*, *j*, *l*, *q*, *s*, *v*, *x*, *y*, and *z*.[5]
Schaaffhausen observes that the labials are especially
difficult to prognathous races.

Shortland asserts that whistling was unknown in New
Zealand.[6] Even the symbols by which the feelings are
expressed are very different in different races. Kissing
appears to us the natural expression of affection. " 'Tis
certain," says Steele, " nature was its author, and it began
with the first courtship." On the contrary, it was entirely
unknown to the Tahitians, the New Zealanders,[7] the
Papuans,[8] and the aborigines of Australia ; nor was it in
use among the Somals,[9] or the Esquimaux.[10] The hill
tribes of Chittagong do not say " Kiss me," but " Smell
me." [11] The Malays,[12] Fijians,[13] Tongans, and many other
Polynesians, always sit down when speaking to a superior ;
the inhabitants of Mallicollo testify " admiration by hissing
like a goose," [14] the sound being perhaps like our " hush,"
a call for silence, and hence a mark of interest ; the mode
of showing respect among the Todas of the Neilgherry
hills is by raising the open right hand to the face, resting

[1] *Garcilasso de la Vega*, Markham's Translation, Author's Preface,
p. x.
[2] Freycinet, vol. ii. p. 757 ; D'Urville, vol. i. pp. 188, 199, 481.
[3] Williams, *Figi and the Figians*, vol. i. p. v. 257.
[4] Ellis, *Polynesian Researches*, vol. i. p. 77.
[5] Brown, *New Zealand and its Aborigines*, p. 100.
[6] *Traditions of the New Zealanders*, p. 134.
[7] D'Urville, vol. ii. p. 561 ; *Voyage of the " Novara*,*"* vol. iii. p. 106.
[8] Freycinet, vol. ii. p. 56.
[9] Burton's *First Footsteps in Africa*, p. 123.
[10] Lyon's *Journal*, p. 353.
[11] Lewin, *Hill Tribes of Chittagong*, p. 46.
[12] Marsden, *Memoirs of a Malayan Family*, p. 37.
[13] Williams, *Figi and the Figians*, vol. i. p. 38.
[14] Cook's *Second Voyage*, vol. ii. p. 36.

the thumb on the bridge of the nose ; at Vatavulu [1] it is respectful to turn one's back on a superior, especially in addressing him.   The same custom occurs [2] in Congo ; Denham found it [3] in Central Africa ; and Speke [4] among the Wahuma in the east.   The people of Iddah shake their clenched fist,[5] while on the White Nile and in Ashantee they spit on you as a compliment.   According to Freycinet, tears were regarded in the Sandwich Islands as a sign of happiness ; [6] and some of the Esquimaux pull noses as a token of respect.[7]   Spix and Martius assure us that blushing was unknown among the Brazilian Indians ; and that only after long intercourse with Europeans does a change of colour become in them any indication of mental emotion.[8]

Again, we find the most striking differences of feeling in the matter of clothing.   The Turk thinks it highly improper for a woman to show her face.   The sculptures on early Indian temples show that a race may attain to a considerable degree of civilization without perceiving any necessity whatever for clothing.   This is the case with the women listening to Buddha while preaching, and even Buddha's wife, and Maya his mother,[9] are habitually so represented ; indeed, Mr Fergusson does not hesitate to say that "before the Mahomedan conquest nudity in India conveyed no sense of indecency."

The ideas of virtue also differ extremely.   Neither faith, hope, nor charity enters into the virtues of a savage.   The Sichuana language contains no expression for thanks ;   the Algonquin had no word for love ; the Tinnè no word for beloved ; mercy was with the North American Indians a mistake, and peace an evil ; theft, says Catlin, they "call capturing" ; humility is an idea

---

[1] *Figi and the Figians,* vol. i. p. 154.
[2] Astley's *Voyage and Travels,* vol. iii. p. 72.
[3] *Travels and Discoveries in Africa,* vol. ii. p. 27, vol. iii. p. 15.
[4] *Discovery of the Source of the Nile,* p. 206.
[5] Allan and Thompson, *Expedition to the Niger,* vol. i. p. 290.
[6] *L.c.,* vol. ii. pp. 542, 589.   [7] Ross, *Baffin's Bay,* p. 118.
[8] Vol. i. p. 376.
[9] See, for instance, Fergusson's *Tree and Serpent Worship.* Pl. lxxiv. and *passim.*

which they could not comprehend. Among the Koupouees the greatest misconduct, says Major M'Culloch, " is to forgive an enemy, the first virtue is revenge."[1]

Among the ancient Greeks, we see in Homer that the deceitful cunning of Ulysses was looked upon with approval.

"Is a man to starve," said an African, indignantly, to Capt. Burton, "while his sister has children whom she might sell?" This sentiment reads at first like the acme of selfishness, but this impression would perhaps be unjust. Marsden records a Sumatran Malay as saying, in admiration of an European watch, "Is it not fitting that such as we should be slaves to people who have the ingenuity to invent, and the skill to construct, so wonderful a machine?"[2]

Chastity before marriage was not reckoned as a virtue by the New Zealanders,[3] the hill tribes of North Aracan,[4] or by many of the ruder inhabitants of Northern and Central America;[5] it was disapproved of, though for very different reasons, by some of the Brazilian tribes, by the inhabitants of the Ladrones, and by the Andamaners. According to Ulloa,[6] the Brazilians do not approve of chastity in an unmarried woman, regarding it as a proof that she can have nothing attractive about her. The inhabitants of the Ladrones,[7] and of the Andaman Islands,[8] come to the same conclusion ; in the latter case, however, for a different reason, regarding it as a proof of selfishness and pride. On the other hand, many races absolutely prohibit a man from marrying a woman of his own family name ; the Abipones thought it a sin for a man to pronounce his own name ; the Tahitians thought

---

[1] *Selection from the Records of the Government of India*, by Major W. M'Culloch, p. 75.
[2] *History of Sumatra*, p. 205.
[3] Brown, *New Zealand and its Aborigines*, p. 35.
[4] St John, *Jour. Anthr. Inst.* 1872, p. 239.
[5] Franklin's *Journeys to the Polar Seas*, vol. i. p. 132 ; Dunn's *Oregon Territory*, p. 92 ; Bancroft, *Native Races of the Pacific States*, vol. i. pp. 123, 242.
[6] Pinkerton, vol. xiv. p. 521.   [7] Freycinet, vol. ii. p. 370.
[8] *Trans. Ethn. Soc.*, New Ser., vol. ii. p. 35.

it very wrong to eat in company, and were horrified at an English sailor, who carried some food in a basket on his head. This prejudice was also shared by the New Zealanders,[1] while the Fijians, who were habitual cannibals, who regarded mercy as a weakness, and cruelty as a virtue, fully believed that a woman who was not tattooed in an orthodox manner during life, could not possibly hope for happiness after death. This curious idea is also found among the Esquimaux. Hall tells us that they tattoo "from principle, the theory being that the lines thus made will be regarded in the next world as a sign of goodness."[2] It seems to the Veddahs the most natural thing in the world that a man should marry his younger sister, but marriage with an elder one is as repugnant to them as to us. Among the Friendly Islanders the chief priest was considered too holy to be married ; but he had the right to take as many concubines as he pleased ; and even the chiefs dared not refuse their daughters to him. In Western Africa the women of the reigning families might have as many lovers as they wished, but were forbidden to degrade themselves by marriage. Among the natives of New South Wales, though the women wore no clothes, it was thought indecent for young girls to go naked.[3]

Many savage races think it wrong for a woman to have twins ; among the Ibos of Eastern Africa, for instance, in such a case the children were exposed to wild beasts, and the mother was driven out of society.[4] There also it is thought unlucky to cut the upper teeth before the lower ones,[5] and "You cut your top teeth first," is the bitterest of insults. I cannot indeed but think that the differences observable in savage tribes are even more remarkable than the similarities.

---

[1] D'Urville, vol. ii. p. 533.

[2] *Life with the Esquimaux*, vol. ii. p. 315.

[3] D'Urville, vol. i. p. 471 ; *Voyage of the "Rattlesnake,"* vol. i. p. 49.

[4] Burton's *Lake Regions of Africa*, p. 90. See, for other instances of this, my *Origin of Civilization*, 2nd ed., p. 25.

[5] This idea is, I find to my surprise, also prevalent among our own nurses.

In endeavouring to estimate the moral character of savages, we must remember not only that their standard of right and wrong was, and is, in many cases, very different from ours, but also that, according to the statements of travellers, some of them can hardly be regarded as responsible beings, and have not attained to any notions, however faulty and undefined, of moral rectitude.[1] But where such notions do exist, they differ widely, as we have seen, from our own ; and it would open up too large a question to inquire whether, in all cases, our standard is the correct one.

In considering the character of women belonging to savage or semi-savage races, we must also remember that savages often regard the white men as beings of a superior order. Thus M. du Chaillu tells us that some of the African savages looked upon him as a superior being ; and the South Sea Islanders worshipped Captain Cook as a deity. Even when they had killed him, and cut him into small pieces, the inhabitants of Owhyhee fully expected him to reappear, and frequently asked " what he would do to them on his return." [2] However absurd and extravagant such a belief may at first sight appear, it must be admitted that it is in many respects very natural. Savages can only raise their minds to the conception of a being a few degrees superior to themselves, and Captain Cook was more powerful, wiser, and, we may add, more virtuous than most of their so-called " Deities." Under these circumstances, although it must be admitted that the chastity of the women is not, as a general rule, much regarded among savages, we must not too severely condemn them on this account. It is not surprising that any connection with white men is regarded rather as an honour than as a disgrace : the Europeans hold, in fact, almost the same position in public estimation as did the amorous deities of ancient mythology.

Again, with savages, as with children, *time* appears

---

[1] See, for instance, Burchell, vol. i. p. 461.
[2] *Cook's Voyage to the Pacific Ocean*, by Capt. King, F.R.S., vol. iii. p. 69.

longer than it does to us, and a temporary marriage as natural and honourable as one that is permanent. Hospitality, again, is frequently carried so far that it is thought wrong to withhold from a guest anything that might contribute to his comfort, and unless therefore he was provided with a temporary wife, hospitality would be regarded as incomplete. This custom is found throughout North America and the South Sea Islands, among the Abyssinians, Bedouins, Kaffirs, Patagonians, and other races. Among the Esquimaux it is considered a great mark of friendship for two men to exchange wives for a day or two. It has been already mentioned that a Kandyan chief, described by Mr Bailey, was quite scandalized at the idea of having only one wife. It was, he said, "just like monkeys." When Captain Cook was in New Zealand, his companions contracted many temporary marriages with the Maori women ; these were arranged in a formal and decent manner, and were regarded, by the New Zealanders at any rate, as perfectly regular and innocent.[1] Regnard[2] assures us that the Lapps preferred to marry a girl that had had a child by a white man, thinking "that because a man whom they believe to be possessed of a better taste than themselves has been anxious to give marks of his love for a girl of their country, she must therefore be possessed of some secret merit." Even in recent years, Lady Duff Gordon told us, in her paper on the Cape,[3] that "there are no so-called 'morals' among the coloured people, and how or why should there ? It is an honour to one of these girls to have a child by a white man." Taking all these facts into consideration, the intercourse which has taken place between Europeans and women of lower tribes must not, I think, be too severely condemned, or rather the blame ought to fall on us and not on them. But, even among savages themselves, we must admit that female virtue is, in many cases, but slightly regarded ; as,

---

[1] Cook's *First Voyage*, vol. iii. p. 450.
[2] Pinkerton, *Journey to Lapland*, vol. i. p. 166.
[3] *Vacation Tourists*, 1863, p. 178.

indeed, is but natural when women themselves are looked upon as little better than domestic animals. Among many tribes, for instance the South Sea Islanders and the Esquimaux, indecent dances are not only common, but are countenanced by women of the highest rank, to whom it does not appear to occur that there is any harm or impropriety in them. Judged by our standards, these facts are very dreadful ; but we must remember they did not entail on savages the same fatal consequences as with us ; and before we condemn them too severely, let us remember our own literature and our own morality, even in the eighteenth century.

The harsh, not to say cruel treatment of women, which is almost universal among savages, is one of the deepest stains upon their character. They regard the weaker sex as beings of an inferior order, as mere domestic drudges. Nor are the labours and sufferings of the women sweetened by any great affection on the part of those for whom they toil. We have already seen that the Algonquins had no word for "love" in their language, and that the Tinnè Indians had no equivalent for "dear" or "beloved." Captain Lefroy[1] says : "I endeavoured to put this intelligibly to Nannette, by supposing such an expression as 'ma chère femme ; ma chère fille.' When at length she understood it, her reply was (with great emphasis), 'I' disent jamais ça ; i' disent ma femme, ma fille.' " Spix and Martius[2] tell us that among the Brazilian tribes the father has scarcely any, the mother only an instinctive, affection for the child. There can be no doubt that, as an almost universal rule, savages are cruel ; but we must remember that they are less sensitive to pain than those who spend much of their time indoors, and that in many cases they inflict upon themselves also the most horrible tortures.

Savages may be likened to children, and the comparison is not only correct, but also highly instructive. Many naturalists consider that the early condition of the in-

[1] Richardson's *Arctic Expedition*, vol. ii. p. 24.
[2] *Reise*, vol. i. p. 381.

dividual indicates that of the race,—that the best test of
the affinities of a species are the stages through which it
passes. So also it is in the case of man ; the life of each
individual is an epitome of the history of the race, and
the gradual development of the child illustrates that of
the species. Hence the importance of the similarity
between savages and children. Savages, like children,
have no steadiness of purpose. Speaking of the Dogrib
Indians, we found, says Richardson,[1] " by experience,
that however high the reward they expected to receive
on reaching their destination, they could not be depended
on to carry letters. A slight difficulty, the prospect of a
banquet on venison, or a sudden impulse to visit some
friend, were sufficient to turn them aside for an indefinite length of time." Even among the comparatively
civilized South Sea Islanders this childishness was very
apparent. " Their tears indeed,[2] like those of children,
were always ready to express any passion that was strongly
excited, and like those of children they also appear to be
forgotten as soon as shed." D'Urville also mentions
that Tai-wanga, a New Zealand chief, cried like a child
because the sailors spoilt his favourite cloak by powdering
it with flour.[3] " It is not," says Cook, " indeed strange
that the sorrows of these artless people should be transient,
any more than that their passions should be suddenly
and strongly expressed ; what they feel they have never
been taught either to disguise or suppress ; and having
no habits of thinking which perpetually recall the past
and anticipate the future, they are affected by all the
changes of the passing hour, and reflect the colour of the
time, however frequently it may vary ; they have no
project which is to be pursued from day to day, the
subject of unremitted anxiety and solicitude, that first
rushes into the mind when they awake in the morning,
and is last dismissed when they sleep at night. Yet if

[1] *Arctic Expedition*, vol. ii. p. 23.
[2] Cook's *First Voyage*, p. 103.
[3] D'Urville, vol. ii. p. 398. See also Burton's *Lake Regions of Central Africa*, p. 332.

we admit that they are upon the whole happier than we, we must admit that the child is happier than the man, and that we are losers by the perfection of our nature, the increase of our knowledge, and the enlargement of our views."

We all know the difficulty which children find in pronouncing certain sounds : *r* and *l*, for instance, they constantly confound. This is the case also among the Sandwich Islanders and in the Ladrones, according to Freycinet ;[1] in Vanikoro,[2] among the Dammaras ;[3] and in the Tonga Islands.[4]

Mr Darwin observed that the Fuegians had great difficulty in comprehending an alternative.

Savages, again, have a great tendency to form words by re-duplication, which also is characteristic of childhood among civilized races.

Again, some of the most brutal acts which have been recorded against them are to be regarded less as instances of deliberate cruelty, than of a childish thoughtlessness and impulsiveness. A striking instance of this is recorded by Byron in his narrative of the *Loss of the "Wager."* A cacique of the Chonos, who was nominally a Christian, had been out with his wife to fish for sea-eggs, and, having had little success, returned in a bad humour. " A little boy of theirs, about three years old, whom they appeared to be doatingly fond of, watching for his father and mother's return, ran into the surf to meet them ; the father handed a basket of eggs to the child, which being too heavy for him to carry, he let it fall, upon which the father jumped out of the canoe, and, catching the boy up in his arms, dashed him with the utmost violence against the stones. The poor little creature lay motionless and bleeding, and in that condition was taken up by the mother, but died soon after."[5]

In fact, we may fairly sum up this part of the question in a few words by saying, as the most general conclusion

---

[1] Vol. ii. pp. 260, 519. [2] Vol. v. p. 218.
[3] Galton, *Tropical South Africa*, p. 181.
[4] Mariner's *Tonga Islands*, vol. i. p. 30.
[5] Byron's *Loss of the " Wager "* ; Kerr's *Voyages*, vol. xvii. p. 374.

which can be arrived at, that savages have the character
of children with the passions and strength of men. No
doubt different races of savages differ very much in
character. An Esquimaux and a Fijian, for instance,
have little in common. But after making every possible
allowance for savages, it must I think be admitted that
they are inferior, morally as well as in other respects, to
the more civilized races. There is indeed no atrocious
crime, no vice recorded by any traveller, which might not
be paralleled in Europe. But that which is with us the
exception, is with them the rule ; that which with us is
condemned by the general verdict of society, and is
confined to the uneducated and vicious, is among savages
passed over almost without condemnation, and treated as
a mere matter of course. In Tahiti, for instance, the
missionaries considered that " not less than two-thirds of
the children were murdered by their parents."

If we now turn to the mental differences between
civilized and uncivilized races, we shall find them very
strongly marked. Speaking of a Bushman tribe, Burchell
observes that " whether capable of reflection or not, these
individuals never exerted it." [1]   The Rev. T. Dove describes the Tasmanians as distinguished " by the absence
of all moral views and impressions. Every idea bearing
on our origin and destination as rational beings seems to
have been erased from their breasts." [2]   It would be easy
to fill a volume with the evidence of excessive stupidity
recorded by different travellers. It may be perhaps
thought that these were rather instances of individual
dulness, than any indication of a national characteristic ;
but in the nature and capacity of a language we find a
test and measure of the higher minds in a nation. Unfortunately, however, travellers have found it difficult
enough to obtain vocabularies of the words in use ; and
it is far less easy to collect information as to those which
they do not possess. Yet there are not a few cases in
which this has been done. I have already mentioned the

---

[1] *L.c.*, vol. i. p. 461.
[2] *Tasmanian Journal of Natural Science*, vol. i. p. 249.

deficiency of some North American languages in terms of endearment ; this fact suggests a melancholy condition of the domestic relations, but it may here be referred to again as an evidence of a low mental, as well as moral, condition. What Spix and Martius tell us about the Brazilian tribes[1] appears also to be true of many, if not of most, savage races. Their vocabulary is rich, and they have separate names for the different parts of the body, for all the different animals and plants with which they are acquainted ; for everything, in fact, which they can see and handle. Yet they are entirely deficient in words for abstract ideas ; they have no expressions for colour, tone, sex, genus, spirit, etc.

The Abipones have no such words as man, body, place, time, never, ever, everywhere, etc. ; nor such a verb as " to be." They cannot say, " I am an Abipon," but only, " I Abipon."[2] The Malay language, also, according to Crawfurd, is very deficient in abstract terms. It contains a word for each colour, but no term for colour itself. The St Petersburg Bible Society endeavoured some years ago to translate the Lord's Prayer and the Ten Commandments into the language of the Tschuktschi, but " partly from the language being entirely deficient in words to express new and abstract ideas, and partly for want of letters to convey the variety of strange and uncouth sounds of which the language itself consists, the translation was wholly unintelligible."[3]

So, again, the Tasmanians had no word for a tree, though they had a name for each species ; nor could they express " qualities, such as hard, soft, warm, cold, long, short, round, etc. ; for 'hard' they would say 'like a stone' ; for 'tall' they would say 'long legs,' etc. ; and for 'round' they said 'like a ball,' 'like the moon,' and so on."[4] According to the missionaries,[5] Fuegians have " no abstract terms for expressing the truths of our

[1] *Reise in Brasilien*, vol. i. p. 385.   [2] Dobritzhoffer, vol. ii. p. 183.
[3] Wrangell's *Siberia and Polar Sea*, p. 121.
[4] Milligan, *Proc. Roy. Society, Tasmania*, vol. iii. p. 281.
[5] *The Voice of Pity*, vol. x. p. 152.

religion " ; and among the North American languages,
" a term sufficiently general to denote an ' oak-tree ' is
exceptional." [1]   Even the comparatively civilized inhabitants of Tahiti had, according to Forster, " no proper
words for expressing abstract ideas." [2]

The names for numbers are, perhaps, the best, or, at
least, the most easily applicable test of mental condition
among the lower races of man.   We have seen that the
Esquimaux can only with difficulty count up to ten, and
that some individuals cannot go beyond five.   The
Abipones [3] can only express three numbers in proper
words.   The Dammaras " in practice, whatever they may
possess in their language, certainly use no numeral
greater than three.   When they wish to express four,
they take to their fingers, which are to them as formidable
instruments of calculation as a sliding rule is to an English
schoolboy.   They puzzle very much after five, because
no spare hand remains to grasp and secure the fingers
that are required for units." [4]   Mr Crawfurd, to whom
we are indebted for an interesting paper on this subject, [5]
has examined no less than thirty Australian languages,
and it appears that none of the tribes in that vast continent count beyond four.   According to Mr Scott Nind,
indeed, the numerals used by the natives of King George's
Sound reach up to five ; but the last is merely the word
" many."   The Cape Yorkers (Australia) can hardly be
said to go beyond two ; their numerals are as follows :

One	*Netat.*
Two	*Naes.*
Three	*Naes-netat.*
Four	*Naes-naes.*
Five	*Naes-naes-netat.*
Six	*Naes-naes-naes.*

The Brazilian Indians also count only up to three ; for
any higher number they use the word " many." [6]

[1] Latham, *Varieties of Man*, p. 375.   [2] *L.c.*, p. 403.
[3] Dobritzhoffer, vol. ii. p. 169.   [4] Galton's *Tropical Africa*, p. 33.
[5] *Ethnological Society's Transactions*, New Series, vol. ii. p. 84.
[6] Spix and Martius, vol. i. p. 387.

Again, in the state of their religious conceptions, still more in the absence of religious conceptions, we get another proof of extreme mental inferiority. The question has been frequently discussed whether there is any race of men so degraded as to be entirely without a religion—without some idea of a deity.[1] The conclusion to be arrived at depends, as it seems to me, very much on the meaning which we ascribe to the term of "religion." If a mere fear of the unknown, if a more or less vague belief in witchcraft, is to be regarded as a religion, it would, I think, be difficult to refute this assertion. But if any higher estimate of religion is adopted, then, so far from this being true, the very reverse is the case. Many, we might almost say all, of the most savage races are, according to the nearly universal testimony of travellers, in this condition.[2]

According to Spix and Martius,[3] Bates and Wallace, some of the Brazilian Indians were entirely without religion. Burmeister confirms this statement, and, in the list of the principal tribes of the valley of the Amazons, published by the Hakluyt Society, the Chunchos are stated "to have no religion whatever," and we are told that the Curetus "have no idea of a Supreme Being." The same is said of the Toupinambas. Bates[4] tells us "that none of the tribes on the Upper Amazons have an idea of a Supreme Being, and consequently have no word to express it in their languages." Azara also makes the same statement as regards many of the South American tribes visited by him.[5] The South American Indians of the Gran Chaco are said by the missionaries to have "no religious or idolatrous belief or worship whatever ; neither

---

[1] I have discussed this question at greater length in my *Marriage, Totemism, and Religion : an Answer to Critics*, Longmans, 1911.

[2] Mr Lang has attempted to show (*The Making of Religion*) that even the lowest races of men believe in an "omnipotent, moral, and eternal Father and Judge." Mr Hartland in *Folk Lore* for Dec. 1898 has, I think, completely replied to his arguments.

[3] *Reise in Brasilien*, vol. i. p. 379.

[4] *Life in the Amazons*, vol. ii. p. 162.

[5] *Voyages dans l'Amér. Mérid.*, vol. ii. pp. 3, 14, 33, 51, 60, 76, 80, 81, 84, 90, 138, 160, 164, 166.

do they possess any idea of God or of a Supreme Being. They make no distinction between right and wrong, and have, therefore, neither fear nor hope of any present or future punishment or reward, nor any mysterious terror of some supernatural power, whom they might seek to assauge by sacrifices or superstitious rites."[1]

Father Baegert, who lived as a missionary among the Indians of California for seventeen years, affirms that "idols, temples, religious worship, or ceremonies were unknown to them, and they neither believed in the true and only God, nor adored false deities";[2] and M. de la Perouse also says that they "had no knowledge of a God, or of a future state." Colden, who had ample means of judging, assures us that the celebrated "five nations" of Canada "had no public worship nor any word for God"; and Hearne, who lived amongst the Northern American Indians for years, and was perfectly acquainted with their habits and language, says the same of some tribes on Hudson's Bay.

In the *Voyage of "l'Astrolabe,"* it is stated that the natives of the Samoan and Solomon Islands, in the Pacific, had no religion, and in the *Voyage of the "Novara,"* the same is said of the Caroline Islanders. The Samoans "have neither morals, nor temples, nor altars, nor offerings, and consequently none of the sanguinary rites, observed at the other groups. In consequence of this the Samoans were considered an impious race by their neighbours; and their impiety became proverbial with the people of Rarotonga, for, when upbraiding a person who neglected the worship of the gods, they would call him "a godless Samoan."[3] On Damood Island, between Australia and New Guinea, Jukes could find no "traces of any religious belief or observance."[4] Duradawan, a sepoy who lived some time with the Andaman Islanders, maintained that they had no religion, and Dr Mouatt believes his statements to be

---

[1] *Voice of Pity*, vol. ix. p. 220.
[2] See Mr Rau's translation, *Smithsonian Contrib.* 1863-64, p. 390.
[3] *Missionary Enterprises*, p. 464.
[4] Juke's *Voyage of the "Fly,"* vol. i. p. 164.

correct.[1] Portman, who lived so long with them, and studied them so lovingly, makes the same statement as regards the native of the Lesser Andamans.[2] Some of the Australian tribes also are said to have no religion.[3] In the Pellew Islands, Wilson found no religious buildings, nor any sign of religion.

Mr Wallace, who had excellent opportunities for judging, and whose merits as an observer no one can question, tells us that among the people of Wanumbai, in the Aru Islands, he could find no trace of a religion ;[4] adding, however, that he was but a short time among them.

The Yenadies and the Villees, according to Dr Shortt, are entirely without any belief in a future state ;[5] and again, Hooker tells us that the Lepchas of Northern India have no religion. Captain Grant could find " no distinct form of religion " in some of the comparatively civilized tribes visited by him.[6] According to Burchell, the Bachapins (Kaffirs) had no form of worship or religion.[7] They thought " that everything made itself, and that trees and herbage grew by their own will." They had no belief in a good deity, but some vague idea of an evil being. Indeed, the first idea of a god is almost always as an evil spirit.

Speaking of the Foulahs of Wassoulo, in Central Africa, Caillié states : " I tried to discover whether they had any religion of their own ; whether they worshipped fetishes, or the sun, moon, or stars ; but I could never perceive any religious ceremony amongst them."[8] Again, he says of the Bainbaras that, " like the people of Wassoulo, they have no religion,"[9] adding, however, that they have great faith in charms.

---

[1] *Trans. Ethn. Soc.*, vol. ii. p. 45.
[2] *J. Geog. Soc.*, Sep. 1888.
[3] Collins' *English Colony in New South Wales*, p. 354.
[4] *The Malayan Archipelago*, vol. ii. p. 280.
[5] *Proceedings of Madras Government*, Revenue Department. May 1864.
[6] *A Walk across Africa*, p. 145.
[7] *Travels in South Africa*, vol. ii. p. 550.
[8] *Travels to Timbuctoo*, vol. i. p. 303.   [9] *L.c.*, p. 375.

Burton also states that some of the tribes in the lake districts of Central Africa " admit neither God, nor angel, nor devil." [1] Speaking of Hottentots, Le Vaillant says : [2] " Je n'y ai vu aucune trace de religion, rien qui approche même de l'idée d'un être vengeur et rémunérateur. J'ai vécu assez longtemps avec eux, chez eux aux sein de leurs déserts paisibles ; j'ai fait, avec ces braves humains, des voyages dans des régions fort éloignées ; nulle part je n'ai rencontré rien qui ressemble à la religion." Livingstone mentions that on one occasion, after talking to a Bushman for some time, as he supposed, about the Deity, he found that the savage thought he was speaking about Sekomi, the principal chief of the district.

Speaking of the Esquimaux, Ross says : " Ervick, being the senior of the first party that came on board, was judged to be the most proper person to question on the subject of religion. I directed Sacheuse to ask him if he had any knowledge of a Supreme Being ; but after trying every word used in his own language to express it, he could not make him understand what he meant. It was distinctly ascertained that he did not worship the sun, moon, stars, or any image or living creature. When asked what the sun or moon was for, he said to give light. He had no knowledge or idea how he came into being, or of a future state ; but said that when he died he would be put into the ground. Having fully ascertained that he had no idea of a beneficent Supreme Being, I proceeded, through Sacheuse, to inquire if he believed in an evil spirit ; but he could not be made to understand what it meant. . . . He was positive that in this incantation he did not receive assistance from anything, nor could he be made to understand what a good or an evil spirit meant." [3]

In some cases travellers have arrived at these views very much to their own astonishment. Thus Father Dobritzhoffer says : " Theologians agree in denying that any man in possession of his reason can, without a crime,

---

[1] *Trans. Ethn. Soc.*, New Ser., vol. i. p. 323.
[2] *Voyages dans l'Afrique*, vol. i. p. 93.
[3] Ross's *Voyage of Discovery to the Arctic Regions*, p. 127.

remain ignorant of God for any length of time. This opinion I warmly defended in the University of Cordoba, where I finished the four years' course of theology begun at Grätz, in Styria. But what was my astonishment when, on removing from thence to a colony of Abipones, I found that the whole language of these savages does not contain a single word which expresses God or a divinity. To instruct them in religion it was necessary to borrow the Spanish word for God, and insert into the catechism ' Dios ecnam caogerik,' ' God, the creator of things.' " [1]

Canon Callaway, in his *Religious System of the Amazulu Kaffirs*, agrees [2] with Casalis, Arbousset, Vanderkemp, and Moffat, that they have " scarcely any notion of a Deity, if any."

We have already observed a case of this kind in Kolben, who, in spite of the assertions of the natives themselves, felt quite sure that certain dances must be of a religious character, " let the Hottentots say what they will." Again, Mr Matthews, who went out to act as a missionary among the Fuegians, but was soon obliged to abandon the hopeless task, observed only one act " which could be supposed devotional." He sometimes, we are told, " heard a great howling or lamentation about sunrise in the morning ; and upon asking Jemmy Button what occasioned the outcry, he could obtain no satisfactory answer ; the boy only saying, ' People very sad, cry very much.' " This appears so natural and sufficient an explanation, that why the outcry should be " supposed devotional," I must confess myself unable to see. Once more, Sir J. D. Hooker states that the Khasias, an Indian tribe, had no religion. Col. Yule,[3] on the contrary, says that they have ; but he admits that breaking hens' eggs is " the principal part of their religious practice." But if most travellers have expected to find a religion everywhere, and have been convinced, almost against their

[1] *L.c.*, vol. ii. p. 57. See also p. 64.
[2] Callaway, *Religious System of the Amazulu*, p. 124.
[3] Yule, *On the Khasia Hills and People*, p. 18.

will, that the reverse is the case, it is quite possible that
there may have been others who have too hastily denied
the existence of a religion among the tribes they visited.
However this may be, those who assert that even the
lowest savages believe in a Supreme Deity, affirm that
which is entirely contrary to the evidence. The direct
testimony of travellers on this point is indirectly corroborated by their other statements. How, for instance,
can a people who are unable to count their own fingers,
possibly raise their mind so far as to realize the difficult
problems of religion?[1] This view becomes less improbable when we consider those races who present us
with what may be called the Dawn of Religion. Fetich
worship, which is so widely prevalent in Africa, can
hardly be called a religion ; and even the South Sea
Islanders, who were in many respects so highly civilized,
are said to have been seriously offended with their deity
if they thought that he treated them with undue severity,
or without proper consideration. According to Kotzebue,
the Kamschatkans adored their deities " when their wishes
were fulfilled, and insulted them when their affairs went
amiss."[2] When the missionaries introduced a printing-
press into Fiji, "the heathen at once declared it to be
a god."[3]

The natives of the Nicobar Islands put up scarecrows
to frighten away the deity,[4] and Burton once heard an old
Eesa woman, who was suffering from toothache, offer up
the following prayer : " Oh Allah, may thy teeth ache
like mine ! Oh Allah, may thy gums be as sore as mine
are now ! "

Savages very generally believe in witchcraft. Con-
fusing together subjective and objective relations, he is a
prey to constant fears.

Perhaps the lowest form of religion may be considered
to be that presented by the Australians, which consists

---

[1] See, for instance, Greg's *Creed of Christendom*, p. 212.
[2] *New Voyage Round the World*, vol. ii. p. 13.
[3] *Figi and the Figians*, vol. ii. p. 222.
[4] *Voyage of the " Novara*," vol. ii. p. 66.

of a mere unreasoning belief in the existence of mysterious beings. The native who has a nightmare, or a dream, does not doubt the reality of that which passes, and as the beings by whom he is visited in his sleep are unseen by his friends and relations, he regards them as invisible.

In Fetichism this feeling is more methodized. The negro endeavours to make a slave of his deity. Thus Fetichism is almost the opposite of Religion ; it stands towards it in the same relation as Alchemy to Chemistry, or Astrology to Astronomy.

A further stage is that in which the superiority of the higher deities is more fully recognized. Everything is worshipped indiscriminately—animals, plants, and even inanimate objects. In endeavouring to account for the worship of animals, we must remember that names are very frequently taken from them. The children and followers of a man called the Bear or the Lion would make that a tribal name. Hence the animal itself would be first respected, at last worshipped.

"The Totem," says Schoolcraft, "is a symbol of the name of the progenitor—generally some quadruped or bird, or other object in the animal kingdom, which stands, if we may so express it, as the surname of the family. Its significant importance is derived from the fact that individuals unhesitatingly trace their lineage from it." Totemism, however, is by no means confined to America, but occurs also in India, Africa, and in fact almost everywhere,[1] often in connection with marriage prohibitions.

Mr Fergusson has recently attempted to show the special prevalence of Tree and Serpent worship. He might, I believe, have made out as strong a case for many other objects. It must be remembered that the savage accounts for all action and movement by life ; inanimate objects, therefore, have spirits as well as men ; hence when the wives and slaves are slain, the weapons also are broken in the grave, so that the spirits of the

[1] *Trans. Ethnol. Soc.*, N.S., vol. vi. p. 36 ; Lafitau, *Mœurs des Sauv. Amér.*, vol. i. p. 464.

latter, as well as of the former, may accompany their master to the other world.

The gradually increasing power of chiefs and priests led to Anthropomorphism and idolatry, which must by no means be regarded as the lowest state of religion. Solomon,[1] indeed, long ago pointed out its connection with monarchical power.

It is important to observe that each stage of religion is superimposed on the preceding, and that bygone beliefs linger on among the children and the ignorant. Thus witchcraft is still believed in by the ignorant, and fairy-tales flourish in the nursery.

As regards pictures, the most curious fancies exist among savage races. They have a very general dislike to be represented, thinking that the artist thereby acquires some mysterious power over them. Kane on one occasion freed himself from some importunate Indians by threatening to draw them if they did not go away. I have already mentioned (p. 524) the danger in which Catlin found himself from sketching a chief in a profile, and thereby, as it was supposed, depriving him of half his face. So, again, a mysterious connection is supposed to exist between a cut lock of hair and the person to whom it belonged. In various parts of the world the sorcerer gets clippings of the hair of his enemy, parings of his nails, or leavings of his food, convinced that whatever evil is done to these will react on their former owner. Even a piece of clothing, or the ground on which a person has trodden, will answer the purpose, and among some tribes the mere knowledge of a person's name is supposed to give a mysterious power. The Indians of British Columbia have a great horror of telling their names. Among the Algonquins a person's real name is communicated only to his nearest relations and dearest friends : the outer world address him by a kind of nick-name. Thus the true name of La Belle Sauvage was not Pocahontas, but Matokes, which they were afraid to communicate to the English. In some tribes these name-

[1] Wisd. xiv. 17.

fancies take a different form. According to Ward, it is
an unpardonable sin for a Hindoo woman to mention the
name of her husband. The Kaffirs have a similar custom,
and so have some East African tribes. In many parts
of the world the names of the dead are avoided with
superstitious horror. This is the case in great parts of
North and South America, in Siberia, among the Papuans
and Australians, and even in Shetland, where it is said
that widows are very reluctant to mention their departed
husbands.

Throughout Australia, among some of the Brazilian
tribes, in parts of Africa, and in various other countries,
natural death is regarded as an impossibility. In the
New Hebrides, "when a man fell ill, he knew that some
sorcerer was burning his rubbish; and shell-trumpets,
which could be heard for miles, were blown to signal to
the sorcerers to stop, and wait for the presents which
would be sent next morning. Night after night, Mr
Turner used to hear the melancholy too-tooing of the
shells, entreating the wizards to stop plaguing their
victims."[1] Savages never know but what they may be
placing themselves in the power of these terrible enemies;[2]
and it is not too much to say that the horrible dread of
unknown evil hangs like a thick cloud over savage life,
and embitters every pleasure.

Nor is the belief in sorcery easily shaken off even by
the most civilized nations. James the First was under
the impression that by melting little images of wax,
"the persons that they bear the name of may be continually melted or dried away by continual sickness."
The belief in witchcraft is not indeed even yet extinct
among us.

The mental sufferings which they thus undergo, the
horrible tortures which they sometimes inflict on themselves, and the crimes which they are led to commit, are
melancholy in the extreme. It must not be supposed
that in the preceding chapter I have selected from various

---

[1] Tylor, *l.c.*, p. 129; Turner's *Polynesia*, pp. 18, 89, 424.
[2] See Brown, *New Zealand and its Aborigines*, p. 80.

works all the passages most unfavourable to savages, and that the picture I have drawn of them is unfair. In reality, the very reverse is the case. Their real condition is even worse and more abject than that which I have endeavoured to depict. I have been careful to quote only from trustworthy authorities, but there are many things stated by them which I have not ventured to repeat ; and there are other facts which the travellers tell us they could not bring themselves to publish.

CHAPTER XVI

CONCLUDING REMARKS

I HAVE already expressed my belief that the simple arts and implements have been independently invented by various tribes, at different times, and in different parts of the world. Even at the present day, we may, I think, obtain glimpses of the manner in which they were, or may have been, invented. Elephants break off boughs to use as fans and scrapers. Monkeys use clubs, and throw sticks and stones at those who intrude upon them. Rengger saw a monkey take a stick and use it to open the lid of a box, and this has since been confirmed by other observers. They also use round stones for cracking nuts, and surely a very small step would lead from that to the application of a sharp stone for cutting. When the edge became blunt, it would be thrown away, and another chosen ; but after awhile, accident, if not reflection, would show that a round stone would crack other stones as well as nuts, and thus the savage would learn to make sharp-edged stones for himself. At first, as we see in the drift specimens, these would be coarse and rough, but gradually the pieces chipped off would become smaller, the blows would be more cautiously and thoughtfully given, and at length it would be found that better work might be done by pressure than by blows. From pressure to polishing would again be but a small step. In making flint implements, sparks would be produced ; in polishing them, it would not fail to be observed that they became hot, and in this way it is easy to see how the two methods of obtaining fire may have originated.[1]

The chimpanzee builds himself a house or resting-place quite equal to that of some savages. Our earliest ancestors therefore may have had this art ; but even if not, when they became hunters, and, as we find to be the case with all hunting tribes, supplemented the inefficiency of their weapons by an intimate acquaintance with the manners and customs of the animals on which they preyed, they could not fail to observe, and perhaps to copy, the houses which various species of animals construct for themselves.

The Esquimaux have no pottery ; they use cup-shaped stones as a substitute ; but we have seen how they sometimes improve upon these by a rim of clay. To extend this rim, diminish, and at last replace, the stone, is an obvious process. In hotter countries, vessels of wood, or the shells of fruit, such as cocoa-nuts and gourds, are used for holding liquids. These will not stand fire, but in some cases by plastering them on the outside with clay they are enabled to do so. There is some evidence that this obvious improvement has been made by several separate tribes even in modern times. Other similar cases might be mentioned, in which by a very simple and apparently obvious process, an important improvement is secured. It seems very improbable that any such advantage should ever be lost again. There is no evidence, says Mr Tylor,[2] " of any tribe giving up the use of the spindle to twist their thread by hand, or having been in the habit of working the fire-drill with a thong, and going back to the clumsier practice of working it without, and it is even hard to fancy such a thing happening." What follows from this argument ? Evidently that the lowest races of existing savages must, always assuming the common origin of the human race,

---

[1] The idea of using fire would also have been suggested by volcanoes, by trees set on fire by lightning, and by the natural fires which occur in hot summers.

[2] *L.c.*, p. 364.

be at least as far advanced as were our ancestors when they spread over the earth's surface.

What, then, must have been their condition ? They were ignorant of pottery, for the Esquimaux, the Polynesians, the Australians, some North and South American tribes, and many other savage races, have none even now, or at least had none until quite lately. They had no bows and arrows, for these weapons were unknown to the Australians and New Zealanders ; their boats for the same reason must have been of the rudest possible character ; they were naked, and ignorant of the art of spinning ; they had no knowledge of agriculture, and probably no domestic animal but the dog, though here the argument is weaker, inasmuch as experience is more portable than property. It is, however, probable that the dog was long the only domesticated animal. Of the more unusual weapons, such as the boomerang, blow-pipe, bolas, etc., they were certainly ignorant. The sling and the throwing-stick were doubtless unknown, and even the shield, as it is only used in war, had probably not been invented. The spear, which is but a development of the knife-point, and the club, which is but a long hammer, are the only things left by this line of argument. They seem to be the only natural and universal weapons of man.

We might be disposed to wonder how man was at first able to kill game ; but we must remember that if man was unskilful, animals were unsuspicious. The tameness of the birds on uninhabited islands is well known ; the wariness of animals and the skill of man must have increased almost *pari passu.*

The same argument may be applied to the mental condition of savages. Our earliest ancestors certainly could not have counted to ten, considering that so many races now in existence cannot get beyond four. It is probable that man originated in a warm climate, and so long as he was confined to the tropics he may have found a succession of fruits, and have lived as the monkeys do now. Indeed, according to Bates, this is still the case with some of the Brazilian Indians. "The monkeys," he says, "lead in fact a life similar to that of the Parárauate Indians." Directly, however, men spread into temperate climates, this mode of life would become impossible, and they would be compelled to seek their nourishment, in part at least, from the animal kingdom. Then, if not before, the knife and the hammer would develop into the spear and the club.

It is too often supposed that the world was peopled by a series of "migrations." But migrations, properly so-called, are compatible only with a comparatively high state of organization. Moreover, it has been observed that the geographical distribution of the various races of man curiously coincides with that of other races of animals : and there can be no doubt that he originally crept over the earth's surface little by little, year by year, just, for instance, as the weeds of Europe are now gradually but surely creeping over the surface of Australia.

The preceding argument assumes, of course, the unity of the human race. It would, however, be impossible for me to end this volume without saying a few words on this great question. It must be admitted that the principal varieties of mankind are of great antiquity. We find on some of the earliest Egyptian monuments, dating back to 4000 B.C., three distinct types : the Semitic on the east and west of Egypt, the Negro on the south, and the Egyptian type occupying a middle place between the two. The representations of the monuments, although somewhat conventional, are extremely characteristic. The statue of Kephren, the third king of the fourth dynasty, who erected the second of the great pyramids of Gizeh, and is supposed to have reigned about 3900 B.C., is a real masterpiece. These distinct types still predominate in Egypt and the neighbouring countries. Thus, then, says Mr Poole, in this immense interval we do not find "the least change in the Negro or the Arab ; and even the type which seems to be intermediate between them is virtually as unaltered. Those who consider that length of time can change a type of man, will do well to consider the fact that three thousand years give no ratio on which a calculation could be founded."[1] I am, however, not aware that it is supposed by any school of ethnologists that "time" alone, without a change of external conditions, will produce an alteration of type. Let us now turn to the instances relied on by Mr Crawfurd.[2] "The millions," he says, "of African Negroes that have during three centuries been transported to the New World and its islands, are the same in colour as the present inhabitants of the parent country of their forefathers. The Creole Spaniards, who have for at least as long a time been settled in tropical America, are as fair as the people of Arragon and Andalusia, with the same variety of colour in the hair and eye as their progenitors. The pure Dutch Creole colonists of the Cape of Good Hope, after dwelling two centuries among black Kaffirs and yellow Hottentots, do not differ in colour from the people of Holland." Here, on the contrary, we have great change of circumstances, but a very insufficient lapse of time, and in fact there is no well-authenticated case in which these two requisites are united. But Mr Crawfurd went, I think, too far, when he denied altogether any change of type. In spite of the comparatively short time which has elapsed, and of the immense immigration which has been kept up, there is already a marked difference between the English of Europe and those of America ; and it would be desirable to inquire whether, in their own eyes, the Negroes of the New World exactly resemble those of Africa.

But there are some reasons which make it probable that changes of external condition, or rather of country, produce less effect now than was formerly the case. At present, when men migrate they carry with them the manners and appliances of civilized life. They build houses more or less like those to which they have been accustomed, carry with them flocks and herds, and intro-

---

[1] Poole, *Trans. Ethn. Soc.*, New Ser., vol. ii. p. 261.
[2] Crawfurd, *Trans. Ethn. Soc.*, New Ser., vol. ii. p. 252.

duce into their new country the principal plants which served them for food in the old. If their new abode is cold, they increase their clothing ; if warm, they diminish it. In these and a hundred other ways the effect which would otherwise be produced is greatly diminished.

But, as we have seen, this has not always been the case. When man first spread over the earth, he had no domestic animals, perhaps not even the dog ; no knowledge of agriculture : his weapons were of the rudest character, and his houses scarcely worthy of the name. His food, habits, and whole manner of life must then have varied as he passed from one country to another ; he must have been far more subject to the influence of external circumstances, and in all probability more susceptible of change. Moreover, his form, which is now stereotyped by long ages of repetition, may reasonably be supposed to have been itself more plastic than is now the case.

If there is any truth in this view of the subject, it will necessarily follow that the principal varieties of man are of great antiquity, and in fact go back almost to the very origin of the human race. We may then cease to wonder that the earliest paintings on Egyptian tombs represent so accurately several varieties still existing in those regions, and that the Engis skull, one of the most ancient yet found in Europe, so closely resembles many that may be seen even at the present day.

Slow and gradual changes, however, still take place, although his " mere bodily structure " long ago became of less importance to man than " that subtle force we term mind." This, as Mr Wallace eloquently says, " with a naked and unprotected body, *this* gave him clothing against the varying inclemencies of the seasons. Though unable to compete with the deer in swiftness, or with the wild bull in strength, *this* gave him weapons wherewith to capture or overcome both. Though less capable than most other animals of living on the herbs and the fruits that unaided nature supplies, this wonderful faculty taught him to govern and direct nature to his own benefit, and make her produce food for him when and where he pleased. From the moment when the first skin was used as a covering, when the first rude spear was formed to assist in the chase, the first seed sown or shoot planted, a grand revolution was effected in nature, a revolution which in all the previous ages of the world's history had had no parallel, for a being had arisen who was no longer necessarily subject to change with the changing universe,—a being who was in some degree superior to nature, inasmuch as he knew how to control and regulate her action, and could keep himself in harmony with her, not by a change in body, but by an advance in mind.

"Here, then, we see the true grandeur and dignity of man. On this view of his special attributes, we may admit that even those who claim for him a position and an order, a class, or a sub-kingdom by himself, have some reason on their side. He is, indeed, a being apart, since he is not influenced by the great laws which irresistibly modify all other organic beings. Nay, more : this victory which he has gained for himself gives him a directing influence over other existences. Man has not only escaped 'natural selection' himself, but he is actually able to take away some of that power from nature which, before his appearance, she universally exercised. We can anticipate the time when the earth will produce only cultivated plants and domestic animals ; when man's selection shall have supplanted 'natural selection' ; and when the ocean will be the only domain in which that power can be exerted, which for countless cycles of ages ruled supreme over the earth."

Thus, then, the great principle of Natural Selection, which is to biology what the law of gravitation is for astronomy, not only throws an unexpected light on the past, but illuminates the future with hope ; nor can I but feel surprised that a theory which thus teaches us humility for the past, faith in the present, and hope for the future, should have been regarded as opposed to the principles of true religion.

I say of hope because we are, I think, justified in

believing that the happiness of man is on the increase. It is generally admitted that if any animal increases in numbers, it must be because the conditions are becoming more favourable to it—in other words, because it is happier and more comfortable. Now how will this test apply to man ?

Schoolcraft estimates [1] that in a population which lives on the produce of the chase, each hunter requires on an average 50,000 acres, or 78 square miles, for his support. Again, he tells us [2] that, excluding Michigan territory, west of Lake Michigan, and north of Illinois, there were in the United States in 1825 about 97,000 Indians, occupying 77,000,000 of acres, or 120,312 square miles. This gives one inhabitant to every $1\frac{1}{4}$ square miles. In this case, however, the Indians lived partly on the subsidies granted them by Government in exchange for land, and the population was therefore greater than would have been the case if they had lived entirely on the produce of the chase. The same reason affects, though to a smaller extent, the Indians in the Hudson's Bay territory. These **tribes** were estimated by Sir George Simpson, late Governor of the territories belonging to the Hudson's Bay Company, in his evidence given before the Committee of the House of Commons in 1857, at 139,000, and the extent is supposed to be more than 1,400,000 square miles, to which we must add 13,000 more for Vancouver's Island, making a total of more than 900,000,000 of acres ; about 6500 acres, or 10 square miles, to each individual. Again, the inhabitants of Patagonia, south of 40°, and exclusive of Chiloe and Tierra del Fuego, are estimated by Admiral Fitzroy at less than 4000, and the number of acres is 176,640,000, giving more than 44,000 acres, or 68 square miles, for each *person*. A writer in the *Voice of Pity*, however, thinks that their numbers may perhaps amount to 14,000 or 15,000.[3] It would be difficult to form any census of the aborigines in Australia ; Mr Oldfield estimates that there is one

---

[1] *Indian Tribes*, vol. i. p. 433.   [2] *L.c.*, vol. iii. p. 575.
[3] *L.c.*, vol. ii. p. 93.

native to every 50 square miles ;[1] and it is at least evident, that since the introduction of civilization, the total population of that continent has greatly increased.

Population, indeed, as a general rule, increases with civilization. Paraguay, with 100,000 square miles, has from 300,000 to 500,000 inhabitants, or about four to a square mile. The uncivilized parts of Mexico contained 374,000 inhabitants in 675,000 square miles ; while Mexico proper, with 833,600 square miles, had 6,691,000 inhabitants. Naples had more than 183 inhabitants to each square mile, Venetia more than 200, Lombardy 280, England 280, Belgium as many as 320.

Finally, we cannot but observe that, under civilization, the means of subsistence have increased even more rapidly than the population. Far from suffering for want of food, the more densely peopled countries are exactly those in which it is, not only absolutely, but even relatively, most abundant. It is said that anyone who makes two blades of grass grow where one grew before, is a benefactor to the human race ; what, then, shall we say of that which enables a thousand men to live in plenty where one savage could scarcely find a scanty and precarious subsistence ?

There are, indeed, many who doubt whether happiness is increased by civilization, and who talk of the free and noble savage. But the true savage is neither free nor noble ; he is a slave to his own wants, his own passions ; imperfectly protected from the weather, he suffers from the cold by night and the heat of the sun by day ; ignorant of agriculture, living by the chase, and improvident in success, hunger always stares him in the face, and often drives him to the dreadful alternative of cannibalism or death.

Wild animals are always in danger. Sir F. Galton, who is so well qualified to form an opinion, believes that the life of all beasts in their wild state is an exceedingly anxious one ; that " every antelope in South Africa has literally to run for its life once in every one or two days

[1] *Trans. Ethn. Soc.*, New Ser., vol. iii. p. 220.

upon an average, and that he starts or gallops under the influence of a false alarm many times in a day." [1]   So it is with the savage, he is always suspicious, always in danger, always on the watch.   He can depend on no one, and no one can depend upon him.   He expects nothing from his neighbour, and does unto others as he believes that they would do unto him.   Thus his life is one prolonged scene of selfishness and fear.   Even in his religion, if he has any, he creates for himself a new source of terror, and peoples the world with invisible enemies.   The position of the female savage is even more wretched than that of her master.   She not only shares his sufferings, but has to bear his ill-humour and ill-usage.   She may truly be said to be " little better than his dog, little dearer than his horse."   In Australia Mr Oldfield never saw a woman's grave, and does not think that the natives took the trouble to bury them.   But, indeed, he believes that few of them are so fortunate as to die a natural death, "they being generally despatched ere they become old and emaciated, that so much good food may not be lost. . . .   In fine, so little importance is attached to them, either before or after death, that it may be doubted whether the man does not value his dog, when alive, quite as much as he does his woman, and think of both quite as often and lovingly after he has eaten them." [2]

Not content, moreover, with those incident to their mode of life, savages appear to take a melancholy pleasure in self-inflicted sufferings.   Besides the very general practice of tattooing, the most extraordinary methods of disfigurement and self-torture are adopted ; some cut off the little finger, some make an immense hole in the underlip, or pierce the cartilage of the nose.   The Easter Islanders enlarge their ears till they come down to their shoulders ; the Chinooks, and many other American tribes, alter the shape of their heads.   Some of the African tribes chip their teeth in various manners, each community having a fashion of its own.   The Nyambanas, a division

[1] *Trans. Ethn. Soc.*, New Ser., vol. iii. p. 133.
[2] *Trans. Ethn. Soc.*, New Ser., vol. iii. p. 248.

of the Kaffirs, are characterized by a row of artificial
pimples or warts, about the size of a pea, and extending
from the upper part of the forehead to the tip of the nose.
Of these they are very proud.[1] Among the Bachapins,
those who have distinguished themselves in battle are
allowed the privilege of marking " their thigh with a long
scar, which is rendered indelible and of a bluish colour by
means of wood ashes rubbed into the fresh wound." [2] In
Australia, Captain King saw a native ornamented with
horizontal scars which extended across the upper part of
the chest. They were at least an inch in diameter, and
protruded half an inch from the body.[3] In some parts of
Australia, and in Tasmania, all the men have a tooth
knocked out in a very clumsy and painful manner.[4]
" The inhabitants of Tana have on their arms and bellies
elevated scars, representing plants, flowers, stars, and various
other figures. They are made by first cutting the skin with
a sharp bamboo reed, and then applying a certain plant to
the wound, which raises the scar above the rest of the
skin. The inhabitants of Tazavan, or Formosa, by a
very painful operation, impress on their naked skins various
figures of trees, flowers, and animals. The great men in
Guinea have their skin flowered like damask ; and in the
Deccan the women likewise have flowers cut into their
flesh, on the forehead, the arms, and the breast, and the
elevated scars are painted in colours, and exhibit the
appearance of flowered damask." [5] The native women in
New South Wales used to tie a string tightly round the
little finger, and wear it until the finger rotted off. Few
of them escaped the painful experience.[6] The American
Indians also inflicted the most horrible tortures upon themselves.[7] In many cases the boys, on arriving at maturity,
are subjected to ordeals which must involve great suffering.

---

[1] *United States Exploring Expedition*, vol. i. p. 63.
[2] Burchell, *l.c.*, vol. ii. pp. 478, 535.
[3] *Narrative of a Survey of the Intertropical and Western Coasts of
Australia*, p. 42. See also Eyre's account, quoted in p. 449.
[4] Freycinet, vol. ii. p. 705.   [5] Forster, *l.c.*, p. 588.
[6] D'Urville, vol. i. p. 406.
[7] See, for instance, Catlin's *North American Indians*, vol. i. p. 170 ;
Azara, vol. ii. p. 136.

These and many other curious practices are none the less painful because they are voluntary.

If we turn to the bright side of the question, the whole analogy of nature justifies us in concluding that the pleasures of civilized man are greater than those of the savage.   As we descend in the scale of organization, we find that animals become more and more vegetative in their characteristics ; with less susceptibility to pain, and consequently less capacity for happiness.   It may, indeed, be doubted whether some of those beings, which from their anatomy we are compelled to class as animals, have much more consciousness of enjoyment, or even of existence, than a tree or a sea-weed.   But even to animals which possess a clearly defined nervous system, we must ascribe very different degrees of sensibility.   The study of the sensory organs in the lower animals offers great difficulties ; but at least we know that they are, in many cases, few in number, and capable of conveying only general impressions. Everyone will admit that the possession of a new sense, or the improvement of an old one, is a fresh source of possible happiness ; but how, it may be asked, does this affect the present question ?   There are no just grounds for expecting man to be ever endued with a sixth sense ; so far from being able to improve the organization of the eye or the ear, we cannot make one hair black or white, nor add one cubit to our stature.   But, on the other hand, the invention of the telescope and microscope is equivalent in its results to an immense improvement of the eye, and opens up to us new worlds, fresh sources of interest and happiness.   Again, we cannot alter the physical structure of the ear : but we can train it, we can invent new musical instruments, compose new melodies.   The music of savages is rude and melancholy in comparison with ours ; and thus, though the ear of man may not have appreciably altered, the pleasure which we may derive from it has been immensely increased.   Moreover, the savage is like a child who sees and hears only that which is brought directly before him, but the civilized man questions nature, and by the various processes of chemistry, by electricity, and magnetism, by a thousand ingenious contrivances, he forces nature to throw light upon herself, discovers hidden uses and unsuspected beauties, almost as if he were endowed with some entirely new organ of sense.

The love of travel is deeply implanted in the human breast ; it is an immense pleasure to visit other countries, and see new races of men. Again, the discovery of printing brings all who choose into communion with the greatest minds. The thoughts of a Shakespeare or a Tennyson, the discoveries of a Newton or a Darwin, become thus the common property of mankind. Already the results of this all-important though simple process have been equivalent to an immense improvement of our mental faculties ; and day by day, as books become cheaper, schools are established, and education is improved, a greater and greater effect will be produced.

The well-known proverb against looking a gift-horse in the mouth does not apply to the gifts of nature ; they will bear the closest inspection, and the more we examine, the more we shall find to admire. Nor are these new sources of happiness accompanied by any new liability to suffering ; on the contrary, while our pleasures are increased, our pains are lessened ; in a thousand ways we can avoid or diminish evils which to our ancestors were great and inevitable. How much misery, for instance, has been spared to the human race by the single discovery of chloroform ? The capacity for pain, so far as it can serve as a warning, remains in full force, but the necessity for endurance has been greatly diminished. With increased knowledge of, and attention to, the laws of health, disease will become less and less frequent. Those tendencies thereto which we have derived from our ancestors will gradually die out ; and if fresh seeds are not sown, our race may one day enjoy the inestimable advantages of health.

Thus, then, with the increasing influence of science, we may confidently look to a great improvement in the condition of man. But it may be said that our present sufferings and sorrows arise principally from sin, and that any moral improvement must be due to religion, not to science. This separation of the two mighty agents of improvement is the great misfortune of humanity, and has done more than anything else to retard the progress of civilization. But even if for the moment we admit that science will not render us more virtuous, it must certainly make us more innocent. Out of 164,000 persons committed to prison in England and Wales, only 4000 could read and write well. In fact, our criminal population are mere savages, and most of their crimes are but injudicious and desperate attempts to live as a savage in the midst, and at the expense, of a civilized community.

Men do not sin for the sake of sinning; they yield to temptation. Most of our sufferings arise from a mistaken pursuit of pleasure; from a misapprehension of that which constitutes true happiness. Men do wrong either from ignorance or in the hope, unexpressed perhaps even to themselves, that they may enjoy the pleasure, and yet avoid the penalty, of sin. In this respect there can be no doubt that religious teaching is much misapprehended. Repentance is too often regarded as a substitute for punishment. Sin, it is thought, is followed *either* by the one or the other. So far, however, as our world is concerned, this is not the case; repentance may enable a man to avoid sin in future, but has no effect on the consequences of the past. The laws of nature are just and salutary, but they are also inexorable. All men admit that "the wages of sin is death"; but they seem to think that this is a general rule to which there may be many exceptions—that *some* sins may possibly tend to happiness—that some thorns may grow grapes, some thistles produce figs. That suffering is the inevitable consequence of sin, as surely as night follows day, is, however, the stern yet salutary teaching of science. And surely if this lesson were thoroughly impressed upon our minds, if we really believed in the certainty of punishment, and that sin could not conduce to happiness, temptation, which is at the very root of crime, would be cut away, and mankind must necessarily become more innocent.

May we not, however, go even farther than this, and say that science will also render man more virtuous? ' To pass our time," says Lord Brougham,[1] "in the study of the sciences, in learning what others have discovered, and in extending the bounds of human knowledge, has, in all ages, been reckoned the most dignified and happy of human occupations. . . . No man until he has studied philosophy can have a just idea of the great things for which Providence has fitted his understanding, the extraordinary disproportion which there is between his natural strength and the powers of his mind, and the force he derives from them." Finally he concludes that science would not only "make our lives more agreeable, but better ; and that a rational being is bound, by every motive of interest and duty, to direct his mind towards pursuits which are found to be the sure path of virtue as well as of happiness."

We are in reality but on the threshold of civilization. Far from showing any indication of having come to an end, the tendency to improvement seems latterly to have proceeded with augmented impetus and accelerated rapidity. Why, then, should we suppose that it must now cease? Man has surely not reached the limits of his intellectual development, and it is certain that he has not exhausted the infinite capabilities of nature. There are many things which are not as yet dreamt of in our philosophy ; many discoveries which will immortalize those who make them, and confer upon the human race advantages which as yet, perhaps, we are not in a condition to appreciate. We may still say with our great countryman, Sir Isaac Newton, that we have been but like children playing on the seashore, and picking up here and there a smoother pebble or a prettier shell than ordinary, while the great ocean of truth lies all undiscovered before us.

Thus, then, the most sanguine hopes for the future are justified by the whole experience of the past. It is surely unreasonable to suppose that a process which has

[1] *Objects, Advantages, and Pleasures of Science*, p. 39.

been going on for so many thousand years should have now suddenly ceased ; and he must be blind indeed who imagines that our civilization is unsusceptible of improvement, or that we ourselves are in the highest state attainable by man.

If we turn from experience to theory, the same conclusion forces itself upon us. The great principle of natural selection which in animals affects the body and seems to have little influence on the mind, in man affects the mind and has little influence on the body. In the first, it tends mainly to the preservation of life ; in the second, to the improvement of the mind, and consequently to the increase of happiness. It ensures, in the words of Mr Herbert Spencer, " a constant progress towards a higher degree of skill, intelligence, and self-regulation—a better co-ordination of actions—a more complete life."[1] Even those, however, who are dissatisfied with the reasoning of Mr Darwin, and believe that neither our mental nor our material organization is susceptible of any considerable change, may still look forward to the future with hope. The tendency of recent improvements and discoveries is less to effect any rapid change in man himself than to bring him into harmony with nature ; less to confer upon him new powers than to teach him how to apply the old.

It will, I think, be admitted that of the evils under which we suffer, nearly all may be attributed either to ignorance or sin. That ignorance will be diminished by the progress of science is, of course, self-evident ; that the same will be the case with sin, seems little less so. Thus, then, both theory and experience point to the same conclusion. The future happiness of our race, which poets hardly ventured to hope for, science boldly predicts. Utopia, which we have long looked upon as synonymous with an evident impossibility which we have ungratefully regarded as " too good to be true," turns out, on the contrary, to be the necessary consequence of natural laws,

[1] Herbert Spencer, *A Theory of Population deduced from the General Law of Animal Fertility*, p. 34.

and once more we find that the simple truth exceeds the most brilliant flights of the imagination.

Even in our own time we may hope to see some improvement ; but the unselfish mind will find its highest gratification in the belief that, whatever may be the case with ourselves, our descendants will understand many things which are hidden from us now, will better appreciate the beautiful world in which we live, avoid much of that suffering to which we are subject, enjoy many blessings of which we are not yet worthy, and escape many of those temptations which we deplore but cannot wholly resist.

APPENDIX

RUNES (*Page* 14)

We do not yet know at what time the use of Runes commenced. The examples found at Thorsbjerg and Nydam carry them back to the second or third century, but they may have begun much earlier. They remained partially in use in out-of-the-way districts of Scandinavia down to the close of the last century. Runic monuments occur in Norway, Sweden, Denmark, England, and, though rarely, in Ireland ; but are more abundant in Sweden than anywhere else. Professor Stephens[1] states that there are three times as many in Sweden as in all other northern countries together, and he estimates the total number in Sweden at not less than two thousand.

The Runic Alphabet, or Futhorc, is as follows :

Ⱶ. ᚻ. Þ. ᚼ. ᚱ. ⱴ. ᛪ. ᚼ. ᛁ. ᛆ. ᛁ. ᛐ. ᛒ. ᛚ. ⱴ.   ᛡ.
F U th O R K H N I A S T B L M (Œ, Y)

There are, however, several varieties ; thus ᛡ sometimes stands for *o*, ᛆ for *n*, ᚼ for *s*, ᛏ for *t*, ᛆ for *d*, and ᛁ for *e*. There is also a class of letters known as tree-runes, which are entirely unlike the rest. The letters given above are those generally used in the engravings on stones in the great tumulus known as Maeshowe, near the Stones of Stennis, in the Orkneys,[2] and are supposed to have been the work of a party of Northmen who broke into the Howe in the ninth century. The numerous variations in the forms of the letters, and the fact that they are sometimes read from left to right, sometimes from right to left, make them at times somewhat difficult to decipher ; but it fortunately happens that we possess no less than sixty-one Runic Futhorcs, so that any inscription which is at all perfect, and not too much abbreviated, can be read with tolerable certainty.

[1] *The Old-Northern Runic Monuments of Scandinavia*, p. 134.
[2] *Maeshowe*, by J. Farrar, Esq., M.P.

OGHAMS

The origin of the Ogham alphabet is as uncertain as that of the Runic. While, however, the Runes occur principally in Scandinavia, and but rarely in Great Britain, Oghams, on the

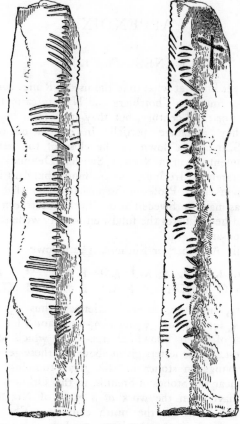

FIGS. 282, 283.—Ogham stones.

other hand, have their headquarters in Ireland, though some few have been discovered in Scotland, and even in Shetland. They are generally intended to be read from below upwards, and the letters consist of mere straight strokes, arranged in groups along a line. This line is very often the edge of the stone, but sometimes a line is cut. In other cases, an imaginary line is supposed to run through the inscription.   Short lines, or notches, stand for the vowels, *a, o, u, e, i,* one notch denoting *a,* two *o,* three *u,* and so on.   Lines on the left of the base line stand for *b, l, f, s,* and *n,* according as they are 1, 2, 3, 4, or 5 in number ; lines on the right of the base line stand in the same manner for *h, d, t, c,* and *q* ; while those crossing the line denote *m, g, ng, st,* or *z,* and *r.* There are some few other characters, which, however, seldom occur.

Almost all the Ogham inscriptions which have yet been read are mere patronymics, containing the name of the person in whose honour the stone was erected.   Thus the above figure (fig. 282) of an Ogham stone found in Kerry reads thus : Nocati maqi maqi ret(ti), *i.e.* (The Stone) of Nocat, the son of Macreith ; the inscription on fig. 283 is, Maqi Mucoi Uddami, *i.e.* (The Stone) of Uddam Mac Mucoi.

Page 51

Staigue Fort, in the county of Kerry, is "an enclosure, nearly circular, 114 feet in diameter, 88 feet from east to west, and 87 from north to south.   The stones are put together without any description of mortar or cement ; the wall is 13 feet thick at the bottom, and 5 feet 2 inches broad at top at the highest part, where some of the old coping-stones still remain, and which is there 17 feet 6 inches high upon the inside.   It has one square doorway in the S.S.W. side, 5 feet 9 inches high, with sloping sides, 4 feet 2 inches wide at top, and 5 feet at bottom.   In the substance of this massive wall, and opening inwards, are two small chambers ; the one on the west side is 12 feet long, 4 feet 7 inches wide, and 6 feet 6 inches high ; the northern chamber is 7 feet 4 inches long, 4 feet 9 inches wide, and 7 feet high. They formed a part of the original plan, and were not, like other apertures in some similar structures, filled-up gateways.   Around the interior of the wall are arranged ten sets of stairs, . . . the highest reaching very nearly to the full height of the wall, and the secondary flights being about half that much ; each step is 2 feet wide ; and the lower flights project within the circle of the higher.   They lead to narrow platforms, from 8 to 43 feet in length, on which its wardens or defenders stood." (*Catalogue of the Royal Irish Academy,* p. 120.)

INDEX